The Therapy of Desire

THEORY AND PRACTICE IN HELLENISTIC ETHICS

*

MARTHA C. NUSSBAUM

PRINCETON UNIVERSITY PRESS

PRINCETON, NEW JERSEY

Library of Congress Cataloging-in-Publication Data
Nussbaum, Martha Craven, 1947–
The therapy of desire : theory and practice in Hellenistic ethics
/Martha C. Nussbaum.
p. cm.
Includes bibliographic references and index.
ISBN 0-691-03342-0
ISBN 0-691-00052-2 (pbk.)
1. Philosophy, Ancient.   2. Emotions (Philosophy)—History.
3. Ethics, Ancient. I. Title.
B505.N87   1994
170'.938—dc20   93-6417

The author's proceeds from the sale of this book will be
donated to Amnesty International

This book has been composed in Sabon Typeface

Princeton University Press books are
printed on acid-free paper and meet the guidelines
for permanence and durability of the Committee
on Production Guidelines for Book Longevity
of the Council on Library Resources

Fourth printing, and first
paperback printing, 1996

Printed in the United States of America

7   9   10   8

The Therapy of Desire

✳

MARTIN CLASSICAL LECTURES

New Series, Volume 2

The Martin Classical Lectures are delivered annually at Oberlin
College on a foundation established by his many friends
in honor of Charles Beebe Martin, for forty-five years a teacher
of classical literature and classical art in Oberlin.

John Peradotto, *Man in the Middle Voice: Name and
Narration in the* Odyssey

Martha C. Nussbaum, *The Therapy of Desire: Theory and
Practice in Hellenistic Ethics*

Josiah Ober, *Political Dissent in Democratic Athens:
Intellectual Crisis of Popular Rule*

Anne Carson, *Economy of the Unlost (Reading
Simonides of Keos with Paul Celan)*

TO THE MEMORY OF GREGORY VLASTOS

✳

Philosophy does not stand outside the world any more than man's brain is outside him because it is not in his stomach; but philosophy, to be sure, is in the world with its brain before it stands on the earth with its feet, while many other human spheres have long been rooted in the earth and pluck the fruits of the world long before they realize that the "head" also belongs to this world or that this world is the world of the head.

(KARL MARX, 1842)

The philosopher desires

And not to have is the beginning of desire.
To have what is not is its ancient cycle . . .

It knows that what it has is what is not
And throws it away like a thing of another time,
As morning throws off stale moonlight and shabby sleep.

(WALLACE STEVENS, "Notes Toward a Supreme Fiction")

✳ *Contents* ✳

CONTENTS

✳ *Acknowledgments* ✳

THIS BOOK BEGAN as the Martin Classical Lectures for 1986. The five original lectures were early versions of chapters 1–2, 4, 8, 10, and 12. I am extremely grateful to the Martin Lecture Committee and the Department of Greek and Latin at Oberlin College for the invitation to present the lectures, and for warm hospitality and stimulating comments during my visit. Preparation of the lectures was very much assisted by the members of my National Endowment for the Humanities Summer Seminar for College Teachers in 1985, where I received extremely tough and searching criticism of drafts and early ideas. Further work on the book began with a sabbatical during 1986–87, supported by Brown University, by a Fellowship from the National Endowment for the Humanities, and by a Visiting Fellowship at All Souls College, Oxford, where I found a stimulating and supportive setting for the expansion of the project to its present scope. Final revisions were completed in the fine facilities and the peaceful environment of the Center for Ideas and Society in the University of California at Riverside.

Many people have helped me in many ways; most of my individual debts are recorded at the ends of the particular chapters. But I would here like to mention especially the help I have received from conversations with Myles Burnyeat, which turned me toward the serious study of Hellenistic ethics in the first place; his work in this area has been an inspiration to me as to so many others, and his tough questions have been invaluable. The triennial Symposia Hellenistica, beginning in 1978, have been a rigorous, and also truly collegial, source of information, argument, and criticism—and, among their members, I would like to thank above all Julia Annas, Jacques Brunschwig, Brad Inwood, G. E. R. Lloyd, Phillip Mitsis, David Sedley, and Richard Sorabji. I have received comments on the entire manuscript from Margaret Graver, Brad Inwood, Richard Posner, Henry Richardson, Richard Sorabji, Cass Sunstein, and two anonymous readers; I am enormously grateful to all of them for the time and effort they have expended and the insights their comments afford. For criticisms and suggestions of many different sorts on individual chapters and issues, I am grateful to Julia Annas, Geoffrey Bakewell, Richard Bernstein, Sissela Bok, Dan Brock, Jacques Brunschwig, Myles Burnyeat, Victor Caston, Abbott Gleason, Michael Gleason, Jasper Griffin, Miriam Griffin, Charles Guignon, Caroline Hahnemann, Stephen Halliwell, David Halperin, Colonel Anthony Hartle, Dolores Iorizzo, Jaegwon Kim, David Konstan, Mary

Lefkowitz, Glen Lesses, Haskel Levi, Geoffrey Lloyd, Mark McPherran, Arthur Madigan, S.J., Gareth Matthews, Giles Milhaven, Joyce Carol Oates, Anthony Price, John Procope, Michael Putnam, James Redfield, Amélie O. Rorty, Stephen Rosenbaum, Christopher Rowe, Malcolm Schofield, David Sedley, Charles Segal, Amartya Sen, Nancy Sherman, Albert Silverstein, Ernest Sosa, Zeph Stewart, Holgar Thesleff, Rex Welshon, Jeffrey Whitman, the late John J. Winkler, and Susan Wolf. I have received many more valuable comments from audiences in the many places where I presented chapters of the book as lectures; I am sorry that I am unable to acknowledge all of those debts individually.

I owe special thanks to Jonathan Glover, who allowed me to be his summer "house-sitter" in Oxford for two consecutive summers, providing an ideally comfortable and undisturbed setting, full of air and light, in which a great deal of the work was done. During these periods Justin Broackes (now, two years later, my colleague at Brown) very kindly lent me a marvelous IBM typewriter, for which I feel great affection.

The cover photograph, for which I thank Rachel Nussbaum, seems to me to capture strikingly some of the imagery of chapter 12: the contrast between a pure white that is linked with death and a green that grows up darkly indefatigably behind it; between clean straight lines and messier shapes of life; between the unsullied blue sky and the strange hot light that cuts straight through both sky and tree, a light coming, as it were, from Medea's countercosmos, set over against the world of Stoic virtue.

One debt stands out above others. For the past fifteen years, until his death in October 1992, I had the good fortune to be a professional colleague and a friend of Gregory Vlastos. His capacity for pursuing philosophical understanding tirelessly and without arrogance or defensiveness, his willingness always to subject his ideas to the searching scrutiny of argument, his combination of exacting textual knowledge with philosophical commitment and of both with social compassion—all this has been exemplary for me, as for so many others. And the warmth and support of his friendship, the way his loving irony could illuminate personal as well as philosophical perplexities—all this supported me in more ways, I imagine, than I know even now. Several months before his death, I asked if I might dedicate this book to him; he agreed. With sadness at the loss of a wonderful friend, I now dedicate it to his memory.

Because the damages caused by anger and hatred in public life cannot be addressed by philosophy alone, the author's proceeds from the sale of this book will be donated to Amnesty International.

Portions of this material have been previously published as follows:

A preliminary version of some of the material in chapters 1 and 4 was published as "Therapeutic Arguments: Epicurus and Aristotle," in *The Norms of Nature*, ed. M. Schofield and G. Striker (Cambridge: Cambridge University Press, 1986), 31–74.

An earlier version of chapter 5 was published as "Beyond Obsession and Disgust: Lucretius' Genealogy of Love," in *Apeiron* 22 (1989): 1–59.

An earlier version of chapter 6 was published in *Philosophy and Phenomenological Research* 50 (1989): 303–51.

An earlier version of chapter 7 was published as "'By Words Not Arms': Lucretius on Gentleness in an Unsafe World," in *Apeiron* 23 (1990): 41–90.

An earlier version of chapter 8 was published as "Skeptic Purgatives: Therapeutic Arguments in Ancient Skepticism," in *Journal of the History of Philosophy* 29 (1991): 1–33.

An earlier version of chapter 10 was published in *Apeiron* 20 (1987): 129–75.

An earlier version of chapter 12 was published in *Pursuits of Reason: Essays in Honor of Stanley Cavell*, ed. T. Cohen, P. Guyer, and H. Putnam (Lubbock: Texas Tech Press, 1993), 307–44.

∗ *Abbreviations* ∗

Fᴏʀ ᴄɪᴛᴀᴛɪᴏɴs from ancient authors whose abbreviations are not included on this list, please see the list of abbreviations in the *Greek-English Lexicon,* 9th ed., edited by H. G. Liddell, R. Scott, and H. S. Jones (Oxford: Clarendon Press, 1968) (abbreviated as LSJ).

Aristotle (Ar.):

DA	*De Anima (On the Soul)*
EE	*Eudemian Ethics*
EN	*Nicomachean Ethics*
GA	*Generation of Animals (De Generatione Animalium)*
MA	*On the Motion of Animals (De Motu Animalium)*
Metaph.	*Metaphysics*
PA	*Parts of Animals (De Partibus Animalium)*
Pol.	*Politics*

Cicero (Cic.):

Fin.	*De Finibus Bonorum et Malorum (On the Ends)*
TD	*Tusculan Disputations*

Diogenes
Laertius (DL): *Lives of the Philosophers* (Book VII on the Stoics, IX on Skeptics, X on Epicurus)

Epicurus:

LHdt	*Letter to Herodotus*
LMen	*Letter to Menoeceus*
LPyth	*Letter to Pythocles*
KD	*Kuriai Doxai (Principal Opinions)*
VS	*Vaticanae Sententiae* (a collection of maxims)
Us.	H. Usener, ed., *Epicurea* (a collection of fragments and reports, Leipzig, 1887)

Galen:

PHP	*De Placitis Hippocratis et Platonis (On the Views of Hippocrates and Plato)*—page numbers as in P. De Lacy edition, Corpus Medicorum Graecorum V.4.1–2, Berlin 1978–80.

Philodemus (Phld.):

O	*On Anger (Peri Orgēs)*
P	*On Frank Criticism (Peri Parrhēsias)*

Plutarch (Plut.):

Adv. Col.	*Against Colotes (Adversus Colotem)*
Comm. Not.	*On Common Conceptions (De communibus notitiis)*
LB	*Live Without Attracting Attention (Lathe Biōsas)*
Non Posse	*On the Fact That If One Follows Epicurus One Cannot Live a Pleasant Life (Non Posse Suaviter Vivere secundum Epicurum)*
St. Rep.	*On Stoic Self-Contradictions (De Stoicorum Repugnantiis)*
Virt. Mor.	*On Moral Virtue (De Virtute morali)*

Posidonius:

E-K	Edelstein-Kidd edition, Cambridge 1972.

Seneca:

Ben.	*De Beneficiis*
Clem.	*On Mercy (De Clementia)*
Ep.	*Moral Epistles (Ad Lucilium Epistulae Morales)*
Ir.	*On Anger (De Ira)*
NQ	*Naturales Quaestiones*

Tragedies:

Ag.	*Agamemnon*
HFu	*Hercules Furens*
HO	*Hercules Oetaeus*
Med.	*Medea*
Oed.	*Oedipus*
Phdr.	*Phaedra*
Phoen.	*Phoenissae*
Thy.	*Thyestes*

Sextus Empiricus:

M	*Against the Professors (Adversus mathematicos)*
PH	*Outlines of Pyrrhonism (Pyrrhoneae hupotupōseis)*

SVF	*Stoicorum Veterum Fragmenta* (4 vols), ed. H. von Arnim, Leipzig 1924.

The Therapy of Desire

✳

* Introduction *

The idea of a practical and compassionate philosophy—a philosophy that exists for the sake of human beings, in order to address their deepest needs, confront their most urgent perplexities, and bring them from misery to some greater measure of flourishing—this idea makes the study of Hellenistic ethics riveting for a philosopher who wonders what philosophy has to do with the world. The writer and teacher of philosophy is a lucky person, fortunate, as few human beings are, to be able to spend her life expressing her most serious thoughts and feelings about the problems that have moved and fascinated her most. But this exhilarating and wonderful life is also part of the world as a whole, a world in which hunger, illiteracy, and disease are the daily lot of a large proportion of the human beings who still exist, as well as causes of death for many who do not still exist. A life of leisured self-expression is, for most of the world's people, a dream so distant that it can rarely even be formed. The contrast between these two images of human life gives rise to a question: what business does anyone have living in the happy and self-expressive world, so long as the other world exists and one is a part of it?

One answer to this question may certainly be to use some portion of one's time and material resources to support relevant types of political action and social service. On the other hand, it seems possible that philosophy itself, while remaining itself, can perform social and political functions, making a difference in the world by using its own distinctive methods and skills. To articulate this relationship, and the conception of philosophy that underlies it, is a central preoccupation of Hellenistic thought, and an area in which Hellenistic thought makes a major contribution to philosophical understanding.

The Hellenistic philosophical schools in Greece and Rome—Epicureans, Skeptics, and Stoics—all conceived of philosophy as a way of addressing the most painful problems of human life. They saw the philosopher as a compassionate physician whose arts could heal many pervasive types of human suffering. They practiced philosophy not as a detached intellectual technique dedicated to the display of cleverness but as an immersed and worldly art of grappling with human misery. They focused their attention, in consequence, on issues of daily and urgent human significance—the fear of death, love and sexuality, anger and aggression—issues that are sometimes avoided as embarrassingly messy and personal

3

by the more detached varieties of philosophy. They confronted these issues as they arose in ordinary human lives, with a keen attention to the vicissitudes of those lives, and to what would be necessary and sufficient to make them better. On the one hand, these philosophers were still very much philosophers—dedicated to the careful argumentation, the explicitness, the comprehensiveness, and the rigor that have usually been sought by philosophy, in the tradition of ethical reflection that takes its start (in the West) with Socrates. (They opposed themselves, on this account, to the methods characteristic of popular religion and magic.) On the other hand, their intense focus on the state of desire and thought in the pupil made them seek a newly complex understanding of human psychology, and led them to adopt complex strategies—interactive, rhetorical, literary— designed to enable them to grapple effectively with what they had understood. In the process they forge new conceptions of what philosophical rigor and precision require. In these ways Hellenistic ethics is unlike the more detached and academic moral philosophy that has sometimes been practiced in the Western tradition.

Twentieth-century philosophy, in both Europe and North America, has, until very recently, made less use of Hellenistic ethics than almost any other philosophical culture in the West since the fourth century B.C.E. Not only late antique and most varieties of Christian thought, but also the writings of modern writers as diverse as Descartes, Spinoza, Kant, Adam Smith, Hume, Rousseau, the Founding Fathers of the United States, Nietzsche, and Marx, owe in every case a considerable debt to the writings of Stoics, Epicureans, and/or Skeptics, and frequently far more than to the writings of Aristotle and Plato. Especially where philosophical conceptions of emotion are concerned, ignoring the Hellenistic period means ignoring not only the best material in the Western tradition, but also the central influence on later philosophical developments.

A few examples will help to make this point vivid to the reader. When Christian thinkers write about divine anger, or about mercy for human frailty, they owe a deep debt to the Roman Stoics. When Descartes and Princess Elizabeth correspond about the passions, Seneca is the central author to whom they refer. Spinoza is aware of Aristotle, but far more profoundly influenced by Stoic passion theory. Smith's theory of moral sentiments is heavily inspired by Stoic models, as is his economic teleology. When Rousseau defends the emotion of pity, he is taking sides in a debate of long standing between Stoics and Aristotelians. When Kant repudiates pity, he joins the debate on the Stoic side. Nietzsche's own attack on pity, coupled with a defense of mercy, should be understood—as he himself repeatedly insists—not as the policy of a boot-in-the face fascist, and also not as an innocuous refusal of moral self-indulgence, but as a position opposed both to cruelty and to deep attachment, a position he derives from his reading of Epictetus and Seneca. When we speak of the influence of "the classical tradition" on the framers of the U.S. Constitution, we must always remember that it is, on the whole, Hellenistic (especially Stoic) ethical thought, via the writings of Cicero, Seneca, and Plutarch above all, that is central to their classical education. Thus the neglect of this period in much recent teaching of "the Classics" and "the Great Books" gives a very distorted picture of the philosophical tradition—and also robs the student of richly illuminating philosophical arguments.

Contemporary philosophical writing has begun to undo these wrongs; in both Europe and North America we have been seeing a flourishing of first-rate scholarship on this material, to which the present book owes a large debt. But there is one reclaiming of Hellenistic texts within philosophy—perhaps the most widely known to the general public—that seems to me, though exciting, also deeply problematic. This is Michel Foucault's appeal to the Hellenistic thinkers, in the third volume of his *History of Sexuality*, and in lectures given toward the end of his life, as sources for the idea that philosophy is a set of *techniques du soi*, practices for the formation of a certain sort of self. Certainly Foucault has brought out something very fundamental about these philosophers when he stresses the extent to which they are not just teaching lessons, but also engaging in complex practices of self-shaping. But this the philosophers have in common with religious and magical/superstitious movements of various types in their culture. Many people purveyed a *biou technē*, an "art of life." What is distinctive about the contribution of the philosophers is that they assert that *philosophy*, and not anything else, is the art we require, an art that deals in valid and sound arguments, an art that is committed to the truth. These philosophers claim that the pursuit of logical validity, intellectual coherence, and truth delivers freedom from the tyranny of custom and convention, creating a community of beings who can take charge of their own life story and their own thought. (Skepticism is in some ways an exception, as we shall see; but even Skeptics rely heavily on reason and argument, in a way other popular "arts" do not.) It is questionable whether Foucault can even admit the possibility of such a community of freedom, given his view that knowledge and argument are themselves tools of power. In any case, his work on this period, challenging though it is, fails to confront the fundamental commitment to reason that divides philosophical *techniques du soi* from other such techniques. Perhaps that commitment is an illusion. I believe that it is not. And I am sure that Foucault has not shown that it is. In any case, this book will take that commitment as its focus, and try to ask why it should have been thought that the philosophical use of reason is the technique by which we can be truly free and truly flourishing.

Writing about this historical period raises difficult organizational questions. The greatest problem for an author who gives an account of Hellenistic practical argument is one of scope. Hellenistic philosophy is hard to study partly on account of its success. The teachings of the major schools, beginning in the late fourth century B.C.E. at Athens, have a continuous history of dissemination and elaboration until (at least) the early centuries C.E. at Rome, where some of the most valuable writings in these traditions are produced and where philosophy exerts an enormous influence on the literary and the political culture. This means that one must deal, in effect, with six centuries and two different societies. One cannot deal exhaustively with all the relevant material, copious and heterogeneous as it is. Any treatment must be a sampling. This, then, will not even attempt to be the entire story of Hellenistic ethical thought; nor will it be a highly systematic selective outline. Instead, it will be a somewhat idiosyncratic account of certain central themes, guided by an obsessive pursuit of certain questions—taking as its central guiding motif the analogy between philosophy and medicine as arts of life.

Even with respect to these questions, it is difficult to find principles of selection. If the major works of Greek Hellenistic philosophers such as Epicurus, Zeno, and Chrysippus had survived, one might decide to limit such a study to the Greek beginnings of the schools, thus to a single culture and period. But the evidence does not permit this. From the vast output of these enormously prolific philosophers, only fragments and reports survive for the Stoics and, for Epicurus, only fragments and reports plus three brief letters summarizing his major teachings, and two collections of maxims. For the arguments of the Skeptics, we are almost entirely dependent on sources much later than the school's beginnings—Diogenes Laertius' *Life of Pyrrho*, and the works of Sextus Empiricus. There is, of course, ample later evidence about the Greek sources; there are also whole original works of Epicurean and Stoic and Skeptic thought from a later period (above all from Rome). The lack of coincidence between early date and textual wholeness makes the task of selection difficult.

But when one turns to later sources, especially to Roman sources, it does not seem sufficient simply to raid them for evidence toward the reconstruction of the Greek sources, as is frequently done. One must face the fact that these Roman philosophical works—works such as the *De Rerum Natura* of Lucretius and the dialogues, letters, and tragedies of Seneca—are themselves complex philosophical and literary wholes, whose practice of "therapeutic argument" cannot be well understood without attending to their overall literary and rhetorical structure, their characteristic patterns of language, their allusions to other literary and philosophical texts. And this is not all: one must attend to their Romanness. For Roman philosophy pursues its questions about the relation of theory to practice while standing in an intimate relation to Roman history and politics. Roman therapeutic argument is more than incidentally the therapy of Romans and of Rome; one cannot completely understand its operations without understanding, as well, the character of the implied interlocutors—of Memmius in Lucretius, of figures such as Lucilius and Novatus in the works of Seneca, and, in all such works, of the implied Roman reader. This means understanding as much as one can of the relevant aspects of Roman literary, political, and social history, of the nuances of the Latin language, as it both translates Greek philosophical terms and alludes to its own literary traditions, and, finally, of specifically Roman attitudes to ethical and social questions. Roman Epicureans and Stoics are Epicureans and Stoics; and as Epicureans and Stoics they are concerned with what they believe to be aspects of our common humanity, as each school understands it. But as Epicureans and Stoics they also believe that good philosophical argument must be searchingly personal, bringing to light and then treating the beliefs that the interlocutor has acquired from acculturation and teaching, including many that are so deeply internalized that they are hidden from view. Many such acquired beliefs are specific to the society in question; so good Roman Epicurean or Stoic philosophy must at the same time be a searching critical inquiry into Roman traditions.

Frequently philosophical scholars neglect this contextual material, producing a picture of Hellenistic ethics as a timeless whole. Typically such approaches will use the Latin texts only as source material for the Greek Hellenistic thinkers, disregarding their specifically Roman literary and social features and the shape of the literary wholes in which the philosophical material is embedded. This book, by contrast, is committed to studying the philosophical arguments in their historical and literary context. Indeed, I shall argue that Hellenistic therapeutic argument is, by design, so context-dependent that it can be fully understood in no other way—even, and especially, when we are trying to understand aspects of human life that are of continuing interest and urgency to us. (This does not imply that there are no transcontextual ethical truths to be unearthed by such a study, as we shall see.) On the other hand, I am aware that to study all of these contextual features completely, in the case of each of the relevant texts and authors, would be the undertaking of several lifetimes, not of a single book. Nor can I achieve complete coverage by limiting my inquiry to a single author, or even a single school; the questions I want to ask require comparing the techniques and insights of the three schools. To make matters more complex still, my own preference for whole texts whose literary form can be analyzed as a part of its argument has drawn me more and more to Roman sources as my work has progressed.

I have therefore found no easy solution to the problems of chronological and cultural range, apart from that of selecting certain topics for discussion and not others, certain works of a given author rather than others—and, in general, focusing on Lucretius and Seneca more than on Cicero, Epictetus, or Marcus. I have begun by limiting my focus to the three major schools in their more or less central and orthodox development, using Aristotle's ethical thought as a background and a foil. I have omitted eclectic schools and the later versions of Aristotelianism. A more problematic omission is that of the Cynics, practioners of a quasi-philosophical form of life that challenged public conventions of propriety as well as intellectual conventions of appropriate argument. The Cynics are certainly important in some way in the history of the idea of philosophical therapy; and the reader of Diogenes Laertius' life of Diogenes the Cynic will find them fascinating figures. On the other hand, there is, I believe, far too little known about them and their influence, and even about whether they offered arguments at all, for a focus on them to be anything but a scholarly quagmire in a book of this type. With some regret, then, I leave them at the periphery.

In the case of each school, I have tried to give some idea of its Greek origins, as well as its Roman continuations. Thus I try to reconstruct the Epicurean practice of therapeutic argument, and to examine Epicurus' own attitudes to fear, love, and anger, before dwelling on the analogous aspects of Lucretius' poem and its therapeutic design. And I attempt to reconstruct Chrysippus' own theory of the passions (concerning which, fortunately, we have an unusually large amount of information) before examining its development in Seneca's therapy of anger and its ambivalent treatment in Senecan tragedy. In each case I have tried to mention at least those portions of the cultural context that seem the most relevant. Although I offer no systematic account of the history of rhetorical practices—again, an undertaking that would require another book—I do consider some portions of

Aristotle's *Rhetoric* in detail, and I attend closely to the rhetoric of particular philosophical arguments. Where my account has gaps, I hope that there is sufficient methodological frankness that the gaps themselves will be visible, in such a way that they can be filled in by others.

At the very least, I hope to have shown—by the incompleteness of my account as much as by what it does succeed in doing—how hard and yet how exciting it is to study the history of ethics in this period, when one understands it not simply as the history of arguments, but also as the history of practices of argumentation and psychological interaction aimed at personal and societal change.

Writing this book has also posed some delicate philosophical problems, which it is best to mention at the start. I undertook this project to get a better understanding of an aspect of Hellenistic philosophy that I enthusiastically endorse—its practical commitment, its combination of logic with compassion. This commitment is to some extent bound up with a more problematic aspect of Hellenistic thought, namely, its advocacy of various types of detachment and freedom from disturbance. The two commitments seem to me to be, in principle, independent of one another; and to some extent this is so also in practice. But it is also plain that one cannot go far in understanding these accounts of philosophical therapy without grappling with the normative arguments for detachment.

When one does grapple with them one finds, I think, three things. First, one finds that to a certain extent the radical social criticism of the Hellenistic philosophers does indeed require them to mistrust the passions: not, that is, to take passion-based intuitions as an ethical bedrock, immune from rational criticism. If passions are formed (at least in part) out of beliefs or judgments, and if socially taught beliefs are frequently unreliable, then passions need to be scrutinized in just the way in which other socially taught beliefs are scrutinized. But this seems to be a wise policy from the point of view of any philosophical view (including Aristotle's) that holds that some ethical beliefs and preferences are more reliable than others.

Second, it becomes clear that at least some of the arguments that Epicureans and Stoics give for radically cutting back the passions are powerful arguments, even to someone who is antecedently convinced of their worth. In particular, their arguments against anger, and their further arguments connecting passions such as love and grief with the possibility of destructive anger, seem unavoidably strong. It is relatively easy to accept the conclusion that in living a life with deep attachments one runs a risk of loss and suffering. But according to Hellenistic arguments that risk is also a risk of evil: at the very least, of corruption of the inner world by the desire to harm. Confronting these arguments should occasion anxiety for any defender of the emotions. This book investigates that anxiety.

Finally, however, one finds in at least some of the Hellenistic texts themselves—especially in Lucretius and Seneca—a greater ambivalence than is at first apparent about the emotions and the attachments that are their basis. Epicurus' commitment to invulnerability is qualified already by the central role he gives friendship. In Lucretius, commitments to the world extend more widely, including, it seems, not only friendship but also the love of spouse and children and city or country. This leads to a complex position, where love, fear, and even anger are concerned. The position of Stoicism is apparently simpler. But Seneca qualifies his anti-passion view in some ways even in his dialogues and letters; and in his tragedies, I believe, one sees a deeper ambivalence, as Stoicism confronts traditional Roman norms of worldly effort and daring. These complexities should be recognized in any critique of Hellenistic norms of self-sufficiency.

Further difficulties are raised by the role of politics in Hellenistic thought. The major Hellenistic schools are all highly critical of society as they find it; and all are concerned to bring the necessary conditions of the good human life to those whom society has caused to suffer. They are, moreover, far more inclusive and less elitist in their practice of philosophy than was Aristotle, far more concerned to show that their strategies can offer something to each and every human being, regardless of class or status or gender. On the other hand, the way they do this has little to do, on the whole, with political, institutional, or material change. Instead of arranging to bring the good things of this world to each and every human being, they focus on changes of belief and desire that make their pupil less dependent on the good things of this world. They do not so much show ways of removing injustice as teach the pupil to be indifferent to the injustice she suffers.

Aristotelianism sets exacting worldly conditions for the good life, making virtuous activity dependent in many ways upon material and educational conditions that are beyond the individual's control. But Aristotle then assigns to politics the task of bringing those conditions to people: the good political arrangement is the one "in accordance with which each and every one might do well and lead a flourishing life" (*Pol.* 1324a23–25). Don't the Hellenistic schools, by contrast, promote what is claimed to be well-being by simply lowering people's sights, denying that material conditions have importance, and renouncing the political work that might effect a broader distribution of these conditions? Epicurus urged a complete withdrawal from the life of the city, Skeptics an uncritical obedience to forces of existing convention. Even among the Stoics, whose commitment to the intrinsic value of justice is plain, we hear less about how to alter the political fact of slavery than about how to be truly free within, even though one may be (politically) a slave; less about strategies for the removal of hunger and thirst than about the unimportance of these bodily goods in a wise life; less about how to modify existing class structures and the economic relations that (as Aristotle argued) explain them, than about the wise person's indifference to such worldly distinctions. In all three schools, the truly good and virtuous person is held to be radically independent of material and economic factors: achieving one's full humanity requires only inner change. But isn't this in fact false? Isn't the inner world itself at least in part a function of social and material conditions? And doesn't the failure to consider this diminish the interest of Hellenistic arguments for contemporary thought? (Consider, in this connection, Marx's shift of allegiance from Epicurus, the topic of his doctoral dissertation, to Aristotle, the classical mentor of his mature work, once the importance of class analysis and of the material conditions of human flourishing became plain to him.)

I shall conclude that this criticism has some merit. But the simple constrast I have just drawn, between material/institutional change and inner change of belief and desire, is too crude to tell the whole story about the relationship between Aristotle and his Hellenistic successors. For in fact both Aristotle and the Hellenistic thinkers insist that human flourishing cannot be achieved unless desire and thought, as they are usually constructed within society, are considerably transformed. (Both hold, for example, that most people learn to value money and status far too highly, and that this corrupts both personal and social relations.) Nor does the more insistent and elaborate attention to such inner changes in the Hellenistic schools seem inappropriate, given their powerful diagnosis of the depth of the problems. Any viable political approach—now as then—must also be concerned, as they are, with the criticism, and the shaping, of evaluative thought and preferences.

Furthermore, the Hellenistic focus on the inner world does not exclude, but in fact leads directly to, a focus on the ills of society. One of the most impressive achievements of Hellenistic philosophy is to have shown compellingly and in detail how specific social conditions shape emotion, desire, and thought. Having shown this, and having argued that desire and thought, as they are currently constructed, are deformed, these philosophers naturally concern themselves with the social structures through which these elements have been shaped, and with their reformation. Above all—like Aristotle, but with more detailed arguments—they are preoccupied with education. Their philosophical therapies both describe and model a new approach to the design of educational practices; and in their representation of the relation between teacher and pupil, they represent, as well, an ideal of community. Here, at least, they appear to achieve an egalitarian result that would have been unachievable in the world around them.

In other respects as well, they reshape social institutions that seem to them to impede human flourishing. Epicurus and Lucretius conduct a radical assault on conventional religion; Lucretius reconstructs social practices in the areas of love, marriage, and child-rearing. Since their arguments claim to be not only correct but also causally effective, they claim to contribute to the revolution they describe. In the Greek Stoics we find ideal political theory that attempts to eliminate differences of gender and class, and even to do away with the moral salience of local and national boundaries. In the Roman Stoics—along with several different types of political theory, both monarchical and republican (the latter very influential in practice, both at Rome itself and in much later republican revolutions)— we find arguments that confront entrenched political realities with bold criticisms, on the topics of slavery, gender relations, ethnic toleration, the concept of citizenship itself. The idea of universal respect for the dignity of humanity in each and every person, regardless of class, gender, race, and nation—an idea that has ever since been at the heart of all distinguished political thought in the Western tradition—is, in origin, a Stoic idea. The relationship of this idea to Stoic detachment needs close scrutiny. But in the meantime, we can say that to study the inner world and its relationship to social conditions is at least a necessary, if not a sufficient, task for a political philosophy that aims to be practical. Hellenistic philosophy gives us distinguished help with that task.

Therapeutic Arguments

I

Epicurus wrote, "Empty is that philosopher's argument by which no human suffering is therapeutically treated. For just as there is no use in a medical art that does not cast out the sicknesses of bodies, so too there is no use in philosophy, unless it casts out the suffering of the soul."[1] The ancient Skeptical teacher, too, portrays himself as a healer of the soul:[2] "Being a lover of humanity, the Skeptic wishes to heal by argument, insofar as possible, the arrogant empty beliefs and the rashness of dogmatic people." As a doctor tries out different remedies on the ailing body and uses the ones that work, so the Skeptic selects, for each pupil, the arguments that are most appropriate and most efficacious for that person's disease (Sextus *PH* 3.280–81). The Stoics vigorously endorse this picture of philosophy and develop the analogy between philosophy and medicine in elaborate detail. The great Greek Stoic Chrysippus, describing his philosophical art, proudly announces:

> It is not true that there exists an art called medicine, concerned with the diseased body, but no corresponding art concerned with the diseased soul.

[1] Epicurus Us. 221 = Porph. *Ad Marc.* 31, p. 209, 23 N: see chapter 4. All translations are my own unless otherwise attributed. On the translation of *pathos* as "suffering" here, see chapter 4, n. 1. "Argument" translates *logos*, which, of course, is a more general term that can also mean "discourse," "speech," "account"—see chapter 2. Chapter 4 shows that Epicurus does indeed focus on argument, basing his therapy on a type of *logos* by then standard in the philosophical tradition. But since his therapeutic discourse is multifaceted, including some techniques not standardly called arguments, it is also possible that a more general reference to therapeutic philosophical discourse is intended here. I have avoided the translation "discourse" largely because it has become an overused term of art in contemporary literary theory and culture studies.

[2] The word "soul," here and elsewhere, simply translates Greek *psuchē*, and, like that term, does not imply any particular metaphysical theory of the personality. It stands, simply, for all the life-activities of the creature; in the case of Hellenistic contrasts between body and *psuchē*, it is especially important to insist that no denial of physicalism need be involved, since both Epicureans and Stoics are physicalists. The contrast is simply between the material constituents of the organism and its life-activities, its states of awareness, and so forth.

Nor is it true that the latter is inferior to the former, in its theoretical grasp and therapeutic treatment of individual cases. (Galen *PHP* 5.2.22, 298D = *SVF* III.471)

Or as Cicero, speaking on behalf of the Stoa, more succinctly puts it:

There is, I assure you, a medical art for the soul. It is philosophy, whose aid need not be sought, as in bodily diseases, from outside ourselves. We must endeavor with all our resources and all our strength to become capable of doctoring ourselves. (*TD* 3.6)

Philosophy heals human diseases, diseases produced by false beliefs. Its arguments are to the soul as the doctor's remedies are to the body. They can heal, and they are to be evaluated in terms of their power to heal. As the medical art makes progress on behalf of the suffering body, so philosophy for the soul in distress. Correctly understood, it is no less than the soul's art of life (*technē biou*). This general picture of philosophy's task is common to all three major Hellenistic schools, at both Greece and Rome.[3] All accept the appropriateness of an analogy between philosophy and the art of medicine. And for all, the medical analogy is not simply a decorative metaphor; it is an important tool both of discovery and of justification. Once one has in a general way understood that philosophy's task is like the doctor's task, one can then rely on that general understanding (further elaborated in a number of general criteria) to find out, more concretely and in greater detail, how the philosopher ought to proceed in a variety of circumstances.[4] And one can appeal to the analogy to justify some new or dubious procedure as philosophically appropriate. The rival schools debate with one another in terms organized by the analogy, commending themselves to prospective pupils as doctors belonging to rival schools of medicine would debate, proclaiming the merits of their differing conceptions of the art. As such debates developed, the analogy became both more complex and more concrete. Specific strategies of the doctor were compared with specific philosophical techniques. And the analogy also generated an increasingly rich enumeration of characteristics that a good "therapeutic argument" should have, traits whose importance could be shown by pointing to the presence, and the importance, of analogous traits in medical procedure.

[3] The Skeptics, strictly speaking, reject the idea that philosophy can be a *technē* of life; on the other hand, they teach strategies of reasoning, and appear to claim that these have causal efficacy toward the good human life. This issue will be investigated in chapter 8.

[4] Of course there are also different schools of medicine; and for the Skeptics especially, distinctions among them will be important in delineating their conception of philosophy.

In short, there is in this period broad and deep agreement that the central motivation for philosophizing is the urgency of human suffering, and that the goal of philosophy is human flourishing, or *eudaimonia*.[5] Philosophy never ceases to be understood as an art whose tools are arguments, an art in which precise reasoning, logical rigor, and definitional precision have an important role to play. But the point of these devices, and of philosophy insofar as it is wedded to them, is understood to be, above all, the achievement of flourishing human lives. And the evaluation of any particular argument must concern itself not only with logical form and the truth of premises, but also with the argument's suitability for the specific maladies of its addressees. I am speaking here above all of ethical arguments; and the schools differ in the ways in which they connect the ethical part of philosophy to its other parts. For Epicureans and Skeptics, the ethical end (the achievement of a certain sort of life) is central in a more obvious way than for the Stoics. But for all three, philosophy is above all the art of human life; and engagement in it that is not properly anchored to the business of living well is regarded as empty and vain.

All three schools, in short, could accept the Epicurean definition of philosophy: "Philosophy is an activity that secures the flourishing [*eudaimōn*] life by arguments and reasonings."[6] And all can agree that a precise, logically rigorous argument that is not well suited to the needs of its hearers, an argument that is simply and entirely academic and unable to engage its audience in a practical way, is to that extent a *defective philosophical argument*. Cicero marvelously expresses this point in the *De Finibus*, criticizing the Stoics for failing, as he believes, in this essential dimension of their job:

> Their narrow little syllogistic arguments prick their hearers like pins. Even
> if they assent intellectually, they are in no way changed in their hearts, but

---

[5] *Eudaimonia* is often rendered "happiness": but this is misleading, since it misses the emphasis on *activity*, and on completeness of life, that is (as Aristotle cogently argues) present in the ordinary use of the Greek term, and wrongly suggests that what is at issue must be a state or a feeling of satisfaction. (Pre-Utilitarian English-language uses of "happiness" had much of this breadth; but in our time the word is unavoidably colored by Utilitarian associations.) One may *argue* that *eudaimonia* is a state or a feeling; and we shall see examples of this. But this is in no way implied in the term itself, and, in fact, it appears that the term as generally used connotes being active: it seems counterintuitive to argue that a non-active state can be equivalent to *eudaimonia*. I shall therefore usually either transliterate the term or use the cumbersome "human flourishing."

[6] Sextus *M* 11.169 = Us. 219. This should not be taken to imply that philosophy is merely instrumental toward a goal that could be completely specified without mention of its activities.

15

they go away in the same condition in which they came. The subject matter is perhaps true and certainly important; but the arguments treat it in too petty a manner, and not as it deserves. (*Fin.* 4.7)[7]

This chapter will characterize Hellenistic therapeutic arguments in a general way, contrasting this approach to ethical philosophizing with other approaches available then and now. I shall propose a schematic account of the properties of a "medical" argument that can be used later on to investigate the particular schools, charting their similarities and divergences. Since Hellenistic therapy is above all therapy concerned with desire and emotion, I shall introduce that topic as well, describing a view all the schools share about the emotions and philosophy's relation to them. Finally, I shall provide a brief overview of the book's argument.

II

The medical model of philosophizing in ethics can be better understood by contrasting it with two other approaches to ethics that were available in ancient Greece: what I shall call the Platonic approach, and what I shall call the approach based on ordinary belief. The former bears some relation to some elements in some arguments of Plato, and I shall in fact illustrate it using a Platonic text. Whether or not it was actually Plato's approach, he was read this way by Aristotle and by others. The latter has sometimes been ascribed to Aristotle, and it does bear some resemblance to some elements in his approach. But the positions of both of these thinkers are subtle and complicated; it is not my intention to suggest that these rather schematic descriptions accurately portray those subtleties. (Indeed, in the case of Aristotle, I shall be arguing that the simple ordinary-belief picture is *not* an accurate characterization of his method.) It is sufficient for my purposes if we can show that these approaches were available in some form in the ancient world—at least as elements in, or simplifications or exaggerations or misunderstandings of, something that was really there. Both approaches are in fact available in modern moral philosophy as well: so a consideration of them will have the additional value of clarifying, for us, the place of the medical model among our actual alternatives.[8]

---

[7] It is difficult to tell how accurate these criticisms of the Greek Stoics are, since we possess so few of their actual words, and the evidence about their use of style is contradictory (see chapters 9, 10, 12). Certainly they were highly concerned with practical efficacy. And the Roman Stoics clearly are not vulnerable to the charge.

[8] I shall not deny, but shall strongly assert, that the medical model in ethics was closely

Consider, then, the picture of ethical inquiry in the central myth in Plato's *Phaedrus*. Souls of many kinds, some mortal and some divine, some with ease and some with difficulty, leave their usual world, their daily pursuits, and walk out to the rim of heaven. There, staring out at the eternal beings that inhabit that "realm above the heavens," they see (some more, some less) the eternal norms that are the true standards for the various ethical virtues. The soul "sees justice itself, it sees moderation, it sees knowledge—not the knowledge that changes and varies with the various objects that we now call beings, but the genuine knowledge seated in that which really is" (247D). In other words, the ethical norms are what they are quite independently of human beings, human ways of life, human desires. Any connection between our interests and the true good is, then, purely contingent. The good is out there; indeed, it has always been out there, even before we began to exist. And no wishing of ours, however profound or urgent, can make it be otherwise. It is not made for us, nor are we made for it.[9] The best life might turn out to be a life that none of us could attain, or even one that none of us could grasp or envisage. (This is in fact the case for most animals—who, unfortunately for them, have the very same standard of good set before them but are too dense to perceive it.) Or, again, it might turn out to be a life that is so out of line with all actual human ways of life, and with all actual human desires, that human beings as they are would find it repugnant, or base, or so boring or impoverished that they would die rather than live it. Such results would indeed be un-lucky for human beings; but they would not constitute any reason to call the account of the good itself into question. It happens that we (or some of us, some of the time) can grasp the true good that is "out there" and, having grasped it, live by it. But we might have been otherwise. Animals are otherwise. And the good—for human beings, for animals, for the universe as a whole—would still have been the same.

Views with this general structure enter the contemporary ethical scene by two very different routes, one scientific, one religious. (Both versions are

---

bound up with the particular cultural and historical circumstances in which philosophy was practiced in the Hellenistic and Roman worlds. Nonetheless, the model itself has a very helpful way of balancing interest in common human problems with attention to concrete context, which we may follow ourselves in order to understand how its contributions may prove illuminating for us in our own contemporary circumstances.

[9] Again, if we put this together with other parts of Plato's writings, we may decide that this simple interpretation is an exaggeration of Plato's actual view. Recollection is not always described as it is in the *Phaedrus*, as purely contingent on some events prior to incarnation that might have been otherwise; and the account of creation in the *Timaeus* implies that our structure is not just contingently related to the structure of the forms—though necessity, as well as intelligence, governs our making.

influenced by Platonism, in different ways.)[10] The scientific version thinks of ethical inquiry as similar to inquiry in the physical sciences—where this is understood in a Platonic way that has by now become deeply entrenched in popular thought about science, if not in the more sophisticated accounts given by contemporary philosophers of science. In this picture, scientists studying nature inquire in a "pure" manner, undisturbed and uninfluenced by their cultural framework, their background beliefs, their wishes and interests. Their task is to walk up to the world of nature (as Plato's souls walk to the rim of heaven), to look at it, and to describe it as it is, discovering its real permanent structure. Their inquiry might lead anywhere at all; it is constrained only by the way things really are "out there." A certain physical theory will be either supported or not supported by the facts. The desires, beliefs, and ways of life of physical scientists—or, indeed, of human beings more generally—must not be permitted to influence their inquiry into its status or their choice of methods of investigation. The idea is that ethics, too, is scientific in just this way. Ethical inquiry consists in discovering permanent truths about values and norms, truths that are what they are independently of what we are, or want, or do. They are set in the fabric of things, and we simply have to find them.[11] (In some variants of this approach, as in contemporary sociobiology, the relation to science is more than analogical: value-neutral discoveries in the sciences are seen to imply ethical norms. This is not the case in the Platonic view I have described, where the fact-value distinction plays no role and the independent norms are norms of value.)

We get a similar picture by a different route in the Augustinian version of Christian ethics. God has set up certain ethical standards; it is our job to do what God wants. But we may or may not be endowed with the capability of seeing, or wanting, what God wants. Truth and God's grace are out there; but the ability to see ethical truth or to reach for grace is not something we can control.[12] There is, therefore, no reliable method by which we can construct an ethical norm from the scrutiny of our deepest needs and responses and desires. For it may perfectly well turn out that a truly good

[10] Nietzsche, for one, saw this connection very clearly: see, for example, "How the True World Finally Became a Fable," in *Twilight of the Idols* (Nietzsche 1888).

[11] For one account of such a view, see Rawls (1980) 518, 554ff., and also Rawls (1971) 48–53. Rawls, of course, does not accept this view: see subsequent discussion.

[12] This does not seem to be the position of the earliest postconversion works, such as *De Genesi Contra Manichaeos* and *De Quantitate Animae*; but it is powerfully developed in *Ad Simplicianum de Diversis Quaestionibus*, and predominates in the *Confessions* and also, it seems, in the *City of God*.

life is so far removed from our present condition and insights that it will indeed strike us as repugnant, or boring, or too impoverished to make life worth living. Here we find ourselves in a far more helpless position than in the scientific, or even the original Platonist, picture. For it is not terribly clear how we can inquire further, or do anything about our cognitive predicament. But the central structural idea remains: the idea of the radical independence of true good from human need and desire. For both Platonists and these Christians, digging more deeply into ourselves is not the right way to proceed in ethical inquiry. For the possibility must always be left open that everything we are and want and believe is totally in error.

This is a powerful picture of ethical inquiry and ethical truth, one that has deep roots in our philosophical and religious traditions. It was known already to the Hellenistic thinkers, through their contact with Platonism. And it is a picture that they want to subvert, with the help of the medical analogy. Consider now a medical inquiry conducted on the rim of the heavens by pure souls, without any knowledge of the feelings, needs, pleasures, and pains of actual living creatures. (Or, if they have such knowledge, they are determined not to be constrained by it.) Think of these heavenly doctors trying to come up with an account of health and the healthy life, independently of any experience they may have of the desires and ways of life of the creatures they are going to treat. They do concede that to *apply* these norms to a group of patients, they will need to know something about their current state. For they cannot treat a disease without recognizing its symptoms and measuring these against their paradigm account of health. What they deny, however, is that the norm of health itself derives in any way from the condition, or the wishes, of the patient. It is "out there" to be discovered and then applied to their case.

These doctors would probably turn out to be very poor doctors indeed. Heavenly physics seems at least initially plausible. But medicine seems to be in its nature an engaged, immersed art, an art that works in a pragmatic partnership with those it treats. It takes very seriously their pains and pleasures, their own sense of where health and flourishing lie. Its aim is to help; that aim can never be completely separated from the patient's own sense of the better and worse. Suppose our heavenly doctor comes down from the rim of heaven and announces, "See this condition of body that you, poor old woman, find intolerably painful and crippling? Well, that's an example of what health is, as I have discovered by consulting the sort of knowledge that resides in true being. You children there: you say that you are hungry; you cry. But that too is health; and you will be making cognitive progress if you learn to see things this way, and accept the wisdom of the universe." Our first reaction it that this "doctor" is sadistic and callous. Our second, however, is that he (or she) cannot be right. These statements are not just brutal, they are false. Health does not have an existence up there in heaven, totally apart from people and their lives. It is not a pure being apart from the patient's becoming. It is a constituent of the form of life of a living species; and it is to the form of life of the species, and the experiences involved in living it, that the doctor must look in constructing a norm.

People can indeed go wrong about their health, in many ways. They can think that they are doing well, when really they are not. This may be because they have an illness that has not yet manifested itself through perceptible symptoms. Or it may be because they have no experience of feeling any better than they now feel—as happens, for example, in pervasive and long-term malnutrition. It may also be because entrenched cultural traditions have convinced them that certain states of weakness that might appear to be ill health for some are just fine, really, *for them*, the best they should look for; this happens frequently, for example, in societies with different standards of flourishing for males and for females.[13] People can also, though less frequently, believe that they are doing badly when they are really doing well. But the sense of any claim that people have gone wrong in one of these ways must be made out in terms of the needs and perceptions of the people themselves. Usually what such a claim means is that the scientist or doctor could show them something about their condition that would convince them that their initial judgment had been wrong, were they to listen and eventually to understand—convince them in terms of some notion of human activity that they share with the scientist, however vaguely they may grasp and articulate it. The person with the asymptomatic illness is shown evidence of her current condition and of the debilitating (and perceptible) consequences to which it can be expected to lead. The malnourished person can be given adequate nutrition (if it is not too late) and can be expected, later on, to compare her later state favorably with her earlier one, recognizing in retrospect the evidence of disease. The person who believes that her condition is just fine for people like her (of her gender, or class, or whatever) will be harder to reach with the evidence. But a combination of medical evidence of the sort produced in our first case with the presentation of comparisons from other cultures (and other individuals in her own), showing, for example, that females are not in general shorter-lived than males, or deficient in stamina—and a combination of both of

[13] See Sen (1985), Drèze and Sen (1989).

20

these, if possible, with the experiential comparisons made possible through some change in the patient's own condition—can be expected, if the claim is a correct one, to elicit from the patient herself a judgment critical of tradition and supportive of the doctor's hypothesis. A recent comparative survey of Indian widows and widowers established that the widows almost always described their health status as "good" or "excellent," even though, from the medical point of view, they were doing rather badly by comparison with the males (who tended to report numerous complaints and to rank their status rather low). Ten years later a similar survey found no significant change in the women's actual health status. But their perceptions of health deficiencies had improved, as a result of education and public information. Now they perceived more nearly what the doctor did, and understood that there was an available norm vis-à-vis which their own condition was seriously deficient.[14]

This, then, is the way in which finding truth in medicine seems to be unlike finding truth in (our simple and schematic picture of) physical science. The patient is essential in the medical case in a way that no human being or human practice seems to be essential in the physical case. Not all actual patients will be convinced by the medical truth about their case: for, as we have suggested, there are frequently powerful obstacles to the perception of such truths. But for it to *be* medical truth, it seems to be necessary, at least, that patients who are adequately informed and attentive, who have the requisite experience of alternatives and have been allowed to scrutinize the alternatives in the right way, should be convinced. This does not mean that the doctor cannot alter people's ideas concerning what health *is*, at the level of more concrete specification. In fact one of her main tasks will frequently be to produce a concrete account of the vague end of health, enumerating its elements. This specification may well clash to some extent with the patient's own prereflective specification—as when, in our example, the Indian widows learn that norms of mobility and stamina for women their age elsewhere in the world are very different from what they have come to expect from themselves. But the challenge of medicine is always to make connection with people's deepest desires and needs and their sense of what has importance. It must deliver to them a life that they will in the end accept as an improvement, or it cannot claim success.

So much, the medical analogy claims, is true of ethics. We do not inquire into the human good by standing on the rim of heaven; and if we did, we would not find the right thing. Human ways of life, and the hopes, plea-

---

[14] See Sen (1985).

sures, and pains that are a part of these, cannot be left out of the inquiry without making it pointless and incoherent. We do not in fact look "out there" for ethical truth; it is in and of our human lives. More than this, it is something *to* and *for* human lives. As in the case of health, what we are looking for is something that we are trying to bring about in human life, something essentially practical, whose point is living and living well. This something is unlikely to be grasped if we detach ourselves completely from our wishes and needs and aims; an intelligent god might not be able to find it. It must be found, if at all, from within ourselves and one another, as what answers to the deepest aspirations and wishes we have for ourselves and for one another. And it is justified as correct by pointing to the fact that it does so answer. As in the medical case, a view of the good human life that seems to human beings, on reflection, to deliver a life that would be extremely painful, or impoverished, or meaningless, not worth the choosing or the living, will be rightly rejected, and rejected not just as difficult to realize, but *as false*. Just as an intolerably crippling condition of body cannot be *what health is*, so an unacceptably monotonous or impoverished or painful way of life cannot be *what the good human life is*.

Are we, then, entitled to speak of truth here? A Platonist might say that we are not. And at least one prominent modern proponent of an account of ethical inquiry that has similar pragmatic elements has concluded that we must jettison the notion of truth in ethics, once we adopt such an account. John Rawls, both in *A Theory of Justice* and *Kantian Constructivism in Moral Theory*, argues that ethical theorizing is essentially a practical matter, a matter not of discovering something that is fixed independently of our wishes, but a matter of constructing a view that we can live by together, a view that answers better than others to our deepest needs and beliefs and desires, once these have been sorted out by a process of reflective scrutiny.[15] But because Rawls is deeply impressed by the contrast this suggests between ethics and physics (which he understands along Platonist lines), he concludes that the notion of truth can be appropriate only in an inquiry that is a search for the nature of an altogether independent reality. Ethical theories, lacking such an independent goal, cannot claim to embody truth.

Both Aristotle and the Hellenistic philosophers (Skeptics always excepted) do claim to pursue and to state truth, even though they also explicitly conceive of ethics along pragmatic "medical" lines. One of my purposes in several chapters will be to ask on what basis and with how much justifica-

---

[15] Rawls (1980) 554ff., Rawls (1971) 48–53. For a contrasting view of the science-ethics distinction, see H. Putnam (1993, and forthcoming).

tion they do so. But here, pursuing the claims of the medical analogy a little further in a proleptic way, I can at least begin to say why this might be a not altogether implausible idea. First of all, we should question the very strong contrast that Rawls draws between ethics and scientific inquiry. It is not clear that any inquiry really does what the Platonist account says physics does, discovering a reality whose structure is altogether independent of human theories and conceptions. Even Aristotelian truth in science may not be conception-independent, as I have argued. And contemporary philosophy of science has gone much further in this direction, finding subtle and impressive arguments against Platonist conceptions of scientific inquiry. But if no inquiry is entirely non-anthropocentric, a fortiori ethics is not either. In this sense, getting clear about the basis for science's claim to truth makes ethics look less disreputably different, makes it seem less peculiar that, speaking from within human life, it should claim truth.[16]

But the medical analogy claims more than this. It claims not only that ethical reality is not altogether independent of human theories and conceptions but also that ethical truth is not independent of what human beings deeply wish, need, and (at some level) desire—a claim that some might defend in physical science, but one that would be controversial there in a way that the analogous claim about medical science would not be. In this sense, even most non-realists in natural science still believe that the aim of science is to discover something—even if our theories play some role in demarcating what it is that can be discovered—while the aim of medicine is to bring something about for people, to answer to people's needs. And so the question still must be, What entitles an inquiry with this sort of practical goal, whose statements are constrained not only by human conceptions but also, in some way, by human desires, to speak of truth?

I can point, proleptically, to three considerations that support this claim. The first is an idea of internal consistency, the second an idea of (a carefully defined kind of) correspondence, the third an idea of broad coherence and fit. First, then, an ethics understood along medical lines still insists on systematizing and rendering consistent the intuitions and desires with which it begins. In fact, a large part of its activity consists in the scrutiny and sorting of beliefs toward the end of consistency. (We shall shortly see that the passions, on account of their propositional content, fall under this scrutiny and must be rendered consistent both with one another and with the patient's other beliefs.) By bringing to light the hidden contradictions and tensions in a system of beliefs (or, really, beliefs and cognitive pas-

---

[16] See H. Putnam (1981, 1993).

sions), a pragmatic medical ethics can claim to be doing something that is, at least, necessary in the search for truth, whether sufficient for it or not. Second, the aim in the end is, in fact, a kind of correspondence: a correspondence of the account produced with the deepest of human wishes and needs and desires—with "human nature," a normative yet empirical notion. It is no simple matter to find out what the deepest parts of ourselves are, or even to draw all the parts to the surface for scrutiny. Thus one can reasonably speak of a kind of discovery here: discovery of oneself, and of one's fellow citizens. And the accounts we are about to study claim that, in seeking correspondence between an ethical theory and the deepest levels of the patients' souls, we shall in fact (wherever and with whomever we begin) arrive at a single, if highly general, theory. So the idea of being constrained by what we discover enters in here, with as much power as it does in the scientific case, if not in the very same manner. Finally, all the theories we shall study (again, Skepticism excepted) insist that the ethical theories we discover must cohere with our best theories in other areas of inquiry— inquiries about nature, for example, about psychology, about the relationship between substance and matter. Thus the results of ethics, like medical results, are constrained not only by internal coherence and psychological correspondence, but also by this broader and more inclusive fit.[17]

III

The medical conception of ethical inquiry opposes itself, as well, to another conception of ethics that stands, so to speak, at the opposite end of the spectrum from Platonism. This is the idea that ethical inquiry and teaching are simply the recording of traditional social belief and have no legitimate goal beyond this. Ethics, in this view, begins from what we might call an assumptionn of social health, the assumption that for the most part people have been brought up to have true ethical beliefs and reliable intuitions, and that ordinary beliefs and intuitions can be treated as criterial of ethical truth and rightness. By asking people what they think or say about a case, or a range of cases, we get reliable data; the task of theory is then simply to find a general account that fits the data. There have been many versions of this idea in the ancient world and after. In one form, it has been

[17] The fit can constrain in both directions; it will be important to ask, in each case, what gives way to what. How far does natural philosophy reach its results independently of ethics, and then constrain ethics? How far, on the other hand, do ethical desiderata constrain natural philosophy?

ascribed to Aristotle—though too simply, as we shall see. Many ancient authors, such as orators and some poets, endorse it in their practice. It probably plays a major role in ancient moral education.[18] More recently, it is embedded in some parts of contemporary "ordinary language philosophy," insofar as that takes ordinary utterances as healthy and normative.[19] Its starting point, if not its end, is central to many forms of Utilitarianism. For while Utilitarianism has a controversial and in some ways counterintuitive account of our ethical end, in terms of the maximization of satisfactions, the material from which it starts is, in fact, the totality of the (expressed or otherwise revealed) desires and preferences of all the people concerned, regardless of the degree of scrutiny to which these preferences have been subjected. The health of these preferences seems to be taken for granted: all alike, they are treated as reliable indicators of where the good for persons lies.[20]

From the point of view of the medical model, clearly, such a picture is not altogether wrong. By looking at what people believe and say, we are looking in the right place.[21] But the medical account of ethics insists on a critical scrutiny of ordinary belief, and gives a place to expert judgment that is absent from simpler versions, at least, of the ordinary belief view. When a doctor examines a patient, she will to some extent trust what the patient says about her condition. But she will also look and see with her own experienced and expertly trained eye, which is likely to be in many respects better than the patient's eye. The patient may well miss something about her condition that the doctor will see; and though she plays a role in determining what condition is and is not health, she may not be able to

---

[18] Consider the portrait of old-time education in Aristophanes' *Clouds*, in the debate between the two *logoi*.

[19] But see Stanley Cavell's attempt to distinguish ordinary-language philosophy from the mere recording of conventions, in Cavell (1979). For an assumption of social health, see also Rawls (1971) 46: "Let us assume that each person beyond a certain age and possessed of the requisite intellectual capacity develops a sense of justice under normal social circumstances." Rawls, however, later denies that his own view of procedure is the ordinary-belief view: rather than "describing a person's sense of justice more or less as it is, although allowing for the smoothing out of certain irregularities," he will confront the person with challenging and possibly distant alternatives, with the result that "a person's sense of justice may or may not undergo a radical shift." This approximates to the distinction between the ordinary-belief view and the "medical" view, as I am trying to draw it here.

[20] Contemporary philosophical versions of Utilitarianism almost all introduce substantial qualifications here, recognizing that preferences formed under certain conditions are not reliable. Economic Utilitarianism usually takes a simpler view.

[21] See the related point about Utilitarianism made in Sen (1982).

articulate a norm of health in the detailed way the doctor can. Furthermore, as the Indian example showed, there may be deep and systematic obstacles to the patient's correct perception and description of her own condition.

This situation is even more acute, clearly, in an ethics modeled after medicine. When a doctor treats a patient, the patient's body is ill; but it is from the patient's beliefs, judgments, and desires that the account of the symptoms is elicited: and these are not the seat of the disease. Medical moral philosophy, by contrast, deals with people whose beliefs, desires, and preferences are themselves the problem. For according to the Hellenistic philosophers, society is not in order as it is; and, as the source of most of their pupils' beliefs and even of their emotional repertory, it has infected them with its sicknesses. The upbringing of young people is held to be deformed in various ways by false views about what matters: by excessive emphasis, for example, on money, competition, and status. These corruptions often go deep; and they will in this way influence any self-description the patient gives the teacher/doctor. Nor, since the diseases are internal, is there even the possibility of an independent examination by the physician: everything depends on the pupil's unreliable report. The philosophical doctor must, then, be even more skeptical than the medical doctor about any report made by the pupil based on her own immediate judgments and perceptions, knowing that the very same parts that produce the report are the ones that are, or may be, diseased. And yet how can the teacher know them, except by asking them to speak?

In many respects, the challenge undertaken by the medical model resembles the challenge confronting a psychologist who tries to deal with mental disturbance or disease. And as we shall see many of the concerns and even procedures of Hellenistic ethics anticipate those of modern psychoanalysis—but with one striking difference. Psychoanalysis has not always been willing to commit itself to a normative idea of health; it is frequently sufficient if the patient is relieved of certain obvious incapacities. The Hellenistic philosophers, by contrast, follow the analogy with physical health more strictly, insisting that they need to operate with a normative idea of the flourishing life that will not be immediately forthcoming from patients who are severely disturbed—even if this model also needs to be justified repeatedly by encounters with patients who will, after prolonged reflection, affirm it.

On the one hand, then, the medical model is committed to trusting the patient at some level: sooner or later, the philosopher hopes that all or most patients will assent to the diagnosis and participate willingly in the cure.

On the other hand, the fact that a corrupt and corrupting society may well have formed the patient's beliefs about the good life, and even about herself, makes it necessary for the philosopher not to be too quickly trusting. She will need to ask, and ask over a long period of time, which parts of the pupil are the healthy parts, the parts that should really be trusted. And frequently, in so doing, she may need to appeal to a normative picture of good ethical judgment, and of the healthy judge, whose procedures and verdicts will be exemplary for the pupil and will guide, at least tentatively, the way the inquiry goes. This judge is not like a Platonic authority, since he or she is a member of the patient's own human community, and is also supposed to represent an ideal of flourishing life to which the patient aspires, however unclearly.

All this suggests that the medical kind of ethics may be inclined—like medicine itself, but even more so—to adopt an asymmetrical model of the relationship between teacher and pupil, doctor and patient. Just as we do not expect a physical patient to be as well informed as the expert doctor about the diagnosis and treatment of her own disease, so too we do not expect the ethical pupil to be able to know her own situation as well as the teacher knows it. The teacher is talking *about her*: and what teaching claims to bring to light is material that, sooner or later, the pupil should be able to acknowledge, sharing the teacher's judgment. But the teacher cannot bring it to light simply by asking the pupil for an account of her current preferences and desires. She must (guided, it seems, by some sort of prima facie normative account) subject the pupil's own beliefs and preferences to searching critical scrutiny, not simply trusting either her general theoretical statements or her judgments about concrete cases.

To illustrate this point, let us return to our example of the Indian women and their incomplete perception of their health status. The medical inquiry did not in any way ignore their perceptions of their situation, their accounts of their pleasures and pains, their beliefs about how things were with them. Nor, however, did it simply trust their first answer to the question about their health. For there was reason to think that answer ill-informed, and biased by the inequities of their traditions. If no amount of further information about health had changed these women's initial perceptions, *and* if there was not ample evidence that women similarly situated in body but with fewer societal and informational impediments perceived things differently, the doctors would have had to begin questioning their prima facie normative judgment that the health status of these women was indeed defective. But making them aware of such facts did change their perceptions, although this was a slow and complex business.

Let us now imagine an analogous case in the ethical sphere. We do not have to go far to do so, for many such cases arise in connection with the same cultural problems. Similar groups of women in India, when polled by the government about whether they feel the need for more education, or believe that more education would be good for them, usually reply that they do not feel this need, or think education would add to their lives.[22] The Platonist I have imagined would think this reply completely irrelevant to the question about what the good for them *really is*. The ordinary-belief philosopher (and, in another way, the economic Utilitarian) would simply accept this preference as given and unassailable. The medical philosopher neither disregards it nor trusts it. Seeing how pervasive are the obstacles to adequate judgment and self-understanding, she would feel the need to engage the women in a more probing and extensive inquiry, confronting them with further information about education and employment, with pictures of alternative ways of life, and with the problematic features of their current situation. She would need to hear a lot about the shape of their deepest aspirations for themselves, encouraging them to consider these in the light of their new information. This may or may not be possible with actual groups of women, given their circumstances; so the philosopher's normative conclusion does not require universal acceptance in order to be regarded as a valid norm. (She cannot, however, wash her hands of the job of engaging their imaginations and their reasoning just because they do not wish to listen to a jargon-laden university lecture on ethics. Her job *as a philosopher*—as Cicero reminded the Stoics—is not simply to give lectures, but to speak to real people.) But the account, whether universally accepted or not, is in principle supposed to be an account of the judgment the pupil herself would give, were she to follow the appropriate critical procedures.

Hellenistic ethics combines immersion with critical distance in something like this way—insisting on the rigorous scrutiny of belief and desire, while insisting, too, that it is to real people and their beliefs and desires that ethics must ultimately be responsible. In order to begin sorting out what the pupil brings forward, it makes use of three closely related ideas, ideas that shape one another and are held together in the therapeutic investigative process:

1. A tentative diagnosis of disease, of the factors, especially socially taught beliefs, that are most prominent in preventing people from living well.

---

[22] For a valuable discussion of literacy debates, see Chen (1983); for a general discussion of perceptual deformations in gender hierarchy, see Sen (1985).

2. A tentative norm of health: a conception (usually general and to some degree open-ended) of the flourishing and complete human life.

3. A conception of proper philosophical method and procedure: what survives the type of scrutiny described in this conception has a prima facie claim to be the norm described in paragraph 2.

The philosophical views we shall investigate fashion comprehensive conceptions by linking these three elements. Each is to some extent independently discovered and supported; but they are also adjusted to one another's requirements, in order to form a coherent whole. The norm shapes and is shaped by the conception of what is disease and deficiency; and conceptions of rational procedure, though they have some independent warrant, are ratified, too, by the satisfactory shape of the results they deliver.

IV

In the course of developing their medical norms of health, the Hellenistic philosophers appeal to "nature" and the "natural." These slippery notions had better be scrutinized, since misunderstanding them could cause serious misunderstanding of the entire medical approach. Now very often the appeal to "nature" or "human nature" in moral philosophy has been bound up with some version of the Platonist/scientific idea: to base ethics on "nature" is to base our norms on an account of some way the world is without human intervention or shaping. This idea, in turn, comes in two forms. In one form, the Platonic one, nature is seen as a repository of extrahistorical transcendent values. Since I have already discussed that idea, I shall say no more about it here. More frequently today (as in sociobiology), nature is seen as a source of value-free facts from which ethical norms somehow follow. Often, in such projects, the appeal to nature is seen as telling us how living creatures operate when human devising does not interfere:[23] to live in accordance with nature would then be to live according to the promptings of instinct, or biology, or whatever we are before we intervene to make something of ourselves. But if that is what "nature" is, it is altogether unclear why we should be moved by it.[24] We do

---

[23] Thus the element common to these conceptions and the one I shall be pursuing is the idea of the removal of some sort of intervention, usually from society. But the interventions removed, and thus the life remaining, are of very different sorts.

[24] For an eloquent critique of the appeal to "nature" in this sense, see J. S. Mill, "Nature," in Mill (1961).

not think it better for a myopic person to use her eyes "in accordance with nature," when human intervention would improve her situation. No more should we suppose that for a person to live as untutored biological instinct prompts is a better thing, when human beings are deliberating ethical creatures who can control their instincts. Sometimes the value-free account of "nature" plays a more modest role, merely suggesting tendencies, constraints, and limits that any ethical view must bear in mind; even here, however, there is a marked tendency for the claims made on behalf of "nature" to overstep their modest bounds and to claim a normative weight that no argument has justified.[25]

The ancient appeals to nature that we shall be considering do not have these features. That is, they do not pretend to derive value-norms from a value-free account of the "scientific" underpinnings of human life. Ancient accounts of "nature," especially of "human nature," are value-laden accounts. They select some aspects of human beings and their lives as especially important or valuable, deciding only then that a certain element should be counted as part of our nature. Frequently, in so doing, they proceed by appealing to the actual sense of value of human beings, asking whether a life without element X, or Y, would be so impoverished that we would be unwilling to think of it as a human life at all. (In this sense, the arguments resemble contemporary arguments about "personhood," more than they resemble biological appeals to facts about humanness.) Norms follow from an account of "nature" because the account is frankly normative to begin with. Second, an account of "nature" is not, or not necessarily, an account of some way things are without human interference. Aristotle argues that we are by nature ethical and political creatures, certainly not implying that this behavior comes about without teaching and development; indeed, he thinks it follows from the central value of these elements in human life that cities should devote much more attention than they currently do to education. Again, for Aristotle the myopic person would precisely *not* be seeing "in accordance with nature," since an account of nature is a normative account of flourishing for some species; medical intervention would bring such a person closer to nature, rather than further from it.

Nonetheless, the appeal to nature usually does suggest the intuitive idea of an absence of deforming or impeding obstacles; it is thus very closely related to a normative notion of health. Just as health, when realized, is the system realizing itself in a flourishing way without disease or impediment,

---

[25] For one valuable critique of sociobiology in this connection, see Williams (1985).

just so the full flourishing of our moral and social nature can be imagined as full activity expressive of our most important capabilities, without impediments that would act as barriers to that self-realization. It is in this sense that nature may still, in the ancient accounts, be opposed to culture: for many cultures are sources of impediments to human flourishing. Thus the Hellenistic philosophers will frequently ask about nature, in the normative sense—about a norm of complete human flourishing—in part by looking at how things are before culture gets to people to deform them. Sometimes they will point to the behavior of infants and of animals as evidence for some way things are prior to culture. But it is important to see what this does and does not imply. It does not, I repeat, imply that we are looking for an account that is value-free: for, as we shall see, what the thought-experiment shows is a possibility of unconstrained flourishing for us that is deemed good. Nor does it imply that we are privileging that which exists without intervention: indeed, philosophy is a set of arts of intervention, closely allied with "nature" in this normative sense. But it does imply that we gravely mistrust society as it is, and would like to scrutinize possibilities that lie outside of it, in search of norms of a flourishing life.

A good introduction to the Hellenistic appeals to nature, which clearly reveals both the normative and the anti-conventional thrust of these appeals, is in the famous lines of Walt Whitman's "Song of Myself" concerning the animal kingdom. (These lines were made the epigraph to Bertrand Russell's highly Epicurean work, *The Conquest of Happiness*):[26]

I think I could turn and live with animals, they are so placid and self-
    contain'd,
I stand and look at them long and long.

They do not sweat and whine about their condition,
They do not lie awake in the dark and weep for their sins,
They do not make me sick discussing their duty to God,
Not one is dissatisfied, not one is demented with the mania of owning
    things,
Not one kneels to another, nor to his kind that lived thousands of years ago,
Not one is respectable or unhappy over the whole earth.

So they show their relations to me and I accept them,
They bring me tokens of myself, they evince them plainly in their
    possession.

[26] Walt Whitman, "Song of Myself," section 32, in *Leaves of Grass*, Norton Critical Edition (New York 1973). See Russell (1955).

What the animals show Whitman is not a value-free realm of life; nor does he learn from them to glorify that which exists without effort or teaching. What he sees is that certain practices that (already) appear to him to impede human flourishing—practices connected with religious fear and guilt, with economic obsession and accumulation, with status and power—need not exist. Moreover, when they do not exist, certain deformations of life—sleepless fear, groveling subservience, anxiety, dissatisfaction—do not exist either. The "tokens of myself" that the animals show Whitman are possibilities for self-respect, self-expression, and social equality that are frequently obscured by the realities of human social life. So too, I shall argue, in Hellenistic appeals to the nature of the child, the nature of the animal: the purpose is to construct a radical norm of true human flourishing. This norm is not value-free or "scientific": it is justified by appeal to deep human desires and judgments, and it is value-laden; but it is highly critical of ordinary belief, and sees many of our ordinary beliefs as impediments to flourishing.

We should note at this point, however, that the schools differ in the degree to which they wish to ground their normative account of nature on an overall teleological view of the world. Epicureans and Skeptics vigorously repudiate any such project, deriving their norms of nature from a consideration of the ways living creatures operate in an indifferent universe. The Stoics, as we shall see, are in a sense closer to the Platonists of my earlier discussion, in that, although their account of nature is certainly value-laden, and does claim to derive both support and justification from the deepest of human desires and aims, they also believe that the universe as a whole is providentially constructed by Zeus, and that norms of human life are part of this providential design. What complicates the matter further is that the essence of the providential design is reason; and reason is the very thing we encounter in ourselves when we scrutinize our deepest judgments. Thus it is no mere accident that self-scrutiny gets things right. In that sense the Stoics are not Platonists: the connection between the deepest layers of our own makeup and the true good is not merely contingent. But a normative ethical structure does pervade the universe as a whole.

V

The medical conception seeks to combine the critical power of Platonism with the worldly immersion of ordinary-belief philosophy. And it adds something further of its own: a commitment to action. The Platonist, having described the good and our distance from it, may or may not develop a further account of how distant pupils may pursue the good. This was a central project in Plato's *Republic*; but one may have an ethical view of a generally Platonist structure and take little interest in education. One might not even believe that there are any reliable procedures human beings can follow to arrive at the good, as we saw in my Augustinian example. And certainly the philosophical procedure that gives the philosopher understanding of the good, being suited to the good rather than to human beings, may itself do little or nothing to put ordinary diseased men and women nearer to the good. In the *Republic*, dialectic is for a few who are already well trained; ordinary citizens do not philosophize, and philosophy does not change them—except through very indirect political strategies, which never bring them all the way to the good life in any case. It can easily seem to the Platonist that one must, as a philosopher, make a choice: either discovery and contemplation of the true good, or service to ordinary citizens, a service that means staying at a lower level of reflection. Knowledge and action are to that extent opposed.

The philosopher who simply records and systematizes ordinary belief is not in this position. But her views, in a different way, also discourage her from thinking that philosophy is and should be committed to action. Her whole procedure rests on the idea that things are more or less in order as they are: that moral education works as currently practiced, that people's beliefs and emotions are pretty free from distortion. Of course, it is possible that people who have correct beliefs and desires will turn out to lack some of the good things that their conception correctly specifies. To that extent ordinary-belief philosophy is compatible with a recognition that some, or even many, people are doing badly. But since it is thought that the defects in their lives—a lack of financial resources, for example, or of friends, or of political rights—have not damaged belief and desire themselves, it also seems that it is not the job of philosophy to deal with those deficiencies. That looks like the job of politics or friendship.

For a medical ethical philosophy, by contrast, the commitment to action is intrinsic. Finding out how human beings are diseased and what they need is a prelude to, and is inseparable from, trying to heal them and give them what they need. The connection is this close, first of all, because the conception of the philosopher's task as a medical one makes compassion and love of humanity central features of it. Having understood how human lives are diseased, a philosopher worthy of the name—like a doctor worthy of that name—will proceed to try to cure them. The whole point of medical research is cure. So, too, the whole point of philosophy is human flourishing. The medical analogy expresses this basic commitment.

But there is another reason as well why the connection between philosophy and action is so intimate. The diseases this philosophy brings to light are, above all, diseases of belief and judgment. But to bring such diseases to light, the philosophers plausibly hold, is a large step toward removing them. Recognition of error is intimately linked to the grasp of truth. Thus philosophical procedure tends in its very nature to make things better, given this diagnosis of the problem. Of course each patient must see her errors, and the truth, individually; so the philosopher's task cannot stop when he or she arrives at a plausible general theory of human diseases. To that extent one might have a fair amount of philosophical truth without having yet healed a very large proportion of the people who are there to be helped. (This, we shall see, is a problem much discussed in the schools.) But it is not the case either that the new case is *simply* a scene for the application of a dogmatic theory. As in medicine, theory must, in the end, be responsible to the cases, and it must therefore be open to the possibility of discovering new symptoms—or even new insights into the nature of health.

A medical moral philosophy is committed to philosophical argument. Indeed it has a very high opinion of the worth of argument. And this is only natural, given its diagnosis. For if the diseases that impede human flourishing are above all diseases of belief and social teaching, and if, as they hope to show, critical arguments of the kind philosophy provides are necessary and perhaps even sufficient for dislodging those obstacles, then philosophy will seem to be necessary, perhaps even sufficient, for getting people from disease to health. But because of the particular way in which this approach to philosophy combines critical detachment from current practices with worldly immersion, it is no easy matter to say what sorts of arguments it ought to use. The philosopher encounters difficulties about using two types of argumentation widely recognized in pre-Hellenistic philosophy—as in much of philosophy today. Platonist philosophy aims at, and can reasonably expect to construct, deductive arguments deriving conclusions from first principles that are true, necessary, and primary. The philosopher's intellect apprehends the first principles, and philosophical logic constructs the ensuing demonstrations. The relation of these arguments to the psychology of ordinary human beings poses no problem, since altering ordinary life is no part of the Platonist philosopher's goal *qua* philosopher. But a medical philosopher who tries to use the same sort of argument is likely to discover, as Cicero said, that deductive argument does little to engage the ordinary hearer, or to probe into and alter the hearer's life. The philosopher who records and systematizes ordinary beliefs can use familiar dialectical arguments. She can elicit the ordinary beliefs by calm questioning, and then do whatever dialectical maneuvering needs to be done to achieve consistency. Medical philosophy cannot take this course either. For its task requires delving deep into the patient's psychology and, ultimately, challenging it and changing it. Calm dialectic does not probe deep enough to elicit hidden fears, frustrations, angers, attachments. If confusions are rooted deeply enough, it will not find them.

Thus medical philosophy, while committed to logical reasoning, and to marks of good reasoning such as clarity, consistency, rigor, and breadth of scope, will often need to search for techniques that are more complicated and indirect, more psychologically engaging, than those of conventional deductive or dialectical argument.[27] It must find ways to delve into the pupil's inner world, using gripping examples, techniques of narrative, appeals to memory and imagination—all in the service of bringing the pupil's whole life into the investigative process. Imagine, for example, how workers from the rural development authority would need to speak to the woman in rural India who says she does not want more education, if they want her to take the idea seriously and care about what they have to say. Clearly, a one-shot logical argument would do nothing to engage her; such a procedure would only reinforce her conviction that education has nothing to do with her. Nor would the exchange get very far if the development workers sat down with her like Aristotle in his schoolroom and asked her a number of calm and intellectual questions about what she thinks and says. But suppose, instead, they spent a long time with her, sharing her way of life and entering into it.[28] Suppose, during this time, they vividly set before her stories of ways in which the lives of women in other parts of the world have been transformed by education of various types—all the while eliciting, from careful listening over a long period of time, in an atmosphere of trust that they would need to work hard to develop, a rich sense of what she has experienced, whom she takes herself to be, what at a deeper level she believes about her own capacities and their actualization. If they did all this, and did it with the requisite sensitivity, imagination, responsiveness, and open-mindedness, they might over time discover that she does indeed experience some frustration and anger in connection with her limited role; and she might be able to recognize and to articulate wishes and aspirations

---

[27] For a contemporary argument along similar lines, see Charles Taylor (1993).

[28] This example is based on the actual narrative of such a process—in Bangladesh, not India—in Chen (1983).

for herself that she could not have articulated to Aristotle in the classroom. In short, through narrative, memory, and friendly conversation, a more complicated view of the good might begin to emerge.

In short, what philosophy needs, practiced in the medical way, is an account of complex human interactions of a philosophical kind. And for this it needs to think about the uses of the imagination, about narrative, about community, about friendship, about the rhetorical and literary forms in which an argument may be effectively housed. Each Hellenistic school does this in its own way. But all agree that philosophy is a complex form of life with complex arts of speech and writing.

Is a procedure so shaped still philosophy? And what are we asking when we ask that question? We seem to be asking, among other things, whether a procedure so committed to the world, and to change in it, can still be that reflective, critical and self-critical, intellectual activity that the intellectual tradition in Greece that began with Socrates and Plato called "philosophy." Socrates turned philosophy toward the world, in a way. But his own aloofness, his lack of affect, and his ironic distance from his pupils preserved for his hearers and later readers the sense that a relatively detached intellectual process was at work, even if one that involved profound sincerity and deep engagement on the part of the pupil.[29] Furthermore, Socrates' view of himself as a gadfly on the sluggish horse of the Athenian democracy set limits to the depth of his critique of ways of life and socially taught norms. Although in many ways his criticisms were profound, he did not suggest that democratic society as a whole was corrupt through and through. (Plato, who did claim this, also felt the need of a starting point for philosophy that was "unhypothetical," radically independent of belief.) And Socrates' very procedures seemed to rely on the intuitions of his interlocutors about concrete cases, though he usually overturned their theoretical pronouncements.[30] Thus he could calmly question them and expect to get *some* reliable answers back. The more radical criticisms of Hellenistic philosophy, and its concomitant commitment to changing the pupil's ways of life, entail the use of more surprising, more interventionist procedures. Philosophy in the hands of the Hellenistic thinkers no longer calmly contemplates the world: it plunges into the world, and becomes a part of it. And this changes philosophy. We must wonder whether it will, in gaining engagement, lose something of philosophy's reflective power. The young Karl Marx reflected on this problem in the introduction to his doctoral dissertation, an account of the practical goal of Epicurean philosophizing:

---

[29] For a wonderful account of all these aspects of Socrates, see Vlastos (1991).
[30] See Vlastos (1983, 1991).

When philosophy turns itself as will against the world of appearance, then the system is lowered to an abstract totality, that is, it has become one aspect of the world which opposes another one. Its relationship to the world is that of reflection. Inspired by the urge to realize itself, it enters into tension against the other. The inner self-contentment and completeness has been broken. What was inner light has become consuming flame turning outwards. The result is that as the world becomes philosophical, philosophy also becomes worldly, that its realisation is also its loss, that what it struggles against on the outside is its own inner deficiency, that in the very struggle it falls precisely into those defects which it fights as defects in the opposite camp, and that it can only overcome these defects by falling into them. That which opposes it and that which it fights is always the same as itself, only with factors inverted.[31]

Marx claims that we must ask whether a compassionate philosophy, in intervening actively in the world, might not lose some of its own critical ability, whether it might not sacrifice the patience proper to philosophy for results, and whether, participating in society, it might not even fall into some of the defects it has identified in society—such as intolerance, lack of reflection, and excessive competitiveness. This question can only be pursued as we examine each case: but we must pursue it. For it is disturbing that there appears, prima facie, to be mutual support between calm meticulous dialectic and the acceptance of the status quo, a prima facie tension between compassion and open-ended dialectical investigation. I believe that Marx is too pessimistic; but the problem arises urgently in at least some of the schools, as we shall see.[32]

VI

Philosophy understood along medical lines deals with both beliefs and emotions or passions.[33] One reason why the tension described earlier seems to arise is that philosophy is asked not simply to deal with the patient's invalid inferences and false premises, but to grapple, as well, with her irrational fears and anxieties, her excessive loves and crippling angers.

---

[31] Marx, in K. Marx (1841).

[32] Although Marx's dissertation concerned only Epicurus (and Democritus), he had a larger plan to write a history of these themes in Hellenistic philosophy generally, and some of his observations reflect this.

[33] On these two words, their etymologies, and their history in the philosophical debates, see chapter 9, n. 4. As explained there, I use them interchangeably, to refer to the genus of which grief, fear, pity, anger, love, joy, and other relatives are the species.

In dealing with these "irrational" elements of the person, in modifying or even removing them, it may well appear that philosophy must cease to reason and argue, and turn to forms of causal manipulation that have little connection with argument. As I understand Marx's argument, this is among the sources of his worry: for he speaks of practical philosophy as "consuming flame"—suggesting, I think, that approaching the inner world as Hellenistic philosophy approaches it requires the deployment of passional energy for purposes of a causal manipulation that is not mediated by argument.

But this argument seems to assume that emotions have little or nothing to do with reasoning. This claim the Hellenistic thinkers reject, with compelling arguments. One reason they believe that philosophy is the art best equipped to deal with human diseases is that they believe that philosophy—reasoning and argument—is what is required to diagnose and to modify the passions. This is so, they argue, precisely because passions such as fear, anger, grief, and love are not blind surges of affect that push and pull us without regard to reasoning and belief. They are, in fact, intelligent and discriminating elements of the personality that are very closely linked to beliefs, and are modified by the modification of belief. (To some extent, as we shall see, this is held to be true even of bodily appetites such as hunger and thirst. This is why we can and should speak not simply of a therapy of emotion but, more generally, of a *therapy of desire.* Unlike the emotions, however, the appetites are thought to be based on innate bodily requirements and to have a relatively low degree of intentional awareness and a relatively crude conception of their object.) I shall study the arguments for this general position later, as I discuss each school; they articulate subtly different conceptions of the relationship between emotion and belief or judgment. But in every case the cognitive dimension of the emotions is stressed, and, in particular, their close connection with a certain sort of ethical belief, concerning what has importance and what not. What I fear, for example, is connected with what I think worth caring about, with the degree of importance I ascribe to unstable things that can be damaged by the accidents of life. Passions may be "irrational" in the sense that the beliefs on which they rest may be false, or unjustified, or both. They are not irrational in the sense of having nothing to do with argument and reasoning.

Both Aristotle and the Hellenistic schools hold, furthermore, that many, if not all, of the passions rest upon beliefs that do not spring up naturally (if any beliefs do this), but are formed by society. They are, in fact, part and parcel of the fabric of social convention; they should be criticized as the rest of that fabric is criticized. (Once again, this is to some extent true even of the bodily appetites, although these, unlike the emotions, are held to be to some extent innate.) Up to a point, they hold, most societies share common errors: so one can expect to find similar emotions turning up at Athens and at Rome, in Asia and in Germany. No actual society they know is without some variety of anger, of fear, of passionate erotic love. On the other hand, they argue that the specific fabric of cultural belief makes the emotional repertory of one society diverge in significant ways from that of another. Thus love at Rome has a distinctive pattern and a peculiar cognitive and narrative history. This means that the philosophical critique of emotion must be highly informed and culture-specific—and, by the same token, that the philosophical critique of a culture is not likely to leave its citizens' emotions and desires unaltered.

In short, medical philosophy can to some extent avoid Marx's problem because what it aims to alter is more reasonable and reasoning than some modern conceptions of emotion might lead us to suppose. To use philosophical argument to modify the passions, the philosopher does not have to turn away from her commitment to reasoning and careful argument: for the passions are made up out of beliefs and respond to arguments. Argument, in fact, is exactly the way to approach them; no less intelligent way will address the root of the problem. Thus in asking philosophy to deal with anger and fear and love, the medical model is not asking it to use devices alien to itself. It can still seek agreement, fit, and truth in the fabric of discourse and belief taken as a whole.

On the other hand, the medical model recognizes that many of the pupil's beliefs—including many of those on which her passions are based—will be deeply entrenched by the time she presents herself for therapeutic teaching. Some socially taught beliefs are internalized at a deep level; they guide many aspects of the pupil's thought and action, often without her conscious awareness. (As we shall see, it is among the greatest distinctions of Hellenistic philosophy to have discovered the idea of unconscious belief and desire; and it has powerful arguments showing the need to recognize such psychological elements, if human behavior is to be convincingly explained.) For the ordinary-belief philosopher, this depth is no problem: for it is assumed that the deeply entrenched beliefs are also healthy, and there is not much need to subject them to critical scrutiny. The medical philosopher does not assume this: some of these beliefs, and some of the associated fears and angers and loves, may well turn out to be false and pernicious. But to alter them will not be the task of a one-shot dialectical argument, clearly. Other techniques of scrutiny and modification will be required to bring these layers of the person to the surface for criticism and to replace false beliefs with true ones.

On the one hand, then, the Hellenistic philosophers develop a conception of the emotions that permits them to treat emotion as a target of philosophical argument, of a piece with the pupil's beliefs and judgments. This conception, and the arguments (both general and concrete) that support it, have enormous power, and are certainly among the most important contributions made by these schools to philosophical understanding. On the other hand, their new recognition of the depth and complex interiority of the personality—of both emotion and belief, as they are actually situated in the pupil's life—implies that the polite surface exchanges of dialectic may not be enough to deal sufficiently with either emotions or other beliefs. The origin of the Hellenistic focus on techniques such as memorization, "confession," and daily self-examination is in this newly complex psychology: not a problem endemic to the emotions as such, but a problem about the cognitive structure of the whole person. No element in the self is impervious to rational argument; but arguments must dig deep in order, as Epicurus puts it, to "become powerful" in the soul.[34]

VII

The purpose of the rest of this book will be to investigate this idea of a compassionate "medical" philosophy by studying its development in the three major Hellenistic schools, Epicurean, Stoic, and Skeptic. The aim will be to understand what philosophy becomes, when understood in the medical way—to understand, in fact, several different conceptions of what its procedures and arguments should be and how they should interact with the pupil's beliefs and emotions, and with the fabric of the social tradition they internalize. All the schools dedicate themselves to the searching critique of prevailing cognitive authority, and to the amelioration of human life as a result. All develop procedures and strategies that are aimed not only at individual efficacy, but also at the creation of a therapeutic community, a society set over against the existing society, with different norms and different priorities. In some cases this is achieved by literal physical separation; in some cases, through the imagination. I shall try to understand the structure of these communities, and the complex interrelationships between the norms implicit in their philosophical interactions and the norms

---

[34] Epicurus, *LHdt* 83: see chapter 4.

for which their arguments argue. Although I shall focus on the ethical aspect of the philosophical views, I shall also ask to what extent their accounts of ethical ends are supported by independent arguments in other areas, and to what extent, on the other hand, those other arguments are themselves shaped (as Marx held Epicurean physics was shaped) by an overriding ethical commitment.

Two of the three schools, Epicureans and Stoics, present impressively detailed conceptions of the emotions; I shall study these also. These analyses, both of the general idea of emotion and of individual emotions (and related desires), are of interest independently of their role within a conception of rational therapy: so to some extent I shall focus on this topic in its own right. But my larger purpose will always be to see how these philosophical analyses are put to work in the amelioration of human life, both individual and communal.

These philosophers do not simply analyze the emotions, they also urge, for the most part, their removal from human life. They depict the flourishing human life as one that has achieved freedom from disturbance and upheaval, above all by reducing the agent's commitments to unstable items in the world. I have recorded in the Introduction my discomfort with this aspect of Hellenistic ethics; and I believe, as I said there, that it is possible to accept many aspects both of their analyses of emotions and of their account of therapeutic procedure without being convinced of the correctness of this normative account of the goal. Indeed, it is very important to the philosophers themselves that this should be so. For they wish to address many people—ordinary people, Aristotelians, and others—who do not share their commitment to freedom from disturbance. It would be an enormous disadvantage to this enterprise if they began by adopting an *analysis* of emotion, or a conception of procedure, that could not be accepted by anyone who did not already accept their normative ethical view. And in fact they go to some pains to show that this is not what they are doing, basing their analyses of emotion on ordinary beliefs, literature, and other evidence, in order to show its strong independent credentials.

On the other hand, it is also of considerable philosophical interest to understand on what grounds compassionate philosophers, committed to the amelioration of human life, did judge that the emotions should be removed from them. Anyone who wishes to take medical philosophy seriously must grapple with these arguments; and anyone who really grapples with them is unlikely to be unchanged by them. In order to get a purchase on this complex issue, I shall begin this book with Aristotle. For Aristotle sketched an account of the emotions and desires that is very close to the more elaborate accounts we find in the Hellenistic philosophers. And yet he did not defend a norm of detachment from the mutable good things of this world. His best human life is a life rich in attachments to people and things outside the self—friendships, family loves, political ties, ties of certain sorts to possessions and property. Thus it is a life rich in possibilities for emotions such as love, grief, fear, and even anger; the study of these connections will shed light, by contrast, on the Hellenistic conceptions.[35]

Aristotle's conception will prove a valuable starting point in another way as well. For Aristotle accepts and develops at length the idea that ethical philosophy should resemble medicine in its dedication to the practical goal of ameliorating human lives. And he develops, in some detail, aspects of the analogy between the philosopher's and the doctor's tasks. And yet Aristotle also criticizes the medical analogy at certain points, arguing that there are some very important ways in which ethical philosophy should *not* be like medicine. And he develops, on this basis, an account of practical procedure that is rather different from those offered by the Hellenistic schools. Measuring them against it is a good way of understanding them, and Aristotle, better. For Aristotle's procedures look philosophically familiar and appealing to us. But if we see what they involve rejecting, and on what basis they may be criticized, our understanding (both of Aristotle and of ourselves) becomes subtler and more complex, and we begin to grasp the motivation for much that at first might seem alien and unphilosophical in the Hellenistic conceptions. On all these issues, then, my aim is not to present an exhaustive account of Aristotle's thought, but rather to present certain parts of his view schematically for the purposes of instructive contrast.

After the background chapters on Aristotle, I shall approach each school in turn. In the case of Epicureanism I shall begin with a general study of the therapeutic community and its conception of medical argument, drawing both on the explicit testimony of Epicurus and on later evidence for the

---

[35] Nothing in my procedure assumes that any Hellenistic thinker is explicitly responding to the text of Aristotle. This is an obscure and controversial matter for the first generations of the Greek schools—though by the time of Cicero Aristotle is widely read, and contrasts between Stoic and Peripatetic positions are frequent. My procedure relies on the fact that Aristotle and the Hellenistic philosophers shared a common culture that, as a culture, understood ethical inquiry in a certain way, as a search for *eudaimonia*. Members of the culture also seem to share certain ethical problems, to which the philosophical views in various ways respond. Aristotle explicitly connects many of his ethical views with widely held beliefs, with good reason; thus in responding to these aspects of common belief the Hellenistic thinkers are setting themselves in a relationship to Aristotle's thought that is, if indirect, still illuminating.

practice of the school. I shall then examine closely three of the emotions that Epicurus claimed to treat: passionate erotic love, the fear of death, and anger. Here, although I shall in each case set out the evidence for Epicurus' own views on the topic, I shall focus on Lucretius' Epicureanism, and therefore on Roman poetry, rather than Greek prose. This is necessary because the Greek evidence is so sparse, and also because understanding a therapeutic argument requires study of its rhetorical and literary form, the devices it uses to get in touch with the desires of the pupil or reader. This cannot be done well dealing entirely with fragments and paraphrases; and it is difficult to go far even with Epicurus' surviving letters, which present his teaching in summary form to pupils who already know it. But it must be remembered that Lucretius' style of therapy is different from any style in which Epicurus philosophized; and the content of his thought as well may be in some ways different, especially where it seems to have been influenced by its Roman context.

The chapter on the Skeptics is a single chapter: for the sweeping rejection of all belief proposed in Pyrrhonian skepticism does not conduce to fine-tuned analyses of individual emotions. I place it after the Epicurean chapters and before the Stoic chapters for purposes of logical sequence and clarity; but it must be remembered that Sextus Empiricus, our main source for orthodox "Pyrrhonian" Skepticism, is a late writer who frequently responds to the Stoics as well as the Epicureans. In this chapter I shall concentrate on Skepticism's procedures and its account of its practical goal—on the way in which, while ostensibly suspending all judgment, the pupil is nonetheless, it appears, invited to aim at an end and to have some views about the causal efficacy of the philosophical life.

Stoicism is an enormously complex and diverse movement in philosophy. It exercised a deep and broad influence on two societies over a period of more than five hundred years, shaping poetry and politics as well as explicitly philosophical thought and writing. And the therapy of desire and judgment is its central focus in ethics. So any treatment of this topic is bound to be highly selective. I shall begin with a general account of Stoic therapeutic strategies, showing how their emphasis on the self-governing and self-critical powers of the soul gives rise to a distinctive conception of philosophical education, aimed at extending the benefits of philosophy to all human beings. Next I shall turn to the Stoic account of the passions and to their arguments for the radical conclusion that the passions are to be extirpated from human life. I shall ask to what degree their therapeutic strategies are independent of the goal of extirpation. A more specific analysis of Seneca's *De Ira* follows, showing how Stoic therapy tackles the role of anger in public life. Finally I shall return to the personal life, investigating the ambivalent portrayal of love and anger in Seneca's *Medea*.

VIII

Therapeutic argument is searchingly concrete. It approaches the pupil with a keen awareness of the daily fabric of her beliefs. And it holds, as well, that this fabric of belief is learned in particular cultural circumstances—so it commits itself to learning about and grappling with those circumstances. The need for historical and cultural understanding makes itself felt even in connection with the emotions, which are sometimes taken to be universal and "natural." For the Hellenistic thinkers insist that they are not "natural" (i.e., innate)[36] at all, but socially constructed and taught. And though there is thought to be much overlap in what different societies teach, there is also significant variation and nuance. This means that to come up with an adequate account of these teachings we must situate the philosophical doctrines in their historical and cultural contexts, Greek and Roman, attending carefully to the relationships between the pupil's diseases and her society, and between the philosophical cure and existing rhetorical and literary forms. This is in fact the only way in which we can get a full idea of what these philosophical teachings have to offer—for central in what they offer is their rich responsiveness to the concrete, and this will be obscured if we characterize their enterprise too timelessly and abstractly.

To imagine how all this works, and to imagine it with some reasonable concreteness, I have chosen to follow the career of an imaginary pupil as she consults, in turn, the different philosophical movements, asking, in each case, how she would be diagnosed and treated by them, how she would be addressed, how she would be "cured." This procedure has several advantages. It will enable us to imagine vividly how each school deals with the concrete problems of an individual case, and how the concrete and the humanly universal are intertwined. It will permit us, too, to describe the structure and activities of each therapeutic community, showing how official philosophical teaching is related to the selection of philosophical procedures.[37] And finally, it will enable us to ask, in each case, *who* can be helped by these means: how inclusive the compassionate reach of medical

---

[36] They will also argue that they are not "natural" in the normative sense I have described, since they impede human flourishing.

[37] We will have to do this in a more complicated way with Lucretius and Seneca, since their writings contain an imagined interlocutor who is distinct from our imaginary pupil.

therapy is. Imagining the career of a female pupil is one good way to see this. So I have chosen to follow the studies of a young woman (perhaps historical and probably fictitious) who is named in Diogenes Laertius as a pupil of Epicurus. Nikidion—for that is the pupil's name[38]—will not retain a fixed historical or social identity across the schools. She will have to be of a social class whose members can be included in philosophizing; and this changes. She will need to move from Greece to Rome, and to change her background beliefs and social status accordingly. In one case at least, she will have to pretend to be a male. But I hope that this will be in its own way revealing, and that Nikidion's polymorphous search for the good life, and for a "little victory" over fear, resentment, and confusion, will make readers attentive participants, until her encounters become her own.

IX

We shall be making complicated comparisons. The idea of ethical argument as therapy is a multifaceted idea, which invites further analysis and subdivision. We need, then, a schematic enumeration of likely characteristics of "medical" argument, to organize our concrete investigations. This list of features is really a list of questions, a list that directs us to look and see whether the arguments we are studying in each case have or fail to have that feature. It is a flexible list; it by no means claims to give either necessary or sufficient conditions for a medical ethical procedure. Nor does it claim to give an exhaustive enumeration of all the features that this conception signals to our attention. Still, given the heterogeneity of the material, it is useful to have such a schematic instrument; and the medical analogy does in fact bring certain features repeatedly to the fore.

If we reflect, then, about the medical analogy, asking what philosophical arguments can be expected to be like if understood in terms of it, the following features emerge, at least initially, for our inspection:

---

[38] DL 10.7 reports, as a story told about Epicurus by the hostile Timocrates, that both Epicurus and Metrodorus had relationships with courtesans, among whom were Mammarion ("Tits"), Hedeia ("Sweety-Pie"), Erotion ("Lovie"), and Nikidion ("Little Victory"). The stories reproduced in this section of the Life are, though slanderous, also full of plausible detail, including apparently authentic citations from treatises and letters. So there is at least the possibility that the name, if not the relationship, is historical. We can see, however, that the beginnings of female philosophizing went hand in hand with the beginnings of sexist "humor" about the character of the women concerned.

1. Arguments have a *practical goal*: they are directed at making the pupil better, and can be assessed for their contribution to this end. (This, as I said, does not entail that the value of argument must be merely instrumental.)

2. They are what we might call *value-relative*: that is, at some level they respond to deep wishes or needs of the patient and, again, are to be assessed in accordance with their success in doing this.

3. They are *responsive to the particular case*: just as a good doctor heals case by case, so good medical argument responds to the pupil's concrete situation and needs.

These three characteristics can be expected to be present, in some form, in any ethical view that takes its lead from the medical analogy. We shall see that not only our three Hellenistic schools, but Aristotle as well, endorse them, though in rather different ways. A second group of characteristics, suggested by thinking further about the medical art, will turn out to be more controversial; and it will be a revealing measure of a view to see how many of them it accepts.

4. Medical arguments, like bodily medical treatments, are *directed at the health of the individual* as such, not at communities or at the individual as member of a community.

5. In medical argument, the *use of practical reason is instrumental*. Just as the doctor's technique is no intrinsic part of what the goal, health, *is*, so too the philosopher's reasoning is no intrinsic part of what the good human life itself is.

6. *The standard virtues of argument*—such as consistency, definitional clarity, avoidance of ambiguity—*have, in medical argument, a purely instrumental value*. As with the procedures of the medical art, they are no intrinsic part of the goal.

7. In medical argument, as in medicine, there is a marked *asymmetry of roles*: doctor and patient, expert authority and obedient recipient of authority.

8. In medical argument, the teacher *discourages the sympathetic dia-lectical scrutiny of alternative views*. Just as a doctor does not urge the patient to experiment with alternative medications, so the teacher does not encourage cognitive pluralism.

Finally we must ask about the relation of medical arguments to themselves. Here the medical parallel can point in more than one direction; so instead of two further features, I shall simply pose two further questions:

9. How do the arguments speak about themselves? In particular, are they *self-praising* (reminding the pupil often of the good that is being done by them), or *self-denigrating* (reminding the pupil of how tentative they are and how much further work remains to be done)? Discourse in bodily medicine is frequently self-praising, encouraging optimism about the cure; but there are times when a modest self-denigration may be preferred, in order not to arouse unrealistic expectations.

10. How do the arguments affect the pupil's need for and ability to take part in further arguments? Are they, that is, *self-enhancing* (making the pupil better and better at arguing the further they proceed) or *self-canceling* (removing the need for and/or the disposition to engage in future arguments? (Ability and motivation are really two separate issues.) Drugs in medicine frequently remove the need for further drugs; and yet some drugs, clearly, are addictive. And some healthful prescriptions (e.g., a healthy diet) become part of a "cured" daily life from then on.

Focusing on this list will not prevent us from following the literary and rhetorical structure of each therapeutic argument as it comes before us. Focusing on it too narrowly would prevent us from seeing a great deal that we ought to see. But regarded with sufficient caution, it will help us to understand the structure of the different philosophical ways of life that our pupil, Nikidion, takes up in search of a good life and freedom from suffering.

Medical Dialectic: Aristotle on
Theory and Practice

I

ARISTOTLE was not the first ancient Greek philosopher to argue that philosophical reflection and teaching on ethical and political topics have a practical goal. And the analogy between philosophy and medicine had been used already to make this point. But with his characteristic explicitness Aristotle set out more clearly the reasons why one should see ethics as practical and not simply theoretical, the contributions theory might make to practice, and the ways in which theory itself might be shaped by the demands of practice. He not only brings the medical analogy forward, he also takes it apart—arguing that in some ways it is a good analogy for ethical purposes, but in other ways potentially misleading. His distinctions will guide us as we ask questions of the more thoroughly "medical" Hellenistic conceptions.[1] And we can understand Aristotle's procedures better as well, once we see what possibilities of human aid they exclude and how a compassionate Hellenistic thinker might criticize them.

II

Aristotle was a great biologist and the son of a doctor. The medical analogy thus has roots in his own experience. But he did not invent it; and he is probably indebted to a long tradition of reflection about the comparison.[2] As soon as there was an expert art of medicine that could, by some precise

---

[1] See Jaeger (1957) for an eloquent account of Aristotle's use of medical analogies. He focused, however, only on the positive use of the analogy, and did not bring out the equally important criticisms of it. See also Hutchinson (1988).

[2] Aristotle probably knew all the authors mentioned in this section; Democritus and the orators were especially well known to him. The *Rhetoric* shows that he has reflected a good deal about popular views of persuasive speech, and their theoretical continuation in the work of figures such as Isocrates.

and teachable procedures, bring relief to the suffering body,[3] it was natural to ask whether there might not be some other art that could in a parallel way handle "diseases" of thought, judgment, and desire. It was also very natural, thinking about experiences of persuasion, consolation, exhortation, criticism, and calming, to feel that the art or arts in question would be arts of speech and argument, of *logos* somehow understood.[4]

In fact, an analogy between *logos* and medical treatment is extremely old and deep in ancient Greek talk about the personality and its difficulties. From Homer on we encounter, frequently and prominently, the idea that *logos* is to illnesses of the soul[5] as medical treatment is to illnesses of the body. We also find the claim that *logos* is a powerful and perhaps even a sufficient remedy for these illnesses; frequently it is portrayed as the only available remedy. The diseases in question are frequently diseases of inappropriate or misinformed emotion. To an Achilles whose heart is "swollen up" with the "bile" of anger (*Il.* 9.946), Phoenix tells the story of the Prayers, divine *logoi* that go behind strife and exercise a healing function (*exakeontai*, 9.503). Much later, Pindar writes of his own poetic speech as a "charm" (*epaoidē*) that can produce freedom from disturbance in the troubled soul (*Nem.* 8.49ff.; cf. *P.* 3.51, *P.* 4.217). The Chorus in the *Prometheus Bound* tells the hero, as a piece of well-known information, that "for the sickness of anger, *logoi* are the doctors" (377); to this Prometheus replies by giving in some detail a theory of the timely (*en kairōi*) application of remedies. As the medical art itself progresses, becoming more detailed and more theoretically sophisticated, and as popular knowledge of it increases, such analogies become more detailed.[6] To give just one example, Empedocles speaks of his philosophical poem as providing *pharmaka* (drugs) for human ills (Diels-Kranz B 111, 112).

Such analogies are already more than decorative: *logos* is being said to play a real healing role, and to heal through its complicated relationship to the intellect and the emotions. But the concept of *logos* is still, it seems,

---

[3] For some of the pertinent background material, see Nussbaum (1986a) ch. 4. A much fuller treatment, discussing the deficiencies of medicine as well as its achievements, is G.E.R. Lloyd (1989).

[4] For pertinent general discussions, see, among others, Rabbow (1954), Buxton (1982), Simon (1978).

[5] Here as in chapter 1, I emphasize that the use of this word implies no particular theory of the personality, and certainly not a non-materialist theory. The Homeric *psuchē* is a material substance.

[6] For further references, see Nussbaum (1986b). See also Buxton (1982) for related discussions.

understood broadly, to include speech and argument of many kinds. Religious and poetic utterances, philosophical arguments, friendly advice—no attempt is made to distinguish these different types of discourse from one another, where the medical analogy is concerned. So far we find no attempt to associate medical functions with a specialized and demarcated art of philosophy. And we therefore see no close attention to the devices that will later seem to constitute speech as philosophical—close argument, sequential reasoning, clear definition of terms.[7] A suffering person in search of "the *technē* of life" would have, so far as these texts are concerned, a number of options.

Philosophy's claim, later on, to be "the art of life" is a defiant and highly contentious claim. It is, in effect, the claim that it can do more for the suffering pupil than other available sources of *logos*, healing the suffering soul in a way that goes beyond the other popular arts and pseudo-arts. Above all, philosophy opposes itself here to superstition and popular religion.[8] For popular religion turns the good life over to prayer, making outcomes neither controlled nor fully scrutinized by human reason. Philosophy will claim to remove that element of darkness and uncontrol from human life, making *tuchē* subordinate to an intelligent and intelligible *technē*.[9] As in medicine, so here: a reasoned procedure takes the place of prayer and wishing. The philosophical schools will later compete vigorously against one another. But it is very important to understand what they have in common. All compete, on behalf of philosophical reason, against other traditional forms of allegedly curative *logos*.[10]

The specifically philosophical form of the medical analogy cannot develop far before there are stable philosophical institutions, offering pupils a definite set of procedures that can be compared with the procedures of medicine and contrasted with popular religion and magic. But we find adumbrations by the end of the fifth century, where, already, the medical analogy is used in contexts where *logos* must mean "argument," and

[7] I do not mean to suggest that these features are nowhere discussed in this period: already in Parmenides, the injunction to "follow by *logos* the very contentious refutation" is set over against other ways of listening and thinking. I am commenting only on the failure to connect the traits of argument with a therapeutic goal—not a surprising absence, considering that little of the surviving early philosophy is ethical.

[8] Each of the schools we shall study has its own religious teaching; even Epicureans are strictly speaking not atheists. But philosophical religion, from Socrates on, is rationalized in a way that requires the rejection of much in popular religious conceptions.

[9] For an excellent discussion of the cultural background, see Sedley (1980).

[10] See especially Vlastos (1991) on Socrates' rationalized religion and its relationship to conventional beliefs and practices.

where some idea of a critical art of reasoned discourse stands in contrast to other ways in which one might speak persuasively. The famous comparison of *logoi* to drugs in Gorgias' praise of Helen probably alludes to persuasive speech in general, not to sophistical or philosophical argument. *Logoi*, he says, like drugs (*pharmaka*) have the power to "stop fear and take away grief and engender joy and increase fellow feeling" (14). There is, however, some movement here in the direction of the later use of the analogy: for his *logoi* are, presumably, neither religious nor poetic nor in any sense traditional. And his entire speech—which clearly attempts, as a whole, to give a demonstration of this part of its content—is an advertisement for a specialized kind of *logos*, one that prominently includes logical (or pseudo-logical) argumentation and is purveyed by specialized professionals to people who want more control over their lives.

It seems to have been Democritus, however, who first really developed the analogy at length in a clearly philosophical context.[11] "Medicine," he wrote, "heals the sicknesses of bodies; but wisdom [*sophiē*] rids the soul of its sufferings [*pathē*]" (Diel-Kranz B 31).[12] And elsewhere as well, he draws attention to analogies between bodily diseases and diseases of thought and desire; he stresses the causal efficacy of his art in balancing the soul and restoring it to a healthy condition.[13] As we enter the fourth century— perhaps as a result of Democritus' influence—such comparisons become increasingly frequent and increasingly elaborate. I shall shortly discuss Socrates' contribution. The orator Isocrates, speaking of his (philosophically influenced) art of political argumentation, alludes to the medical analogy as to an already familiar idea, and develops it at length: "For sicknesses of the body, medical men have discovered many and varied forms of therapeutic treatment; but for souls that are sick . . . there is no other drug but *logos* that will forcefully strike those who are in error" (*Peace* 39). He continues with an elaborate analogy between medical cut-

---

[11] The outstanding edition of the fragments and testimonia is by Luria (1970)—though the translations and commentary are in Russian. (Luria published most of his works in German or English, but this, his magnum opus, was a posthumous publication.) I wish to give warm thanks to Abbott Gleason for translating the relevant portions of Luria's excellent commentary for me. On the transmission of the ethical fragments (with grave doubts about their authenticity), see Stewart (1958).

[12] As Luria convincingly shows, *sophiē* is Democritus' characteristic word for philosophy; material containing the word *philosophia* must be spurious, or a later paraphrase.

[13] See, for example, the reference to a canker in Diels-Kranz B 281; also 231, 224, 285, which contain striking parallels to Epicurean views on the limits of desires. Luria's discussions are always valuable.

tings and burnings and harsh or grating forms of argument: to get well, people are going to have to hear arguments that will give them distress (40).

Throughout the late fifth and early fourth centuries, then, Greek thinkers and writers were finding it increasingly easy to think of ethical/political argument as similar to medicine and to look to it for "healing" when confronted with seemingly intractable psychological afflictions. The analogy becomes more and more detailed, more closely linked with specifically philosophical uses of *logos*. But if this had been all there was to the medical analogy, we would be entitled, perhaps, to think of it as a vague commonplace, without much serious philosophical weight. These increasingly detailed uses, however, contain an implicit challenge to dig deeper, to say what work the analogy actually does and what ethical conception or conceptions it expresses. So we would expect to find, sooner or later, in this culture already deeply committed to argument and to critical discourse about the quality of arguments,[14] attempts to delineate, for ethics as well as for science, some criteria of appropriate procedure when applying *logos* to souls, criteria that would enable the ethical practitioner to distinguish between *logoi* that are merely forces[15] and *logoi* that are in some sense truly rational. Gorgias has compared *logos* with drugs, which exercise causal power without the patient's critical participation. We might expect someone to say, in reply, that this is not the only way that *logos* can work in the soul: that there are also *logoi* that are practical, and yet rational; *logoi* that work not just by being causes, but by giving reasons. This would be a particularly important task for a philosopher who was anxious to distinguish his professional activity as ethical *logos*-giver from that of the unreliable rhetorician or the practitioner of mere eristic (contentious disputation). He would need to develop these distinctions if he wanted to win respectability for his philosophical art in a culture grown suspicious of the uses and abuses of argument.[16]

[14] On the work being done in this period to distinguish superstitious from rational uses of *logos*, see G.E.R. Lloyd (1981).

[15] The limiting case of such a *logos* would be a magical incantation; but many *logoi* that are taken in by some sort of cognition still do not elicit active critical reasoning, and it is this contrast that is my primary focus.

[16] In many respects this history is being repeated, in the interaction between some parts of contemporary literary theory and the law. Here we find, once again, the Gorgianic claim that all speech is power, and that there is no criterion that reliably distinguishes causes from reasons. See, above all, Fish (1989).

This challenge was taken up, in different ways, by three great moral philosophers: Socrates, Plato, and Aristotle. And it was in their hands that the medical analogy really began to be a rich and illuminating guide to certain aspects of ethical philosophizing. The Socrates of Plato's early dialogues develops a conception of the health of the soul, and of procedures of philosophical *elenchos* as linked to that health. I shall not discuss these important contributions to the history of practical philosophy, since they have been amply discussed in Gregory Vlastos' fundamental study.[17] Plato's complex contribution has also received much outstanding discussion;[18] in dialogues as diverse as *Protagoras, Republic, Symposium, Phaedrus,* and *Sophist,* he develops a complicated account of the soul's health and of the role of rigorous critical philosophical argument in securing it. In these discussions we see many elements of the later Hellenistic use of the medical analogy already in place: a focus on false beliefs (and the associated passions) as an origin of the soul's misery; the insistence that philosophy knows systematic procedures of therapy that can produce psychic health; the idea that critical and self-critical arguments, in particular, are tools by which experts can probe deeply into the personality and rid it of diseased elements. And these discussions had considerable influence on the Hellenistic thinkers.

It still seems fair to say, however, that it was Aristotle who first developed a detailed and explicit account of the potentiality and limitations of a medical conception of ethical argument, setting out what work the analogy could and could not do.

III

We now turn to our pupil. And we must ask what she must be like in order to be received by Aristotle *as* a pupil. The name Nikidion, "little victory," is probably the name of a *hetaira* or courtesan. And in the world of fourth-century Athens, *hetairai* would be more likely than other women to be literate, and to have the freedom to move around at their own discretion. Although there are reasons to doubt the historicity of Diogenes' list, given its connection in the text with slanders against Epicurean hedonism, it is

---

[17] Vlastos (1991).

[18] For therapeutic aspects of Plato, see Kenny (1973), Sinaiko (1965), Simon (1978), and, most recently, Price (1989, 1990). I discuss some of the issues, with regard to *Protagoras, Symposium,* and *Phaedrus* in Nussbaum (1986a).

worth bearing in mind that a recent papyrus discovery has confirmed Diogenes' report—long dismissed—that Plato taught two courtesans in his school.[19] Whether or not Nikidion's particular name is historical, a woman like her could, then, have enrolled in Plato's Academy, and also in any of the three major Hellenistic schools. The career of Pericles' mistress Aspasia illustrates the degree of sophistication and intellectual influence a woman of the *hetaira* class could achieve, even in a culture as restrictive of women as Athens.[20]

The first thing we must record, then, is that in order to study ethics with Aristotle, Nikidion would probably need to disguise herself as a male. Aristotle's is the only major philosophical school for which we have no evidence of female pupils.[21] His philosophical views, according to which women are incapable of practical wisdom, appear to support this practice.[22] We should also bear in mind, however, that to include women in ethical/political instruction at Athens would have been a most unconventional step, bringing the practitioner public ridicule and criticism (as we know it did in the case of Epicurus). Aristotle, as a resident alien at Athens, without any civic, religious, or property rights, twice forced into exile by political opponents suspicious of his Macedonian connections,[23] was not in a position to make surprising gestures—whereas Plato's wealthy aristocratic family protected him from abuse. There are philosophical reasons for Aristotle's exclusion of women; but there may be political reasons as well.

Nikidion, then, disguises herself as a male. She must not be too young: for Aristotle insists that lectures on ethics and politics should not be at-

[19] See DL 3.46, and discussion in Lefkowitz (1986).

[20] Consider Plato's *Menexenus*, a fictional conversation between Aspasia and Socrates. (For historical background, see Guthrie [1975].) In the *Apology* (41C), Socrates mentions his intention to question women in the underworld after death—where, presumably, their movements would be less restricted than at Athens.

[21] Evidence about the Stoics is unclear until Roman times, but it is plain that the ideal cities of Zeno and Chrysippus promote equal citizenship and education for women. There is little evidence for the skeptical academy per se, though it seems reasonable to suppose that it continued the Platonic tradition. Women achieved particular prominence in neo-Pythagorean circles, and fragments of some of these works survive.

[22] See *Pol.* I.13, 1260a13. G.E.R. Lloyd (1983) argues that Aristotle's view of women's capabilities lags well behind that of other intellectuals of his day; see Salkever (1989) for a more positive estimation. See also the misogynistic views in the fragments of "On Marriage" by Aristotle's pupil Theophrastus.

[23] See Düring (1966); Owen, "Philosophical Invective," in Owen (1986); and, on the resident alien question, Whitehead (1975, 1977).

tended by the young person (*neos*, *EN* 1095a2, on which see subsequent discussion). Two reasons are given for this: a young person lacks practical experience, and this is a necessary basis for understanding the content and point of the lectures (1095a2–4). Furthermore, a young person is likely to have, still, a rather unsettled ethical life; such a person will derive little practical benefit from the lectures, whose entire point is "not knowledge, but action" (1095a4–6). This is clearly less a matter of chronological age than of moral development.

In real-life historical terms, what this probably means is that Nikidion would have to give the appearance of a young male beyond the ephebe stage (the stage of preliminary military duty), already bearded, already embarking on a political career. She would have to give the appearance of self-discipline and a settled pattern of life. To have the free time to get such an education, she would need to be from the leisured propertied class—not, for example, from a rural farming family.[24] Such a relatively prosperous youth would have received a good deal of preliminary education. "He" would be literate, well versed in poetry and in the city's moral and political traditions, competent in rhetoric and some aspects of musical performance, with a smattering of mathematics and science.[25] Above all, "he" would have to have some firsthand experience of the city's daily life, its religious and civic institutions, its assemblies and lawcourts, its tragic and comic festivals. "He" would have to have participated in the group activities proper to "his" age and status, including military activities. "He" would have to have listened to political discussions of older men, who would provide living examples of something like practical wisdom. "He" would very likely have had the tutelage and protection of an *erastēs*, an older male lover who would have contributed to "his" moral and civic development, while receiving sexual favors.[26] Above all, as Aristotle insists, "he" would need to have had, from the beginning, parents who treated "him" like a future adult citizen, imparting instruction in the virtues by precept, praise, blame, and, above all, love, encouraging "him" to think of citizenship as "his" future sphere, practical wisdom as "his" goal.[27] All this, Nikidion would have to simulate. You will say that all this

---

[24] This point is stressed in the *Politics*, where Aristotle recommends that farmers, sailors, and craftsmen be excluded from citizenship because they lack the leisure requisite for education.

[25] See Marrou (1956).

[26] See Dover (1978), Halperin (1990), Winkler (1990); on the ideal of male citizenship, see Winkler (forthcoming).

[27] See Nussbaum (1986a) ch. 12, Sherman (1989).

would have been impossible for a real-life Nikidion at Athens, even if she were a courtesan and not a citizen wife or daughter—no matter how clever she was, or how well disguised. This seems true. It is a part of what we must see about Aristotle's program. It includes only those whom society already includes and favors.

This does not mean that Aristotle takes no thought for the situation of the excluded. He does, as we shall see. But his philosophical practice, beginning, as it does, with the demand for *paideia* and leisure, can do nothing, in and of itself, to improve the situation of individuals whom politics has not already helped. These individuals must be helped, he holds, by political and institutional designing—which is what these more privileged characters are learning how to do. Once people have been raised in a situation of exclusion, philosophy as such can do nothing for them.

Nikidion arrives, then, at the Lyceum, well disguised and putting on an impossibly good performance. Much of her time there will probably be spent in non-ethical studies, in logic, metaphysics, biology, astronomy, the general study of nature and explanation.[28] All this she pursues (as far as she does pursue it) for its own sake, as well as for its practical implications. On the practical side, part of her time will be spent doing research in political history. Along with other students, she will be helping Aristotle to complete the collection of detailed accounts of the 158 "constitutions," or forms of political organization, that provide background material for Aristotle's constructive political theorizing.[29]

Although Aristotle's surviving lecture manuscripts (which, as edited much later by others, constitute the treatises of the corpus) do not tell us much about classroom procedure, there is reason to think that students attended in relatively large groups and took notes, in a way not too far removed from customs in modern universities.[30] Almost certainly there was discussion and debate during and/or after the lecture. We know what the purpose of the ethical lectures is supposed to be, because they tell us. Their purpose is to effect the dialectical clarification of each pupil's ethical beliefs and responses—of Nikidion's beliefs, then, as one part of the larger community of listeners, who in turn view themselves as members of the larger community of their city. The presence of the group, and the identi-

---

[28] See, however, *PA* I.1, which makes it clear that young gentlemen do not need to go on very far in the sciences.

[29] On the constitutions, see especially Newman (1887–1902); for a famous and idiosyncratic account of their role, see Jaeger (1934).

[30] See Düring (1966) on the practices of the school generally; for an appealing reconstruction of the lecture room from indications in the texts, see Jackson (1920).

fication of each individual with a group, are very important parts of the process. What is sought is a clearer view of a common goal. Teacher and pupil are not just seeking what will satisfy each of them singly, but for what they can live with together in community. This is so, above all, because their ultimate goal will be to legislate for such a community; a central reason for reflecting about the good life is to give direction to that task (*Pol.* VII.1). A desire for agreement is thus presupposed, and regulates their procedure inside the inquiry itself. When alternative views are described, they do not consider the possibility that one person will opt for one view, another for another. What they are always after is the view that does best as a view that all can share.

On the other hand, such references to "community" should not make us think of this process as narrowly Athenian, or in general as specially attached to the local traditions of any particular community. Pupils came to Athens from all over the Greek-speaking world, bringing with them different local traditions, different accounts of the good. Aristotle deliberately augmented the school's store of information about ethical and political alternatives through his cross-cultural research programs. Guided by the view that "all people seek not the way of their ancestors, but the good" (*Pol.* 1269a3–4), he views the different traditions as contributions to a common project, whose aim is to define and defend a general account of human functioning and human flourishing that can guide ethical choice and political planning in any human community.

Nikidion will be told that the purpose of pupil and teacher in ethical inquiry is "to set down the appearances, and then, first working through the puzzles, to go on to show, if possible, the truth of all the things we say concerning these matters; if not, the truth of the greatest number and the most basic" (*EN* 1145b2–7; cf. *EE* 1216b26ff., to be discussed).[31] Appearances are what people say, perceive, believe. So the aim overall is a thorough sifting and scrutiny of the experience and beliefs of the group, one that will effect a consistent ordering (an ordering free of "puzzles") that preserves the greatest and deepest part of the original material. Aristotle's lectures offer one example of how this winnowing might be accomplished. But the dialectical process he constructs is open-ended. It tells pupils that they are supposed to go on being actively engaged in the sorting, making their own varied contributions to the conversation. In this larger dialectical enterprise, Aristotle's own lectures will be just one offering, no matter how complex they are, and no matter how much they represent a previous

---

[31] See Owen, "*Tithenai Ta Phainomena*," in Owen (1986).

winnowing of experience.[32] Aristotle says as much: after offering an especially important set of arguments about human functioning, he remarks:

> So much for our outline sketch for the good life. It would seem to be open to anyone to take things further and to articulate the good parts of the sketch; and time is a good discoverer and ally in these things. That is how progress takes place in the sciences [*technai*] too: it is open to anyone to supply what is lacking. (*EN* 1098a22–26)

Although Aristotle will certainly try to persuade the pupils that his is the position that best preserves the appearances, there is no reason to suppose that they might not lead him to change his mind. He is committed to taking their contributions seriously as material toward truth—and to revising his own view if another one emerges that does the job better. "For everyone has something of his own to contribute to the truth," he writes, "and it is from these that we go on to give a sort of demonstration about these things" (*EE* 1216b1–2; cf. section V).

IV

Now we turn to the medical analogy itself, trying to describe Nikidion's education more concretely by looking at each of our schematic points, in connection with Aristotle's explicit remarks about medicine and other methodological observations. He connects his use of the medical analogy with an explicit endorsement of the first three points in our list of medical characteristics. Ethical arguments have a *practical goal*; they are and should be what I have called *value-relative*; and they should be *responsive to the particular case*. I shall examine each of these points, then turn to areas in which Aristotle is critical of the analogy.

1. *Practical goal.* The philosophical study of ethics, the exchange of arguments about the good human life, is practical. Unlike many other studies in which a philosopher might engage, this one has as its goal, he insists, not just theoretical understanding, but also the improvement of practice.[33] These arguments must be *chrēsimoi*, "useful," have an *ophelos*,

[32] One might observe in this connection the large amount of disagreement between Aristotle's successors, Theophrastus and Strato, and Aristotle himself: the authority of the founder seems to have less weight here than in any other Hellenistic school.

[33] *EN* 1095a5, 1103b26 ff., 1143b18 ff., 1179b35 ff.; *EE* 1214b12 ff., 1215a8 ff. In fact, there is reason to think that we should not use the term "theoretical understanding" at all for what Aristotelian ethics achieves—not if that translates *epistēmē* or *technē*. For the denial

58

"helpful contribution."[34] And ethical arguments are appropriately criticized as *useless* if (as Aristotle thinks about many of Plato's) they have no helpful bearing on any important practical end.[35]

In *Eudemian Ethics* I.5, Aristotle uses the medical analogy to underline this point about the practical goal of ethics. Some sciences, he writes, for example astronomy and geometry, have only knowing and understanding as their proper ends (1215b15–17). There are, on the other hand, other forms of inquiry whose proper end is something practical over and above the knowledge gained through inquiry: such studies are medicine and politics (of which ethics is a branch). "For we aim not to know what courage is but to be courageous, not to know what justice is but to be just, just as we aim to be healthy rather than to know what health is, and to be in a good condition rather than to know what good condition is" (1216b22–25).

Aristotle is not saying that the practical sciences should not acquire knowledge or that the natural sciences cannot have practical application. He explicitly asserts the latter point (1216b15–18), and the former he clearly believes. What his talk of the *telos*, or proper end, of a discipline seems to mean is that this is the primary thing we are going for in pursuing the discipline, the thing that gives that discipline its point and importance in our lives. We would, and do (as he insists in *Metaphysics* I), pursue the study of astronomy and mathematics with intense concentration for the sake of understanding alone. We do not demand of mathematicians that they improve our lives. Although they might incidentally do so, our assessment of them as good or bad mathematicians is based solely on their contribution to the advancement of understanding. This is not true of medicine. We judge doctors good as doctors, not only on the grounds that they are knowledgeable or get theoretically elegant results—although this is certainly part of their preparation—but on the grounds that they are good at curing, or have made some valuable contribution to future cures. (Notice that we cannot even say what a significant result *is*, in medical science, without talking about people.) We give their science as a whole its place of respect in our community because of its contribution to health, a practical goal. So much, Aristotle now claims, is true of ethics: if it makes human lives no better, it will be deservedly ignored.

To say this is not to say that the contribution of ethical study must be

---

that practical matters fall under a *technē*, see *EN* 1103b34 ff., cited later; for the denial that practical wisdom is *epistēmē* (because of the role particulars play in it), see *EN* 1142a23–24, discussed in Nussbaum (1986a) ch. 10.

[34] *EN* 1143b13; *EE* 1217b23, 1218a34, 38; *EN* 1103b29.

[35] *EN* 1096b33; *EE* 1217b25–26, 1218a33–34, 1218b1–2, 9–10.

merely instrumental toward an end that can be completely specified and aimed at apart from the study, any more than it is to say that the medical art cannot tell us more concretely what our vague end of health *is*, as well as give us instrumental means to it (cf. chapter 1). The medical science of Aristotle's day did investigate and debate the question what health *is*; and indeed, it knew it had to, before it could go on to devise concrete instrumental means to health. So when Aristotle makes ethics practical he is not making it the mere tool of established conceptions of ends. It will be permitted to ask (of a very general conception of good functioning that is broadly shared) what, more precisely, it comes to, what its parts are. This is what his own lectures are doing throughout; he indicates that this is one of their salient contributions.[36]

What is the practical contribution of ethical lectures to someone who already has a thorough moral education, a relatively disciplined plan of life, and some experience of decision making? With what goal or goals in view does Aristotle speak of his contribution as "very helpful" (*poluōpheles*, *EN* 1095a11), even as "making a great shift in the balance where life is concerned" (1094a22–23)? The help offered Nikidion, as I have already suggested, seems to be of two closely related kinds: individual clarification of ends and communal agreement concerning ends. These two goals are usually conflated in Aristotle's ways of speaking, in that what the individual sees more clearly is a conception of the human good that is to form the basis for shared life and for social planning; and the communal agreement is, as *Politics* VII stresses, above all an agreement about the conditions of the good human life for "each and every" citizen.[37]

Early in the *Nicomachean Ethics*, he uses an image from archery to illustrate the practical contribution of his arguments: "Won't knowledge of it [sc. the good] make a great shift in the balance where life is concerned, and won't we, like archers with a target before us, be more likely to hit on what is appropriate?" (1094a22–24). Ethical inquiry does not *supply* a target where one was previously altogether absent; this was ruled out in the description of the pupil. The use of target language in Book VI (1144a7) suggests that adults trained in the virtues are already aiming at some target (cf. also *EE* 1214b7 ff.); what is lacking, it seems, is a clear *view* of the target, an articulation of *eudaimonia*, our shared end, into component

---

[36] See, for example, *EN* 1097b22–25. This question is elegantly discussed in Austin (1961).

[37] *Pol.* VII.2, 1324a23–25. On the desire for agreement about *eudaimonia*, cf. for example *EN* 1095a17–22, 1097b22–24. *Politics* IV–VI, however, discusses strategies for achieving stability in situations where different classes have different ends.

parts. Philosophical lectures contribute to this articulation of the parts and of their interrelationships. This will improve practice in the way that a clear view of a target makes it easier to hit: we become more discriminating, more confident, more reliable in choice.

Nikidion's philosophical education, then, will contribute to her life with her fellow citizens by prompting a comprehensive type of reflection that her previous life probably did not encourage. This will make her a better choice-maker both in her personal life and in her political interactions.[38]

2. *Value-relativity.* How close is this reflective enterprise to the systematization of ordinary beliefs described in chapter 1? To what extent does it contain possibilities for criticism of the status quo? And, insofar as it is critical, is the criticism performed in the name of some independent Platonic reality, or by appeal to some deeper layer of human experience? This is a very large topic, which the purposes of this chapter require me to treat more briefly than it deserves.

All Aristotelian inquiries, ethics included, are bounded by the "appearances"—by human experience. In none does there appear to be the possibility of confirming results by comparison to an altogether extraexperiential reality. On the other hand, Aristotle does not mourn the absence of such standards: for the boundaries of experience are also, he holds, the boundaries of discourse and thought. The search for truth is the search for the most accurate account of the world, as we do (and shall) experience it. But this is unqualifiedly a search for *truth*; and no apologies need be made for using that word.

Ethics, however, relies on human experience in a stronger sense. First, what it aims to describe is the good life for a particular species: and in so doing it must consider that species' characteristic capabilities and forms of life. The good human life must, in the first place, be such that a human being *can* live it: it must be "practicable and attainable for the human being" (*EN* 1096b33–35). This is no trivial requirement. And in fact, Aristotle seems to hold something far stronger: the good life must be "common to many (*polukoinon*): for it is capable of belonging to anyone who is not by nature maimed with respect to *aretē*, through some sort of learning and effort" (*EN* 1099b18–20). (It is important to bear in mind that in Aristotle's view not many people are so "maimed": nothing like a view of original sin plays any role in his thinking.) He rejects the view that

---

[38] Close to these formulations, with explicit reference to Aristotle, is the conception of ethical method in Rawls (1971, 1980); they differ, however, on the question of truth—see chapter 1 and later discussion in this chapter.

the good life is primarily a matter of luck or innate talent—and rejects these views as *false ethical views*—not on the grounds that some independent cosmic evidence refutes them, but on the grounds that such a view would "strike too false a note" (1099b24–25), be too out of line with people's aims and hopes.

The corresponding passage in the *Eudemian Ethics* makes it perfectly clear that the ethical truth is constrained, and appropriately constrained, not only by what we *can* do and be, but also by our desires, what we will consider worthwhile and worthless:

> For if living finely is one of those things that comes about by luck or by nature, it would be unhoped for by many—for its attainment would not be secured by effort and would not be up to the people themselves and their own activity. But if it consists in being of a certain sort oneself, and in actions that are in accordance with oneself, the good would be both more common and more divine—more common because more people could share it, more divine because *eudaimonia* would then be available for those who work in order that they and their actions should be of a certain sort. (1215a13–19)[39]

What, more concretely, does this mean? On the one hand, it clearly means that we must reject, *as false*, conceptions of the good human life that strike us (or a sufficient number of reflective people) as such as to make life not worth living. Among these would be lives too full of suffering, he argues: for suffering does in fact cause people to throw life away (1215b18–22). Such too is the sort of life that a child lives: "for no sane person could endure to go back there again" (1215b22–24)—though related lives have had their unreflective philosophical defenders.[40] So too, again, are lives in which a person experiences neither pleasure nor pain— or pleasure only of an ignoble kind (1215b25–27). And furthermore, the sum total of things that we experience unwillingly, whether pleasant or not, will not suffice to make us choose life, even if infinitely prolonged; nor would a life given over to the sort of mindless and choiceless pleasure of which animals are also capable, or to the pleasures of sleep (1215b27– 1216a10). Nor, he elsewhere argues, would a life suffice in which one had

---

[39] "More divine" presumably suggests that the universe as a whole looks more just and in better order if it seems that the good life is in fact broadly available by effort.

[40] See, for example, the discussion of a simple form of hedonism early in the *Nicomachean Ethics*, where Aristotle's opponents defend "choosing the life of dumb grazing animals" (1095b20); in a related discussion of hedonism in Plato's *Philebus*, the life is said to be suited to a shellfish.

all the other good things, but was utterly without friends (*EN* IX.9). In short, a human life, in order to be even a starting-gate candidate for the *true* normative account, must be chosen from among the lives that human beings would willingly choose as preferable to not being alive. And this rules out, in fact, some accounts of the good (such as extreme forms of hedonism) that had found theoretical backing. Ethics, like the medical art, must give its patient a life she could swallow.

But human desires constrain ethical truth in a much more exacting way. For it turns out that the true account of the good human life must describe a life that contains ends that human beings choose for their own sake (as well as the willing choice *of* the ends); and it must, apparently, be inclusive of all such ends, lacking in nothing which, being added, would make the life in question better or more complete. This famous and much discussed requirement[41] leads Aristotle, among other things, to rule out accounts that narrow the good life to that which can be completely controlled by the individual's own agency. For he argues that a life containing only (the state of) virtue, but no action from it out in the world (where the agent's efforts encounter the buffetings of chance), will not be judged by a reasonable person to be complete and lacking in nothing. In fact, says Aristotle, nobody would hold the view that the state of virtue is sufficient for *eudaimonia*, "unless he were defending a theoretical position at all costs" (*EN* 1153b16–21; cf. 1096a1–2).[42] And in general, if it can be shown, for a putative constituent of the good life, that a life that has the other good things and lacks that one thing is seriously incomplete, this will give the element in question a claim to be admitted as a constituent. Judgments of completeness are formed by consulting reflective desire (e.g., *EN* IX.9). Such thought experiments involve complex imaginative and comparative activity; the desires they elicit and consult are not brute or untrained, but heavily shaped by argument and deliberation. But they are judgments that a god who lacked experience of human life and its forms of desire could not form. And it is with reference to such judgments that ethical truth is justified.

The good life is constrained by desire in one further way. We have already said that a solitary life would be rejected as not worth the living. And elsewhere Aristotle stresses that a life in community with others is the only life that will be accepted as complete by a being who identifies itself as

---

[41] *EN* 1097a15–b21; see the excellent analysis in Ackrill (1980), Williams (1962).

[42] Notice that Aristotle is here dismissing what seems to have been the position of both Socrates and Plato, as well as the Stoics. On Socrates, see Vlastos (1991).

human.[43] From this it is taken to follow that a *true* account of the good human life must deliver not a life that is "self-sufficient for the person all by himself, living a solitary life," but self-sufficient "for the person along with parents and children and wife and in general loved ones and fellow citizens" (*EN* 1097b8–11). A certain kind of community—including not only friendship, but also the nuclear family in some form and broader ties of citizenship—is built into the very requirements of the ethical method, as part of the most general description of what it is seeking. This rules out from the start, *as ethically false*, views of the human good that do away with broad ties of citizenship, or with the nuclear family.

When Aristotle's method asks about desire and permits itself to be constrained by what people want and choose, it does not simply record the status quo, or commit itself in any simple way to preserving ordinary beliefs. Aristotle is not the ordinary-belief philosopher of our first chapter, because he refuses any simple majoritarian principle for sorting appearances, insisting on a deeper and more critical scrutiny. Appearances about ethics contain contradictions and ambiguities. The job of inquiry is to listen to every pupil's contribution, along with previous theories and information about other societies—but not to stop there. Puzzles must be perspicuously described, ambiguous terms must be investigated, contradictions must be eliminated. (This may seem obvious, but it is far from obvious, and the Skeptics will insist that it is wrong.) The cross-cultural nature of the social data-gathering project guarantees that we will have plenty of discrepancies on the table. Participants must now be asked what they believe are the deepest and most indispensable appearances, the ones they can least live without. And when this sorting is performed, the procedure calls upon, or tries to emulate, a kind of expert judge, the person of practical wisdom—whose well-informed, sensitive, and experienced discriminations are normative for the correct solution. Once again, the heterogeneous nature of the ethical data, combined with the ethical heterogeneity of Aristotle's group of pupils (since many come, like Aristotle, from non-Athenian backgrounds) will guarantee a rich debate about what lies deepest, and even about what faculties and procedures to trust.[44]

The accounts of the good that emerge in the existing works are, as we

---

[43] For discussion of the evidence, see Nussbaum (forthcoming b).

[44] For Aristotle's interest in intuitions about the good life in a variety of societies there is ample evidence: above all, perhaps, the practice of constitution-gathering, and the study of varied forms of social life in *Politics* II. Here Aristotle follows a tradition of ethically motivated ethnography that begins with Hecataeus and Herodotus (perhaps even with Anaximander).

might by now expect, far from being uncritical records of ordinary belief. They are, in fact, extremely critical of many of the popular views they record: critical, for example, of the views allegedly held by most people about the importance of money, about bodily pleasure, about status and reputation, about anger and revenge (cf. chapter 3). In no case is Aristotle's account simply neglectful of tradition. But it claims to be deeper and more synthetically coherent; it aims to say what an informed and reflective sorting of all the relevant beliefs would say. Not all people are able or willing to perform such a sorting; but the resulting account will nonetheless be true *for them*, as well as for those who do participate.

For this procedure does claim to arrive at truth, despite the medical nature of its operations. Some reasons for this should already be evident. It insists on a rigorous scrutiny of appearances and on the fundamental role of consistency. It claims correspondence, too, with the deepest human beliefs and desires. And one further point should now be stressed. Results in ethics must be consistent, not just internally, but also with everything else held to be true: with the best accounts, then, of the universe, the soul, substance, and so forth. Exactly how far this will constrain the ethical account can be seen only concretely; and Aristotle never states that where there is a prima facie tension, ethical intuitions must yield to metaphysical or psychological appearances. But his demand for overall consistency helps to justify his use of the word "true" in the ethical case, encouraging the idea that we are not just looking into ourselves, but also coming to grips with the world as a whole, as we experience it. All this Nikidion will learn, as, in discussion with her teacher and fellow students, she searches for ethical health.

3. *Responsiveness to the particular case.*[45] Most of the sciences, as Aristotle understands them, deal with what is so always or for the most part. Their principles will therefore often be highly general. Medicine, however, on account of its practical commitment, must strive for a fully adequate perception of the particular cases before it, regarding any general guidelines as aids to perception of the actual. The doctor's primary responsibility, Aristotle writes, is to "the health of this person: for he treats them one by one" (*EN* 1097a12–13). The doctor may appropriately learn, and be guided by, general formulations written down in advance. But these formulations will often prove inadequate to the complexities of the concrete case at hand—either because, designed to cover many particulars, they lack sufficient concreteness, or because they fail to anticipate some

---

[45] This is the focus of the fine discussion of the medical analogy in Jaeger (1957).

feature or group of features that the case actually presents. In such situations, the doctor's primary responsibility is to what is there, in all its complexity. He must be flexible and attentive; if he simply insisted on going by the book, his treatment would be crude and medically irresponsible. The same, Aristotle argues, is true in ethical reasoning. General principles are authoritative only insofar as they are correct; but they are correct only insofar as they do not err with respect to the particulars. And it is not possible for a general formula intended to cover many different particulars to achieve a high degree of precision, even when it is not actually wrong. For this reason, "Among statements about conduct . . . the particular ones are more true—for action is concerned with particulars, and statements must harmonize with these" (*EN* 1107a29–32).

Nor is this just a corrigible defect of actual principles. It is in the very nature of ethical life. "The error is not in the law or in the legislator, but in the nature of the thing, since the matter of practical affairs is of this kind from the start" (1137b17–19). In a famous use of the medical analogy, Aristotle develops the point further:

> Let this be agreed on from the start, that every statement about practical matters ought to be said in outline and not with precision, as we said in the beginning that statements should be demanded in a way appropriate to the matter at hand. And matters of practice and questions of what is advantageous never stand fixed, any more than do matters of health. . . . For such cases do not fall under any science or under any precept, but the agents themselves must in each case look to what suits the occasion, as is also the case in medicine and in navigation. (*EN* 1103b34–1104a10)

The general account, in ethics as in medicine, *ought* to be put forward as an outline or set of guidelines, not as the precise final word. And this is in the nature of the subject matter, not just a deficiency in current practice.

This brief passage suggests three distinct reasons for this judgment. First, both ethics and medicine—unlike, for example, mathematics—concern themselves with mutable creatures and their world. A system of rules set up in advance can include only what has already been seen, just as a medical treatise can only summarize the cases that have been recorded. But the world of change confronts human beings with a bewildering variety of new configurations: in medicine, ever new combinations of symptoms, in ethics, ever new situations for choice. A doctor whose only resource, confronted with a case unlike any that had been previously described, was to turn to the authority of Hippocrates would not give adequate treatment. (Nor would he be doing what Hippocrates himself did, that on account of which he is respected as a medical authority.) In just this way a person of practical wisdom must be prepared to encounter new cases, with responsiveness and imagination, using what she has learned from her study of the past, but cultivating as well the sort of flexibility and perceptiveness that will permit her, in Thucydides' words, to "improvise what is required."[46] Aristotle tells us that "the person who is good at deliberation without qualification is the one who improvises according to reason at the best for a human being in the sphere of things to be done" (*EN* 1141b13–14); he associates this ideal closely with the observation that practical wisdom is concerned with particulars and not with general rules alone (1141b14–16).

It is not only change over time that concerns Aristotle here; it is also the context-sensitivity of good ethical choice. In a related discussion in *Nicomachean Ethics* V, he uses the word *aoriston*, "indeterminate" or "undefinable," in connection with statements very similar to those he made in the passage that introduces the medical analogy. The word *aoriston*, applied to practical matters, is hard to interpret; but an example elsewhere makes Aristotle's meaning clearer. There is no definition (*horismos*) of good joke-telling, he writes, but it is *aoristos*, since so much is a matter of pleasing the particular hearer, and "different things are repugnant and pleasant to different people" (1128a25 ff.). Extrapolating from this case, we may say that excellent ethical choice cannot be captured completely in general rules because—like medicine—it is a matter of fitting one's choice to the complex requirements of a concrete situation, taking all of its contextual features into account. A rule, like a joke manual (like a medical textbook) would do both too little and too much: too little, because the rule (unless carefully qualified) would imply that it was itself normative for correct response (as a joke manual would have you tailor your wit to the formulae it contains); this could impinge too much on the flexibility of good practice.

In the context of love and friendship, it is possible that Aristotle may recognize particularity in a yet stronger sense, recognizing that some valuable forms of ethical attention and care are not even in principle universalizable. The love of a particular child or friend includes not only the highly concrete (but in principle replicable) history of the friendship; it also includes the thought that a substitute with the very same descriptive features would not be acceptable as a replacement. Criticizing Plato's proposals for holding spouses and children in common, Aristotle points out

[46] Thucydides I.138, of Themistocles.

that close particular attachments are fundamental to familial and political motivation. "There are two things above all that make people love and care for something: the thought that it is all yours, and the thought that it is the only one you have" (*Pol.* II.4, 1262b22–24). A person motivated in this way is unlikely to view her own particular spouse or child as simply the object of universalizable ethical obligations. Parental education is superior to public education, Aristotle argues, because it begins from a grasp of the child's particularity, and is thus more likely to hit on what is appropriate (1180b7 ff.).

In all these ways, general principles, if seen as normative for correct practical judgment, prove insufficient. Nor, for related reasons, is there any general algorithm that will suffice to generate, in each case, the virtuous choice. For one thing, such algorithms have a marked tendency to reduce the many intrinsically valuable things recognized in an Aristotelian account to one thing, varying in quantity only; for another, they simply seem to impose too much on judges in advance. Situations must be grasped with an "eye" for all their complexities: in short, as Aristotle twice remarks, "the discrimination lies in perception" (*EN* 1109b18–23; cf. 1126b2–4). Perception is not a mysterious *sui generis* visionary ability. Like the doctor's clinical ability (and like the ability of a good judge in the Anglo-American common-law tradition), it is steered by general learning, principles, and history. But the ability also requires a resourceful imagination, and an ability to confront the new case, picking out its salient properties. This ability, Aristotle plausibly insists, must be learned through experience—for only experience of particulars yields an eye for what is salient and an ability to seize the occasion (*kairos*, 1096a32, where medical imagery is used again).

If we now return to Nikidion, we find that this third and crucial medical element is harder than the others to see in operation in the lecture room, since it is hard to exemplify it at all in general lectures, except by pointing, as Aristotle so frequently does, to its importance. (In this task the medical analogy plays a valuable guiding role: for what is difficult to communicate in other ways may be easier to grasp through analogical reasoning.) But general lectures are hardly the whole of Nikidion's education. She will be pursuing research into concrete issues of political history—and no doubt also studying works of literature in which complicated cases are displayed.[47] And, given that she holds that the goal of theory is good practice,

---

[47] Aristotle frequently uses literary examples in the *Nicomachean Ethics* to illustrate his points about the virtues. For just a few characteristic examples, see *EN* 1109b9; 1111a10 ff.; 1116a22, 33; 1136b10; 1145a20; 1146a19; 1148a33; 1151b18; 1161a14.

she will also be putting Aristotle's lectures to work in her life, sorting out concrete situations of choice with reference to the account of the good evolving in the lectures, and using her experience, in turn, to assess their claims. Education is a two-way process of mutual illumination between experience and a general view or views of human life—which never claims finality, and sends her back again to experience as the scene of practical judgment.

V

Aristotle has used the medical analogy to depict a philosophical approach to ethics that is practical, fruitfully related to human hopes and beliefs, responsive to the complexities of cases. But his conception of practical philosophy makes him turn away from the analogy at a crucial point, so that he rejects a group of "medical" traits of philosophy that the Hellenistic schools will in many cases defend.

We can begin with two passages in which Aristotle explicitly breaks with the medical analogy, and then use related passages to develop the view of ethical argument on which this criticism relies. In *Eudemian Ethics* I.3 (1214b28 ff.), Aristotle gives his reasons for excluding children and insane people from the range of those whose ethical opinions will be surveyed. He says that such people have many beliefs that no sane person would consider seriously. Then he adds what appears to be an argument for omitting the holders of these opinions from the philosophical process in which teacher and pupil are now engaged: "They are in need not of arguments, but, in the former case, of time to grow up, and, in the latter case, of either political or medical chastisement—for the administering of drugs is a form of chastisement no less than beating is." Here Aristotle speaks of medical treatment as a causal technique for the manipulation of behavior; he links it with beating and sharply dissociates it from the giving and receiving of arguments among reasonable people. Similarly, in *EN* X.9, he speaks of irrational people whose condition yields not to argument but only to "force" (*bia*, 1179b28–29). Medical treatment, the conjunction of the two passages implies, is a form of *bia*, of external causal intervention. Argument is something else, something apparently gentler, more self-governed, more mutual. The former sort of thing is suitable for young and/or seriously disturbed people, the latter for reasonable adults. I turn now to Aristotle's other explicit criticism of the medical parallel.

In *Nicomachean Ethics* VI.13, Aristotle confronts an opponent who charges that the intellectual element in ethics is useless. If practical knowledge aims not at theory but at practice, the objector charges, then someone who already has a reasonably good character has no need of any further intellectual study of goodness. The objector uses Aristotle's own characteristic parallels from the practical arts. The *study* of gymnastic *theory* does not improve gymnastic practice. The *study* of medicine does not make the patient better: "If we want to be healthy, we do not learn medical science" (1143b32–33). So too in ethics, if you *are* good, you don't need the study; if you are not good, it will not help you become so. In either case, then, study and intellectual grasp are useless from the practical point of view.

Aristotle does not dispute the opponent's point about medicine; he implicitly grants that medicine has an intellectual asymmetry about it. Its practical benefits require that the doctor should know, but not that the patient should know; its *logoi* are authoritative and one-sided. He does, however, go on to dispute the claim vigorously for ethics, arguing that study and the application of intellect have a practical value for everyone in this area. Ethics appears to be less one-sided, more "democratic," than medicine is: the benefits of its *logoi* require each person's active intellectual engagement. (We now notice that even the positive use of the medical analogy at 1104a was strained: for it compared what *each* person ought to do in ethics with what the good *doctor* does in medicine.) This observation fits well with the contrast, in the *Eudemian Ethics* passage, between force and argument: ethical *logoi* are unlike medical treatment, in that they involve a reciprocal discourse in which the pupil is not ordered around by an authority figure, or manipulated by coercive tactics, but is intellectually active for herself. But in order to understand the view of argument and its benefits that lies behind this contrast, we need to turn to some related material in which the medical contrast is not explicitly present.

Aristotle repeatedly claims (as we saw, discussing Nikidion) that the proper recipient of ethical arguments and lectures must already be a person of a certain maturity, who has been well brought up and who has both some experience and some passional balance. The need for experience flows, we now see, from the positive side of the medical analogy: ethical *logos* deals with particulars, and only experience can deliver a good grasp of these. Therefore, though a young person might already do well at mathematical arguments, he should not study the *Nicomachean Ethics* (1095b4–5, 1094b27 ff., 1179b23 ff.; cf. 1142a12 ff.). Balance is necessary because disorderly people are ill-equipped for the give and take of rational argument, and they will "listen badly." Their condition requires something more compelling—the element of force supplied by discipline—to bring it into order (1179b23 ff.). For this reason, an intellectual study of ethics will be of no use to such a person (1096a4, 9–10).

This claim is easy enough to understand if we think of the *Nicomachean Ethics* or the *Eudemian Ethics* as our model of an ethical argument. We can agree with Aristotle that a very disorderly person, either young or older (cf. 1095a6–7, 9), will not get much out of a study of this book. Indeed, it is fiendishly difficult to teach even to very bright and highly motivated under-graduates, for the reasons Aristotle gives. But as the Hellenistic writers know, and many in the philosophical and literary traditions before them, there are many kinds of ethical argument. We might say that for any condition of soul we can always find *some* therapeutic *logos*, and probably even one that we would call an argument. If a pupil should prove unable to attend to the *Nicomachean Ethics*, she may well do better with a simpler or more dramatic or more rhetorically colorful work. The real question seems to be why Aristotle opts for the sort of discourse that is gentle, compli-cated, reciprocal, and quite unlike force and drug treatment. On what grounds does he insist, as he repeatedly does, that there is an important sort of practical benefit to be gained from the very sort of *logos* that does *not* therapeutically treat the character but requires its antecedent ordering? Why, in other words, should ethical philosophy not be really like medicine?

I shall be pursuing that question throughout the book; but I can begin to sketch an answer here, on Aristotle's behalf. I have said that the practical goal of Aristotelian ethics is individual clarification and communal attune-ment. In both cases, getting a clear view of the "target" makes practice more discriminating and more reliable. We can now connect this to Aris-totle's criticism of the medical analogy. In *Nicomachean Ethics* VI, he answers the opponent who claimed that intellectual grasp is useless by insisting, in fact, on the great practical value of clarity. We do not pursue our own health by studying medicine, he grants: but we do go after ethical and political goodness by pursuing the intellectual study of ethics— because through the intellectual scrutiny of our ends we get a clearer *vision* of what pertains to the end, that is, of the constituents of the good human life and how they stand to one another. He insists that although virtue alone may aim us at the target, we need intellect and teaching to get it correctly articulated (1144a7–8); practical wisdom, an intellectual virtue, is the "eye" of the soul. We already know that practical wisdom requires experience and moral education. What Aristotle now insists is that it is also importantly developed by philosophical teaching.

The task demanded of *logoi*, being one of clarification and articulation, requires clarity and articulateness in the *logoi* themselves: "We will have spoken sufficiently," he elsewhere writes, "if we make things clear as far as the subject matter permits" (*diasaphētheiē*, 1094b11–12).[48] The *Eudemian Ethics* makes this requirement even more evident. To live well, we must have our lives ordered toward some end of our choice (1214b7 ff.). But then, "it is most especially important first to demarcate within oneself [*diorisasthai en hautōi*], neither hastily nor carelessly, in which of the things within our power living well consists" (1214b12–14).[49] This careful clarification is contrasted with the "random talk" (*eikēi legein*) in which most people usually indulge on matters ethical (1215a1–2). Then, in a most important passage, Aristotle tells us that this enterprise, and its related goal of communal attunement, are best served by a cooperative critical discourse that insists on the philosophical virtues of orderliness, deliberateness, and clarity:

> Concerning all these things we must try to seek conviction through arguments, using the appearances as our witnesses and standards [*paradeigmasi*]. For it would be best of all if all human beings could come into an evident communal agreement with what we shall say, but if not, that all should agree in some way. And this they will do if they are led carefully until they shift their position. For everyone has something of his own to contribute to the truth, and it is from these that we go on to give a sort of demonstration about these things. For from what is said truly but not clearly, as we advance, we will also get clarity, always moving from what is usually said in a jumbled fashion [*sunkechumenōs*] to a more perspicuous view. There is a difference in every inquiry between arguments that are said in a philosophical way and those that are not. Hence we must not think that it is superfluous for the political person to engage in the sort of reflection that makes perspicuous not only the "that" but also the "why": for this is the contribution of the philosopher in each area. (1216a26–39)

Aristotle here accepts, once again, a part of the medical analogy: for he insists that the touchstone and standard of ethical argument must be the appearances—a term that means, in the ethical case, the particulars of human ethical experience—supplemented by general ethical theories and traditions.[50] But he shows us clearly, too, his reasons for breaking with that

[48] Cf. *diasaphēsai*, 1097a24, *dioristhōsi*, 1098b6, *enargesteron*, 1097b23.

[49] Note here, again, the stipulation that the true account of living well must make it "within our power."

[50] The use of the word *paradeigma* surely invites comparison with Plato, who had insisted that the "standards" ethics requires must be in a realm of eternal being situated over against the "appearances" of perception and belief.

analogy. The goals of personal clarification and communal agreement require a progress beyond the hasty and confused modes of ordinary discourse, toward greater coherence and perspicuity. But this, in turn, requires
the sort of argument that sorts things out and clarifies, that leads people to
shift their alleged ground by pointing to inconsistencies in their system of
beliefs and, in the process, makes evident not only the fact of our commitments, but also their "why," that is, how they contribute to one another
and to the good life in general.[51] Aristotle tells us unabashedly that to give
this sort of *logos* is the business of the professional philosopher, and that
this is why the philosopher is a useful person to have around and to
emulate.

Shortly after this, he goes on to warn the reader that clarity and elegance
are not by themselves *sufficient* for practical value in ethical argument. You
have to be on your guard, he says, against the sort of philosopher who
argues clearly but is lacking in the proper connectedness to human experience. And some pupils are led astray by such people, thinking that "to use
arguments and to say nothing at random is the mark of the philosopher"
(1217a1–2); they thus allow themselves to be influenced by jejune and
irrelevant glibness. Clarity, deliberateness, and logical consistency are not
enough: arguments must also be medical in the good way, rooted in the
particulars and attentive to them. But we should not let the empty glibness
of some philosophers give ethical philosophy a bad name. We should not
disdain the specifically philosophical contribution to ethics or think of the
moral philosopher as a superfluous person. He is useful both because of his
similarity to the doctor and because of his difference from the doctor.
Unlike the doctor, he engages you actively in the "treatment," taking your
view of things as seriously as his own; he leads you on through the interchange of calm and clarifying argument to what he hopes will be an
articulated picture of the good.

We can now return to Nikidion and to our schematic list of medical
traits. We shall see that Aristotle's criticisms of the medical analogy lead
him to reject from her education a second group of characteristics—in
order to achieve the practical benefit that is, in his view, distinctive of
philosophy.

4. Medical treatment is *directed at the health of the individual*, seen as a
separate unit. Aristotelian ethical argument, by contrast, addresses individuals as members of familial and political communities, separate units,

---

[51] On the "that" and the "why," see *EN* 1094b4–8, and the discussion in Burnyeat
(1980b).

but bound to one another by shared ends and ties of affection and concern. Its participants identify themselves as essentially social and political beings: so to look for the good life for Nikidion is to look for a life that she can share with others, and achieving her own good involves working for the health of the community.

5. In medicine, *the characteristic procedures of the art are purely instrumental* to the production of an end, bodily health, that can be fully characterized without mention of practical reason. In a medical or therapeutic ethics, then, argument would serve a productive and instrumental role. But in Nikidion's education it is also of high intrinsic value. Activity in accordance with complete virtue is also an activity of practical reason. And thus what she does when she discusses Aristotle's lectures and goes over arguments about the good is not just instrumentally useful, it is also valuable for its own sake. Without it life will be less good and less complete, even if it has every other good thing.

6. *The standard virtues of philosophical argument*—logical consistency, definitional clarity, and so forth—*are treated as merely instrumental* in the medical analogy, and perhaps even (like the techniques of the doctor) dispensable, if a cure were found that short-circuits them. But they are absolutely central to the practical benefits sought for Nikidion, and central not only as invaluable instruments but, apparently, as ends in themselves. Aristotle insists that we move beyond the muddle of daily life, and come into agreement with one another, only by ferreting out inconsistencies and seeking clarity in all our discourse; and both consistency and clarity appear to be valuable for their own sake, as elements in the exercise of practical wisdom and intellectual excellence.

7. The medical analogy creates a sharp *asymmetry of roles*: doctor and patient, authority and recipient of authority. Aristotle has criticized the analogy on precisely these grounds. Aristotelian ethical argument involves authority in a sense, for the professional philosopher claims that his superior experience in the criticism of argument and in giving perspicuous accounts gives him a claim to be heard by the political person. But the denial of the analogy in *Nicomachean Ethics* VI shows us that Nikidion will not be a passive recipient of this expertise. She is to emulate the philosopher, entering actively into the give and take of criticism, being not subservient but independent, not worshipful but critical. The teacher and the pupil are involved in the very same activity, each as an independent rational being; it is only that the teacher has done it longer and can therefore offer a kind of experienced guidance. It is no accident that near the beginning of the *Nicomachean Ethics* Aristotle gives an example of how to

regard the authority of one's teacher. When he begins his devastating criticism of Plato, he says that it may be difficult to criticize the views of those who are dear to us: but we must put the truth first, "all the more since we are philosophers" (1096a11 ff.). Nikidion is encouraged to think this way about Aristotle.[52]

8. The medical analogy *discourages the sympathetic dialectical scrutiny of alternative views*. The doctor goes on with his own way. It is at best peripheral, at worst confusing and dangerous, to instruct the patient in other available ways. But this respectful dialectical scrutiny is a fundamental part of Aristotelianism. What we are after is to find out more clearly what we share or can share. And this requires a patient and non-hasty working through of the available accounts of the subject, accounts, as Aristotle says, of both "the many" and "the wise." Aristotle's position is that each person has something to contribute to the ethical truth. As he remarks of some of the alternatives he is examining, "Some of these things have been said by many people over a long period of time, others by a few distinguished people. It is reasonable to suppose that none of them has missed the mark totally, but each has gotten something, or even a lot of things, right" (1098a28–30)."[53] (Here we find another source of the teacher's claim to teach: for the Aristotelian philosopher knows more political history and more history of ethics than most people, and therefore can bring alternatives to bear on the common project in an especially perspicuous way.) Nikidion will study, both critically and respectfully, many books in philosophy and history. She will learn a great deal about the arguments of Socrates and Plato; she will do research in the comparative study of constitutions; she will learn to compare Aristotle's views of the good life and of political arrangement with those of other philosophers, other communities, and also with her own and those of her friends. And she will regard all these alternatives sympathetically, with imagination, seeing them as serious candidates for truth.

9. What, finally, will Aristotelian arguments have to say about them-

[52] When I was taken to visit the tomb of Confucius in 1987, my Chinese host Li Zhen, an Aristotle scholar, pointed to the throng of worshipful pilgrims who were there in order to venerate Confucius as a divine thinker, and said: "There you see the difference between Confucius and Aristotle. Aristotle never would have permitted himself to be treated in that way." With Epicurus, as we shall see, things are otherwise.

[53] Compare the introduction to the account of mathematical entities in *Metaphysics* XIII, 1076a11–16, where Aristotle says that we should study the writings of predecessors in order to avoid making the same mistakes over again and to avail ourselves of their valid contributions: we should be content if we say some things a little better than they, and other things no worse.

selves? It follows from the considerations advanced in point 8 that they will usually be somewhat tentative and respectful of other possibilities. Insofar as they have done their historical and experiential work, they will be somewhat confident—they will not expect to be overthrown completely—but they leave open the possibility of revision and correction. And in any case, the pupil is to regard the general account presented in these arguments as a guide to future cases, not as altogether legislative for practice. She is learning to trust her own increasingly refined ethical faculties, rather than to rely on Aristotle's text. In short: the lectures do not claim finality, and they repudiate dogmatic and subservient praise.

10. Nikidion's relationship to the Aristotelian arguments can be expected to be increasingly strong and enthusiastic. The more she reasons in the Aristotelian way, the better she will become at doing so. And the more she does it well, the more she is likely to see its benefits in her life and therefore to desire more eagerly to do it.

VI

We have now identified some medical and some non-medical or even anti-medical elements in Nikidion's education. The point of singling out this last group will become clear when we reach Epicurus, who, using the medical analogy in these cases as well, argues for a view very different from Aristotle's, and creates a different sort of therapeutic community.

In these educational procedures we find much that has become deeply rooted in Western philosophical practice, much that we have come to value in teaching and writing. Those of us who teach moral philosophy in universities are likely to recognize in this account of the teacher-pupil relationship ideals that we, too, try to exemplify in some way. These ideals also have deep roots in American society more generally, in norms of personal separateness and active critical practical reasoning that are an important part of its liberal democratic traditions. Hellenistic procedures, by contrast, will in some cases seem foreign and even alarming. Since one point of this inquiry is to wrestle with the liberal ideals exemplified in these elements of Aristotle by coming to terms with a deep challenge against them, I want to end this chapter by starting to ask some troublesome questions about Nikidion's Aristotelianism and the assumptions that lie behind it.

This account of ethical inquiry as a *winnowing* and a *sifting* of people's opinions—what does it assume about the relationship between these opinions and the correct account? Several things, plainly. First, that truth is there in the sample of opinion to be tested. And Aristotle seems to be committed to something still stronger: that each questioned person's beliefs contain at least some truth. So far, as we shall see, he is on common ground with all exponents of a "medical" account of ethics; I have suggested that such an assumption is a defining feature of such conceptions, by contrast to various forms of Platonism. But, second, Aristotle must believe that the procedures of intellectual questioning standardly used in his writing and no doubt in his lecturing as well, practiced in a context of calm intellectual study, are sufficient to elicit from Nikidion whatever true beliefs she holds, to guarantee that they are out there among the intuitions she brings forward for ethical scrutiny. Third, he must believe that his procedures of working through puzzles, clarifying definitions, and so forth, are sufficient to guarantee in a reliable way the separation of the true beliefs from the false: when pupils see the conflict of appearances and go to work on it in the Aristotelian way, they will regularly throw out the false beliefs and keep the true.

What does someone who believes all these things have to think about ordinary (even well-educated) human beings, about their health, about the health of their society? Doesn't he have to have views about social health that are, to say the least, controversial, and perhaps incompatible with the searching criticism of existing practices and institutions? Doesn't he, in addition, have to have views about the transparency of the personality that might be false, and are certainly not justified by any argument Aristotle presents? And even if he is right about the abilities of the pupils he teaches—given that these have been carefully selected to conform to his specifications—what becomes of the ones he does not and cannot teach? Such as Nikidion, if she takes off her elaborate and impossible disguise? Isn't he so busy perfecting the already blooming ethical and psychological health of privileged young gentlemen that he has nothing to offer to her diseases, to her lack of citizen experience, and the suffering of her excluded state? Looked at in this way, isn't this apostle of fine-tuned perception a politically and ethically smug and self-satisfied character?

This question will return regularly, with each Hellenistic challenge against conventional philosophical practice. But we can pose it more precisely, if we now turn to Aristotle's account of the emotions and their training.

✳ CHAPTER 3 ✳

Aristotle on Emotions and
Ethical Health

I

Nikidion is an emotional person. She loves her friends and feels joy in their presence, hope for their future. If one of them should die, she weeps and feels great grief. If someone should damage her, or someone dear to her, she gets angry; if someone should help her out, she feels gratitude. When others suffer terrible harms and wrongs, she feels pity for their suffering. And this means that she feels fear as well, since she perceives that she has similar vulnerabilities. She is not ashamed of these emotions. For the city in which she was raised endorses them, staging tragic festivals that encourage citizens to feel pity at the unjustified suffering of others, fear for their own similar possibilities. How will Aristotle deal with these aspects of her character?

The Hellenistic thinkers see the goal of philosophy as a transformation of the inner world of belief and desire through the use of rational argument. And within the inner world they focus above all on the emotions—on anger, fear, grief, love, pity, gratitude, and their many relatives and subspecies. In Aristotle's ethical thought we see, on the one hand, a view about the nature of the emotions that adumbrates many ingredients of the more fully developed Hellenistic views. Emotions are not blind animal forces, but intelligent and discriminating parts of the personality, closely related to beliefs of a certain sort, and therefore responsive to cognitive modification. On the other hand, we find a normative view about the role of the emotions inside the good human life that is sharply opposed to all the Hellenistic views, since it calls for cultivation of many emotions as valuable and necessary parts of virtuous agency. Nikidion's education here will not seek to "extirpate" the passions, though it will modify them; and it may even need to cultivate them further, should her dispositions in this regard prove deficient. For this position Peripatetics will be sharply attacked by Hellenistic thinkers, who view the Aristotelian position as a cowardly halfway measure that fails to address the most urgent human problems.

Why, then, does Aristotle adopt an analysis of emotion that resembles that of the Hellenistic thinkers, while at the same time advancing a very different normative view of their role? And what does this mean for Niki-dion's philosophical education? We can understand the Hellenistic thinkers better if we grasp some features of the conception against which, increasingly as time goes on, they direct their assault.

II

According to some influential modern views that have left a deep mark on popular stereotypes, emotions like grief, anger, and fear come from an animal irrational side of the personality that is to be sharply distinguished from its capacity for reasoning and for forming beliefs. Emotions are simply bodily reactions, whereas reasoning involves complex intentionality—directedness toward an object, a discriminating view of the object. Emotions are unlearned or innate, whereas beliefs are learned in society. Emotions are impervious to teaching and argument, beliefs can be modified by teaching. Emotions are present in animals and infants as well; belief and reasoning belong to mature human beings alone. These are some of the common clichés about emotion—whether or not they reflect or have ever reflected the ways in which people actually talk about specific emotions when they experience them in life.[1]

Such views have had a profound influence on the science of psychology, until very recently.[2] They have had a profound influence on the ways in which people think and talk about emotion when they discuss standards of reasoning and argument in philosophy and public life. Appeals to emotion are frequently depicted as altogether "irrational" in the normative sense, that is, inappropriate and illegitimate in discourse that claims to engage in persuasive reasoning. In a famous discussion of philosophical speech, John Locke compares the emotive uses of language to the wiles of a seductive woman: delightful when one wants diversion, pernicious when one is on the track of the truth.[3] One still finds many similar statements, even though

---

[1] For criticism of the clichés, see, in very different ways, Lutz (1988), Kenny (1963).

[2] For a history of the field in this regard, see Lazarus (1991); also Oatley (1992). Lazarus notes that the field of psychology has just managed to win its way back to the position that Aristotle already defended in the *Rhetoric*.

[3] Locke (1690): *Essay* III ch. 10. An excellent recent treatment of the whole topic is De Sousa (1987). I discuss contemporary legal debates about emotion in Nussbaum (forthcoming a).

the analysis of emotion that supported Locke's view of argument no longer wins broad acceptance.

This, however, was not the view of the emotions held by any major ancient Greek thinker. If we schematically lay out the common ground of their agreement, we will be in a better position to appreciate Aristotle's specific analyses:

1. Emotions are forms of *intentional awareness*: that is (since no ancient term corresponds precisely to these terms), they are forms of awareness *directed at* or *about* an object, in which the object figures as it is seen from the creature's point of view. Anger, for example, is not, or not simply, a bodily reaction (such as a boiling of the blood). To give an adequate account of it, one must mention the object to which it is directed, what it is *about* and *for*. And when we do this, we characterize the object as it is seen by the person experiencing the emotion, whether that view is correct or not: my anger depends upon the way *I* view you and what you have done, not on the way you really are or what you really have done.[4]

2. Emotions have a very intimate relationship to beliefs, and can be modified by a modification of belief. My anger, for example, requires a belief that I have been deliberately wronged by someone in a more than trivial way. Should I decide that this belief was false (that the alleged wrong did not in fact take place, or was not in fact a wrong, or was not done by the person in question, or was not done deliberately) my anger will be removed, or shift its target. At this point, positions diverge, some claiming that the belief in question is a *necessary condition* of the emotion, some claiming that it is a *constituent part* of the emotion, some that it is both necessary and *sufficient* for the emotion. The Stoics, as we shall see, claim that the relation is one of *identity*: the emotion just is a certain sort of belief or judgment. The logical relationships among these positions, and the arguments for and against different combinations, will be further addressed in chapter 10. But the weakest thesis that seems to be accepted by any major Greek thinker, from Plato on, is the thesis that belief(s) of a certain sort are a *necessary condition* of the emotion in each case.[5]

3. All this being so, emotions may appropriately be assessed as *rational*

---

[4] From this follows the possibility of directing emotions toward items that are not really there, whether absent or imagined. On the notion of "freedom of content" in the analysis of intentionality, and for an excellent overall treatment of the topic of intentionality in Aristotle's thought, see Caston (1992).

[5] Posidonius' position on this question is unclear, and he comes closer than any other to a non-cognitive view of emotion; but even he believes emotions can be modified by cognitive therapy.

or *irrational*, and also (independently) as *true* or *false*, depending on the character of the beliefs that are their basis or ground. Thus, rather than having a simple dichotomy between the emotional and the (normatively) rational,[6] we have a situation in which all emotions are to some degree "rational" in a descriptive sense—all are to some degree cognitive and based upon belief—and they may then be assessed, as beliefs are assessed, for their normative status.

Now, however, we shall turn to Aristotle, seeing how he develops this area of agreement and puts it to work in the analysis of specific emotions.

III

Even the bodily appetites—hunger, thirst, sexual desire—are seen by Aristotle as forms of intentional awareness, containing a view of their object. For he consistently describes appetite as *for, directed at*, "the apparent good." Appetite is one form of *orexis*, a "reaching out for" an object; and all the forms of *orexis* see their object in a certain way, supplying the active animal with a "premise of the good."[7] In other words, when a dog goes across the room to get some meat, its behavior is explained not by some hydraulic mechanism of desire driving it from behind, but as a response to the way it sees the object. Aristotle also holds that appetite—unlike, for example, the animal's digestive system—is responsive to reasoning and instruction (*EN* 1102b28–1103a1). He is talking about human appetite here, but he recognizes much continuity between humans and other animals, with respect to the capacity for acting from a (modifiable) view of the good.

Where specifically human appetite is concerned, the case for intentionality and cognitive responsiveness is clearer still. Aristotle's account of

[6] I include this qualification since, in both ancient and modern discussions, the terms "rational" and "irrational" (and their Greek counterparts) are used, often confusingly, in both a descriptive sense (meaning, often, "cognitive" and "non-cognitive") and also in a normative sense (meaning "conforming to [some] normative view of the right way to reason.") The Stoics will hold that all emotions are "rational" in the descriptive sense (all are judgments), but "irrational" in the normative sense (all are unjustifiable and false judgments). Galen tries to convict them of absurdity by pointing to this twofold use of the word *alogos*, but all he succeeds in showing is that there is a delicate terminological issue that needs attention.

[7] See *De Motu Animalium* ch. 7; this whole issue is discussed in Nussbaum (1978), commentary and essay 4, and in Nussbaum (1986a) ch. 9. For recent defenses of this way of viewing Aristotelian desires, see Richardson (1992) and Charles (1984).

the virtue of moderation, which is concerned with the proper management of the bodily appetites (the appetites, he frequently says, that humans share with other animals), shows that he believes suppression is not the only way to make appetite behave well. Indeed, suppression could produce at best self-control, and not virtue. The virtue requires psychological balance (*sumphōnein*, 1119b15), so that the person does not characteristically long for the wrong food and drink, at the wrong time, in the wrong amount (1118b28–33). But this is achieved by an intelligent process of moral education, which teaches the child to make appropriate distinctions, to take appropriate objects. The object of well-educated appetite, he holds, is the "fine" (*kalon*, 1119b16).[8]

All types of desire are responsive to reasoning and teaching, then, to some degree. But it is in connection with the emotions, rather than the bodily appetites, that Aristotle develops the role of belief in desire most clearly.[9] A number of texts in the ethical and psychological writings give us help here, especially in determining the normative role of emotion within the good human life. But it is above all in the *Rhetoric* that we find Aristotle's detailed analysis of emotions such as anger, fear, pity, and friendly love. Although much of the ethical material in the *Rhetoric* cannot be used directly to reconstruct Aristotle's own ethical views—since it provides the young orator not with Aristotle's considered view but with popular views of ethical matters that would be likely to prevail in his audience[10]—the material on emotion is not similarly circumscribed. For Aristotle's project in these chapters is to enable the aspiring orator to *produce* these emotions in an audience (*empoiein*, 1378a27). For this to succeed, he needs to know what fear and anger really *are*, not just what people think they are. If the popular view held that anger was a brutish unreasoning bodily appetite, a fire in the heart, and the truth about anger was that it was a complex cognitive disposition resting on beliefs of several kinds, then it would be the latter view, not the former, that the orator would need to know, since his aim is not to talk about anger but to produce it. He does not need to know whether the things that usually make people angry ought to do so, or

[8] On the discriminating character of Aristotelian moral education generally, see Sherman (1989), Sorabji (1980); on the appetites and moderation, see Price (1989), Young (1988). Price makes an especially good case for the educability of sexual desire.

[9] For an excellent account of this issue, see Leighton (1982); see also the earlier influential account in Fortenbaugh (1975). There are excellent accounts of the cognitive structure of pity and fear in Halliwell (1986), and of anger in Aubenque (1957). Cf. also Fillion-Lahille (1970).

[10] Notice, however, that, given Aristotle's ethical methodology there is much continuity between the two.

82

whether their beliefs about what is fearful are in fact true: that indeed is the business of the ethical writings, and we shall turn to these in due course. But he needs to know what really produces emotion; and it seems to be the underlying assumption of the whole rhetorical enterprise that belief and argument are at the heart of the matter. For the orator does not have the opportunity to work on people's physiology, to give them drugs or light a fire under their hearts. If there is any hope of rhetoric's doing what Aristotle wants it to do, it had better be the case that emotions can in fact be created and taken away pretty reliably by discourse and argument. And this is what Aristotle now attempts to show. I shall focus on the cases of fear and pity, since these provide an excellent place to begin examining the contrast between Aristotle and his Hellenistic successors, who will revive Platonic attacks on fear and pity to which Aristotle already responds. I shall begin from two important passages in the psychological works, and then turn to the detailed analyses in the *Rhetoric*.

Fundamental to Aristotle's analysis is a distinction between *fear* and *fright* or *being startled*. In two texts analyzing the building blocks of action,[11] he notes that a loud noise, or the appearance of enemy troops, may produce a startling effect, even on a brave person. The person's heart may leap from fright or startling, without its being the case that the person is really afraid (*DA* 432b30–31; cf. *MA* 11). (The *De Motu* discussion adds a parallel example: sometimes the appearance of a beautiful person may produce sexual arousal, without its being the case that the person has sexual emotion of the sort that would really lead to action.) But if the person is only startled and not afraid, it is clear that he will not run away: as the *De Motu* argues, only a part of the body will be moved, and not the entire body. The *De Motu* analysis suggests that we see in such cases the effect of *phantasia*, or "appearing," without any concomitant *orexis*, reaching out, or desire.[12] (Emotion is a subclass of *orexis*.) The question must now be, What would have to be added to this being startled, in order to turn it into real *fear*?

The example resembles another one used by Aristotle in the sphere of perception, where he distinguishes simple *phantasia*, appearing, from belief or judgment.[13] The sun, he says, *appears* a foot wide: it has that *look*. But at the same time, we *believe* that it is larger than the inhabited world. Here we could expect a related consequence for action: if I have only the

[11] *DA* III.9, *MA* ch. 11.
[12] For this interpretation, see Nussbaum (1978) ad loc.
[13] *DA* 428b2–4; cf. *Insomn.* 460b19.

"appearance" that the sun is a foot wide, I won't be so likely to act on it. Here it is clear that the something that needs to be added, in order to turn the mere appearing into the usual sort of basis for human action,[14] would be an element of conviction or acceptance. It is in this that mere *phantasia* differs from belief. Although the contrast between *phantasia* and belief in Aristotle is sometimes depicted as one between non-propositional and propositional cognitive attitudes, it is clear that this cannot be quite the right story for our case. For the *phantasia* of the sun as a foot wide involves, at the very least, *combination* or *predication*. It is a little hard to see where to draw the line between this and the "propositional." The real difference between *phantasia* and belief here seems to be just the difference that the Stoics will bring forward as the difference between *phantasia* and belief: in the former case, the sun strikes me as being a foot wide, but I don't commit myself to that, I don't accept or assent to it. In the latter case, I have a conviction, a view as to how things really are.

The very same contrast seems to be at work in our emotion examples. The loud noise strikes the brave man as something terrible, but, being a brave man, he doesn't accept that it is in fact terrible; he judges that it is not so terrible.[15] So he stands his ground. The ancient commentator Michael of Ephesus analyzes the *De Motu*'s sexual case in a similar way, using the Stoic terminology of assent: the alluring object appears, and appears alluring: but, being a temperate man, the person in the example does not "assent to"

---

[14] I say "usual basis" because, as the Skeptics will show (chapter 8) it is perfectly possible for a human being to act without conviction or belief, simply going with the causal pressures of appearances as they strike him. This is how they think animals move: for a related interpretation of animal motion in Aristotle, see Sorabji (1993) chs. 2–4. On Sorabji's account, Aristotle permits animals emotions, and these emotions are based on *phantasia* alone, without *pistis* (conviction based on persuasion). Sorabji points out that, although later Stoic-influenced commentators on Aristotle assimilated the distinction between *phantasia* and *pistis* or *doxa* to the distinction between mere appearing and appearing plus assent, Aristotle may have meant something subtly different: a distinction between an appearance plus a certain sort of unreflective assent and assent based on persuasion by argument. I agree that this would solve the problem of how Aristotle can grant emotions to animals without granting them belief (though we must remember that the evidence that he really does so is slight and largely in passages in which he is reporting popular views); on the other hand, I am not altogether convinced of this account of the distinction between *phantasia* and *doxa*: for there are many beliefs that Aristotle will call *doxai* that are not the result of persuasion by argument. In any case, the question is, I think, irrelevant to the interpretation of the *Rhetoric*, which appears innocent of these technical distinctions, and indeed of comparative biological thinking.

[15] In this case, Aristotle does not raise the question whether the brave man feels some real fear; as we shall see, he later does raise it and, for certain cases, answers it in the affirmative.

the suggestion that this particular object is in fact alluring. He refuses it, and so we get just momentary arousal (an "involuntary erection," Michael writes), not emotion and not action. It seems, then, that Aristotle is agreeing with an analysis already suggested by Plato in *Republic* II–III: in order to have emotions such as fear and grief, one must first have beliefs of a certain kind, beliefs that terrible things may befall beyond one's own control.

But we need to proceed cautiously: for the analysis of fear in the *Rhetoric* begins in an ambiguous manner. "Let fear be, then, a certain sort of pain and disturbance [*tarachē*] out of the appearance [*phantasias*] of an impending bad thing, either destructive or painful" (1382a21–3). And again, below, "It is necessary that those things are fearful that appear to have [*phainetai echein*] a great power to destroy or to harm in a way that leads to great pain" (1382a28–30). These passages might seem to connect fear with simple *appearing*, rather than with belief or judgment.[16] Then, if our analysis has been correct, fear would here be analyzed very differently, and connected with a mere impression as to how things are, rather than with a real conviction or commitment. Further pursuit of the question shows clearly, however, that no technical distinction between *phantasia* and believing is at issue in any of these analyses of emotion: *phantasia* is used, in the rare cases where it is used, simply as the verbal noun of *phainesthai*, "appear."[17] The passage contains no suggestion that *phantasia* is being distinguished from *doxa*, belief.[18] And indeed Aristotle feels free to use belief-words such as *dokein* and *oiesthai* in connection with his analyses of emotions.[19] In other words, what is stressed is the fact that it is the way

[16] So they have been interpreted by David Charles, in a fine paper delivered to the 1991 Helsinki conference on Aristotle's *Rhetoric*.

[17] See for example *DA* 402b22–24, where the philosopher's project of speaking *kata tēn phantasian* about the attributes of soul is clearly the project of giving the best account he can, the one that makes the best sense of the evidence. It would be absurd to think of his project as that of producing an account "in accordance with" mere impressions, as opposed to conviction or belief. The verb *phainesthai* plus the infinitive means "seems to be such-and-such"; with the participle it means "is evidently such-and-such," and indicates a more confident sort of belief.

[18] The distinction between *phantasia* and *doxa* seems to be introduced in one passage in Book I (1370a28), but is altogether absent from Book II. In general, the account shows no awareness of the more technical psychological distinctions of the *De Anima*.

[19] The words in question are *oiesthai, nomizein, logizesthai*, and *phainesthai* plus infinitive; also verbs of remembering and expecting. See 1385b17, 21, 22, 24, 32, 35; 1386a1–2, 26, 30–31, etc. The word *phantasia* occurs only twice more in Book II: once in the analysis of fear, once in that of shame (1383a17, 1384a23). When the noun does occur it is surrounded

things are seen by the agent, not the fact of the matter, that is instrumental in getting emotions going. Intentionality, not absence of commitment, is the issue.

Aristotle has, in fact, a lot to say about the beliefs that are requisite for fear. The object of a person's fear must, he says, be an evil that seems capable of causing great pain and destruction, one that seems to be impending, and one that the person seems powerless to prevent. (Thus, he notes, we do not typically have throughout life an active fear of death, even though we know we shall die, since death usually seems far away; nor do we fear becoming stupid or unjust, presumably because we think this is within our power to prevent [1382a23].) What makes a person fearful is now given in a complex series of reflections, representing the sorts of judgments that might be involved in different cases of becoming afraid: for example, the thought that some other person has been insulted and is waiting for the opportunity to take revenge (1381a35–b4). In general, Aristotle continues, "since fear is with the expectation that one will suffer some destructive affect [*phthartikon pathos*], it is evident that nobody is afraid who thinks [*oiomenoi*] that he can suffer nothing" (1382b30–32). The belief is now out in the open, and is made a necessary condition of the emotion. Further, fear is said to be increased by the belief that the damage, if suffered, will be irreparable (1382b23), and that no assistance will be forthcoming. It is removed by the belief that (*nomizontes*) one has already suffered everything bad there is to suffer.

In short: fear, as described in this chapter, is a peculiarly human experience with a rich intentional awareness of its object, resting on beliefs and judgments of many sorts, both general and concrete. Phrases such as "They do not fear if . . ." and "the one who fears must . . ." indicate that these beliefs, or some of them, are necessary conditions of the fear. And, indeed, this suggestion also seems to be contained in the original definition, which uses the preposition *ek*, "out of": the distress and pain are not independent of the judgment, but result *from* it. Thus if the judgment changed, we could expect the feeling itself to change—as Aristotle himself insists, when he speaks of the conditions under which fear will be removed.

Let us now turn to pity. Pity is another painful emotion—*lupē tis*, a certain sort of pain. What sort of pain? "Pain at [*epi*] an appearing evil, destructive or painful, belonging to one who does not deserve to have it happen—the sort of evil that one might expect oneself to suffer, or some

---

by occurrences of either *phainesthai* or other belief-verbs; the definitions of anger, shame, pity, and spite all use forms of the verb.

member of one's family" (1385b13–15). Three cognitive conditions for pity, suggested already in this opening definition, are unpacked in the analysis that follows. First, the person pitied must be thought to be undeserving (*anaxios*) of the misfortune. The word *anaxios* is given tremendous emphasis in the passage as a whole.[20] Aristotle remarks that the pitier must believe "that there are some good people; otherwise he will not pity, because he will think that everyone deserves the bad things that happen to them" (85b34–86a1). The (believed) goodness of the individual object of pity is also important: for it reinforces the belief that the suffering is undeserved (86b6–8). Such undeserved sufferings appeal to our sense of *injustice* (86b14–15).

Second, the person who pities must believe that he or she is vulnerable in similar ways. People who think that they are above suffering and have everything will not, he says, have pity. Aristotle is not at all friendly to this state of mind: twice he refers to it as *hubris* (85b21–22, b31). And third, the pitier must believe that the sufferings of the pitied are significant: they must have "size" (86a6–7; cf. the comparable requirement for fear at 82a28–30). His list of the likely occasions for pity bears a close resemblance to his own list of significant impediments to good action in *Nicomachean Ethics* I (1099a33–b6). It includes death, bodily assault or ill-treatment, old age, illness, lack of food, lack of friends, having few friends, separation from one's friends, ugliness (which impedes friendship), weakness, being crippled, having your good expectations disappointed, having good things come too late, having no good things happen to you, having them happen but being unable to enjoy them (86a7–13).

Pity and fear are closely connected: what we pity when it happens to another, we fear lest it should happen to ourselves (86a27–28). The perception of one's own vulnerability is made, indeed, a part of the definition; so it follows from the logic of pity that the pitier will have self-directed fear as well (though not necessarily at the same time—for 86a22 notes that a good deal of self-directed fear can temporarily knock out pity). Most occasions for fear will also be occasions for pity, and indeed Aristotle asserts the other half of the biconditional at 1382b26–27; but in fact this is a slight overstatement, since some listed occasions for fear are occasions

---

[20] Either it or its contrary (negated) occur at 85b14; 85b34–86a1; 86b7, b10, b12, b13. The judgment is repeated in the *Poetics: peri ton anaxion dustuchounta*, 1453a4, and *eleos men peri ton anaxion*, 1453a5. On the *Poetics* treatment of these emotions, see Halliwell (1986), Nussbaum (1992).

where one knows that one has done something wrong and fears (deserved) punishment; these will not be occasions for (other-directed) pity.

In short, these emotions have a rich cognitive structure. It is clear that they are not mindless surges of affect, but discerning ways of viewing objects; and beliefs of various types are their necessary conditions. But we can now say more. For we can see by looking at Aristotle's accounts that the beliefs must be regarded as constituent parts of what the emotion *is*. Fear and pity are both painful emotions. Nowhere in his analyses does Aristotle even attempt to individuate emotions by describing different varieties of painful or (as the case may be) pleasant feeling. Emotions, instead, are individuated by reference to their characteristic beliefs. We cannot describe the pain that is peculiar to *fear*, or say how fear differs from grief or pity, without saying that it is pain *at the thought of* a certain sort of future event that is believed to be impending. But if the beliefs are an essential part of the definition of the emotion, then we have to say that their role is not merely that of external necessary condition. They must be seen as *constituent parts* of the emotion itself.

And we can go further. It is not as if the emotion has (in each case) two separate constituents, each necessary for the full emotion, but each available independently of the other. For Aristotle makes it clear that the feeling of pain or pleasure itself depends on the belief-component, and will be removed by its removal. He uses two Greek prepositions, *ek* and *epi*, to describe the intimate relationship between belief and feeling: there is both a *causal* relationship (fear is pain and disturbance "out of"—*ek*—the thought of impending evils), and also a relationship of *intentionality* or *aboutness*: pity is defined as "painful feeling *directed at* [*epi*] the appearance that someone is suffering . . ."). In fact, both relationships are present in both cases, clearly: for it is equally true that pity's pain is produced by the thought of another's suffering—Aristotle's rhetorical analysis relies on this—and also that fear is pain *directed at* the imagined future evil.[21]

Are the beliefs *sufficient* as well as *necessary* conditions for the full emotion? (Since they are clearly sufficient conditions for themselves, what we are asking here is whether they also are sufficient causes of the other constituent in the emotion, the feeling of pain or pleasure.) We do not get altogether clear information on this from the text. Throughout the chapters on emotion, we do find sentences of the form, "If they think X, then

---

[21] See also 1378a20–23, where Aristotle defines passions as *followed by* pain and pleasure, as if the feeling were not even a proper part of the passion. The "followed" also gives some indication of the sufficient-condition view: see subsequent discussion.

they will experience emotion Y"; this strongly suggests a sufficient-condition view. In one case, Aristotle may even state the view: "It is necessary that people who think they are likely to suffer something should fear, and fear those people at whose hands they think they will suffer and those things they think they will suffer and at the time at which they think they will suffer" (1382b33–35). And in general, the whole point of telling the aspiring orator so much about the beliefs of emotional people is that he should have a reliable set of devices for stirring up these emotions. The orator, Aristotle writes, must know the targets and occasions of anger: "For if he should know one or two of these, but not all, he will be unable to produce anger [empoiein], and similarly with the other passions" (1378a24–28).

Our passage from the *De Anima* might have seemed to give a counterexample: the brave man has the same thought as the coward, but does not feel fear. We should, however, question whether the belief is actually the same. The brave man says to himself, "The enemy is approaching." He does not, I think, say to himself, "A terrible future evil is approaching, one capable of causing great pain and destruction." Or if he does say this, it seems reasonable to suppose that he will already be afraid. (Brave men, at least in the *Nicomachean Ethics*, do feel fear at the thought of death.) In short: if we get clear about exactly what the thought is—with all its evaluative elements—the alleged counterexamples are less weighty. We shall see that this is an important issue in the Stoic theory as well, where the evaluative content of the emotional person's judgment is salient. We can conclude, I think, that although evidence of a sufficient-condition view is not clear, Aristotle has to believe that at least much or most of the time the belief does sufficiently cause the complex passion, or he could not take the pride he does in his rhetorical technique.

I have focused on these two emotions for reasons that will shortly become apparent: they provide an especially clear illustration of the normative structure of Aristotelian emotion, and the connection of that structure to Aristotle's anti-Platonic views on luck. But other emotions that will be important for us in this book are given a similar sort of analysis. Anger is especially complex: for it has both a pleasant and a painful feeling-component, these being associated with different, though closely related, sets of beliefs. It requires, on the one hand, the belief that one (or someone dear to one) has been slighted or wronged or insulted in some serious way, through someone else's voluntary action (1380a8); this, Aristotle insists, is a painful experience. (Once again, the pain is not a separate item directly caused by the world itself; it is caused by *the belief that* one has been slighted. If the belief is false, one will still feel that pain; and if one has been slighted without knowing it, one will not have it.) Once again, these beliefs are necessary constituents in the emotion. Aristotle makes it clear that if the angry person should discover that the alleged slight did not take place at all, or that it was not deliberately performed (80a8–10), or that it was not performed by the person one thought (78a34–b1, 80b25–29), anger can be expected to go away. So too, if one judges that the item damaged by another is trivial rather than serious (*peri mikron*, 1379b35, and cf. 1379b31–32). But Aristotle holds that anger requires, as well, a wish for retaliation, the thought that it would be good for some punishment to come to the person who did the wrong—and the thought of this righting of the balance is pleasant (1378b1 ff.). The orator's whole effort—whether in inspiring anger or in calming angry people down (II.3) is directed toward this complex cognitive structure.

The subject of love is a highly complex one in Aristotle's thought. But since love, and its relation to anger, will be a major theme of the Hellenistic philosophers, the background for those discussions should be briefly set forth. The general rubric under which Aristotle analyzes love is that of *philia*, which, strictly speaking, is not an emotion at all, but a relationship with emotional components. But the fact that he analyzes it together with other emotions in the *Rhetoric* shows his recognition of the importance of those components. The relation itself requires mutual affection, mutual well-wishing, mutual benefiting for the other's own sake, and mutual awareness of all this. Both in the *Rhetoric* and the *Nicomachean Ethics*, the cognitive content of *philia*'s emotions is made overwhelmingly clear, since Aristotle informs us in detail that people who love one another do so on the basis of a certain conception or description of the object, and on the basis of their belief that the object has the feature or features in question—as well as their further beliefs that the object is well disposed to them, and so forth. It is perfectly clear that if any of these central beliefs turns out to be false, or becomes false, love will itself cease—unless it has in the meantime developed some other basis. (Thus a love based on a conception of the other person as pleasant to be with may, Aristotle holds, evolve over time into a love based on respect for good character.)[22] Erotic love is treated as a special case of *philia*, characterized by a special intensity. Usually it begins with a conception of the other party as pleasant; but it may mature into a *philia* that is based on character. Or if it begins asymmetrically, as a desire of one party for the other—so that it doesn't properly count as *philia* at

---

[22] See the excellent treatment of these issues in Price (1989) ch. 4.

all—it may, as the parties come to have more knowledge of one another, develop in the direction of greater mutuality, and come to be *philia*.[23] In any case, the description under which the parties perceive one another, and the beliefs they have about one another, are indispensable grounds of the emotion.

IV

On further inspection, the beliefs involved in the central cases of emotion have one general feature in common, as Socrates and Plato already observed.[24] All, that is, involve the ascription of significant worth to items in the world outside of the agent, items that he or she does not fully control. Love, most obviously, is a profound attachment to another separate life,[25] which must remain as a separate center of movement and choice, not being engulfed or fused, in order for the relationship of love to be possible at all. And in the loves Aristotle values most highly, the participants view one another as good characters, therefore as fully independent choosers of the good; if one controlled the other, even to the extent that a parent does a child, the love would apparently be less good as love. But then, as Aristotle knows, it is perfectly possible for the relationship to be broken off— whether by death or separation or betrayal. So loves of a more than casual sort require a belief in one's own lack of self-sufficiency with respect to some of the most important things in life.

In pity and fear, there are related beliefs. For one who does not attach importance to things that can be harmed by the world will have nothing to fear—and so too, no reason to pity others when such things are damaged in their case. The listed occasions for pity—losses of friends and children, health problems, losses of opportunities, and so forth—all of these will give rise to pity only if those items are to some extent esteemed. Aristotle singles them out because he does esteem them (as we shall see); he does not say that one pities someone for losing a nail, or fears the destruction of a hairpin. In pity and fear, we acknowledge our vulnerability before the circumstances of life; we have those emotions, he makes plain, only if we really do think that life can do something to us, and that this something matters. Anger is closely related: for in anger we acknowledge our vul-

---

[23] See Price (1989) for relevant passages in the logical works.

[24] On Socrates on anger, see Vlastos (1991).

[25] I leave to one side here the case of "self-love" (*philautia*), which is usually not treated as a case of genuine *philia*, and is given separate analysis.

nerability before the actions of other people. Again, if we judge that the slight is trivial, we do not become angry.

As this suggests, the beliefs that ground the emotions are bound up with one another, in the sense that any deep attachment to uncontrolled things or persons in the world can provide the basis for any and all of the major emotions, given the appropriate changes in circumstance. Once one cares about a friend or family member, for example, one has, in addition to love itself, a basis for fear if that person is threatened, of grief if the person should die, of pity if she suffers undeservedly, of anger if someone else harms her. Love provides anger with a different kind of basis too: for as Aristotle notes, we expect those we love to treat us especially well, so if they do not, their slights seem all the more cutting, and we get angry at them more than at strangers (1379b2–4).

Believe now, with Socrates, that "a good man cannot be harmed" (*Apology* 41D, and cf. 30CD). Or believe, as the Socrates of Plato's *Republic* continues the argument, that "a good person is completely sufficient to himself for good living" (387–88). (This is so, according to Socrates, because virtue cannot be damaged by external contingencies, and virtue is sufficient for *eudaimonia*.)[26] If this is right, as the *Republic* goes on to argue, there will be no room for the emotions of pity, fear, and grief. For nothing that is not a lapse in virtue is worth taking very seriously; and a lapse in virtue, by definition under the person's own control, is an occasion for blame and reproach, not for pity. The things that are usually taken to be occasions for fear and pity—losses of loved ones, losses of fortune and political standing—are not really so: for "nothing among human things is worth much seriousness" (*Rep.* 604B12–C1). Tragic poetry, which displays such things as if they did have great significance, is to be dismissed from the city, for it "nourishes the element of pity in us, making it strong" (606B). Although Plato's guardians are permitted to retain a certain sort of anger—directed at the enemies of the city—it is obvious that most occasions for anger, too, are removed by the removal of vulnerability: the good person has no need for revenge, since the slights that others take to be harms and damages trouble him not at all.[27] And though love of a sort is present in the city of the virtuous, it is far from being the sort of love that tragedy depicts and that many people value. For it is based on the norm of

[26] See Vlastos (1991).

[27] Thus Vlastos' (1991) claim that among Socrates' greatest achievements is to have transcended the morality of revenge needs some qualification: he transcends it, to be sure, but only by doing away, in the process, with the bases of love and pity as well. See Nussbaum (1991b).

virtuous self-sufficiency, and on the teaching that the good person "has least of all people any need for another person. . . . Least of all, then, is it to him a terrible thing to be deprived of a son or brother or . . . anything of that sort" (387DE).

Set over against the love and grief and pity of ordinary mortals is the ideal of the "wise and serene character, always consistent with itself" (604E). Plato remarks that it is difficult to represent such a figure in the theater, since audiences are used to more emotional volatility. Plato's dialogues, however, do represent such a figure: a Socrates who cares little for the prospect of his own death and who pursues his philosophical search regardless of his external circumstances. The *Phaedo* begins from a story that has all the ingredients of tragic emotion: its interlocutors remark that, accordingly, they expected to feel pity. But they did not, for Socrates' attitude to his impending death discouraged this response (58E, 59A). Xanthippe is sent away for her tears, Apollodorus sternly admonished for "womanish" behavior (60A, 117D). Socrates, by contrast, pursues the search for understanding without fear, resentment, or mourning.

What all this brings out is that emotions, while not "irrational" in the sense of being non-cognitive, are based on a family of beliefs about the worth of externals that will be regarded as both false and irrational (in the normative sense) by a large segment of the philosophical tradition. This anti-tragic tradition will reach its fullest development in the Hellenistic schools, and especially in the Stoa.

V

Unlike the Socrates of the *Republic*, Aristotle does not believe that the good person, the person of practical wisdom, is "sufficient unto himself" for *eudaimonia*, and therefore impervious to grief and fear. According to him, it is *right* to grieve at the death of a friend, since that is an acknowledgment of the importance of the tie and the person. As for fear: in *Nicomachean Ethics* I, he makes room for the appropriateness of fear, by insisting on the possibility of calamities so great that they can dislodge the person who was doing well from *eudaimonia* itself.[28] Later, in his account of proper courage, he makes this explicit, insisting that the courageous person will indeed feel fear and pain at the prospect of death, on account of the value that he rightly attaches to his own life. Defining fear in the same way as in the

---

[28] *EN* I.11, esp. 1101a9–14.

Rhetoric (1115a9), he insists that not all fears are appropriate. (For example, one might fear a mouse, and this is treated as something so absurd as to be pathological [1149a8].) On the other hand, "there are some things that one must fear, that it is noble to fear, and not to do so is shameful" (1115a12–13). As objects of proper fear he mentions disgrace, assault on or the killing of one's children or wife, and, above all, one's own death. The brave person fears death, but "in the appropriate way, and as reasoning instructs, he will stand his ground for the sake of the fine" (1115b11–13). In fact, Aristotle adds, a person will be "more pained at the prospect of death the more he has complete virtue and the more *eudaimōn* he is . . . for he will be aware that he is being deprived of the greatest goods, and this is painful" (1117b10–13). A person who is completely without fear does not strike Aristotle as virtuous (which would imply the possession of practical reason) but, rather, as unbalanced. "The person who is excessive in fearlessness has no name, but he would be a kind of mad or insensitive person, if he feared nothing, not earthquakes or waves, as they say about the Celts" (1115b24–27).

Pity is less frequently discussed in the ethical writings, since they focus on virtues one should cultivate within oneself more than on responses to the actions and fortunes of others. The discussion of reversals of fortune in *Nicomachean Ethics* I, however, implies that Aristotle does recognize as legitimate a number of occasions for pity, the same group on which the *Rhetoric* focused in its account of that emotion. And in the discussion of voluntary and involuntary action, Aristotle speaks of pity in connection with actions that are involuntary on account of non-culpable ignorance— the sort of action he imputes to Oedipus in the *Poetics* (*EN* 1109b30–32, 1111a1–2).

In short, there are things in the world that it is right to care about: friends, family, one's own life and health, the worldly conditions of virtuous action. These can sometimes be damaged by events not under one's own control. For these reasons it is right to have some fear. The good person, rather than being a fearless person, is one who will have appropriate rather than inappropriate fears—*and* not be deterred by them from doing what is required and noble. The objects of fear are appropriate objects of pity when they happen to someone else. Education in proper fear and pity would consist in learning what the appropriate attachments are, and what damages one can reasonably expect in a variety of circumstances.

Anger is treated in a similar fashion. On the one hand, Aristotle clearly believes that many people get angry too much and for insufficient reasons. His choice of the name "mildness" (*praotēs*) for the appropriate virtuous

disposition in this area reflects his conscious decision to pitch things rather toward the unangry than toward the angry end of the spectrum (1125b26–29). The virtuous person, he writes, gets angry only "in the manner that reason instructs, and at those people and for that length of time" (1125b35–1126a1). If anything, he errs in the direction of the deficiency— "for the mild person is not given to revenge, but is inclined to be forgiving [*sungnōmonikos*]" (1126a1–3). Reason, however, does tell this person that there are some very good reasons for getting angry, in connection with damages to things that it is really worth caring about:

> The deficiency, whether it should be called unangriness [*aorgēsia*], or whatever, is blamed. For those who do not get angry at the people at whom they should get angry seem dense, and also those who do not get angry in the manner they should and at the time and for the reasons they should. For they seem to be without perception or pain. And a person who is not angry will not defend himself; but to allow oneself and one's loved ones to be trampled underfoot and to overlook it is slavish. (1126a3–8)

To be a slave, according to Aristotle's account, is to be at the disposal of another, the "living tool" of someone else's plan of life, lacking the integrity of one's own choice (*Pol.* I.4). Aristotle is then saying here that, assuming one has made deep commitments to people and things that can be damaged by another, not to defend those commitments is to lose one's own integrity. Anger is said to be a necessary motivation for defending things that are beloved—presumably because anger is seen as an acknowledgment that the item damaged has importance, and without that acknowledgment one will have no reason to defend it. The belief in the item's importance, together with the belief that the slight or damage was voluntary, was held to be (usually) a sufficient condition for anger. So if anger is not on the scene, one would be led to the conclusion that some of the relevant beliefs are probably not on the scene. If the agent believes that there has been a damage and that it was voluntarily inflicted, but is not angry, then, if we follow Aristotle's account, we will have to conclude that the agent did not think the damage very important. It is this conceptual connection between anger and the acknowledgment of importance that explains why Aristotle holds it to be necessary for defensive action—not because it plays some mindless hydraulic role. The point is that if one does not have the beliefs that are involved in anger, it is hard to see why one would risk one's life, or even make painful effort, to defend the item in question. (This problem will surface in the Epicurean and Stoic accounts— chapters 7, 11, 12.) The mild person is not especially given to revenge, as

Aristotle has said. But in the case of the deepest commitments, not to take some action seems to show a lack of "perception"; and if one has those practical perceptions, then one seems bound to be angry. Anger, in these cases, is a recognition of the truth.

Emotions, in Aristotle's view, are not always correct, any more than beliefs or actions are always correct. They need to be educated, and brought into harmony with a correct view of the good human life. But, so educated, they are not just essential as forces motivating to virtuous action, they are also, as I have suggested, recognitions of truth and value. And as such they are not just instruments of virtue, they are constituent parts of virtuous agency: virtue, as Aristotle says again and again, is a "mean disposition" (disposition to pursue the appropriate) "with regard to both passions and actions" (*EN* 1105b25–26, 1106b16–17, etc.). What this means is that even were the apparently correct action to be chosen without the appropriate motivating and reactive emotions, it would not count for Aristotle *as a virtuous action*: an action is virtuous only if it is done *in the way that* a virtuous person would do it. All of this is a part of the equipment of the person of practical wisdom, part of what practical rationality is. Rationality recognizes truth; the recognition of some ethical truths is impossible without emotion; indeed, certain emotions centrally involve such recognitions.

VI

The person of practical wisdom, then, will approach a concrete situation ready to respond to it emotionally in the appropriate ways. What is appropriate is given by the general ethical theory, in the role it ascribes to external goods that can be damaged. This ethical theory is critical of much that Aristotle's society teaches. People often value too many of these external things, or value them too highly, or not enough. Thus they have too much emotion in connection with money, possessions, and reputation, sometimes not enough in connection with the things that are truly worthwhile. An important role for philosophical criticism is to insist on the central role of virtuous action, which can usually be controlled by one's own effort. But this control is not, and should not be, absolute. The emotions recognize worth outside oneself; in so doing, they frequently recognize the truth.

In Nikidion's education at the Lyceum, emotional experience can be expected to play a central role. If our account so far has been correct, a detached unemotional intellectual survey of all the true opinions seems impossible: in avoiding emotion, one avoids a part of the truth. In the process of sorting beliefs and intuitions, then, Nikidion and her fellow students will rely on their emotional responses and on their memory of emotional experience, as guides to ethical truth. When confronted with a question such as, "Would a life without friends be complete or incomplete?" and "Is this a case of courageous action or not?" she will deliberate in an immersed way, consulting her fear and love and grief, along with other pertinent judgments. Her deliberation will for this reason be (according to her teacher) more and not less rational. And as Aristotle's view of moral development implies,[29] the same process of scrutiny will also refine the emotions, as it refines and educates all the involved elements of practical reason, making them more discriminating and responsive, better at confronting new situations in the future. Furthermore, the life Nikidion and her fellow students construct, as they work out a specification of their "target," will contain emotional experiences of certain types inside it, as valued elements in virtue. By relying on and further cultivating the emotions, they are trying, we might say, to keep themselves in health, and even to become healthier.

There seems, however, to be a tension in Aristotle's position. On the one hand, he describes the emotions as closely bound up with judgments, and therefore as capable of being modified by the modification of judgment. This picture implies not only that emotions can play a role in rational deliberation, but also that they can be changed as beliefs of all sorts can be changed, *by* deliberation and argument. On the other hand, as we saw in chapter 2, he makes a sharp distinction between character training and the philosophical study of ethics, on the grounds that emotions need to be balanced *before* the student can get anything much out of his philosophical arguments. Why, taking the view of emotion that he does, does he appear to insist on a separation between character training and philosophy? Why can't philosophical argument itself shape character? This question is of clear importance for philosophy's range and medical usefulness: for it was the demand for antecedent *paideia* that made the Lyceum an inhospitable place for the real-life (undisguised) Nikidion.

First we must make this contrast subtler. Clearly none of the schools can hope to help someone whose life is so disorderly that she cannot follow any sustained course of study or participate in the give-and-take of argument. Epicurus requires of any pupil a willingness to do hard intellectual work, even if his approach requires less dialectical independence than does Aris-

---

[29] See Sherman (1989).

totle's; much the same is true of the Skeptics; and the Stoics will require far more. So if Aristotle is talking only about the person who is too disorderly to study and argue at all, they can agree. On the other side, Aristotle clearly does think that his arguments can modify many beliefs, among which will be some on which various fears and angers are based. In this sense, even he must allow that, insofar as arguments like his have a practical value, they influence the passions in the process. The student who works through the *Nicomachean Ethics* in a serious way, starting from the position of the average educated young gentleman in Aristotle's Athens, can be expected to emerge with somewhat different angers and fears, and different selections in the area of love and friendship.

But this does not remove the distinction; and we should investigate it further. Why should Aristotle insist on a firm basis of good character *before* the application of philosophical medicine? Where does he think this basis comes from, and why does he think it different in kind from the other beliefs and judgments that are formed and modified by teaching?

First, in many passages where Aristotle discusses non-intellectual training and the need for discipline, he is probably thinking, above all, of the bodily appetites, which do have a substantial non-cognitive component, though to some extent also they are responsive to reason. He does seem to believe that young people have difficulties of ethical inconstancy that come from their appetites, especially sexual appetite (see *Rhet.* II.12, 1389a3 ff.). For these desires, it appears that time to grow up is essential; without allowing for this, and also providing some early non-philosophical training, we will never get people who are stable and undistractable enough for philosophy.

Second, Aristotle believes that the emotions, unlike many other beliefs, are formed above all in the family, in the child's earliest interactions with parents and other loved ones. The parent's love and the child's gratitude for the parent's love are fundamental to motivation and passion of all sorts in later life—as Aristotle argues against Plato. Here we see a reason why, while still holding a strongly cognitive picture of the emotions—love and gratitude are said to be based on certain perceptions and thoughts, whose absence in Plato's city is said to lead to an absence of care—Aristotle could think that philosophizing with adults can do little to change such basic patterns. Take someone raised in Plato's city, without a family, and it may be impossible in later life to instill the thoughts and attachments proper to the family. On the other hand, the early life in the family paves the way for future attachments to friends and city, in a manner that lies so deep in the personality that one might question how far philosophical examination can reach in altering those structures, even should they be judged to be defective.[30] It may be for this reason that in the *Nicomachean Ethics* Aristotle frequently refers to the emotions as "irrational"—though, strictly speaking, his theories do not entitle him to use that word of them in either of its recognized senses: for they are (in his view) neither non-cognitive nor (normatively) unjustified and false. They may, however, be more resistant to modification by teaching than other beliefs and judgments, on account of their history.[31] While depending on belief and judgment, the emotions may depend upon a type of belief and judgment that is less accessible to dialectical scrutiny than are most of the person's other beliefs.

Here Aristotle has touched on something extremely important. He has not fully made out his case. More than a few anti-Platonic assertions are needed to show *how* the emotions have their origins in childhood, and to what extent, this being the case, they remain accessible to therapeutic persuasion. This insight, if pursued all the way, would change philosophy: for it implies that philosophy, if it wishes to grapple with emotions effectively, must gain access to depths in the personality that calm dialectic cannot touch. The Hellenistic thinkers will develop the insight and take up the challenge.

VII

But Aristotle's insight suggests something more. It suggests that philosophy is not self-sufficient as a shaper of souls. Prior to her encounter with philosophy—prior to any encounter she could conceivably have with any conceivable philosophy—Nikidion has a material and institutional and relational life. And this life shapes her, for good or for ill. She is the child of her parents: their love and care, or the absence of it, shape her. She is the child of material circumstances of need or plenty; she is healthy or ill, hungry or full: and this, once again, shapes her—shapes not only her health, but her hopes, expectations, and fears, her capabilities for reasoning. She is the child of her city and its institutions: and these institutions shape her capacity for shame and self-esteem, for stinginess or generosity,

---

[30] All this is analyzed extremely well, in much detail, in Sherman (1989).

[31] For emotions as *aloga*, see for example *EN* 1102a28, b29–34; 1111b1; 1168b20. Usually in such discussions the emotions are grouped together with appetitive desires. In *DA* III.9, Aristotle is highly critical of the Platonic division of the soul into the *alogon* and the *logon echon*, which makes his uncritical use of it in the *Nicomachean Ethics* somewhat surprising.

for greediness or moderation. This shaping reaches deep into the soul, profoundly affecting what, even with philosophy, it can become.

And this creates another job for philosophy. This job is political. Philosophy can deal with students one by one, refining their capacities for the good life. But it can also, and perhaps more urgently, reflect about the material and social conditions of their lives, so as to design institutions that will allow people to be such that they can, if they wish, be further perfected in the philosophical way. Aristotle's students pursue not just their own *eudaimonia* but that of others: for they think about the design of political institutions, starting from the idea that the best political arrangement is the one "in accordance with which anyone whatsoever might do best and live a flourishing life" (*Pol.* VII.2; see previous discussion). Aristotle's critique of other political arrangements in *Politics* VII devotes much attention to the conditions that shape emotions; so too does his own sketch for an ideal city in *Politics* VII–VIII.

In short: the apparent conservatism of Aristotle's dialectical education of Nikidion is only apparent. Radical change is excluded from the part of his educational scheme that deals with her as an individual. But that is not all that philosophy does. The individuals who do come to share in it partake in a task that is both radical and far-reaching: the design of a society in which money will not be valued as an end, in which honor will not be valued as an end, in which war and empire will not be valued as ends—a society in which the functioning of human individuals in accordance with their own choice and practical reason will be the ultimate end of institutions and choices. Granted that Nikidion must be a member of an elite in order to profit by the arguments Aristotle designed; still, the aim of her education is to make her capable of bringing the good life, by politics, to distant others.

But the ideal city—even Aristotle's—is still a city in the heavens.[32] No existing city comes close to winning Aristotle's approval. And so, to a compassionate Nikidion, reflecting on this conception of philosophy, it might begin to seem to be a recipe for continued misery. What does one do with the real people of the world, while waiting for politics to become rational? It may be true that philosophy can speak to the design of institutions; but it can rarely do anything to make its conceptions reality. Alex-

[32] In *Politics* II Aristotle criticizes Plato's *Laws* for introducing constraints that make the city "impossible"; his own ideal, described in *Politics* VII–VIII, is clearly intended to be possible, and to give direction to legislators for the improvement of actual cities. But the point remains: what does philosophy do, while the slow and uncertain processes of political change go their way?

ander the Great was not a good Aristotelian pupil, and that was a better shot at shaping the world than most philosophers ever get. Must philosophy then simply abandon the lives of those who live under defective institutions? Aristotle's account of the emotions seems to provide material for helping real people. If emotions are shaped by beliefs, and not through some other mindless process, then it seems possible that those beliefs can be reached and modified in each individual case, with or without radical political change. Should a compassionate philosophy not follow that lead?

In short: if one agrees with Aristotle, then philosophy can do little for the real misery of the world. It can refine already refined and lucky young gentlemen. It can point the way toward an ideal that may or may not have any chance of being realized in any place at any time. These are the limits of its practical efficacy. If, however, one conceives of philosophy as a medical art for the human soul, one is unlikely to accept this as the last word. For medicine would be no good as medicine if it simply gave vitamins to the healthy and designed impracticable schemes for ideal health insurance. Its job is here and now, with this patient's actual sufferings. If it does nothing for these sufferings, it does nothing at all. The Hellenistic philosophers think this way about philosophy. That is why they feel they must leave Aristotle behind.

Epicurean Surgery: Argument and Empty Desire

> Criticism has plucked the imaginary flowers from the chain, not in
> order that man shall bear the chain without caprice or consolation but
> so that he shall cast off the chain and pluck the living flower.
>
> (Marx, "Toward a Contribution to the Critique of Hegel's
> *Philosophy of Right*")

I

EPICURUS wrote, "Empty is that philosopher's argument by which no
human suffering is therapeutically treated. For just as there is no use in a
medical art that does not cast out the sicknesses of bodies, so too there is no
use in philosophy, if it does not throw out suffering from the soul."[1] He
also said, "What produces unsurpassed jubilation is the contrast of the
great evil escaped. And this is the nature of good, if one applies one's mind
correctly and then stands firm, and does not go walking about [*peripatēi*]
chattering about the good in an empty fashion" (Us. 423 = Plut. *Non Posse*
1091B). The conjunction of these two utterances, the second of which
seems to be a swipe against Aristotelian (Peripatetic) ethical argument,
suggests the following criticism. Aristotelian ethical arguments are empty
and useless because they are not adequately committed to the only proper
task for philosophical argument, namely, the relief of human misery. They
are insufficiently practical, or practical in an insufficiently effective way. I
shall now try to establish that this was in fact Epicurus' view, to investigate
his charge, and to study the character of his therapy.

Aristotelian dialectic, as I have argued, makes several controversial assumptions about the nature of the ordinary person's ethical beliefs. It
assumes that these beliefs are essentially healthy: truth is in there, along
with whatever is false, and in such a way that, in the process of scrutiny, the

---

[1] Us. 221 – Porph. *Ad Marc.* 31, p. 209, 23 N. *Pathos*, of course, can mean "feeling,"
"affect," or, especially, "emotion" (see chapter 10). But Epicurus wants to "cast out" all and
only the painful disturbing affects; this does not include all emotions (see chapter 7), and
includes much else (as will be noted). For this reason "suffering" seems preferable. But we
should remember that not all *pathē* treated by Epicureans are felt as pain (chapter 5).

true beliefs will turn out to be the "greatest number and the most basic." Since the beliefs in question are for the most part socially taught, the procedure also assumes the relative health of the surrounding society. Moreover, the method assumes that the most important beliefs lie close to the surface of the interlocutor's reason in such a way that they can be elicited by calm dialectical questioning. And finally, the method appears to assume that everyone who *ought* to be helped by the dialectical process *can* be so helped: it points to no troublesome gap between the availability of rational "therapy" and the needs of its intended recipients.

Such assumptions seem to Epicurus at best naive, at worst obtuse and callous. He invites us to look at ourselves, at our friends, at the society in which we live. What do we see when we look, and look honestly? Do we see calm rational people, whose beliefs about value are for the most part well based and sound? No. We see people rushing frenetically about after money, after fame, after gastronomic luxuries, after passionate love— people convinced by the culture itself, by the stories on which they are brought up, that such things have far more value than in fact they have. Everywhere we see victims of false social advertising: people convinced in their hearts that they cannot possibly live without their hoards of money, their imported delicacies, their social standing, their lovers—although these beliefs result from teaching and may have little relation to the real truth about worth. Do we, then, see a healthy rational society, whose shared beliefs can be trusted as material for a true account of the good life? No. We see a sick society, a society that values money and luxury above the health of the soul; a society whose sick teachings about love and sex turn half of its members into possessions, both deified and hated, the other half into sadistic keepers, tormented by anxiety; a society that slaughters thousands, using ever more ingeniously devastating engines of war, in order to escape its gnawing fear of vulnerability. We see a society, above all, whose every enterprise is poisoned by the fear of death, a fear that will not let its members taste any stable human joy, but turns them into the groveling slaves of corrupt religious teachers.

Again, do we see people who know what they believe and desire, who can say so when questioned by the straightforward procedures used by Aristotle? No. We see, wherever we look, people who are profoundly ignorant of what they believe and what motivates them. When questioned, they might give answers that show fearlessness and optimism. But their anxious frenetic activity betrays them: the fear of death is deeply planted within their hearts, an "unseen goad" prompting action, "though the person himself is unaware of it" (Lucr. III.873, 878). What can calm dialectic do in this situation? Can it cut through the distorting power of greed, dismantle the edifice of false belief and desire erected by all the resources of a diseased culture? Can it gain access to the powerful motivations that come from unconscious belief and emotion?

Finally, whom does this dialectic help? The answer seems all too obvious. It helps those who are already well off. For it offers itself only to those who have already had *paideia*, a "liberal education."[2] This excludes everyone who was never offered such an education on account of existing social arrangements. Aristotle is so good as to announce openly that not only all women and slaves, but also tradesmen, sailors, and farmers will be excluded. And this dialectic is elitist in its content as well. Respecting the beliefs of the elite whom it interrogates, and turning these social dogmas, through a sort of critical scrutiny, into "truth," it will inevitably perpetuate the values of the status quo, dooming the excluded to further misery—a strange alchemy, that takes some diseased beliefs, subjects them to some polite sifting, and claims to have converted them, thereby, into "the practical truth."

Epicurus challenges us, then, to recognize that Aristotelian dialectic may be powerless to help where help is most urgently needed, powerless to criticize where the need for philosophical critique is greatest. A philosophy that stops here is not only impotent but also callous: a tool of exploitation, an accomplice of misery. This powerful challenge compels us: can we recognize both the depth of social ills and the delicate complexity of the human psyche and still remain believers in the calm give-and-take of "Aristotelian" ethical argument?

II

As Epicurus sees it, human beings are troubled and driven creatures. Their bodies are vulnerable to numerous pains and diseases. Those assaults of worldly contingency we can do little to avoid or control, except insofar as the medical art has found remedies. But bodily pain, in his view, is not especially terrible as a source of general unhappiness;[3] and even this pain, as we shall see, can be mitigated by philosophy. Worse by far is the disturbance of the soul. Most human souls are, quite needlessly, in a state of

[2] See Marrou (1956), Sherman (1989).

[3] See especially *KD* 4, where Epicurus makes the famous claim that intense pain is brief and that long pain can be made endurable.

painful stress and disturbance, buffeted as by a violent tempest (*LMen* 128). Needlessly, because the causes of the disturbance can be removed. For the causes are false beliefs about the world and about value, along with the "empty" desires that are generated by false beliefs. Epicurus sees people rushing about after all sorts of objects of desire: wealth, luxury, power, love, above all immortal life. He is convinced that the central cause of human misery is the disturbance produced by the seemingly "boundless" demands of desire, which will not let us have any rest or stable satisfaction. But, fortunately for us, the very same desires that cause anxiety, frenetic activity, and all sorts of distress by their insatiable boundlessness are also the desires that are thoroughly dependent on false beliefs, in such a way that the removal of the belief will effectively remove the desire, hence the trouble. What he needs, to make this diagnosis compelling and to commend his cure, is, first, a procedure for separating good desires from bad, healthy from sick; then, a diagnosis of the genesis of bad desires that will show that and how they are based on false belief; finally, a therapeutic treatment for false belief that will show us how, through a modification of belief, we may get rid of bad desire.

Epicurus' procedure for separating healthy from sick desires is of interest to us: for we shall later see to what extent the values embodied in this procedure influence the structure of his philosophical method. We can note, first, his generic terms of classification: on the one hand, we have empty desires (*kenai epithumiai*), on the other, those that are "natural" (*phusikai*).[4] This tells us that the desires Epicurus will consider healthy and non-empty are the ones that belong to our nature; but nature is treated as a normative notion—opposed not to artifice, but to that which is puffed up, excessive, that which might well impede healthy functioning. His procedure for identifying the natural desires confirms this idea and develops it.

Like Plato and Aristotle before him,[5] Epicurus selects a creature who would seem to be a reliable and uncorrupted "witness" of the good or flourishing life, and asks what that creature goes for. Any desires not found in that creature are suspect: there is a prima facie case for regarding them as corruptions. The desires that are present in this unimpeded creature are themselves, prima facie, taken as healthy. But who should this creature, this model of unimpeded selection, be? For Aristotle, the reliable witness was the person of practical wisdom, immersed in the commitments of an active

---

[4] For the Epicurean classification of desires, see *LMen* 127; *KD* 15, 26; *VS* 21, 23, 35, 59; Cic. *Fin.* 2.26 ff., etc.

[5] For Plato, see subsequent discussion; Aristotle's "witness" is discussed in this paragraph.

social existence. We can guess that Epicurus would be suspicious of this choice: for such a person, if his society is corrupt, can all too easily be the dupe of its fantasies, the apostle of its deformed preferences. For Epicūrus, the only reliable witness in this sense will be the creature who has not been corrupted by social teaching, who bears human capabilities for flourishing ("nature" in that normative sense) unimpeded by the reduced or inflated expectations engendered by the surrounding culture. To give this idea a vivid realization, Epicurus refers frequently to the child not yet corrupted by teaching and discourse—and also to the healthy animal, seen as a way of looking at our sensuous and bodily nature as human animals.

Diogenes Laertius tells us what Epicurus hoped to accomplish, using this uncorrupted witness as a guide. It is nothing less than a demonstration of his claim about the true end of human life:

> As a proof [*apodeixis*] for the fact that pleasure is the end, he points to the fact that animals, as soon as they are born, are well contented with pleasure and fight against pain, naturally and apart from discourse [*phusikōs kai chōris logou*]. For we flee pain by our very own natural feelings [*autopathōs*]. (10.137)

The same account appears, with slight variations, in Sextus Empiricus and Cicero:

> Some people who come from the school of Epicurus like to say that the animal feels pain and pursues pleasure naturally and without teaching [*phusikōs kai adidaktōs*]. For as soon as it is born, when it is not yet a slave to the world of opinion [*tois kata doxan*], as soon as it is slapped by the unaccustomed chill of the air, it cries out and bawls. (Sextus *M* 11.96; cf. *PH* 3.194–95)

> Every animal as soon as it is born pursues pleasure and delights in it as the chief good, while it flees pain as the chief evil and pushes it from itself as far as possible. And it does this when not yet perverted [*nondum depravatum*], with nature herself doing the judging in an uncorrupted and unblemished way [*incorrupte atque integre*]. (Cic. *Fin.* 1.30)

In all three passages (which probably derive from a common source), we find a recurrent opposition: between "nature"—apparently some healthy unimpeded condition—and corrupt social teaching. The reference to animals does not obscure the fact that it is some healthy part of us that we are asked to consider: for the first passage slips into the first person, while

Sextus describes the cries of human infants at birth.[6] Epicurus is suggesting that we come into the world as healthy living creatures, our faculties operating reliably and without blemish. But shortly after this we encounter external forces that corrupt and confuse us. These influences take hold of us: and yet they are not really us. They are not "our very own feelings," but something from the world outside; and they enslave us as time goes on. We know already what some of these influences are: religious superstitions that teach us fear of the gods and of death; love stories that complicate our natural sexual appetite; conversations all around us glorifying wealth and power. Epicurus' core idea seems to be that if in imagination we can catch the human animal before it gets corrupted, see what inclinations it has before these insidious social processes have deformed its preferences, we will have an authentic witness to the true human good, and a way of isolating, among our own desires, those that are healthy.

If society is unreliable, Epicurus reasons, the reliable testimony about the end is the testimony of the senses and the bodily feelings, separated from teaching and belief.[7] That, in effect, is what the appeal to the child provides. Cicero's interlocutor Torquatus makes this explicit:

> So he denies that there is need for argument [*ratione*] or dialectical reasoning [*disputatione*] to show that pleasure is to be pursued and pain avoided. He thinks these things are perceived by the senses [*sentire*], the way we perceive that fire is hot, that snow is white, that honey is sweet. None of these things needs to be supported by fancy arguments [*exquisitis rationibus*)—we only have to draw attention to them. . . . Nature herself must be the judge of what is in accordance with or contrary to nature. (1.30)

Torquatus' peroration makes the same point about self-evidence:

> If the things that I have said are clearer and more luminous than daylight itself; if they are entirely drawn up from the spring of nature; if our whole discourse relies for confirmation on the senses—that is, upon witnesses that are uncorrupted and unblemished [*incorruptis atque integris testibus*]; if children who cannot yet speak, if even dumb beasts almost cry out, prompted by nature's guidance, that nothing is good but pleasure, nothing bad but pain—and concerning these things they judge without perversion or corruption [*neque depravate neque corrupte*], should we

---

[6] *LMen* 128 shifts in the other direction, from "us" to "the animal."

[7] See Long and Sedley (1987) 87–90.

107

not have the greatest gratitude to the man who heard the voice of nature
and understood it so firmly and fully that he has guided all right-minded
people into the path of tranquil, calm, and happy life? (1.71)

Epicurus' account of the ethical end is inseparable from his general
epistemology, according to which the senses are themselves entirely reliable, and all error comes from belief.[8] This epistemology supports his
choice of an ethical witness; but it is also supported by his analysis of
ethical disease; it is because society and its teaching are found so sick and
unreliable that we need to rely on a judge that stands apart from its teaching. And Epicurus shrewdly grasps the implications of his moral epistemology for philosophical method. A claim about the end is not something to be
demonstrated by subtle argument, because subtle argument is not the
reliable cognitive tool some think it is, but something easily perverted by
culture; instead, we should assess it by consulting our senses and feelings.
The uncorrupted human creature, using its very own unimpeded faculties,
does not see worth in wealth, power, love, the immortal life of the soul.
When it has secured the removal of pain and impediment, it lives in a
flourishing way. We, in turn, looking at the uncorrupted creature with our
very own faculties, see that this is the nature of true good.

And since the uncorrupted creature is simply a device to isolate a certain
part in us, Epicurus confirms his choice by a further thought experiment. If
we can really get ourselves to imagine a (mature] human being for whom
all disturbance and impediment are removed—for whom the child's desires are truly satisfied—we will see, he claims, that this person lacks
nothing and has no need to go after more:

> When once this [sc. freedom from pain and disturbance] is secured for us,
> the entire tempest of the soul is undone, in that the animal does not have to
> go off as if in search of something that is lacking and to look for something
> further with which to fill up the good of the body. (*LMen* 128; cf. *Fin.*
> 1.40, and the test for desires in *VS* 71)

The uncorrupted creature is a reliable witness because it is what, at
some level, we *are*—because, when we think without social impediment,
we find ourselves endorsing the thought that the freedom from pain and

---

[8] See also Cic. *Fin.* 3.3: "Epicurus himself says that there is no necessity to argue about
pleasure, since the judgment is situated in the senses, so that it is sufficient to remind us, and
teaching is irrelevant"; cf. also *Fin.* 2.36. For further discussion of Epicurus' view of error, see
chapter 5; also Long and Sedley (1987) 78–86, C.C.W. Taylor (1980).

disturbance that this creature pursues is our own complete flourish-ing.[9]

We must be careful to say what this procedure does and does not imply. It does imply that anything that cannot be seen and desired as good by the uncorrupted creature, using its untutored equipment, is not a part of the human end. Thus, if the child does not go for logic and mathematics (and Epicurus, unlike Aristotle, seems to believe that it does not), logic and mathematics are shown to have, at best, an instrumental value. *Ataraxia* (freedom from disturbance and anxiety) in the soul and freedom from pain in the body: these are the uncorrupted creature's goals. We should not, however, conceive of these goals in a purely negative way. What the healthy creature goes for, according to the texts, appears to be not a zero state, a state of stagnant inactivity; such a state, indeed, would be death for the organism. The goal seems to be something more substantial and more positive: the continued undisturbed and unimpeded functioning of the whole creature. Thus Epicurus' account of pleasure—which he identifies with freedom from pain and disturbance—seems to be very close to the account given by Aristotle in *Nicomachean Ethics* VII: "the unimpeded activity of the natural condition."[10] The pictures of fulfillment we get in the text are not at all negative or dead: they show the creature actively using all its faculties, albeit in a way not strained or impeded by hunger, disease, or fear. This being the case, it is plausible that a certain sort of reasoning, too, is included as a part of the end: for a complete paralysis of mental function-ing would surely be a grave impediment or disturbance, for a human creature. But what apparently would not be a part of the end would be any specialized or socially tutored use of reason, anything beyond its healthy functioning as a faculty of the human animal. This ordinary use, Epicurus frequently suggests, is closely tied to bodily functions and usually would consist of awareness of and planning for bodily states.[11]

---

[9] On Hellenistic appeals to the behavior of children, see the illuminating discussion in Brunschwig (1986). I am in agreement with Brunschwig in insisting that Epicurus does not propose a simple return to the life of nature. But I would still ascribe importance to the fact that the child is taken to be a reliable and sufficient witness of the end.

[10] *EN* 1153a15; on the Epicurean view of pleasure, for a similarly positive account, see Mitsis (1988a), Rodis-Lewis (1975), Long and Sedley (1987) 123, with additional references. We should notice that Aristotle's characterization of pleasure as the activity of a *hexis* or settled condition is close to Epicurus' conception of the central type of pleasure as "ka-tastematic," that is, pertaining to a settled systemic condition.

[11] Numerous passages insist that for Epicurus the pleasures of the mind that have more than instrumental value are limited to forms of awareness of bodily functioning: cf.

Again, the procedure does seem to imply that no faculties or procedures not available to or used by the uncorrupted creature are necessary for recognizing the true final good. This seems to limit us to the bodily senses and feelings, and to the low-level use of practical reason that might be characteristic of a young child. Epicurus' insistence on this point amounts to an (probably deliberate) inversion of Plato, according to whom the only reliable witness to the end or good is the philosophical reason, purified of its bodily attachments by years of mathematical and dialectical training.[12] Epicurus and Plato agree in rejecting as unreliable the cultural attachments of the people in whose midst they live, and also such emotions and desires as go with the culture (for example erotic love and the fear of death). But Epicurus finds truth in the body, whereas for Plato the body is the primary source of delusion and bewitchment, and clarity comes only from separating oneself, through intellect, from its influence.

It is not easy to find any argument in the text for Epicurus' claim that the end for a human creature can be apprehended without teaching and training (and therefore contains nothing that it would take teaching and training to perceive). His conception of nature is normative: he does not make the mistake of approving of something just because it comes about without intervention, as his treatment of bodily pain makes clear. Nor does he believe that any providential design in the universe is at work in the creation of our bodily faculties. In fact, Lucretius ascribes to him the view that the world works pretty badly, where human beings and their lives are concerned. So it is not terribly clear why he should think that the human creature is fully equipped to perceive the good as it comes into the world, without teaching and training. And since this claim plays such a large role in his conception of the place of philosophy in human life, we would have wished for more substantial discussion here. We understand his motivations much better, I think, when we look at the contrast between the social and the unimpeded in the specific cases of love, fear, and anger. For now we can say that the texts present a powerful intuitive picture of a creature that is well equipped to pursue its own satisfaction in an exuberant healthy way, and for whom the recognized forms of social teaching seem to be sources of constraint and impediment.

Epicurus' position does not imply, however, that human beings should

---

Us. 409.70 = Athenaeus 546F; Cic. *Fin.* 2.69; and esp. Plut. *Non Posse* 1088E, 1089DE, 1090A. Plutarch insists that (unlike Aristotle and Plato) Epicurus does not include the love of reasoning in his account of human nature (1093D ff.).

[12] See Nussbaum (1986a) chapter 5, and Vlastos (1991) on mathematics in Plato's development.

try to live the lives of untutored children, or that such a life would be best for us now. It is not best, for two reasons. First, as we now are, we are products of our society. We have deeply internalized fears and desires that need long-term therapy. This therapy works, as we shall see, through a philosophical use of reasoning and argument. Second, the uncorrupted creature, while capable of apprehending the ultimate end, is not very good at discovering instrumental means to it. Even if we suppose it to be free from all anxieties of soul, it will still be vulnerable to bodily need, pain, and disease. A tutored use of reason can help the adult to avoid these pains: by providing sources of food, drink, and shelter, by finding medical treatment, by forming friendships that provide further support, even by using happy memories to counteract bodily pain. If Epicurus had been childlike, he would not have been happy on his deathbed. But he claims that despite the intensity of his pain, he does have a net balance of pleasure over pain because he has managed to diminish his awareness of pain through joyful memories of philosophical conversations with friends.[13] Thus, though an untutored child can apprehend the end correctly, the tutored adult is far more able to get the end.

Using his intuitive picture of health and impediment as a guide, Epicurus now divides human desires into two basic groups: the "natural" and the "empty." The natural are those whose appropriateness is witnessed by their presence in the uncorrupted creature.[14] The empty are products of teaching and acculturation, absent from the uncorrupted condition. They are called "empty" (or sometimes "empty-striving," *kenospoudon*) be-

---

[13] DL 10.22: "Going through this day of my life, which is at one and the same time blissful and my last, I write this to you. My sufferings from kidney stone and dysentery keep me continual company, lacking nothing of their natural force. But over against all of these I set joy of the soul [*to tēs psuchēs chairon*] at the memory of our past discussions." VS 41 similarly speaks of a pleasure (*to terpnon*) in philosophical learning and arguing. Long and Sedley (1987) 156 argue that this is not katastematic pleasure, but the "kinetic" pleasure of restoration from a disturbed condition. This is unclear: for the philosopher's *soul* will not be troubled by bodily pain, if he is well trained; so his mental activity is just the healthy activity of that part of him that is not disturbed by the (ongoing) pain. It is probable that Epicurus would not have taken the katastematic pleasure of the soul to include elaborate philosophizing or, indeed, much more than happy memory and awareness of bodily health: cf. *KD* 11 and my subsequent discussion. But the deathbed passage does not imply that the memories contain any technical philosophical material: they may be simply of friendly conversation, and perhaps such memories are included in the healthy functioning of the mind.

[14] Since sexual desire is counted as natural (see chapter 5), and since there is no sign of a belief in infantile sexuality, we can conclude that Epicurus is thinking of the entire career of an uncorrupted creature, not just its infancy.

cause they are infected with the falsity of the evaluative beliefs that ground them; and also because they tend to be vain or self-defeating, reaching out for a "boundless" object that can yield no stable satisfaction. Epicurus takes these two features to be connected. For, pointing to the uncorrupted creature, he argues that the "natural" operations of desire "have a limit"— that is, they can be filled up, well satisfied, they do not make exorbitant or impossible demands.[15] Their end is simply the continued healthy and undisturbed operation of the body and soul of the creature. But this, Epicurus believes, can be achieved with finite and usually modest material resources that are usually ready to hand.[16] False social beliefs, on the other hand, teach us not to be content with what is ready to hand, but to long for objects that are either completely unattainable (immortality) or very difficult to procure (luxuries and delicacies) or without any definite limit of satisfaction (the money-lover will never be satisfied with any definite amount of wealth, the lover will never enjoy the possession he desires). The nature of empty longing is, then, not "limited," but "goes off into infinity" (*LMen* 130, *KD* 14, Sen. *Ep.* 16.9).[17]

Let us look at some examples. The natural desire concerning food is a desire not to be hungry or malnourished. Put more positively, it is a desire for the continued healthy operation of the body. But this desire can be satisfied with a modest amount of food. This food needs only to have a certain nutritional balance, not to be especially luxurious or well prepared. "Frugal meals deliver a pleasure that is equal to that of an expensive diet, when once all the pain of need is removed; and bread and water give the very summit of pleasure, when a needy person takes them in" (*LMen* 130). "Send me a little pot of cheese," Epicurus writes to a friend, "so that I may have a luxurious feast whenever I like" (DL 10.11). Cravings for unlimited quantities of food and drink, for meat, for gastronomic novelties, for exquisite preparations—cravings all not natural but based on false beliefs about our needs—obscure the desire's built-in limit. "It is not the stomach that is insatiable, as the many think, but the false belief that the stomach

---

[15] On the "limit" in natural desire, see for example *KD* 15, 18, 20, 21. This idea is already present in Aristotle, who holds that the limit of desirability for external goods is given by the correct picture of *eudaimonia* as activity in accordance with complete excellence: see *Pol.* I.8 on false accumulation, VII.1 on external goods in general.

[16] Cf. Us. 469 = Stob. *Florileg.* 17.23: "Thanks to blessed Nature, because she has made the necessary things easy to procure, and the things difficult to procure she has made unnecessary." Also *VS* 20, *LMen* 130, *KD* 26, etc.

[17] Cf. also *VS* 68, Us. 473, and, on wealth, *VS* 25, Us. 478, 479, 480.

needs an unlimited amount to satisfy it" (*VS* 59).[18] Again, the longings associated with erotic love are held to result from a belief-based corruption of sexual desire, which itself is easily satisfied. The desire for immortality—and all the other complex human pursuits that can be diagnosed as stemming in various ways from that desire—derive from false belief about the gods, the soul, and personal survival. In short, the healthy desires are also the ones that are reliably easy to satisfy; much of our pain and all of our anxiety come from corrupt ways of thought.

Sometimes false belief infects desire in a subtler way: not by changing its view of its object, but by teaching the creature to have an anxious intensity about the goal that is not itself characteristic of the uncorrupted creature.[19] Epicurus finds this sort of corruption especially in the realm of the "natural" but "non-necessary" desires, that is, those that are present in the uncorrupted creature, but whose object is not necessary for continued life or painlessness. The most prominent example of such a desire, he seems to believe, is sexual desire; we shall discuss its corruptions in chapter 5.

The relationship between empty desire and false belief is very intimate. Epicurus holds that the belief is the basis and necessary condition of the desire. Its presence generates the desire (or emotion) in the first place, and its removal removes not simply the justification or rationale for the desire or emotion, but the desire or emotion itself:

> Correct apprehension of the fact that death is nothing to us makes the mortality of life enjoyable, not by adding on some limitless time but by taking away the passionate longing for immortality. For nothing is fearful in life to the person who is genuinely convinced that there is nothing fearful in not living. (*LMen* 124)

Similarly, *KD* 20 tells us that "Reason . . . by driving out the fear of eternity, makes life complete." *VS* 21 speaks even more boldly of an *elenchos*, a "refutation," of inappropriate desires.

---

[18] Cf. *VS* 25, 33, 67, 68; DL 10.11; Us. 189 = Stob. *Florileg.* 17.34; and, on meat-eating, Us. 464 = Porph. *De Abstin.* 1.51–52. "The cry of the flesh," says *VS* 33, "is: not to be hungry, not to be thirsty, not to be cold. Someone who has these things and has the hope of having them in the future might rival Zeus in *eudaimonia*."

[19] *KD* 30: "Whenever, among those natural desires that do not lead to pain if they are not fulfilled, an intense eagerness [*spoudē suntonos*] is present, they too are the products of false belief. And it is not on account of their own nature that they are not dispelled, but on account of the human being's empty believing." Cf. chapter 5 and notes, and also, for a different view, Konstan (1973).

Epicurus, then, seems to share Aristotle's view that beliefs are necessary conditions of emotions such as fear, love, anger; he extends this view to many other desires as well. His talk of the desires as "products of" false belief suggests that he may also hold that certain beliefs are sufficient conditions of desire: and this we shall see in some of our examples in the later chapters.[20] Unlike Aristotle and the Stoics, he does not make the distinction between emotions (fear, anger, love, grief, envy, gratitude, etc.) and appetites (hunger, thirst, sexual desire, desire for warmth and shelter) a central theoretical distinction; his own distinctions between the "natural" and the "empty" and between the bodily and the mental cut across it. For many appetites have a "mental" component, while many emotions have a close connection to a bodily condition. And many appetites are "empty," resting on false beliefs about items that are neither necessary nor even important for well-being; and at least some emotions may be based on beliefs that are not false but true. (The salient example given by Philodemus is what is called "natural anger": anger, apparently, based on the true belief that pain is bad.)[21]

Epicurus' diagnosis implies that there is a job of great urgency to be done. And since false belief is the root of the illness, the curative art must be an art that is equipped to challenge and conquer false belief. It must, then, be an art of reasoning:

> It is not drinking and continual feasting, nor is it enjoyment of young men, or women, nor of fish and the other things offered by a luxurious table, that make the pleasant life; it is sober reasoning [*logismos*] that searches out the causes of all pursuit and avoidance and drives out the beliefs from which a very great disturbance seizes the soul. [*LMen* 132][22]

---

[20] See, however, Philodemus, O XLIX–L, where he may deny that belief that one has been wronged is a sufficient condition of anger; the text is difficult, and he does appear to take very seriously the possibility that the belief may after all be shown to be a *drastikē aitia* (productive cause, perhaps sufficient condition of the emotion). See also O fr. 4 and col. VI. On Epicurean emotions in general, see Annas (1992).

[21] On natural anger, see Philodemus, O XXXVII, XLI; and see further in chapter 7. Although Philodemus says that this anger arises from seeing how the nature of things is, he also seems to think that its object is usually a person: so we might conjecture that it is most often felt on occasions when a person causes physical pain to the agent, or denies him the object of some necessary desire.

[22] I discuss this passage, with its (to us) odd list of enjoyings, in Nussbaum (1990c). The passage is frequently mistranslated, obscuring both the reference to males and the parallelism of sexual and edible objects.

Since false belief is an illness with which we are all in one or another way afflicted, this art will be necessary for a good life for each of us.[23] Since the removal of false belief by reasoning is thoroughly effective in driving out disturbing desire, an art that effectively treats belief will also be sufficient for securing the happy life.[24]

This art uses reasoning as its tool. It also needs to deal with many of the traditional concerns of philosophy: nature, the soul, the value of ends. It therefore seems to Epicurus appropriate to give this saving art the name of philosophy; and, furthermore, to insist that this saving art is what, properly understood, philosophy *is*. Sextus tells us that Epicurus defined philosophy as "an activity that secures the flourishing life by means of arguments and reasonings."[25] But if philosophy is necessary for the good life, and if Epicurus is, as it seems, committed to securing the good life for people of many talents and circumstances, then it would seem that he will have to make philosophy over into something that can in fact bring each and every person to his or her end—not only young gentlemen who have already had a liberal education, but farmers, women, slaves, people undereducated and even illiterate. For philosophy is indeed for everyone, everyone with an interest in living well. The *Letter to Menoeceus* begins:

> Let nobody put off doing philosophy when he is young, nor slacken off in philosophy because of old age. For nobody is either too young or too old to secure the health of the soul. And to say that the proper time for doing philosophy has not yet come, or has already gone by, is just like saying that the time for the flourishing life [*eudaimonia*] has not yet come or has already gone by. (*LMen* 122)

This medical conception can be expected to shape Epicurus' conception of the "arguments and reasonings" through which philosophy "secures the flourishing life."

III

What, then, *is* philosophy, when practiced in the Epicurean way? How does it approach its recipients, and what sorts of arguments does it use? In

---

[23] See, e.g., Cic. *Fin.* 1.63–64, *KD* 22, *VS* 54.

[24] E.g., *LMen* 135, and see the end of section III.

[25] *Tēn philosophian energeian einai logois kai dialogismois ton eudaimona bion peripoiousan,* M 11.169 = Us. 219; cf. Us. 227 = Schol. D. Thr.: *methodos energousa tōi biōi to sumpheron.*

answering these questions, Epicureans relied heavily on the medical analogy, which permeates the tradition as a metaphor, and more than a metaphor, for the philosophical endeavor. We have already seen Epicurus use it to insist that the only proper mission for philosophy is the curing of souls. This passage suggested that Epicurean philosophical practice will be circumscribed by the analogy in a way that Aristotle's is not: arguments aimed at other ends will be called empty. Again, we have seen the *Letter to Menoeceus* use the analogy to insist that philosophy is for all ages and persons: this, too, sets constraints on philosophy, of a kind Aristotle would not have thought appropriate.[26]

But the medical analogy was more prominent and pervasive in the Garden than the surviving words of Epicurus alone would make clear to us. The first four of the *Principal Opinions* (*KD* 1–4) were known to pupils as the *tetrapharmakos*, the fourfold drug.[27] And in the writings of the Epicurean Philodemus, Cicero's contemporary—especially the *Peri Orgēs* (*On Anger*) and the *Peri Parrhēsias* (*On Frank Speech*)[28]—medical imagery abounds. Despite the notorious difficulty of working with these lacuna-laden papyrus fragments, we can extract a rich complex account of the Epicurean view of therapeutic *logos*. Philodemus not only uses the image of doctoring as his primary and guiding image for Epicurean philosophizing throughout both of these texts; he also develops the analogy with painstaking detail, comparing different types of arguments to different types of medical procedures, different problems faced by the working philosopher to analogous problems faced by the doctor. The appropriateness of the analogy, assumed from the start, can be used to justify a controversial element in Epicurean practice. This fascinating material, probably not original with Philodemus, refers constantly to the authority and practices of Epicurus, cites known writings of Epicurus as exemplary of types of therapeutic *logos*, and in general indicates its close relationship to the practice of Epicurus himself, as well as that of later Epicurean commu-

[26] Cf. also *VS* 54: "We must not make a show of doing philosophy, but really do philosophy: for what we need is not the appearance of health, but real health." Similar language can be found in *VS* 64, *LHdt* 35, Cic. *Fin.* 1.59, Us. 224 = *Florilegium Monac.* 195, Us. 471 = Porph. *Ad Marc.* 27, p. 208 N. Us. 471 = Porph. *Ad Marc.* 27, p. 208 N compares the soul of a person suffering from empty desires to the physical state of a feverish body. For other medical references, see Clay (1983b).

[27] For this title, see *Pap. Herc.* 1005, col. 4. See Bailey (1926) 347.

[28] For the *Peri Orgēs* (*O*) I use the edition of Wilke (1914); for the *Peri Parrhēsias* (*P*), the edition of Olivieri (1914). There is an excellent study of these fragments in Gigante (1975), with extensive discussion of ancient uses of the medical analogy, to which I am indebted. See also Clay (1983a), Frischer (1982).

nities.[29] In Diogenes of Oenoanda as well—another not very original Epicurean writer—highly specific medical images are used to characterize arguments, and the whole purpose of "publishing" his huge philosophical *logos* is described in terms of the medical parallel (see section IV).

How, then, does the medical analogy both express and justify a distinctive attitude to philosophical argument? Let us pursue this question by returning to Nikidion, who began searching for a good life inside the city, in the company of well-bred young Aristotelians. We can begin by pointing out that her name—that of a woman and a courtesan—may well be the real name of an Epicurean pupil, as it could never be of one of Aristotle's. The fact that she has grown up outside the wealthy propertied class, that her education has been uneven,[30] that she may be illiterate,[31] that she has certainly not been trained for a future as citizen, leader, person of practical wisdom—none of this disqualifies her from Epicurean therapy, or therefore from Epicurean *eudaimonia*, as it would surely have disqualified any real Nikidion from Aristotelian dialectic and Aristotelian *eudaimonia*. The radical step Epicurus took in opening his school to the real Nikidions of the world[32] both influenced and was influenced by his conception of what philosophy should be.

On the other hand, Epicurus does not teach vast groups of pupils or

---

[29] Philodemus' source in *P* is Zeno of Sidon, an Epicurean of c. 100 B.C.E. Zeno's work is a probable source for *O* as well—see Wilke; it is clear, however, that some of the material on anger is eclectic, influenced by Stoic discussions also. See Wilke (1974), Fillion-Lahille (1984).

[30] Much depends on how we situate her; if she is a *hetaira*, as the name suggests, she will have had, probably, more education than a citizen wife or daughter; but not all *hetairai* were Aspasias.

[31] On the distribution of literacy by class and gender, see the forceful arguments in Harris (1990); again, *hetairai* would be better off than citizen wives.

[32] Even if the names of *hetairai* cited in the passage that introduces Nikidion are not authentic, surviving fragments of letters attest securely to the presence of women in the school; in one case, a married couple (Leontius of Lampsacus and his wife Themista, DL 10.25) seem to have been his associates; she receives letters from Epicurus (DL 10.5), and they name their child after him (10.26). Leontion the courtesan, too, seems to have been active in the philosophical life of the school, and receives letters from him (10.5); there were probably others. Plutarch (*LB* 1129A) mentions as a piece of common knowledge the fact that Epicurus sends his books and letters "to all men and women" (*pasi kai pasais*). We should not consider Epicurus a complete social radical: his will frees (then and only then) his male and female slaves—here he and Aristotle are alike; and although he provides funds for the support of Metrodorus' daughter as well as his sons, only the sons are enjoined to do philosophy, while she will be given in marriage, when she is old enough, to a husband selected from among the members of the school. (In fact, this makes her more expensive, and Epicurus provides her with a dowry [DL 19–20].)

teach them in public. It is a prerequisite for being an Epicurean pupil that Nikidion be able to leave her usual occupations in the city and enter the Epicurean community, in which she will live from then on. Although little is known about the financial structure of the community, Epicurus' will mentions that pupils have supported him from their private resources (DL 10.20). He expressed opposition to the idea that the property of the community should be held in common, saying that it showed a lack of trust (10.11). Although he began relatively poor—he may have been the son of a schoolmaster (DL 10.1–4)—by the time of his death he was evidently prosperous, with funds that he generously bestows on the future of the school and the support of his friends.[33] We may, then, conjecture that the situation was rather like one we observe in many religious communities, where the pupil may enroll and be supported on condition of making a donation to the central treasury, and perhaps also showing a willingness to support communal life in other ways. (VS 41 mentions *oikonomia*, housework or household management,[34] as among the regular features of an Epicurean life. And a letter of Epicurus to Idomeneus requests an "offering" of agricultural produce [Plut. *Adv. Col.* 1117E, discussed later].) Thus although the community draws pupils from every social class and from both sexes, there are implicit restrictions. Nikidion will probably have to bring her savings and her jewelry with her; and if she has any children, she will probably be urged to leave them behind.[35]

Let us imagine this friend of ours, then, as she really might have been: smart but ill-educated, relatively weak in intellectual discipline, fonder of poetry than of Plato. Her soul is full of unbounded longing. She is ambitious for influence, prone to passionate love, fond of exquisite food and clothing, deeply afraid of death. Philodemus tells us that women offer more resistance to Epicurean argument than men do, since they dislike receiving the sort of "frank criticism" of belief that, according to Philodemus, was Epicurus' stock-in-trade [P col. XXIb). Let us, then, imagine her somewhat

---

[33] Note especially the insistence that "as many as have provided necessary support to me in personal life and have demonstrated their thorough goodwill and have chosen to grow old with me in philosophy, should lack none of the necessities, so far as is in my power" (10.20).

[34] *Oikonomia* means, centrally, running the household; but Xenophon's account of the young wife's pursuit of this job shows that it involves not only ordering servants around, doing the accounts, and so forth, but also supervising the cleaning and doing light cleaning, such as dusting, herself.

[35] On children, see chapter 5. For further discussion of the structure and economic arrangements of the school, see Clay (1983a, 1983b, 1984a, 1986), Frischer (1982), De Witt (1954), Fauth (1973), Longo Auricchio (1978). Philodemus P 55 states that the teacher deserves to receive property because of the good he has done.

vain, and more than a little stubborn—for this will give us a chance to speak of the therapeutic techniques that are applied to the recalcitrant pupil, an especially fascinating part of our subject. On the other hand, she has deep intuitions about a healthy untroubled life that waits for her, for each human being, the other side of longing, anxiety, and care. She connects this dream, perhaps, with memories of a carefree, healthy childhood—although it is not exactly to that childhood that she wishes to return.

Nikidion arrives, then, at the Garden. It is an enclosed therapeutic community, at some distance from the city. It is rather self-sufficient economically; its members have few reasons to be in contact with their former associates in the city. She has probably made the decision to enroll before having personal contact with its leaders, attracted by its promise of a life free from stress.[36] Perhaps she has heard of, or even read, some of Epicurus' voluminous publications—whose bulk and renown, says Plutarch, undermines his claim that he is seeking to "live unknown."[37] In going to the Garden she has decided to separate herself from her old way of life in the city and, so long as she is there, to live a life devoted entirely to the philosophical community itself. Its members become her new family.

And there can be no question as to who the head of this family is: for its members even wear images of Epicurus on their rings and put his portrait on their drinking cups (Cic. *Fin.* 5.1.3, Pliny *NH* 35.5). They refer to Epicurus as their "savior" and celebrate him as a hero, during common feasts, with acclamations similar to those that would, in the world outside, be used of a divinized hero such as Heracles, with whom Epicurus is favorably compared by Lucretius. Plutarch speaks of "your 'roars of applause' and 'ecstatic cries' and 'tumultuous clappings' and 'reverencings' and 'adorations,' in which you supplicate and celebrate the man who calls you to pleasure" [*Adv. Col.* 1117A]. The "hero cult" of Epicurus is the Garden's analogue for civic religion.[38] Entering the community, Nikidion agrees to recognize a new "savior."

---

[36] For a controversial discussion of Epicurean recruitment—allegedly through statues depicting a calm undisturbed visage—see Frischer (1982), reviewed critically by Clay (1984b).

[37] Plutarch, *Lathē Biōsas* 1128–29; cf. Clay (1983a, 1984b). It seems to me that this evidence shows that we do not need to invoke the somewhat dubious evidence of portrait sculpture to explain the procedures of Epicurean recruitment.

[38] See Clay (1983, 1984a, 1986); also Plut. *LB* 1128–29. It is difficult to know how much of this veneration went on during Epicurus' lifetime. There is also some evidence for allusions or links to mystery religions—Plut. *Adv. Col.* 1117B.

She enters, then, a placid, cheerful, apolitical world, a world devoted to the values of friendship and solidarity, a world in which, to use Metrodorus' words, members may "sink away" from dangers and disturbances "by means of fellow feeling" [*tais homoiopatheiais*; Plut. *Adv. Col.* 1117B); a world suspicious of all external ties, suspicious above all of *paideia* and the values involved in it. This world is self-sufficient not just economically but spiritually as well. It has its own ordered structures of daily life, its own "religion," its own replacements for familial, societal, and civic relationships. It is most important to think of this philosophy as structuring not only periods of formal instruction, but the entirety of an alternative way of life. This is probably a large difference from Aristotelian practice. Aristotle does not need to give his pupils a new community, since he assumes the relative health of the one they are in. Epicurus thinks otherwise. In his will, he speaks of the decision to join the community as a decision "to spend one's time there continuously, in accordance with philosophy" [*endiatribein kata philosophian*, DL 10.17), and says of pupils that "they chose to grow old with me in philosophy" (10.20; see n. 35).

What arguments does Nikidion encounter, and what makes them therapeutic? We turn now to our schematic list of features, asking how Epicurus stands toward them.

1. *Practical goal.* The most general and indispensable characteristic of the arguments in which Nikidion will participate is that they are indeed designed to achieve a practical goal, namely, to bring her closer to *eudaimonia*. Arguments do not simply provide her with reasons to live thus and so. They may do this; but their task is, above all, to act as *causes* of good living. A valid, simple, elegant, but not causally effective argument has no more use in philosophy than a nicely colored, fragrant, but ineffective drug has in medicine. The promise to Nikidion is the promise to Menoeceus: "Go over these things . . . and you will never be disturbed, waking or sleeping, and you will live like a god among humans" [*LMen* 135). If the course of treatment is a good one, she can write home to her family what Epicurus apparently wrote to his mother: "O mother, be of good cheer. . . . Consider that each day I advance toward greater *eudaimonia*, acquiring some further helpful benefit."[39] Arguments are "useful" items that "will continuously come to the aid" of the aspiring pupil.[40]

Epicurus' devotion to a practical goal thus far resembles Aristotle's. But

---

[39] *Letter to Mother*, ed. Chilton (1976). For some of the controversy over the contents and argument of this letter, see Clay (1983a).

[40] *Chrēsima ta dialogismata, LPyth* 85; *sunechōs boēthēsei, LHdt* 83.

it turns out to be far more all-embracing. For Aristotle, ethics and politics have a practical end, but other branches of philosophy have a purely theoretical end, and theory is worth pursuing for its own sake. For Epicurus, every branch of philosophy must be assessed for its contribution to practice. If it makes none, it is empty and useless.[41] Nor does he seem to believe, as does Aristotle, that theoretical reasoning, undertaken for its own sake, can be practical simply by being an intrinsically valuable constituent part of the best human life. Mathematical, logical, and scientific studies are not themselves part of the end, of what it is to be in an undisturbed condition. Philosophy narrows to whatever serves the master art of living. As Cicero's Torquatus puts it:

> He seems to you lacking in education. The reason is that he thought no education worthy of that name unless it contributed to our training for happy life. . . . Was he to occupy himself, like Plato, in music, geometry, arithmetic, and astronomy, which, starting from false premises, cannot be true and which, even if they were true, would not help us live more pleasant, and therefore better, lives? Was he, I say, to study those arts and neglect the great art of living, which requires so much effort and is correspondingly so rewarding? (1.17)

Many parts of the traditional curriculum, unlike mathematics, will still justify themselves as helpful to the art of life; but even here there is a shift in their function. Ethics becomes architectonic over all uses of reason.

We can add that the practical aim to which Epicurus dedicates both ethics and philosophy of nature is characterized in a markedly un-Aristotelian way: for it involves nothing less than the complete removal of *tuchē*, of vulnerability to events beyond our control, from the pursuit of *eudaimonia*. Aristotelian ethics does not give *tuchē* unlimited power; in fact, it insists that the most important things in human life are not very vulnerable to reversal. But Aristotle would never have written what Metrodorus writes:

> I have gotten in ahead of you, O Tuchē, and I have built up my fortifications against all your stealthy attacks. And we will not give ourselves up as captives to you or to any other circumstance. But when necessity leads us out, spitting a lot on life and those who emptily cling to it, we will go out from life with a fine song of triumph, stating that we have lived well. [*VS* 47)[42]

---

[41] This was the central argument of Marx's doctoral dissertation (Marx 1854), which contrasts Epicurus, in this regard, with Democritus.

[42] On the authorship of *VS* 47, see Clay (1983a) 260ff., who argues that the practices of emulation and imitation in the Epicurean community make it impossible to give a clear-cut

This commitment, too, shapes Epicurean arguments, as we shall see.

2. This brings us to the medical property of *value-relativity*. We saw that for the Aristotelian, what will count as health must have some connection with the pupils' own antecedent ideas of health. The cure cannot look to them like a state not worth enduring: indeed, they must recognize it as something that answers to their deepest and most central desires. All this Epicurus develops further. However revisionary his inquiry may be, his challenge, as he portrays it, is always to get the pupil to see that what he delivers to her *does* in fact fulfill her desires, at least the deepest and most central.[43] She may in the process alter her ideas concerning what her desires are, and which of them are deepest; but in the end the therapist must make the connection.

Philodemus makes it clear that this was a much discussed problem in Epicurean therapy. For often, especially at the beginning of treatment, the pupil will refuse to admit that her "empty" desires are in fact bad, and in consequence may not be disposed to accept the result of therapeutic argument as an improvement in her condition. Nikidion may enjoy being in love; she may be attached to her wardrobe, to her wines, even to her religion. It is essential, Philodemus tells us, that the therapeutic teacher should at an early stage do what a good doctor similarly does for a patient who refuses to acknowledge her physical illness. Just as the doctor will try, through vivid description of the disease in frightening language, to make the patient see its danger and enormity, so the philosopher must present the pupil's current condition to her in language that "causes a great shudder" and place the "size" of the illness "before her eyes" in an unavoidably clear way (O cols. III–IV). For only that shudder and that vision show Nikidion that the end of therapeutic argument does after all hook up with what she really wants for herself: only then will she "turn round and get herself ready for treatment" (IV).[44] An alternative technique is positive. The

---

answer to the question whether Metrodorus or Epicurus was the author. "In this context, individual features tend to blur, but a distinct physiognomy begins to emerge for the group itself" (261). Cf. Epicurus, at Us. 489 = Porph. *Ad Marc.* 30, p. 209,12 N: "Wisdom has no association with *tuchē.*"

[43] It appears that Epicurus and Aristotle have different intuitions about what is likely to be deepest and most central. Aristotle, on the whole, believes that reflective evaluations based on education and communal experience are more reliable than is untutored desire; Epicurus sees reflective evaluation as full of delusion and has, as we have seen, more confidence in untutored desire.

[44] See also P 1, 3, 67. And cf. Augustine, *Conf.* 9.16: *et videbam et horrebam, et quo a me fugerem non erat.*

teacher holds up, as does Cicero's Torquatus, the picture of the happy godlike sage as a sign of the good things in store. He tries to get the pupil to recognize that image as one to which she has a deep antecedent attraction. And these procedures are not just heuristic devices: as is plain from our prior discussion of the "proof" of the end, they are also tools of justification for the view of the good.

Thus this ethical view is pragmatic in some of the same ways that Aristotle's is. But there are some differences that make the use of pragmatic constraints in Epicurus' case seem more disturbing. The first and most obvious difference is that Epicurean ethics is revisionary to a degree that Aristotle's is not.[45] From the beginning it discounts a large number of the "appearances" embodied in Nikidion's beliefs as empty and unreliable. And it seems to know pretty clearly which ones these are, in advance of asking Nikidion herself to sort them out. Epicurus' choice of the untutored human being as a "witness" does not help here, since it is frankly normative, laden with peculiarly Epicurean values; it would hardly be accepted by Aristotle, who thinks of the child as an example of incomplete life and reasoning.[46] Furthermore, even what one sees in the untutored human being depends so much on what one already thinks important. Aristotle discovers in children a love of distinction-making, a reaching out for knowledge (*Metaph.* I.1). Epicurus sees only the desire for freedom from pain and disturbance. The difference seems to be, however, that Aristotle shows respect for and seriously investigates his pupils' full experience of value, viewing all that as material toward the ethical truth. We feel that it is an open question what conception they will choose. This seems less clearly the case with Epicurus. Nikidion is there not to pursue an inquiry but to be converted.

The second difference is in the extent of the pragmatism. For Aristotle, results in ethics must cohere, in the end, with results in psychology, science, and metaphysics. These other inquiries range far beyond the human case and are undertaken for their own sake, apart from a consideration of human needs and purposes. That is why coherence across inquiries may give us additional confidence in the rightness of our ethical view. For Epicurus, *every* inquiry (as Marx argued well) has ethical constraints. "If we had never been burdened by suspicious fears about things in the heavens, and about death, lest it might be something to us, and by not

---

[45] Philodemus speaks (in a manner reminiscent of Plato) of "turning the reason around" (*tēn dianoian apostrephesthai*, P 22); cf. P 13, which claims that education involves character change.

[46] *EN* 1111a25–26, 1144b8, 1176b23.

apprehending the limits of pain and desire, we would not have had any need of the science of nature" (*KD* 11; cf. 12). But this means that a science of nature that delivered disturbing rather than calming stories of how things are would not have fulfilled the purpose for which we need a science of nature, and would justly be dismissed as empty. The fruit of "a continuous study of natural science" is "a calm course of life" (*LHdt* 37). The summary of physical teachings "will continuously aid" a pupil, giving her a "strength" incomparable with that of others (83). The letter's conclusion refers to its contents—the central surviving teachings of Epicurean philosophy of nature—as "the things that are most important for calming the mind" (83). Again, the *Letter to Pythocles* about celestial phenomena is described as "reasonings concerning the things that conduce to the happy life" (84); and Epicurus' first instruction to Pythocles is: "In the first place, remember that knowledge of celestial phenomena, like everything else, whether taken along with other subjects or in isolation, has no other end than freedom from disturbance and a secure state of conviction" (*LPyth* 85).

This material gives evidence of a fundamental Epicurean belief: freedom from disturbance requires having a firmly defended view about physical matters that bear on our ethical ends. In this sense we require not only appropriate physical dogma but also close and convincing physical arguments. Otherwise an opposing set of arguments might throw us into disturbance. But it would be a serious mistake to think that the school was especially scientific or given to the dispassionate study of nature for its own sake. In fact, by comparison to Aristotle's school, where firsthand research in biology and history was continually going on and where astronomical research, if not firsthand, was drawn from the most up-to-date independent research of Eudoxus, the Epicurean school was very unscientific. Cicero's Torquatus grants this, and pleads, in reply, the supremacy of ethics. The physical theory of Epicureanism has a lot of internal elegance and some brilliant argumentation; but there seems to have been no attempt to test it against observed nature with an open mind in the Aristotelian way. The point is to convince people of its truth; and its practical contribution is again and again brought forward as a reason for our commitment to it. With this theory we need have no fear of the gods or of death; we can prove the mortality of the soul.

So Epicurean philosophy is not only value-relative where ethics is concerned; it is value-relative through and through. All its truths must support its view of happiness. It is not altogether an accident that all and only the disturbing views of the universe turn out false.[47]

---

[47] We can connect with this Epicurus' insistence, in *LPyth*, that in many cases we should

3. Epicureans pride themselves on the *responsiveness of their ethical arguments to particular cases and situations.* The philosophical teacher, like a good doctor, must be a keen diagnostician of particulars, devising a specific course of treatment for each pupil. Here Philodemus makes his most extensive use of medical imagery. Some arguments, like some drugs, are "bitter" or "biting"; some are gentle. Epicurus will treat Nikidion as gently as he can in curing her of her bad desires, for such a teacher is "the mildest and most evenhanded of people" (*O* XLIV). (Pythocles is mentioned as a person whom Epicurus addressed with mild critical therapy [*P* 6].)[48]

The doctor will, then, "do therapy with moderate discourse" (*P* 20) as long as this works; but he also has at his disposal harsher and stronger remedies. If he uses "bitter" argument, Philodemus stresses, it is not from bad temper or ill will, as some people think (*P* 54); it is good contextual medical judgment. Operating like a doctor who decides "through plausible signs" that a certain patient needs a purgative, he will administer an argument that has a similarly evacuating effect—presumably, some devastating critique of Nikidion's former attachments and ways of life. (We might think, for example, of Lucretius' scathing attacks upon love; cf. chapter 5.) And if the purge does not work the first time, he will try his harsh treatment "again and again" (*P* 63–64), so that if it does not accomplish its *telos* one time it may the next (64). (So Lucretius piles argument on argument, beating down the resistance of even the most stubborn devotee of that virulent disease.) Epicurus said, "Let us altogether chase out our bad habits, like evil men who have long done us great harm" (*VS* 46). Purgative arguments, repeatedly applied, are the doctor's remedy of choice for deeply entrenched habits of believing and valuing. At the same time— since the teacher is not a one-sided character and his "devotion to his *technē* is many-colored"—he will "mix in" with his harsh medicine some good-tasting stuff, for example, some "plentiful words of praise"; and he will "encourage her to do good things" (*P* 86). (Even so, Lucretius "mixes in" some helpful accounts of non-disturbing procreative sex.) So young Nikidion will find herself swallowing a heady mixture of praise, protreptic, and caustic reproof, designed and mixed especially for her—and, we now add, administered by a doctor who knows how to spot the critical moment (*kairos*) for its administration, as he takes note of the *akmē*, or most acute state, of her condition (*P* 22, 25, 65).

---

accept multiple explanations of phenomena; but we do not do this where the choice among explanations has serious consequences for our *eudaimonia*. See *LPyth* 86–87, Long and Sedley (1987) 45–46.

[48] Gentle treatment is much stressed in *P* as the most desirable strategy: see 6, 8, 9, 18, 26, 27, 71, 85–87, col. I. Cf. Gigante (1975).

Now it may turn out that Nikidion, being a woman, will prove resistant even to the strongly purgative or abrasive sort of medicine. Even words that are analogous to wormwood in their power have no effect (*P* 68). (Some people, said Epicurus, find truth all on their own; some need a guide, but follow well; those in a third group have to be driven.)[49] Then, says Philodemus, the teacher/doctor has no choice but to opt, very reluctantly, for surgery. Like a "wise doctor," he will operate at just the right time, and "out of well-wishing" (*O* XLIV, *P* col. XVII; cf. Gigante). It is hard to know what the surgical form of argument would be. Philodemus calls it a "reproof" (*nouthetein*). This suggests that the teacher would express strong disapproval of the pupil's beliefs and conduct, giving reasons for this disapproval. One student's words, reported by Philodemus, suggest that the criticism was felt as an aggressive invasion of personal dignity: "I fell of my own will into the ignorance of youth; and on account of that he had to give me a whipping" (*mastigoun m'edei*, *P* 83). Athenian male citizens were, we know, obsessive about preserving the integrity of their bodily boundaries; one might beat a slave, but one could never so much as lift a hand to a free citizen.[50] If, then, this criticism is felt as analogous to a beating, it must have been some humiliating invasion of what the pupil would see as her private space: perhaps, a public exposure of her weaknesses and bad thoughts. This would fit well with the community's practice of "confession," which I shall shortly describe.[51]

Particularity plays different roles in Epicurean and Aristotelian practice. For Aristotle, the ethical adult, the person of practical wisdom, is like a doctor in her relation to new cases and situations: context-sensitive, ready for new features, flexible and responsive. Ethics is medical because rules are not good enough. Epicurus uses the medical model to describe, instead, the relationship between the ethical *teacher* and the sick *pupil*. The teacher is quite literally a doctor, who must deal with the vicissitudes of illness in the individual soul. But there is little if any stress on the idea that the healthy cured life will employ forms of reasoning that focus on the particular. In fact, Epicurean normative ethics looks, from the surviving texts, rather dogmatic and given to general rulelike formulations. "The wise man will be a dogmatist and will not be at a loss" (DL 10.120).

---

[49] Sen. *Ep.* 52.3. On this passage, see Clay (1983a) 265.

[50] See Dover (1978), Halperin (1990).

[51] On the stubborn pupil, see also O XIX, XXXI–XXXII; P 6, 7, 10, 30, 59, 61, 63, 67, 71, col. II, col. XIV. Stubbornness is connected with reliance on things external (*P* 30), with youth (*P* 71), with *paideia* (O XXXI–XXXII).

We seem to be in danger of losing touch with argument. For our account has led us into areas of psychological interaction that do not look much like the give-and-take of philosophical discourse. It is tempting at this point to imagine that we have in some of this material about purgation and surgery interesting information about the extracurricular life of the Garden, but that the real hard-core philosophical activity was something else. (For after all, the extant writings of Epicurus look like philosophical arguments of a recognizable kind, detailed, systematic, frequently sophisticated in their strategies against the opposition.) We must resist this temptation.

First, all this therapy is conducted through argument. Just as the illnesses Epicurus describes are illnesses of belief, often nourished by philosophical doctrine, so the cure must of necessity come through philosophical arguments. The elaborate apparatus of medical imagery is illustrative of the many ways in which the philosopher practices his own distinctive activity, "using reason and *logos*." The job is to root out false beliefs; for this we need arguments that discredit the false and leave the true in place. Philodemus frequently cites actual writings of Epicurus as examples of the therapeutic practices he has in mind. Only a complex system, carefully argued, will give the patient a way to account for everything; and only that will calm her anxiety.

Furthermore, we must also insist that what all argument *is*, in this community, is therapy. "Purgation" and "drugging" are not ancillary to philosophy; they are what, given its practical commitment, philosophy must become. Whatever parts of traditional philosophy are omitted are just those that are taken to be empty. Thus we should not be surprised that there seems to be a thoroughgoing interpenetration of philosophical activity and daily human interaction in this community; for interaction is mediated above all by philosophy, and philosophy is aimed entirely at the amelioration of daily practice. Epicurus insists on this intermingling in the strongest terms: "We must at one and the same time laugh and do philosophy and do our household tasks and use our other faculties, and never leave off proclaiming the sayings of the correct philosophy" (*VS* 41). We are not to imagine Nikidion (like one of our students) going to class for several hours and then living the rest of the day as if the class did not exist. She lives in this community; all her activities are governed by its goals and by the guiding presence of Epicurus, revered as a savior. Her life is suffused with philosophy, as the philosophy she learns is suffused with life.

But if we feel that there is something more than a little odd about calling the whole of this therapeutic interchange philosophy, and its tools arguments, we will not be wrong. Our uneasiness can be further explored if we now turn to our second group of "medical" attributes.

4. Nikidion's arguments are not just suited to her concrete situation: they are fundamentally *directed to her health as an individual*, rather than to any communal end. Although fellow feeling and friendship are absolutely central to the therapeutic community, it looks most of the time as if its end is the health of each taken singly, friendship being only an instrumental means. Since the evidence on that point is complex, I defer it to chapter 7; what is clear, however, is that, where Epicurus himself is concerned, the larger political community is no part of the goal; and even marriage and family ties are discouraged (chapter 5). Lucretius may take a different view.

5. In these arguments, unlike Aristotle's, the *use of practical reasoning is merely instrumental*. I have already argued that this is true of scientific reasoning; the same obtains in ethics. *KD* 11 (quoted previously) links the two together: fears coming from false beliefs about desire are our reason to philosophize about desire, just as fears about the heavens are our reason to philosophize about the heavens. The *Letter to Menoeceus* tells us that the reason to go in for philosophy is "to secure the health of" the soul. It promises Menoeceus a godlike life as the reward for studying it. Suppose we had a special drug that could make Nikidion instantly forget all her false beliefs, while retaining the true beliefs: we have no reason to think Epicurus would not have used it, provided that it did not impede the other instrumental functions of practical reason, such as the discovery of means to food and shelter. Therapy must go its arduous and difficult course through argument only because no such drug exists: our only access to the ills of the mind is through its rational powers. But the arguments that work through these powers have no intrinsic human value.[52] We are never safe from bodily ills: so we need arguments around to counterbalance them should they arise. Nor can false beliefs be permanently put to rest, so deeply are they fixed in people who have grown up in a conventional culture; so we need to counter them continually by going over Epicurean arguments. But arguments are with us as handmaids only: useful, even necessary, but not valuable in themselves. Among the uses of practical reason, only its daily use in providing for basic wants has a chance of counting as a constituent part of the end.

[52] Similar issues seem to be at stake in some contemporary debates about the relative merits of psychoanalytic and chemical treatment for psychological problems: for one must ask, among other things, whether the psychoanalytic process of self-scrutiny has an intrinsic worth, independent of the worth of the "cured" state to which it leads.

6. The Epicurean teacher therefore gives *the standard virtues of argument* a purely instrumental role. Consistency, logical validity, clarity in definition—all these clearly have a high instrumental value. But, as Torquatus informs us, Nikidion would be taught to have contempt for those who study logic and definition *for their own sake*.[53] She probably will not even pursue them for their own sake for a while, so as to be better prepared to apply them to practical arguments later on: Stoics claim a major difference between their school and Epicurus' here. Nikidion will learn just as much analytic rigor as she needs to go over the arguments that bring calm and to appreciate their superiority. Frequently this is quite a lot. As Lucretius writes, the clarity of Epicurean argument is like sunlight dispersing dark shadows. But these virtues are servants only. If Nikidion shows daily progress toward *ataraxia*, and if we can be sure that she will continue safely to do so, defended against opposition, the fact that she cannot always distinguish a valid from an invalid argument, a clear from an ambiguous definition, will not trouble the teacher's calm.

Nowhere is this more obvious than in the role of epitomes and summaries in Epicurean practice. Epicurus recommends that all pupils, including those who do not have the time or the experience to work through the detail of his arguments, digest and memorize epitomes of the most important Epicurean conclusions. The surviving three letters are such epitomes. All three begin by announcing Epicurus' decision to prepare a brief and easily remembered summary of the principal doctrines on a topic; and this summary of "elements" is explicitly directed to the pupil who does not go further, as well as the one who does. Even for the one who does, it has a value, "For a general overview is often needed, the details not nearly so often" (*LHdt* 35). Aristotelians that we are, we would shrink back in distaste from giving one of our philosophy students such a summary of doctrine. For we tend to think, with Aristotle, that this short-circuits the whole point of the enterprise, which is the distinction-making use of practical reason. It would be like giving a math student a list of answers. It would not be philosophy at all. If we do divulge to students the conclusions in ethics we believe to be true, we also indicate clearly that they are worthless without the reasoning that leads to them. For Nikidion's teacher, this is not the case. And this difference seems comprehensible, given that his driving aim is to help all unhappy people. To help not just the Brown undergraduate, whose talents and prior acculturation make an analytical approach to

---

[53] Cf. DL 10.31 = Us. 257, Cic. *Fin.* 1.63 = Us. 243; and see Long and Sedley (1987) 99–100.

philosophy possible, but the unleisured, the uneducated, the poor. To help Nikidion, even if she is who she is.

At this point, looking ahead to our discussion of Skepticism, we must insist on one more point. A certain sort of overall coherence is extremely important instrumentally in the Epicurean practice of philosophy. The system, to use Lucretius' image, is a well-fortified stronghold inside which the pupil is protected from all challenges. But this means that the system must have, instrumentally, a high degree of order and elaboration. Nikidion may not hear the same teaching Epicurus gave Herodotus; more sophisticated diseases require more elaborate remedies, and if she shows no signs of worry about Aristotle's criticisms of Democritus, she is not going to be taught the theory of minimal parts. But the whole of the system is there waiting in the wings, should the pupil's state require it.

7. The medical model creates a sharp *asymmetry of roles*: doctor and patient, active and passive, authority and obedient follower of authority. Philodemus stresses that the teacher must continue to work and to receive criticism—presumably from himself or fellow teachers.[54] But nonetheless the pupil is encouraged to follow the example of medicine and to put herself entirely in the power of the doctor. She must "give (her)self over to," put (her)self into the hands of" the teacher (cf. O IV, P 40). She must even, says Philodemus, citing the medical parallel, "throw (her)self, so to speak, into the hands of the leaders and depend on them alone" (P 39).[55] Before embarking on the course of therapy, he continues, the pupil might recite to himself or herself the tag from the *Iliad* that goes "with him at my side." This passage is one in which Diomedes asks to have Odysseus as his protector on the night expedition: "With him at my side, both of us could come back from the blazing of fire itself, since his mind is best at devices" (10.246–47). Philodemus says that the pupil, reciting this, acknowledges the teacher as the "only savior," the "one correct guide of correct speech and deed."

Accordingly, all ancient accounts of Epicurus and Epicureanism agree in depicting an extraordinary degree of devotion and deferential obedience toward the master. The pupils, from Lucretius to Cicero's Torquatus, concur in celebrating him as the savior of humanity. He is revered as a hero, even as a god. Plutarch reports that one day, while Epicurus was lecturing about nature, Colotes fell at his feet, seized him by the knees, and performed a *prokunēsis*—an act of obeisance appropriate to a divinity or a self-deifying monarch (*Non Posse* 1100A, *Adv. Col.* 1117B); he quotes a letter from master to pupil in which Epicurus recalls the incident with

---

[54] See P 46, 81, col. VIII.
[55] Here see Gigante's revision of Olivieri's text: Gigante (1975).

approval, stressing that Colotes "seized hold of (him) to the full extent of the contact that is customary in revering and supplicating certain people" (*Adv. Col.* 1117BC = Us. 141). Epicurus makes the vague claim that he would like to "revere and consecrate" Colotes in return—presumably a wish that Colotes should eventually attain his godlike condition. But this just further underlines the asymmetry of the give-and-take of argument: either you are a god or you are not. If you are not, your proper response to the arguments of the one who is, is acceptance and worship. In a letter to Idomeneus, Epicurus makes a request: "Send us, then, an offering of first-fruits for the care [*therapeian*] of our sacred body [*hierou sōmatos*], on behalf of yourself and your children" (Plut. *Adv. Col.* 1117E). Philodemus tells us that the student's fundamental attitude is: "We will obey the authority of Epicurus, according to whom we have chosen to live" (*P* 15). We have already seen evidence (supported by Diskin Clay's new work on the papyri—Clay 1986) that Epicurus established a hero cult of himself as a focus of the pupils' communal attention. Try imagining Aristotle taking this role, and you will have some measure of the distance we have traveled. Seneca tells us that the Stoics, too, reject the Epicurean conception of philosophical authority: "We are not under a king. Each one claims his own freedom. With them, whatever Hermarchus said, whatever Metrodorus said, is ascribed to a single source. In that band, anything that anyone says is spoken under the leadership and command of one alone" (*Ep.* 33.4; cf. chapter 9).

8. Had Nikidion gone to Aristotle's school, she would have been exposed to a number of alternative positions and taught to examine their merits sympathetically, using her critical faculties. Epicurus' school, governed by the conviction that most available views are corrupting, proceeds otherwise. Nikidion will be saturated with the correct ways of thought and kept away from alternative views—except for the purposes of learning how to refute them. The fact that the whole process of argument is often called *diorthōsis*, "correcting," shows us how little concern there is for any sort of dispassionate evenhanded scrutiny of the opposition. But after all, no doctor tells you to take three medicines simultaneously and see which one works: their effects could block one another. Even so, Epicurus urges Nikidion to avoid competing influences, both from the general culture and from other philosophical schools. He writes to Apelles, "I congratulate you, O Apelles, because you have embarked on philosophy pure of all *paideia*" (Us. 117 = Athenaeus XIII p. 588).[56] He writes to Pythocles,

---

[56] Wachsmuth's text; others conjecture *aikia*; but Plutarch's paraphrase (*Non Posse* 1094D), which uses the word *mathēmata*, supports Wachsmuth's choice.

"Happy man, hoist sail and flee from every form of *paideia*" (Us. 161 = DL 10.6). Even if rival philosophical views are not the same as *paideia*, they are all, in Epicurus' view, infected with the false values of *paideia*. And we may note that this is especially true of Aristotle's view.

These features of therapeutic argument lead to the establishment of certain practices associated with arguing that mark off the Epicurean school from all other schools of the day. These practices are: memorization, confession, informing. Nikidion wishes the correct Epicurean teaching to rule her life and soul. But the stubbornness of her bad habits can be overcome, Epicurus holds, only by daily repetition. The *Kuriai Doxai* were to be learned by heart by all pupils. The epitomes in the surviving letters are also designed for memorization and repetition, so that pupils can "on every occasion help themselves in the most important matters" (*LHdt* 35, cf. 36; *LPyth* 84, 116; *LMen* 135). The *Letter to Menoeceus*, for example, ends by enjoining its recipient: "Practice these things and things similar to these night and day, saying them to yourself and to someone similar to yourself."

This emphasis on memory and repetition is neither fortuitous nor peripheral. Epicurus offers at least three reasons why it is essential. First, memory is the student's way of taking the teaching inside himself or herself, so that it will "become powerful" and can help her in the confrontation with error. If she has to look up writings each time for refutation of false doctrine, she will often be caught unprepared. (Pythocles complained of the difficulty of remembering Epicurus' views on important matters [*LPyth* 84].) If she internalizes the teaching, she will, like Menoeceus, "never be disturbed either awake or asleep" (135; cf. 123).

Second, memory of a compendium provides a comprehensive grasp of the structure of the whole system; this shows the student just how safe and complete a structure it really is, how neatly all its pieces fit together. This Nikidion could not have, Epicurus thinks, by simply working through all the details of the written treatises:

> Even in the case of the perfectly accomplished student the most crucial element in the clarification of every particular problem is the ability to summon concepts up rapidly and (this is impossible unless) these concepts have been reduced to elementary propositions and simple formulations. For there can be no adequate condensation of the complete round of the general truths of nature if it fails to encompass in concise formulations the potential explanation of problems of detail as well. (*LHdt* 36, trans. Clay 1983a)

Even an immature student such as Nikidion will in this way be enabled "in silent fashion and as swiftly as thought to make the circuit of the doctrines most essential for a calm state of mind" (*LHdt* 83).[57] Here Epicurus, with considerable originality, acknowledges that reading, being done aloud, is public and discursive. The grasp we want is an internal private overview that takes no time; memory provides it.

Why does he insist on this sort of internal grasp? This brings us to our third and deepest point, the point that reveals Epicurus' greatness as a psychologist. This is his understanding that the false beliefs that cause disturbance in life do not all lie on the surface of the self, ready for critical and dialectical scrutiny, as the Aristotelian seems to think. They lie deep in the soul, exercising their baneful influence, often beneath the level of consciousness. Epicurus, in short, discovers the unconscious—a discovery after which Aristotelianism cannot ever look the same. Most of the evidence for this insight is in Lucretius, and I shall discuss it in chapter 6. But there are enough signs of it in the writings of Epicurus himself that we are entitled to attribute the discovery to the teacher. Two passages connect Epicurus' emphasis on memorization with the consequence that the pupil will not be disturbed *when asleep* (*LMen* 135, noted previously; DL 120). To Herodotus, as we have seen, Epicurus emphasizes that memorization and practice make the argument "become powerful" (*dunatos, LHH* 83) in the pupil's soul—implying that it is only by driving it down deep and rooting it firmly that it will get the sort of power that it needs to defeat its opponents.

This view of the person has large consequences for philosophical method. If we are not transparent to ourselves, but are frequently motivated by beliefs we do not know we have, then the operations of dialectic do not go deep enough. They may help in some cases to uncover beliefs the pupil did not know she had; but they are unlikely to bring to the surface beliefs she has suppressed on account of their troubling character, beliefs she has a stake in not knowing she has. To counter those voices deep in the breast, we need to drive other voices deep down, so that they will speak to Nikidion even in her dreams.

But before we can even get to this point, we have another problem: how to discover the patient's real disease. Aristotelianism appears to assume that if we ask Nikidion what she believes and desires, she will tell us correctly. Epicurus suggests that such an approach will merely graze the surface. To find out what she believes deep down, the teacher will have to

---

[57] See the valuable discussion of this issue in Clay (1983a).

see what she does and how she does it. And if he cannot do this by
following her around every day, how will he get his data?

A natural soluton is the use of narrative. Like a modern psychoanalyst,
the teacher must get Nikidion to make her symptoms available by telling
him the story of her actions, her thoughts, her desires, even her dreams—so
that he will be as well placed as the bodily doctor is to grasp the totality of
her symptoms and to make an appropriate diagnosis. And Epicurus confronts the problem in just this way. For we find in the school the first record,
in the Greek philosophical tradition, of an institution of confession or
personal narrative. The importance of this fascinating material from the
Peri Parrhēsias was first seen by Sudhaus in 1911,[58] although he did not
cite all the relevant fragments, and although he assimilated the practices in
question too closely, I think, to Christian practices from which it is important to distinguish them. Philodemus tells us that Epicurus "praised Her-
acleides, because he considered that the reproaches he would receive on
account of what he was going to bring out into the open were less important than the help that he would get from them: so he divulged his errors[59]
to Epicurus" (*P* 49). Philodemus concurs with his teacher in judging that
Epicureans should "become accusers [*katēgorous*] of ourselves, if we err in
any respect" (51). And in a passage I have already mentioned, he gives the
point of this practice in terms of the medical analogy:

> The pupil must show him his failings without concealment and tell his
> defects in the open. For if he considers him the one guide of correct speech
> and deed, the one whom he calls the only savior and to whom, saying
> 'with him at my side,' he gives himself over to be therapeutically treated,
> then how could he not show the things in which he requires therapeutic
> treatment, and receive his criticism? (*P* 39–40)

This passage, not used by Sudhaus, shows us that concepts of sin and
absolution are not the most revealing tools for the understanding of Epicurean "confession," which is a matter of bringing the symptoms into the
open for analysis and diagnosis.[60] It is close to some of the ideas and

---

[58] Sudhaus (1911) 647–48.

[59] *Hamartias*, wrongly rendered "Sünden" by Sudhaus. "Sin" usually implies that the
defects in question have a basis in our original human nature; this all Hellenistic thinkers
vigorously deny.

[60] Cf. *P* 28: "if we show by argument that, while many fine things come out of friendship,
none of them is as great as having someone to whom one can speak what is in one's heart, and
to whom one can listen when he speaks. For nature intensely desires to reveal what one thinks
to others." Also *P* 41: it is unfriendly to act in secret. For other evidence on confession, see
Plut. *Col.* 1124D; cf. *Mor.* 566F.

procedures of modern psychotherapy: before the therapist can form a hypothesis about the material, including unconscious material, that is causing disturbance in the patient's life, he needs a story of the patient's life and thought that is as complete as possible.[61] Narrative permits him to inspect the pupil's solitude, her dreams, her secret moments.

But Nikidion, we have supposed, is a recalcitrant pupil who does not like to receive criticism. She may be unwilling to tell the history of her love affairs; she may conceal her craving for oysters, her longing for the social life she left behind. She is in the community because she wants to be there; even so, she may have difficulty bringing herself to tell what needs to be told. This is a large problem in modern psychotherapy: for even if a patient is in treatment voluntarily and wishes to be honest, she also wants to make a good impression on the doctor; she has various sources of resistance and reticence; and she herself may not be aware of what is most relevant to her cure.

The orthodox psychoanalyst has no resource here but prolonged contact with the patient herself. Because of the limitations of this procedure, many therapists deviate from orthodox Freudian practice and meet with the patient's family and friends. This is what Epicurus apparently did, drawing on the resources of his close-knit community to solve the problem. Philodemus reports that there was a certain Polyaenus who, seeing that Apollonides was "slackening" in his pursuit of Epicureanism, "went" (or "wrote"—the text is corrupt here) to Epicurus. The next fragment continues the saga: "For if a person desires his friend to attain correction, Epicurus will not consider him a slanderer, when he is not this; he will consider him a person who loves his friend [*philophilon*]: for he knows the difference well" (*P* 50). Another fragment reports that on account of the activity of friends, "the person who doesn't come forward is clearly seen to be concealing, and . . . not one thing has escaped notice" (*P* 41; cf. 8). We can see how these practices, once again, get their support from the medical model: for an undeclared non-evident symptom cannot be therapeutically treated. One might well offer such assistance to a friend or relative who was in danger of losing all good functioning because of a hidden ailment. And although we would have to confront difficult issues of privacy in so assisting, the urgency of the patient's need might well cause us to get round these, in a protected therapeutic context. For the Greeks, who were far less attached to the value of privacy than we are, this problem would have seemed less grave.

---

[61] There is also some evidence that the very idea of Epicurus' watching one is supposed to inhibit future transgressions: see Seneca, *Ep.* 24.4–5, "Do everything as if Epicurus were watching." For further discussion of the modern psychoanalytical parallel, see Nussbaum (1993c).

9–10. The arguments Nikidion hears frequently comment on their own efficacy: the pupil is constantly reminded that they are both necessary and sufficient for saving her. (Nowhere is there a starker contrast to Aristotle, whose modesty and disclaimers of completeness are closely connected with the value he ascribes to the pupil's independent contribution.) Epicurean practice is rigorous; it involves the surrender of much that was previously valued, and a kind of disciplined study for which many of Epicurus' pupils would have been unprepared. To encourage them to keep with philosophy, an argument must mix exhortation and self-advertisement with its reasoning.

The effect of the arguments on Nikidion's ability and motivation to engage in them is a complex matter. On the one hand, as she becomes more deeply immersed in the Epicurean system, Nikidion will become both more zealous about the system and more competent in going through *its* arguments. But it may well be that she will in some sense get worse *at arguing* generally. The Aristotelian pupil becomes a better Aristotelian *by* becoming better at taking charge of her own reasoning; the same, as we shall see, is true of the Stoic. The Epicurean pupil is not encouraged to bring objections of her own against the system, or to argue dialectically; and as she becomes more dependent on the text and doctrines of the master, she may be less adept at reasoning for herself.

IV

Now we have a sketch of Nikidion's philosophical education. Its features are not all equal in their importance. Dominant, for any good Epicurean, is always the keen sense of drastic illness and the need for cure. The practical goal, then, is what gives the medical analogy its purchase and motivates the other more specific features of the therapy. We can see, for example, that a conflict arose at times between the urgency of the practical goal and the claims of particularity: to cure effectively all the "sick" who need cure, the doctor cannot always take time to make a careful individualized prognosis for each patient. In an epidemic, the urgency of need dictates less finely calibrated and more general remedies. Epicurus, though he confined his personal teaching to the immediate community, nonetheless wrote and circulated an extremely large number of works. It seems implausible that the only purpose of these works was to advertise his teaching to those who might then come to the school in person as pupils, and far more likely that he took the written works themselves to have some independent therapeutic value, even though addressed to human beings in general.[62] The second-century C.E. Epicurean Diogenes of Oenoanda goes even further, insisting that the epidemic nature of the belief-disease in his time requires the construction of a single, non-specific, and highly permanent *logos*. The huge stone inscription he put up on the border of his estate in Asia Minor, near the public road—one of the largest Greek inscriptions ever unearthed, containing a compendious summary of Epicurean argument on all major issues—explains its own provenance as follows:

> If it was one only, or two or three or four or five or six or however many more than that you want, O human being, but not a very large number, who were in a wretched condition, then calling them one by one . . . [Here there is a gap in the inscription.] But since, as I said before, most people are sick all together, as in the plague, of false opinion concerning things, and since they are becoming more numerous—for on account of their reciprocal emulation they get the disease from one another like sheep—in addition to the fact that it is *philanthrōpon* to help strangers who pass by the way—since, then, the aid of this piece of writing goes out to many, I have decided, using this stoa, to put out in public for all the drugs that will save them [*pharmaka tēs sōtērias*]. (III–IV, Chilton 1971)

This shows us to what extent the practical need for curing is, for the good Epicurean, dominant over all other considerations about philosophical argumentation. The inscription of Diogenes does contain arguments; it is far from a billboard saying "Jesus Saves." On the other hand, it is equally far removed from the *Summa Theologica* of Thomas Aquinas, probably the most widely influential "saving drug" of Aristotelianism. Mutuality, critical activity, even the pupil's particular needs and motivations may be jettisoned, when this seems necessary to establish saving contact with a soul.

V

In many ways the Epicurean use of the medical analogy appears continuous with Aristotle's: for it demands, as does he, arguments that are genu-

---

[62] Plutarch's unfriendly interpretation is that writing is an attempt to gain personal fame: "If it is to good people that you offer the advice to escape notice and live unknown, then . . . to you yourself, in the first place, Epicurus, you are saying, 'Don't write to your friends in Asia. Don't enlist recruits from Egypt. Don't send presents to the young men of Lampsacus. Don't send books to all men and women [*pasi kai pasais*] advertising your wisdom'" (*LB* 1128F–1129A).

inely practical in their design and effect, responsive to antecedent values, hopes, and desires, flexibly attentive to the nuances of concrete cases. Aristotle and Epicurus agree that the art of the ethical philosopher, like that of a good doctor, requires attentiveness to the patient's hopes and fears, and a flexible seizing of the occasion. But at this point they part company. Aristotle has claimed that the activity of ethical argument is essentially dialectical and mutual; that its success requires a community of more or less equals, all of whom are both doctor and patient. He has argued that the practical benefit of ethical argument is inseparable from the dialectical scrutiny of opposing positions, from mutual critical activity, and from the essential philosophical virtues of consistency, clarity, and perspicuous ordering. Qualify his position as we may, it is clear that Epicurus does not have exactly the same commitment to these non-medical procedural virtues.

Epicurus has charged that these dialectical commitments are callous, when there is another sort of philosophy available that can minister more broadly to human need. A compassionate philosophy will make itself over into whatever answers that need. This charge should worry us, since we ourselves live in a world in which philosophical education of the Aristotelian sort cannot be very broadly distributed, requiring, as it does, an antecedent educational and motivational background that is strongly correlated with class membership (and local or national traditions). Aren't we all, in effect, empty and useless, insofar as we do not reach out, with our teaching and writing, to address the needs of the world as it actually is?

The Aristotelian should begin by conceding that Epicurus is right about the narrow reach of analytic and dialectical philosophy. But she insists that this sort of philosophizing contributes a distinctive sort of practical benefit, one that we will not get from anything less comprehensive, less rigorous, less dedicated to clarity. The fact is that whatever is great and memorable in Epicurean philosophy is so because it does meet those standards; and to treat them lightly is to forget about the practical value of *good philosophy*—in really getting to the most powerful and justifiable pictures of human excellence, human functioning, human social justice. Such philosophical accounts are not at all useless: for once they are worked out, they can offer a great deal of guidance to public life—to judges, legislators, economists, policy-makers of many kinds. Those people will not themselves all *be* philosophers; but they will be able to use the results of philosophical inquiry to design social institutions better. And in that way they will bring the benefits of philosophy to many people who are never going to study philosophy at all, thus helping in their own way the very people

Epicurus claims the Aristotelian cannot help.[63] Epicurus should not have neglected this possibility; and insofar as he did neglect it, he seems to have sold both philosophy and society short, for the sake of preserving the *ataraxia* of a small group of individuals. Epicurus might argue that the judges and legislators are all part of the corrupt system anyway, and therefore will not listen to the arguments of good philosophy. But he has not shown that this must be so, and insofar as there is any hope of such an effect, it is surely important to attempt it.

Epicureanism goes beyond Aristotle in several ways: in the precision and depth of its analysis of emotion and desire, in its recognition of unconscious layers of motivation, in its penetrating critique of the construction of desire and preference in a society obsessed with wealth and status. We shall see in the following three chapters just how probing its inquiries, in these areas, are. And we shall see, as well, that many of the arguments actually used in Epicureanism do in fact meet high standards of rigor, perceptiveness, and even dialectical mutuality. To some extent, then, our anxieties about the practice of philosophy in the Epicurean community will be allayed.

But we should continue to scrutinize the procedures closely with the example of Aristotle in mind. Our inquiry suggests that any relaxation of the commitment to dialectical argument is a move not to be taken lightly or unreflectively. For it is always possible, and in fact all too easy, to turn *from* calm critical discourse to some form of therapeutic procedure, as Epicurus himself turned from his Platonist teacher Nausiphanes to his own way. But once immersed in therapy it is much more difficult to return to the values of Aristotelian critical discourse. The passivity of the Epicurean pupil, her habits of trust and veneration, may become habitual and spoil her for the active critical task. Diogenes reports[64] that someone once asked Arcesilaus why it was that many people moved from other schools to the Epicurean school, but no Epicurean pupil ever moved to another school. Arcesilaus replied, "Because men can become eunuchs, but eunuchs never become men." Even if Nikidion notes that Arcesilaus seems to have forgotten her presence in the Epicurean school, she may sense that his too-narrow metaphor contains a profound criticism, applicable to herself.

[63] For one example of an attempt to bring a neo-Aristotelian position to bear on issues of poverty and inequality in developing countries, see Nussbaum and Sen (1993). But of course the position need not be an Aristotelian position in order to perform the functions Aristotle had in mind: Kantian and Utilitarian positions have also made valuable contributions to the contemporary debate.

[64] DL 4.43.

Beyond Obsession and Disgust: Lucretius on the Therapy of Love

> And so sexual love and the intercourse between the sexes is apotheosized to a religion, merely in order that the word religion, which is so dear to idealistic memories, may not disappear from the language.
> . . . The possibility of purely human sentiments in our intercourse with other human beings has nowadays been sufficiently curtailed by the society in which we must live. . . . We have no reason to curtail it still more by exalting these sentiments to a religion.

> (Friedrich Engels, *Ludwig Feuerbach and the End of Classical German Philosophy*)

I

THE POET Titus Lucretius was born. Later on he went mad from drinking a love potion. In the lucid intervals of his insanity he wrote several books, which were later edited by Cicero. Then he died by his own hand at the age of forty-four."[1] Jerome's famous story bases itself upon two evident facts about Lucretius' poem: that its poet-speaker claims to speak to us out of an intense personal experience of love; and that this same speaker, allegedly from the point of view of lucid rationality, condemns and assails love with a bitterness seldom equaled in poetry. But Jerome's story does not simply record these facts. It constructs a piece of biography to explain them. The biography informs us that Lucretius' criticism of erotic love was caused by his experience of love; and, furthermore, that this experience, and the criticism that arose from it, were highly atypical and peculiar. The madness of love was not any ordinary erotic experience: it was a compulsive state induced by a drug. And the condemnations of love that were written in the "lucid intervals" can, in consequence, be seen as outpourings of bitterness and misery produced by an unwilling addict, rather than as rational criticism constructed through reflection by a free thinking being.

---

[1] The story is given in Jerome's additions to Eusebius' Chronicle under the year 94 (or possibly 93). For discussion of the problems of dating, see Bailey (1947) vol. I, 1ff.

The ensuing suicide story completes the picture. We are led to believe that in Lucretius' poem we have not arguments worthy of respect and close study, but the last words of a desperate and despairing mind, a mind in whose condition none of us would choose to be, and whose condition cannot possibly be favorable for reflection. There is a further moral. One could infer from Jerome's account that for someone who gets to the point of making these criticisms, there is no way back to a happy life. The story of madness not only casts doubt upon the arguments, it urges us to reject them as a danger. In short: we need not, and even should not, study Lucretius' attack on love seriously. We are permitted to pity him; but we have nothing to learn from him on this subject on which he addresses us with such interesting violence.

The story, with its edifying conclusion—which fits in far too well with the spirit of Christian polemic against atheism and materialism not to be deeply suspect as biography[2]—has served for centuries as an informal blueprint for the interpretation, not only of Book IV's attack on love, but of the *De Rerum Natura* as a whole. In consequence the poem has been read as personal poetic expression more frequently than as philosophical argument, more frequently as irrational symptom than as rational therapy.[3] Its moral challenge has been evaded, even while its poetic excellence has been acclaimed—as if, indeed, Lucretius were a poet for whom poetry had any other legitimate function than the clarification and liberation of human lives.

In this century, scholarship has begun to undo these wrongs. Interpretations that take the poem's therapeutic and anti-religious purpose seriously have become less the exception and more the prevailing norm. And discussions of many different types—from George Santayana's lucid account of Lucretius' aims in *Three Philosophical Poets* to Cyril Bailey's magisterial commentary to Diskin Clay's recent book on Lucretian therapy[4]—have stressed the harmony between the poem's moral purpose and its poetic design, treating both as deliberate creations of a rational mind.[5] Clay has

---

[2] For criticism of the Jerome story as biography, see Ziegler (1936), Kenney (1977), Classen (1968), Betensky (1980), Wormell (1960). There is now a general consensus that the story is not literally true.

[3] For a few recent examples of this approach, see Logre (1946), Perelli (1969). Patin (1883) influentially developed the thesis that Lucretius' psychology and deeper motivations conflict with the Epicurean teaching he expounds, so that we can see in the poem many signs of an "anti-Lucrèce chez Lucrèce." This thesis still has numerous defenders and followers.

[4] Santayana (1910), Bailey (1947), Clay (1983).

[5] For this approach, see also Kenney (1977), Classen (1968); we still find an emphasis on

convincingly argued that the poem is carefully crafted so as to lead an imagined reader through the process of Epicurean therapy, step by step. And he has offered a detailed, if not in every way persuasive, account of how this aim is carried out. We are a long way, clearly, from Jerome's pity and condescension.

This progress toward acknowledging Lucretius is clearly connected with the prevalence, in our time, of secular and materialist views of human life, accompanied by critical attitudes toward established religion. Lucretius' views about the world of nature and the soul now seem not mad but eminently sane—far saner, frequently, than the views they were invented to replace. Several years ago it even happened that an eminent British moral philosopher, invited to deliver a lecture in a venerable series dedicated to the topic of the soul's immortality, found that the best way to make both philosophical and intuitive sense on this topic for a contemporary audience was to turn the topic on its head and to lecture, with reference to Lucretius, on the soul's *mortality*, and why that is not a bad thing.[6] In fact, all of Lucretius' assaults on traditional belief now look like a part of our own traditions of belief. They can be read, at any rate by many people, without surprise, without a sense of threat, without a feeling that something precious is being violated in a sudden and shocking manner.

All assaults, with the exception of one. For love is widely revered; in fact, for many people it has the status of a secular religion. And people often prove far more willing to give up god or gods than to stop making gods of one another. Love was religious even in Lucretius' religious time, as he himself tells us: a condition taken to be caused by a god, godlike in its power, linking the lover to a beloved who is appropriately seen as an embodied divinity. But in our time, when religious sources of individual salvation are widely mistrusted, personal erotic love (along with other secular sources of value) has come, even more intensely, to bear the weight of many people's longings for transcendence, for a perfection more than earthly, for mysterious union with that perfection. And non-religious contemporary readers who revere love may identify themselves with their erotic aims more fervently, even, than does Lucretius' imagined reader—since all of the hope and desire which for that reader flows also toward the heavens must, for the contemporary reader, be poured into fragile human and worldly projects. So Lucretius' assault on those projects threatens in a way that his other attacks no longer do.

---

the "mind" of the poet in Bailey (1938) and Wormell (1960), though with caution. For another major account of Lucretius' poem as rational therapy, see Schrijvers (1969, 1970).

[6] See Williams (1973), discussed in detail in chapter 6.

We see this clearly in the response that greets Book IV. The Christian response to Lucretius' atheism, in the Jerome story, was not an open expression of anger and fear. It was, instead, pity and condescension. From within religion, these anti-religious arguments look silly and mad, rather than dangerous. So much is true now for the love arguments. To the lover of love, they can easily seem perverse and embarrassingly weak, creations of an embittered and despairing mind, rather than rational proposals that we should seriously consider. And in fact most serious philosophical accounts of Lucretius' materialism spend little or no time on them. Two major book-length studies, those of Clay and M. Bollack, give them hardly a mention; and E. J. Kenney's effective summary of recent scholarship, sympathetic to Lucretius' atheism, conspicuously avoids commitment on the subject of love. Santayana, though he does not analyze the passage, accuses Lucretius of having an impoverished sense of human value because of his negative attitude to love.[7] When the passage is discussed in detail, it is usually treated either biographically (even Bailey at this point permits the insanity explanation)[8] or from the point of view of the history of literature—as if, at this point, Lucretius ceases to be a philosopher and becomes merely ornamental and a collection of symptoms. Such readers read, in short, with the confident superiority of true believers, who know already how wonderful erotic/romantic love is, and how impoverished a life without it. The voice that denounces it sounds like a mad voice, the voice not of a doctor but of a patient.

If we follow this line of thought, it is natural to return to the Jerome story, looking at it in a slightly different way. For if we read the story not as Christian moralists, but as lovers of love (whether ancient or modern), the story itself begins to look suspiciously like a love story. Obsession, madness, attempted escape, suicide—all the ingredients of romantic/erotic love are there, ingredients that have provided the plot of love stories from *Aeneid* Book 4 to the *Sorrows of Young Werther*—and of countless stories

---

[7] Clay (1983); M. Bollack (1978); Kenney (1977); Santayana (1910) 205.

[8] Bailey, commentary on IV.1058: "It has often been thought that his vehemence is due to his personal experiences, and Jerome's story of the love-philtre is quoted in support of this view. Of this we cannot be sure, but the disproportionate length and the violence with which he urges his plea lend colour to the suggestion." Logre (1946) diagnoses Lucretius as a manic-depressive, primarily on the basis of the love passage; Perelli (1969) speaks of his obsessive revulsion with sex and his inclination to sadism. Major exceptions to this style of "interpretation" are the new commentary by Godwin (1986), and especially the first-rate book by Brown (1987)—published after this chapter had gone to press as an article, and thus without influence on its main line of argument, but admirable throughout. See also the articles by Fitzgerald (1984) and Betensky (1980): the latter provides an especially helpful account of the positive side of the poem.

both before and after these. Across the differences in the cultural experiences of love that separate ancient Rome from contemporary North America and Europe, these basic features have remained more or less constant, and are a major source for the continued power of Latin poetry to move and engage us. Looked at in the light of the traditions, of storytelling about love, Lucretius' philosophical attack on love looks like just one episode inside his own tragic love story. It can hardly provide a serious, cogent attack upon that passion, since, merely by existing inside that story, it offers proof, if we needed it, of love's power over the creative intellect. The more vigorously he argues, the more he betrays himself. The more he undercuts, the more he glorifies. This romantic rereading of the Jerome story is, like the moralizing reading, a recipe for evasion. It allows us to attend to the poem only by granting, ahead of time, that it has nothing to teach us.

Such responses are very natural and very tempting. For this reason, if we have followed Nikidion's therapeutic education this far, we should suspect them. Epicurean therapy does not waste time on illusions that are no longer powerful. It aims at the bad ones that provide the very structure of Nikidion's daily life—at the bad habits that, "like bad friends," have been leading her into distress and error for years. Only that which threatens holds the promise of true therapy. And true therapy, as Epicurus insists, is painful. So we must ask Nikidion to consider a possibility. We ask her (and we should also ask ourselves) to take absolutely seriously the possibility that Lucretius is right: that erotic love, as most people know and live it, is bad for us, and that human life will be richer and better without it. We shall see later that Lucretius has a lot to say about the motivations that most people have, in their experience of love, for embarking on the course of therapy. We shall see in detail how he motivates his imagined reader. But for now we ask our pupil to approach the poem with the door open a tiny crack, allowing, simply, that it might have something to say to her, not only in a seminar room, but in her life. Love might not be so very wonderful.

And in fact I believe that these arguments are of great worth to believers in love and in love stories. They are therapeutic, I believe, not in a nihilistic sense, but in a humane and constructive way. I shall argue that they lead us not into an impoverished world but into a world more richly human. They do this by exposing myths and delusions that constrain us and prevent us from dealing with one another in a fully human way. They teach us to acknowledge one another, and ourselves, as human beings—that is, as beings both natural and social—in one of our most important and intimate activities. Through their complex and carefully crafted structure, they lead us to a world beyond the religion of love, beyond that world's emotions of vain longing, of awe and obsession, of disgust with the body and its limits, into a world both natural and rational. Not a world of colorless atoms,[9] but a world in which we see and care for one another, without religious interference, as the very beings we are.

To see how all this works, we must study in detail both the arguments and their poetic expression, asking how the poetry is constructed, how it addresses its interlocutor and readers, from what perspective or perspectives it asks them to examine the phenomenon of love. Lucretius tells us that Epicurus is a hero greater than any hero of legend, since he conquered no mere imaginary monster, but the real monsters that now tear human beings apart: vain longing, anxiety, fear, arrogance, wantonness, anger, gluttony (5.45–48). And he conquered these monsters of belief and desire without imitating the aggression he opposed: for he used words, not arms, as his weapons (*dictis non armis*, 49–50; cf. chapter 7). We are, then, invited to examine closely the poetic words that Lucretius chooses for his adversarial task. And this is especially crucial where love is concerned. For love, more than any of the other false beliefs examined by Lucretius, is itself the creation of poetic words. Through poetry and its stories, his reader learned its characteristic structures, its "plot," its shades of feeling.[10] And poetic love stories, once learned, serve the reader as paradigms to which actual experience is referred, and on which it is modeled. So poetry against love will have to have a peculiar relation to its own traditions. It must turn poetry against itself, asking it to undo, using its own devices, some of its most cherished and most alluring structures. I shall follow Lucretius as he artfully pursues this task, commenting on his writing as he writes. And I shall hope in this way not only to develop a general account of the structure of the argument, but also to come up with answers to some structural and technical questions that have bothered serious literary readers of Book IV. For example, why is the story of erotic disillusionment immediately followed by a discussion of female desire? Why is the very end of the book preoccupied with marriage? Why do its last lines seem so terribly prosaic, so inferior in poetic power to Lucretius' finest moments?

II

The philosopher who writes about sexual love faces a troublesome question: what point of view is the reliable one from which to describe and discuss this phenomenon? And how can this point of view be defended *as*

[9] See my criticism of Clay (1983a), in section VII.
[10] See especially Lieberg (1962), Kenney (1970).

the reliable and appropriate one? Love, perhaps more than almost any other part of our lives, looks different from different angles. We can examine it from within, from the point of view of immersed experience. We can look at it from the point of view of its ending, or its failure. We can try to capture it from a detached or scientific perspective that stands outside of both the experience and its ending. Again, we can consider it as a social and political phenomenon, with an eye to more complex human interests. Each of these perspectives is, in turn, a multiplicity. The inside of love's experience has many stages, and comes, as well, in many kinds: happy and unhappy, gentle and violent, relaxed and possessive, confident and insecure, and so on. There are equally many responses to the ending of love. The scientific perspective is, itself, multiple. The scientist may speak reductionistically, seeing humans and animals, for example, as mere congeries of atoms whose large-scale structures have no explanatory significance. Or he or she can accept the significance of the larger forms and adopt the perspective of an Aristotelian science of nature. Again, the scientist may or may not accord independent significance to the psychological and intentional elements in natural reality: to feelings, desires, thoughts, pains, pleasures. The social and political perspective is in turn many, since there are many rival accounts of good society, of its proper interests and goals, of the role of marriage and family in relation to those goals. All of these viewpoints were available to Lucretius through his literary and philosophical heritage. He had to select from among them. Some of the points of view are complementary, or at least compatible; others are not. How can the philosopher of human life find a perspective or perspectives that will win conviction as truly rational, truly appropriate for the task of addressing us about our deepest concerns?

We have seen that the Epicurean doctor, at the beginning of his treatment, insists on establishing contact with the pupil's own current standpoint or standpoints, with her own sense of health and disease. Where love is concerned, and where the teacher's end is critical and negative, he will have one great disadvantage and one great advantage. The disadvantage is the obvious one: that love is so widely and deeply loved. The inner perspective of Nikidion's own experience is almost certain to endorse it as extremely important, as beautiful, wonderful, even as divine. Any perspective from which it does not appear as real, and as good, looks to her immediately suspect. When the Epicurean argues against the fear of death, he can begin his argument from inside ordinary experience. For though most of us believe this fear to be justified, most of us also find it highly unpleasant. Certainly it holds no positive allure. Again, when he argues against anger

146

he can count on the fact that most of us dislike being angry, and dislike, too, the effects of anger that we see in public life: murders, assaults, persecutions, wars. With love, things are more complex. Most pupils will say, and consciously believe, that they value love, however much their anxious behavior might cast doubt on this. The difference is reflected in love's mythology. For Venus/Aphrodite and Eros are major, attractive, and well loved, whereas Eris (Strife) and Phobos (Fear) are hateful and minor. There are no poems beginning "Immortal Fear, throned in many-colored splendor." Nor is any young hero brought low for his failure to worship strife. How, then, can the Epicurean attacker find a beachhead from which to lauch his verbal invasion?

His situation is less hopeless than this description makes it seem. For if Nikidion is almost certain to have a strong sense of love's beauty and wonder, she is almost equally certain to have experienced, as well, the ending of love, with its enervating anxieties, its crushing grief, and, quite frequently, an ensuing period of disillusionment and critical assessment. All this is also a part of love's mythology—so even in that personal experience she will think of love as a dangerous source of madness and constraint.[11] She will be aware that love brings pain as well as pleasure; and she will also have seen that it brings a shifting of perceptions. From the point of view of the ending of love, both the loved one and the love frequently look different. Deprived of the radiance they seemed to wear within the perspective of desire and fascination, they look ordinary and unremarkable— frequently even unworthy or repellent. And this perspective of the end of love has a way of vouching for itself as the sane or rational one, of turning against the internal vision and attacking it as delusion and fantasy.[12] Nikidion has almost certainly inhabited, in turn, love's internal perspective and the perspective of this criticism; so she has almost certainly experienced, in her own life, a "rational" critique of love, and has felt the strength of her own motivation to conduct such a critique.

Lucretius will exploit this double orientation, giving his critique intuitive force by imitating this familiar movement in and out of love. I shall argue that his purpose is, ultimately, to move us beyond both love's peculiar exaltation of its object and disillusionment's bitterness toward the object, to a perspective that, being constrained by neither of these, is free to perceive a partner clearly and with genuine affection. He will be assisted in this task by two further perspectives in which he involves the reader: the

---

[11] See especially "The Constraints of Eros," in Winkler (1990), and Halperin (1989).
[12] Consider the first two speeches in Plato's *Phaedrus*.

147

perspective of nature and the perspective of society. He first asks the interlocutor to look beyond his own immediate human concerns to the way things go on in the world of nature as a whole, seeing himself as a part of the world of nature. Knowing the atomic theory is an important part of inhabiting this perspective; but the perspective, I shall argue, is not eliminative, or reductionistic.[13] It contains complex biological forms; and it contains intentions, thoughts, and desires. The second reminds the reader that, unlike other natural beings, he[14] lives in society, and that society is very important to his happiness. (Precisely how this is so emerges only in Book V; but the general conclusion of that book is presupposed throughout, in that it is assumed that the health of the reader's whole society is a legitimate and important concern.) It asks him to reflect on the implications of various forms of action, and especially of various forms of belief, for social health.

Later I shall try to show in detail how the movement in and out of these perspectives advances Lucretius' therapeutic argument in Book IV. Now I want to suggest in a general way that the use of these multiple perspectives is essential to Lucretius' procedure for two reasons. First, it gives his argument greater therapeutic *power*. Through the use of these different viewpoints, he can inspire self-examination and self-discovery in the interlocutor, who has occupied all these different perspectives at one time or another, but who has never worked systematically through the full range of his own antecedent concerns, and who will frequently find, when he does so, that his current beliefs and ways of life do not do justice to the full range of those concerns. And this procedure also gives Lucretius' arguments, I think, a strong claim to be rational, in a sense that would impress even those who are dedicated to the openness of Aristotelian dialectic and suspicious of Epicurean dogmatism. What Lucretius does, in subtle and complicated ways, is to ask us how we see a topic when we have examined it completely from as many perspectives as are relevant. The totality of the perspectives is supposed to give us, correctly put together, an accurate view of the whole of the object. This gives Lucretius a good reply to some of the charges we have leveled against Epicurus in the previous chapter. He can claim that he has not ignored our intuitions, forced an alien view down the pupil's throat, or imposed on him a mindless process of behavioral conditioning. He is asking for a balanced and thorough view rather than the

---

[13] Here my interpretation is in harmony with recent work by David Sedley: see Sedley (1983b) and Long and Sedley (1987).

[14] On the gender of the interlocutor, see subsequent discussion.

narrow and partial view we usually have when we are immersed in some cherished activity. And isn't this exactly what good Aristotelian dialectic aims to achieve? Not all perspectives are equally fundamental, or equally legitimate; and Lucretius will say this. But when we have surveyed them all and seen how they stand to one another, we can claim to have satisfied, within an Epicurean framework, many of Aristotle's requirements.

III

Of Epicurus' teaching on love and sexual desire, little survives.[15] This teaching was apparently, however, an important part of his work. A treatise *On Love* (*Peri Erōtos*) is the third item in Diogenes Laertius' list of Epicurus' works—just after the magnum opus *On Nature* and another work that must have been of fundamental importance, *On Atoms and the Void* (DL 10.27). Since the list appears to have been composed, at least in part, according to someone's ideas of importance, we may cautiously suppose that *On Love* was no minor work. Again, it is clear that sexual desire was discussed in the famous and fundamental work *On the End* (*Peri Telous*) and also in the *Symposium* (see subsequent discussion); it probably figured as well in the *Opinions Concerning the Passions: Against Timocrates* (10.28). Sexual matters form an important part of Diogenes' summary portrait of the Epicurean wise man (10.118–19). The Epicurean definition of *erōs* is well known in later antiquity and is frequently contrasted with Stoic definitions. Yet, with all of this, so little concrete evidence remains that we are forced to reconstruct Epicurus' views from a handful of sentences. We must do this, before we can assess Lucretius' contribution; yet we must remember that we are in an unusually bad position to compare the two thinkers. Let us get as much out of the evidence as we can.[16]

Toward erotic love, or *erōs*, Epicurus is unremittingly hostile. "They believe that a wise man will not fall in love [*erasthēnai*]," Diogenes tells us. "Nor do they believe that love is something sent by the gods" (10.118 = Us. 574). Epicurus' definition of *erōs* was, apparently, "An intense [*suntonos*] desire for intercourse, accompanied by agony and distraction" (Us.

---

[15] Compare Brown (1987) 101–22, a comprehensive and valuable discussion.

[16] Here I am not, of course, examining the much richer evidence on *philia*; see chapter 7 for some discussion of this. I shall consider here Epicurus' views on marriage and children—which Lucretius will connect with *philia*.

483 = Hermeias *In Plat. Phdr.* p. 76).[17] Ancient commentators who contrast Epicurus with the Stoics point out that this definition, unlike the Stoics', makes *erōs* bad *simpliciter*, bad in its very nature.[18] Epicurus himself, speaking more generally of all desires with this intense and agonizing nature, issues a stern warning to young people to avoid them absolutely: "For a young person the portion of safety is to guard your youth and ward off those things that pollute everything in accordance with agonizing desires [*epithumias oistrōdeis*]" (VS 80).[19]

On sexual desire and sexual relations,[20] the record is more complicated. We have many reports of sexual enthusiasm and sexual indulgence in the Garden; but most of these come from witnesses hostile to hedonism and are not to be trusted. In this category are Timocrates' slander that Epicurus and Metrodorus had intercourse with *hetairai* named Mammarion, Hedeia, Erotion, and Nikidion (DL 10.7), and Carneades' story (reported by Plutarch) that Epicurus kept a diary of his wine-drinking and lovemaking (Plut. *Non Posse* 1089C). But we also have more reliable evidence that points in the same direction. There is Epicurus' letter to young Pythocles, described by Diogenes as "beautiful," which says: "I shall sit here and wait for your divine and much longed for arrival" (DL 10.5: *himertēn* strongly connotes sexual longing). We have, above all, the famous and frequently quoted fragment of *On the End*: "I have no idea what I should consider good, if I take away the pleasures of smell, take away the pleasures of sexual intercourse [*aphrodisiōn*], take away the pleasures of sound, take away the pleasures of beautiful shapes."[21]

On the other hand, we also have evidence that suggests an austere and negative attitude toward sexual intercourse and the desires that prompt it. "Intercourse [*sunousia*] never helped anyone, and it's lucky if it does no harm." This saying, quoted by Diogenes (118) and Clement as a general Epicurean saying,[22] is firmly ascribed to Epicurus' *Symposium* by Plutarch

---

[17] The Greek: *suntonos orexis aphrodisiōn meta oistrou kai adēmonias.* On this and other related evidence, see Brown (1987) 113ff., who points out that Epicurus is in this respect developing a prominent strain in Greek popular thought.

[18] Cf. Hermeias; also schol. Dionysii Thr. BAG p. 667, 13; Alex Aphrod. *In Arist. Top.* p. 75; Cic. *TD* 4.70—all cited in Us. 483.

[19] Cf. also Plat. *Tim.* 91B, where Plato writes of the genitals that they *pantōn di'epithumias oistrōdeis epicheirei kratein.*

[20] The pertinent Greek terms are *aphrodisia* and *sunousia.*

[21] Us. 67: the full cited text is given twice in Athenaeus (XII p. 546e, VII p. 280a), and part by Athenaeus at VII p. 278f and in DL 10.6; cf. also Cic. *TD* 3.41, *Fin.* 3.7, 20, and several other passages cited in Usener.

[22] See Us. 62; Clem. *Alexandr. Paedag.* 2.10 p. 84; Galen *Art. Med.* c. 24 t. I p. 371 K;

(*Qu. Conviv.* 3.6 = Us. 62). A Vatican Sentence that probably originated as a letter conveys the same message:

> You tell me that the movement of the flesh has made you excessively preoccupied with achieving sexual intercourse [*aphrodisiōn*]. So long as you do not break any laws, or upset customs that are well designed, or offend any person around you, or harm your health, or waste your property, you may indulge your inclination[23] as you wish. But in fact it is impossible not to run up against one of these obstacles. For sexual intercourse never did any good, and it's lucky if it does no harm. (*VS* 51)

This does not amount to an absolute prohibition but is strong instrumental dissuasion.

To get further, we must understand where Epicurus places sexual desire in his classification of desires. For empty desires, as we saw, are thoroughly based on false belief, and the removal of false belief is a sufficient condition for their removal. Desires that are natural and necessary, on the other hand, are to be fulfilled up to the limit set by our nature. The activities that fulfill them will be, I have argued, constituents of the end, of the undisturbed way of life. If sexual desire is, on the one hand, not banished completely and, on the other, severely constrained in its expression, this strongly suggests that it belongs to neither of these two groups, but to the third major group of Epicurean desires: those that are natural and non-necessary. These desires have their origin in our natural constitution, not in social teaching; but they can be neglected without jeopardizing our happy undisturbed condition.[24]

There is evidence that this classification is the one Epicurus intended. Only one source explicitly makes the connection: a scholion on Aristotle's *Nicomachean Ethics* III gives desire for intercourse as its example of the Epicurean natural but non-necessary class, giving the desires for food and clothing as examples of the natural-necessary, and the desires for this

---

Galen in *Hippocr. Epidem. III Comm.* I 4 t. XVII p. 521. See also Us. 62a: when asked when to have intercourse with a woman, Epicurus answers, "When you wish to become weaker than yourself" (*Gnomologion Monacense* 194).

[23] The word is *prohairesei*; the implication presumably is that the path of sexual intercourse is, on account of the young man's current state, his *preferred* way. (Compare our phrase "sexual preference," also used without any implication that the person has the power to choose this way rather than some other.)

[24] For Plato, in the *Republic*, sexual desire figures, instead, in the class of "necessary" desires, which are to be allowed satisfaction "up to the point of health and well-being"; it is treated the same way as the desire for food (*Rep.* VIII.558D–559C). The *Phaedo* takes a more negative view: the philosopher will not be at all concerned with sex (64D).

particular drink or this particular clothing as examples of the empty.[25] This is thin support, but we can add to it. First, we notice that no Epicurean passage speaking of what nature requires makes mention of sexual fulfillment. The "voice of the flesh" asks for an end to hunger and cold (*VS* 33; also Bailey fr. 44). A fragment cited in Stobaeus (Us. 181) says that bodily pleasure is made complete by water and bread. The *Letter to Menoeceus* (132) includes intercourse with young men and women as one of the items that does *not* go to make the pleasant life. The passages I have already quoted clearly say that intercourse is not necessary for happy life. On the other hand, the *Peri Telous* fragment includes intercourse in a list of basic pleasures that do have some intimate relation to the good. The best explanation of this seems to be that the pleasure of intercourse, like two other pleasures mentioned in that fragment—the pleasures of sound and shape—is natural, but non-necessary. This means that we should indulge ourselves sexually only when the structure of the rest of our pleasures makes this prudent and unproblematic. If Epicurus thinks that on the whole it is not prudent to have intercourse, this is not because he thinks that the desire for it rests on false belief. It is, as *VS* 51 explicitly says, because of the frequently adversarial relationship between sexual indulgence and the orderly conduct of the rest of life.

We must add that the Garden, centered as it is around the happiness of each individual, teaches no strong positive motive for sexual activity. Epicurus apparently did not encourage marriage, though his precise position is in doubt because of an unfortunate textual crux in Diogenes.[26] And

---

[25] Cited in Us. 456: the same point seems to be made by Plutarch *Grylli* c. 6 p. 989b, also cited in Us. 456. See also Brown (1987) 108ff.

[26] At DL 10.119, the reading of the MSS is *kai mēn kai gamēsein kai teknopoiēsein ton sophon hōs Epikouros en tais Diaporiais kai en tais Peri phuseōs kata peristasin de pote biou gamēsein.* In other words, translated as best one can: "And indeed the wise man will marry and have children, as Epicurus says in the *Problems* and the *On Nature*. But on occasion he may marry, owing to particular circumstances of his life." There are two problems with this. First, it is internally incoherent: the contrast between the first and the second halves of the sentence is unintelligible. The person who has done best to make sense of it is Bailey, with "Moreover, the wise man will marry and have children. . . . But he will marry according to the circumstances of his life." This version, however, omits the important word *pote*, "at some time" or "on some occasion." What the sentence clearly requires is a contrast between a general prohibition of marriage and an exception or exceptions made owing to occasional special circumstances. Second, the sentence as in the MSS contradicts all our other evidence about Epicurus' views on marriage and children. Epictetus repeatedly asserts, as if referring to a famous (or, from a Stoic point of view, infamous) position, that the Epicurean will neither marry nor have children (*Disc.* 3.7.19, 20; 1.23.3; 1.23.7); he condemns this teaching as ruinous for the city, and exclaims that Epicurus' parents, even had they known he was

although there is some evidence that there were at least some children in the Garden, Epicurus is said to have agreed with Democritus that children.are a bad thing for the wise man, on account of the "many displeasures and distractions from more necessary things" that they occasion (Us. 521 = Clem. *Strom.* 2.232). An Epicurean with a stronger sense of transgenerational obligation[27] or a greater interest in the family as a central political institution might easily reverse Epicurus' instrumental conclusion, arguing that intercourse, properly managed, has a usefulness that outweighs its risks. This is what happens, I believe, in Lucretius.

What turns this desire for intercourse, harmless in itself, into dangerous, agonizing *erōs*? The answer seems to be, the influence of false belief. There is a difficult *Principal Opinion* that appears to say just this:

> Whenever, among those natural desires that do not lead to pain if they are not fulfilled, an intense eagerness [*spoudē sontonos*] is present, they too are the products of false belief. And it is not on account of their own nature that they are not dispelled, but on account of the human being's empty believing. (*KD* 30)[28]

This fragment speaks of a transformation that sometimes takes place in a natural non-necessary desire. (The words are almost exactly those used to describe that class of desires in *KD* 26.) This alteration brings about

---

going to say this, would not have exposed him (1.23.10). Seneca reports the same view, with a slight qualification: the sage will marry only *raro*, "since marriage is mixed up with many inconveniences" (fr. 45 Haase). And Clement concurs, ascribing to both Epicurus and Democritus a rejection of both marriage and childrearing (*Strom.* 2.23.138). (Cf. Us. 19, 521, 523.) Epicurus himself, the paradigmatic wise man, did not marry. We may add that the context of the DL passage is clearly corrupt; the second half of the sentence in question, which makes some remarks about drunkenness based on Epicurus' *Symposium*, makes very little sense at all. For all these reasons, scholars ever since Casaubon and Gassendi have felt that this text must be emended; Casaubon's conjecture, changing *kai mēn kai* to *kai mēde* makes the sentence read: "And the wise man will not marry. . ." (Usener, Bailey, and Diano all retain the MSS reading, whereas Hicks accepts the emendation.) There is a comprehensive and excellent discussion of the problem in Chilton (1960), who makes a solid case for the emendation. We should certainly recognize that the sense of the passage must be that conveyed in the emendation, whether or not we accept this particular proposal. Brown (1987) 119–20 is aporetic and, I think, underestimates the evidence of textual corruption in the passage as a whole.

[27] See, for example, Diogenes of Oenoanda frr. III–IV Chilton (1971): "for they too are ours, even if they have not yet been born."

[28] My translation here is similar to that of Arrighetti (1960). A different account of the sentence is given in Konstan (1973). On the word *suntonos* and its implications, see chapter 8. Philodemus uses the word of the sort of anger the Epicurean will avoid.

(1) strained or intense eagerness, and (2) an unsatisfiable, unlimited character (*ou diacheontai*, they are not dispelled, a point of repletion is not reached). Epicurus is saying that whenever you see these two characteristics in a desire with a natural basis, what you have on your hands is a hybrid; the corruption of a basic natural impulse at the hands of false belief. Love, we recall, is by definition an intense, *suntonos*, version of the desire for intercourse, itself (we have argued) a natural non-necessary desire. So it seems that we can conclude, on Epicurus' behalf, that erotic love is the product of a corruption of natural sexual impulses by false beliefs. I believe that this is roughly the story that Lucretius tells. Although he gives a much more generous account of the role of sexual desire in human life, and a more richly social account of our human sexual aims and ends, his story in many respects fleshes out these Epicurean distinctions. And he will offer us a detailed account—whether based on Epicurus or not we shall never know—of the way in which sexual desire becomes corrupted and loses its proper limits.

We know little about Epicurus' views about the cure for love. One surviving remark is disappointingly superficial. "Take away looking and association and daily encounters, and the passion of love [*to erōtikon pathos*] is undone" (*VS* 18). This sounds like behavioral therapy, rather than the cognitive methods we expect from Epicureanism. And it does not seem properly appreciative of the depth the passion has in many lives. A particular love might be ended this way; but that is hardly a cure for the soul attached quite generally to the passion. Another remark, however, is more characteristic, and serves as a good introduction to Lucretius' therapy. "By a passion for true philosophy [*erōti philosophias alēthinēs*] every disturbing and burdensome desire is undone" (Us. 457 = Porph. *Ad Marc.* 31, p. 209, 21). One sort of *erōs* drives out the other. The cure for bad desires comes through a love of arguments that dispels illusion and leaves us with truth.

IV

Epicurus did not write poetry. Indeed, there is evidence that he was hostile both to poetry and to forms of education that nourish a desire for it. He himself wrote in a rough inelegant prose that seems abrupt, harsh, and, frequently, ill-constructed, beside the smoothness of Plato, or even Aristotle's lucid economy. It is likely that he deliberately chose to express, in the style, a disdain for his culture's aristocratic norms and a commitment to an ordinary man's plainness of speech. ("He used the ordinary terms for things," says Diogenes, 10.13.) His anti-Platonic saying, "I spit on the *kalon*,"[29] has stylistic, as well as ethical, implications. It rejects aristocratic fantasy in diction, just as his philosophy rejects aristocratic fantasy in thought. And since it is obvious that most conventional poetic genres are deeply committed in their very structure to the very desires and emotions that Epicurus denounces as empty—to fear, love, pity, and anger—Epicurus has a strong additional reason, while avoiding elitism in language, for avoiding poetic language in particular. Even popular and non-elite poetry would fall under this critique—a point already seen by Plato in his attack on epic and tragedy, and by Aristotle in his defense.

Lucretius, a devout follower of Epicurus, writes an epic poem. And the choice to write poetically is itself a subject of the poem. From the very opening lines, Lucretius encourages us to think about the choice and about the desires aroused by poetic writing—at the very same time that we are also asked to think about the character of desire in nature as a whole. For after calling on Venus as the principle of sexual desire in all of nature, the principle that explains animal fertility, he invokes her as the ally of his poetry (*sociam*, 24), the one who can give a pleasing character to his words. And later in the first book he explains to us why this pleasing character is so important.[30]

With strong mind [*mente*][31] I travel through the pathless haunts of the Pierides, places never trodden by any before. It is a joy to approach these fresh springs and drink, it is a joy to pluck new flowers and to seek a distinguished crown for my head from that place whence before this the muses have never wreathed any man's temples—first because I teach about great things and hasten to free the mind from the tight bonds of religion; then, because on this dark subject I put forth verses so full of light, touching everything with the muses' charm. For this too is seen to be not without a reasoned plan [*ratione*]. But as doctors, when they try to give bitter wormwood to children, first touch the rim all around the cup

[29] For the various sources of this fragment, see Us. 512, and, among these, esp. Athenaeus XII p. 547a; the full statement seems to have been, "I spit on the *kalon* and on those who wonder at it in an empty fashion—whenever it does not produce any pleasure." For other evidence concerning Epicurus' view of poetry, see Classen (1968) and Segal (1990), with additional secondary references.

[30] On this passage, and in general on Lucretius' attitude to the didactic function of poetry, see Clay (1976, 1983a), Classen (1968), Brown (1987) 127–43.

[31] Here as in chapter 6, I translate both *mens* and *animus* with "mind," but include the Latin word in the case of *mens* to remove ambiguity.

with honey's tawny sweet liquid, so that the children's unforeseeing youth might be tricked as far as the lips, and they meanwhile may drink the bitter drink of wormwood down, and, though taken in, should not be held fast, but should instead be restored in this way and become healthy—just so I now, since this reasoned argument [*ratio*] often seems forbidding to those who have not tried it, and the many shrink away from it, have decided to explain our reasoning [*rationem*] to you in a sweetly speaking poetic song, and, so to speak, to touch it with the sweet honey of the muses, to see if perchance by this reasoned plan [*ratione*] I could hold your mind on our verses, while you survey the whole nature of things, its structure and form. (I.925–50)

Lucretius depicts himself as an innovator in that he is writing Epicurean poetry. This is innovation both from the point of view of Epicureanism[32] and from the point of view of poetry, which has not treated these important subjects except in the way of traditional anthropomorphic religion. He tells us that his "reasoned plan" for using poetic language was inspired by practical and medical motives. In order to engage the reader in a process of therapy leading to health, he will provide the inner argument of the poem, its *ratio*, with a pleasing sweet surface. The "reasoned plan" (*ratio*) of his poem is this combination of argument with poetic surface.[33] The truths of Epicureanism are difficult and, from the perspective of the pupil, unappetizing, in that they will require him to detach himself from much that he deeply values. Therefore this healthful medicine needs a "coating"; and by describing poetry as providing a coating or surface, Lucretius implies that the argument itself will not be corrupted by its commerce with poetry.[34]

This image suggests an account of poetic pleasure, or some poetic pleasures at any rate, that would make those pleasures acceptable to the Epicurean. For the sweet taste of a delightful thing is a legitimate, though nonnecessary, Epicurean pleasure, not itself connected with empty desire or false emotion. It can, then, be selected whenever its instrumental relation to freedom from disturbance is good. And yet, by reminding us so forcefully that poetic words arouse and shape desire, Lucretius invites us to conduct a critical examination of poetry, and of this poem as it goes on, asking whether all the desires inspired by poetry in general and this poem

---

[32] Philodemus' poetry is not closely linked to his Epicureanism as Lucretius' is: see Segal (1990).

[33] On this point I have profited from an unpublished paper by A. Lowell Bowditch.

[34] Note that once one gets beyond the initial stage, Epicurean arguments themselves cease to be unappetizing and become nectar-filled (III.11); on this see Graver (1990).

in particular are in fact benign, whether poetry might be the ally not only of legitimate pleasure but also of empty love. Venus is the accomplice of Lucretius' poetic project; she will turn out to be a complex and ambiguous figure in the poem.

As we follow Lucretius' poetic argument, we must temporarily turn away from the career of Nikidion. For the reader and pupil addressed in the poem is a male; he is identified with Memmius, Lucretius' aristocratic patron.[35] Many of the arguments against love assume the male point of view, and assume, as well, that the pupil is a citizen active in his country's political and military affairs. To understand what Lucretius is doing, we must follow the education of this reader. But this does not mean, as we shall see, that the poem takes no account of female experience and has nothing to say to a female reader. At the end we shall return to our pupil, asking in what way, for her as well, this poem might be therapeutic.[36]

V

Any study of Lucretius' arguments on love and sexual desire had better begin with an account of the first appearance of love and desire in his poem—that is, with his proem addressed to Venus.[37] The proem is important for the poem as a whole; but it is of special relevance, clearly, to Book IV, since it gives an account of the role of sexual desire in the world of animal nature—a perspective to which the arguments on love will return at two crucial points.

[35] On the portrait of Memmius, and Lucretius' poet-speaker's attitude to him, see Clay (1983a) and Classen (1968). Brown (1987) 122ff. convincingly argues that the entire discussion of love is written from a male perspective, but is less convincing when he asserts that the "sexual and emotional needs" of women are not taken into account: his own later account of the passages on mutual pleasure and marriage contradicts this. For further references to discussions of Roman sexual attitudes and practices, see Brown, 123 n. 64.

[36] There is no barrier to imagining Nikidion as a Roman pupil. The educational and social position of a Roman woman of the appropriate class background is somewhat more favorable to philosophical education than is women's position at Athens, where citizen wives, at any rate, would not commonly have studied philosophy; see de Sainte Croix (1981) 108–10 and Pomeroy (1975). On Roman proposals for women's education, see chapter 9. And the availability of Lucretius' poem would have guaranteed access to Epicurean philosophy even for those who could not read Greek. (In other respects, however, Lucretius relies on a more elite audience than does Epicurus.) On Lucretius' relation to his Roman context, see Fowler (1989).

[37] The literature on the proem is vast; for just two examples of helpful and illuminating discussion, see Classen (1968), Brown (1987) 91ff.

There is another more urgent reason to focus on Book I before turning to Book IV. A major recent interpretation of the poem by Diskin Clay has suggested that the relationship between Book I and Book IV is not complementary at all, but strongly adversarial. Book I's proem records and plays upon an anthropomorphic religious mythology about love that Book IV will destroy, showing the reader that what nature really contains is just congeries of atoms in motion. The point of Book IV is to lead the reader to this stark reductionist view of love and sexuality, in which not only the anthropomorphism of popular religion, but also, apparently, our everyday habit of viewing one another as complete organic forms with thoughts, emotions, and desires, are all to be replaced by materialist talk of atoms in a void. Book I begins where the naive reader is. Book IV shows him what Venus *really* comes to.[38]

I believe that this stark reductionist reading cannot survive a close examination of Book IV's arguments (arguments that Clay does not examine). I shall argue that Lucretius does not reject a human and intentional view of desire in favor of a reductionist view. He rather tries to create, or rediscover, a human view by rejecting the superstitions and mythologies of the popular religion of love. In this task the perspective of nature, first developed in Book I's proem, is extremely important. So I believe that, while Book I does not emerge unscathed from Book IV's critique—its Venus-Mars story in particular, will need critical scrutiny—it is in many ways a valuable basis for Lucretius' further arguments, both critical and constructive. And it would be more in keeping with Lucretius' therapeutic practice if this were so. For he uses proems, in each book, to show Memmius (and his readers) something good, something that should motivate them toward therapy, something that is correctly seen as a goal and promise of therapy. Let us see how this works in the Venus proem itself.

Before she is seen in the midst of nature, Venus is addressed in her connection with a particular human society. She is, in the poem's opening words, *Aeneadum genetrix*, parent of the race of Aeneas, that is to say, of the Roman people. This phrase sets up complex associations that will reverberate throughout the poem. Quite a few of them concern love. The reader thinks of the love of Venus for Anchises, a love in which a mortal satisfied the desire to make love with the perfect goddess of beauty. He would also think, inevitably, of the Trojan War. Sexual desire can be fertile and benign, as when Venus' desire for Anchises created the reader's nation; certainly it is essential for the nation's continuity. But it can also be destruc-

---

[38] Clay (1983a).

tive of a society—for example, through jealousies that lead to war. Memmius is urged to ask what makes it turn destructive, rather than benign. (He will later be told that the answer has much to do with the apparently benign story that a human being can love and win a goddess.) From the beginning, then, the addressee (who will shortly be seen to be a political and military man) is assumed to be a human social being, an animal different from every other animal, who is and ought to be concerned with Rome and Rome's traditional aspiration to social order and social justice. He is invited to look at sexual desire in this social perspective.

Venus is next invoked as "the pleasure (*voluptas*) of men and gods." This, I think, casts doubt from the start on Clay's claim that Venus is destined to "disappear" from the poem, to be replaced by pleasureless, intentionless, atomic motions. For Lucretius names her as identical with the highest good in an Epicurean life, a good that it will be his poem's task both to describe and to produce. Nature is always "barking" at us, the poet says in Book II, one single message: that the body should be free from pain, the mind delighted by joyful sense-perceptions (*iucundo sensu*), freed from anxiety and fear (II.16–19). The greatest problem with Clay's book as a whole is its omission of the joyful side of life that is so much emphasized in Epicurean teachings—of the relief and delight that come when one is liberated from all religion and all stress. Here Venus is identified with that delight.

Now Memmius' perspective is opened up: he sees himself and the Roman people as a part of a larger order in nature, as Venus is next invoked as the principle of fertility in the world of living things as a whole. Having seen himself first as a member of the line of Aeneas, he is now asked to see himself, and all humans, as members of the whole kind or class of living things, *genus omne animantum*; and living things, in turn, as parts of the larger natural world, a world that also includes sun and wind and cloud and earth. He is asked to see that desire is a unifying principle of and in that world, the explanation of its continuity, and also of much of its joyfulness.

For the world of nature, as this proem depicts it, is a joyful world. It is springtime. The earth is pleasant (*suavis*, 7), full of color; the waters laugh, the sky is peaceful, the winds are gentle and benign. The animals who respond to the pull of Venus are full of a strong vital energy that is exuberant, playful, and non-conflicted. Sexual desire has great force: their hearts are "struck" (*perculsae*, 13; *incutiens*, 19). They are so aroused that they can cross wide spaces, swim across swollen rivers (14–15). Venus' power is felt in the sea, in the mountains, in swelling brooks, in the leafy homes of birds, in the green fields (17–18). But it is a joyful power, not anxious, compulsive, or painful: they "jump across the fields" (15); "seized by delight they follow you eagerly [*cupide*] whenever you lead" (15–16). If forceful, this Venus is also gentle (*blandum . . . amorem*, 19); it is not tainted with any kind of sadism or possessiveness. If we contrast this picture with other related poetic depictions of animal nature—for example, with the account of animal desire in Virgil's *Georgics* (a comparison effectively pursued by Philip Hardie in his recent book)[39] we see that Lucretius has constructed a very positive picture of the animal world, showing the sexual energy of that world to be pleasant and benign. There is no madness here, no cruelty either to self or other.

If we already have the Trojan War story in mind, we cannot help noticing that there is also no being in love. There is none of the obsessive focusing on a single object that gives rise to jealousy and its associated violence; none of the thought of the beloved as a god that motivates obsession and (as we shall see later) prevents acknowledgment of the other as a bodily being. Not coincidentally, there are no wars here, and no murders. We cannot help noticing, then, that nature is in order as it is and, in some sense, in better order than we are. We are invited to ask what makes the difference, and to look to love for an understanding of the difference.

At the same time, we are told in no uncertain terms that we too are a part of this nature. We share the sexual instincts of our *genus*, and it is plausible to suppose that our conduct in sex and love is originally motivated by the very same force of sexual attraction that functions in the rest of the natural world. When Lucretius asks us to take up the perspective of nature, there is usually a deflationary purpose in view. A certain sort of conduct is thought by humans to be very special—either itself divine, or sent and controlled by divinity; in any case, not susceptible of ordinary natural and physical explanation. Love is one such phenomenon (recall Epicurus' opposition to the popular view that it is god-sent). The poem discovers many more. The strategy of the deflationary argument is to place before us some behavior in animal nature that looks very similar to our behavior; to offer a convincing naturalistic explanation for the animal conduct; and then to imply that if we cling to the basic rational principle that similar things ought to have similar explanations (a principle explicitly endorsed by Lucretius, and used in many passages), we are led to apply the straightforward naturalistic explanation to our own conduct, in preference to the complex or special non-natural explanation. In this case, we find exactly as much "divinity" in

---

[39] Hardie (1986). Lucretius has certainly accentuated the positive and attractive aspects of animal life here, and is silent about aggressive competitiveness for females and other violent aspects of animal mating.

our own conduct as we do in that of the animals—that is to say, an imma-
nent naturalized "divinity," a Venus that is identified with the natural
sexual instinct. This same deflationary strategy is used to great effect by
Hume in the remarkable sections of the *Treatise of Human Nature* that
concern animals ("On the Reason of Animals," "On the Pride and Humility of Animals," "On the Love and Hate of Animals"). He uses it for the
same purpose, namely, to puncture the pretensions of theological and
metaphysical explanations of natural conduct, and to lead us toward a
natural history of the human being.[40]

But at the same time the social perspective, present from the beginning
and explicitly recalled in the ensuing address to Memmius (41ff.), reminds
us that we are not simply like the other animals, and that the solution of the
problems posed by human desire cannot lie in anything so simple as a
return to animal nature. We are animals and not divinities: but we are also
social creatures, for whom life in complex forms of community appears to
be essential to flourishing life. There is reason to suppose that our Venus is
friendly to these more complex forms of animal bonding as well: for she
uses her charms to divert Mars from making war, thus giving peace to
Rome (*quiescant*, 30, is a strongly positive Epicurean word). At the same
time she gives Lucretius space to compose his poem with a quiet mind (41–
42), his reader space to study it without abandoning the common good
(43). But if Venus is to play a positive role in our human lives she will need
to be a more intelligent, more complex force than the force that leads the
animals in their cheery jumping and skipping.

And it is very clear, from Book V, that human Venus *is* different, that the
development of human forms of association requires an evolution in the
form of Venus. Venus, in the lives of the earliest humans, is just the Venus of
Book I's animals: a strong force of animal attraction that ensures the
reproduction of the species, through that mutual pleasure that is, Lucretius
insists here as in Book IV, a necessary condition for healthy sexual functioning in nature generally (V.849–54). The first human beings, tough and
hardy, had no settled dwelling places (I.932), no love for their offspring, no
ability to think of the common good (958), no morals and laws. They lived
by instinct, on whatever came their way (960–61).

And Venus joined the bodies of lovers in the woods. For each woman was
made receptive either by mutual desire or by the violent force and over-

---

[40] Hume (1739–40) Book I, Part III, sect. XVI; Book II, Part I, sect. XII, Part II, sect. XII. For
some examples of Lucretius' insistence that similar *explananda* must have similar explanations, see *pari ratione*, IV.191; *necessest consimili causa*, IV.232; *simili ratione*, IV.750–51.

whelming sexual energy of the male, or by a price—acorns and arbute-berries, or choice pears. (962–65)[41]

These people are living, as Lucretius indeed says, *more ferarum* (932), in the manner of the beasts. And he makes clear that in one sense this is a far better life than ours: for if these people lack many means of self-protection, if they die helpless, overwhelmed by beasts, still they lack, as well, the slavery to religion that torments us, the scourge of war, the corruptions of luxury (cf. 188ff., 1161ff.; cf. chapters 6 and 7). And they lack, as well, we see, the ills caused by *erōs*—to which Lucretius points when he says that they had no reason to cross the sea, and connects crossing the sea with the thought of war (999–1001). But he also makes it very clear that this life is not a complete life, this Venus not a complete Venus, for human beings; that human affection and desire must evolve in order to include the tenderness toward others, the concern for laws, institutions, and the common good, that are essential for truly human happiness.

Lucretius shows us the first stage in this evolution (1011ff.). It consists in the establishment of households and families, and some sort of institution of marriage. This, he says, makes people see, or acknowledge, that their children are theirs, created out of them; and this sense of family connection, together with the appeal of a stabler sexual relationship (in which there is probably more time for enjoyment than in those sudden encounters in the woods) begins to "soften" the previously toughened race. Parents formerly hard now feel tenderness for their children; and we may assume that this same tenderness and friendliness now also characterizes the relation between husband and wife. For this Venus is now said to "soften" their force, much as love of children does (1017–18). These "softenings" are the necessary preconditions of promises and contracts, of community, of law. Hence, in Lucretius' view, they are necessary for a full flourishing human life. Venus does not "disappear" from Lucretius' poem. She becomes civilized.

These reflections are not pursued in detail until Book V. But the proem to Venus with its appeal to the social perspective establishes from the beginning some constraints in the mind of the pupil who is thinking of Venus, showing him some considerations to which any acceptable account of human love and sexuality would have to respond.

Lucretius distances human Venus from that of the beasts in yet another way: he reminds us that we are the creatures who produce poetry and philosophy, and that one of our greatest delights is to understand things

---

[41] For further discussion of this material, see chapter 7.

about ourselves, including our capacity for pleasure and delight. For he next invokes Venus as the colleague of his poetic enterprise (*sociam*, 24), as we have seen—the one who can give a delightful character to his words. He uses, for delight, the same word he had used for the sexual pleasure of animals (*lepore* 15; *leporem*, 28). Where animals find *lepos* only in bodily contact, we find it also in words and thoughts. This tells us that human delight, even in its sensuous aspect, is intimately bound up with mind. Just as words can be, for us, more heroic weapons than arms, so too they can be objects of a pleasure that is held to be central in giving the reader a happy life.

What the reader is led to expect from a good account of sexuality is, then, a sexual life that is, on the one hand, natural, partaking of the freedom from anxiety and disturbance that Lucretius discovered in the life of na-ture; that is, on the other hand, rational, both expressing and gratifying our human love of reasoning and language, and making room for the friendly, tender, and social aspects of human life that are essential for speaking and reasoning beings. A sexual life that is, we might say, naturally human. Lucretius' reader will tend to associate the specifically human in desire with the obsessions and torments of erotic love. The challenge of the poem will be to demonstrate that the way of erotic love is not the only way to form a specifically human sexual relationship; that, indeed, erotic love pollutes sexual relationships with quasi-religious illusions that prevent us from acknowledging one another as human beings.

Venus makes one further appearance in the proem; and this appearance, though apparently benign, gives Memmius his first explicit introduction to the diseases that will be diagnosed in Book IV. We see Mars reclining in Venus' arms, "conquered by an eternal wound of love" (34). "And so, looking up with his shapely neck thrown back, he feeds his hungry eyes with love, gazing ardently at you, and as he lies back his breath hangs on your lips" (I.35–37). It is a tableau, depicted in painterly fashion. Readers will easily recall similar scenes in both poetry and painting, scenes that have shaped their understanding of the meaning and structure of love.[42] The picture is one of male obsession with a female divinity. The poem's opening recalled Venus' seduction of a wise and fine mortal. Now we learn that such a divine woman can distract even a god, to the extent that he forgets his proper business, content to feed on the non-food of looks and glances. This poetry is meant to be very familiar, almost a cliché. It is a

---

[42] On the wound imagery and its use in the Hellenistic epigram, see Kenney (1970), with references.

picture of love that animates the religion of love; and love poetry reveals itself as a traditional ally of that religion.

So far the mythology looks benign, since this particular distraction has the good effect of postponing war, even of making this poem possible. But if we think back to the poem's opening, we might recall that the Trojan War, and no doubt many others as well, have been products of exactly similar obsessions. We might recall, too, that the love of Mars and Venus was itself by no means unproblematic. It undermined a marriage; and the jealousies it aroused created strife among the gods. These reflections might or might not be aroused so early in the poem;[43] but they will return later, when we learn at what cost to men, to women, and to society men and women follow this paradigm in their lives.

VI

Book IV is cleverly constructed so as to prepare for the attack on love. The interlocutor is so attached to love that he must be led into the attack gently, indirectly, with a good deal of oblique but vital preparation. Hence three-fourths of the book are not about love at all. They are occupied with analyses of perception, perceptual error, and dreaming that are of no obvious relevance, as one first reads them, to questions about *erōs*. But, while these discussions are of general importance to Lucretius' philosophical project, they also do work that will be of special relevance to the later love arguments.[44] Above all, they get us to accept the fact that not everything we see is really as it is; to see that a realist causal theory of perception such as Epicurus', and an Epicurean defense of perception as criterion of truth, are fully compatible with the claim that many of our perceptual experiences are delusory and misleading. In particular, we are shown how our habits and habitual beliefs can distort our relationship to the objects of perception around us, even though those objects have a real character that can be correctly grasped by a healthy perceiver. The arguments are dense, and it is beyond the purposes of this chapter to investigate them in detail. But we can summarize the points in Lucretius' analysis that will prove of greatest importance for his subsequent attack.[45]

---

[43] They are more likely to be aroused if we retain here lines 44–49, a contrasting description of the peaceful life of the Epicurean gods, not touched by anger; I argue for their retention in chapter 7.

[44] On the unity of Book IV, see Brown (1987). On perceptual relativity, Graver (1990).

[45] This section of the poem is very well analyzed in Bailey (1947).

1. *Perceptions are not always veridical.* Simulacra, or visual effluences, are real, but are caused in many ways that do not truly reflect the nature of the object. Some are spontaneously generated in the air; some are composites of pieces coming from other objects; some have been damaged by their passage through a medium; some have gotten exchanged for other images; still others are non-representational in other ways. Any perceptual experience should be scrutinized and criticized by mind, attending to these possibilities of error. Only then can perception be trusted. (735ff., 818–22).

2. *Desire and perception influence each other.* The lover thinks of his desire as being aroused by the sight of the beloved. Lucretius tells us, however, that perception is also determined by desire. Out of the many visual effluences, or simulacra, that are at any one time present in the air around us, we single out for perceiving those that correspond to our antecedent desires and concerns. Perception is a form of *attention to*; it misses what it does not make the object of attention; and what we single out for attention at any time depends on a great deal else about us, especially what we wish to see (779ff.).

3. *The mind extrapolates rapidly from its perceptions*, building up a whole picture from small signs, instead of attending closely to all the perceptual evidence that is actually available (814–17).

4. *Our physiological state influences desire—and, through this, attention and perception.* When our body is in a state of depletion, we feel pain, hence desire for what will cause the end of that pain—for example, food. And it is at this point that we would tend to focus on food as an object of perception or thought. When we are satisfied, we think about the corresponding object far less (858ff.).

5. *Habit influences perception.* In sleep (but by extension also in waking life) our habitual pursuits influence what we see—presumably through the same mechanism that we described previously under (1). Forms of habitual activity contain characteristic structures of pleasure and attention (*studium atque voluptas*, 984), which influence thought even at the unconscious level. Thus lawyers dream of pleading cases, generals of fighting battles (962ff.). As for Lucretius, he writes, "I do this, continually investigating the nature of things at all times and, when I find it, setting it out in my native language" (969–70).

At this point Lucretius makes a particularly effective use of the perspective of nature. Dream visions are widely believed to have a supernatural significance. But if we show that non-human animals have the same experience and exhibit the same dream-behavior, and if we all agree that the best explanation for that behavior is natural rather than supernatural, then for reasons of consistency and economy it should be chosen in the human case as well. Animals, Lucretius now asserts, do display all the behavioral signs of a dream-life that recreates habitual scenes of daily life. Horses sweat and pant, dogs move their legs and sniff the air, wild beasts and birds are equally stirred, as if by images of their prey (986–1010). In short, the experience belongs "not to humans alone, but in truth to all animals" (986). Lucretius even illustrates the general proposition with human as well as non-human evidence, underlining the point that we are all animals in common (1011ff.). But then it is most rational to view this psychological mechanism as natural, not supernatural.

These observations, taken together, prepare Memmius to understand how the mythology of love that permeates his society can corrupt not just the conscious but even the unconscious life of each person; and to see this influence as a natural, not a supernatural or god-sent process. They prepare him, too, to understand how one might begin to counteract that influence. One way will surely be to do what he is doing, spending his time reading and thinking about Lucretius' poem. Poetry reaches deep into human lives; it shapes the images people see, even in their dreams. So it must be approached with caution, clearly. For reading love poems will give Memmius, waking and sleeping, the images of love, the paradigm of Venus that he then will carry into his life, looking for signs of the beautiful goddess in the woman he sees and extrapolating freely from these signs, ignoring the rest of what she actually is. Lucretius tells him here that reading his poem will have an opposite and therapeutic effect: it will not only conduct a critique of illusion, it will also cause Memmius, at the deepest level, to spend his mental time in a rational reflection that criticizes illusion. He will get not just a one-time grasp of an argument and its conclusion but, if he properly attends, new habits of vision, new patterns of desire.

VII

The discussion of erotic love develops out of the passage on dreaming through a series of subtle and carefully crafted transitions. This transitional passage prepares the reader to see love as illusion and, at the same time, to understand that it has a natural psycho-physiological basis. The reader is first led up to the topic of sexual desire through the discussion of dreams. Describing, now, dreams that have their origin in actual bodily appetites, he gives three examples: (1) a thirsty man dreams of a river or fountain—in his dream he gulps it down (1024–25); (2) a fastidious person, feeling a need to urinate, dreams he is urinating into a chamber pot, and actually wets himself and his expensive bed clothes (1026–29); (3) an adolescent boy dreams of a beautiful person,[46] and ejaculates, staining[47] his clothes (1030–36).

The examples all have several things in common. In all, there is an element of delusion. No real river or pot is there, and the thought of a lovely face or form is caused by simulacra coming in "from any and every body" (1032). In all, the vision is occasioned in large part by actual bodily needs that have caused the dreamer to fasten on these simulacra rather than others. In none of the three cases, finally, is the need appropriately satisfied. In the first there is no actual satisfaction; in the second and third, there is a kind of satisfaction (though not of the dream-desire with all of its intentional content); but because of the delusion, the satisfaction takes a ridiculous and inappropriate form. From the perspective of waking life, the dreamer feels shame and disgust for what he did. He wishes that he had not been taken over by the delusion.

All of this we readily grant when dreaming is in question—even a young person's erotic dreaming. What we shall soon see (and what the analysis of error has permitted us to see, with its easy movement between waking life and dream life) is that all these features can be present, as well, in waking experience. And all are present in the experience of erotic love.

Lucretius will be attacking a much-loved and central part of Memmius' (and most readers') life. So his procedure is more indirect and less confrontational than it is in his assault on fear, where the unpleasantness of the experience is agreed, and only its veracity and value remain to be examined. Having quietly laid the groundwork for his assault through the whole account of perception, having prepared it even more nearly by the three dream examples, Lucretius does not, even now, come right out and say directly, "Love is an illusion, just like that dream." Instead, he permits Memmius and the reader to laugh at the three dreamers without being aware that the argument is about to turn on them.[48]

---

[46] The dream-object is not specified as to gender: it has, only, "a gorgeous face and a beautiful coloring," and it is produced by *simulacra* coming in "from any and every body." Later the object is said to be either "a young man with womanish limbs" or a woman (1053), though the rest of the argument concerns love of women. It is noteworthy that Lucretius thinks human desire must always have a particularized object.

[47] The word is *cruentent*, which usually denotes spilled blood. Brown (1987) discusses the line well, suggesting that "Lucretius has boldly extended the normal meaning by subordinating the primary connotation of color to that of staining or pollution."

[48] Compare Brown (1987) 62ff., who stresses the passage's "clinical" tone.

At the same time, throughout the entire passage on dreaming, Lucretius has prepared Memmius to be led along by adopting an authoritative, magisterial tone, distancing himself from him and asking him, "You: give me your fine ears and your intelligent mind [*animum*]. Do not say that the things I call possible are impossible. Do not depart from me with a heart [*pectore*] that rejects the truth I speak, when you yourself are in error and cannot grasp it" (912–15). He portrays his distance from Memmius as the distance of a mind that ranges over all of nature and is able to grasp it, from a weak and error-prone but still intelligent mind that is likely to miss the truth unless it follows humbly along. He tells Memmius, in effect, not to trust his intuitions where this topic is concerned, but to be more than usually subservient to his guidance.[49]

After the three dream examples, Lucretius turns to waking sexual life, as if this discussion followed naturally upon the account of the erotic dream.[50] Love is not yet mentioned, nor is it yet apparent that some of the interlocutor's most cherished beliefs are scheduled for criticism. The poet begins, here, to use the first-person plural, including Memmius (and the reader) in the argument, reminding Memmius that both he and the poet are human and subjects of similar experience. From the comfortable on-looker's position from which he had been permitted to watch the three ridiculous dreamers, Memmius has now moved to the center of the stage— or, we might say, of the operating theater—as the poet, at once surgeon and (former) patient, prepares for surgical argument.

The calm discussion of erotic desire that follows contains nothing that seems immediately threatening or negative. It is a simple straightforward description, in the style of many descriptions in the earlier part of the book, of the complex interaction between physiology and psychology in sexual longing. Sexual desire is in part a physical impulse, produced by an accumulation of seed and requiring a certain stage of bodily maturity and readiness. But it has, as well, a complex psychology: for not just any chance cause will produce the excitation. "Only the attractive force of a human being draws human seed from a human being" (1040).[51] The body seeks to

---

[49] See the useful discussion of the changing modes of address to the interlocutor in Clay (1983a).

[50] For the connection, see Brown (1987) 76, 82ff., who correctly points out that passion for Lucretius is not like real eating or drinking, but like dreaming of eating or drinking: one makes contact only with *simulacra*.

[51] Brown (1987) ad loc. notes that the gender neutrality of this passage leaves room for the effect of young men on men as well as women on men, and perhaps even men on women, given the belief in female seed.

discharge seed not into any chance receptacle, but into a human body; and not into any chance body, but into the body "whence the mind [*mens*] is wounded by love" (1048). Thus in its very nature human sexuality is not just physical but at the same time mental; not only a bodily urge to discharge but a form of selective intentionality. We cannot define it without mentioning its object, under an intentional description. It is the desire to perform a bodily act with another human being whom the perceiver sees in a particular way.[52] Of course the intentional content is also, at bottom, something physical. There are no supernatural entities here, clearly. But Lucretius shows no tendency, either here or later, to reduce sexual intentions and perceptions to atomic motions, nor does he indicate that our humanistic and non-reductionistic language is the culprit in our problems concerning love. Lucretius summarizes his complex physical/psychological description of sexual phenomena with a statement that strongly indicates his approval of the account he has just given. He commends to the reader: *Haec Venus est nobis; hinc autemst nomen amoris* (1058). "This is what our Venus is. It is from this, however, that we get the name of love."

Diskin Clay has argued that this passage marks the disappearance of the anthropomorphic Venus from the poem. At this point the pupil learns that he has been wrong to speak of love and desire in the anthropomorphic terms taught in popular mythology. From now on, he must learn to speak a strange and stern new language, the language of atomic physiology. That—a motion of atoms—is all that our Venus is. I have already indicated that I find this reductionism highly peculiar as a reading of a passage that prominently and centrally uses intentional psychological language.[53] In

---

[52] *Amore* here should probably be read weakly, not as implying the presence already of the particular sort of love that is based on false belief—for that is not a necessary condition for sexual arousal. The rest of the poem informs us that arousal is fully compatible with a veridical relation to the object. Lucretius' problem is that the language gives him no word for that veridical relation. The passage would then mean "a person whom the perceiver's mind sees as desirable." This would be in keeping with the naturalistic and deflationary use of the conventional "wound" imagery later in this passage (1049, 1053), where the clichés of love poetry are used as naturalistic description. See Kenney (1970) for an excellent discussion of Lucretius' strategy here, and especially p. 254 on 1049ff.: "The conventionally prettified and, so to say, exsanguinated image is transformed so as to illuminate in the most crudely physical terms Lucretius' physical conception of love and hence to devalue the current romantic conception." On the military imagery, see also Fitzgerald (1984). The same thing happens to the imagery of liquids—see subsequent discussion.

[53] Thus it is strange that Kenney (1970) should characterize the desire described by Lucretius in this passage as "a desire, prompted by a physical stimulus in which the mind has no

fact, so committed is Lucretius to erotic intentionality that he appears to insist that human erotic desire always has a particular human object: accumulation of seed does not lead to orgasm without fantasy. Nor does the Venus of intentionality in any sense disappear from the poem. In Book V Venus is invoked in connection with the transition from brute violence to the more tender desires in marriage, desires that make community possible. And even in Book IV itself she appears again, unreduced. Intentional language continues to be used, furthermore, both with and without the name of Venus, for conduct that Lucretius approves. The passage on mutual desire, for example, to be analyzed later, is surely one of the most empathic and positive in the book (1192–1207). And yet it is full of intentional language: of desire, pleasure, seeking, aiming, thinking. It even uses the name of Venus for the intercourse that is the outcome of this desire.[54]

But Clay is, I think, on the right track. *Something* is being rejected and unmasked in this passage. *Something* is being said to be all there "really" is to sexual experience. It is only a matter of getting the two precisely characterized and distinguished. I think we should say that what is kept is the full richness of naturalistic explanation—including all the language, both physical and psychological, that we would wish to use in talking about ourselves as complex natural beings with a physiology and a mentality that stand in a complex relationship to one another.

What is rejected is, so far, far less obvious. But we do notice the absence from the approved description of several ingredients that we associate with the popular mythology of Venus, as typefied by the Venus-Mars story in Book I and in the love poetry to which the poet will shortly refer: the exaltation of the object of love into a kind of deity and an object of obsession and worship; the aim to become one with the object, so seen; the thought that love is something godlike or god-sent, something in and

---

part, to transplant seed from one body to another" (255); this is surely an odd paraphrase of *mens unde est saucia amore*. The same unjustified reductionism appears in the otherwise helpful discussion quoted in n. 49. Fitzgerald (1984) and Betensky (1980) also give reductionistic readings of these lines.

[54] It is useful to compare the judgment of Commager (1957), summarizing his study of Lucretius' deviations from Thucydides in the narrative of the plague: "These changes betray something more than the carelessness, poetic elaboration, or the inevitable consequence of writing in Latin rather than Greek. We have seen Lucretius describe physical ills in a psychological vocabulary, treat clinical phenomena as emotionally motivated actions, change medical data to ethical commentary, and broaden the plague's area in defiance of physical fact. In simplest terms his additions and alterations display a marked tendency to regard the plague less in physical terms than in emotional, moral, and psychological ones." This passage is discussed in Wormell (1960). See also Brown (1987) 95.

through which we transcend our mere humanity. The people in the approved description want physical satisfaction and pleasure (1057). They are attentive to one another and, like the animals of the proem, they are struck by one another. They are selective and reflective in their behavior, seeking out the one person who is the source of their being struck. But they are not obsessive and possessive. This, Lucretius now tells us, is the original or natural Venus. This is where we get the name of love. This is the original source of the sweetness that love drips into our hearts, the sweetness that is followed by chill anxiety.

The transitions here are difficult. We move from what is apparently the natural basis of love, from a form of sexual behavior to which no criticisms seem to be attached, to a conventional form of anxious and unhappy love, described in the commonplaces of poetic language. This unhappy form Lucretius will soon reject; and he will inform us that it is not an inevitable or natural outgrowth of the natural form. In this passage Lucretius moves us along from one to the other, without marking the boundary very clearly; and this is, I think, deliberate. Having acquainted Memmius with the whole terrain of love, so to speak, he will then go on to show very clearly what the differences are between natural Venus and sick *amor*, showing him that we need not move (as perhaps he thinks he must) from here to there. Since these explanations remain to be given, the interpretation of these three lines depends to a certain extent on hindsight. But I believe that it ought to focus on the distinction between *haec* and *hinc, this* and *from this. Haec Venus est nobis:* this, the natural complex we have just described, is what Venus genuinely, or truly, is in human life. *Hinc autemst nomen amoris: from this*, however, we derive the name of love; we apply the name of love, with all its conventional associations, to the experience that has this natural basis. *Autem*, usually left untranslated, probably indicates an opposition between the original thing and what has been derived from it.[55] *Hinc illaec primum Veneris dulcedinis in cor / stillavit gutta et successit frigida cura.* From this that old familiar drop of erotic sweetness (*illaec . . . gutta*) dripped into our hearts—and chill care ensued. In other words, that's the innocuous basis for the painful experience described in those familiar clichés.[56] That's the origin of that mythology.

---

[55] Brown (1987) ad loc. points out correctly that *autem* is not invariably adversative, though it always marks a contrast of some sort. He does not, however, offer any argument against an adversative reading or in favor of his own "furthermore."

[56] On these lines, see Kenney (1970) 255–57, who makes the same point about *illaec*, and adduces examples of the poetic clichés in question. Fitzgerald (1984) points usefully to the implicit contrast between *muta cupido* (1057) and the view of the world created by poetic

Slyly and almost imperceptibly, with the detachment of one who has heard those old poetic phrases one time too many, Lucretius has moved us into a critical examination of erotic love.

VIII

In the section that immediately follows, Lucretius gives more information about the difference between love, the sick or bad form of sexual interaction, and the more natural and fruitful form that he recommends. The bad form, he says (confirming suggestions made earlier in the poem), is obsessively focused on a single person (1066), religiously attentive to that person's form and even name (1061–62), tormented by an anxiety that eats away at the lover like an ulcerous sore (1068–69); it is a madness that grows day by day (1069). We are not yet told what this madness is about, or how it arises. For the person who avoids this love, on the other hand, there is available a pure form of sexual pleasure (*pura voluptas*, 1075) that is not marred by these pains.

We now need to be told precisely what is bad in the structure of love; for only when we have grasped the analysis can we fully understand what relationships Lucretius is and is not condemning. And if we are attentive readers of Epicurean arguments, we expect the analysis to bring forward false beliefs that are responsible for the bad form. The belief that through love we are vulnerable to loss does not seem to be a promising candidate for the false belief in question. For any good reader of love poems is prepared for a certain amount of anxiety and pain, and perhaps he will even see this as a sign of the depth of his love. Lucretius' argument would be blatantly circular if he seized upon vulnerability as the central false belief; for if it is false inside an Epicurean conception of good, it is true inside most of the conceptions that his readers would be likely to hold. Such an argument would hardly achieve the goals of therapy.

Accordingly, Lucretius does not stop with vulnerability to loss. In the remarkable account of sexual intercourse that follows, he offers a complex criticism of the cognitive structure of love, assailing both love's beliefs about its aim and its conception of its object, and describing the conse-

---

language. Betensky (1980) oddly takes these lines to supply a condemnation of the *natural* Venus, as well as the poetic view of love: "This is *our* Venus . . . devoid of any personality or divinity, causing only waste and destruction" (292). On the pun between *amor* and *umor* throughout the passage and the attempt to derive one etymologically from the other, see Brown (1987) 64–65.

quences, both internal and external to the sexual relationship, of pursuing that aim and having that view of the object. The passage is detached and scathing in tone. It describes lovemaking as one might describe the behavior of an alien tribe engaging in a strange ritual. And yet, at the same time, it vouches for its own subjective origins, since the poet (or so it seems) can have known in only one way what goes on in bed, and how intense, how mad, that is. He speaks as one who has known the most intense depths of passion and has survived to regain his sanity. If Memmius is or has been himself in the position of the lovers in bed, he would feel the poet looking down on him as from a great height, and telling him with his clear eye exactly what he sees. The poet's critique has force with him both because he sees himself in the lovers described, and is convinced that the poet has been there and known what he knows, and also because the poet, as poet, now stands above it all and sees as Memmius will readily grant he does not see himself. The origin of Jerome's story is in this complex and deliberate poetic design.

What are these lovers trying to do, the ones who make love with the intensity of people "in love with" one another, squeezing, grasping, biting (1079ff.)? Lucretius' first point against them, in this extraordinary passage, is that they do not *know* what they are up to. Their passion "fluctuates in unsure wanderings [*incertis erroribus*]" as they "cannot decide what they should enjoy first with eyes and hands" (1077–78). They "wander, unsure [*incerti*], over the whole body" (1104); "unsure [*incerti*], they waver, weakened by a hidden wound" (1120). It is no wonder that they cannot decide. For the aim that becomes evident from their behavior, the aim that they are actually pursuing in their actions, is one so strange that they could not own it consciously without convicting themselves of absurdity. The natural human lover, like the animals of Book I, aims at pleasure—in fact, at mutual pleasure, as we shall be told. This aim may or may not be combined with various other aims, such as friendship, marriage, reproduction. The person in love, however, aims at something far odder: at union or fusion with the object of his desire. This is the origin of the intensity of these lovers' efforts, the explanation of their frenzied biting and grasping (1056ff.).

But this aim cannot be achieved, because the person never can be taken in.[57] Even if little bits of flesh could be rubbed off (cf. 1103, 1110); or even if, being a woman, or a male having intercourse with a male, one does take in something from a partner—still, this does not fulfill love's aim, since the

[57] One might usefully compare Aristophanes' story in Plato's *Symposium*.

aim is to possess or devour the person and the person, as we know, is so much more than pieces of matter.[58] Lovers must feed themselves on perceptions, and on these alone (1095–96). The separateness of the other, the fact that contact is possible only through perception, by responding to perceptible signs, all this is not delight to these lovers, but a painful frustration of their dearest wish, which is to eat the other sexually, feeding on that other mind and body and having it completely.[59]

But why, one might ask, does the lover form this peculiar and impossible goal? One might seek fusion as a special pleasure or a supreme ecstasy. These lovers, however, seek it out of pain. Feeling their erotic desire as a source of weakness and instability, an ulcerous sort in the self, they seek to put an end to the pain and even shame of this vulnerable condition by a complete possession of the other that would put an end to all desire, all unseemly openness. Lucretius' poem in this way sets itself in the context of popular thought about love, according to which erōs is a source of constraint and unmanly infirmity that gives rise to an urgent desire to constrain and immobilize the source of the weakness through possession.[60] The lover, out of desperation about his passivity, forms the false belief that through sex he can put an end to the longing that undermines him, getting complete control over its excruciatingly separate and uncontrolled source.

We can understand the aim even more fully, I think, if we connect it to Lucretius' accompanying diagnosis of love's false beliefs about the properties of its object. This diagnosis is explicitly given only later, but it has been suggested ever since the Venus-Mars passage in Book I. Why does love want to devour this person—this one and no other? Because this person is

---

[58] Even the physiological wishes are confused: at 1105–11 the wish to ingest the beloved is combined in a confused way with a wish to enter the beloved's body and get lost inside it. This, Lucretius hastens to point out, is equally impossible.

[59] This view of the aim of desire is still defended: see Scruton (1986), who writes that the goal is "to aim one's words, caresses and glances, as it were, into the heart of the other, and to know him from the inside, as a creature who is part of oneself."

[60] See especially "The Constraints of Desire: Erotic Magical Spells" in Winkler (1990). Winkler surveys the history, from Hesiod through the second century C.E., and especially in popular magic spells preserved in the so-called Magical Papyri, of the idea that erōs is a disease, a "victimization by unwanted invasive forces," whose cure consists in binding and possessing its source. Many of the magic spells he studies use imagery that is closely connected to Lucretius' account of erotic sadism. (For just one example: "If she wants to sleep, put thorn-filled leather whips underneath her and impale her temples with wooden spikes.") Winkler perceptively summarizes: "The control exercised by the agent is in some part a control over his own desperation . . . and puts him in a role opposed to that of the erotic victim he 'actually' is." One might also usefully compare Sartre's account of sex in Being and Nothingness, where the lover's goal is that the loved one relinquish freedom to him.

seen to be perfect, divine, the only one, the one he has to have. (Maybe, too, his passport to happiness, his stairway to the stars, all of these.) Lovers are so hooked on the stories and clichés of love, Lucretius argues, that they hardly look at the actual person when they love. They glimpse a few signs and (in the manner described in the account of perceptual error) make up, attribute (*tribuunt*, 1154) the rest, "blind with desire" (1153). Where does the extrapolation, the fiction come from? The famous satirical passage about men's false romanticized view of the women they love makes the origin plain: the made-up inflated picture comes from culture and, in particular, from our popular poetic culture, which is in this matter an accomplice of religion.

> Men, blind with desire, attribute to women excellences that are not really theirs. And thus, we see women who are in many ways misshapen and ugly being the objects of great delight, and of the highest honor. And each man laughs at others, and urges them to make amends to Venus, since they are sick with a base love—while, poor wretch, he often cannot see his own trouble. A black woman is called "honey-skinned" [*melichrus*],[61] an unwashed and smelly woman "unadorned" [*acosmos*], a grey-eyed woman "a veritable Pallas," a wiry and twiglike woman "a gazelle" [*dorcas*], a tiny dwarfish woman "one of the Graces" [*chariton mia*], "all pure salt," a giantess is "a wonder" [*cataplexis*] and "full of majesty." If she stammers and cannot speak, she "has a lisp" [*traulizi*]; if she is dumb, she is "modest"; the fiery spiteful gossip is "a flaming torch" [*lampadium*]. She becomes "a slender darling" [*ischnon eromenion*] when she cannot live from undereating; if she is on the verge of death from coughing, she is "fragile" [*rhadine*]. The fat bosomy woman is "Ceres nursing Iacchus"; the snub-nosed is "a female Silenus" or "satyress." The thick-lipped is "a living kiss" [*philema*]. It would be tedious to try to relate other examples of this sort. (1153–70)

Each of the inflated false descriptions is a poetic cliché.[62] The large number of Greek words makes this point especially clear. Some explicitly deify the

---

[61] See the convincing discussion in Brown (1987) ad loc. Bailey (1947) translates "honey-gold," understanding its derivation differently.

[62] See the excellent treatment in Kenney (1970), who emphasizes the Hellenistic epigrammatic tradition, and also suggests that Lucretius may be aiming at Catullus, who sets himself in that tradition. We should probably not confine ourselves to the epigram, since much of the lyric tradition that would have been important for the Roman Neoteric poets is lost to us. See also Bailey (1947) ad loc., Brown (1987) 78–79, 127–43, 280–83, and the excellent translation by Humphries (1968), who finds suitable English equivalents for the clichés. For an exhaustive study of the poetry of the "divine" mistress, see Lieberg (1962). For the use of

woman, some only make a natural quality into a perfection. Lucretius is showing us how the lover's perception, guided by stories and poetic myths, extrapolates from the signs that are actually before him. Poetic descriptions provide ready vehicles and paradigms for the erotic imagination, which tends, in all these cases, to make a real woman into a Venus. The lover's desire for complete possession can now be seen as a desire to possess something of the more than human, to devour the divine. It would be no pain at all not to possess an ordinary human being: but the divine goddess causes a running sore of longing.

The poet, before and after this passage, enumerates the bad consequences of this sort of love-illusion. For despite its internal incoherence and the impossibility of its goal, love can be and is lived, so incoherence and impossibility had better not be the only arguments against it. The consequences he mentions are of two sorts: external, that is, the areas of the lover's life outside the erotic relationship; and internal to the relationship itself. The external consequences are familiar and can be briefly mentioned: waste of strength and force; loss of control over the rest of one's life; damage to fortune; damage to political activity; damage to reputation (1121–32).[63] The internal consequences are more striking. Love's possessive aim and its inevitable frustration produce, within the sexual relationship itself, three pernicious consequences that Lucretius scathingly describes, appealing again to that combination of experience with detachment which we have found so persuasive.

First, these lovers suffer, in the act of lovemaking and in the larger relationship of which lovemaking is the center, from a continuous sense of frustration and non-fulfillment. This, Lucretius suggests, is an inevitable result of the impossibility of their project. Because they cannot devour and possess, they struggle ever more frenetically and insatiably to do so, spurred on and then left hungry by their illusory pictures of union:

> At last when, limbs clasped, they enjoy the flower of their maturity, when already the body can taste the joy ahead and Venus has reached the point of sowing seed in the woman's furrow, eagerly they nail their body to the other's and mingle the moisture of mouths and breathe deeply, clenching the other's lips in their teeth—all for nothing, since they cannot scrape

---

Greek by educated Romans, cf. Juvenal 6.187–96. On the relationship of this passage to Plato *Rep.* 474D, see Godwin (1986); Brown (1987) 128–32, 280–83.

[63] These points are common in ancient criticism of love: for two salient examples, see the first two speeches of Plato's *Phaedrus*. Brown (1987) 77ff. comments well on the passage's condemnation of love's obsessiveness: the main point, he argues, is "to expose the hollowness of a one-sided, materialistic relationship."

anything off, or penetrate and get their body lost in that body.[64] (1105–11)

Even at the best of times, in the midst of such pleasure as intercourse does offer, "some bitterness rises up to torment them even in the flower of their enjoyment" (1134). To the frustration caused by the impossibility of possession Lucretius now adds the closely allied frustration of jealousy—of a word that stabs like a weapon and lives, burning like a fire, in the heart (1137–38); of glances at others, or hidden smiles, that remind the lover of his incomplete possession (1139–40). These torments, as well as the simpler frustrations, arise from the lover's aim, which does not tolerate the other person's separate life.

And it is not surprising that his aim has bad consequences for the other person as well. The aim to possess leads to suspicious anxious behavior that can hardly be either pleasant or just to its object; it does not foster a disinterested concern for the object's good. The lover's obsessive focusing on his own aim and on the meaning of each casual remark or smile or glance for the status of that aim is not conducive even to a correct perception of the loved one's actual properties, much less to conduct that seeks the good of the other so qualified. The other disappears almost entirely, becoming merely a vehicle for the lover's personal wish and, at the same time, a permanent obstacle to its fulfillment. Even in the intimacy of intercourse, the real life of the other is ignored in the lover's frantic pursuit of his aim of union. For instead of thinking about his partner's experience and aiming at her separate pleasure, he devotes all his attention to the grabbing, biting, and scratching that are vain expressions of his desire to control and immobilize, and of the vindictive impulses produced in him by the pain of longing. The partner is punished, in effect, for her very otherness, for resisting an incorporation that would remove love's bondage:

> What they have grasped they press tight and cause pain to the body, and often drive their teeth into little lips and batter them with kisses, because their pleasure is not pure, and there are hidden stings that goad them to hurt that very thing, whatever it is, that is the source of those seeds of madness. (1079–83)[65]

---

[64] For further discussion, see chapter 7, where I argue that this is written from the point of view of males collectively. See also Brown (1987) ad loc.

[65] See Brown (1987) ad loc. for excellent discussion. He notes the harsh contrast between the diminutive noun (*labellis*) belonging to the language of love and the violent verbs. On the ambiguity of "they," here as in 1005ff., see chapter 7 n. 26, where I argue that it probably refers collectively to male lovers, not to pairs of male and female.

If she is going to go on feeling separately, if she obstinately resists being devoured, then pain is what she's going to feel.

This account of love's psychological consequences suggests one further criticism. Love's desires, it now appears, are not just painful for both lover and beloved, they are also self-defeating. For it appears that the desires generated by love's project of union lead to results that inhibit such union or harmony as might actually have been achieved; the jealous desires generated by the aim to possess lead to an increasingly agonized sense of non-possession, and to an increasing opposition between lover and beloved. In Book III, appropriately, Lucretius compares the lover's agonies to the punishment of Tityos in the underworld, as his liver is devoured by vultures; even so, the lover's own anxieties tear and devour him.

Finally, Lucretius argues, such a lover, armed with such aims and obsessed with the overestimation of the loved one that is a part of that project, will prove unable to tolerate the evidence of the woman's everyday bodily existence. This passage, which follows the satirical description of the lover's overestimation, forms the climax of the therapeutic argument, and it needs to be analyzed in detail:

> But let her be as fine of face as she can be and let the power of Venus arise from all her limbs, still . . . she does just the same in everything, and we know it, as the ugly, and reeks, herself, poor wretched thing, of foul odors, and her housemaids flee far from her and giggle in secret. But the tearful lover, turned away from her door, often smothers the threshold with flowers and garlands, and anoints the proud doorposts with marjoram, and plants kisses, poor wretch, on the door. Yet if he were finally let in, and if just one whiff of that smell should meet him as he came in, he would think up a good excuse to go away, and his deep-drawn lament, long planned, would fall silent, and on the spot he would condemn his own stupidity, because he sees that he has attributed more to her than it is correct to grant to any mortal. Nor are our Venuses in the dark about this. That's why they are all the more at pains to conceal the backstage side of their lives from those whom they want to keep held fast in love. All for nothing, since you can still drag it all into the light in your mind [animo], and look into the reasons for all this laughing, and, if she has a good mind [animo],[66] and is not spiteful, overlook all this in your turn, and yield to human life [humanis concedere rebus]. (1171, 1174–91)

[66] Bello animo here implies character as well as intellect; see also Brown (1987) 305. Bellus is pointedly transferred from its usual reference to physical beauty.

The passage begins like one more satirical maneuver. Appealing to ridicule and even disgust, it asks the lover to look behind love's radiant appearance to see what is really there. It tells him that if he does so, he will find things that repel him. We are now confronted with a stock scenario from Latin love poetry: the lover standing outside his mistress's door.[67] The reader is invited simultaneously to be that lover (since he has been promised an exposé of his own mistress's practices) and also to go behind the locked door where unadorned daily life is going on. In front of the door the lover places sweet smelling flowers on the posts and kisses the door his divine mistress has touched. Inside we find foul odors and knowing giggles. The reader's inside surrogates, the serving maids, free from all illusion, run off to avoid the odor and laugh at their mistress. It is clear that the only reason the lover behaves in that worshipful fashion is that he is not standing where they are. If he could go behind the scenes, he would quickly invent some excuse to go away, and he would forget his artfully composed speech of love. He would regret the time he spent in worshipful behavior, seeing that he has falsely attributed to this woman properties that do not belong to a mortal.

What is going on here? The passage has mystified commentators through the ages. Some of their more remarkable interpretations are ridiculed by Housman in a learned note whose sexual frankness is inseparable from its elegant Latinity.[68] Lambinus, he says, claims to be totally at sea. Two later commentators conjecture that the woman is dirty and is attempting to cover herself with perfume. But this cannot be right: as Housman points out, we are not talking here of the *immunda* and *fetida* whom the blind lover calls *acosmos*; we are talking about the one whom we have allowed to be as beautiful as a woman can be. Furthermore, putting on perfume could hardly be described as *se suffit . . . taetris odoribus* ("reeks . . . of foul odors"). Lachmann's conjecture is more remarkable still. The woman, he says, has been having intercourse with another lover, and wants to cover up *that* smell with perfume. As Housman says, *taetris* still presents difficulty on this reading, which, furthermore, attributes to the lover a most remarkable olfactory competence: "miror amatoris sagacitatem, qui una suffitamentorum aura offensus continuo intellegat amicam cum alio consuevisse."[69] Besides, the Lucretian lover's concluding reflection, that he has

---

[67] On this poetic convention, see Brown (1987) 297ff., with references, and especially Copley (1956).

[68] Housman (1972) 432–35.

[69] "I am amazed at the sharpness of the lover, who, struck by one whiff of those effusions, immediately guesses that his lover has had intercourse with someone else."

attributed to the woman more than it is appropriate to attribute to any mortal, fits badly with the suggestion that it is simply fidelity that he has falsely attributed to her. Housman concludes: "nimirum Lachmanno, vir sanctissimo, accidit ut in his vitae postscaeniis parum feliciter versaretur."[70]

What we need is an interpretation that makes sense of the fact that the odors coming from the woman are bad (*taetris*); that they are coming from her against her will (*miseram*, 1175, not undercut by *se suffit*, which means "covers herself with" in the sense of "exudes"); that the odors are natural (yielding to them means yielding to "human things"); that they are funny (the housemaids laugh); that the lover's romantic image of the woman excludes them. Housman's suggestion is that the woman is afflicted with flatulence.[71] (He elegantly expresses this thought in both Greek and Latin.) This fits the criteria rather well. The only problem is that this is not a particularly *female* affliction: and "she does just the same in everything as the ugly" suggests that a specifically female secret is being unmasked. Nor does flatulence seem the sort of predictable and lasting occurrence that could have led the woman to exclude the lover ahead of time. We might therefore conjecture[72] that what is at issue is the smells associated with the menstrual period—surely more difficult to control in times before disposable paper products, and the subject, in all times, of intense negative concern and superstitious misogynistic loathing. This conjecture would make more sense of the lover's period of exclusion, as also of the idea that the affliction is evidence of her female humanness. On this account, the servants are laughing because someone who gives herself airs and pretends to be a race above them is now clearly revealed to be exactly the same animal as they are.

A new alternative has now been proposed by Brown.[73] He suggests that *se suffit* refers to medical fumigation, widely practiced as a treatment for

[70] "Evidently Lachmann, that very pious man, had some rather unhappy experiences in this backstage side of life."

[71] Housman (1972); his view is accepted by Godwin (1986). One might compare Semonides fr. 7W on the weasel woman, who makes the man who comes near her sick. (Weasels were notorious for flatulence.) For more general complaints about women's smelliness, see Alcaeus 347.4, Aristophanes *Equ.* 1284–85, Juv. 6.131–32. For a number of these references I am grateful to Mary Lefkowitz.

[72] I advanced this interpretation independently when this chapter was first published as an article in 1989. I am indebted to Brown (1987) 296 for pointing out that it was also advanced, though without argument, in Brieger (1908) 1625: "Kein Mediziner wird hier etwas anderes finden als 'male olet ex mensibus.'" As a parallel Brieger cites Casanova, *Mémoires* II.1.

[73] Brown (1987) 296–97.

certain gynecological complaints. Fumes—sometimes containing bad smelling substances such as sulphur, urine, and excrement—were applied to the nostrils and, through a tube, to the vagina. Lucretius' point would then be that even the beautiful woman has bodily afflictions that lead her to use disgusting remedies. This reading seems to me possible—though I think it does less well than mine in explaining how every lover could be certain that his mistress produces the foul odors—for surely not all women regularly used these treatments. Furthermore, they are on this account *not* natural (although the complaints they address might be said to be). Nor does Brown have any cogent argument that *se suffit* must have the technical medical sense: he admits that in its one other occurrence in Lucretius (II.1098) it does not. And his evidence for the practices in question is mostly Greek rather than Roman. Still, if we accept his view, the basic point is close to the one I find: something about the way the female body typically works, once inspected, produces male disgust.

Whether we accept my suggestion or Brown's, or even Housman's, then, the girls laugh at the way in which nature gives the lie to their mistress's pretenses. The man, who has focused all the energy of his love on the denial of this woman's ordinary humanness, has or would have a far more profound reaction. Because he has worshiped at her door, because he has attributed to her more than it is just to attribute to a mortal, his reaction to this ordinary mortal event must be disillusionment, disgust, and repudiation. In this way, Lucretius continues, male illusion forces the female too to live a dishonest life, staging herself as in a theater, and concealing the stage machinery.[74] Since this lover has been brought up on myths of Venus, a Venus is what he must see.[75] And so the poor human women ("our Venuses," says Lucretius with irony) must strain to give him what he wants, even if it means concealing themselves.

But it doesn't work, Lucretius tells them. Even if you can't get into the house in fact, you can go backstage in your mind at any time, drag everything out into the light, and—

And what? We expect, if we have followed this far, that the next stage for the lover/reader will be rejection and disgusted scorn. The passage so far has had the deflationary and negative structure of the passage on made-up characteristics quoted earlier. And like that passage, which moves the lover from worship to ridicule, this one has moved him from obsessive love to scorn and disgust, from the ritual of adoration to a flight from bad odors.

---

[74] On the theatrical terminology, see Brown (1987) 303–4.
[75] See Brown (1987) 80 on "the theme of romantic apotheosis."

But: that is not where the therapeutic argument ends. The argument now takes a sudden and surprising turn, as the poet moves us beyond disgust as well, to an attitude altogether new: "If she has a good mind and is not spiteful, overlook all this in your turn, and yield to human life." *Humanis concedere rebus.*[76] How did we get to this point, from the moment of unmasking and disillusionment? And what does the cryptic advice mean?

What has happened, I think, is that Lucretius, by writing a surprise ending to the lover's story, has forced us to reflect on the oppositions contained within that story. He invites us to see that these opposites depend on one another. If there is no illusion, there is no moment of disillusionment. If there is no glamorous onstage show, there is no backstage that looks, by contrast, mean and poor. If the loved one is not turned into a goddess, there is no surprise and no disgust at her humanity. The really cured state would not be the state of the disgusted lover. It would be a condition beyond both obsession and disgust, in which the lover could see the beloved clearly as a separate and a fully human being, accurately take note of the good properties she actually does possess, and accept both her humanity and his own. Love's fantasies constrain and enclose both men and women, dooming the former to an exhausting alternation between worship and hatred, the other to a frantic effort of concealment and theater, accompanied by an equal hatred of everyday human things.[77] They are both in the grip of an old and deep picture, and until they stop seeing themselves in the terms of that picture, they will not have a chance to have a genuine human relationship.

The injunction to yield to human things is followed by an argument about female pleasure—a passage that has often been thought to be a loosely connected postscript. Bailey writes, "Lucretius now leaves the sarcastic comments on the passion of love and returns for the remainder of the book to certain physiological details."[78] But the passage on mutual pleasure is, on its face, no mere detail. The existence of female sexual pleasure is

---

[76] See Brown (1987) 306–7: "The condemnation of overconcession to a mortal is now replaced by a recommendation to make such concessions as the human condition calls for . . .; *humanus* is a warmer adjective than *mortalis* (1189) and this heightens the contrast."

[77] This argument, as I have interpreted it, can usefully be compared with the various arguments of Nietzsche in many works throughout his career concerning the way in which religion inspires intolerance of everyday bodily humanity, and concerning, also, the way in which a criticism of one pole of an opposition should end by freeing us altogether from our adherence to the polarities themselves, and the view of the world they construct.

[78] Bailey (1947) III.1312. Contrast Brown (1987) 60ff. and 307ff., who appropriately stresses the organic interconnectedness of the attack on love with this and other biological/psychological discussions.

argued for eloquently, with an appeal to the perspective of nature whose language, describing the behavior of animals, is deliberately close to the language that described the lovers in the passage immediately preceding (*Veneris compagibus haerent*, 1205, 1113). And the conclusion of the argument is asserted with as much rhetorical force as any conclusion in Lucretius: "Again and again I say, there is pleasure on both sides" (1207). Furthermore, we are invited to see the argument as tightly linked with what immediately precedes it. For it opens with a connective *nec*: "Nor does a woman always simulate pleasure." So: what is the point of the passage, and what the connection?

I believe that the passage is, in fact, very intimately linked to the preceding discussion of staging and unmasking, and that it is an application of the new positive attitude of acceptance and acknowledgment that Lucretius now recommends. In the religion of love, men are obsessed with aims that have little to do with *giving* pleasure. (Does a goddess have needs?) They go through intercourse in the grip of the picture of sublime union, mad with desire for a quasi-mystical experience in which there would be no separate pleasure of the woman to consider in any case, since at the climactic moment all sensations would be fused. This picture makes them forget, or actively deny, the fact that there is another separate sentient being there, whose pleasure is a separate thing and does count for something. Even the very rushed and frantic character of male sexual behavior, as Lucretius describes it, is badly suited to the fulfillment of another person's separate needs. But once we get rid of both divinization and the aim of fusion, the ground is clear for a new understanding of intercourse, one that makes its aim the giving and receiving of pleasure on both sides. It is only at this point in the poem, when human things have been accepted by the reader, and the woman is present to him as a whole human being, with a mind and body of her own, that the question of her pleasure can be fruitfully considered. And Lucretius tells us that, once we seriously consider it, we will find that in all nature this pleasure is evident and is essential to the explanation of animal behavior. For animals (this argument tacitly assumes) do not have the sick motives for intercourse that human women have: the aim to be seen as a goddess, the aim to get power over the man, the aim to get revenge for the denials men inflict on her. So if female animals engage in intercourse willingly, as they do, the explanation must be quite simply that they enjoy it.[79] And this motive is available to human beings too, once the therapeutic

---

[79] The enjoyment of the animals is obscured by Bailey's translation, which renders *retractat* (1200) as "accepts reluctantly" (III.1313). This, however, makes nonsense of *laeta* imme-

argument is complete. So it is one more advantage of Lucretian therapy that it clears the way for men and women to see something true about the bodies and responses of women, something that would not have been seen had therapy not prepared readers to see women, and men as well, in the perspective of nature.

These arguments are impressive. We tend sometimes to believe that it was the feminist movement in the 1960s that invented this critique of male behavior, of the roles it makes women assume, and of the connection between male illusion and an inept and ignorant treatment of women as sexual partners. We tend to think that female pleasure was a recent discovery, and the injunction to care about it as a separate thing, a contemporary feminist piece of advice. But in fact there is a long and rich debate on this subject in antiquity, a debate in which writers as disparate as Lucian and Ovid are active participants, defending relationships based upon mutual pleasure over one-sided relationships, and stressing that mutual pleasure is especially likely to occur in male-female (as opposed to male-male) relationships—if the capacity of the female for pleasure is sufficiently recognized.[80] Lucretius' critique of love seems to play a leading and formative

---

diately before. His slightly different translation in the facing-page version in vol. I, "with reluctant joy," makes it clear that he is having difficulty with the line. But here, as in the parallel passage at 1270, where what is at issue is the movements human women make out of pleasure during intercourse, Lucretius is describing the thrusting of the female away from the penis in order to receive its thrust again. Fitzgerald (1984) and Godwin (1986) both argue well that *re-tractare* should be regarded as having a double sense: both "withdraw" and "feel again." Godwin notes that *Venus* is used with the meaning "penis" at Martial 3.75.6, Juv. 2.167. Brown advances a similar view. He notes that *laeta* marks the equal sexual eagerness of the female. The talk of the "trap" of pleasure at 1207 does not undercut Lucretius' claim that the pleasure is real and mutual. As Godwin insists, we are meant to think not of any deception, but simply of "the closely locked position of the animals during intercourse." (We should also note, however, that there is some confusion in the text at this point. The order of the lines is uncertain, and the transition from *quod facerent numquam, nisi mutua gaudia nossent* to *quare etiam atque etiam, ut dico, est communi' voluptas* is smooth, and is disrupted by the presence of the intervening line.)

[80] On the pleasure of the female in intercourse, see (for a few characteristic examples) Aristophanes *Lys.* 163; Aristotle *GA* 727b9–10, 727b35–36, 739a29–35; Xen. *Symp.* 8.21; Ovid *Ars Amatoria* 682–84; Plut. *Mor.* 769EF; Lucian *Erotes* 27; Achilles Tatius 2.37. These and other related passages are discussed well in Halperin (1986, 1990), Brown (1987) 307–8. See also Dover (1974) 101, Pomeroy (1975) 146ff. Some of these passages (Xenophon, Ovid, and Lucian in particular) contrast heterosexual intercourse, in this respect, with male-male intercourse, where the younger is said not to derive any pleasure. On this see Dover (1978) especially 52, 91–103. Perhaps Lucretius' interest in mutual pleasure—in addition to his evident interest in marriage and children—helps to explain why male-male desire, after having been briefly introduced at 1053, is not mentioned in the rest of the book.

role in this tradition of argument, anticipating later arguments in every major point, and with greater depth, in that he traces the "diseased" form of erotic desire to a more fundamental denial, on both sides, of human things and human limits.

Book IV ends with a series of observations about marriage and fertility. And this is appropriate, in two ways. The social perspective that has been present since the poem's opening should return explicitly at this point, now that the perspective of nature has been duly investigated, reminding the reader of its requirements and assessing our developing account in the light of these. And it is only at this point in the poem that the social perspective can return. For love, as Lucretius has argued, is subversive of society: it engenders anxious cares that distract the lover from politics and community; and the relationship itself, with its instability and its mutual sadism, cannot be the basis for a marriage that would, by raising children in an atmosphere of tender concern, promote the ends of community. Marriage, as Book V shows, requires both stability and tenderness. And now we see that it requires something more. It requires the ability to see, every day, the other's daily "backstage" life, and to see this without disgust or even boredom, without a constant implicit contrast to some other wonderful excitement. To attend to the everyday, and to make it an object of delight. Of *voluptas*, intentional and mutual. The goal of Lucretian therapy is to make a good marriage possible.[81]

---

[81] See also Brown (1987) 87–91, 371–80, who correctly notes that the remarks about promiscuity at 1065–66 are a temporary expedient to break obsession's hold, not Lucretius' final positive recommendation. Twice during this discussion, Lucretius insists that a good marriage or long-term relationship requires discarding the *religion* of love: we should not believe that either conception or marital affection require divine interference (*nec divina . . . numina*, 1233; *nec divinitus*, 1278). There may seem to be a problem in reconciling these conclusions, and the section of the poem on which they are based, with Lucretius' later remarks about sex and fertility. For he urges the married lovers to adopt positions and motions that are most favorable for conception, and tells wives not to express pleasure (*laeta*, 1270) by wiggling motions that will prove contraceptive, presumably by causing the male to ejaculate outside the woman's body. These motions, he says, are chosen by prostitutes both for contraception and because they think men find gymnastics interesting—but "our wives" have no need of them. These observations might be taken as evidence that there is a tension among the ends pursued in marriage, and that mutual pleasure is to be subordinated to reproduction. This, I think, would be wrong. Lucretius plainly does not think these motions necessary for female pleasure—for he shows us the pleasure involved in reproductive animal intercourse. All he says is that prostitutes think they add to *male* pleasure; but the primary aim is contraception, and that is apparently why they try to give pleasure in that particular way. It would be implausible to suggest that mutual pleasure requires, or is even enhanced by, *coitus interruptus*. Brown (1987) 361–62, cites the evidence for *coitus interruptus* and other

The end of Book IV may strike the reader as boring. It says that a woman who is not divinely beautiful can still be loved—and not by divine interference. You just get used to her and learn to value her, her deeds, her efforts, the habits of sharing daily life with her. The poet leaves us with a question: doesn't habit affect desire in just the way that water wears away a rock (1278–87)?

This ending is likely to startle and disappoint. For although it is in the style of many naturalistic explanations elsewhere in the poem, it is singularly lacking in poetic appeal if we are expecting love poetry of the traditional sort. In fact, we notice that its simple naturalistic image rewrites the dramatic imagery of love poetry: instead of love's drop of chill care, we have a drop of fluid that works slowly and undramatically,[82] effecting its positive result by means that have little to do with the traditional poetic intensities of love. Memmius would expect a poem about love to end with a death; or with anger and bitterness: at the very least with some strong upsurge of intense joy. We wonder what it means that Lucretius leaves him like this, with words that do not even impress us as effective poetry, since they are not particularly arresting, or vivid, or dramatic. As readers, we begin to become aware of our own problematic relationship to our everyday life and its routines—including its routines of affection and concern. We begin to see the way interest in these daily repeated patterns is undercut by romantic longing and by the poetic language in which that is so frequently expressed and taught. I shall soon return to this topic.

This therapeutic argument has many traits in common with the model of Epicurean therapy described in chapter 4. But its multiperspectival character has given it, as I already suggested, a dialectical openness that did not seem characteristic of Epicurus' own procedure, so far as we were able to reconstruct it there. Lucretius has led us through alternative ways of viewing and characterizing sexual phenomena; and he has even considered, with considerable power, the view of the opposition. Without arousing or instilling the very emotions he criticizes, he has shown us the life of love in vivid and intimate detail, and shown us something of what it is like to live that life. This procedure, like the use of multiple perspectives in general, gives his argument dialectical power.

---

related contraceptive practices in antiquity, though he nonetheless—I think without sufficient argument—reads the passage as subordinating other sexual goals to reproduction. For the proverbial gymnastic practices of ancient prostitutes, see references to the visual evidence in Winkler (1990) and Halperin (1990); one may well doubt whether any woman in the bizarre positions often depicted on vase paintings could be experiencing any pleasure other than that of athletic accomplishment.

[82] See Brown (1987) 64–65, 378–79.

And its dialectical character, itself perhaps a departure from Epicurus, leads it to some apparently non-Epicurean conclusions. For its concerns for the social perspective leads it to take up a position on marriage and on sexual intercourse that is decidedly more positive than Epicurus', just as Book V is, for similar reasons, more positive on children. These "distractions" are now held to be very valuable; indeed they may even be given intrinsic worth here, as expressions of our political nature. Furthermore, this new attachment to marriage and the family leads Lucretius to defend as valuable a way of life that does not seem to be the one best suited for individual *ataraxia*, since it includes many risks and possibilities for loss and grief. Far from being value-relative in any viciously circular way, these arguments investigate as openly as many of Aristotle's the pupil's own conception of the parts of human happiness, asking—apparently without any prior acceptance of individual *ataraxia* as the supreme value—just what living well consists in.[83] This same tension exists clearly, in Epicurus' account of *philia*, as we shall see further in chapter 7. But by describing a marital relationship that is, in effect, a form of *philia*, Lucretius has considerably widened the sphere of the good person's need and interdependency. One could not claim that the Epicurean commitment to *ataraxia* does not color and shape many aspects of Lucretius' argument; and chapter 6 will show just how deep this commitment is. But the arguments concerning love, especially where they seem to depart from Epicurus, seem independent of a narrow commitment to that end, and seem dedicated to a dialectical consideration of certain putative constituents of the human end. And this new openness about the contents of the end—expressed and also further produced by the dialectical openness of the procedure—seems to give Lucretius' argument a very strong claim to be rational, and to be doing methodological justice to deep-seated intuitions about the ethical value of practical reason.

We have, then, an argument that is both radical and rational; that asks us to alter our beliefs through a process of rational criticism. The critique is, like an Aristotelian critique, internal: it appeals, throughout, to the pupil's own experienced sense of life. And yet it leads to conclusions that would have been accepted by very few readers at the start, conclusions that look radical even in our own time. If we have allowed the argument to work with us, we now stand differently toward some of our most cherished beliefs, and to the cultural paradigms of love that are their basis.

---

[83] Here Lucretius' Romanness makes itself felt more keenly than elsewhere in the poem. He is clearly thinking of Roman ideals of marriage and is not even attempting to discuss marriage as Epicurus would have known it. On this, see Classen (1968) 342; and, on the positive elements in the marriage discussion, see Betensky (1980), Brown (1987) 87–91.

X

What are we to make of this: how good are these arguments? And how can lovers of love attempt to answer them? Lucretius' general account of the relationship between emotions and stories is, I think, a very powerful one. Lucretius deepens the Epicurean account of emotion and belief when he claims that the beliefs that ground emotions are frequently taught through stories, pictures, poems—through representations to which we later refer, using them as paradigms that guide our understanding of the signs we perceive in life. Especially as an analysis of the origin and nature of love, this account in terms of stories and their stereotypes is persuasive. And yet the partisan of love will raise some objections.

Lucretius argues that the central aim of people in love, the aim that they are trying to gratify in intercourse, is union or fusion with the beloved. This diagnosis is a central part of his argument, as we have seen. But is he correct? There is every reason to think that he is correct about love's frequent overestimation of its object, and the problems attendant on that. But is love really, in its nature, based, as well, upon the idea of fusion? We could grant to Lucretius that this mistake is sometimes made, and yet insist that the proper or true aim of love, an aim well expressed in lovemaking, is not fusion, but intimate responsiveness. What the lover wants is to be extremely close to the person he or she loves, to be close enough to perceive and respond to every movement and every perceptible sign. In that closeness, the lover wants to achieve the other person's pleasure and his or her own—and, at the same time, to achieve a kind of knowledge of the other person, the sort of knowledge that consists in awareness and acknowledgment of every perceptible portion of that person's activity. For this sort of intimate responsiveness, fusion or union is neither necessary nor sufficient. Not necessary, because lovers can respond to one another as separate persons, without ever denying that they must always remain apart. (And respond better, in fact, if they do not distract themselves from the project of attending and responding with fantasies of fusion or union.) Not sufficient, because even if a lover could, *per impossibile*, take his lover's body and mind into himself, making them parts of him, that would be, precisely, not to respond to them as hers, not to seek to please her as someone with a separate life, whose projects and aims are distinct from his own, whose inner awareness of life is forever beyond his reach. The same can be said of the knowledge of one another that lovers seek to achieve. Fusion would be neither necessary nor sufficient for it, since it is a kind of attunement to the separate, not a having of the same. It is, we might argue, this desire for closeness, attunement, and responsiveness that explains the way lovers hold, bite, and squeeze one another—not the impossible thought of union or fusion. We do not need to posit that error, even at the unconscious level.

This objection says important, and rather Lucretian, things about love and sexual intimacy. But is it really an objection to Lucretius? Lucretius does not say that the fusion error is necessary to intercourse. Indeed, he denies this. Nor does he say that it is necessary to a concerned and affectionate relationship between a man and a woman who are sexually attracted. This, again, in his portrait of a "cured" sexuality, he denies. What he is saying is that lovers for whom deep need of another is felt as torment and unmanly weakness will seek to defeat the separateness that gives rise to their weakness, and will believe that they can achieve this through sexual incorporation. He suggests that this error is the best explanation for the jealousy and sadism that impair many erotic relationships, and also for the male's frequent neglect or denial of the woman's pleasure. Is he wrong about this? Like Proust, whose Marcel keeps Albertine a prisoner and wishes to immobilize her completely, hating the pain of need she awakens in him, Lucretius sees that human beings (and perhaps especially males in cultures that associate masculinity with self-sufficiency) find it difficult to be needy, and wish to punish the source of their incompleteness. The fact that this is not a universal or necessary truth about human love should not mask from us the depth and the pervasiveness of the phenomenon he describes. Lucretius could cite further evidence to show this—not only the countless instances of jealous possessive self-centered behavior that make up much of love's history, but also the total denial, by whole societies and groups, of the reality of female pleasure, even in the face of the evidence from nature that Lucretius himself brings forward, evidence that anyone who looks can see. This corruption of perception is surely connected with fear of female separateness; it is just a more sophisticated and unconscious version of practices of mutilation through which other societies continue to express the desire that the woman should have no separate pleasure, but should be simply a part or extension of the male, completely controlled by him. By connecting the lover's error to the infliction of pain, Lucretius' argument suggests a persuasive diagnosis of much of male violence toward women, and even of violent pornography, which is frequently obsessed with the idea that the woman should be converted into a machine for the use and control of men.

Lucretius is right: the history of our failures to attend to the humanity of those we love is long, as long as our unwillingness to live as incomplete beings. [84] The account of love's aim that he offers as a replacement for the love error is the one my imaginary objector has also put forward. If the objector can accept that account and live with it, then he does not need Lucretius' argument; he is, to that extent, cured. But as a cured person he should endorse the argument as an argument that most people need to consider.

And yet there remains something disturbing about Lucretius' account. The poem insists that with the removal of illusion all the mystery, wonder, and more than daily excitement of *erōs* must go. Lucretius seems to believe that these come entirely from quasi-religious illusions and from hatred of one's personal neediness Cured, he suggests, we will have deliberately arranged will-governed friendships, with sexual pleasure and child-rearing added in; these will contain the risks and vulnerabilities proper to friendship, but no deeper erotic excitement.

In other words, Lucretius fails to ask whether there might not be intense excitement and beauty precisely in being needy and vulnerable before a person whom one loves. He fails to ask whether a certain sort of deep sexual excitement might not come precisely from the surrender of control and the acceptance of the intense importance of another separate person for one's entire life. This was already seen by Plato in the *Phaedrus*, I think, in his insistence that love's beauty consists in part in its "madness," in its sense of being taken out of one's own control, and in the experience of receptivity to the influence of the other over all of one's body and soul. In such a love, the separateness of the other person is not hated and opposed; it is made, at one and the same time, the source of risk and the source of joy. Nor, in such a love, are the particular characteristics of the other person ignored or deformed: for the joy Plato describes consists precisely in being receptive to a person whom one sees as good and as aiming at one's own good in certain ways. The accurate perception and the mutual generosity of these lovers are central constituents of their passionate arousal.

If Lucretius cannot envisage this possibility, and I think it is plain that he cannot, it may well be because he has not seen his therapeutic idea through to the end. The people he criticizes are doomed, in love, by their obsession with completeness and control. But cured Epicureans still cling to these goals. They may not insist on controlling and immobilizing their erotic partners. But this is not because they have actually learned to be humanly incomplete and needy without resentment; it is, I think, because they have become internally godlike in the Epicurean way, with no deep needs from

---

[84] For related observations, see Cavell (1969, 1979).

the world or from one another. What neither the sick patient nor the cured pupil have found, it seems, is a way in which being simply human can be a source of erotic joy.

And this sheds light, too, on Lucretius' relationship to his own poetic tradition. The suggestion of his flattened anti-poetic poetry is that once the illusions of love are removed, there is no love poetry to write. There is no positive literary account of the interest and excitement of a good Epicurean marriage to offer—presumably because it would contain too little drama and too little affect. But one might question this: for one might recall the remarkable literary power of the *Phaedrus'* description of the power and joy of a long-lasting erotic love that is free from the desire to control or incorporate. One might consider the way in which much of the most powerful erotic writing in the Western tradition, from John Donne through Emily Brontë and beyond, focuses on the experience of exposure, need, and receptivity, seeing that itself as a source of erotic excitement and wonder. (And perhaps the joy derives precisely from the fact that, in a love of this sort, one reconfigures as generous and benign a neediness that in childhood is at first experienced as terror.) Lucretius cannot understand this joy: for, in the end, he is an Epicurean, and as an Epicurean, he cannot permit himself, beyond a certain point, to follow his own advice to "yield to human life." Such neediness before the world would be hateful and terrible to the Epicurean. He does not yield; he demands the life of a self-sufficient god. He says, "I have gotten in ahead of you, O Tuchē, and I have built up my fortifications against all your stealthy attacks."[85] Is this the attitude of a cured lover, or is it simply a new form of the disease that Lucretius' therapy was supposed to cure?

[85] *VS* 47; see chapter 4, p. 121.

✳ CHAPTER 6 ✳

Mortal Immortals: Lucretius on Death
and the Voice of Nature

Mortals [are] immortal, immortals mortal, alive with respect to
mortals' death, dead with respect to their life.

Heraclitus

Divinity must live within herself:
Passions of rain, or moods in falling snow;
Grievings in loneliness, or unsubdued
Elations when the forest blooms; gusty
Emotions on wet roads on autumn nights;
All pleasures and all pains, remembering
The bough of summer and the winter branch.
These are the measures destined for her soul.

Wallace Stevens, "Sunday Morning," II

I

EPICURUS WRITES: "The correct recognition that death is nothing to us makes the mortality of life enjoyable, not by adding on an infinite time, but by removing the longing for immortality" (*LMen* 132).

But Nikidion might think incorrectly. For she might, as often happens, take a walk at dawn in the early spring. She might feel the knifelike beauty of the morning. See leaves half unrolled, translucent, their sharp green still untouched by life; the sun striking sparkles on the moving surface of a stream. And she would listen, then, in the silence to the sweet and deadly music of time.

Images summoned by the smell of new spring air might spin before her then, crowding and overlapping: images of faces loved and mourned, of childhood and home, of play and hope and new desire. She would see that morning through the images, until each tree looked not only like itself but like many things that are gone, and each of her steps was taken in company with the dead. The beauty of things would appear to her under the aspect of mourning, and become, for this reason, the more beautiful and lordly, the more human, the more terrible. She walks, in time, exile from a thousand times, transient on the way to no time at all. No animal could see so beautiful a morning.

If Nikidion saw and felt all this, she might also wish to immobilize the present moment, to fix or devour it—indeed, to hold and seize each thing and activity and beauty that she loves. For it occurs to her that no human being is ever really in possession of any joy at all, not even during a moment. A moment is itself the gathering place for a thousand other moments, not one of which can be inhabited again; it is also composed of projects that point beyond it to moments not known. Even as itself, each time is vanishing as one tries to grasp it. And any one of the projects that inhabit these moments can at any point be cut short, made vain and pointless, by the world, closing itself against her totally as it has closed already on so much that she has loved and will not do again. Death appears to her as the limiting constraint, the culmination of temporal losses. She sees that she will do the things she loves only a small and finite number of times more. Some she will not finish doing, even once. It is beauty itself, and the sense of joy, that make these thoughts so terrible to her; and the thought of the end flows terribly back upon the experience of beauty, making it keener and more astonishing.

This condition does not seem to her acceptable. It is an illness that must, she thinks, have a cure. Perhaps some deeper grasp, some more profound reflection, would protect her. Perhaps indeed there is some way to freeze all of life within life; to immobilize the most important things, and to rise above this condition of abject helplessness before time; to create, within mortal life, some analogue of a god's non-finite completeness. Above all, not to be at the mercy of the thought of death.

It seems to her that philosophy ought to contain the answer to this problem.

The first humans, as Lucretius describes them, found life sweet. They left the "sweet light of life" with sadness and looked to that departure with fear (V.988–93). The love of life, Lucretius claims, is natural in all sentient creatures, and so all creatures go to death with reluctance. But these first humans do not stop, as she has stopped, to reflect on their finitude. They do not wonder about their own fragility, or find agony in the mere knowledge of the "mortality of life." The Epicurean gods, on the other side, have reflection without vulnerability, thought about the universe without anxious fear and concern. In between are actual human beings, the only beings both vulnerable and reflective, who go through life in the grip of a fear of the natural condition of their own existence, straining to understand and also to improve their condition through the reflective capacity that is also the source of much of their agony. Lucretius' ambition is to show Nikidion a way in which reflection on death can remove fear and the sense of fragility, rather than increasing them: to take her, by therapeutic argument, from that spring morning to a position like that of the gods, untroubled by change, understanding and accepting the ways of nature.

Lucretius (or rather the poet-speaker in his poem) is no stranger to Nikidion's experience. In fact, this speaker refers to similar moments twice, in terms that suggest an acquaintance with their power. And yet the tone of both references is scathing and critical. Once he speaks of a man who gets drunk and then begins to weep, saying, "We poor little humans [*homullis*] have only a brief enjoyment [*fructus*] here. Soon it has already been, and one cannot call it back" (III.914–15). This man says what most of us seriously believe—yet he speaks in a silly, sloppy, drunken way, like someone out of control of himself and his thought. Lucretius suggests that the thought of life's brevity is self-indulgent, sloppy, self-pitying thought; he urges the reader to view it with detachment and distaste. Later, again, the poet speaks of the way in which people

> feed, always, the ungrateful nature of the mind[1] and fill it with good things, but never satisfy it—as the seasons of the year do, when they come round again, bringing their new growth and their varied delights; nor are we ever filled up with the fruits [*fructibus*] of life. (1003–7)

This is Nikidion's experience: and the poet lets the reader know that he has known it. And yet he stands aside from it now, detached, critical of the sense of life from which it springs. We must try to discover how the poet-speaker can know these moments so well and yet mock them, how philosophy has taken him beyond them, to a place in which he claims to find both a divine life and a life according to nature.

I shall focus here on this dual aim of Lucretius' Epicurean therapy: the aim to make the reader equal to the gods and, at the same time, to make him[2] heed nature's voice. We shall see that these two aims are actually in a profound tension with one another; and I shall make a proposal for the resolution of that tension. In the process, I shall need to investigate the suggestion planted in my description of Nikidion's experience: that much

---

[1] Throughout I translate *animus* as "mind"; occasional occurrences of *mens* are also so translated, but with the Latin given in parentheses.

[2] Once again, as in chapter 5, I shall focus on the way the poem addresses itself to its male interlocutor; but I shall not ignore the implications for Nikidion's therapy. Gender differences do not seem to play a role in Epicurean diagnosis of the fear of death.

of the human value of human experience is inseparable from the awareness of vulnerability, transience, and mortality.

II

How bad is the fear of death? It is the job of Epicurean argument to remove false beliefs and the desires that causally depend on them. But Epicureans do not go about removing any and every false belief the pupil might have. They focus on beliefs that impede flourishing. We need natural philosophy only insofar as we are impeded; falsity will count as disease only if it can be shown to block *eudaimonia*. If Nikidion falsely believes that the ratio between a circle's circumference and its diameter is 3.14152, rather than 3.14159, this is not likely to become a major target of therapy.

But the fear of death (and the associated longing for indefinite prolongation of life) are alleged by Epicureans to have a violently disturbing and impeding role. "In its empty way it causes pain," writes Epicurus in the *Letter to Menoeceus* (125). The many fear death as the "most terrifying of evils" (125), and this belief about its supreme badness allegedly causes disturbances that are correspondingly great. Philosophical reasoning, the letter continues, has as its task to "drive out those beliefs from which the greatest upheaval seizes the soul." Lucretius speaks even more strongly:

> That fear of Acheron must be hurled out headlong, that fear which shakes human life at its very foundations, covering everything over with the blackness of death, and which does not leave any pleasure fluid and pure. (III.37–40)

Lucretius' complex diagnosis of this fear's disturbing effects is a very important part of his argument against it. For he wishes to show that its consequences are so bad and so pervasive that we have reason to get rid of it even independently of its false basis: indeed, that it is a central cause in many of the worst human ills.

To establish this, the Epicurean doctor cannot simply look at what most people say about their lives when asked for their ordinary intuitions. For most people, as Lucretius recognizes, do not admit to a fear of death—and there is no reason to think these denials insincere, as far as they go. Those who do admit to the fear will not concede that it plays a very influential role in their lives. Nikidion may confront the fear of death on a certain sort of spring day; she will be unlikely to admit that it is with her in most of her actions. So if the Epicurean teacher wants to establish the badness and causal power of the fear of death, giving Nikidion a diagnosis that will motivate her to seek his treatment, he must elaborate a conception of fear (and the beliefs that ground it) that does not make fear simply identical with conscious fearful sensations and thoughts. He must present an argument that will convince the pupil to acknowledge the presence, and the causal role, of unconscious elements in fear, connecting them to perceived bad things in a compelling way.

Lucretius undertakes this task in the complex diagnostic portion of his argument. Recall that a central difficulty for the Epicurean doctor is, frequently, to convince the pupil of the existence and the gravity of her illness.[3] It was to this end that the teacher would undertake a prolonged and systematic examination of the pupil's soul, urging her to bring all her symptoms, her thoughts, desires, and activities, into the open before him. In Lucretius' treatment of the fear of death, we have our clearest example of the way in which such a diagnosis would proceed.[4]

The diagnostic argument has four parts:

1. A description of a pattern of behavior that seems to lack adequate explanation. It will be argued that the most powerful explanation of these symptoms is fear of death.

2. A description of a subjective condition which, although not consciously felt as fear, lacks, as described, adequate explanation. Again, it will be argued that the fear of death is the best explanation of these inner symptoms.

3. A description of occasions of confession or acknowledgment: situations in which the patient, dropping her habitual defenses, will grant that fear is in fact what she feels.

4. In the background, a normative picture of the healthy unconstrained person, a person whose life is not burdened by fear and who lacks, in consequence, the bad symptoms associated with it.

Let us examine each of these parts of the argument in turn, seeing how they give rise to Lucretius' powerful explanatory hypothesis.

The *behavioral symptoms* are many and diverse; and their evident bad-

---

[3] This evidence is not discussed by Segal (1990), who argues that Lucretius' vivid portrayal of the anxieties and pains of dying derives from his poetic background and goals, and is in tension with his philosophical mission. I believe that Lucretius' vivid use of language is clearly in harmony with Epicurean practices of therapeutic argument.

[4] This material concerning the unconscious is present only in Lucretius; but there are reasons to suppose that the recognition of unconscious beliefs and desires belongs to Epicurus as well—cf. chapter 4 ; the presence of similar material in the *Axiochus* (see further) confirms this.

ness plays a central role in getting Nikidion to identify the fear that causes them as disease. They can be divided, in turn, into four distinct categories.

First, the fear of death produces subservience to religious beliefs and religious authorities. This bad consequence of the fear of death is identified from the poem's very opening, with its grim account of the sacrifice of Iphigenia (I.80ff.). It is seen to be very prevalent in human life. Its role is stressed again in Book III, as Lucretius tells us how unhappy people, wandering far from their homes, still cling desperately to religious custom:

> And wherever these wretched people go they sacrifice and slaughter black cattle and send them to the spirits of the world below, and in adverse fortune turn their minds far more sharply to religion. (III.51–54)

Religious belief is bad, Lucretius persistently argues, because it is superstitious and irrational, built upon false and groundless beliefs about the gods and the soul. It is also bad because it makes people dependent upon priests, rather than on their own judgment. And priests stimulate human fears further, increasing dependence (I.102ff.). It is bad, above all, because it causes people to harm one another, committing "criminal and impious deeds" (I.82–83)—for example, Agamemnon's slaughter of his own child.

Second, the fear of death interferes with the enjoyment of such pleasures as mortal human life does offer. We have already seen that Epicurus believes we must banish this fear in order to make "the mortality of life enjoyable": and Lucretius has claimed that the fear interferes with life from its foundation on up, leaving no pleasure undisturbed. He shows us, too, people who never find satisfaction in any activity, since no activity succeeds in gratifying their thirst for immortal existence (III.1003ff.), and people who move on from a hatred of the end of life to a hatred of life itself:

> And often, on account of the fear of death, such a hatred of life and of seeing the light seizes human beings that, in their state of agony, they commit suicide, forgetting that it is this fear that is the source of their anguish. (III.79–82)

We saw the germs of this agony in Nikidion. Lucretius' claim is that, unchecked, it poisons everything as life goes on.

Closely connected to this is a kind of aimless and restless frenetic activity that has no point at all, other than the avoidance of one's own self and one's own finite condition:

> If only human beings, just as they seem to feel a weight in their minds that wears them out with its heaviness, could also grasp the causes of this and know from what origin such a great mountain of ill stands on their chest,

they would hardly lead their lives as we now often see them do, ignorant of what they really want, and always seeking a change of place as if they could put down their burden. Here's a man who often goes outside, leaving his house, because he's tired of being home. Just as suddenly he turns back, since he feels no better outdoors. He rushes off in haste to his country house, bringing his slaves, as if the house were burning down and he had to bring help; he turns back again, as soon as he touches the threshold; or, heavy, he seeks forgetfulness in sleep; or, full of haste, he charges back to the city. Thus each person flees himself. But in spite of all his efforts he clings to that self, which we know he never can succeed in escaping, and hates it—all because he is sick and does not know the cause of his sickness. (1053–70)

This symptom is closely connected to the preceding one, since self-avoidance, proving, as it always does, impossible, generates self-destructive rage. Notice, here, that Lucretius is claiming that the unconscious nature of the disease is a large part of its destructive power. Awareness is already progress toward cure.

Finally, and very ambitiously, Lucretius links the fear of death with a large number of activities destructive either of self or of others, all of which allegedly give expression to a thirst for some sort of continued existence: "These wounds of life," he writes, "are fed in no small part by the fear of death" (III.36–40). The greedy accumulation of wealth makes its possessor feel further from death, since poverty seems to be a slipping toward death (59–67). The same can be said for the "blind lust for honors and power" (60) in which people pursue an immortality of reputation. These two passions, in their turn, cause many criminal acts, ruptures in families, enviousness of others, betrayals of friendship, betrayals of civic duty (III.59ff.).

This bad behavior is in many cases not accompanied by a subjective awareness of fear. But the symptoms do have their *subjective side*. Lucretius here puts before us people who never experience unalloyed enjoyment; who feel driven and stung by an "unseen goad beneath their heart" (873–74); who feel a weight in their soul, a mountain of misfortune sitting on their chest. And, feeling this, they also feel that they must do what they can to throw it off—whether through crime, through an exhausting round of empty diversions, or through sleep and oblivion. So it is crucial to Lucretius' diagnosis that the subjective condition of the patient is, if not readily identifiable as fear, still painful and debilitating, and intelligibly seen as the cause of bad actions.

By bringing together this collection of symptoms, outer and inner, and by showing persuasively how they might be understood to be caused by the fear of death—whereas, as described, they appear to lack any other adequate explanation—Lucretius has advanced a forceful theoretical hypothesis that might well convince the pupil just on account of its simplicity and its power. But this is not the full extent of his diagnostic argument. And this is fortunate: for without any further evidence such an all-purpose explanation for human miseries might seem unconvincing. The further evidence comes from a valuable source, the patient. For Lucretius claims that the same people who usually deny that they fear death, or that this fear plays a large role in their lives, can be brought to see this and acknowledge it, under certain circumstances. The correctness of the explanatory hypothesis is established by the fact that the patient herself will vouch for its truth:

> It is more in times of danger that one can really look into a person and know, in his adversity, who he is: for then, at last, the true voices are drawn forth from the depth of the breast. The mask is torn off; the fact remains. (III.55–58)

A similar argument can be found in the Pseudo-Platonic dialogue *Axiochus*,[5] which can be traced (in part) to Epicurean origins. Axiochus has spent most of his life denying that death is bad, even denying this with the aid of philosophical argument. But, he says, "now that I am right up against the fearful thing, my brave and clever arguments steal off and breathe their last" (365B–C). The Epicurean claim is that such moments of direct confrontation with the facts of our human situation are moments of truth. We can rely on the statements produced in such moments, when the life is laid bare to its own inspection by the force of an event (or imminent event) whose sharpness simply cuts through habits and rationalizations. And these statements are taken to be accurate, not only about that moment's condition, but about what has been the case all along in the person's soul. Epicurus' attack on the deluding power of habit and convention is linked, plausibly enough, to a belief in the veracity of that which emerges when habit is suddenly broken down and the soul is left raw and unprotected, simply perceiving itself. In this he resembles Proust; and his argument has comparable psychological power.

These three parts of the diagnosis—outer symptoms, inner symptoms, and moments of acknowledgment—are now drawn together by the explanatory hypothesis: it is our fear of leaving life and its good things that produces so much evil and distress. Despite the difficulties attaching to any

---

[5] On the *Axiochus* and its authorship, see Furley (1986), and the edition by Hershbell (1981).

such global explanation, I think we should view the Epicurean hypothesis with sympathy both because of its psychological plausibility and because of the complex argument through which he has commended it to us. This hypothesis is linked to a vague and as yet unspecified conception of a *human health* that is not plagued by these ills, a condition that Nikidion can imagine as possible for herself, and in contrast to which she will view her present condition as diseased. It may have been a central job of Epicurean confession to show her the pattern of her symptoms, together with the hypothetical explanation, and to provoke a confrontation of the sort that would allow the "true voices" to be heard. Such a confrontation would naturally be accompanied by a portrayal of the *eudaimonia* that a cured Epicurean can achieve.

It is important to grasp the relationship of this diagnosis to the religious beliefs it criticizes. One might suppose that, for Epicureans, the fear of death is the creation of religious teaching, and that it does not exist in the natural prereligious condition of human life. Frequently Lucretius' arguments are, in fact, portrayed as if their target were religion alone, and as if a sufficient cure for the fear were a rejection of religion.[6] The text refutes this. Book III already suggests that the dependence on religion is a consequence of the fear of death, not fear's origin. And Book V explicitly confirms this. In the course of criticizing the hypothesis that the gods created the world, Lucretius asserts that the love of continued life is universal in living things: "Whatever has been born must naturally desire to remain in life, as long as sweet enjoyment [*blanda voluptas*] holds on to it" (177–78). His later account of the first humans confirms this: for before religion's origin they hate death, and die with reluctance:

> Nor was it much more common then than now for mortals to leave the sweet light of life with laments. For then, each one of them, caught, used to provide living food to the beasts, devoured by their teeth. And, seeing his own guts buried in a living grave, a person would fill up the groves and mountains with lamenting. (988–93)[7]

Indeed, he later argues, it is men's perception of their own vulnerability before death, and their perception that the gods lack their own weakness and fear (*mortis timor*, 1180) that is one of the primary causes of the invention of worship and religious subservience.

Lucretius tells us that religion has made our relation to our death far worse than it was before, filling us with terror of the afterlife and causing us

---

[6] See, for example, Shibles (1974).

[7] Translation cannot convey the gripping alliteration of the original: *viva videns vivo sepeliri viscera busto.*

to become far weaker than we already were, as "a certain hidden force saps human affairs" (V.1233–34). He tells us that the first humans, while they feared and lamented, did not engage in the ambitious schemes of military conquest and seafaring through which contemporary man tries to grasp immortality (V.949–1006). But the fact remains that the fear was there before, as a direct response to the natural love of life and to our human sense of life's beauty and value. Thus, in extinguishing fear Lucretius cannot claim simply to be returning human beings to some uncorrupted pre-religious condition or, as in the case of love, to be undoing deep religious/cultural constructs. He must acknowledge that he is attacking a deep and fundamental part of "natural" human life, a part closely related, as he himself stresses, to the structure of the human sense of value. This sense of value is empirical and not a priori, clearly: it is a response to human experience of the world. And yet it lies deeper than any particular culture, deeper even, apparently, than culture itself; deeper, then, than the errors that culture manufactures. This means, as well, that Lucretius' arguments will not be truly therapeutic if they deal only with those errors about death that have their origin in cultural or religious teaching—in a concern about the afterlife, or the fiction of posthumous survival. Such arguments would not even remove religion, since its underlying causes would be left in place. His therapy must also deal with what Plutarch calls "the longing for being, the oldest and greatest of all forms of *erōs*" (*Non Posse* 1104C). And in dealing with this longing they must focus above all on our relation to the things we love and find delightful: for our fear is, above all, a fear of losing, as Axiochus says, "this light and the other good things" (365 B–C). Fear is a response to value.

III

Lucretius' poem contains three central arguments aimed at showing the reader that it is irrational to fear death. The first and most important is also found in Epicurus, and is the explanation of the famous Epicurean claim that "death is nothing to us." It goes as follows:

1. An event can be good or bad for someone only if, at the time when the event is present, that person exists as a subject of at least possible experience, so that it is at least possible that the person experiences the event.[8]

---

[8] On experience and possible experience, see the sympathetic and lucid reconstruction of Epicurus' argument in Rosenbaum (1986). Epicurus sometimes seems to state premise 1 in terms of actual experiences (e.g., *KD* 2, perhaps *LMen* 124); but *LMen* 125's famous formu-

2. The time after a person dies is a time at which that person does not exist as a subject of possible experience.

3. Hence the condition of being dead is not bad for that person.

4. It is irrational to fear a future event unless that event, when it comes, will be bad for one.[9]

5. It is irrational to fear death.

Much of the poem's attention is devoted to establishing premise 2, by showing that the person, identified with a certain complex of body and soul, must end his or her career at death. This argument is important to both Epicurus and Lucretius, since it is sufficient to remove fear of the afterlife, which, in their view, plays a large part in the fear of death. But Lucretius is aware that there are many people who believe in the mortality of the person and who nonetheless fear death. To these he commends his first premise. Many such people, he perceptively points out, are in the grip of an inconsistent mental picture of death. Although they actually believe that the person ends at death, they also imagine a surviving subject who is pained and grieved by damage to his corpse, and by the loss to himself of the good things in life—of children, home, various delights and activities (III.870–911). The basis for the subject's grief is that he is dead; yet, by imagining himself grieving, he endows himself with life. It is Lucretius' suggestion that only such an illogical fiction, subconsciously held (*inscius*

---

lation, "When death is there, we are not, and when we are there, death is not," makes, it seems, the stronger claim that the subject is not there at all, as a subject of even possible *aisthēsis*; and we could take *LMen* 124's "Death is the privation of *aisthēsis*" to be making this stronger point as well. Lucretius' argument concentrates on establishing the stronger claim: it is not only actual perception that is extinguished by death, it is the very possibility that this subject could ever, under any circumstances, exist again as a subject of experience numerically identical with the former subject (esp. III.845–69). Epicurus' argument, to be plausible, requires a focus on this stronger claim: for if he is taken to insist that nothing can be good or bad for one who does not have actual experience of it, his claim will be open to many obvious and plausible counterexamples of the sort that Nagel brings forward (see further). See also J. Bollack (1975).

[9] *LMen* 125: "Whatever, being present, does not produce impediment or annoyance, is an object of (merely) empty pain when it is expected." It is perfectly clear that it is the state of being dead, not the process of dying, that is the focus of Epicurus' concern. On this see Rosenbaum (1986, 1987); all major interpreters agree. Epicurus does not seem to have thought that a painful process of dying was an appropriate object of fear either: and his remarkable deathbed letter, declaring that day the "happiest day of my life," despite the intense pain of kidney stone and dysentery, shows how he would argue this. He claims that the happy memory of conversations with his friends is more than enough to offset the bodily pain (DL 10.22, quoted in chapter 4). On dying, see also Segal (1990), who concludes that dying is painful only to the uninstructed.

ipse, 878), makes the fear of these people at all plausible.[10] Every reader, he believes, will endorse premise 1; and once he is made to realize that he is not entitled to his absurd belief that death is a loss that can be experienced by the subject, he will naturally concede the truth of the Epicurean conclusion.

Three supplementary arguments can be introduced at this point. One, which I shall call the symmetry argument, is closely related to the first. It points out that the time before we were born is, as all will agree, a time that is of no concern to us: not in the sense that now, during our lives, we do not take an interest in the events of history, as we clearly do, but in the sense that then, we did not suffer either good or ill, even if good or bad things were then happening, since we were not even in existence. So too, the argument continues, if we take away the illicit fiction of the survivor, we will see that the time after our death is, equally, of no concern to us, in the sense that it is a time during which we can suffer neither good nor ill, no matter what events are going on, since we will not even exist.[11] I shall return to this argument when I discuss the first argument.

A third argument is placed by Lucretius in the mouth of Nature (931ff., esp. 938–39). It urges us to realize that life is like a banquet: it has a structure in time that reaches a natural and appropriate termination; its value cannot be prolonged far beyond that, without spoiling the value that preceded. Mortals should therefore not strive to prolong their lives indefinitely, since this will just spoil the pleasure of the life they have. This argument looks importantly different from the other two; and it is, in ways that we shall shortly examine.

A fourth argument, also spoken by Nature, follows closely on the third (963–71). I shall call it the population argument. Nature points out that if

---

[10] For the self-contradiction involved, consider especially *vivus . . . in morte* (879–80), *in vera morte . . . vivus* (885–86), *stansque iacentem* (887).

[11] This argument is suggested at 832–42, 852–61, 972–77 and also *Axiochus* 365D–E, on which see Furley (1986) 78. As Furley correctly notes, the reference to our lack of concern about the Punic Wars is not, as some have believed, a statement about our current feelings about either past or future events. The point is, rather, to insist that a subject must be on the scene at the time when an event takes place if that event is to be either good or bad for her. (Furley [1986] 76–78; contrast Kenney [1971] 193.) For a recent reconsideration of the symmetry argument, and a probing analysis of the relevant texts, see Mitsis (1988b) and the comments of Striker (1988). Mitsis points out, correctly, that 972–77 is concerned with the rationality of our present attitudes to death in a way that earlier passages are not; and yet, this does not undermine Furley's account of the argument, since, as our analysis of the central argument shows, the conclusion about the non-existence of the subject is Epicurus' basis for the further conclusion that our present fears are irrational.

there are births but no deaths, the world will become unlivable. There is need for the old to die eventually, so that the young may live. This argument, like the banquet argument, seems different in strategy and conclusion from the central argument; and we shall see, when we examine it later on, to what extent this is so.

IV

Epicurus' central argument has been, in recent years, the subject of intense philosophical debate. In fact, there is no aspect of Hellenistic ethics that has generated such wide philosophical interest, and produced work of such high philosophical quality.[12] Major interpreters agree, on the whole, in finding the argument insufficient to establish its radical conclusion. On the whole they have focused their attacks on premise 1. But there is little agreement about what is wrong with this premise, or about why the fear of death is, after all, rational.

For Thomas Nagel, the problem lies in premise 1's focus on possible experience. He argues that a person is not simply a subject of experience, even possible experience: "Most good and ill fortune has as its subject a person identified by his history and his possibilities";[13] and to a person, so identified, much good or ill can befall beyond the boundaries of awareness. A person may be betrayed and never know it; nonetheless, this betrayal is a loss to him. Moving to a case closer to Lucretius',[14] a person may lose all higher mental functioning in an accident: and this loss, which he cannot now even possibly grasp, is still a loss for him—and not only on account of pain that he now feels; for we can imagine a case in which the damaged person lives like a contented child. Indeed, Nagel, continues, it is evident

---

[12] Philosophical discussions focusing on the interpretation of Epicurus' views include Furley (1986), Long and Sedley (1987), Miller (1976), Mitsis (1988b), Rosenbaum (1986, 1987), Sorabji (1983) 176ff., Striker (1988). More general philosophical articles including substantial discussions of Epicurus or Lucretius include Green (1982), Luper-Foy (1987), Nagel (1979), Silverstein (1980), Sumner (1976), Williams (1973). For philosophical discussions related to this debate but not concerned directly with Epicurus, see Brueckner and Fischer (1986), Feinberg (1977), Murphy (1976), Partridge (1981), Pitcher (1984), A. Rorty (1983), Yourgrau (1987). Most of the articles discussing Epicurus reject his conclusions in various ways; Rosenbaum offers an eloquent and acutely argued defense.

[13] Nagel (1979) 5. At this point in the argument, Nagel (1979) is attacking only the focus on actual experience; but he later insists that possible experience is not the appropriate focus either.

[14] Nagel (1979) 5–7.

204

that the "him" for whom the diminished state represents a loss is not the damaged individual who survives in a childlike condition, feeling no pain or frustration. The loss is loss for the intelligent adult who was and is no longer. So it appears that losses do not even have to be located within the temporal career of the subject for whom they are losses, but are to be assessed in terms of their relationship to that person's possibilities during his career. Death is bad because it deprives the agent who was of the fulfillment of all his possibilities.

This is, obviously, a strong and interesting argument. Certainly it moves in the right direction, when it asks us to look at the person's whole history and the trajectory of that history through time, and to see death as a termination of something that was under way, projecting toward a future. But it leaves some difficulties remaining, as Nagel himself observes. First there is a problem with the notion of possibilities: it is left rather unclear how these are to be located, and how we go about determining just what possibilities death has actually frustrated.[15] Equally important, the somewhat static notion of "possibility" does not, Nagel recognizes, do enough to bring out a life's unidirectional temporal movement: for it may be insufficient to show what is wrong with the symmetry argument.[16] We might, argues Nagel (developing a suggestion made by Robert Nozick), imagine a case in which an unborn creature (in the example, a spore waiting to hatch) lived on with unactualized possibilities, and was prevented from fulfilling these by not being born; we would have to grant that this was extremely close to the death case, described in terms of possibility-frustration. And in both, something essential about our fear of death seems to be omitted.[17]

Furthermore, Nagel does not make it clear exactly how an event located completely outside a life's temporal span diminishes the life itself. The cases he actually analyzes are not by themselves sufficient to show this, since in each of them a subject persists, during the time of the bad event, who has at least a strong claim to be identical with the subject to whom the bad event is a misfortune. In the betrayal case, this subject is clearly the very same, and is a subject of possible, if not actual, experience in relation to

---

[15] See the criticism by Furley (1986) 88. I become particularly uncomfortable when Nagel (1979) 10 speaks of "indefinitely extensive possible goods" and denies that a person's own experience of his life contains any idea of a "natural limit."

[16] See Nagel (1979) 8, n. 3: "I suspect that something essential is omitted from the account of the badness of death by an analysis which treats it as a deprivation of possibilities."

[17] Cf. n. 3 again: "I conclude that something about the future *prospect* of permanent nothingness is not captured by the analysis in terms of denied possibilities."

that event. In the second case, it is hard not to feel that the continued existence of the damaged person, who is continuous with and very plausibly identical with the former adult, gives the argument that the adult has suffered a loss or at least a part of its force. Where death is concerned, however, there is no subject at all on the scene, and no continuant. So it remains unclear exactly how the life that has ended is diminished by the event.[18]

A different approach is suggested by Bernard Williams in his article "The Makropulos Case." He begins by assuming that the satisfaction of desire is good. But not all desires are conditional (as Epicurus may suppose) on being alive at the time relevant to satisfaction. For, Williams argues, there are some desires, which he calls "categorical desires," that propel an agent on into life explaining his or her willingness to continue living. These desires may be of many different kinds; we will discover what they are if we imagine the question of suicide arising, and ask what desires would thwart it. These desires cannot, then, be contingent on continued life; and death frustrates the fulfillment of those desires.[19]

This argument does more than Nagel's to take account of the temporal structure of a life, the way it projects beyond its present states toward the future, the way in which death cancels a fulfillment that is specifically future. So, although Williams does not discuss the symmetry argument, his argument is well equipped to handle it: the unborn have no desires for fulfillment, a fortiori no categorical desires; and so the badness of death is not to be found in their case. But in another way Williams' argument does less than Nagel's: for Williams' case against death, unlike Nagel's, is based upon a contingent fact about most people, namely, that they have desires of this sort. It does not show that to have such desires is an essential feature of human life—although Williams, recognizing that his argument is in this way less strong than Nagel's, suggests that one might persuasively argue for that position.[20] Even more important, it does not show that such

---

[18] A further problem in Nagel's argument as a critique of Lucretius is that he relies, for his criticism, on ordinary intuitions. Epicurus would no doubt agree that intuitions have the content that Nagel describes; but he would insist that we can show those intuitions to be corrupt, based on socially taught false beliefs. See Rosenbaum (1986), Silverstein (1980), and my discussion in chapter 4.

[19] Williams (1973) 85–87.

[20] Williams (1973) 88: he describes his argument as "more Utilitarian" than Nagel's, and says that "there are strong reasons to adopt his kind of consideration as well." Williams believes that his argument is stronger than Nagel's, in the sense that it will be likely to persuade a Utilitarian person, whereas Nagel's may not. But for us, since we have insisted from the beginning of this book that uncriticized desires and preferences are not reliable guides to ethical value, an argument that is based on them alone is actually weaker.

desires are in any way good or rational; and so it does not really meet the Epicurean critique. Lucretius' answer would certainly be that one cannot defend the rationality of one desire by pointing to its intimate relation with another desire—unless one has already established that this desire itself is rational and worth keeping. If both are irrational, therapeutic argument could just take for itself the larger task of removing them both. This, in effect, is what Epicurean therapy attempts, as we shall see. Williams expresses sympathy, at this point, with Nagel's more objective argument, and suggests that he might be willing to move in that direction; but such suggestions remain undeveloped.[21]

A further difficulty is created by the use of "categorical desires" to explain why death is bad. It is not clear why the badness of death should be explained by pointing to the frustration of this narrow group of human desires, and this group alone, when there is so much of human life— activities, projects, desires, hopes—for all of which death is the unwelcome end. Suppose that a desire is not, for the agent, such that all by itself it would suffice to propel him on to continued life. Does this show that the frustration of this desire by death is not a loss to the agent?

A valuable recent discussion of Lucretius' argument by David Furley[22] has suggested a somewhat different and promising way of looking at the badness of death, in its relation to the life that death terminates. Death is bad for the person who is no longer, because it makes empty and vain the plans, hopes, and desires that this person actually had during life. Furley uses the example of a person who plans for his future life in ignorance of the fact that he is soon to die. To the relatives and friends who know this, his hopes and projects for the future seem, right now, particularly vain, futile, and pathetic, since they are doomed to incompleteness. Furley then argues that removing the knowing relatives does not alter the case. Any death that frustrates hopes and plans is bad for the life it terminates, because it reflects retrospectively on that life, showing its hopes and projects to have been, at the very time the agent was forming them, empty and meaningless. Our interest in not dying is an interest in the meaning and integrity of our current projects. Our fear of death is a fear that, right now, our hopes and projects are vain and empty.[23]

---

[21] A particularly clear statement on this point is in Striker (1988); for related considerations, see Brueckner and Fischer (1986), Sumner (1976).

[22] Furley (1986).

[23] Furley (1986) 89–90. A similar line of thought is pursued by Murphy (1976), whose discussion is, however, weakened by his explicit and undefended assumption that the central element in human rationality is self-interest (191). Pitcher (1984) gives a different account of

This argument succeeds in refuting Lucretius' contention that our fear of death is in every case based on the irrational fiction of a surviving subject who grieves for his loss. It shows how death reflects back upon actual life; and in so doing it gives us a vivid way of making sense of Nagel's point that an event may be bad for a life even if that life does not survive at the time of the event. In its sensitive depiction of the structure of future-oriented desires and projects it is, moreover, well suited to counter the symmetry argument: the unborn have no projects and hopes that will be made futile and empty by delayed birth.[24] But there is something troublesome, still, in the weight that is placed on the agent's present desires, hopes, and plans. Most people do, of course, project themselves toward the future in the way that Furley describes. Most people do live in such a way as to leave themselves open to emptiness and frustration. But we may not be convinced that this is the only way for a human being to live. Epicurus will suggest another way, as we shall see. And we all know people who plan and hope less than most, who have fewer hostages to the future. So Furley's argument, like Williams', needs supplementation. We need to be told whether the way of living that death makes vain is or is not a good and rational way of living. Like Williams', the argument does not go far enough because it stops with desires, without saying whether, or why, they are good.

We can begin to extend Furley's argument by pointing out that among the many available human activities, the activities and relationships that human beings usually value most have, in more or less every case, a temporally extended structure. All seem to involve planning for a future that may or may not come, forming hopes that may be dashed, moving through a temporal sequence of changes that may be cut arbitrarily short. A parent's love for a child, a child's for a parent, a teacher's for a student, a citizen's for a city: these involve interaction over time, and much planning and hoping. Even the love or friendship of two mature adults has a structure that evolves and deepens over time; and it will centrally involve sharing future-directed projects. This orientation to the future seems to be inseparable from the value we attach to these relationships; we cannot imagine them taking place in an instant without imagining them stripped of much of the human

---

the way in which death can cast a "backward shadow" on life. The related issue of whether one can have interests that extend beyond one's death and can, therefore, be frustrated by occurrences after one's death is sensitively and acutely pursued in Feinberg (1977); see also the critical discussion of Feinberg's position in Partridge (1981).

[24] On this see also Sorabji (1983), who argues that our asymmetrical preferences and our sense that life has a unidirectional movement are "deeply human" and not adequately criticized by the Epicurean argument.

value they actually have. In fact, what can take place in an instant could hardly be called love at all. For love is not, or not only, a feeling that can be had in a moment; it is a pattern of concern and interaction, a way of living with someone. Similar points can be made about hope, grief, and several other emotions.

Much the same, too, can be said of individual forms of virtuous activity. To act justly or courageously, one must undertake complex projects that develop over time; so too for intellectual and creative work; so too for athletic achievement. And in these cases, again, the temporally extended character of the pursuits is an important element in their value. Even such a simple human experience as Nikidion's spring walk has the beauty and value it has for her because of the way that the experience itself extends over time, and involves her in projects for future times. Her hope might only be to have that experience again next year, or to have the experience of summer after the experience of spring. The fact remains that her delight in the seasons' cyclical changes involves an awareness that this is not an isolated event in her life, but a part of a natural pattern in which she, too, plays her evolving and changing role. So death, when it comes, does not only frustrate projects and desires that just happen to be there. It intrudes upon the value and beauty of temporally evolving activities and relations. And the fear of death is not only the fear that present projects are right now empty, it is the fear that present value and wonder is right now diminished.[25]

This argument will be sufficient to make the fear of death rational for anyone who still has valuable activities underway—who still loves, works, chooses, enjoys beauty. Death will be most terrible when it is, in conventional human terms, premature; for then the value of many preparatory activities—activities involving training oneself so as to be able to act in some valued way in future—will be completely lost, in that they will never lead on to the fruition that gives them their entire point. To devote a large part of one's life to merely preparatory activities is characteristic of youth. But the elderly, too, have valuable lives; and their activities, too, are inter-

[25] Stephen Rosenbaum has suggested to me in correspondence that perhaps Epicurus can reply by saying that all we need, in order for our present projects not to be vain, is that they are based upon reasonable beliefs about the future. I note that Epicurus did not avail himself of this reply; and I think he was right not to do so. Beyond the enormous difficulty of saying what a reasonable belief is in this world of accident, the reply does not seem adequate to the difficulty. A young person who dies in an accident was planning for the future in accordance with beliefs as reasonable as any; and yet it is in this sort of case that we feel most keenly the emptiness and fruitlessness of the dead person's preparatory activities. On doing valuable things, see Striker (1988).

rupted by death. It would perhaps be irrational for an elderly person to devote the whole of his or her time to activities whose value is entirely preparatory and instrumental; but even the activities that are constitutive of a good life can, as we have said, be interrupted. And even if there should be a person for whom death arrives just as all current projects are, for the moment, complete and at a standstill—if such a thing ever happens for a person who loves living—still, the bare project to form new projects is itself interrupted; and it seems that this project is itself a valuable one in a human life, and a deep part of what Lucretius will call, critically, "the ungrateful nature of the mind."

This argument captures quite a lot of what we mean when we say that death is a loss for the person who dies. But, in its focus upon the interruption of projects and activities, it may seem incomplete. For even when a project or pursuit is for the time complete, still, we feel that it is frequently a loss in value to the person that he or she had a life that stopped short at that moment of completion, not permitting her to pursue different future projects, or to undertake that one again. And we do not have to believe that a young person is living in a primarily preparatory or future-directed way—many, of course, do not—in order to feel a tragedy in premature death. At this point, however, we should consider that there are actually two different sorts of interruption in human life: or rather, that interruption can occur at two different levels. We have focused so far on cases in which the interruption is internal to a single pursuit or project. But there are, in human life, many projects that involve the plan to do a certain activity repeatedly, over the course of a complete life. A good marriage, for example, as Lucretius himself depicts it in Book IV, has this shape: it is not a single isolated act, but a pattern of daily acting and interacting, extended over time, in which the temporal extension, including the formation of patterns and habits, is a major source of its value and depth. Thus even if death does not catch the spouse poised in the midst of some specific act or concrete plan that is cut short by the death, there is a larger and deeper sort of interruption here: the interruption of the project of being married, and leading the way of life characteristic of marriage, with its habits, its vague and concrete plans, hopes, wishes. At the deepest level, there is, when death arrives, the interruption of every one of these patterns of life—of work, of love, of citizenship, of play and enjoyment: the interruption, then, of a project that lies, however vaguely and implicitly, behind them all: the project of living a complete human life. This project need be nothing so formal as a life plan; it may consist only of vaguer hopes, expectations, an implicit sense of human life's expected unfolding and duration. Most deaths interrupt this complex activity, and are bad for that reason, even if for no other.[26]

This argument, furthermore, is already made by Lucretius himself, in Nature's banquet image. This argument tells us that life, like a meal, has, or is, a temporally unfolding structure. Nature uses it to counter the wish for indefinite prolongation of life; and this use we shall examine later. But now we can see that it also supports the judgment that death can come too soon and, in effect, almost always does. For it almost always cuts short, before the point of repletion and satiety, the temporally extended process of living a human life that seems to be admitted, within the argument, to be a good thing. If one dies prematurely—for example, before reaching the main course—this will be the worst sort of death; for it will make fruitless those "courses" in the meal whose primary function was to prepare appetite and palate for the main course. (One would have eaten differently had one known the main course was not going to arrive.) But the argument suggests, as well, that just so long as eating is a good and a pleasure for the eater, just so long death will be, in another way, premature, and bad for the subject because of its interruption of a process of living in the usual human temporal way, a process that is, like a banquet, good. When we now turn to Epicurean criticisms of our own argument about temporal extension, we

---

[26] Silverstein (1980) suggests, in his very interesting argument, that we should regard our lives in a four-dimensional framework, treating time as we now treat space, and concluding that temporally distant events can make a difference to the goodness of the subject's whole life just as spatially distant ones can, insofar as they affect its shape seen as a whole. He concludes: "In short, it is the four-dimensional ability to understand life in durational terms, to view one's life as a temporal whole and to make evaluative comparisons between it and alternative possible life-wholes, which ultimately accounts for the fact that statements of the form, 'A's death is an evil for A' are commonly regarded as not merely intelligible, but true" (424). Silverstein's argument is further discussed in Yourgrau (1987).

The argument given here, based, as it is, on the activity of "living a life," interpreted to include some sort of planning, hoping, and wishing for the future, might seem to have the consequence that deaths of extremely young children are not bad for the subject—though of course they may still be bad in some other way, or bad for the subject for some other reason. This consequence is, in fact, frequently accepted in the medical ethics literature, which distinguishes the interruption of the life of a person from other deaths, at both the beginning and the end of life. See the excellent survey of these arguments in Brock (1993), and the discussion of the demented elderly in Brock (1986). I am not, however, happy with this consequence where infants are concerned, since I think that the presence of basic human capabilities, of a functional organization such that, with adequate support, human planning and acting of many kinds would in time take place, already makes death an interruption of a life that is projecting toward a future; the case of the elderly who have lost these capabilities is not symmetrical.

should not forget that our argument is itself, apparently, Epicurean, and placed in the mouth of Nature herself.

V

Epicurus has an answer ready. It is that the values to which we point are false values. Moving from desire to value does not really help, since reflective evaluation is at least as likely to be corrupt. We do not need to hold on to these fear-producing values; and if we do they block our enjoyment of mortal happiness, precisely by convincing us that death is a loss. The wise Epicurean will identify herself completely with godlike pleasures that do not derive their completeness from a temporally extended structure, that do not link her thus to a world of transient things and to her own transience. For Epicurus does not endorse the sort of hedonism that approves of all satisfactions, and counts as supremely good the enjoyment of whatever it is that people happen actually to enjoy.

True pleasure, as Epicurus describes it, is, first of all, not additive: having more, or having a longer episode of it, does not make it better or more valuable; nor does the sheer number of episodes of it add to its worth. Lucretius' Nature tells the reader that there is nothing new that she can devise that will increase the worth of her life (944–45). Many sayings of Epicurus insist on this: when once *ataraxia* and *aponia* are attained, the agent is at the top of life, and nothing—not even prolongation or repetition of the same—can add to the sum of her pleasures. Cicero summarizes the matter well:[27]

> Epicurus denies that length of time adds anything to living happily [*beate*, Cicero's rendering of *eudaimonōs*]. Nor, in his view, is less pleasure felt in a brief span of time than if it were everlasting. . . . He denies that in a life of infinite duration pleasure becomes greater than in a finite and moderate time. . . . He denies that time brings increment to the highest good. (*Fin.* 2.87–88)

This is a promising critical point, so far as it goes. It does indeed seem plausible that the value of pursuits is not like the value of commodities, is not heaped up in such a way that more is always better. But, first of all, this does not show that it is not better to be able to choose a valued activity again (to go on having the capability to choose such activities when one

[27] See also Furley (1986) 81.

wants), or that the life in which that option exists is not superior to a life in which it does not. The woman who wants another child need not be making the error of supposing that having more children is always better. She may just be thinking that to occupy oneself by raising children is a very valuable thing to do, and that the value of the activity gives her a good reason for performing it again. The scholar who wants to write another book after the last can, similarly, be motivated by her belief in the value of the activity that she performs; she need not be thinking that books are like coin. If this is so, then it seems that death, or any other accident that deprives the individual of the capability of choosing a valuable action, does remove something of value—whether or not the accident takes place after the activity has been once performed.

Moreover, even if we should dialectically grant to Epicurus that more is *never* better, this would not suffice to give him his radical conclusion that death is never a loss in value to the one who dies. For, returning to the interruption argument, we can remind him that even a single valued activity may have itself a temporally extended structure; and that death can interrupt that structure, diminishing its value. It can in this way remain tragic that death cuts short love, child-rearing, working, planning, in mid-course.

Perfect Epicurean pleasures, however, do not have a temporally extended or limited structure. They are, like Aristotle's *energeiai*, complete in a moment, complete once we do or act at all.[28] Healthy undisturbed life, Epicurus insists, is not a process on the way to some further goal beyond itself, vulnerable to interruption before it might reach that goal. If it is there it is there, and nothing beyond that, but that itself, is the end. By urging us to revise our scheme of values and to attach ourselves to pleasures which have this self-sufficient structure, Epicurus claims to put us beyond the accidents of life. So it is no good objection to his theory, he claims, that it

---

[28] See Furley (1986) 81, Diano (1974), Mitsis (1988b). Furley gives a good account of the tensions in Epicureanism on this point, marshaling evidence that Epicurus allows a certain sort of concern for the future to affect the agent's present state. In particular, a necessary condition of complete Epicurean happiness seems to be the secure expectation of future freedom from pain (e.g., VS 33, Plutarch Non Posse 1089D). On Aristotelian *energeiai*, compared by Furley and Diano to Epicurean complete pleasures, see also Nussbaum (1986a) chapter 11, where I argue that in Aristotle's view *energeiai* can be impeded, though not cut off in mid-course, by accidents beyond our control. For example, myopia can cause a person to see less well every time she sees, even though, in the Aristotelian sense, seeing is complete in an instant and does not require a temporal sequence. Later in this discussion I shall give reasons for seeing some of the activities Aristotle called *energeiai*—for example, intellectual work— as involving a temporal sequence of stages.

does not fit with many of our current thoughts about value. For Epicurus will give us new values, within which death will indeed be non-fearful, in precisely the way that he says. Within this new scheme, furthermore, the symmetry argument will hold, as it does not for mortals who think badly. True pleasures do not project forward in time; so the termination of death is exactly symmetrical to the threshold of birth.

This reply, however, points to a deep tension within Epicurean thought, one that surfaces in many parts of his theory, as we began to see in discussing love, but causes special difficulty for the arguments about death. This is the tension between the perspective of nature and the perspective of the god. On the one hand, Epicurus repeatedly urges us to live as mortal beings within the limits of nature, listening to nature's voice and relying on perception, a natural animal faculty, as our criterion of truth. He describes the goal of his entire enterprise as one of "making the mortality of life enjoyable." And Lucretius follows him, urging the reader to reject the teachings of convention and to adhere, instead, to a form of life that is truly human and natural. In this case, we are to leave aside our culturally taught longings for immortality. But Nature's voice in Book III, while it rejects the search for outright deathlessness (a point to which I shall return), and rejects, too, excessive greed for life among the elderly, still suggests that life and its value, like the banquet described, does have a temporally extended structure, a sequence of interrelated parts building over time and appropriately terminating at one time rather than another. The banquet image is introduced by Nature in order to show that it can be too late to die; but it implies, just as surely, that it can be too soon—while delightful and valuable projects are still under way, before repletion has made feeding a burden. It suggests, furthermore, that the value of any part of a life derives in part from its place in the whole sequence, just as the value of dessert derives from the way in which it complements and follows the main course. A premature termination will then affect, retrospectively, the value of the parts that have been lived, just as an appetizer that is never followed by anything becomes, by that fact, less valuable as what it is. All this accords well with our argument, but badly with Epicurus' emphasis on godlike pleasures. And this is no isolated passage in Lucretius' poem. For we recall that the love of continued life and enjoying are, for the poet, natural desires in all that have life; in the human case they take the form of judgments about beauty and "sweetness" that are the basis for a set of "natural" and transsocietal human values. They can hardly be criticized as empty constructs of this or that society.

But on the other side, as we have begun to see, there is an equally deep strand in Lucretius' Epicureanism that urges us to leave our mere mortality behind us and to live like gods. The *Letter to Menoeceus* concluded with the promise of a godlike existence: "You will live like a god among humans. For a human being who lives in deathless goods is in no way similar to a mortal animal" (135). And if we recall Epicurus' letter to Colotes about Colotes' act of *proskunēsis*, we see how deep in the daily practice of Epicureanism was the promise to raise the pupil above her finitude.

This appeal to divinity as an image of the good life is also a pervasive feature of Lucretius' poem; and Lucretius makes it clear that the pursuit of this goal requires us to transgress boundaries or limits set up in Nature herself. The extrahuman goal is present from the poem's opening, in which mortals, victims of disturbance (32) are immediately contrasted with the Epicurean gods, who live without grief, without change, without need, without gratitude or anger (I.44–49 = II.646–51). If there should remain any doubt that this portrait of the god is a goal held up to those of us who seek to cure ourselves through philosophy, this doubt is removed in the ensuing description of Epicurus' achievement. Epicurus is the foe of conventional religion; but he is also, in the encomium, the foe of nature and nature's limits. His mind's excellence is stirred up

> so that he, first in history, desired passionately to burst through the narrow confines of the gates of nature. Therefore the keen force of his mind conquered,[29] and he advanced far beyond the blazing walls of the universe and traversed the immense whole with his mind and soul, whence, a conqueror, he brought back to us the account of what can arise and what cannot, and by what rational principle each thing has its power bounded, and its deep-set boundary stone. Therefore religion is abased and trampled underfoot, and he makes us, with his victory, equal to the heavens. (I.70–79)

In this description of philosophical heroism, the endorsement of appropriate natural limits is juxtaposed to the praise of a bold transgression of limit. The true Epicurean learns nature's boundaries; at the same time, she is enabled, by Epicurus' victory, to move beyond them.

The proem to Book II, similarly, promises the diligent reader a life that is in no respect significantly different from the lives of Epicurean gods: a life detached from human care, looking down (*despicere*, 8) upon the world of mortal things without worry or tension. Here the imagery of boundaries takes one more turn: philosophy is said to build round the pupil a wall that

---

[29] Note, again, the alliteration: *vivida vis animi pervicit*.

sets her off from other mere humans, until she inhabits "the lofty serene temples of the wise, well fortified by doctrine" (7–8). In Book V we learn that our ability to resemble the gods who "look on all with a mind [*mens*] at peace" (V.1203) will depend on bounding ourselves off from the temporally extended desires of mortals, which rest upon a perception of incompleteness. For we are told that those who are completely self-sufficient have no desire for any change at all (V.168–72); so in their world there will probably be no sense of temporal extension at all, and surely no sense of temporal development with respect to value. And at this book's opening, Lucretius emphatically insists on the transgressive character of Epicurean longing. "He was a god, a god, distinguished Memmius" (V.8), the poet exclaims, by his epithet, opening to his pupil the possibility of a similar elevation, even as he has nourished the same hope for himself, asserting that nobody "born from a mortal body" could worthily praise Epicurus' achievement (6). This achievement was, to "take life out of such great waves and shadows, and to set it up in such tranquillity and such clear light" (11–12).

And at the opening of Book III itself, just before giving us the arguments that are supposed to remove the desire for godlike immortality and to reconcile us to nature's limits, Lucretius makes a similar claim. Epicurus' words are "most worthy of eternal life" (13), "born from a divine mind [*mens*]" (15). They make the "walls of the world stand aside," until we, godlike ourselves, can see the void, the "peaceful homes of the gods" (16–22). Even the poet's emotions, as he pursues his task, are a strange mixture of the mortal and the immortal:

> At these things I am seized by a kind of divine pleasure and horror, seeing that thus nature, by your force, lies so open to view, uncovered on every side. (28–30)

In these famous lines[30] Lucretius lets us see very clearly that Epicurean reflection is an assault on the secrets of nature, an insertion of the human into the realm of the gods. But the claim is not simply the claim that science is in itself transgressive, that the ambition to know the whole is a kind of ambitious human violation of the mystery of the whole. That point could have been made by many thinkers who would not urge the human to become divine through detachment from human things. What Lucretius is saying in these passages is that the grasp of the whole takes the knower permanently and decisively beyond the mortal condition, into the value

---

[30] On which see Schrijvers (1970).

system, therefore the security, of the god. Knowing limits delivers an unlimited life, through the particular sort of shift in values that is commended, and effected, in Epicurean teaching. Epicurean science is transgressive not only because it gives a bounded being knowledge of the whole but, above all, because the content of Epicurean scientific knowledge teaches her to see and care in such a way that she really is no longer bounded.

VI

This shift over to a godlike life and a godlike self requires enormous revision in human patterns of desire and of value. We are asked not to alter reactions that we have and regard neutrally, but to alter evaluative judgments that we endorse on reflection as giving us a correct account of what constitutes mortal good life. We were told that this shift is commanded by nature, that it is a shift away from a religious view of life toward a life lived within the limits of a finite being. But on deeper inspection it appears that the goal of the shift is, in fact, different: to rise above mortality altogether and to make ourselves into gods. But isn't this the religious view of life once again, in a slightly different form, furnished with a new conception of the divine and a new Hercules (cf. V.22ff.), but still feeding the same old longing for transcendence? We begin to suspect that instead of taking on the task of making us not hate who and where we are, Epicurus has taken on the easier task of shifting the ground of our religious otherworldly longing, until it finds a home in thisworldly detachment. This question arose in our analysis of the love arguments; it arises now in a more general and inclusive form. So we wish to know what Lucretius can say to Nikidion to defend his radical assault on beliefs of hers that are both deep and, by his own admission, a natural part of the human response to the conditions of life.

At this point, however, Lucretius can justly charge us with neglect of some of his arguments. If we believe that there is a contradiction between the advice of nature and the aspiration to divinity, this is, he might well object, because we have not attended sufficiently to the whole of nature's speech, or to the complex critique of the structure of mortal values that follows it. These parts of Book III have been unjustly omitted in most philosophical accounts of Lucretius' argument, perhaps because of the vivid dramatic force of their poetic expression. Even Furley says that the portions omitted by his analysis are "more rhetorical, poetic, or satirical than philosophical"—assuming distinctions that our analysis of Epicurean therapy has given us much reason to question. The passage between lines 931 and 1052, beginning with nature's speech and ending with the interlocutor's critical speech to himself, contains two powerful arguments that are intended to dislodge the reader from comfortable acceptance of human temporal values and to commend, in the name of Nature herself, the godlike values that Epicureanism recommends. The first argument attacks mortal values as self-defeating and therefore peculiarly unnatural. The second asks the reader to view his life, and death, from the point of view of the natural universe taken as a whole.

First, then, Nature's voice, and Lucretius' subsequent commentary, urge us to see that there is much in the structure of our current value system that is actually contrary to nature in the sense of being internally perverse or self-defeating. Four different errors about value are identified and attacked. First is the mistake we have already discussed: the mistake of treating life's valuable things like commodities of which more is always better. This attitude is condemned by Nature on the grounds that it betrays inattention to the structure of the good things that nature actually offers. She suggests, further, that it actually undercuts our attempt to realize value in our lives, since the repeated accumulation of enjoyments leads to satiety and non-enjoyment. "There is nothing new that I can devise or invent to please you," she says to the accumulator. "Everything is always the same" (944–95)—implying that the search for more enjoyment will lead inevitably to boredom, undercutting itself.

Next, Lucretius identifies several other forms of corrupt evaluation and activity, associating each one with one of the proverbial torments of the underworld, and claiming that they distort life on earth, making earthly life a hell. There is in real life no Tityos who lives in a perpetual state of being devoured by vultures: but there is the erotic lover, whose very project entails anxieties that devour him and tear him apart (984–94). As Lucretius shows in Book IV, the lover's very pursuit of an impossible goal gives rise to anxieties that undercut love and impede his other projects. Again, in real life there is no Sisyphus pushing his boulder vainly up a hill whose top he will never reach. But there is, says Lucretius, the vain pursuit of political power, which guarantees by its own internal structure that the power-seeker's desires will never attain their end (995–1002). The power-seeker, as Lucretius sees it, dooms himself to an endless futile struggle and ensures, by his choice of that way of life, that he will never get the goal that he seeks within it. Here again, Lucretius' point seems to be not only that the goal—the stable possession of power—is one that can never actually be achieved (*nec datur umquam*, 998), but also that the desires and pursuits generated within that way of life produce an instability that contributes to the frustration of the power-seeker's aims.

Finally, there are Nikidion's pleasures:

> Then, to feed, always, the ungrateful nature of the mind and to fill it with good things, but never satisfy it—as the seasons of the year do, when they come round again, bringing their new growth and their varied delights, nor are we ever filled up with the fruits of life—this, I think, is just the same as those young girls they tell about, who pour water into a sieve that could by no stratagem ever be filled up. (1003–10)

Here the activity chosen by the maidens—pouring water into a sieve—guarantees the frustration of their goal, which is to hold and carry some water. Just so, it is claimed, the usual mortal pursuit of earthly beauty and value guarantees the frustration of our mortal aim—which, if we read the parallel strictly, seems to be to hold on to some beauty and value.

These are significant arguments, since they raise against the mortal values we defend the charge of internal self-negation. Our most cherished activities pursue ends that are rendered unachievable by the nature of the activity itself. Such arguments might well convince Nikidion that mortal values are in a significant sense unnatural; for she is likely to believe that nature is not in this way self-frustrating. She may be induced to see her cherished pursuits as not just difficult or risky, but also warped or perverted in their very structure; and she may then believe that the godlike life of Epicurean detachment is the one in which true natural human value is to be found. If successful, these arguments bridge the gap between the two parts of Lucretius' strategy. But how telling are they?

The error of addition, with its self-undermining effort, is a real error made by some people. But I have argued that a human life can avoid that error while still remaining committed to temporally extended values. We have been given no good reason by the addition argument to believe that the activities of such people are vain and self-defeating. Much the same can be said for the critique of Tityos' activities. For, as Book IV clearly shows, one can avoid the peculiar self-negating kind of love attacked by Lucretius, while still loving another human being in a way that evolves over time and makes the lovers vulnerable to loss. Not all human love is self-negating, nor does Lucretius think that it is. His own account of love in marriage stressed temporal development as essential to the value of the relationship, and yet showed, too, how that love avoids the self-negation of *erōs*. The lover who seeks fusion does pursue an aim both impossible and self-defeating (in the sense that the pursuit of the aim makes him less united with and more at odds with the object, prone to anxieties that undercut his project). But the lover who seeks mutual pleasure, affection, and conversation seems not only not to undercut but actually to augment his own activity by his choice of ends. For conversation and pleasure, in a Lucretian marriage, get better as one pursues them more and longer, since one then responds more aptly and with deeper habits to one's partner's character, tastes, and desires. This would be even more true, I think, if we allow the lovers to be even more humanly needy and less self-protective than Lucretius suggests.

Again, a certain type of power-seeking may indeed be Sisyphean, damning itself to frustration by its very choice of the goal to be pursued. Plato's account of the self-undercutting life of the tyrant (*Rep.* IX), in which the striving for absolute control leads to ever new insecurities and vulnerabilities, gives us a persuasive image of what Lucretius has in mind. But there are other political activities that, while depending for their completion on temporal extension, seem to lack a Sisyphean structure: the effort to make just laws, to advance the well-being of one's city, to improve the well-being of its citizens. These goals are neither impossible nor negatively related to the activities that pursue them. And we can enumerate many other valued pursuits whose aims are attainable, and whose activities really do promote (or even help to constitute) that aim: the activities of friendship, of child-raising, of many kinds of work and social and virtuous activity.

The Danaids are a more persuasive image for many mortal pursuits: for we may grant to Lucretius that many of the activities that we value most, and in which we take most delight, do have an internal structure of need and repletion, absence and presence. They are like pouring water into a sieve in the sense that the value is moving and changing even as it arrives, and depends for its worth on this temporal sequence that begins in, and returns to, emptiness. But the fact that an antecedent lack gives point and vividness to a pursuit does not mean that the pursuit itself has a merely need-relative value, like that of scratching an itch; nor does it imply that this activity is somehow absurd, and that a life without both need and activity would be somehow better and more respectable. We value activities such as eating and sex not just as scratches that appease itches, but as forms of human expressive activity, connected with other valued ends, both social and personal. Again, the fact that the beauty of spring is related to the contrast between spring and winter, and indeed to our sense of finitude and mortality itself, does not imply that spring is not really beautiful. A changeless being could not, perhaps, see or respond to that beauty. But this does not mean that it is not beauty, all the same. The Danaids are absurd and self-defeating, because what they are trying to do is to *hold* some water; and the activity by which they attempt this project—pouring water into a sieve—is one that guarantees the frustration of this aim. We object that this is not what the mortal being usually attempts. The person who eats does not aim at eliminating all hunger forever; and her desire is really satisfied, though hunger returns as certainly again. The person who seeks sexual pleasure does not usually attempt to hold on to the condition of satisfaction forever, freed from all desire; indeed, he or she would prefer that the desire should renew itself again. She is satisfied, and satisfied in part on account of the fact that the condition of satisfaction is not permanent. Nikidion, again, does see beauty and loves the beauty that she sees, even though this beauty is changing and moving off even while she sees it— or rather, in part because it is so moving: change is a part of its beauty. All of Lucretius' tormented people are tormented because they are trying to immobilize something, to hold on to something absolutely and forever. This project not only is doomed to failure; it also generates frustrations that impede its own pursuit. But suppose one were to try not to hold and keep, but simply to live: what would Lucretius say then?

We see here again the tension between the two parts of Lucretius' project. From the point of view of nature, the argument has made a deep criticism of the activities and values of some people—the ones who are in the grip of the idea of immortality. The answer to their hellish predicament would be, it seems, to live in and according to nature—that is, to value life's goods without trying to immobilize them, even noticing how their transience shapes the value we find in them. But that is not the conclusion Lucretius draws, here or elsewhere. Instead, he seems to draw a more sweeping conclusion, rejecting these mortal and transient pursuits altogether in favor of the godlike pleasures of Epicurean wisdom. From the point of view of a being whose pleasures are unchanging, and valuable precisely on that account, the transactions of mortals with changing nature look like silly futile attempts to have stable and unchanging pleasures—attempts always doomed to frustration by the nature of the chosen pursuits, with their cycle of need and repletion. Lucretius seems to assume that a pursuit has true value, and avoids hellish futility, only if it can be detached altogether from change and vulnerability and seen as valuable from something like a god's-eye view on nature.[31] A deep intolerance of nature and temporality betrays itself in Lucretius' words about the seasons: for what is being attacked is

---

[31] For discussion of some vary similar arguments in Plato's *Gorgias* and *Republic*, see Nussbaum (1986a) chapter 5.

nature itself, the way change goes on and the way in which it evokes love and hunger from the mortal soul.[32] But isn't this judgment a repudiation of the mortality of life, and isn't that hatred of mortality exactly the disease that therapeutic argument was supposed to cure?

Lucretius has one more argument in this section of the poem, however. And we must grasp it before we can finally evaluate his therapy and propose a modified therapy of our own. The argument, spoken, once again, by Nature's voice, asks us to look at our personal situation from a wider viewpoint, the viewpoint of the lives and interests of all living things, both present and future. When we look at the natural world with love and concern for it as a whole, and consider our own life or death in this perspective, as one life within that whole, two things happen. First of all, our own personal anxieties look small. We think, why should we spend our lives preoccupied by the thought of our own death, when there is so much in the universe to consider? Others have died; birth and death are both universal and necessary; ours is no special case. The windows of our thought open out. To use Lucretian images, the shadows that bound our vision to our own narrow surroundings now lift, and the whole of our mind's vision is flooded with the clear light of the universe. Contemplating and caring for the whole, we are ashamed to be wrapped up in ourselves; and the shameful obsession is itself dissipated by the engrossing interest of the reflection in whose light it is revealed as shameful. As George Santayana summarizes this part of the poem, "One who lives the life of the universe cannot be much concerned for his own."[33]

Second, when we look at our death in the light of the whole, we understand that it is necessary for the continued health and life of the whole.

> There is need of matter, so that future generations may grow. They too, having lived out their lives, will follow you. Generations before this perished just like you, and will perish again. Thus one thing will never stop arising from another. Life is nobody's private property, but is everyone's to use. (967–71)

In short, says nature: this life to which you so stubbornly cling is not only not a very large part of the whole, it is actually required back from you, if the whole is to live well. If people never died, that would bring all nature to a halt: no room for new birth, no resources for the newly born. Clinging to

---

[32] Cf. also III.936–37, where the same image of pouring liquid into a vessel full of holes is used by Nature herself.

[33] Santayana (1910) 56.

life (beyond a reasonable limit) is selfishness and callousness toward other natural beings.

The assumption behind the argument is that the world's resources are not indefinitely expandable. Even if the world could support some increase in population, it could not support an indefinite increase. New people will be born naturally, in the normal course of events. And if there are no deaths we will have, sooner or later, a situation in which some of the existing ones, or all, will lack resources. Indeed, Lucretius seems to imagine that the burden of scarcity will fall most heavily on the new: for the people already around, who already command resources, will cling to them tenaciously. Life will be like a university faculty with no retirements, in which the old, tenaciously clinging to their tenured posts, will prevent the entry of an entire generation of young people. What Lucretius says to those aging professors is: it is selfish and callous to cling to your position at such a cost. Move out and make room for someone else. This does not mean that the current retirement age is just, or that some other much longer term of service might not be made compatible with the entry of the young, if resources were better marshaled and arranged. It just says that the pro-longation cannot be indefinite, without squeezing out the new, and that you yourself, seeing that, should modify your attitude to your own departure accordingly.

This argument is strong. Unlike the arguments about self-negating de-sires, it does not spring from intolerance of change. Instead, it asks from us a deeper and more consistent love of life and change, a love that is willing to confront one's own small place in the whole. It does not ask us not to think untimely death a tragedy; or even to stop fearing our death, as a loss, at any time. It reminds us, however, that this loss is someone else's good, that what you wish most to avoid is necessary and good for unborn others, that nature's structure contains an always tragic tension between the desires of the part and the requirements of the whole. And this thought, while it does not remove either the fear of death or its appropriateness, does diminish the sense of injustice that frequently accompanies the thought of death. It sternly tells Nikidion not to make herself a special case, not to think herself the center of the universe, or to ask for favors that would diminish it. And this injunction, followed, may transform the experience of fear.

Nikidion might make two objections to this argument. The first would be to ask why she herself should not be an exception. Universities can still do well if they have a handful of really permanent positions. So too in the case of life: one person's immortality, or even many people's, would not suffice to do harm. Here Nature will remind her that in adopting the perspective of nature, a perspective that she herself has agreed to as partly constitutive of rationality, she has agreed to consider herself as one among others; and this seems hard to reconcile with the application, here, of special principles to her own case. Furthermore, Nature will point out that it is not the case that nobody suffers as the result of her choice. Even if the young do not suffer, Nikidion will be wronging other members of her own generation, who will have to move on, and perhaps even move on more quickly, as a result of her permanent tenure, in order to support her continued life. Like Euripides' Admetus, she has allowed someone else to die in exchange for her life: and this act of self-promotion and cowardice (whether or not it actually shortens the life-span of the one who dies for her) will color the rest of her life.

But she may, if she is resourceful, attempt a more general reply. For it may seem that the non-death of the elderly is a problem only if the birth rate is more or less constant, or increasing. Why, on the other hand, couldn't we get the same balance by lowering the birth rate drastically, so that a substantial portion of our population remains frozen in years of adulthood, never moving off, but the new people are so few in number that no one ever lacks resources? Contemporary society does this to some extent already, seeking a birth rate that will be appropriate to available resources, given the lengthened life-span.

The objection is not easy to rebut; for if to Lucretius it would have seemed fanciful, it seems to us eminently practical. To some extent, we must concede that the objector is right: given the claim that the already living have to continued life, it seems morally correct (though not uncontroversial) to prolong those lives as long as we can, devoting our resources to that first of all, and to limit birth accordingly. But the proposed alternative of an almost total freezing of the population raises new moral problems that the objector does not consider. We shall later speak about the problems it raises for the frozen person herself and the value of her life. For now, we shall focus on the problems it raises for the community. A university faculty that is frozen at the top—as many in fact are today—lacking any positions for young entering people, lacks a crucial element of the value of such an institution. It lacks the value, for both parties, of the interaction between young and old, the education of young people by the experience and wisdom of the old, the stimulus for the old of the young people's fresh ideas and approaches. So, too, a world without young people would lack much that we currently value in our own world: new birth, the growth and rearing of children, the special types of love that bind the generations, the freshness of young energy and thought, the stimulus of generational interaction in creative projects of many kinds. The person who chooses the frozen world has opted out of much of life's actual beauty.

And we can add one thing further: he or she is a parasite on the very system she seeks to subvert. For in growing up to the point of frozenness that she now proposes, she has profited from the old system, from the love and care of parents, the concern of teachers. In opting for a world that no longer contains these structures, she seems to be opting for a world in which she could never have come to be exactly as she is. Since a person who values herself and her life so highly as to seek to freeze it values, as well, on pain of inconsistency, the conditions that made it what it is, and since there is no reason to suppose that a life of similar structure and value could have come about in any other way, she is, in urging the rejection of the intergenerational way of life, very likely to be inconsistent with herself.

So the argument appears to survive Nikidion's objections, and to do so with its force broadened and clarified, rather than diminished. But notice that, like the banquet argument, it does so not by uprooting mortal temporal values but by affirming them, and showing their importance.

VII

We have a complex result. On the one hand, we have an impressive argument that does, to some extent and in some ways, therapeutically treat personal fear by appealing to wider cares. This argument allows us to preserve, as rational, our belief that death is a loss of value to the person who dies. But it balances this belief against other concerns. On the other hand, we have a further therapeutic argument assailing the belief; but this argument seems to be less powerful, inspired by rage against mortal life itself, and in tension with the description of mortal value offered in Nature's voice. No argument in this poem has so far persuaded us that the fear of death is irrational, or that the values to which this fear is a response are not genuinely good.

At this point another argument comes forward—an argument that Lucretius himself is prevented from making because of his own commitment to godlike detachment, though it is suggested in Nature's banquet argument and in some of Lucretius' examples of the bad attitude to earthly value. It is an old argument, at least as old as myths and stories about mortals who become immortal, and the immortals who fall in love with mortals. It consists in pursuing seriously the thought that the structure of human experience, and therefore of the empirical human sense of value, is inseparable from the finite temporal structure within which human life is actually lived. Our finitude, and in particular our mortality, which is a particularly central case of our finitude, and which conditions all our awareness of other limits, is a constitutive factor in all valuable things' having for us the value that in fact they have. In these constraints we live, and see whatever we see, cherish whatever we cherish, as beings moving in the way we actually move, from birth through time to a necessary death. The activities we love and cherish would not, as such, be available to a godlike unlimited being. I have already argued that friendship, love, justice, and the various forms of morally virtuous action get their point and their value within the structure of human time, as relations and activities that extend over finite time. I used this observation to explain why the abrupt termination of these activities and relations by death is appropriately seen as tragic for the person who has been pursuing them. But we can now turn this consideration around and suggest that the removal of all finitude in general, mortality in particular, would not so much enable these values to survive eternally as bring about the death of value as we know it.

This is so far a general claim. It needs to be further explored. It is a claim about our empirical concept of value: so the investigation that pursues it will have to be empirical, bringing forward parts of human experience and using them (rather than some alleged a priori principles) to establish that our concept of value is in fact as we say it is. But it will also need to be deep and probing, going beneath first thoughts and automatic everyday responses, to elicit deeper judgments about what matters. We need for this purpose complex fictions, works of literature that give us stories of immortals and of mortals, imagining in detail what can and cannot go on in those respective lives and convincing us, by this means, of the relationship between mortality and human value. Here I shall do something simpler and more preliminary, telling a schematic philosopher's story, but with reference to some literary data that are pertinent for our purposes.

Bernard Williams pursued a related plan in "The Makropulos Case."[34] Considering the life of Janacek's heroine, who had lived for three hundred years, frozen always at the age of forty-two, he argued that this woman's eventual boredom and frozenness, her loss of desire and her eventual suicide, were inevitable results of the attempt to prolong human desire so far beyond its natural limits. This interesting and convincing case leaves a number of questions unanswered. For example, how far did the result depend on the fact that she was alone in her predicament? That she was

[34] Williams (1973).

brought up to form the desires characteristic of a mortal? And does her case give us any reason not to try to cultivate, in ourselves and in others, desires that would sustain an immortal existence? In keeping with my emphasis on value and on good reasons, I shall select a slightly different case and try to confront these worries.

We give the proponent of immortality the strongest case, I think, if we imagine the immortal human as non-isolated, so that the pain of difference does not, by itself, blight her life, and as having lived this way all along, or at least since earliest childhood, so that a jarring discrepancy between expectation and result does not spoil it either. (We can even suppose her immortal in both directions, so that she has no childhood.) And let us choose a minimal change where vulnerability is concerned, removing death alone without removing pain and other related limitations on her physical power.

This thought experiment has already been performed, by Homer and by Greek culture as a whole: it is the story of the Olympian gods, frozen immortal anthropomorphic adults.[35] The question we want to ask is, How many of the virtues and values we prize turn up in their unbounded lives? In removing death from these humanlike creatures, note, we have made two changes: a change concerning risk, and a change concerning time. The gods live forever, and on this account there is a marked limit to the risk they can undergo.

The first thing we notice about the gods is that they cannot have the virtue of courage, as we know and honor it. For courage consists in a certain way of acting and reacting in the face of death and the risk of death. A being who cannot take that risk cannot have that virtue—or can have, as we in fact see with the gods and their attitude to pain, only a pale simulacrum of it.[36]

This means, as well, that the component of friendship, love, and love of country that consists in a willingness to give up one's life for the other must be absent as well—indeed, must be completely mysterious and obscure to people whose experience does not contain the sense of mortality. Thus, as in fact we see in Homer, there is a kind of laxness and lightness in the relationships of the gods, a kind of playful unheroic quality that contrasts sharply with the more intense character of human love and friendship, and

[35] The gods do have birth, and thus are immortal in only one direction; but in many cases their childhood is not an important topic of myth, and they are imagined as if permanent adults.

[36] This will vary, however, with the amount and type of pain we allow them. Prometheus' suffering is in certain ways worse because eternal.

has, clearly, a different sort of value. In heaven there is, in two senses, no Achilles: no warrior risking everything he is and has, and no loving friend whose love is such that he risks everything on account of his friend. Friendship so differently constituted will not be the same thing, or have the same value.

Beyond this, we begin to discover that many of the virtues we prize require an awareness of the limits and needs of the human body that will be absent, as such, from a being who can never die. Moderation, as we know it, is a management of appetite in a being for whom excesses of certain sorts can bring illness and eventually death; who needs to deal with other beings similarly constituted, for whom the stakes are similarly high. Political justice and private generosity are concerned with the allocation of resources like food, seen as necessary for life itself, and not simply for play or amusement. The profound seriousness and urgency of human thought about justice arises from the awareness that we all really need the things that justice distributes, and need them for life itself. If that need were removed, or made non-absolute, distribution would not matter, or not matter in the same way and to the same extent; and the virtue of justice would become optional or pointless accordingly. Aristotle is right to say that the idea of debates about justice and contract among the gods is a ridiculous idea (*EN* 1178b10–16). The closer we come to reimporting mortality—for example, by allowing the possibility of permanent unbearable pain, or crippling handicaps—the closer we come to a human sense of the virtues and their importance. But that is the point: the further mortality is removed, the further they are.

These changes change still further the structure of personal, family, and social relationships. If parents are not necessary to enable children to survive and grow, if a city is not necessary for the life of its citizens, if altruistic sacrifices of what one actually needs cannot be made, then human relationships would more and more take on the optional, playful character that Homer, depicting the gods, so marvelously shows us. And of course the absence of temporal limit, and the changed attitude this brings toward intergenerational relationships (if generations remain in any form), toward birth and growth (if there is any), toward all relationships whose structure and point is connected with growth, change, and process, would lead to still more remarkable changes, difficult even to imagine. We cannot suppose that the precise pleasure of Nikidion's spring morning would be found, even as a solitary event, in the life of an immortal being; for part of her understanding of and joy in nature and its finite temporal movement derives from her own self-understanding as a natural being related to nature and to other finite human beings in certain concrete ways, moving as nature and other human beings are moving, and partaking of a similar fragility. It is hard to imagine Apollo taking such a walk.

Now, returning to our criticism of Lucretius' therapy of love, we can see the issue in a deeper and more general way. The depth of erotic neediness and vulnerability that seems to be omitted from Lucretius' account of "cured" mortal love may itself be connected obscurely with the awareness of mortality and finitude. Without this, we will have the pleasant sexual play of two self-sufficient gods, but not everything that gives human sex its interest.

And, in general, the intensity and dedication with which very many human activities are pursued cannot be explained without reference to the awareness that our opportunities are finite, that we cannot choose these activities indefinitely many times. In raising a child, in cherishing a lover, in performing a demanding task of work or thought or artistic creation, we are aware, at some level, of the thought that each of these efforts is structured and constrained by finite time. And the removal of that awareness would surely change the pursuits and their meaning for us in ways that we can scarcely imagine—making them, perhaps, more easy, more optional, with less of striving and effort in them, less of a particular sort of gallantry and courage. Gods are, as Heraclitus observed, in a paradoxical way finite; for they are dead to, closed off from, the value that we see, the beauty that delights us. From the haunting beauty of Nikidion's morning; from the embrace of a parent and a child; from the struggle to do good work inside the constraints of a finite human life. There would be other sources of value, no doubt, within such an existence. But its constitutive conditions would be so entirely different from ours that we cannot really imagine what they would be.

We are judging the gods' life from the point of view of our empirical human sense of value. This may seem, in a sense, unfair—unfair in particular to Epicurus, who insists that we cannot rely on uncriticized intuitions. But recall what we are attempting to show. We are not attempting to show that an immortal existence could not have value, beauty, and meaning internal to itself. Unlike Williams, I believe that we do not have good reason to say this; and that we have, of necessity, far too little understanding of the structure and the "language" of such a life even to investigate that question well. What we are attempting to show is the extent to which *our* values would be absent in that life; and that is the thing most relevant to a therapeutic treatment of our always impossible wish to have that life in place of our own. It is, as well, the only perspective on value from which we can coherently proceed, in asking a question for ourselves: for in asking about ourselves there is not much point in asking whether a certain life seems good from the point of view of creatures that we have no chance of ever being, or rather creatures becoming identical to which we would no longer be ourselves. When Epicurus asks us to look critically at intuitions, he does not require such a total departure; if he did, he would not be the interesting philosopher that he is. He asks us, rather, to conduct a more profound and searching inquiry into the totality of our thought about ourselves; and this we can claim to be doing when we think as we have.

In Wallace Stevens' poem "Sunday Morning,"[37] the female speaker, looking in nature for some paradise, some transcendence, finds that the conventional images of paradise do not, in fact, contain the mortal beauty that she loves:

> There is not any haunt of prophecy,
> Nor any old chimera of the grave,
> Neither the golden underground, nor isle
> Melodious, where spirits gat them home,
> Nor visionary south, nor cloudy palm
> Remote on heaven's hill, that has endured
> As April's green endures; or will endure
> Like her remembrance of awakened birds,
> Or her desire for June and evening, tipped
> By the consummation of the swallow's wings. (IV)

Her attempt to imagine an enduring value cancels, paradoxically, the very sort of enduring that she prizes: the enduring that is inseparable from transience and motion, and from her own awareness of her own transience. (For what she finds wonderful expresses, clearly, her own sense of her finite time.) She calls out again for immortality, saying, "But in contentment I still feel / The need of some imperishable bliss" (V) (the need that Epicurus allows, and claims still to satisfy). The answer comes back directly:

> Death is the mother of beauty; hence from her
> Alone, shall come fulfilment to our dreams
> And our desires. (V)

Finally she hears, in the silence, a voice that seems to tell her that real value is not beyond this world in some separate spiritual realm; it is in living a life that ends in the grave. The poem ends with an account of the

---

[37] Stevens (1954).

place in which we live, a place of death and mutability, in which we find whatever value we find:

> We live in an old chaos of the sun,
> Or old dependency of day and night,
> Or island solitude, unsponsored, free,
> Of that wide water, inescapable.
> Deer walk upon our mountains, and the quail
> Whistle about us their spontaneous cries;
> Sweet berries ripen in the wilderness;
> And, in the isolation of the sky,
> At evening, casual flocks of pigeons make
> Ambiguous undulations as they sink,
> Downward to darkness, on extended wings. (VIII)

The geography of our world is structured by its ending; the light appears as light against that darkness, the graceful motion of its life against the void that contains no motion.

This argument does not oppose Nikidion's fear of death. It tells her that fear is appropriate because based upon true beliefs about death's badness and life's value. But it reminds her of the positive role of that fear, as an appropriate expression of her awareness of the constitutive conditions of human finite value. It tells her not to hate her fear, not to use it as an excuse to flee from human things, but to see its just cause, instead, as one condition of her best possibilities. When the spring brings round its sequence of beauties and pains and fears, she will, following this argument, embrace the pain and fear along with the delight; for she will see how they are connected. She will not avoid circumstances that evoke fear, or try to fashion herself a life without it. For she will know how fear is linked with a conception of the good that, on reflection, she endorses. We must emphasize that this does not mean that she will view death as a good thing, or cease to struggle against it. For death would not be the sort of value-constituting limit it is in human life, if it were a limit to be embraced with equanimity. It is better called the stepmother than the mother of beauty. She will continue to fear and to avoid it, and she will believe it rational to do so. It does mean that in fearing and avoiding it she will not condemn the whole condition of mortality itself, or imagine the condition of gods as superior in worth.

If she should find herself dying prematurely, this argument has little to say to her. Such a death is a terrible thing, and is a reason for rage as well as for fear. As she reaches the time normally associated, in her historical time, with the vague idea of "a complete life," the time vaguely, but implicitly, involved in her planning for a life, she might view the advent of death with somewhat less negative emotion. And yet, so long as she still has valuable activities under way, she will be justified in fearing death.

The argument is incomplete. For it should, ultimately, investigate not only death, but other limits as well: the human being's susceptibility to pain and disease, our need for food and drink, our proneness to accidents of various kinds, our birth into the world as vulnerable babies who depend absolutely on the love and goodwill of those outside of us, our need throughout life for the support and love of others. All these things are, seen in one way, limitations; and yet all might plausibly be seen as necessary conditions of some type of specifically human value; perhaps, in some cases, as something more—as a constituent part of the valuable relation or activity. All this would be an appropriate and natural continuation of this therapeutic argument, although I cannot pursue these further issues here.[38]

In this argument, together with the population argument, we have the basis for a truly naturalistic therapy for the fear of death. It is the appropriate development of the naturalistic portions of Lucretius' argument, separated loose from its conflicting commitment to transcendence. It can claim to do what Epicurus said he wanted: to "make the mortality of life enjoyable, not by adding on some infinite time, but by removing the longing for immortality." The truly naturalistic pupil of Lucretius should, I suggest, prefer this therapy—which does not remove fear, but balances and opposes it with other reflections that ought to diminish its immobilizing power.

VIII

But these balancing and alleviating arguments do not, like Lucretius', banish all fear; and Lucretius has argued that so long as the fear of death is not

---

[38] This further argument would have implications for the question of premature death. For we would have to reflect that human life is not only a place of death, it is also a place of accident. There is in real life no such thing as the "normal life-span," except as a statistical artifact. Premature and accidental deaths are an ubiquitous fact of human life. We cannot be sure, without a great deal of further reflection, to what extent this fact affects the constitution of mortal values. Suppose all lives were of the same duration, and ended in a predictable way, without Nature's caprice and inequity. This seems to be a good situation; and indeed it is one we try to bring about in many ways. But we need to look more deeply before fully accepting that conclusion, asking what human life would be were Nature really under our control to that degree.

completely banished it will cause many bad consequences in human life. Now, therefore, we must return to the Epicurean diagnosis, asking whether the bad consequences of fear will appear in Nikidion's life, should she choose to listen to our revised therapy.

The bad consequences of the fear of death were of four kinds: dependence upon religion; inability to enjoy other pleasures (culminating, in the extreme case, in a total hatred of life); pointless frenetic and anxious behavior, together with the subjective feeling of a great weight or burden; and, finally, various forms of harmful and immoral behavior aimed at seizing a kind of worldly immortality in the form of money, power, and reputation. These categories are closely related. Religion, for example, is condemned not only because it is false and irrational, but also because it makes us hate our human activities, and inspires various forms of immoral action. Immoral behavior increases fear of the gods and therefore, in turn, our dependence on religion. Frenetic behavior is prompted by a desire to flee oneself, thus by a hatred of our merely mortal existence; thus it is closely linked to the inability to enjoy. What will Nikidion's relation be to this web of consequences?

Subservience to religion, in Lucretius' persuasive analysis, was prompted not so much by the fear of death *simpliciter* as by the belief that this fear is a weakness, and that the gods live better because they live without it. By inspiring in Nikidion a love of the fragile and the human in human life, a love, however unstable and uneasy, of the very limits that separate her from godlike beings, the revised therapeutic arguments ought to work against the turning to religion, making it possible for us to live where we are, with joy rather than hatred. Indeed, it can be claimed that only this revised therapy really breaks the hold of religion: the Lucretian therapy simply turns us over to a new image of divinity, a new form of self-hatred. Nikidion's concern for the whole of nature ought to undercut still further the role played by otherworldly religion in her life. For she will suspect (following Lucretius' other arguments about mind and religion) that it is neither consistent with a true account of the whole nor good for the life of the whole.

Much the same can be said of the relationship between fear and her other pleasures and activities. Because Nikidion does not connect the fear of death with a weak or bad condition, a condition to be transcended at all costs, she will not let it cancel her joy in the various beauties that human life contains. Indeed, she will observe reflectively, as previously she did not, how deeply the joy and the fear are interrelated; and she will therefore not be inclined to turn aside from her pleasures in an anxious search for an end to fear. Here again, we might say that this therapeutic argument does better than Lucretius' own: for he requires Nikidion to turn aside from most of her previous values, pleasures, and activities in the name of godlike life. (This shows us a further reason why our critical argument must be concerned with value, as well as with structures of desire: for only a defense based on value will reveal how much Epicurus has in fact diminished Nikidion's life.) The perspective of the whole will, in general, enhance and not undercut Nikidion's pleasures. It will take away such pleasures as come from damaging the whole, or denying the importance of the whole. But this seems to be a good rather than a bad consequence. And it will add to her life the great joy and value of understanding the world, perhaps one of the greatest pleasures available to a human life; and all the greater, it seems, for a human life that places itself within the world, rather than apart from it.

The feeling of being burdened and the associated frenetic activity were caused, above all, by ignorance and denial of oneself and one's real condition. Nikidion's therapy not only removes the ignorance, it also removes the hatred of human limits that causes the denial. A person who loves herself, and her limits as constitutive of herself, has no motive to flee herself. And here once again we can say that only the revised therapy really goes to the root of the problem. Epicurus permits us to hate and flee ourselves. He promises a secure and peaceful destination; but there is no doubt that it is the terminus of a flight, a shore where one watches, with relief, the other poor mortals who go on being themselves. Since our arguments have not canceled fear, and have insisted on the human value of this pain and restlessness, there will remain in Nikidion's life some restless, striving activity. She will not achieve, or strive for, complete *ataraxia*. But this seems both good and human. And it does not look pointless or hollow, once it is seen, as the therapy sees it, as a natural and valuable part of human life.

Finally we turn to the ways in which mortals seek worldly immortality, and the forms of damage and immorality that result. This appears to be the most difficult Lucretian charge for us to answer, since it might be thought that by confining the human being to the human world, by denying her Epicurean as well as religious transcendence, and leaving her with the sense of pain at her own finitude, we have greatly increased her motivation to undertake these harmful actions—whereas the Epicurean life, if non-human, is also benign.

Here we must point out, again, that the proposed therapy is evaluative, not simply concerned with the description of human desires. And it is part of a more general evaluative inquiry, which would include a scrutiny of the value of money and power in human life. Because of this, this therapy, unlike an account that limited itself to an analysis of desire, can point out, as it goes along, that among the human ways of struggling against human limits, some are better and more valuable than others. The ways of power, reputation, and money are among the most prudentially unsound—in that they base the effort of human striving and imagining on goods that are both external and unstable. But they are also unsound in a deeper way: because they attempt to extend a person's life beyond itself using vehicles that are, in their impersonal nature, unsuited to express the identity of the person who is trying to project herself through them. And they are also among the most evaluatively impoverished, since they pour the intensity of human activity into an external thing that cannot really be more than a means to activity.

At this point we notice something striking: in his survey of consequences, Lucretius has completely failed to consider the possibility that the fear of death may have, as well, some good consequences in human life. First of all, in a very obvious way, this fear is conducive to our self-preservation: for it motivates prudent and cautious behavior, toward ourselves and toward others, just as the ability to feel pain motivates behavior that avoids bodily harm.[39] It is likely that creatures who lacked this fear completely would come to grief. Epicurus will point out that self-preservation is a good consequence only if death is bad, which is just what he denies. But still, our ability to manage our lives in a stable and self-preserving way does seem to be linked to other valued Epicurean (and Lucretian) ends, such as the formation of political communities, of the bonds of family and friendship, and indeed the attainment of freedom from pain itself—for creatures without self-preserving caution will get injured more often and suffer more pain. So it is not obvious that Epicurus can dismiss this consequence as morally irrelevant, even within his own conception of the good.

More important still, Lucretius' argument, in speaking of the ways in which people try to become immortal in this life, has omitted many forms of expressive human activity that humans have chosen as vehicles for their own continuation. It has, that is, omitted all those forms that seem benign or even very good, all the forms described by Plato's Diotima, in her reflection about the way in which the awareness of mortality stimulates a desire to beget value.[40] These include the creation and rearing of children;

---

[39] This is the central thesis of A. Rorty (1983); a good deal of work has been done on animal fear, leading to the same conclusion: see Lazarus (1991), Oatley (1992), De Sousa (1987).

[40] *Symposium* 206C–212A, on which see Kosman (1976).

the creation of works of art; the creation of good political conditions and systems of laws; the creation of ideas and scientific or philosophical inquiries; in short, the creation of all worldly beauty and value that expresses the creator's own identity, and in which she can, in a specifically human way, live on in the world after her death. The Epicurean agent must reject this search for a historically evolving and human immortality, just as he rejects the search for immortality in possessions. The only immortality that can count for him is that of the single moment's godlike thought. Like a god, furthermore, he is required to "look at all things with a calm mind": all things, including human suffering, including injustice, including the absence of beauty. So even if he were not forbidden to seek this sort of continuation of himself, he would lack the other motives for creation that most people have. Nikidion's fear and discontent, combined with her love of and concern for human things, will, by contrast, provide her with a powerful set of motives toward the creation of worldly value.

Describing the contribution of the dead Keats in *Adonais*, Shelley writes that through his work Keats has achieved a continuation in the world of nature, as an ongoing part of that world.[41] The poet-speaker realizes, with great joy, that in this particularly appropriate and human way, Keats has not died:

> He lives, he wakes—'tis Death is dead, not he;
> Mourn not for Adonais.—Thou young Dawn,
> Turn all thy dew to splendour, for from thee
> The spirit thou lamentest is not gone. (XLI)

Nikidion can respond to this joy; and, responding, seek in her own life to make a similar contribution to the changing world. This need not be in the form of great masterpieces. It might perhaps simply be by living in a family and a community, and giving to these, that she gives herself to the whole— as, in Stevens' poem, people living together in nature and in society

> . . . shall know well the heavenly fellowship
> Of men that perish and of summer morn. (VII)

If we believe that this is a good way to live with ourselves and with others, we have good reason not to choose the Epicurean therapy.

The population argument increases her motivation for creative activity. For it tells Nikidion that she should live her life in a spirit of concern for the

---

[41] I do not, of course, mean to deny that the poem also pervasively expresses an interest in Platonic transcendence; it is not entirely clear to me how its conceptions of immortality are related.

other members of her kind and for other living beings. Thinking this way, she will be less likely to go toward death in silence; for she will want, before death, to give something of herself to the whole and the future, in whatever way best suits her nature: as a parent, a scientist, a poet, a just legislator. Her other-regarding and self-regarding motives fit well together. Just as she seeks for herself continuation in history and in nature, so at the same time she will seek to give to history and nature. The Epicurean, by contrast, armed with a concern for the whole, but too godlike to have the motives for creation that come from the fear of death, will not give her own other-regarding goals the best sort of service.

We can, I think, go further. It is not at all clear that the kind of concern with the whole that the voice of Nature urges is even compatible with the godlike perspective on life that Lucretius elsewhere recommends. Standing so far above and beyond mortal troubles, the cured Epicurean seems to have no reason to meddle in the world, no more reason than do the Epicurean gods; and certainly they have no concern with alleviating the suffering of others by creative activity. Both fellow feeling and a sense of one's own finitude are, according to the Epicurean account of the gods, motives for creation on behalf of others that are lacking in the gods' lives. So it is not clear that the Epicurean can heed Nature's voice to even a limited extent, caring for the whole and its beings, present and future.

It is very revealing that when Lucretius speaks of his own poetic vocation he alludes to both of these non-Epicurean motivations:[42] to fellow feeling in Book I, when he speaks of nature's Venus, goddess of "the whole class of living things," as the patron of his poetic efforts; to the desire to leave a mark on human life when, in both Book I and Book IV, he speaks of his longing for appropriate praise, a longing that "strikes my heart with a sharp Dionysian thyrsus" (I.922–23), leading him to "seek a distinguished crown for my head from a place from which the Muses have never previously crowned anyone's temples" (I.929–30 = IV.4–5). This is not, clearly, the bad love of fame and power that Lucretius assails in his attack on fear: for the poet makes it abundantly clear that what he wants is fame for good activity, and for helping others who need help. His desire would not be satisfied by any fame not so earned. But it is, still, a creative and other-

---

[42] See the sensitive discussion of these passages, and of the evolving stance of the poet-speaker, in Segal (1989), who finds here a profound tension between Lucretius the poet and Lucretius the Epicurean philosopher. Although I find Segal's discussion excellent, and an invaluable basis for further work on these questions, I am more inclined than he is to find this tension in Epicureanism itself, as a tension between its aspiration to give us a natural life and its aspiration to give us a godlike life. See also Segal (1990).

regarding aim that fits oddly with the Epicurean project of detaching the agent from concern with the human world and its accidents. If it seems in many ways to be the appropriate fulfillment of the demand of Lucretius' voice of Nature, it also reveals to us as clearly as anything in the poem the depth of the tension between that voice and the voice of godlike transcendence. And the fact that a poet officially committed to godlike transcendence cannot, or will not, explain his own actions to us in terms of that commitment shows us just how difficult it is to see that transcendence as sufficient for a good human life.

"By Words, Not Arms": Lucretius on
Anatomy and Aggression

I

If from the earth we came, it was an earth
That bore us as a part of all the things
It breeds and that was lewder than it is.
Our nature is her nature. Hence it comes,
Since by our nature we grow old, earth grows
The same. We parallel the mother's death,
She walks in autumn ampler than the wind
Cries up for us and colder than the frost
Pricks in our spirits at the summer's end,
And over the bare spaces of our skies
She sees a barer sky that does not bend.

II

The body walks forth naked in the sun
And, out of tenderness or grief, the sun
Gives comfort, so that other bodies come,
Twinning our phantasy and our device,
And apt in versatile motion, touch and sound
To make the body covetous in desire
Of the still finer, more implacable chords.
So be it. Yet the spaciousness and light
In which the body walks and is deceived,
Falls from that fatal and that barer sky,
And this the spirit sees and is aggrieved.

Wallace Stevens, "Anatomy of Monotony"

I

Battle. Chariots equipped with scythes slice off the limbs of the enemy.
Legs and arms lie warm on the ground, still trembling in their blood. One
man charges eagerly forward, unaware that his left arm is being trampled

239

by the horses. Another presses on without his right. A third tries to rise without a leg, while the toes of his severed limb lie twitching on the ground. A head cut from the warm trunk preserves the look and gaze of life. (III.642–55)

Forest. An unarmed man is seized in the jaws of a wild beast, who begins to devour his still-living meal. The man fills the woods and mountains with his cries, as he watches his own insides being interred, still living, in a living grave. (V.988–93)

Bed. Lovers grasp their partners fiercely, causing pain. They dash mouth against mouth, biting the soft lips, urged on by a desire to hurt the object that has caused their frenzy. (IV.1079–83)

Battle. Bulls, boars, and lions, guided by their human trainers, advance against the human enemy. Smelling hot blood they go wild, making no distinctions. A lioness, hurling her body with a leap, tears the face of an advancing soldier. Another seizes an unwary man from behind, ripping him with curved claws. Bulls tear open the soft bellies of horses. Boars chew on their former masters, spilling blood on their unused weapons. Everywhere wounds noise flight terror tumult. Did this happen? Didn't they foresee the disaster that would ensue? Perhaps it is best to say that it happened in some possible world, not in this one. But if it happened, they did it not so much to win a victory, as to inflict the greatest possible pain on the enemy and despairing, to perish themselves. (V.1308ff.)[1]

Anger is a less overtly central theme in Lucretius' poem than are fear and love. No book of the poem, no extended discussion, is devoted to the diagnosis of the passions that prompt aggressive behavior, or to their therapy. And yet scenes of brutal aggression fill the work, drawing the reader's attention repeatedly and obsessively to the pervasiveness of violence in human life. The poem begins with, and owes its origin to, a temporary respite from war—as Venus, deflecting Mars from slaughter, permits the poet and his pupil Memmius to turn from the crisis of the Republic and fix their thoughts on philosophy (I.41–43). It ends with a fierce quarrel over corpses dead in the plague (VI.1278–86). And throughout the poem aggressions' damages assail the reader's sensibilities in language more graph-

---

[1] These are close paraphrases, with some material omitted. The second and third passages are quoted in chapters 6 and 5 respectively; the last is quoted in full later in this chapter.

240

ically physical than any devoted to the description of fear or grief. "Everything naked and unarmed yielded easily to everything that is armed" (V.1291–92): and the poem is obsessed with scenes of ripping, gouging, tearing, scenes in which what is soft and without protection yields to the intrusions of the tough and hard. If a central function of Epicurean therapeutic argument is to portray the soul's diseases in vivid frightening language, there is no disease to which more attention is given. The human body is presented to the reader as a soft unarmed thing, defenseless in the world of nature, subject to violence of many kinds. And the human soul, being not an immutable bodiless substance but a soft and divisible physical object, can itself be ripped, and lives unsafely. At the same time, however, the human being is a most dangerous being, more violent than any tough wild beast, a being who can create nightmarish horrors of destruction. The aggressive passions that tear this being's soul from within (V.45–46)— more hideous by far, according to Lucretius, than the monsters of myth and the beasts of nature—make it lash out at the world, a danger to itself and to others.

Above the slaughter, delicate and yet invulnerable, touched by neither gratitude nor anger, live the Epicurean gods, in a life of supreme peace. The peace of the gods rests upon their complete safety. Because they are not in and of this world, they can afford to be soft rather than tough, serene rather than aggressive, mildly idle rather than artfully resourceful. But their situation is not ours. Is there, then, any way in which human beings can live in peace, protecting the weak without violence, giving and receiving love and pleasure without aggression, gentle in an unsafe world?

I shall try to show the deep and organizing importance of this question for the De Rerum Natura as a whole. I shall examine Lucretius' contrast between the situation of the gods and the human situation, asking how he connects these metaphysical observations with an account of aggression's origins. Aggressive violence is mixed in complex ways with many human pursuits and with other complex passions; so I shall next examine more closely two of these connections—the aggressions connected with the fear of death and the aggressions of erotic love. I shall then examine Lucretius' account of the origins of aggressive behavior and warfare in the famous passage on the origins of civilization in Book V, concluding with the alarming passage about wild beasts at war. Lucretius shows here how human attempts to protect the body's fragile boundaries can lead, on the one hand, to tenderness, pleasure, and justice—but, on the other hand, and in other ways, to sadism and to slaughter. Finally, I shall try to uncover Lucretius' therapeutic recommendation—following his account, and his poetic embodiment, of philosophy's gentle war against violence, its war conducted "by words, not arms"—the only war through which a Roman citizen, it is claimed, can win a true triumph.

II

Before we approach Lucretius' depiction of anger, we need a sense of its philosophical context. The Epicurean view on which he bases his account is a distinctive one, one that causes his account of anger's therapy to diverge, in some respects, from parallel Stoic and Aristotelian accounts. But it also shares with these other accounts certain features that may initially strike a modern reader as peculiar. For both of these reasons, we need to examine it carefully, to see to what extent it is at odds with our own intuitions.

Most of Epicurus' known remarks about anger are made in connection with the portrayal of the gods. But these brief remarks suffice to give us a general idea of how he understood the passion and its connection with aggressive behavior. This account is confirmed and supplemented by the *On Anger* of Philodemus, one of our major sources of information concerning Epicurean emotion theory.[2]

The Epicurean analysis of anger focused, apparently, on the connection between anger and beliefs about the value of external items that can be damaged by another's agency. As in Aristotle's analysis, anger is seen to be associated with certain characteristic feelings—above all, for the Epicurean, feelings of heat, swelling, and irritation (Phld. O VIII.20–27); but its cognitive structure is seen as far more important, the ground of the feelings and the target of therapy. For if one does not think that external things that can be damaged are of very great importance, one will not believe that damages, when they occur, are of very great importance; and then, Philodemus argues, one will either not have anger at all, or will have only brief and light anger (O XLII, XLIV, XLVII–XLVIII, XLIX). In this way, anger is seen to rest upon a condition of exposure and weakness, in which the person, having invested a great part of herself in the vulnerable things of this world, is correspondingly subject to reversals of fortune. And anger is very closely connected, in its cognitive basis, to a group of other passions. Its nearest relative, both Epicurus and Philodemus stress, is gratitude. For the very same attachments that give rise to anger, should the

2 See Annas (1992).

actions of others prove maleficent, give rise to gratitude,[3] should they happen to behave well. The two passions are counterparts both in nature and in degree (O XLVI): if you have one, you will have the other; and if you have only a small amount of one, you will have a correspondingly small amount of the other (XLVIII). The gods, being in a condition of self-sufficiency, have neither one nor the other (Epicurus KD 1). The *Letter to Herodotus* adds that susceptibility to anger and gratitude is connected with both fear and need (77).

I have spoken of anger. My topic, however, is not only anger but also aggression. And, in fact, all major ancient analyses of *orgē*, or *ira*,[4] understand the passion to be, or to involve, not only the reactive emotion that we most often think of when we think of anger, but also a component of active aggression. For they hold that a wish for the suffering of the original aggressor is an essential part of what anger itself *is*. Aristotle defined anger in terms of two beliefs: the belief that one has been wronged, and the belief that retaliation would be a good thing; the former is accompanied by painful feeling, the latter is accompanied by pleasure. For the Stoics, who classify passions according to whether the judgments involved relate to the present or the future and according to whether the situation in view is perceived as good or bad, anger is not, as we might most naturally suppose, classified as a judgment concerning a bad present state of affairs. It is, instead, put in the good/future category, as a form of longing for a future good, namely for the punishment of the aggressor.[5] The Epicurean analysis of anger, too, makes the desire for the suffering of the damager an essential part of what anger itself is. Philodemus insists that the angry person thinks that the aggressor's suffering is good, even good in itself.

How do these connections work? It is not, clearly, a simple matter of automatic physiological reaction, an invasive stimulus provoking, mechanically, a defensive counterassault. The connections are made on the cognitive level. Philodemus' account gives us the following picture. If I believe that A has voluntarily inflicted a substantial damage on me, it is natural to feel that it would be a good thing for A to be punished, to suffer for what

---

[3] Some translators render *gratia* and Greek *charis*, in these contexts, with "favor"; but this fails to bring out the symmetry with anger: both are emotions based upon beliefs about the importance of externals.

[4] For the Greek and Roman anger-vocabulary, see the Stoic taxonomies presented in *SVF* III.397–38 and in Cic. *TD* 4 (pertinent sections excerpted in *SVF*). The large number of anger-words seems to be evidence of an intense interest in this passion in both the Greek and Roman worlds; no similarly elaborate taxonomy is given for varieties of fear, or love.

[5] For anger as a form of *epithumia* (i.e., desire for a future good), see *SVF* III.397.

she has done. Similarly, on the side of gratitude, the thought that A has gone out of her way to help me is naturally linked with a thought that it would be nice for good things to befall A; and Philodemus seems to hold that this wish is a part of what gratitude is. Aristotle urged that failing to form the wishes and projects characteristic of anger is a sign of "slavishness": allowing oneself to be "kicked around" by others without in some manner retaliating shows a deficient sense of one's own worth (*EN* 1126a3–8). Anger he construes as some form of retaliatory self-assertion; it involves, in itself, a counterassault. Epicurus (as Philodemus reports him) appears to agree, analyzing the retaliatory element as a wish that the aggressor be punished.

To Christian and post-Christian readers, these connections seem suspect—for we have become so accustomed to the idea of turning the other cheek to aggression that it might at first seem natural to suppose that one could be very angry, even justifiably so, without wishing to do harm in return.[6] I believe, however, that the ancient analyses are not, after all, so remote from our own beliefs, if we examine them further: that if it is really anger we are dealing with, and not simply an awareness that one has been wronged, this does involve a negative wish directed back at the aggressor. But before we can see this, we need to make some qualifications. First, it is important to bear in mind that anger need not be acted on to have the feature in question. What the analysis requires is a wish for the other's suffering, not retaliatory action, which one might for many reasons decide not to pursue. The claim is, simply, that to be angry at someone is not only to blame them for having done a voluntary wrong, it is also to wish them ill. Second, the ill that is wished may not be anything so dramatic as death or bodily torture. It may be far subtler: punishment by the law; punishment by god in the afterlife; a life that does not turn out well, and in which the world recognizes the person's badness; the suffering of recognizing the terrible wrong one has done; or even, perhaps, just the ill of going on being the sort of bad person the person actually is (the basis for Dante's picture of hell). Once we understand that ill-wishing may take all these complex and subtle forms, the claim that some ill-wishing is essential to anger seems far more plausible. Third, a diagnosis of anger and ill-wishing may turn out to

---

[6] For a valuable analysis, and related observations about the Christian tradition, see Murphy and Hampton (1988). They agree with this analysis in preserving the conceptual connection between anger and ill-wishing—and agree with the Hellenistic traditions that the real question should be whether it is right to be angry. They stress that the role of forgiveness in the Christian tradition is precisely that of overcoming angry resentment *and* the ill wishes associated with it, not that of driving a wedge between anger and ill-wishing.

be as complex and long-term a matter as is, in Lucretius' view, the diagnosis of the fear of death. Although Lucretius' analysis does not mention unconscious beliefs explicitly in connection with anger, except insofar as it is analyzed in connection with the fear of death, there is no reason why one could not extend the analysis to cover anger more generally—interpreting an extended pattern of behavior as revealing desire for the other's suffering, even though this desire was not at first transparent even to the agent. Finally, anger may arise in the context of an ongoing love, and thus its wishes may prove extremely hard to disentangle from other more pervasive wishes for the object's good.

With these qualifications in mind, in order to assess the distance between the Epicurean conception and some of our own—and thus to understand it better—let us consider several putative counterexamples to the Epicurean claim that anger involves a wish for ill to the damager. Or, rather, let us imagine how Nikidion might consider them, as she ponders the Epicurean definition at the beginning of her philosophical education. But since here, once again, we shall be imagining her as at Rome,[7] and since the topic of anger seems to have assumed a special prominence in Roman Epicureanism,[8] in the light of characteristically Roman concerns, let us now imagine Nikidion pondering the definition in the light of Roman examples.

Imagining this transition also requires us to imagine her in a world in which aggressive behavior is much admired, in which military might and the daring of the good commander are central human virtues, and sluggish inactivity the most contemptible choice. It is a world in which the human being defines itself as superior to the beasts by striving for victory, by hard work in agriculture, seafaring, military affairs—in short, by practical enterprises, usually of a competitive sort, rather than by any more leisured or reflective exercise. In this world, Lucius Catilina, the notorious subversive of Lucretius' lifetime, can hardly be described as a villain by the historian Sallust (a valuable source for ordinary moral beliefs of the first century B.C.E.), without also being described as a hero. His capacity for labor and endurance, his "great vigor of body and mind," his "daring, flexible, cunning mind" with its intensely aggressive desires for whatever is high (cf. Sallust *Cat.* 5)—all these traits, essential to his alleged villainy, also mark him, for a Roman audience, as a seductively attractive figure. In fact, one

---

[7] On Lucretius' Roman milieu, and Roman Epicureanism generally, see Bailey (1947) I.5ff., and Grimal (1963).

[8] Philodemus also wrote, at Naples, in a Rome-influenced context, though no doubt his circle was quite different from those of Lucretius and Seneca at Rome. For a comprehensive account of Hellenistic treatments of anger, see Fillion-Lahille (1984).

has only to read Sallust's enumeration of common moral opinions at the opening of his work to be brought up short by the enormous attention given to aggression and the military virtues. For, having given an eloquent abstract argument that human beings should distinguish themselves from the beasts by seeking virtue, especially virtue of mind, the historian then continues, without any break: "But for a long time there has been a big argument among mortals as to whether military affairs progress better by force of body or virtue of mind" (1.5). The point of the earlier praise of virtue, then, seems to have been to prepare the way for an analysis of military might. In this world, heroes are generals, not philosophers. And the more successfully aggressive they are, the better.[9]

Imagine Nikidion, in this world, confronting the definition that links the reactive passion of anger with a wish for harm to the wrongdoer. It is likely to seem less problematic to her, given her context, than it does to us. But this will not prevent her, if she is an apt philosophical pupil, from considering counterexamples. In fact, Romans who wished to defend anger as a military motive often wanted to deny that it had any bad consequences. So if she is already interested enough in Epicurus' view to believe that harming others is morally suspect, she will want to ask whether anger, by itself, does really commit the angry person to wishing some sort of harm. She imagines four cases:

Case 1. She imagines a woman who is a slave, who is mistreated by her masters, subjugated both to hard labor and to sexual service. This woman may, she imagines, be so exhausted in spirit that she not only takes no action against the masters, but does not even dream it or wish it. Nikidion may think, considering this woman, that one of the awful features of this woman's situation is the absence of any such self-assertive response.

Here, clearly, Nikidion should judge that the slave woman is not really angry at her master. Like the "slavish" people described by Aristotle, she is

[9] Sallust's other heroes are military as well: Jugurtha, Marius; see Syme (1964). Sallust's enterprise in the *Catiline* is to vindicate his own career by aligning himself with a rigorous form of traditional moral judgment: see Syme. This goal makes him a good source for traditional values. Greek values are not altogether different; there too, outside the philosophers, there is great emphasis on a norm of the citizen as stouthearted soldier: see Winkler (1990). But the emphasis on the leisured life of the Athenian gentleman that we find in both philosophical and non-philosophical writers does suggest a difference of emphasis, at least. Leisure is not inactivity; but it is incompatible with being always on campaign, a natural state for a Roman hero. And Lucretius plainly identifies the peaceful value of philosophy with its Greek origins; he is concerned (as is Seneca later) to show that adherence to philosophy can be made consistent with what is deepest in a Roman reader's beliefs, even though it entails revising many of them. See Classen (1968), Grimal (1963).

allowing herself to "be kicked around." Anger would have been, by contrast, a response of self-assertion and self-defense.[10] The Epicurean analysis holds that if anger had been there, the wish that the masters be in some way punished would also have been there; and this seems very plausible. Furthermore, the Epicurean analysis gives insight into what has gone wrong. For it appears that the slave woman really does not believe in the worth of her own bodily integrity. Thus, she really does not believe that what has been damaged is of very great value. It is this that prevents anger from getting off the ground.

Case 2. Nikidion now thinks of a man powerful in political life, a man accustomed to the aggressive struggle for honor and fortune, but increasingly troubled, and deprived of joy by his own insecurity. Like the tyrant in Plato's *Republic*, he becomes the prey of fears and anxieties that undo his capacity for competition and even, eventually, for action. Harmed by others, he no longer wishes them ill, but hides away. In the end, he hates the outdoor active life he formerly prized and, hating his anxieties and fear, he also hates himself. If Nikidion has read Lucretius' poem already she knows that Lucretius describes such a person in Book III: a person whose hatred of insecurity causes him to wish ill, not to his rivals, but to his own life.

This depressive reaction to damages and uncertainties is prominently recognized in Lucretius' analysis—not only in the passage we have mentioned but also, as I shall argue, in the strange passage on wild beasts at war. What Nikidion should say here is that there is anger in the story, and aggression as well—in the form of a desire for the suffering of the one responsible—only this one is believed to be oneself, seen as finite, needy, insecure; and aggression is then turned inward. The political man does indeed wish himself suffering—at the limit, Lucretius points out, even death.

Case 3. Nikidion now imagines a case closer to home—a case that, as we can tell from Musonius Rufus' writings on women and philosophy,[11] must have been rather common in the Roman family. It may be the story of several of her friends. She imagines a Roman wife and mother who is told by her husband that she must not go in for "higher education," that is, for philosophical study—for, he says, it will distract her from her tasks as mother and manager of a household. This appears, to Nikidion at any rate, to be a damage, for the woman is being deprived of what both Stoics and

[10] See also Murphy and Hampton (1988), especially Murphy's "Forgiveness and Resentment."

[11] See Musonius Rufus, "That Women Too Should Do Philosophy?" ed. Hense (1905)—on which see chapter 9.

Epicureans hold to be necessary for achieving the human end, *eudaimonia*. And yet it seems easy to imagine this woman loving her children and her husband, and forming no ill wish against them.

Cases like this one cannot be well understood without a much more elaborate analysis of a long-term pattern of behavior and thought. Perhaps Nikidion will find out that the wife is not angry: insofar as the situation damages her, she perceives the damages as light or trivial. Perhaps, indeed, despite her awareness of philosophical views about philosophy's importance, she does not share these views, holding consistently that her own life is fine. Perhaps, on the other hand, it will emerge on further inspection that she is very angry—perhaps without being fully aware of it—and that she manifests in many ways the wish that others should suffer for having caused her unhappiness. There are many subtle ways in which aggression can manifest itself in family life; frequently it is hard to recognize it, without a long-term pattern—all the more since it can be counteracted by love. As with the fear of death, we would need to bring together patterns of behavior, unexplained symptoms, and moments of acknowledgment, before we could be at all confident of a diagnosis. But if Nikidion were convinced that the wife really recognizes that she has been deliberately wronged by her husband, it will be natural to look for such a pattern of aggression, or at least of spiteful ill-wishing, which for our purposes is aggression enough. What is far less likely is that we could reach an explanation of the case in which we ascribe to the wife a belief that she has been seriously damaged by her husband's voluntary actions, *and* ascribe to her anger in connection with this belief, without at the same time ascribing to her the view that it would be a good thing if her husband suffered in some way for what he has done. The ascription of anger does seem to depend, Nikidion would be likely to conclude, on the discovery, or the postulation, of some sort of negative wish—although, as we have said, that wish may take many forms.

Case 4. Nikidion now imagines another common sort of domestic anger: a parent becoming angry at a child who misbehaves. (She could equally well have thought of temporary and localized angers between loving spouses.) The mother, she imagines, really loves the child; she goes on loving the child and wishing it well, even while she is angry. She is really upset, she really does believe that the child has deliberately offended her, she does take it seriously. But does she of necessity wish the child *harm*, in a way that conflicts with her overall good wishes?

A number of different possibilities must be distinguished here. First, it seems perfectly possible for her to wish some corrective punishment for the child without being really *angry*; and very often we do feel that parental irritation stops short of being full-fledged anger, inasmuch as the parent does not react to a child's misbehavior as a threat to her own important ends.[12] Often, too, the response falls short of being anger because the child's wrongdoing is not seen as fully voluntary.[13] But suppose real serious anger is on the scene, anger involving the unbalancing sense that one's own aims have been seriously compromised by another's actions. Then it does seem plausible to think that the parent wishes something bad to happen to the child—some suffering, some constraint in the pursuit of the child's own interests. Often enough love will temper this wish, prevent it from being acted on, or convert it to a wish for a punishment that is gentle and educative rather than a real harm. But it would, I think, seem plausible to Nikidion that the wish of anger by itself is aggressive—that the real imbalance in the parent's sense of self would give rise to a wish that is itself unbalanced, and possibly difficult to govern. This is why anger is found so frightening by children: fear is the appropriate response to the perception of anger's aggressive wish. And this is why anger might seem to be always a danger in domestic life.[14]

Thinking about the Epicurean definition in this way, Nikidion would probably feel convinced that *ira* was a problem worth worrying about for anyone who was concerned about the various forms aggressive behavior may take, in personal relations and in society. The Roman civil war would give her obvious motives for such concern. Not simply a harmless reaction, anger is the cause of damages. And, by examining the definition along with her, we have been able to see, I think, that the Epicurean account is not as completely foreign to our own intuitions about the relationship between anger and aggression as we might initially have supposed, but a reasonably good place for the citizen of a very different, but comparably militaristic and aggressive, nation to begin.

One remedy for the damages of anger, according to Epicurus, is complete self-containment and self-sufficiency. The wise man, the *Letter to Herodotus* informs us, will avoid being in any condition of weakness or need toward his fellow humans; in this way, he will manage to avoid both

[12] As we shall see, it is this attitude that Seneca recommends for the punisher in general.

[13] On the voluntary actions of the child in a process of moral education, see the study of Aristotle's views in Sherman (1989).

[14] Child abuse is recognized as a cause of moral deformity by Aristotle in *EN* VII.5; cf. Price (1989).

anger and gratitude. Philodemus tells a similar story. The wise man, who does not think external things very important, will sometimes feel brief or light anger—probably, although this is not made clear in the text, in connection with damages to things he does (as an Epicurean) appropriately cherish, such as his health or his life or, perhaps, his friends. But most offenses will meet a calmer and more humane response. Being, Philodemus says, the mildest and most gentle of men (O XLIV), he will view an offense as a remediable defect in the offender, and, if he seeks a punishment, he will regard it not as something good or enjoyable, but as necessary for correction or improvement (O XLIV, cf. DL 10.121).

We can see why cutting ties to the external world might be sufficient for the avoidance of anger and aggression; but we might want to know whether so much is really necessary. For the Epicurean proposal, at least as described in the passages we have mentioned, seems to get rid of too much. In particular, it seems to get rid of the element of protectiveness and loyalty that is a major part of most ordinary forms of human affiliation and love, which we might think of enormous importance. Some of these, moreover, are recognized as very important by Epicurus himself—for, although it is difficult to reconstruct his view with confidence, given the slim and apparently contradictory nature of the evidence, friendship may be, in his view, not only a major instrumental good but also an end in itself.[15] There seems to be something cold and even brutal in the wise man's self-sufficiency, in the hardness with which he denies his need of others and limits his investment in their lives. It is difficult to tell how Epicurus solves this problem; but we shall see that Lucretius confronts it, presenting a complicated picture of our human goal, where anger is concerned. He will give an account of the therapy of anger that aims at a familial and communal, not a solitary, self-sufficiency, fostering, rather than eradicating, ties of interdependence and mutual need among human beings.

---

[15] See the extensive account of these issues in Mitsis (1988a). One especially vexing problem is textual: the claim that every friendship is "through itself *aretē*" has been found corrupt by some editors, who have emended to "through itself choiceworthy" (*hairetē*). Mitsis defends the emendation and places some weight on the passage. It seems to me that it is not clearly corrupt as it stands, and that, in any case, no such conjecture should bear much weight in settling a question of this magnitude. (Furthermore, the idea of "for its own sake" would more usually be expressed with *heneka* plus the genitive: *dia* is more regularly causal.) See my discussion in Nussbaum (1991a), where I argue that, although this passage by itself does not settle the issue, the evidence of Cicero's *De Finibus* does lend further support to Mitsis' interpretation. The case for this is strengthened if we think of Epicurean pleasure as unimpeded natural activity: for then the interactions of *philia* can count, themselves, as constituents of the end.

III

"The blessed and immortal has no troubles itself and causes no trouble to any other, so that it is constrained neither by anger nor by gratitude. For all this sort of thing resides in weakness" (*KD* 1). In this way the first of Epicurus' *Principal Opinions*—first, then, among the sayings that pupils were to memorize and repeat as their "fourfold drug"—connects the strength of self-sufficiency with the absence of anger. And a central purpose of Epicurean religious teaching was to attack the idea that the gods have the motives for angry punishing action toward humans—or, for that matter, for gratitude and favor—that popular religion ascribes to them. The gods are complete: that is what it is to be divine, to be without limit or need. But, being complete, they have no interest in our world and no needs from it. Therefore, nothing we do in our world (and, indeed, nothing that takes place in theirs) can be an occasion for rage. Anger is an outgrowth of weakness and "does not harmonize with the condition of blessedness" (*LHdt* 77).

Lucretius accepts this characterization and develops it, using the peace of the gods as a foil for the aggressions of the world we live in. Indeed, the trait of the gods that he most persistently emphasizes is their freedom from the constraints of anger. And he invites the reader to reflect about the connection between this freedom and the gods' secure and replete life, the connection between both of these and their soft delicate natures. Near the opening of the first book, just after appealing to Venus to give Rome a temporary respite from war, allowing Lucretius to write his poem and Memmius to attend to it, the poet describes the nature and situation of the gods. The juxtaposition has sometimes been found harsh, and the lines (repeated in Book II) removed;[16] but their pertinence to the troubles of Rome and the situation of poet and pupil is plain:

> For it is necessary that all the nature of the gods should enjoy immortal life with the highest peace, set apart from our affairs and a long way separated. For free from all pain, free from danger, flourishing with their own resources, in no way in need of us, they are neither constrained by gratitude nor touched by anger. (I.44–49 = II.646–51)

Their situation stands in dramatic contrast with that of the Roman Republic—needy, endangered, rent by civil conflict. It is natural to ask how that peace might be ours, and whether philosophy can give it.

[16] See Bailey (1947) ad loc., where he criticizes his earlier decision (Bailey [1900]) to omit the lines from Book I. See also chapter 5.

The poem's other discussions of the gods' nature reinforce and further develop this picture. In Book II (1090ff.) the poet proclaims that the Epicurean view has freed nature from harsh and arrogant masters. The gods really dwell in "tranquil peace" (1093), living a "placid and serene life" (1094)—and they lack all interest in controlling the world of nature, or in using nature to punish us. Again, completeness and tranquillity are linked; and both are linked with an absence of aggression. Elsewhere we are told that the gods did not design this world for us: its goods are not benefits, its bad features not damages (V.156ff.). Book VI, again, reminds the interlocutor of the foolishness of imagining that the gods' "very great power" can ever be assailed in such a way that they would be led to "seek harsh punishments out of anger." They live "inactive in calm peace," and to suppose that they "roll toward us great billows of anger" is to disturb oneself needlessly (VI.71–79).

Book V informs us that the gods are not secure on account of being fortified, hard, or tough: indeed, they are extremely light and delicate, so delicate, in fact, that they can be apprehended only by our minds, not our senses. Furthermore, unlike Plato's forms or Aristotle's god, they are physical beings, composed of atoms and void, divisible and, at least in principle, changeable like everything else in nature. Thus the account of their invulnerability emphasizes features that make them safe in the world of nature: both the fineness of their physical composition, which eludes blows, and the secure non-aggressive character of their surroundings. They can be gentle, apparently, because they do not live in our exposed situation in our risky world. Their homes are far removed from us—indeed, from any usual sort of world, since they apparently reside in the *intermundia*, the space between worlds—and are very different from our surroundings, being delicate and light as their bodies are light (V.146–55). In that world they are entirely free from trouble:

> The divinity of the gods is revealed, and their peaceful home, which no wind shakes, no clouds wet with storms, no white falling snow violates, frozen together with harsh frost—and always the cloudless air covers it, and smiles with widely diffused light. Nature, furthermore, supplies everything, nor does anything erode their peace of mind at any time. (III.18–24)

We are told relatively little about the physical nature and the physical environment of the gods. We do not know what it *is* that nature supplies to them—what supplies, if any, they require (note also the emphasis on resources in I.48–II.650), and how their divisible physical being is, if at all, nourished and sustained. But we are made to understand that their delicate non-aggressive nature is connected with the fact that—though physical and thus in principle destructible—they live in a world perfectly suited to their mildness, a delicate supportive world in which neither climate nor enemy poses a threat of violence.

I have based this account of the Epicurean gods on what Lucretius himself tells us. On several difficult questions I have taken no stand.[17] Do the gods have a substantial form of their own, or are they simply identical with the stream of *simulacra* that is the object of our awareness? If the former, how do they replenish themselves, given that *simulacra* are constantly peeling off? What resources do they have for this in the *intermundia*, and how, without trouble or action, do they secure these? If the latter, what sort of existence, what sort of self-sufficiency, is this? How is this life supposed to be a life of serene peace? And a further question now arises: are we to understand (on the latter account) that the gods are, in effect, simply our mental constructs? This view has recently been vigorously defended by A. A. Long and David Sedley, who claim that the gods function as human constructions of an ideal of blessedness and self-sufficiency. Humans intensify or perfect actual features of human existence, and it is this imaginative enhancement of what we know that gives rise to the *simulacra* of large beautiful self-sufficient humans that we call gods.[18]

Lucretius' poem does not settle these issues. On the one hand, like the Epicurean interlocutor in Cicero's *De Natura Deorum*, Lucretius' poet-speaker seems to want Memmius to believe in the real existence of gods with the characteristics described. And Book V's account of the origins of religion appears to endorse, as evidence of this reality, early humans' pre-conceptions of the gods' beauty, self-sufficiency, and immortality—though it is by no means easy to tell which features of these imaginings the poet approves. On the other hand, the function of gods in the poem is, above all, to exemplify self-sufficiency and peace, and to undermine religious doc-

---

[17] For representative discussions of entirely different sorts, see Long and Sedley (1987) and Rist (1972), the latter with extensive discussion of the views of others. The central text from Cicero's *De Natura Deorum* is well analyzed by Pease (1955).

[18] Long and Sedley (1987) 139–49. The view has, I think, problems, despite its attractiveness. It requires placing a good deal of weight on a passage from Sextus Empiricus, who probably should not be regarded as a very reliable authority in such a matter. And their contention that each human constructs an image of divinity in accordance with his or her own personal norms makes the view far more subjectivistic than the evidence allows: for Epicurus plainly believes that he can criticize many widely held views of divinity as false and inappropriate; and he also thinks that it is the striking consensus on certain features of divinity that provides some evidence for the validity of those features.

trines that are a threat to peace. In any case, the choice between the Long-Sedley view and other more conventional views does not affect the point in which I am most interested here: namely, that the self-sufficiency of the gods is a condition that depends upon their peculiar situation. Whether we say that they are really self-sufficient because they dwell in a non-threatening home that somehow enables them to resist decay, or whether we instead say that people cannot imagine an ideal of complete self-sufficiency in anthropomorphic form without imagining it in conditions very different from the ones that obtain in our world, the contrast between divine and mortal situations remains, and its implications for anger.

Contrast, then, our world. This world, Lucretius argues, could not have been made for our benefit, because it is, from our point of view, so grossly defective (V. 199). Half of it is made uninhabitable by mountains, by woods teeming with wild beasts, by rocks and swamps and seas that greedily possess it (V. 200–203). Of the rest, two-thirds are made useless for us by excessive heat or cold. The arable part is covered with shrubs and undergrowth, unless humans labor hard to plow it. Even when we do plow, the crops are often killed by drought or storms or frost or wind (204–17). Furthermore, the world is full of wild beasts, "hostile to the human race [genti]," the "horrifying race [genus] of wild beasts," which the world nourishes and supports on land and sea (218–20). The changes of season bring disease; premature death stalks us (220–21). The earth itself, meanwhile, is aging, losing the vital energy that is the source of our sustenance. And the beasts—on whose ubiquity as a threat to our weaker bodies the poem repeatedly insists (e.g., V. 39–40, V.998ff.)—live better lives in this dangerous and imperfect world than we do. For they are naturally more protected than we are, and have less need of covering:

> The human child,[19] like a sailor tossed out from the fierce waves, lies naked on the ground, speechless, in need of every sort of aid to stay alive, when first Nature brings it forth by labor from its mother's womb into the shores of light. And it fills the place with a mournful crying, as is appropriate for one who has such troubles ahead in life. But the various sorts of cattle and wild beasts grow up and have no need of rattles, nor does anyone have to speak to them in the gentle broken speech of the fostering nurse, nor do they look for different clothing for the changes of season. Finally, they have no need of arms, or of tall walls, to protect their own, since the earth itself supplies everything to all of them, and Nature the artful maker of things. (V. 222–34)

[19] For puer as child of either sex, cf. 3.447 and Bailey (1947) ad loc.

In other words, this world is a world in which beasts are at home, and live, more or less, in a godlike situation, Nature supplying everything they need. The invulnerability of the gods is delicate and soft; the beasts' invulnerability is their toughness. Armed by Nature against the weather, equipped to sustain themselves in the hunt for food and their struggles against one another by "either guile or strength or mobility" (V.857), they are, though mortal, at least relatively self-sufficient. Though they are, in a sense, aggressive, and although their heat and ferocity is invoked elsewhere to explain part of the Nature of anger (III.288ff.), there is a sense in which they lack the conditions for full-fledged anger. For they are not depicted as conscious of voluntary damages that do them substantial harm: nor are they desirous of inflicting punishments. They are not only dull in awareness—they are not, in fact, terribly needy, being well equipped by Nature and at home in it.[20] And their aggressive behavior, though we anthropomorphize it, looks, when we scrutinize it more closely, more like a part of their natural equipment than like the expression of a complex learned cognitive/ethical disposition. They are not grateful to Nature for her benefits; no more are they angry at assaults. When they attack us, they are simply after a meal.

Epicurus and Lucretius thus continue an ancient tradition according to which the human being is situated in Nature between the beasts and the gods; Lucretius follows this tradition in showing, too, that the beasts and the gods have a certain surprising resemblance to one another. Both are in their own way self-sufficient; neither needs the social or political virtues. Epicurus' gods, being more radically self-sufficient than the gods of myth, appear to be even more radically asocial. They have no responsiveness, it seems, to anything outside themselves, probably not even to one another; certainly they have no compassion for our suffering. In this they resemble the beasts; and their gentle softness is not so unlike the others' hardness, given the change in surroundings.

Indeed, Lucretius' gods are even closer to the beasts than the gods of previous versions of this tradition. For they are not only not like us in respect of their bodily nature, they also seem, so far as Lucretius' own portrayal is concerned, to lack thought, speech, and action. The characteri-

---

[20] This does not mean that a particular animal could not be aware on a particular occasion of some pain or deprivation, and have some disturbance as a result. Philodemus thinks that the animals have at least analogues of some of our emotions: see *De Dis* 11.19–20, 28–34; 13.30–31, 34–35; 14.7–8, 21–28, 29–30; on all of this, see Sorabji (1993). What they seem to lack is the awareness of the voluntariness of a damage that is essential for full-fledged anger, and the belief that the wrongdoer should be *punished*.

zation of their life is almost totally negative. We hear of freedom from care and want, of peace, of freedom from fear, of perfect self-sufficiency—but not of any activity, even mental activity, issuing from this. The account of early human dreams in Book V (1161–82) adds several of the features that the later Epicurean tradition stressed: as in Cicero's account, the gods are anthropomorphic, large, and beautiful. Lucretius reports that humans endowed them (*tribuebant*, 1172) with sense-perception, since they seemed to move and to speak—but the extent of his endorsement is unclear, and *tribuo* is the term used in Book IV for unwarranted extrapolation. The claim that they "seemed in dreams to do many wondrous things without any effort" (1181–82) is similarly unendorsed. Certainly there is here no trace of the elaborate positive account of the gods' eating, drinking, and other activities that we find in Philodemus' *De Dis*.[21]

At any rate, even if we give these lines the most positive possible reading and supplement them with the portrait of the gods in Cicero, Lucretius' gods clearly do very little. As Cicero's Cotta says: "God does nothing, is involved in no ties of occupation, plans no projects, takes delight in his own wisdom and virtue" (51). And Lucretius fails conspicuously to stress in his own voice this wisdom and virtue, stressing, instead, only the absence of vice. Clearly his gods lack the usual motives for worldly action, including, it would seem, most ethically virtuous action; in this, Epicurus would be agreeing with a number of earlier thinkers, including Aristotle.[22] But Aristotle's god was a thinking being, and thinking was taken by both Plato and Aristotle to be something one could love and choose, even without awareness of any incompleteness, or pressure of any need. This is not so in the Epicurean tradition. Epicurus defines philosophical thinking in terms of its practical goal: "Philosophy is the art that secures the happy life by means of reasonings and arguments. This means that a creature whose happiness is permanently complete has no motive to pursue it (cf. also *KD* 11). The secure life is also the life without philosophy.

In short: the gods are models, but in a negative way. They lack our rage and our weakness, but they also seem to lack, therefore, many of the arts we have contrived to deal with our weakness—among these, social morality

---

[21] Rist (1972), who ascribes to Epicurus an elaborate positive account of the gods' nature and activities, is frustrated at Lucretius' failure to mention which parts of mortal dreams he endorses and which he does not: he is also inclined to trust parts of the evidence of Philodemus' *De Dis*, which many scholars regard as distant from the original Epicurean position.

[22] Aristotle *EN* X.1178b10–16. Similar views are present in Xenophanes and, perhaps, in Heraclitus.

and philosophy. They do mirror, in a sense, the self-sufficiency of the beasts; and, like them, lack the cognitive basis of anger. But they lack this because they lack a certain sort of investment in the world and its events that may be inevitable, and even good, in a human life. We are already invited to ask whether human beings can or should set themselves toward the goal of divine happiness—and whether complete freedom from anger, in their case, is not connected with other absences, of friendship, poetry, argument.

In between these two realms of self-sufficiency, in a world made, so to speak, for the wild beasts, lives a being whose soft nakedness links it to the world of the gods. "Naked and unarmed," the human being, however, lives in a world that is not suited to its needs, a world that confronts its nakedness aggressively. What to the beasts is just sun and rain is, to the unprotected human child, a deadly assault. Even the process of birth is like a violent exhausting tempest. And, once born, the child finds Nature full of violence. Lucretius describes the menacing face of the world of Nature as if the elements themselves were willing aggressors: mountains and woods "greedily hold" our land; heat and cold "rob" us of our living; Nature "by her force [vi] obscures with undergrowth" the arable land; rain, wind, and sun "kill" and "vex" our crops; the world "feeds and nourishes" our enemies, the beasts. From the human viewpoint, the earth is a hostile invading army, aggressively directing its weapons against the delicate boundaries of the child's body. And the aggressive violence of beasts, in league with Nature, makes the unarmed human, often, little more than a "living meal" (V.991).

In the passage about the human child, Lucretius mentions two responses to the danger in which humans find themselves: counteraggression and society. Weapons, arms, walls, towers are our devices to give ourselves the security the beasts have already. As we shall later see, these stratagems are two-edged: they provide a certain security, but they also increase insecurity and thus nourish future aggression. There is, however, another response depicted: the tenderness of the nurse, the compassion that leads to the protection of the weak. The two responses are certainly not incompatible. Both seem to have their origin in a reasonable desire for self-preservation, the continuation of that which is oneself and one's own.[23] And both have a good deal in common: for a nurse protects a child by giving it a certain sort

---

[23] Although, unlike the Stoics, Epicurus does not make the desire for self-preservation the basic desire of the child, he does recognize such a desire, by recognizing a class of "necessary desires," among them desires for things necessary for life.

of armor—clothing, a safe room to sleep in, guardians to watch over it. Both responses seem necessary, to some degree, in any human community. But there are also tensions between them; for a human being who is fully armed, and thus self-sufficient like a beast, has little need of others, little motive to treat others gently; the gentle interactions between nurse and baby require an absence of defensive hardness.

Three further points emerge in this passage. First, the human being is not by nature a ferocious or aggressive being. The human child is shown as weak, needy, and rather sad; but it is not hostile.[24] Lucretius does not try, here or elsewhere, to explain aggression as the outgrowth of an instinctive desire; this is consistent with what we know about Epicurus.

But, second, we can also see that aggression does not require any particular bad social formation in order to arise. Arms—and the desire to use them—are a reasonable response to a correct perception of the situation one is in, the fragility of one's boundaries. All that needs to be added to this perception is an attachment to one's own life as a thing of value—and this Lucretius takes to be both universal and legitimate. "Whatever is born appropriately wants to remain alive, as long as sweet pleasure holds on to it" (V.177–78). The correct perception of life's worth is the origin not only of fear, but also of anger. Something further is needed, to be sure, to convert a threatening situation into one eliciting anger: for, to give rise to anger, damages must be seen as voluntarily inflicted. Thus if a human being lived alone in a natural world that threatened him, but without any superstitious or religious views about how the world operated, and without any deliberate human aggressors, he could have fear without having anger. And, as we shall see, the "first mortals" even used weapons against the beasts for self-protection, apparently without anger—for they did not, apparently, see the damages as deliberate, or think of themselves as inflicting punishment. But, given our ungodlike situation of general danger and scarcity, we would expect the competition for resources and survival—and thus the roots of aggression—to be present in any human social group. And philosophy will not be able to achieve the complete eradication of anger unless it eradicates, as well, either these dangers or the reasonable fear for one's own safety and the safety of others.

Third, we should notice that there is a striking difference between the two responses, with relation to the cosmology Lucretius has mapped out. The response of arms and counteraggression consists in turning oneself into a quasi-beast, devising the tough armor and imitating the ferocity that

---

[24] For a similar view, see Mitsis (1988a).

beasts show already by nature. We might also say that such a response, if successful enough, can give the human being an almost godlike life, in which nothing threatens it and it has whatever it needs. The social response, however, is unavailable to both beasts and gods; for in those realms of self-sufficiency there is no understanding of mutual dependence, no tenderness, no compassion. The possibility is held out that, by gentle interdependence, human beings can live safely without rage, calling on one another rather than on arms, becoming not beastlike but more communally human.

Is this a genuine possibility? What does it depend on, and how far does it solve our problems? Is the compassion of the nurse an alternative to wars and arms, or only the preparation of future warriors? Isn't communal anger, too, a possibility—and a more dangerous one, perhaps, than the individual's rage? We can begin answering these questions only when we have studied some cases of human aggression and ferocity, understanding their psychological structure.

IV

I have said that anger and aggression are seen by Epicureans to be closely related to other passions. Before he presents his picture of the origins of civilization, which provides Memmius with a picture of the gradual development of both aggression and community, Lucretius has shown him two case studies of aggression in the contemporary Roman world, cases that begin to uncover the psychology of aggression and to show its self-increasing patterns. Both passionate love, in Book IV, and the fear of death, in Book III (which I shall here treat together with Book V's account of religious fear and dependence) reveal a common pattern in our most violent desires and actions, tracing the origins of aggression to a fear for the safety of one's own bodily boundaries, combined with a set of beliefs—mostly false and sometimes very elaborate—about what has damaged those boundaries, and what will suffice to protect them.

Lovers inflict pain on one another (IV.1079–83). They do so because they perceive their desire for the other person as a source of pain—a wound or ulcerous sore in the self (IV.1068, 1069, 1070). Their condition of neediness is experienced as an open hole, a lack of self-sufficiency, accompanied by weakness (*tabescunt vulnere caeco*, 1120). In sexual intimacy they seek to heal these wounds—or, as Lucretius also puts it, to extinguish the fire that burns them (1086–87), thus achieving a condition of self-sufficiency. In part they pursue this aim in a disordered way, uncertain of what they are after—madly biting and scratching in a way that indicates their wish to take revenge on the source of their weakness. In part, as I have argued, they are animated by a more specific, though hidden, aim—the aim to defeat the source of their pain by achieving incorporation or fusion with the object to which they have ascribed such exalted importance. Becoming totally merged with that body, they would no longer be agonized by the pain of desire for it: so this wish for fusion seems to be one version of their more general wish for an end to vulnerability and weakness. Their frenzied biting and grasping is both an attempt to achieve that aim, and—as they realize, increasingly, that they will not achieve it—an expression of rage against the separateness of the other person, which is an obstacle to the fulfillment of their wish. Throughout, the other person is seen as a voluntary aggressor, in that she has damaged the self-sufficiency they wished to achieve by inflicting the debilitating and even shameful wounds of desire and need. Desire and rage race with one another, unlimited, generating ever more obsessive projects of domination and punishment.[25]

This spiral, we have said, is not necessary; Lucretius shows that the lover's aims are based upon false beliefs about what will restore one's mastery and self-sufficiency. And he suggests that a "pure pleasure" is available that avoids these false beliefs. There are also some suggestions in the poem that female sexuality, even in the current culture, is somewhat less aggressive than male sexuality.[26] This would be no great surprise, since the

[25] Good general discussions are in Godwin (1986) and Brown (1987). Brown convincingly shows that the violence in Lucretius' description of erotic biting is in striking contrast with other references to such bites in Latin poetry, where they are usually playful and non-painful.

[26] In the discussion of mutual pleasure, the woman's embraces are described in language that implicitly contrasts them with the painful embraces earlier described. "Embracing the body of the man, she joins it to her own body and holds him, wetting his mouth with kisses and sucking his lips" (IV.1193–94) contrasts with "What they seek they press tight and cause pain to the body and often drive their teeth into little lips and batter them with kisses" (1079–81). The "they"s in the latter passage are ambiguous: usually read as describing the behavior of pairs of male-female lovers, they can equally well, and even better, be read distributively, as about what each male lover does to and with his own mistress. Similar plural subjects, this time clearly male, are in evidence at 1121ff. and 1153ff. At 1121 (immediately after the passage on intercourse), the people who expend much trouble and labor in love must be males—who are, in any case, the ones being given advice in the section as a whole. And within the passage on intercourse itself, at least two passages are much more easily read taking the subjects as all male: 1086–87 (where the lovers desire to extinguish the flame of their desire *inside* the body of the one who caused desire), and 1107, where intercourse has reached the point of "sowing seed in the woman's furrow"). The lovers mentioned in 1077 (*amantum*) and 1101 (*amantis*) could well be all male. The one potential difficulty is in *membris collatis* (1105), which is

ambitions connected with self-fortification and self-perpetuation are, throughout the poem, illustrated with male examples, whereas females— Venus in the proem, the nurse and the mothers of Book V—usually turn up in less aggressive and less anxious postures. Lucretius lets us see possibilities, then, for the avoidance of erotic aggression; but by linking this aggression to deeply rooted anxieties, he also shows his interlocutor that avoidance will not be easy.

Similar problems arise, Book III shows, in human beings' relation to their own death. For, once again, their experience of their own incompleteness and vulnerability leads them to create elaborate stratagems of self-protection that are believed to shore up these boundaries against assault. These stratagems are never successful, since death and finitude are never defeated. This leads, once again, to an increasingly frenzied attempt to secure the bounds of the self, which involves the agent in increasing aggression against others: this opens up, in turn, new types of vulnerability, new sources of anger.

Lucretius has linked a number of different pursuits with the fear of death, as people try to use the world to place barriers between themselves and all the incursions that might cause their end. A major stratagem is, of course, the turning to religion, which Lucretius connects with aggressive behavior in no uncertain terms from the beginning of the poem. He carefully shows how images of angry punishing divinities—created initially as support for human incompleteness—both increase fearfulness and dependence, and also engender, possibly by imitation, ferocious acts such as the slaughter of Iphigenia, in which priestly commands prevail over parental love and compassion (I.80–101; cf. III.51–54, V.1194ff.). Religion promises to turn the needy incomplete being into a being as secure as the gods are seen to be (V.1169–85). It does not work. And its consequence is, in fact, an increase in weakness, a "hidden force" that saps human strength, engendering self-contempt and acquiescence in the (frequently aggressive) projects of priests (V.1233–40).

Two other devices for warding off death are prominently identified in the poem: the pursuit of wealth and the pursuit of power and honor. Both are believed (falsely and irrationally) to be ways of keeping death at bay, since

---

usually taken to mean that the pairs of male-female lovers wrap their limbs *around one another*: but it seems perfectly possible to take it as meaning that each of the male lovers in question wraps his limbs around those of his mistress. Consider also that in 1192ff. the poet speaks as if the question of female erotic desire has not yet been raised: this would be odd indeed, if the eager parties in the earlier section included women. See also Brown (1987), who stresses throughout the fact that the passage is written from the male viewpoint.

the neediness of poverty and low status is thought to be a state bordering on death, and the rich and powerful person feels, by contrast, an almost godlike security (III.59–69). These pursuits lead the person into competition and aggression against others. The mere fact of another's possession is viewed as a damage, since it keeps from the wealth-seeker what he thinks he needs to save himself. Some "build up their fortunes by civil war and greedily redouble their riches, piling slaughter on slaughter. Cruelly they delight in the sad burial of a brother" (III.70–72). Others are devoured by anxious resentment of the powerful and, "sweating out their own blood," struggle against others on the narrow path of ambition (V.1131–32).

In all these cases, an initial sense of incompleteness leads to an attempt to secure oneself against threats and wounds. But such attempts involve competition and thus easily lead to angry aggressive behavior toward others, who are threats on account of their very presence. Furthermore, since the fortification sought is never sufficient to yield the protection that is really desired, the agent forms even more exaggerated and unlimited desires for the goods in question, desires that are colored already by envious resentment against others who possess some of what is desired. These desires lead directly to the desire to hurt, kill, rob, humiliate those who are seen as obstacles to the fulfillment of an essentially impossible project. The minute one sets out to protect oneself by honor and wealth, hostility inevitably follows:

> Men wanted to be distinguished and powerful, so that their fortune could remain on a stable basis and they could live, in prosperity, an untroubled life—in vain, since by competing to get to the highest honor they made the way hostile for themselves, and in spite of everything they are struck and hurled down from the summit, as by a lightning bolt, by envious resentment, which hurls them in scorn to foulest Tartarus—resentment which, like lightning, most often sets ablaze the highest things and whatever stands out above others. (V.1120–28)

The origin of this hostility is in the nature of their project. Because they wanted to be safe at all costs, and to need nothing, they are not satisfied with what is available, and embark on schemes that are not only dangerous to others, but also the source of new dangers from others, and from the world of nature.

All of these factors are at work in Lucretius' account of war. The poem draws the reader's attention repeatedly to the phenomena of warfare, situating itself in a brief respite of peace in the midst of civil upheaval, returning, even when the argument does not require it, to the incursions of war against the soft human body. The passage from Book III that describes the limbs severed by scythe-bearing chariots is one of many proofs in that book of the divisibility and the mortality of the complex of body and soul. No reference to war was, strictly speaking, necessary in order to complete the argument. And yet the poem dwells on the details of violence in an almost morbid manner, forcing the reader to see the damages of anger.[27] The very violence of Lucretius' descriptions, here and, even more, in the horrifying account of the beasts at war (which I shall analyze later) cuts through the interlocutor's defenses and presents to him, as the Epicurean tradition of therapy urges, the horrifying face of his own disease.

Wars, as Book III has claimed, are fought for honor and for possessions. They are also fought, clearly, out of the aggressive and envious rage generated in the struggle for honor and possessions.[28] The mention of the Trojan War in Book I invites us to look for connections, as well, between war and erotic jealousy. War is an attempt to inflict damage and pain on an enemy who is seen as a threat—sometimes to life and safety, far more often to the (false) safety of wealth and power. The first humans, who worry only about defending themselves against beasts, do not engage in warfare; but as soon as any luxury is found, it introduces envy and strife. The coat of animal furs lies "torn apart among them, spoiled with much blood" (V.1421).[29] In those days it was furs, the poet comments, in ours gold and purple, that "wear out human life with care and exhaust it with war" (1423–24). War is presented as the more or less inevitable outcome of the fear of death and as closely bound up with the other ambitions that grow out of that fear. It increases itself without limit, beginning with the simplest weapons— "hands, nails, teeth, and stones, and branches broken off in the forest" (V.1283–84)—and proceeding on, through bronze and then iron weapons, to the complex horrors of modern warfare:

So did sad discord beget one thing from another that would be fearful to human nations in warfare [armis], and day by day gave increase to the terrors of war. (V.1305–7)

These reflections invite the reader—informed from the poem's beginning that peace is an urgent concern—to search in the poem for some sign of a limit or stopping place. The poet connects war with ignorance of limits, which "little by little has carried life out onto the deep seas and has

---

[27] Cf. Segal (1990).

[28] On the poem's attitude to war, see Segal (1986b, 1990).

[29] Segal (1986b) provides an excellent discussion of the use of "blood" and related words in the poem.

moved from the depths the great tides of war" (V.1434–35).[30] What, then, is the stopping place? What leads from reasonable self-defensive action to atrocity? And where might we find the place in the history of the human race to draw the line, saying, *here* society should have stopped, *here* anger can stably rest, consistently with virtue? I shall now argue that no such stable stopping point is offered us by Lucretius' poem—that new arts of defense and cooperation are connected always with new incitements to aggression, in such a way that a gentle disposition is a precarious and unstable achievement.

V

Lucretius' account of the origins of civilization in Book V has the appearance of a history. But, like many such accounts in ancient literature, its primary function is less literal reconstruction than ethical analysis. By presenting a sequence of forms of life, and examining in quasi-temporal terms the consequences of a "new" art or stratagem for life as a whole, it dissects the interlocutor's own complex life for him, showing what goes with what, what costs might be entailed by what simplifications, what benefits are conferred by something that is also the source of great danger.[31] The account has frequently been approached in the light of an excessively simple set of questions. Is this a story of progress or a story of decline? Is Lucretius a progressivist or a primitivist? And so forth. Fortunately, recent scholarship, including work by David Furley, David Konstan, and Charles Segal,[32] has begun to remedy this situation, seeing the account as telling a far more complex story in which there are elements of both improvement and decline, often closely linked. The history of aggression in the narrative has just such a complex structure.

Lucretius has connected anger with our softness, our tendency to lash out at others with our perception of ourselves as weakly defended for-

---

[30] For this translation, see also Costa (1984). Bailey (1947) wrongly takes *in altum* to mean "to a high point," which misses the sense of risk and exposure contained in the lines, and confuses the patterns of imagery. Costa appropriately compares Epicurus' reference to the soul's tempest in *Ep. Men.* 128, and *belli/miscebant fluctus* at 1289–90.

[31] For some excellent general observations about such stories, see Sihvola (1989).

[32] Furley (1978); Konstan (1973); Segal (1990); see also Long and Sedley (1987) 125–39; for analysis of the primitivist-progressivist debate, see Blundell (1986) with bibliography. For an excellent treatment of this sort of narrative generally, with particular reference to Hesiod and Plato's *Protagoras*, see Sihvola (1989).

tresses. It is significant, then, that the history of civilization begins with a human race whose most salient characteristic is its hardness:

> But that former human race, on the land, was much harder—as was appropriate, since the hard earth had given birth to them—equipped with bigger and more solid bones within, strung with strong sinews running through their flesh. Nor could they be easily gripped by heat or cold, nor by strangeness of food, nor by any bodily disease. Through many shinings of the sun rolling through the sky, they led their nomadic life in the manner of the wild beasts. (V.925–32)

These people are human; yet Lucretius, with "that former human race" (*illud genus humanum*) makes it perfectly clear that they are a different race or kind from us. These humans resemble, in their toughness, the beasts of Book V's earlier description. The vulnerable naked child, object of solicitude and protection, does not appear here, and the emphasis on the creation of this human race from the earth (rather like the Sown Men of Greek legend) makes us imagine them as never children, never in a state of softness or dependence. In other ways as well, their self-sufficient lives resemble the lives of beasts. They gather their food from the trees and the ground, they sleep with only the protection of caves and forest. They lack all sense of the common good, all morality, all law (V.958–59); they live each one for himself, in single self-sufficiency. Sex joins them: but this joining, too, is animal-like, unmediated by Memmius' concern for the future of a community, by Book IV's concern for the good mind and heart, even by the concern already mentioned in Book V for the child's defenseless nakedness (V.962–65). To the reader of Book IV—and, in general, to a Roman reader concerned with marriage, children, and community—this will seem an unattractive type of hardness. If it lacks some of the problems Lucretius has found in human love, this is because all humanity is lacking.

There is aggression, in the lives of these hard humans. But it is close to the heedless aggression of beasts, who also subdue their mates and hunt their prey. Lucretius, while never suggesting that there is a separate natural aggressive instinct in human beings, suggests nonetheless, as earlier in Book V, that aggressive behavior is a plausible and prudent response to the perception of one's limited situation, and to the thought that it is a bad thing to die (cf. 988–93, where the man being eaten alive weeps for his loss of the "sweet light of life"). Male aggression subdues an unwilling woman, procuring both sexual satisfaction and the survival of the species. The aggressions of hunting, described in adjacent lines, subdue dangerous enemies with rocks and clubs, and procure food as well. Because of the hardness and the brute simplicity of these people, aggression remains limited, in both areas. They do not make love sadistically; and they do not make war or, apparently, use any force against one another. In fact, so little thought is in their force that it is hard to know whether we should even speak of anger, or a desire to inflict pain; the text gives no evidence that these wishes and emotions are present. And yet the limited aggressiveness of this life is not exactly praised: indeed, it is shown to be inseparable from the general brutishness of the life, and its total lack of major ethical and communal goods.

"Then for the first time the human race [*genus humanum*] began to grow soft" (1014). Settled dwellings, clothing, and fire lead to a physical softening, as they can no longer so easily endure the rigors of the outdoor life (1015–16). But this softening—which brings new physical needs and fears—is also necessary for stable bonding in marriage and the family. Only in the indoor non-nomadic life can family units be formed. Sexual relations in marriage now diminish the violent aggressiveness of the male; and children, securely perceived as belonging to a single couple, "with their charms easily broke the arrogant disposition of the parents" (1017–18). At this point, a more general social bond can be formed, based on the idea of protection for the weak and the renunciation of aggression:

> Then neighbors eagerly began to make contracts of friendship,[33] agreeing among themselves neither to hurt nor to be harmed, and they entrusted children and women to one another's care, when, with inarticulate utterances and gestures they signified that it was appropriate to have compassion[34] for anyone weaker. Harmony could not be brought about in every way, but for the most part they properly kept their agreements. (1019–25)

This famous passage has frequently been studied as a source for Epicurean thought concerning the contractual nature of justice.[35] But it needs to be studied in its context, as one stage in the analytical "history" Lu-

---

[33] *Amicitiem iungere*. Mitsis (1988a) argues that *amicities* is altogether distinct from *amicitia* and has, here, the sense of contract rather than the sense of affectionate friendly relationship. It seems to me that a distinction of this sort will not survive an examination of Lucretius' use of fifth-declension variants of first-declension nouns; it is a fairly common practice in the poem, and one does not find systematic distinctions of meaning. See Bailey (1947) I.74. Of course there is a sense here of a contractual relationship; but that is supplied by *iungere*, not by the word *amicitiem* alone.

[34] *Miserier*. Note the Epicurean endorsement of pity or compassion, which the Stoics will utterly condemn.

[35] Most recently by Mitsis (1988a).

cretius is narrating. It is not an account of the way society currently is. Its function is to show how elements of society that we value are connected with other ways in which our life differs from that of the beastlike first humans. It should be read closely with the account of that earlier race, and its contrasts understood as showing the complex relationship of one change with other changes.

So read, the passage tells a very complex story. The softening of the human being is, by contrast to the hardier and harder form of life previously depicted, in one way surely a weakening. And we are already aware that it is out of a keen sense of one's weakness that angry passions arise. Beasts do not take revenge, nor are the first humans sadists. We are invited, then, to suppose that the softening has laid the ground for these more complex and dangerous attitudes. And if we begin thinking along these lines, we cannot fail to notice that here for the first time we hear of the aggression of one human being against another, and also of certain causes of aggression—garments, houses, family relationships, sexual monogamy—that play such a large part in other Lucretian accounts of the bases of rage. (The cloak of skins lies "torn apart among them, spoiled by much blood.") The necessary conditions for war, for murder, for erotic sadism, begin to be set in place.

On the other hand, the softening is instrumental in producing creatures who are recognizably human rather than bestial, who are capable of gentle concern, responsive love, and stable moral dispositions. The reader—especially the Roman reader, but indeed any sympathic reader of Book I's Roman proem, or Book IV's account of mutual pleasure and of marriage—could not fail to find the account of human softening attractive. Indeed, the reader of Book IV would be very likely to recall, especially, its descriptions of the soft and liquid motions of the female in sexual relations aimed at mutual pleasure. The assimilation of the male to the softness of the female seems, in this connection, an admirable development.

What Lucretius shows in this way is something complex and disturbing: that the original bases of gentleness and of rage lie very close in the soul, and that the very softening that makes community and mutual responsiveness possible also introduces new dangers, new potential incentives to violence. The combination of vulnerability with awareness that marks our non-bestial humanness contains the roots for these opposed responses.

The pattern continues throughout the book. Language (V.1028ff.) makes possible new dimensions of loving and friendly recognition—including, of course, the peaceful and peacemaking art of philosophy. And yet it lets in, too, we know, the false arts of love and religion, each a source of new forms of rage. Book IV has made clear that the destructive forms of love owe their dissemination and their structure to language and to art; the same is evidently true of the domination of priests, and of their crippling myths of the afterworld. Next rage is moderated by laws and institutions, new forms of admirable and virtuous human connection (V.1145–50).[36] But these institutions augment envious resentment and the competitive struggle for power and position. And this new complexity in civilization feeds, as well, the desire for and the possibility of war. The development of weapons is apparently a preoccupation of the human race only in its more settled condition (1281ff.): before, people simply protected themselves with whatever was ready to hand.

It appears, then, that no development in the direction of a gentler and, in a sense, less bestial life—no advance toward more responsiveness to the claims of others, to more complex forms of interdependence—is without its cost. For each new softening brings new fears and dependencies; and each new complex device of protection generates attachments that lead the soul into increasing anxiety for itself and its own—and, from anxiety, all too often, into competitive and hostile raging. False religion's origin lies in the true perception of our human weakness and the gods' invulnerability (1175–82). The origin of the bad form of love is in the true perception that in love one is especially soft, especially dependent on another for one's own completion. The bestial life was unappealing, but it had a certain stability and a certain internal logic. The softer life is more human, but, in its deep needs both from other humans and from the world, it appears to be inherently unstable. The instability has its source in the fact that each individual still reasonably cares about his or her own life, bodily integrity, freedom from pain. Thus each, entering into bonds of friendship, love, and social compassion, both seeks and at the same time compromises his or her own safety. Without the search for safety, the softer human being is simply torn apart: "Everything naked and unarmed yielded easily to everything that is armed." The search for complete individual safety brings, as we have seen, an ever-ascending spiral of violence. Between these two extremes is the life—or, rather, the several lives, according to the further arts and complexities we choose to introduce—of humans in community, protecting and depending on one another. But it is made clear that these peaceful forms of interaction are unlikely to be, for a large group at any rate, stably or

[36] On language, see especially Konstan (1973). For the way in which laws and political institutions contain a rage whose violence was wearing people out, see 1145–50: especially *defessi vi colere aevum* (1145), *pertaesum vi colere aevum* (1150). For a good general approach to the ethical assessment of these transitions, see Furley (1978).

permanently isolated from the destructive forms. In the softness that is the strength of friendship are also the seeds of fear.

VI

This connection between protection and insecurity is made clearer and deepened by Lucretius' analysis of the passions of the individual soul[37] in the proems to Books V and VI. In both cases, he stresses that a certain diminution of external threats has been accompanied by an increase in the disorderly and ferocious possibilities of the soul itself. And in both cases he points to philosophy as the only help we have against this violence.

In Book V, the exploits of Hercules against the monsters of the external world are vividly described. Indeed, the poet grants, they have made the earth in certain ways safer—but by now these monsters could not harm us much in any case because we have progressed so far in the arts of bodily self-protection. The hero's exploits have not, however, dealt with the most dangerous monsters we have to face, the ones that assail us continually, cutting us up inside and producing aggression against others. These monsters are the soul's desires, especially fear and sexual longing:[38]

> If the heart [*pectus*] is not purged, what battles and dangers must we not endure against our will?[39] In that case, how many sharp anxieties of passion cut a person up, tormenting him, and how many fears? What of arrogance, filthy avarice and lust, what of insolence? What slaughters these cause! And what luxury and idleness? (V.43–48)

The human soul is now seen as not only the origin of aggression but, itself, its battleground and its victim. In fact, it is impossible to tell, here, whether the "battles" and "dangers" are external or internal. The image of desire's aggression against the soul suggests that the surrounding words refer to internal violence and danger; but since we are well aware, too, that here lies

---

[37] Although I continue to use "mind" for *animus*, I shall use "soul" here as the more inclusive word, taking in thoughts, desires, and their bodily basis. Epicurus does not entirely identify the bad desires with thoughts; and it seems significant that Lucretius in these passages uses several words like *pectus* and *vas*, rather than *animus*.

[38] The word used, *spurcitia*, is pejorative even in ordinary discourse, as *amor* is not: it is usually translated as "filthy lust," or the equivalent. We might say that Lucretius, through his analysis of *amor* as disease, has earned the right to call it by this pejorative name.

[39] *Ingratis*: cf. VI.15 (on which see subsequent discussion). In both passages the word emphasizes the external genesis of these passions, which constrain the true self. See chapter III.1069.

the source of external war and slaughter, we are encouraged to give the words a double reference. The violence with which passion attacks the soul is artfully expressed in the construction of the poetry, as the word *scindunt*, "cuts," itself cuts the line sharply in two (45). The soul's openness to and need from the world calls up, in the soul itself, violent and destructive movements—not only against the world, but against itself, as the soul appears to punish itself for its exposed and needy condition.

To nourish such desires and fears, Lucretius suggests, is a form of self-hatred: for what these "monsters" rely on is the belief that one is no good without external things that one cannot fully control. In a similar way, Lucretius has already linked the longing for immortality with self-contempt, and even with suicidal depression and the complete hatred of life (V.1233–40, III.79–81; cf. chapter 6). Love's anxieties have been connected with similar, though often weaker, responses. Perceiving the terrible precariousness of one's own situation, and longing, in vain, for a world that would remove it, leads in the end to a hatred of what one is. "What wonder if human beings hate and despise themselves" (V.1238; cf. also VI.53, *depressosque premunt ad terram*). Self-hatred is not incompatible with hatred of and violence against others. Indeed, as this passage suggests, the two go so closely together that we cannot easily tell them apart.

The proem to Book VI, in a similar manner, contrasts our external safety with our internal violence and disorder, and goes further, suggesting that the two are in certain ways causally linked. For the items that are now said to have given the Athenian people an externally "safe life"—riches, honor, praise, pride in one's own fame and that of one's children (VI.11–13)—are the very things that the poem has already identified as causes of boundless desire and of aggression. And Lucretius soon makes the presence of these bad desires explicit:

> No less did each person, at home, have an anxious heart [*corda*], and this vexed their lives against their will [*ingratis*] without any respite, and forced them to rage in hostile quarrels. He [Epicurus] understood that the defect was in the vessel itself, and that because of its deficiency all the things that come in from without, even good things, were corrupted—in part because he saw that it was leaky and full of holes so that it could in no way ever be filled up; in part, because he perceived that it tainted everything it received with a foul taste. (VI.14–23)

The soul, once again, is a scene of aggression—whether directed in toward itself or out toward others, or both, it is once again difficult to tell. (Shortly after this Lucretius makes reference to the soul's depressed condition in the

270

light of its fear of death.) The soul's aggressive tumult is caused by anxious awareness of its own insecurity—made not better, but, perhaps, worse by the new securities of civilization. And Lucretius shows, once again, how the soul's war inside itself poisons life and makes it hateful.

I now want to suggest that it is in the light of these connections that we should read the famous, and infamous, passage concerning the wild beasts at war. It comes almost at the end of Book V, as the climax of a series of discussions of the advancement of warfare and weapon-making. But its nightmarish quality, and the poet's own strange comments about his own story, suggest that we are being offered not only a narrative of events in the external world but also, and perhaps more deeply, an image of the soul's own unbridled and self-destructive violence. The passage must be quoted in full:

They even tried out bulls in the service of war, and attempted to send fierce boars against the enemy. And in some cases to send strong lions on before them, with armed trainers and fierce teachers who could restrain them and hold them in chains—in vain, since once they were warmed with the mingled blood they raged fiercely through the ranks, making no distinctions, shaking their terrifying manes from side to side. Nor could the cavalry calm the hearts of their horses, terrified as they were by the roaring, and turn them back against the enemy. Lionesses threw their angry bodies with a leap in every direction, and sought out the faces of those who came at them, or ripped from behind those who were unaware and, tearing them, threw them to the ground conquered by their wounds, grasping them tight in their strong jaws and their curved claws. Bulls threw their own men down and trampled them with their feet, and gashed open the sides and bellies of the horses with their horns, and pawed the earth with menacing intent. Boars killed their allies with their strong teeth, fiercely staining the men's unused weapons with the men's own blood, and caused a confused rout among the infantry and the cavalry. . . . If there were any animals whom they believed sufficiently tamed at home, they saw them boil over in action, with wounds clamor flight terror tumult. Nor could they bring back any of their own—for the mixed races of beasts all fled—as often, now, badly mauled elephants in battle scatter, after doing much violence among their own troops. If that is how it happened. But I can hardly bring myself to believe that they did not manage to foresee and anticipate this foul and general disaster before it happened. And you might perhaps say that it took place in some one of the various worlds created in various ways, than that it was done in any one definite world. But they wished to do this not so much because they hoped to win, as in order to inflict pain on the enemy, and to perish themselves, because they had no confidence in their numbers or their arms. (V.1308–49)

The fantastic nature of this passage has caused great consternation among Lucretius' commentators.[40] Bailey suggests that we do see here evidence of the poet's insanity; and the lack of any parallel for this story in ancient literature and history has certainly made the passage seem to be a nightmare peculiar to the poet. The odd sequence of thought in the closing section has also been found puzzling: the poet first doubts the actuality of what has occurred, then proceeds to analyze the motives of the parties as if it had.[41] I suggest that we best understand the complexity of Lucretius' design if we read it in the same double manner in which we have been forced, by the ambiguity of the text, to read the passages from the two proems. The story of horror is a story not just about what human beings do to one another in war, but also, and more importantly, a story of the self-destructive violence of the soul against itself.[42]

A number of features of the passage itself invite this reading. For the story is presented by the poet not as a fact, but as a possibility, and set in some indefinite possible world, not in ours. And when the motives of the humans are analyzed, their undertaking is presented as wish, rather than as deed: "They *wished* to do this because . . ." (This shows us a way of reconciling the possible with the actual: as external action the events look at most possible; as wish, they can be described as actuality.) Furthermore, the events of the passage are connected in a number of concrete ways with events in the human soul. The lion is a beast who has already been connected with human aggression (III.288 ff.); and the wild boar has been said to be *like* the primitive human (V.970). The proem of Book V has already invited the reader to view aggressive desires as monsters in the soul, linking inward and outward aggression. And the book will end on a related parallel, as the mind's absence of true knowledge "little by little has carried life out onto the deep sea and has moved from the depths the great tides of war" (1434–35)—a war that is at once an external danger and a tempest in the soul (cf. *LMen* 128). Again, the "terrible headgear" of the lions is described in the same words as the headgear of human priests in Book II

---

[40] For a review of critical opinion, with references and ample citations, see Segal (1986b).

[41] See the good analysis by Costa (1984).

[42] This line of interpretation is briefly suggested in Segal (1986b). Cf. *Republic* IX, in which the angers and appetites of the soul are compared to a lion and a many-headed beast.

(632). The phrase "warmed by mingled blood" (*permixta caede calentes*) is repeated from Book III's account of an all-human war (643). And the account of the lion ripping her prey from behind recalls the language of Book III's account of the way in which death stalks the unsuspecting human (959).[43] The description of the beasts' biting and grasping reminds the reader of the biting of the human lovers in Book IV. We seem to have, then, not only a nightmarish tale about a possible war employing wild beasts— which by itself would show the self-defeating lengths to which human aggression can go—but also a true story of the real structure of human wishes, the self-defeating lacerations of longing and fear. In their frenetic search for invulnerability, humans press into service instruments that lead to their own destruction: religious fears, angry desires to harm, ferocious longings for the possession of one another, the thirst for honor and power. Such aggressive stratagems, the poet concludes—though in one sense very logical—are so self-defeating that it is a wonder people choose them at all. At most they can succeed in inflicting pain on others (the opposing army being, in this reading, the analogue of the external world); but at the same time they turn on the self and bring about its ruin. Aggression, unbounded, is suicidal. Wholeness can be preserved only by a gentle disposition.

VII

But the monsters of the soul have an enemy. That enemy is Epicurean philosophy. And the life of Epicurus is the only turning point in the complex history of the human being that makes possible any real amelioration in our condition, where anger is concerned. The poem repeatedly compares Epicurus' encounter with humanity to a war—but a war in which the enemy is aggression itself, and in which the weapons are the gentle, and even pleasant, weapons of words and arguments. In his account of Epicurus' achievement, Lucretius offers Memmius and the reader new images of heroism, of war, and of victory to replace the traditional aggressive norms cherished by Roman society.

In Book I, the description of Rome's brief respite from war is followed by the description of another and very different type of warrior. Epicurus, not named, but called "a Greek human being" (66)—introducing already a contrast between words and arms, Greek reasoning (the *vivida vis animi*) and Roman might—dared to oppose religion, and to conquer, on our

---

[43] Cf. Segal (1990).

273

behalf, an understanding of Nature. He now returns, as a Roman military hero conducting a triumph:[44]

> From there [sc. the universe] he brings back to us, as a victor, what can happen and what cannot, and by what principle (*ratio*) each thing has its power limited and its deep-set boundary stone. Religion, cast down, is crushed underfoot in its turn, and with his victory he makes us equal to the heavens. (75–79)

These images of victory and triumph announce in no uncertain terms that the Greek arts of (poetry and) philosophy must replace Roman military might if Memmius, and Rome, are truly to emerge victorious. Greece is the source for many of the bad arts of the soul—for the Athenian art of moneymaking and the pursuit of honor, for the love-poetry that gives the Roman soul its bad images of desire, for the priestly slaughter of Iphigenia and perhaps, therefore, for much of Roman religion. But it is also from Greece that philosophy arises—and only from this comes the possibility of peace. Book V insists that Epicurus is the true hero, since he has conquered the really dangerous monsters, the soul's desires—and conquered them *dictis, non armis*, with words, not arms. Book VI, similarly, portrays Epicurus as the giver of the one art by which the soul's fears and angers can be cured. And in Book III, portraying his own relationship with Epicurus as a non-competitive and non-aggressive love ("not desirous of competing, but out of love," III.5), Lucretius also replaces, for the reader, the love of gold by the love of the "golden words" (*aurea dicta*) of Epicurean philosophy, which "set to flight the terrors of the mind [*animi*]" (III.16).

Philosophy's first and most general task, in the war against anger and fear, is to make things clear—to give the soul an understanding of its own situation and its possibilities. This is repeatedly stressed: the anxiety that gives rise to strife can be put to flight only by knowledge and self-knowledge, *naturae species ratioque*. Anxiety is the soul's darkness, philosophy its light. Clearly Lucretius believes that confronting one's desires is a long step in the direction of making them more healthy.

In a number of specific areas, this idea works to contain aggression. The arguments concerning love, as I argued, reveal to the lover the futility of his projects and the falseness of the beliefs on which they are based, clearing the way for a more fruitful relationship with one's lover and family, in which the other's separateness can be a source of pleasure. The arguments concerning death set a limit, in a similar way, to the boundless desire for

---

[44] Cf. Sykes Davies (1931–32) on the triumph imagery.

life, convincing the pupil of the futility of attempts to achieve complete deathlessness. In general, the account of the non-teleological character of the world, and of our place in it, convinces the pupil not to make impossibly high demands that, being frustrated, will give rise to new rage and new aggression. It also convinces her to interpret the world's damages not as voluntary assaults from gods or nature—but as simply there, the natural conditions of her life, thus as occasions for effort and resistance, but not for anger. The triumph of philosophy, in short, is a triumph not through political action, about which the poem is remarkably silent, but within each human soul in relation to itself—as the soul learns to acknowledge its humanness and that of others. Ironically, then, the way of becoming more integrated and less an object of the world's rage is not to defend oneself at all costs, but rather to understand and accept the ways in which a human life is necessarily vulnerable and incomplete, to be willing to live as a soft body rather than an armed fortress. Book IV's injunction to "yield to human life"—however ambivalently pursued in the arguments about death and love—shapes the poem as a whole, and its conception of the goal of therapy.

In procedural terms, this therapeutic transition will not be accomplished quickly. We can assume that any Roman pupil will require years of assiduous and patient therapy to defeat these monsters of the soul. The therapy would begin (and continue) with confession, as the teacher would listen to Nikidion's account of her life, her anxieties and ends, her religious attitudes, her view of the cosmos, her loves—in order to understand how, and in what areas, she requires therapeutic treatment. During her course of study, the repeated teaching of Epicurean physics and ethics would alternate, one supposes, with personal analysis—so that she would, at one and the same time, increase the grasp of the arguments over her waking and sleeping life, and also bring the arguments into vivid confrontation with her own symptoms and behavior, as she carries on her daily life with others. She would be presented with the general analysis of anger contained in this poem; and she would learn to see the same patterns in her own life. (In much the same way, Seneca examines himself at the close of each day, scrutinizing his behavior for the seeds of anger, and giving himself criticism from the point of view of Stoic ethics.[45] But in the Epicurean case, one imagines that the teacher would continue to play a central role.) Meanwhile, if she were living in an Epicurean community, she would receive instruction, as well, from the daily behavior of the members of the school,

[45] Seneca *De Ira* 3.36, on which see chapter 11.

and the example of their non-competitive friendship. The search for the gentle disposition can be expected to be a lifelong matter, accomplished only through patient attention to Epicurean teachings, to oneself, and to one's friends.

There are tensions in this teaching. As we have seen throughout these chapters, there is in Lucretius' Epicureanism a deep attachment to godlike self-sufficiency that pulls against the injunction to live in accordance with nature, accepting the limits of a finite life. This tension surfaces, as well, in the treatment of anger. For the most part, Lucretius' poem appears to urge the pupil, in this area, to "yield to human life," accepting the fact that her boundaries are porous rather than hard, that her life is unstable and incomplete rather than godlike. But we have already seen that he appears to treat the condition of the gods as normative for a kind of self-sufficiency that humans can also appropriately seek. And elsewhere as well, he expresses an aspiration toward complete invulnerability: most famously, in the proem to Book II, in which Epicurean philosophy is depicted as a fortress of peace from which one may look down on the suffering of others (7–8). In one way, the search for invulnerability and the search for an acceptance of one's human limits cohere. For the one who accepts limits is free of many vulnerabilities and anxieties that afflict the ambitious. One who inhabits the fortress built by *doctrina* has less need than others to build the fortresses of war. And yet one feels, as well, a tension in these lines—for it is not clear that the fortified condition *is* really one that accepts a finite nongodlike life.

This same tension is present in the poem's attitude toward friendship and justice. The gods, as we saw, lack strong attachments to others; neither just nor unjust, they simply live on, invulnerably. And the poem offers Nikidion the hope of a godlike life. On the other hand, as we have also seen, the poem invites its reader, from its very opening words, to develop a broader set of attachments, caring deeply about spouse and family, and even about city and country. In its portrayal of family love, and of the poet's and Memmius' concern for Rome, it strongly indicates that these attachments are not simply instruments of personal safety, but are valuable as ends in themselves. The poet and Memmius share "the hope of sweet friendship"; Epicurus is a father, and the object of the poet's love; both the poet and Memmius are permitted to be passionately concerned for the future of Rome. Furthermore, the poem seems to endorse pity or compassion for the needs of other weak humans (*miserier*; see 1019–25); this passion the Stoics, more thoroughly committed to invulnerability, sternly denounce.

276

Thus the poem seems to leave its reader not only with an absence of greedy striving, but also with a good deal of strong positive concern for the well-being of others.[46] And it suggests, in its portrayal of family life, that such strong bonds are an essential part of the development of the passion for justice. Unlike Stoic accounts, Lucretius' therapy does not attempt to derive just conduct from the sense of duty alone; nor does it appear to motivate it entirely out of a concern for one's own safety; it allows it to rest upon love and compassion. Where friendship and civic attachment are concerned, Lucretius proves more willing to accept the neediness of our mortal condition than in his arguments about death and erotic passion. The finitist side of his argument appears to prevail, at least on balance, over the immortalist side. He gives philosophical therapy in this area a human, rather than a divine, goal, and promises it, where anger is concerned, a human triumph.

And yet, how complete can this triumph actually be? The poet reminds us that philosophy operates patiently on the souls of individuals; the majority shrink from it (I.944–95). But this means that the philosopher depends to a great extent on chance for the opportunity of engaging in the exchange of arguments and forming the bonds of friendship. The poem situates itself in a temporary chance-given respite between battles, reminding us that the individual soul remains susceptible to the incursions of the world around it. Even the closed Epicurean community is not altogether safe; but Lucretius strives, on Memmius' behalf, for a Roman Epicureanism, a philosophy not severed from the city—and that opens him, and his pupil, to far greater dangers. And aren't we led to see, too, that even a good friendship is always, in this sense, a chancy business? For how high is the likelihood that two gentle non-aggressive characters—characters whose attachments and passions are only those recommended by Epicurean philosophy—will meet up in Rome, or, meeting, avoid disaster?

Furthermore, even the soul of the good Epicurean may not be stably safe from monsters. For the basis of aggression still remains, in the entirely reasonable concern one has for one's own life, safety, and freedom from pain. This basis has now been extended to include care for the safety of family, friends, even country. "One must not think," writes the poet in Book III on the subject of anger, "that the evils can be rooted up and removed completely" (310). The *vestigia*, however small, remain—here Lucretius' Epicureanism differs from Stoicism, presumably in keeping with

---

[46] The elimination of greedy desire for more does, however (as had been argued already in Plato's *Republic*), remove most of the actual motivations people have for injustice.

the greater importance it attaches to such worldly goods as the health and integrity of the body, marriage, friendship. Do we know, then, that there are no circumstances in which an attack will provoke a violent response?[47] People invented and used weapons because they had to, because it was no good sitting around waiting to be slaughtered. Nakedness looked like foolishness, when the enemy could cut you open (V.1291–92). Can even the Epicurean find a sure remedy or limit for this reactive rage?

There are images of gentleness in the poem. They are, typically, brief, and soon eclipsed by darkness. The nurse, talking to her infant charge, is swept from the scene by wild beasts, who have no need of baby-talk. The neighbors who make a contract for protection of the weak, and usually keep it, disappear from view, as language, religion, and ambition complicate and corrupt their simple compassionate life. The liquidity of sexual embraces aimed at mutual pleasure lives, in the poem, under continual threat from erotic insecurity and its attendant violence. The good death of Epicurus, who calmly accepted nature's limits and was kind to his friends until "the light of his life had run out" (III.1042–43) is surrounded by other less satisfactory deaths: of kings, of military leaders (III.1024ff.), of ignorant fearful masses in the plague, as the living quarrel fiercely over the corpses of the dead (VI.1276–86).

But there is one sustained example of gentle human social interaction from which one might derive some hope for the soul. This is the poem itself, the therapeutic argument it offers to its interlocutor and its readers. I have said that the aggression in the poem is a part of its therapy, aimed at motivating the readers and the interlocutor, through a shock of self-recognition, to become involved in philosophy. Once they are involved, they will discover in the imagined relationship between poet-speaker and interlocutor (and between interlocutor and readers) a beneficent concern that is neither envious nor self-protective—for the poet expends much labor for his creation and insists that he will get no popular approval as a result. They will discover a friendship that is, while at first asymmetrical, increasingly mutual, and inspired by hope of a still greater equality. Not poisoned by the spirit of competition, it aims to provide pleasure as well as illumination, as poetic language and rigorous argumentation combine in a way unprecedented in the Epicurean tradition.[48] The poem conducts the

---

[47] It is true that later on the poet holds out some hope that even the roots of anger can be eliminated some day by philosophy. But the vagueness of this hope, and its failure to come to terms with the problems the poem has repeatedly identified, make it seem more a distant wish than a real possibility.

[48] Other Epicurean poetry was clearly less philosophical: Philodemus' poems have little connection with the rigor of philosophical argument. Cf. Kenney (1970).

interlocutor's soul gently from the recognition of his diseases to a clear grasp of truth, showing at every stage an affectionate concern for his needs and his pleasure. In all these ways it is as dissimilar as possible to the war from which it calls Memmius' attention: and its existence as actuality provides a vision of what may be possible for individual souls, if not for societies. For its composition is also a way of life, extending, Lucretius makes clear, deep into the soul and shaping even its dreams.

It is not clear—perhaps by accident, probably by design—how the therapeutic relationship with Memmius, and with the reader, is intended to end within the poem. The abruptness of the ending of Book VI—in which angry strife over corpses has the last word, and there is no concluding summary to Memmius, no message of optimism or encouragement for the reader—has led critics for centuries to hold that the poem as it stands is unfinished. Recently the tendency has been, instead, to accept its bleak and sudden ending.[49] At any rate, we must surely say that the poem, as a therapeutic argument, presents itself to us in an incomplete condition; and that if, as seems likely in the absence of evidence to the contrary, Lucretius planned this conclusion, it is an ending that presents the therapeutic argument as itself without a closure or a happy end, as subject always to sudden incursions of fear and of anger. The task of therapy is always incomplete while the roots of these passions remain in the soul—as they do remain, in any human life that cherishes itself and knows itself to be incomplete. The war of philosophy cannot be finished on the page—but only, if at all, in each reader's daily life, in each day's efforts to build kindly affectionate relationships with friends, children, spouse, society, in each day's vigilant efforts to limit and manage one's own desires—and all this, preferably, without being torn apart or bitten or trampled by the hostility of others. Ending the poem on a scene of strife, Lucretius leaves his readers with a solemn warning—and turns over to them the dangerous and delicate job of living well.

[49] Cf., for example, Clay (1983a), Segal (1990).

Skeptic Purgatives: Disturbance and the Life without Belief

So FAR, in describing Nikidion's education, I have emphasized the differences between Epicurus and Aristotle. One is more revisionary, the other more inclined to trust appearances; one uses practical reason to produce freedom from disturbance, the other values it for its own sake; one may deprive the pupil of autonomous intellectual activity, the other insists on the value of that autonomy. It is now time to insist that, along with these differences, they have some very important traits in common. For both believe that human health requires having many definite beliefs, including ethical beliefs. Aristotle's attitude to ethical belief is less dogmatic and more open-ended than Epicurus'; but he too feels that the good life cannot be lived without beliefs—some of which will be so deeply held that they will be the basis for the person's self-conception. Both agree that Nikidion must go through life with some well-defined views about how the world operates, about what sort of creature, in that world, she is, and also about what she is aiming for. Though no single belief of hers will be treated as entirely unrevisable in Aristotle's program—with the exception of the basic principles of logic that ground all coherent discourse—at any point she must hold at least some beliefs firm and use these as a basis from which to ask questions about others. In Epicurus' school, of course, she will become profoundly committed to the entirety of a system; and she will regard that system as an absolutely necessary basis from which to venture into life. We might say, using Lucretius' image (II.7–8), that Epicurus' belief-structure has the character of a solid impregnable fortress, whereas Aristotle's is more like a ship that gets rebuilt gradually as it sails along. No single plank is irreplaceable (with the exceptions we have noted); but at any one time there must be enough of a structure there to keep the vessel from foundering. Both, then, believe that the human being needs to go through the natural world housed in a more or less safe structure, and that this structure is built up out of beliefs, including beliefs about ethical value.

I

But, someone might say, the trouble with any fortress is that it invites attack. The trouble with any ship is that the waves beat against its hull (in a way that they do not beat against a non-rigid object, like a piece of sea-weed). No fortress is forever impregnable; the ship that appears most unsinkable frequently ends up on the ocean's bottom. And in general: when with human art we pit ourselves against nature, intending to conquer our natural vulnerability to chance, this very ambition makes us vulnerable. What creature escapes being wrecked in a tempest? The creature who goes through life as natural instinct prompts it, without ambitious enterprises, without oppositional structure: the fish swimming with the current, or the land creature who never ventures out beyond the land to take up a hopeful dangerous form of life. What group of people escape being beseiged and conquered? Not builders of fortresses—but nomads, who move along grazing here and there as natural need dictates, flexibly seeking satisfaction.

All of this is metaphorical. But it brings out the fact that, in claiming to give Nikidion a life according to nature, Epicurus, just as surely as Aristotle, has encouraged her on the path of a life that—insofar as it has a definite fixed structure of belief and claims through belief to manage natural contingency—is a life set against nature, a life that challenges, opposes, wards off natural accidents. A life that will not permit her to move flexibly anywhere at all, as impulses and appearances dictate. In short, a dogmatic life. A life that says that this is right and this is wrong, this true and this false, and asks her to care deeply about these distinctions.

But the other face of commitment is vulnerability. If she cares deeply about rightness, she will be deeply disturbed if something happens that is not right according to her view. And if she identifies herself with a view about how things are, she will be shaken in her whole being if an impressive argument challenges the view that she believes to be true. Perhaps she will do better, then, living a life that is more truly according to nature—a life in which a fixed oppositional structure of belief plays no role at all; a life most like that of the freely swimming fish, who listens only to the promptings of instinct and perception. A life without commitment. This is the life that our next school, the Greek Skeptics, wish to offer Nikidion.

Let us make the problem more concrete. Nikidion is now a well-trained Epicurean. She knows the system thoroughly, and she has internalized it through years of practice. She feels freed from most of her anxiety about death; she does not form attachments of a sort that will cause stress. Happy thoughts about the community and her friends distract her from pain when she is physically ill. But, or so the Skeptics claim, two residual sources of anxiety spoil her carefree life. First, consider her encounter with bodily pain. This pain cannot be avoided. To some extent she will be able to ignore it through pleasant thoughts and memories. But Nikidion has mastered, and is committed to, an ethical theory that teaches her that pain is an intrinsic evil; and not just an intrinsic evil, but the intrinsic evil. So, in addition to the natural creaturely perception of pain, she cannot help having, as well, the thought, "The bad is now with me." Surely this thought will not make her pain lighter. The added element of belief will, in fact, intensify her agony. Take that belief away, and "she will remain unaffected in matters of belief, and will endure only moderate suffering in respect of what she can't avoid" (Sextus *PH* 3.235–36).

Again, suppose that a friend of hers is in pain. If she had no general ethical beliefs, this would be unlikely to cause her profound distress—or only the sort of distress that an animal feels, out of creaturely sympathy and fellow feeling. But since she has the general theory that pain is the bad, she will, once again, have the thought, "The bad is now at hand." And this thought cannot occur to her, it is claimed, without generating anxiety. Indeed, "to have an additional belief of this sort is worse than the suffering itself, just as sometimes those who are having surgery or suffering something else like that endure it, while the bystanders faint away because of their belief that something awful is going on" (*PH* 3.236–37).

Consider, too, another source of anxiety. Nikidion is convinced that Epicurus' doctrine is correct—so convinced that she has staked her whole life on its correctness. She is living in accordance with his theory as to how things are. Suppose, now, that an equally dedicated adherent of an opposing view, say a Stoic, confronts her. (Notice that this problem, unlike the first, requires some break in the isolation of the Garden, or some serious failure to maintain a harmonious climate of belief within it.) This Stoic mounts a strong, well-argued attack on the Epicurean view that pleasure is the only intrinsic good, appealing to some residual intuitions about the intrinsic worth of virtue and reason that Epicurus has subdued but not completely eliminated. Since Epicurus' is a highly revisionary view, there will probably be some chink in every Epicurean's armor: some feeling, some picture, left over from childhood, from the experience of stories or theater or history, using which the opponent can get inside her defenses. The opponent uses examples, familiar to her from her upbringing, that get her to recall (for example) the powerful appeal of selfless courage, of stalwart endurance, displayed as part of a rational soul whose thoughts are dominant over impulses and inclinations. She is unprepared for this challenge—all the more since Epicurus has not encouraged her to understand sympathetically the motivations behind Stoicism, or to work her way non-polemically through the arguments that support it. Nikidion finds the sympathetic portrayal so intuitively appealing, the arguments so solid and so powerfully connected to one another, that she is thrown into sudden uncertainty. The discrepancy is alarming. The views appear to be of equal force. Which one is really correct? Since she has been encouraged to care about truth and correctness, she must press this question: which one is really true? Obviously, the answer matters very much. For if Stoicism is correct, she is living a bad life, and she is full of false beliefs—just the thing she most wants to avoid. But she is unable to find a decisive way of resolving the debate; there appears to be no criterion that is not biased in one direction or the other. Epicurus asks her to consult perception; the Stoics urge her to listen to the voice of reason. So even the proposals about how to resolve the conflict are in conflict; and no decision procedure is forthcoming.

Now what happens, ironically, is that this very thought makes it impossible for Nikidion to go on living a good life in the Epicurean manner. For she cannot help being anxious and distressed, being a person who wants always to be in the right. She knows she is not the virtuous person described by the Stoics; and she probably could not become one without years of deconditioning and relearning. But the moment this distress of mind assails her, she is not a good Epicurean either. Then in no way is she living a good and happy life.

Notice that this problem can arise for Nikidion in many areas—not only through a challenge made against her system of ethical beliefs. For Epicureanism is a complex system, all of whose pieces hang together; so a serious challenge to any one of those pieces brings disturbance. An opposing view about the soul, about the gods, about matter, about natural phenomena—any of these could give rise to alarm, on account of the threat they represent to Epicurean ethics. And furthermore, quite apart from the relationship of these views to her ethical beliefs, Nikidion cares about all or some of them. Most people have views about body and soul, about what a person is, about the parameters of life and death, about the structure of the universe, the continuity of bodies—views to which they are attached in such a way that a challenge brings anxiety and disturbance. If they actually become convinced that there is no justification for the belief that effect follows cause of necessity; or that physical objects persist unobserved; or that temporal succession is a real property of the natural world—all of this is disturbing, and not a matter of indifference. Nikidion is no different. As many commitments as she has to the truth of any claim, so many sources of anxiety. As many planks as are in her boat, through so many cracks the water can force its way.[1]

---

[1] On the range of Skeptical argument, there has been a vigorous debate in recent years. For two opposing viewpoints, see Burnyeat (1980a, 1984) and Frede (1979, 1983). Burnyeat argues that the Skeptic's aim is the elimination of all belief from the pupil's life; Frede argues

We must also insist that Nikidion is not invulnerable to disturbance if the opponent finds her before she enters Epicurus' school, or some other philosophical school. Epicurean theoretical dogmatism sharpens, but does not create, her problem. It is not only beliefs held in a special way, or as part of a philosophical theory, that make the holder subject to anxiety.[2] For even before Nikidion went in for philosophy, she had some definite view about how to live, and about many other matters concerning which philosophers make theories. And if she is at all like most of us, it was very important for her to be right about these views. (If she had not had opinions, Epicurus would not have been needed.) Most people hold many of their beliefs about the world firmly and dogmatically, even without the guidance of the philosopher. That is, they think it is important to get the truth, to be right; and they get deeply attached to what they take to be the right story about the way things are. Such attachments need not be explicit; Nikidion may not be able to articulate them in a theoretical form, or perhaps even to state them at all. But they ground her actions and her choices and thoughts nonetheless; she will feel adrift without them, and anxious when they are challenged.

In short, says the Skeptic, Epicurus is correct that the central human disease is a disease of belief. But he is wrong to feel that the solution lies in doing away with some beliefs and clinging all the more firmly to others. The disease is not one of *false* belief; belief itself is the illness—belief as a commitment, a source of concern, care, and vulnerability.

In this chapter, we shall see how Greek Skepticism, attaching itself to the

---

that he aims only to remove a class of beliefs restricted both by their content (they are beliefs about theoretical entities, and/or about the real natures or essences of things) and by the way in which they are held (they are held dogmatically, in the manner of one who attaches himself to a philosophical position). Frede's Skeptic has little to say to the ordinary non-theoretical person, except in areas such as ethics and religion, where, according to Frede, the ordinary person does hold his beliefs dogmatically; Burnyeat's Skeptic radically challenges the ordinary person's way of life, asking him not to have any commitments as to the way things are. For an attempt to adjudicate the dispute, see Barnes (1982b). Burnyeat, it seems to me, has successfully argued that the Skeptic is attacking all the pupil's attachments to the truth of a claim, and that the ordinary person is deeply attached to many views about the way things are, not only in ethics and religion, but in many other areas as well.

[2] Again, I am in agreement with Burnyeat (1980a) about the way in which ordinary beliefs are held: most people do hold to their beliefs in a way that will give rise to *tarachē* should a challenge make itself convincing. And this is all that is required in order to make those beliefs the target of Skeptical argument. Glidden (1983) 239 remarks that in this sense Sextus' claim that Skepticism follows and defends ordinary life is somethat disingenuous: "The farmer does not bring his harvest of wheat into shelter from an impending storm simply out of habit, but because it is going to rain."

medical analogy, commends this diagnosis and proposes a radical cure: the purgation of all cognitive commitment, all belief, from human life. The Skeptic, "being a lover of his fellow human beings, wishes to heal by argument, insofar as he can, the conceit and the rashness of dogmatic people" (*PH* 3.280). Why does he want to do this, and how does he attempt to do it? I shall first give a brief description of the general nature and procedures of Greek Skepticism, as described by Sextus Empiricus. I shall then examine in more detail its conception of its own motivation and its end, arguing that there is, despite Sextus' many denials, a quasi-dogmatic element within Skepticism, one commitment that the pupil is not allowed to let go or even to question. I shall ask how this fact affects Sextus' attitude to the therapy of ethical belief in particular. Finally, I shall study Nikidion's therapy, comparing its medical properties with those of Epicureanism. And I shall ask how a person thus treated would live, what feelings and desires she would have, what attitudes toward herself and others.

Although Skepticism is a complex philosophical movement with a long history, I shall focus for these purposes on the account of Skepticism offered by Sextus,[3] which seems to represent an attempt by later Skepticism to return to its Pyrrhonist origins, or at least to what it takes the life and practices of Pyrrho to represent.[4] I shall not ask here about the extent to which the Academy in the intervening period, under Arcesilaus and Carneades, did or did not diverge from these ideas.[5]

II

Skepticism, as Sextus reports its self-definition, is "an ability [*dunamis*] to set up an opposition of appearances and thoughts, in any way at all, an ability from which we come, through the equal force [*isostheneia*] of the opposing statements and states of affairs, first into suspension [*epochē*], and after that into freedom from disturbance [*ataraxia*]" (*PH* 1.8). This account is revealing; each of its terms needs to be scrutinized. Skeptical

---

[3] On Sextus' life and how little we know about it, see House (1980); on the history of the school, see Sedley (1980) and also (1983a). For related historical background, see De Lacy (1958), Long (1981).

[4] See Sedley (1983a)—who qualifies this observation by pointing to the interest of later Skepticism in the procedure and structure of argument, an interest that it is hard to trace back to the practices of Pyrrho. On Pyrrho, see also Flintoff (1980).

[5] Here see Sedley (1980), Striker (1980), and Burnyeat (forthcoming b).

therapy, first of all, is an ability or capability, a *dunamis*. This claim is significant because it implicitly denies what will later be denied explicitly: that Skepticism is a *technē*, and art or science, an organized body of knowledge. How can Skepticism be anything, one might ask, if the Skeptic has no beliefs? What is one learning, when one learns to be a Skeptic? Sextus' cogent answer is, one is learning a capability, a know-how; one learns how to do something, namely, to set up oppositions among impressions and beliefs. "In any way at all," can, Sextus says, be taken in several ways. It tells us that the ability is not a special recondite faculty, but just an ordinary or natural capability. It can also refer to the variety of the types of opposition in which the Skeptic engages, opposing impressions to thoughts and each to one another. Finally, it also tells us that there is no special preferred procedure for setting up oppositions, but that it may be done in any manner: the Skeptic, then, is not procedurally dogmatic, any more than she is content-dogmatic. We shall later be returning to this claim. Equal force, *isostheneia*, is the apparently equal persuasiveness or plausibility of the opposing claims where "neither of the contending discourses lies ahead of any other as being more convincing." Suspension, *epochē*, is "a standstill of reason through which we neither deny nor assert anything." Freedom from disturbance, *ataraxia*, is "the unburdened and tranquil condition of the soul" (*PH* 1.8–10).

We must now note an ambiguity in the definition. How are we to understand the connection of the clause beginning "from which" ("from which we come, through the equal force . . . first into suspension, and after that into *ataraxia*") to the earlier part of the sentence? Two possibilities appear open. First, we might treat the clause as a non-restrictive modifier. The full definition of Skepticism is, "Skepticism is the ability that sets up oppositions of impressions and thoughts"—and it is then added that Skepticism, so defined, in fact happens to lead to equipoise, suspension, and *ataraxia*. In this case, Skepticism would apparently be any old *antithetikē dunamis*, and it just happens to lead to these results. The second possibility is that the modifier is restrictive, the results a part of the definition. Skepticism is a particular *antithetikē dunamis*, namely, the one from which we come into suspension, equipoise, *ataraxia*. The Skeptic is not operating correctly as a Skeptic unless he is aiming his know-how at those results, or at least practicing his know-how in the particular way that would produce those results. We shall later see that the ambiguity is no accident: that Sextus wants and needs to claim the first understanding but is forced continually toward the second, with results that we shall soon observe.

How do oppositional procedures produce their results? Here is the story

Sextus tells us in his chapters on the starting point (*archē*) of Skeptical inquiry (*PH* 1.12) and on its end or goal (*telos*) (*PH* 1.25–30). The explanatory starting point of Skeptical inquiry, its *archē aitiōdes*, is, he says, the hope of achieving freedom from disturbance. For, he continues, "great-natured people," that is, presumably, people of energy and ability, being disturbed by the discrepancies and contradictions they encountered and being at a loss as to what view to take up, embarked upon inquiry into the truth about things—thinking that if they settled what was true and what was false they would be free from disturbance. The turn toward Skepticism begins when they discover, as they inquire, that to every argument another argument of equal strength is opposed. So Skepticism has the same original motives as the dogmatic search for truth; it is a result of the failure of that search (1.12).

This interesting story is told again several chapters later, in the discussion of the end (*telos*) of Skepticism:

> We say up to the present[6] that the end of the Skeptic is freedom from disturbance [*ataraxia*] in matters of belief and moderate affect [*metriopatheia*] in things necessary. For, beginning to philosophize with the idea of sorting out impressions and grasping which are true and which are false, so as to be free of disturbance [*hōste ataraktēsai*), he fell into disagreement, with equal weight on both sides. Being unable to sort this out, he suspended judgment; and as he was suspending judgment, there followed, as it just happened [*tuchikōs*] freedom from disturbance in the sphere of belief. . . . The Skeptic's experience is, in fact, the same as what is reported about the painter Apelles. For they say that as he was painting a horse, and trying to represent the foam on its coat, he was so unsuccessful that he gave up and flung at the picture the sponge on which he had been wiping the paints off his brush. And the sponge made the effect of the horse's foam. So, too, Skeptics used to hope to get freedom from disturbance through sorting out the discrepancies in impressions and thoughts; but proving unable to do this, they suspended; and as they were suspending, freedom from disturbance, as if by chance [*hoion tuchikōs*], followed them as a shadow follows a body. [*PH* 1.25–29]

Let us return to Nikidion's experience. Sextus' claim is that her original motive for philosophizing was to attain freedom from disturbance by the resolution of troubling contradictions and discrepancies; she thinks that

---

[6] This way of talking is chosen characteristically by Sextus to indicate that even his central philosophical claims are not dogmatic assertions, but simply reports of how things strike him.

latching onto some definite truth about the world will put her mind at rest. He seems to be correct about the motives of the Epicurean pupil, at least, though he neglects the role the particular content of Epicurean teaching might play in getting that tranquillity. We philosophize, he claims, so as to be at ease and safe in the world. But—as our Nikidion story, anticipating his argument, suggested—this aim is not always fulfilled. Belief brings not only the anxiety of selection, but all the other difficulties we have mentioned. Commitment makes a contrary result more difficult to tolerate and generates anxieties about an uncertain future. Philosophy is an extension of Nikidion's ordinary tendency to cling to her beliefs; it exacerbates the problems caused by that tendency.

Nikidion will fail to get what she wanted from philosophy. But, Sextus claims, in the very failure, in the paralysis of reason by its own oppositional activity, she gets what she wanted all along. In short: the Skeptical suspension is a more efficacious route to the very same end the dogmatist goes for; it answers, far better than his own original methods and procedures, to the need that led Nikidion to undertake philosophy in the first place.

This passage describes a Skeptic's initial experience. The experience happened, the first time, by mere chance. But the Skeptical ability seems to be the ability to go about deliberately setting up such oppositions, in such a way that the happy chance happens regularly, with respect to every subject—ethical and non-ethical, ordinary and philosophical—on which Nikidion thinks it important to get the truth, with respect to every area in which she has cognitive commitments or searches for commitment.[7] Skeptical ability releases reason from these burdens and these vulnerabilities. Since the disease is a disease of reason, its cure comes through reason and argument—from a philosophical school that traces its history back to Socrates and appears in many respects to provide a systematic rational education. Since, however, the disease is not so much *of* reason and belief as it is reason and belief themselves, the cure, being itself an operation of reason, involving—at least temporarily—belief, will be likely to have a peculiar relation to itself. It will wish to take itself out of the pupil's life along with the commitments it purges.

The Epicurean sets up as the goal of natural human life a complete painlessness in both body and mind. It chooses this goal relying upon the natural creature as a guide. The natural creature seems to pursue this goal.

---

[7] Here I am in agreement with Barnes (1982b); but see my qualification, p. 299. Notice that the Modes and Tropes, as reported by Sextus, contain no restriction of subject matter, but range very widely over many areas in which pupils can be expected to have beliefs.

But this means that nature itself has disease in it, in a sense. For the natural creature, uncorrupted by belief, does not always, or even regularly, get what it wants. Although nature is the standard, reason—and even a special philosophical use of reason—proves necessary as a remedy for ills that are present in nature itself. Only Epicurean thoughts can take an uncorrupted creature from the condition of nature to its own proper end. We can expect the Skeptic to take a different tack. For the Epicurean analysis of the end commits the pupil to a life of belief, a life that the Skeptic has argued to be diseased and anxious, ultimately self-defeating. The Skeptic, then, will do well to aim at a target that does not require belief for its attainment. This means renouncing the Epicurean hope of opposing bodily pain through philosophical reflection. Consequently, the Skeptic does not express objections to natural and necessary bodily pain. What, after all, is the point of having objections to something that we cannot help? (And, recall, we really do not help them by belief, since belief, it has been claimed, causes more problems than it solves.) Pain is a part of nature; the real disease is the setting oneself up against nature, the theorizing about pain that sooner or later compounds pain. So, instead of complete painlessness, the Skeptic adopts as his end a target that is readily available in nature, without the agency of dogma: complete freedom from disturbance in matters of belief, and moderate affect, *metriopatheia*, in necessary physical sufferings. "For inasmuch as he is a human being, he will suffer through his senses [*aisthetikōs*]; but if he does not in addition have the opinion that what he suffers is bad by nature, he will suffer moderately" (*PH* 3.235–36; cf. *PH* 1.25, 30; *M* 11.118, 141.) Again, he argues: "For he who has no additional belief about pain being bad is gripped by the necessitated motion of the pain; but he who in addition imagines that pain is the only evil, the only thing discordant with our nature, doubles the burden that comes from its presence through this opinion" (*M* 11.158–59).[8] Against Epicurus' claim that belief assists us in our struggle with pain, Sextus claims that "in the person who is burdened by hunger or thirst it is not possible to engender the conviction through Skeptical argument that he is not so burdened" (*M*

---

[8] This particular example, which seems to refer to the Epicurean theory of good, may suggest that the pupil's problem arises only because she accepts a *philosophical* theory of the good. But many other examples, and the general tenor of Sextus' discussion of ethical commitments, make it plain that his concern is not limited in this way. And we can easily imagine the same point made about the belief that "pain is a bad thing," a belief that all ordinary people share, as Sextus' audience, whatever its philosophical persuasions, would agree. Epicureans defended their position on pain by pointing to its roots in ordinary belief and behavior. See Mitsis (1988a).

11.149)—so the best we can aim at is to remove all disturbances of belief. The continuously active vigilant Skeptic (cf. *PH* 1.1–4), always on guard against a relapse into dogma, can live, thus, at the very summit or end.

Nor, I think, is this merely a verbal difference with the Epicurean, in which the Skeptic calls "end" what Epicureans would call a falling off from the perfect end. There is a point to speaking of this middle condition as the ultimate end. It is (as we have suggested already) that if we make the end (the focal point of our intentions—cf. *PH* 1.25) the way things actually go on, and let our desires flow toward that, then we can just go on living as nature takes us, without a definite view about how things ought to go on, without constantly trying to force nature around to our demands— without, therefore, the anxiety and pain that comes from that effort. Not anything that lies beyond this, no, this—the way life actually goes in nature—this is the end. The Skeptic gives up all commitments that take him beyond the way life actually goes; he has no theory that makes him fight the ordinary, nor does he require theorizing because of some commitment to fight against the ordinary.[9] He can relax, and let life happen to him. It is an important part of Sextus' distinction between the Skeptical way of life and its rivals in ethics to insist that he alone does not teach a *technē*, a systematic art of life that gets people intensely worked up about some end, in such a way that they are upset when they don't have it. Intense pursuit and avoidance is, as even the Epicurean (using the same word, *suntonos*, has agreed)[10] an evil. To be *suntonos* about something is to stretch or strain toward it. (The word is used of the taut string of a musical instrument, of muscular tension, of the constant stress of an unleisured life.)[11] But this intensity of pursuit and avoidance, the Skeptic claims, is at the root of all disturbance (*M* 11.112). To have a *telos* or goal in the usual

---

[9] This use of "ordinary" is one-sided and somewhat tendentious—see subsequent discussion and n. 2; but the Skeptic would reply that this is because the ordinary person is full of dogmatic commitments that press beyond the way life ordinarily goes. In spite of this fact, we can, especially from our dealings with animals and children, recognize a sense of ordinariness and naturalness that does correspond to what the Skeptic is talking about. For a study of the expressions the Skeptic uses to describe his allegiance to ordinary life, see Barnes (1982).

[10] For the Epicurean use of *suntonos*, see *KD* 30, the definition of *erōs* at Us. 483, and many uses in Philodemus' *Peri Orgēs*.

[11] For representative examples, see Aristotle *Pol.* 1337b40, 1370a12; *GA* 787b12. The last passage is of particular interest. Aristotle explains that the fitness of certain animals for movement is caused by the *suntonia* in their muscles. The young don't have it yet, and the old have lost it. He then adds that castration produces a general loss of *suntonia* in the animal, and that this explains vocal and other changes. It is useful to think of the Skeptic's use of the imagery of castration in this connection.

way—to strain the bow of one's life toward it as a target[12]—is a recipe for disturbance. What the Skeptic has done is not so much to introduce a rival account of the *telos* as to undermine the whole notion of reaching for a *telos*. What is the end of human life? Oh, just life, the way it actually goes on—if you don't mess up its flow by introducing beliefs. This is not an answer to that question: it is a way of telling the questioner not to go on pressing that question, not to care about the answer.

As she lets herself go, Nikidion will not be altogether inactive. For in doing away with all belief, all commitment to get it right about how things are, she has not eliminated motivation. Intensity requires belief and commitment; mere action does not, as we can readily see by looking to the lives of animals. From Aristotle on, as we saw in chapter 3, it has been an agreed position in Greek thought about action that living creatures can in fact be motivated to move and act without belief—by merely a combination of impressions (*phantasiai*) as to how things are, and desires. *Phantasiai* or *phainomena* are the ways the world looks to us, what we see it as, the ways it strikes us.[13] They are different from beliefs because they involve no commitment as to the way things really are; so, when they oppose one another, there is no contradiction.[14] An object appears now one size, now another: there is no problem in this, if I do not start worrying about how it really is. *Phantasiai* involve operations of the cognitive faculties, both senses and intellect; but they involve no attempt to sort out and coordinate the different impressions, arriving at a general view.[15] Even with respect to a single time, the person who reports a *phantasia* can perfectly consistently go on to say, "But of course, I have no idea how the matter really stands, and I don't care." Thus, animals who have *phantasiai* but neither memory

[12] The target image appears prominently as an image for the *telos* in both Aristotle (*EN* 1094a22–25, *EE* 1214b7 ff.) and the Stoics (e.g., Cic. *Fin.* 3.22, Plut. *Comm. Not.* 1071A-E)—who stress, against Aristotle, that *eudaimonia* consists in straining toward it, not in hitting it. See Striker (1986), C.C.W. Taylor (1987), Irwin (1986), Inwood (1987).

[13] See Nussbaum (1978) essay 5, which argues against the prevalent tendency to translate *phantasia* as "mental image." The same criticism can be made of translations of Sextus and his Stoic opponents: on Sextus, see Frede (1979), Striker (1980), and on the Stoic notion of *phantasia*, Annas (1980). Frede argues that for Sextus there is no salient distinction between *phantasia* and *phainomenon*. The Stoic idea of assent to a *phantasia* may be subtly different from Aristotle's idea of belief, but for our purposes we may treat the two together.

[14] Thus this is a non-epistemic appearing—see chapter 3 and Nussbaum (1978), Burnyeat (1980a); it does not imply judgment, or even a tendency to believe.

[15] Aristotle explicitly contrasts *phantasiai* with general principles at *EN* 1147b4–5. *Metaph.* 980b26 contrasts *phantasia* with experience and memory. See also Sorabji (1993) chs. 2–4.

nor belief will just move as things strike them at the moment; they can have no general views of any sort, including ethical views. If we add memory to *phantasia* but stop short of belief, we will get richer temporal connections and the possibility of being moved by habits, traditions, know-how, even principles acting as causes of action, but we will still stop short of any assent to a view that such and such is actually the case. Animals who operate on this basis have plenty of causes of action. What they do not have is reasons for action, that is, views they are committed to as correct.

This, says the Skeptic, is how humans can move and act without belief.[16] They go on using their faculties. The world strikes them now this way, now that; they are influenced by their desires, their cognitive activities, even their memories. But they do not bother inquiring into truth or sorting things out. They neither assent to nor refuse the appearances that strike them.[17] They just allow themselves to be swayed:

> Clinging to appearances [*phantasiai*], then, we live without belief, according to the practices of life [*tēn biōtikēn tērēsin*], since we cannot be altogether inactive. And it looks as if these practices of life are of four sorts. The first lies in the guidance of nature, the second in the necessity of the feelings, the third in the transmission of laws and customs, the fourth in the instruction of the arts. By guidance of nature, I mean that according to which we are naturally perceiving and thinking creatures; by the necessity of the feelings I mean that according to which hunger sets us on the road to food, thirst to drink; by the transmission of customs and laws I mean that according to which we accept in a practical way [*biōtikōs*, i.e., so far as living our lives is concerned] that it is good to perform conventional religious observances and bad to disregard them; by the teaching of the arts, I mean that according to which we are not inactive in the arts that we take up. But all this we say without belief. (*PH* 1.23–24; cf. also 1.17, 22, 229, 231; 2.244, etc.)

We have here four motivating forces, four ways life can strike or impress us, which are sufficiently powerful, either singly or in combination, to

---

[16] On the challenge raised against the Skeptics by their opponents—that Skepticism makes action impossible (the *apraxia* argument)—see Striker (1980), Burnyeat (1980a), McPherran (1987).

[17] The Skeptical argument is couched, on the whole, in the language of Stoic psychology of action (cf. chapter 10 and Inwood [1985]); but their reply follows lines mapped out by Aristotle in his account of the movement of animals: see Nussbaum (1978). See Cic. *Acad.* 2.104, and Striker (1980).

engender movement.[18] We use the senses and the reasoning powers we naturally have—going as thought-impression or sense-impression strikes us, without commitment.[19] It would be artificial to close our eyes, to shut off the perception of a tree, the thought of food and drink; so we go on as is most natural. Again, we go by our natural bodily feelings and desires, listening to hunger not as a signal of "the bad" but as a push from our instinctual nature. And, perhaps the most interesting part of Sextus' claim, we are guided by the habits we have formed and the skills we have acquired—allowing all of this, insofar as it is already internal to us (in memory and habit) to move and sway us. We do not resist the push of habit when it does push; but all of this is done without the concern for rightness and truth that makes the ordinary person so strained and anxious about action.[20] Nikidion will acquire no new ethical beliefs. But she will also not struggle against the ones she has. She will simply stop caring about whether they are true, treat them as impressions whose truth value is indeterminate—as motives that are simply there, parts of naturalized life. But viewed in this way, they cease to *be* beliefs.[21]

The same, we now discover, applies to her verbal behavior. Although the Skeptic does not, Sextus insists, assert anything at all in a full-fledged sense, making a claim (explicit or implicit) as to how things are, she may of course utter many things as they strike her, including the ideas of Skepticism themselves.[22] Many of her utterances will have the grammatical form of

[18] On the fourfold *biōtikē tērēsis*, see Burnyeat (1980a) and Barnes (1982b), who stresses that it does not involve believing. It should be stressed that it is the performance of conventional religious observances that Sextus includes here, and not, as Bury's translation suggests, religious beliefs. On the "necessity of the feelings," see Stough (1984), who stresses that Sextus' examples here and elsewhere are all sensory; she suggests that there is an implicit contrast with belief and judgment, which are not deemed necessary or necessitating (*M* 11.156–57). See *M* 11.143, 157, 148, 152, 156; *PH* 3.123, 238; sensory responses are described as *alogon, abouleton, akousion* (*M* 11.143, 148, 152–53, 156, 161).

[19] On the associative sign, see Burnyeat (1982), Stough (1984), and Glidden (1983)—who suggests, unconvincingly in my view, that the Skeptic's allegiance to it is an insincere ploy used inside an ad hominem argument. Of course there are limits to the "sincerity" of any Skeptical utterance, since, as he himself says, the Skeptic has no belief-commitments; but the associative sign is a psychological procedure in accordance with which he naturally goes on, not a belief he asserts.

[20] Thus Stough (1984) is, in my view, mistaken in assimilating the good Skeptic as closely as she does to ordinary practical reason in its action-guiding role.

[21] On belief and the varieties of assent, see Sedley (1983a).

[22] On non-assertion, see Stough (1984), McPherran (1987), Barnes (1982b). Barnes makes a helpful comparison to Wittgenstein's observations about pain-behavior in *Philosophical Investigations* I 244 and *Zettel* 549.

assertions. But whenever she says something—including any of the maxims proper to Skepticism itself—then, Sextus tells us, "in bringing these utterances forward she is telling what strikes her [*to heautōi phainomenon*] and reporting her experience without belief, not making any firm claim about anything outside of this" (*PH* 1.15). Again, "This she does, telling what strikes her about what is at hand, in the manner of someone making a report—not with belief and conviction, but going through what she is experiencing" (1.197). Diogenes says that Skeptical utterances are "confessions" or "avowals" (*exomologēseis*, 9.104). This sort of remark is repeated over and over again by Sextus,[23] on his guard lest he seem to dogmatize and aware that ordinary language is, as ordinarily used, a committed and dogmatic instrument. It shows us what Nikidion might expect to say as she is being cured—and also what she can expect to hear from her doctor.

III

Nikidion arrives, then, at the Skeptical school. We have, unfortunately, more or less no information about how the later Pyrrhonist Skeptics lived, what sort of philosophical community they created, who their pupils were, and how they interacted with them.[24] Their attitude to habit makes them less dependent upon isolation than were the Epicureans; they liked to stress that a good Skeptic can look like anybody else and live successfully among non-Skeptics; so it seems likely that they did not attach the importance the Epicureans did to creating an entire counter-culture that will fill every corner of daily life with correct philosophizing. They may well have operated more like a regular school, offering instruction and argument in their own particular way, but leaving the pupil's activities unconstrained when instruction was not in process. As to the range of pupils, the Skeptic neither requires nor rejects *paideia*: whether you are a well-educated young gentleman or a courtesan, you can find something there to suit you. And Sextus sometimes explicitly stresses that the Skeptic can deal with pupils who have a wide range of intellectual abilities and backgrounds, so long as he does not try to instruct them all in a group. Even in Plato's day it is probable that

[23] See *PH* 1.4, 15, 187–91, 197, 200, 203; for parallel passages in Plotinus, see Barnes (1982b) 22, n. 24.

[24] House (1980), after sifting the available evidence, urges suspension of belief; the time and location of the school are wildly uncertain, and it is not clear that there was an organized school at all in the late Pyrrhonist period, as opposed to individuals teaching groups of pupils.

the Academy admitted female pupils; so I see no reason why Nikidion, just as she is, could not go there.

She arrives, then burdened by all her struggles of belief and emotion. She finds that here, as in her other schools, imagery of doctoring is prominently used to explain philosophy's practical contribution and to justify particular practices. What is more, she will probably find among her teachers a connection to the practice and theory of actual medicine that was not present in the Garden. Sextus himself was probably a doctor[25] and Skeptical teachings are prominent in two of the three major schools of medicine in his day: the empirical and the methodical schools. Galen preserves for us a debate between a dogmatic and a Skeptical doctor that evidently was staged before prospective pupils;[26] and Sextus, despite his name, takes care to tell us that it is the Methodist and not the Empiricist school of medicine that is the truly Skeptical school.[27] For the Empiricists positively assert that we cannot know what is not evident to the senses, thus taking up a dogmatic position in the theory of knowledge. The Methodists, by contrast, following "the common practice of life" (*ho bios ho koinos*) simply allow themselves to be guided by what they experience, without any commitment to any particular method of procedure or view of knowledge. They are naturally moved, in a way that is mediated by their professional training but does not involve any thick commitment to or belief in its rightness, to counter an observed alien symptom with a remedy. "It is evident that conditions that are naturally alien to us compel us to move toward their dissolution—for even a dog, when it is pricked by a thorn, proceeds to remove it" (*PH* 1.238–39). This is how the Methodist doctor practices bodily medicine, using the techniques he has learned because they come naturally to him, not because he thinks they are right. And this is how the philosophical doctor will proceed to heal Nikidion.

It is likely that Nikidion will begin by describing to the teacher the dogmatic beliefs that have failed to bring her comfort. She will display her situation by revealing as many cognitive commitments as she cares about, and by showing the degree of refinement and sophistication with which she

---

[25] On the evidence, and its uncertainty, see House (1980); on Sextus' use of medical analogies, see Barnes (1982b).

[26] For examples of such a debate, see Barnes (1982a).

[27] *PH* 1.238–39; on the Methodists, see Frede (1982). The conflicting evidence concerning Sextus' Empiricist or Methodical affiliation is reviewed by House (1980). Hossenfelder (1968) argues that if he was already an Empiricist doctor when he became a Skeptic, Sextus might have felt no reason to switch: he might have continued to practice his profession but in a new spirit. See also Edelstein (1967).

grasps the arguments both for and against them. The teacher will now proceed through her beliefs, bringing forward counterarguments like those organized in the extant Modes and Tropes.[28] In each case, he will try to take her into the condition of equipoise. Nikidion will find each of her arguments opposed by a counterargument that is designed to seem to her equally persuasive. And so, again and again, through the entire range of her beliefs she will be led into suspension—until there is no thesis she cares to defend, no belief (as Sextus says) whose answer means more to her than the answer to the question whether the number of the stars is odd or even.[29] They will all seem just that unimportant, and just that remote.

Now we need to examine the teacher's arguments more closely, using, once again, our ten points as a guide. For as we do so, we will begin to see some remarkable similarities with the Epicurean practice of argument— but also some equally striking differences.

1. The Skeptic's arguments, like the arguments used by Epicurus, are good therapeutic arguments only if they are well directed toward their *practical goal*.[30] We have already seen the Skeptic claim that by opposing an equal argument to every argument he can bring either himself or another into equipoise and thence to suspension; and that *ataraxia* follows upon suspension. We have seen that he claims to have discovered more effective means than the dogmatist to attain the dogmatist's own end, namely, freedom from disturbance. And all through his work Sextus repeats these claims of causal efficacy. In a passage that we shall shortly examine, he describes the good Skeptical teacher as a doctor who, basing himself on the evidence before him, selects precisely the right remedy for the particular patient's disease (*PH* 3.280). Again, he tells us that the follower of the Skeptic way in ethics "will live happily [*eudaimonōs*] and free from disturbance, not being lifted up by the good as good, nor oppressed by the bad" (*M* 11.118). In the ethical sections especially but also elsewhere—for example, the early section on the end of Skepticism—he gives us a detailed account of how and why this improvement in Nikidion's life takes place. Suspension frees her, first of all, from the burden of worrying about what is true and right; it frees her, second, from belief in a view of what is good—a belief that adds to her torment when the thing deemed bad is present. It will release her, as well, from all the evils that come from

---

[28] On the Modes and Tropes, see Annas and Barnes (1985), Striker (1980).

[29] Epictetus *Disc.* 1.28.3; cf. Cic. *Acad.* 2.32, *PH* 2.97, *M* 7.393, 8.147, 317; see Burnyeat (1980a), 40 n. 35.

[30] Cf. *PH* 2.90, 97; *M* 7.393, 8.147, 317; and see Burnyeat (1980a), Barnes (1982b).

the intense pursuit of any practical goal "with eager conviction" (*meta sphodrou peismatos,* M 11.121).

These evils prominently include emotion: arrogant confidence and a restless excessive joy when the good is present (*PH* 3.235 ff., *M* 11.115ff.); a gnawing fearfulness and watchfulness lest it vanish; a distressingly intense desire for the good before it is present (*M* 11.116); if it should be absent, a grief intense because based on an evaluative belief, and even a fantasized sense of guilt—the feeling that she is in a bad way because the Furies are punishing her for something she must have done (*PH* 3.235 ff.).[31] The Skeptic shares with the other schools of his day [32] (at least for the purposes of argument) the view that all these emotional states, including the uncertain kind of joy that is based upon the presence of unstable externals, are bad things to have in one's life, because of their disturbing character. So it is a major part of his claim of causal efficacy to assert that his arguments get rid of these, while those of his opponents do not, even if they believe that they do. These emotions are based upon ethical belief; and Sextus suggests that only the complete extirpation of belief gets rid of them. The dogmatists all have one thing in common: all urge the intense, committed pursuit of some end. But this means that they cannot really cure our diseases:

> To say that one should avoid this as base, but incline to this as nobler, is the way of men who are not undoing disturbance, but are simply changing its position . . . so that the philosopher's discourse creates a new disease in place of the old one . . . not freeing the pupil from pursuit, but only shifting her over to a different pursuit. As, then, the doctor who in doing away with pleurisy creates pneumonia, or in curing brain fever creates lethargic fever, does not remove the danger, but changes it around, so the philosopher, if he brings in another disturbance in place of the former one, does not come to the aid of the person who is disturbed. (*M* 11.134–37)

Only Skepticism gets rid of the burden altogether: "therefore, it belongs to Skepticism to secure a flourishing life [*to eudaimona bion peripoiein*]."[33]

[31] The Skeptics are unusual among Hellenistic schools in recognizing this retrospective emotion and its importance. The Stoic taxonomies divide emotion into the present-oriented and the future-oriented—see chapter 10.

[32] On Epicurus, see chapters 4–7; on the Stoics, chapter 10.

[33] In order to avoid the misleading implications of "happiness" as a translation of *eudaimonia,* I shall use transliteration as often as possible; where a translation is required to

These claims are repeatedly made; and yet there is need for caution. For it is an official and a much repeated part of the Skeptical way that the Skeptic's claims are subject, themselves, to their own scrutiny. The Skeptic cannot exactly assert what Epicurus asserts: that his way will bring *eudaimonia*. For, strictly speaking, he can have neither a committed view as to what *eudaimonia* is, nor a committed causal belief as to what does or does not secure it. He can use such language ad hominem against his opponents—but if he were to get enmeshed in it himself, he would be just as diseased as they. So he must have toward his own philosophical practice, and display to Nikidion, the attitude that he found in the Methodist doctor. This is how I go on, he can say, this is what my experiences cause me quite naturally to do; and this is what I have so far observed to result from these doings. See what happens in your own case. See whether, like the dog with the thorn in its foot, you too are naturally moved to go on in this way, opposing argument to argument. Is this enough to say to someone who is not already habituated in the Skeptic way? Doesn't the Skeptic centrally, and illicitly, trade on a more dogmatic set of attitudes? I shall pursue this worry when I discuss end-relativity. But first I turn to the third medical characteristic.

3. The arguments addressed to Nikidion will be *responsive to the particular case*, chosen on account of her particular situation. Again, as with our other two schools, this point is stressed through use of the medical analogy. It is made in the Epicurean, rather than the Aristotelian way: that is, the emphasis on attention to particularity comes in the context of attention to the pupil's particular pathology, not in the context of elaborating a norm of practiced wisdom or health. The Skeptic, claims Sextus, will argue in exactly the way suited to the nature of the pupil's disease. In the fascinating section of the *Outlines of Pyrrhonism* entitled, "Why the Skeptic sometimes deliberately puts forward arguments that are weak in persuasive power" (*PH* 3.280), he argues that a good doctor will not give the patient an overdose but will carefully calibrate the dose of medicine to the magnitude of the disease. Even so, the Skeptic will carefully gauge the degree to which the pupil has been infected by the disease of belief, and will choose the weakest and mildest remedy that will knock out the obstacles to *ataraxia*. Sometimes, then, his arguments will be "weighty"; but sometimes "he does not shrink from propounding some that are evidently less forceful." In short, the arguments must balance the degree and location of Nikidion's commitment, so as to bring her into equipoise in each case.[34] If

---

[34] Barnes (1982b) uses this observation to solve the problem of the range of Skeptical argument.

she is vulnerable to persuasion and commitment, a good strong argument might sway her too much, convincing her that its conclusions were true—causing her, say, to overbalance from Epicureanism into Stoicism. The object is to get her to stop right in the middle. We may add that as Nikidion becomes more and more used to the Skeptic way she will, quite possibly, come to hold all of her convictions more and more lightly; so she will need, progressively, weaker and weaker arguments. Argument gradually effects its own removal from her life. At the end, I imagine that the bare posing of a question will already induce a shrug of indifference, and further argument will prove unnecessary.[35]

It has been suggested by Jonathan Barnes that the teacher will give Nikidion antithetical arguments only in areas where she already feels a disturbance caused by conviction.[36] This, I think, is not so clear. For in his section on the Skeptical phrase, "to every argument an equal argument is opposed," Sextus remarks that some Skeptics utter this expression in the form of a hortatory address: "let us oppose." "They address this advice to the Skeptic," he continues, "lest, being misled by the dogmatist, he should give up the search concerning arguments, and thus miss through haste that freedom from disturbance that appears to the Skeptics, which they think arises concomitantly with[37] suspension concerning all things" (PH 1.204–5). A later passage remarks that we ought to subject to antithetical argument not only ethical beliefs on which contrary claims already exist, but also all those on which some counterargument might someday arise. For we might have supposed that all people agree in judging incest with sisters to be a bad thing, if we had never heard of Egyptian customs—and then we would have been thrown into anxiety when we did hear about them. "Even so, concerning those practices where we know of no discrepancy, we should not assert that there is no disagreement—since it is possible, as I said, that in some nation unknown to us a conflicting view may exist" (PH 3.234). I take this passage to imply that the Skeptic does not only treat actual disturbances in Nikidion's belief structure; he addresses himself to all her convictions across the board, wherever there might possibly arise a conflicting view that would generate anxiety. (This would also be required by Sextus' arguments about the way in which belief, even without conflict,

---

[35] See also Burnyeat (1980a).

[36] Barnes (1982b) 18–19.

[37] The verb is paruphistēmi, suitably vague for the Skeptic's purposes. R. G. Bury's "believe to be dependent on" in the Loeb Classical Library translation (Cambridge, Mass., 1936) gives a clear causal sense that the Greek does not have. On the word and its use in Stoic accounts of thought and language, see Caston (forthcoming).

produces disturbance in good times and in bad.) He practices preventive medicine; and to do this he must assault all of her convictions without exception. Particularity is still there in the dosage of argument judged relevant in each case. But every pupil must hear arguments on all topics on which they have any beliefs at all; so there will be a great deal of overlap in the instruction. (This position of the Skeptic's explains, I think, why he can link continued vigilance and searching[38] with continued calm in the way that he does: for only vigilance does in fact guarantee calm.)

2. Now we can no longer avoid the deepest problem we have in understanding the Skeptic's therapeutic practice: that is, to assess the degree and the nature of its *value-* or *end-relativity*. The Skeptic asserts that neither he nor his pupil is to be committed to anything—not, then, to any ethical end, and not even to the belief that their reciprocal procedures are productive of any good end. And yet he advertises his therapy by pointing to its efficacy in achieving a certain very particular end, namely, freedom from disturbance, or *ataraxia*. He says he has no commitments—he just goes along with life. But can he in fact avoid all commitment here?[39]

The Skeptic's official answer goes like this. *Ataraxia* just comes by chance, *tuchikōs*, as the result of a process he is following out of some non-dogmatic motivation—say, because it is his trade. He does not seek it out, he does not believe in it: it just happens to him. Since it happens as an unexpected result, we do not have to attribute any commitment to him in order to explain his actions. Apelles did not have to have a desire to make a certain sort of effect by tossing the sponge. He just threw it out of frustration, and the effect came by lucky coincidence. Just so, *ataraxia* comes to the Skeptic: it is like a shadow that follows the suspension of belief (DL 9.107, *PH* 1.29). He is passive to it. As for his treatment of Nikidion, he will presumably say that he goes on in the way that a Methodist doctor goes on, because experience and his perception of her situation suggest to him the idea of proceeding as he does. He has no belief that this or that is healthy, no belief that a certain procedure will produce a certain end; he

---

[38] The name *skeptikos* ("inquiring") is indicative of the school's emphasis on this point: see Sedley (1983a). The Skeptics also call themselves *zētetikoi*, "searchers"—again emphasizing the fact that their school always inquires into the arguments and never settles on any dogma.

[39] On the history of this problem in the school, see Sedley (1983a), and also Burnyeat (1980a). Burnyeat sees dogmatic commitment to the end only in the early Skeptics, and particularly Timon. But see also Cic. *Acad.* 2.77, which attributes to Arcesilaus the view that the life without belief is "honorable and worthy of the wise man"; and the later Skeptics' reliance on Pyrrho as a practical model is another indication of the central role played by *ataraxia* in the practice of Skepticism.

just goes on. If it causes *ataraxia* in her, and if she likes that result, very well. But he could not and would not choose to do this or that for the sake of *ataraxia*—either his own or someone else's. For this would be to be committed; and to be committed is to be liable to disturbance.[40]

Notice, however, how emphasis on the value of *ataraxia* keeps coming back. For why does the Skeptic have a Skeptical attitude to *ataraxia*? According to him, because he must have this attitude, if he is to avoid disturbance and attain *ataraxia*. We are invited, then, to press our suspicions further, asking whether, in spite of his official line, the Skeptic does not have, and have to have, a more than Skeptical attitude toward this one end—and perhaps toward his own procedures as causally linked to that end. As we inquire, we notice, first of all, that the Skeptic frequently says things that have a dogmatic flavor. We have seen that the very definition of Skepticism contains an ambiguity: is productivity of *ataraxia* part of the definition of the process, or not? A similar ambiguity appeared in the characterization of the pre-Skeptical dogmatist in the chapter on the end: for he was searching for the truth "so as to be free of disturbance" (*PH* 1.26). The Greek contains a result clause and not a purpose clause, in order to give the impression that we need not ascribe any purpose connected with *ataraxia* to this person: it just falls out as a result. But we just saw that in order to translate it coherently we are more or less forced (given that the verb is a verb of searching) into using the language of purpose. And elsewhere Sextus himself unambiguously uses such language. The starting point of Skepticism is "the hope of achieving *ataraxia*" (1.12). And, having first defined *telos* or end as "that for the sake of which everything is done or considered, but not for the sake of anything else" (*PH* 1.25), he goes on to say that Skepticism's end is *ataraxia* in matters of belief, moderate affect in necessary suffering. To be sure, he qualifies this by saying, "We say up until now that . . ."—but even the "up to now" impression or appearance that one in fact has an end or goal to which all one's activities are directed seems to be more than the Skeptic should have.[41]

And the dogmatic element returns again and again—wherever Sextus needs to proceed against an opponent who promises a practical benefit; whenever he needs to explain why his own way beats all such opponents at their own game. The dogmatic element, as we said, comes in two parts: first, in a claim that *eudaimonia* is equivalent to *ataraxia* (or *ataraxia* along

---

[40] See Burnyeat (1980a).

[41] Sedley (1983a) accurately captures the notion of *telos* when he says that it is the "ultimate focus of all his [sc. the Skeptic's] desires and intentions."

with *metriopatheia*); second, in a causal claim that this end is reliably secured by the Skeptic way. As examples of the first, consider the following:

> All unhappiness [*kakodaimonia*] comes through some sort of disturbance. But all disturbance [*tarachē*] comes to humans either through intensely [*suntonōs*] pursuing something or through intensely avoiding something. (*M* 11.112)

> *Eudaimōn* is the person who lives out his life free from disturbance and, as Timon says, situated in a state of calm and repose. (*M* 11.141)

For examples of the second—or, really, the first combined with the second, consider:

> Those from the Skeptical way, not affirming or denying anything rashly, but leading everything into Skeptical examination, teach that to those who believe that there is something by nature good and bad there follows unhappy living (*to kakodaimonōs bioun*], while to those who refuse to define, and suspend, "The most carefree life among humans is theirs." (*M* 11.111)

> If someone should refuse to say that anything is more worthy of choice than of avoidance . . . he will live in a flourishing way and without disturbance [*eudaimonōs kai atarachōs*] (M 11.118)

> And to teach this [viz., not to assert of anything that it is good by nature] is peculiar to the Skeptical way. Therefore it belongs to that way to secure flourishing life [*to eudaimona bion peripoiein*]. (*M* 11.140)

> Therefore, he who suspends concerning everything in the realm of belief reaps the most complete *eudaimonia*; and in involuntary and irrational movements he is disturbed—"For he is not made of ancient oak or from rock / But sprung from the race of human beings"—but nonetheless he is only moderately affected. (*M* 11.161)

It will strike the reader that these dogmatic passages are concentrated in the ethical section. But this is not surprising, seeing that it is here that Skepticism has to fight its most intense battle for the souls of pupils—for it is fighting here against rivals who also claim to deliver a practical benefit. We found the dogmatism elsewhere, too, in the general remarks about Skepticism's origin and end; and these later passages, though surrounded with specifically ethical discussions, are themselves perfectly general. They state that the Skeptical position involves suspension about all beliefs, and it is this total suspension that they connect with the practical benefit.

But still: suppose Sextus slips up from time to time, carried away by his own rhetoric against his rivals or, perhaps, deliberately using their own rhetoric against them. Is this any reason to think that the Skeptical position requires a more than Skeptical attachment to *ataraxia*? Yes, I claim. First, he has to say things like this in order to display the value and point of his therapy—in order to display the value that he himself attaches to his therapy. The Skeptic prefers his way to the dogmatic way; he recommends it. He can qualify the recommendation in many ways; but if he qualifies his interest in the end of *ataraxia*, or fails to make it clear that this end is better than *tarachē*, or fails to display a certain sort of confidence in the causal relation between his method and *ataraxia*, then the whole enterprise will look hollow and pointless. If he wrote without an element of dogmatism, Nikidion would only learn that it appears to someone that on some occasions a non-dogmatic procedure has produced *ataraxia*, which might seem to someone to be a good thing. But if neither she nor her teacher had an attachment to *ataraxia* that went beyond suspension, she would probably go on being dogmatic after receiving this information—for it is simpler and more habitual to be a dogmatist than a Skeptic. Again, if no further support were given for the Skeptical procedures beyond my imagined non-dogmatic claim, then she would have no reason to make an effort to turn from her habitual dogmatic ways into those procedures. The Skeptic says that he wants life just to go on; but he is in the business of making converts, of turning people away from cherished habits. He cleverly does so by preaching that his therapy delivers the same end the competition goes for, but more effectively. This teaching is essential to his function; and to perform its role, it must be put forward dogmatically.

Consider, too, the role played by *ataraxia* in ordering the whole Skeptical enterprise. Suppose the connection between equipoise and *ataraxia* was, as Sextus says, discovered by chance in the first place. (And even here, Sextus' story informs us that it was discovered by chance while the pupil was already searching committedly for *ataraxia*. Since this was so, the result was directly recognized as the result that was wanted. Apelles, similarly, liked the effect of the sponge because he recognized it as the very thing he had been going for.) Well, what happened next? Does the Skeptic now argue any old way, and wait for *ataraxia* to strike him if and when it may chance to do so? Did Apelles go back to his brushwork and wait until the next episode of frustration caused him to throw another sponge? Of course not. Apelles, we may suppose, used his sponge from then on, whenever he wanted that effect. And the Skeptic devises, with care and ingenuity, patterns of argument—the modes and tropes—that can be used by himself or another to bring any person into equipoise about anything whatever. We know that with each particular pupil he calibrates his arguments with care, in order to achieve precisely the same result each time. There is nothing accidental about this—no matter what form of words the Skeptic may use to suggest that there is. The structure of the whole is incomprehensible except on the supposition that the practitioner believes *ataraxia* is an end worth going for by some sort of deliberate effort, and believes that these procedures have a connection with *ataraxia* that other available procedures do not. Skepticism, we recall, is a *dunamis antithetikē*, a capability whose point is to set up opposition—not simply to let them happen should they happen.

Finally, we notice that there is one major ethical thesis that is never put through the Skeptic's antithetical procedures, one of Nikidion's beliefs that will not be subjected to opposition until equipoise results. This is, of course, the belief that *ataraxia* is an important end (or even the end). Suppose we imagine the following application of Skeptical therapy. Some people, says the teacher, regard freedom from disturbance as the highest end or good, finding disturbance—produced by intensity—the greatest evil. But, you know (he says to a Nikidion who is eagerly nodding her head), there are many others who like intensity, and don't very much mind the disturbances it lets them in for. This is a plausible position; it was around in Nikidion's culture. With some qualifications and more positive content, it is Aristotle's position.[42] The Skeptic could quite well give such a lesson; indeed, given his account of his own method, he seems duty bound to do so. He does not give it; we nowhere find any mention of this very obvious idea. We can see why, if we imagine what would follow from such a lesson. For then, since *ataraxia* (so he has claimed) is supported by Skepti-

---

[42] *Suntonos* itself does not seem to be a positive word in Aristotle's moral psychology; but his account of the way in which a good life strains toward its *telos* expresses a very non-Skeptical intensity of focus and commitment; and the word *spoudaios* has connotations of deep and serious commitment to one's beliefs. The Aristotelian feels that an insoluble or unsolved intellectual challenge is like being in chains (*Metaph.* 995a30 ff.); and he is right to feel this way, since Aristotelianism encourages him to care deeply about the truth. In ethics, getting it right about how one should live is, for Aristotle as for Plato, "no chance matter" (*Rep.* 352D), but a matter of the highest importance, about which it would be right to be intense. And in general Aristotelianism encourages the agent to form ties to friends, city, and the conditions of action that are sufficiently intense to be the occasion for great grief when things go wrong; for such ends the good person will risk not only comfort, but life itself—and this is painful (*EN* 1117b10–16, 1169a18–26).

cal procedures, and since the intense pursuit of value is, as a way of life, supported by other, more dogmatic (or at least Aristotelian) procedures, then, together with the opposition of ends, the teacher will have to arrange for Nikidion, as well, a full-scale opposition of methods and procedures. If she is to be really neutral about *ataraxia*, the teacher must arrange for her to shift from being the pupil inside chapter 8 to being the audience for chapter 2, so that she will end up, as it were, suspended between chapter 8 and chapter 2. And even this will not be fair, since suspension, as a result, is linked to the values of chapter 8 and not those of chapter 2. The only truly fair procedures would be ones that would leave her (alternately?) both suspended and not suspended. Such thoughts are not thought in Skepticism; such oppositions are not tried. The reason can only be that one goal is held fixed, so that we are entitled to use only the method linked to that one. The message that I have been arguing for all along in this book is that there is no value-neutral procedure in ethics. Sextus cannot have a single definite procedure without having some values. He can conceal the value-commitments of his own procedure only by concealing the alternatives to *ataraxia* as an end, refusing to allow its rivals (and their associated methods) to appear on the stage.

What can the Skeptic say in reply to our charges? I think he would now answer that yes, after all, an orientation to *ataraxia* is very fundamental in his procedures. But the orientation to *ataraxia* is not a belief, or a value-commitment. It has the status of a natural inclination. Naturally, without belief or teaching, we move to free ourselves from burdens and disturbances. *Ataraxia* does not need to become a dogmatic commitment, because it is already a natural animal impulse, closely linked to other natural impulses that are part of the "observances of life"—for example, to hunger and thirst, which "set us on the road" to that which will preserve us. Just as the dog moves to take a thorn out of his paw, so we naturally move to get rid of our pains and impediments: not intensely or with any committed attachment, but because that's just the way we go. Animal examples play an important part in Skepticism, illustrating the natural creature's orientation to freedom from disturbance, and the ease with which this is attained if we only can, in Pyrrho's words, "altogether divest ourselves of the human being" (DL 9.66). The instinctive behavior of a pig, calmly removing its hunger during a storm that fills humans with anxiety, exemplifies for the Skeptic the natural orientation we all have to free ourselves from immediate pain. It also shows that this is easily done, if we divest ourselves of the beliefs and commitments that generate other complex pains and anxieties. Pointing to that pig, Pyrrho said "that the wise man should live in just such an undisturbed condition" (DL 9.66). So *ataraxia* is not like the other ends we go for, with the help of belief; it is just there for us as things flow along. If you take away everything but nature, you get the orientation to that end and no other. Asked whether the Skeptical wise man, like his dogmatic counterparts, avoids the bad by deliberately controlling bad desires, Sextus answers that the wise man doesn't need to control an inclination to believe things, since he has no such inclination naturally in him:

> Just as you would not call a eunuch self-controlled with respect to sexual intercourse, nor the person who has a stomach upset self-controlled with respect to eating (for there is not in them any inclination at all for these things, over which they would need to exercise control), so the wise man should not be called self-controlled, since that over which he would need to exercise control does not arise in him. (*M* 11.212)

The urge to believe can be cut out; it leaves behind the inclination to *ataraxia*, which is of a different, more fundamental nature. Nikidion encounters the eunuch image for the second time in her philosophical education; I shall return to it, and to this Skeptical reply. But first, we must continue our examination of the other medical aspects of Nikidion's therapy.

4. Sextus' arguments, like Epicurus', focus on Nikidion's *individual health*. And they do so even more markedly than do Epicurus'. For the goal of argument is her own personal health—and there is no reason to think *philia* a component part of that end. And there is also, apparently, no prominent communal aspect to the therapy itself. She could heal herself, if she learns the knack. (Diogenes says that once Pyrrho was "discovered talking to himself. When asked the reason, he replied that he was training to be good" [9.64].) The claim of the teacher to be *philanthropos*, and to heal on this account, is nothing she can stably rely on. For he just goes on in the way things strike him; and if there is an end to which he is committed, it is his own *ataraxia*, not hers. No connection has been made out between helping others and being free of disturbance oneself. Furthermore, even where Nikidion does retain some of the habits and practices characteristic of her community, she does not retain them in a way in which they would prove effective bonds to the community; for she doesn't really believe in them or commit herself to them in the way that others around her do.

5 and 6. *Reason and reason's virtues are purely instrumental*—and far more blatantly so than in Epicureanism, where the demand for coherence and clarity in the system as a whole brought in, instrumentally, a high degree of careful argumentation. Here we are told that the aim is the

complete paralysis of rational commitment by reason itself,[43] that the process of arguing is (as we shall shortly see) a drug that must expel itself along with the bad bodily humors. At the end, the Epicurean must retain the rational powers that will enable her to counteract pain by thought; but the Skeptic is to end up without argument, with only the natural uncommitted use of reason that is part of the "observances of life."[44] So she does not need to hold on to careful logic. As for the virtues of reason, they are blatantly treated in an ad hoc and instrumental way. An argument should be only as sound and as well executed as it needs to be to counter what is, or might be, in the pupil's soul.

There are several implications here. One, obvious in any case from Sextus' practice, is that the premises of opposing arguments should be chosen not for their truth, but for their acceptability to the interlocutor. Thus it is perfectly all right for the Skeptic to rely, in one argument, on premises that he himself will undermine in another. Since he himself is committed to none of the premises, it should not matter to him whether they are consistent across the board, so long as each argument does its job. Persuasiveness here and now to the pupil simply replaces logical validity and soundness as the desideratum. And if equivocation, question-begging, and other logical sins seem useful on a particular occasion, then nothing at all holds the teacher back. (Even when Sextus is discussing frankly this aspect of his practice, recall, he does not use pejorative words like "ambiguous" and "invalid"; instead, he says, "weak in persuasive power.") The Skeptic makes it one of his central tasks to ridicule and subvert the whole idea of inference and proof (see *PH* 2.134–203, *M* 8.300–481);[45] and to the charge that in arguing against proof he, by using proof, grants what he attacks, he has a most interesting reply that we shall examine when we reach point 10. It is not a reply that concedes the charge.

There is, however, one area in which the Skeptic's attachment to logic may have to be deeper than his official policy states. This is the area of contradiction. For the Skeptic never opposes the principle of non-contradiction: the principle that contradictory claims cannot be true together. In fact, there are many passages where he appears to endorse it (e.g., *PH* 1.88, 3.182; *M* 11.74, 115). Could he do otherwise? His entire enterprise relies upon the idea that a contradiction is a problem; that it must be

---

[43] See Burnyeat (1980a).

[44] See also Annas and Barnes (1985), Annas (1986).

[45] See also the attack on truth, *M* 8.2–140, *PH* 2.80–96. On the criterion of truth, *M* 7.1–446, *PH* 2.14–79; on definition, *PH* 2.205–12; on inference from signs, *M* 8.141–299, *PH* 2.97–133; on the method of division, *PH* 2.212–13.

resolved, if truth is what we are after. Indeed, it is because contradictions seem not susceptible of resolution that the Skeptic gives up on finding truth. He cannot say, faced with an opposition, "Let's have both. Both are really true." This would short-circuit his project, for it would simply be to deny the discrepancy (*anōmalia*) that it is Skepticism's business to treat. Even he, then, accepts the ordinary person's cognitive commitments, to this extent. Even he will not suspend what Aristotle calls "the most basic principle of all." He allows us, apparently, to keep this one feature of our cognitive humanity—without which our troubles would not exist, and he would not be necessary.

Even here, however, the Skeptic has a partial reply to make. He must concede that the principle of non-contradiction is a fundamental psychological principle, one that is regulative for the entire Skeptical enterprise as well as in the rest of human life. It is a trait of our cognitive machinery that we go on in this way, and that, in a way unparalleled in other areas, we are unable to cope with opposition to this way of going on. And yet, to go on in accordance with this principle is not the same thing as believing it to be true, or believing that it is the way things are. The Skeptic assents, then, in a non-epistemic way, accepting the principle's authority but not that this authority is justified by the way things are. Accepted in this way it is very deep, perhaps uniquely deep; but it is not a threat to his Skepticism.[46]

7. The *asymmetry of roles* that we noticed in Epicureanism seems at first to be present in the Skeptical school as well, when Sextus portrays himself as a doctor who cleverly diagnoses and treats an apparently passive patient. However, Skepticism has in it none of the dogmatic sense of correctness and authority that shape Epicurean society. Since what we all aim at is to go on in the flow of life, free of belief's crushing weight, then none of us is any higher or better than any other; there is nothing one knows or has that another lacks. Some are more burdened than others, some are freer; some have arrogant false beliefs, some just go along in the ordinary practices; some have the knack of shaking off their burdens, others have still to learn it. But this does not make the freed ones into authorities or saviors; that is the last thing a freed person would want to be. Furthermore, the teacher will be even less likely than the pupil to lay claim to knowledge and expertise. If the Skeptics act as doctors, it is because it just naturally occurs to them to do so; but Skepticism is a knack, and anyone can learn it. Nikidion might remain for a long time in a close relationship with a

---

[46] On the role of non-contradiction in Skepticism, see Burnyeat (1980a) and McPherran (1987). For a distinction between two types of assent, see Frede (1984) and Stough (1984).

Skeptical teacher; more likely, she would soon pick up the know-how and practice it on her own. One of the great benefits offered by Skepticism, Sextus implies, is that we are no longer subject to arrogant grandiose claims, our own or another's. Doing away with truth does away with reliance on authority.

8. The treatment of various viewpoints in Skepticism is about as far away as we can get from Aristotle's dialectical way (although it has its roots in an "eristic" and sophistical use of pseudo-dialectical reasoning that Aristotle was very concerned to avoid). There is no respect for the views of others as truth or partial truth; they are from the beginning treated as diseases, sources of vulnerability to disturbance; and the aim from the beginning is to subvert them, knock them out. This is so not because, as in Epicureanism, the teacher claims to have the truth already—but because truth is not sought, from any source. When a view comes forward it will not be investigated as to its motivations in human experience, as to its weight, its degree of practical truth, its relation to well-established beliefs and intuitions. It will be scanned only to ascertain the nature and degree of its power over the pupil; and then it will be tossed into the contradiction-mill like everything else. This procedure looks objectionable. But this, the Skeptic will say, is because we are still in the grip of the old idea of truth as a goal. The absence of respect for alternatives is not only what follows when we do away with truth. It is also a tool to prise the pupil loose from her old picture of the goal of inquiry. Nikidion must be taught the uselessness and the impotence of belief before she will be ready to leave her old dogmatic ways behind. She is taught it, by the Skeptic's unsympathetic and anti-dialectical procedures.

9 and 10. Aristotle's arguments expressed respect for argument, but gestured toward their own incompleteness, out of their respect for particulars and for the judgments of each person. Epicurus' arguments praised their own completeness, and their sufficiency for human good living. What will Nikidion's attitude to her Skeptical procedure be? We know already: she will have to subject it to its own critique. She cannot have faith in it, or think it true: for this would itself contradict what the method says; and, more important, it would leave her prey to disturbance in future. She also will not reject it, or hold it to be false: for this too would be dogmatism. Other philosophies, the Skeptic charges, just shifted the disease from one place to another; Skepticism purges it completely. And here is where Skepticism makes its most famous and vivid use of the medical analogy. Skepticism describes its own way, its characteristic arguments. But, says Sextus, "We must grasp the fact that as to their being true we make no assertion at all [*pantōs ou diabebaioumetha*], inasmuch as we say that they are capable

of being confuted by themselves, seeing that they themselves are inscribed together with the things of which they are said—just as purgative drugs do not only take away the humors from the body, but eliminate themselves too, along with the humors" (PH 1.206; cf. DL 9.76, PH 2.188). To the opponent who charges that, in using argument to attack argument, the Skeptic tacitly concedes what he explicitly assails, the probative value of argument, Sextus repeats this point:

> There are many things that produce on themselves the same effect that they produce on other things. For just as fire, having destroyed fuel, destroys itself as well; and just as purgative drugs, having driven the fluids out of bodies, remove themselves as well; so the argument against proof both abolishes every proof and also inscribes itself together with them [sumperigraphein]. And again, just as it is not impossible for a person who has climbed on a ladder to a high place to overturn the ladder with his foot after he climbs it, so it is not unlikely that the Skeptic, getting to the establishing of his claim that there is no proof by an argument that shows this, as by a ladder, should then turn and abolish this very argument. (M 8.480–81)

This passage adds to the purgative drug image the famous image of the ladder. But Skeptics seem to prefer the image of the purgative, which is present more often and in more sources. It is, perhaps, a more accurate image for their purposes, since it displays the near-simultaneity[47] of Skeptical self-inscription, in which arguments inscribe themselves "together with" (sumperigraphein) the arguments they oppose. Skeptical arguments start by attacking the claim of other arguments, just as purgatives go to work on the antecedent contents of the body. But by the time that process of treatment is complete, the purgative drug itself is gone, eliminated from the system along with the obstacles it opposes. So too the Skeptical argument does not really require an extra stage of argument against itself in order to remove itself. At the very same time that it is removing the pupil's commit-

---

[47] Sextus still uses temporal language in talking of the purgative: both the tenses and the use of meta ("after") indicate that some sort of sequence is still envisaged. But the purgative image suggests greater closeness and overlap between the stages than does the ladder image, and sumperigraphein definitely points to the fact that the argument acts on itself along with the other arguments it opposes. The term sumperigraphein presumably designates the self-referring property of the argument: it "writes a circle around itself" along with the other things it "circles" as unfounded or unsupported. One might usefully compare Jacques Derrida's practice of marking an X through a term that he must continue to employ, even though his arguments have robbed it of its backing.

ments to her beliefs, it is loosening her attachment to argument, therefore to itself as well. At the end of the Skeptical process (should it ever be finally ended—a thing the Skeptic doubts), Skepticism itself has vanished.

Strictly speaking, Skeptical argument opposes only that which has been asserted and believed—and the Skeptic tells us that he asserts nothing. So Skeptical arguments do not oppose themselves in exactly the way in which they oppose dogmatic arguments—just as purgative drugs do not need to loosen themselves while they are loosening the rest of the contents of the digestive system. They need to oppose themselves only to the degree that the pupil, being human, is inclined to rely on them as she proceeds. This degree of reliance will weaken over time, as the pupil's detachment becomes greater across the board. Properly received, they need not struggle against themselves; they need only slide along out of the mind, not pausing to lodge there.[48]

IV

Can Nikidion live like this?[49] I see no reason why she cannot, provided that she allows herself the principle of non-contradiction to organize her thoughts, and provided that she allows herself a commitment to *ataraxia* sufficient to organize her involvement with Skeptical procedures. At first, I think some rather intense longing for calm might be required to overcome the hold of dogma, to propel her from Epicurus' school into the hands of the Skeptical teacher. But an intense attachment to the absence of intensity is a funny sort of desire, a desire born of troubles. Once disturbance begins to be removed, we can expect the calm of her life to diminish all her intensities, even the intensity of the longing for calm. And then, relaxing into the flow of life, the play of appearances and the push of instincts and habits, she will go on in the Skeptical way—first, perhaps, out of a gratitude for what it has given her and a fear of lapsing again into disturbance; but later (since gratitude and fear both rest on belief)

[48] On self-inscription, see McPherran (1987), who argues that Skepticism does not refute itself so long as its claims are put forward in a non-assertive way. McPherran also argues for a two-stage interpretation of Skeptical *peritropē*, pointing to Cic. *Acad.* 2.95 (the Skeptic weaves and unweaves his web like Penelope) and Stob. *Florileg.* 82.13 and Plutarch *Comm. Not.* 1059E (Skepticism is a polyp that eats its tentacles after they have grown) as additional evidence. Note that these additional parallels are not Pyrrhonian, and elide possible differences between Academic and Pyrrhonist Skeptics.

[49] See Burnyeat (1980a).

in a more relaxed way, because it is her habit and her natural inclination. As time goes on, she will need less and less motivation; she will be increasingly emptied of powerful emotion, of intense commitment; so she will need less and less to organize her life in the face of these. As her attachments weaken all round, so too will her attachment or commitment to Skepticism. But this will not matter, since by now it will be a habit, and she will just go on.

I see no reason why a human being could not live like this. The Skeptic makes a strong case that it is possible, and practically coherent. Empirically, we do not need the rather fanciful *Life of Pyrrho* to make the case for us, since Skeptical practice has a great deal in common (and may be influenced by) Eastern therapeutic philosophies, which provide us with many empirical examples of a detached mode of existence like the one Sextus recommends.[50] The plausibility of his case rests on the psychological claim about our natural inclination to remove disturbance. But this claim has been found plausible by many people; it is well buttressed by appeal to the behavior of animals and non-dogmatic humans; and it may well be true. Given all this, the Skeptic seems to me to offer a viable alternative to Epicurean dogma, one that may, as he says, prove more effective in getting to a similar end.

But one reason why the Skeptical procedure is so plausible is that it is frank about the radical alteration in life-style[51] that it asks of us. Pyrrho talks of "altogether divesting ourselves of the human being"; Sextus describes the Skeptic as a eunuch with respect to rational desires. This is revealing talk: for it concedes, perhaps, that even if what we have left is a part of our natural constitution, what we have cut off or purged away is also a part of what it is to be naturally human. Our choice is to follow a part of nature by ridding ourselves of another part. And the eunuch image, like the similar image used of Epicurus, implies that the choice, once made, cannot be reversed. So we are entitled to ask more questions about Nikidion's way of life after the change; about what attitudes toward self and others will be possible for her. And the Skeptic answers such questions for us with unusual honesty and imagination.

Much has been made of the Skeptic's passivity, of the strange sense (or lack of sense) of self that would go with seeing oneself as the play of appearances and giving up the Aristotelian idea of unifying appearances

---

[50] On a possible connection between Pyrrho and Indian philosophical procedures of Pyrrho's time, see Flintoff (1980) and Sedley (1983a).

[51] Annas and Barnes (1985) use "life-style" to translate *agōgē*, with much plausibility.

through the active exercise of reason.[52] I think some of these points are well taken; but I see no reason why Nikidion, as a prospective pupil, should be excessively troubled by them. To someone to whom practical reason is a source of painful vulnerability, a little disunity and passivity (the animal use of reason that we see in some higher creatures) would be very welcome. If she is living a life closer to that of a child at play—or of a dog or a bee—so much the better. So I want to concentrate, in concluding, on the emotional and desiderative attitudes that will be open to her, seeing whether in this way we can give her a more vivid idea of what she is giving up.

Nikidion will come to lack all the emotions canonically so called—that is, all desiderative attitudes that are based upon belief, all attitudes such as anger, fear, jealousy, grief, envy, passionate love. This will be so because these all rest (as the Skeptic and his opponents seem to agree) upon belief; and she will have no beliefs. Many texts stress removal of emotion as an advantage of the Skeptical life; stories told about Pyrrho confirm this.

There will be other surprising benefits. The Skeptic stresses that the removal of belief removes arrogance and irascibility, which now create barriers between her and others. Dogmatists, they insist, are self-loving, rash, puffed up (e.g., *PH* 1.90, 1.20, 1.177; 2.258); Skeptics, by contrast, are calm and gentle. Pyrrho used to be hasty and irascible in his youth, Diogenes writes (9.63); Skepticism taught him composure and good temper. In fact, Diogenes tells us revealingly, some Skeptics actually say that their end, *ataraxia*, can also be called gentleness, *praotēs* (9.108).[53] Again, dogmatists are imagined as interfering with others, imposing their own way on others; the Skeptic, by contrast, is tolerant. He keeps to himself (9.68), and lets others go their way. Nor is he a slave to social prejudices as to who should do what. Pyrrho, who lived with his sister, did not mind if he was seen doing the housecleaning[54] and taking the pigs to market; "they say he even showed his indifference by washing a pig" (65–66). This absence of sex role and class consciousness was evidently shocking; but to Nikidion (to us) it could be a deeply attractive result.

But another side of this "indifference" is more disturbing. Even those of us who might accept a life without emotion are likely to be disturbed at the

[52] See especially Burnyeat (1980a): and on parallel criticisms of the self in Indian thought, see Collins (1982).

[53] On the role of *praotēs* in Skepticism, see Morrison (1990); and on Skeptical gentleness in the later history of political thought, see Laursen (1992).

[54] All forms of indoor housework would be considered deeply shameful for a Greek male. Marketing is not a gender but a class issue: even in a moderately comfortable family, this would be done by slaves.

degree to which this life lacks commitment to others and to society. The Skeptic tries to insist that Nikidion will live just like anyone in her world, on the outside, allowing herself to be motivated by habits of virtuous action and social observance in which she was raised. But they know, too, that they have removed the intensity of commitment to virtue that makes people risk their lives for justice, or endure hardship for those they love. Consider Sextus' profoundly ambiguous answer to the charge that the Skeptic will not be able to make a choice if ordered by a tyrant to do something "unspeakable":

> When they say this, they do not understand that the Skeptic, though he does not live according to a philosophical account (for he is inactive so far as that is concerned) is perfectly able to choose some things and avoid others according to the unphilosophical practices of life. So if he is compelled by a tyrant to do one of the unspeakable things, in virtue of his thinking according to the ancestral laws and customs he will perchance choose the one and avoid the other. (*M* 11.165–66, cf. DL 9.108)

Is "perchance" (*tuchon*) enough for us? for Nikidion? And the Greek is no clearer than my English about which alternative will "perchance" be chosen. Yet the Skeptic must be like this: for she will go with the play of forces upon her, and she cannot guarantee ahead of time which force will push stronger.

The same casualness will appear in her relations with individual others. (Here I think it is helpful to think of the related ideal of being "laid back" and not "uptight" in our recent culture—which has some of the same consequences, both good and bad.) As a Skeptic, she will sometimes do nice helpful things, when it occurs to her; she may give Skeptical argument to others; she may do a friend's housework, or even wash her pig. But none of this can be done out of any serious commitment or even emotion; so it is likely that it will not carry her so far as to endure risk or hardship for another's sake.[55] Customs of friendly and marital loyalty will be observed when it is easier; but the commitment that underwrites them is shrugged off as a form of antiquated uptightness. "And once, when Anaxarchus fell into a slough, Pyrrho passed by without helping him; and while others blamed him, Anaxarchus himself praised his indifference and his freedom from emotion" (DL 9.63).

---

[55] Much depends here on one's estimation of the intensity of untutored instinct in animals and humans: for the Stoic will allow the pupil to keep any ways of acting that are based on instinct and "nature" rather than belief.

Does Nikidion want this life? In the 1960s and 1970s one knew many people who aspired to this indifference, motivated by a hatred of aggression, of the committedness that leads into war, into personal jealousy, into rigidity of all kinds. But can it ultimately satisfy as a whole way of life? Even Pyrrho had his limits. In one of his most revealing and remarkable anecdotes, Diogenes tells us that once a man insulted Pyrrho's sister Philista; and he allowed himself to get enraged on her behalf, saying "that it was not over a helpless woman[56] that one should make a demonstration of one's indifference" (DL 9.66). Some love, not altogether cut away, prevents the complete triumph of philosophy. Pyrrho could have replied that this was the natural animal level of concern for others and so consistent with his Skepticism; his reply suggests instead that he sees his action as an exception to Skepticism, because of the level of emotion and concern it requires.

And here we see at last how deeply Skepticism cuts into nature—even while claiming that it restores us to the ordinary. It seems opposed even to the nature of the animal, since animals are not always calm, and they do defend their mates and children. But it is all the more opposed to human nature, one of whose distinguishing marks is to be a social being, one among others, and to be able to form stable commitments to others, both individually and as a group. It is reported that Timon "kept to himself and was fond of cultivating his garden" (DL 9.112). The image of the garden, which Voltaire may have drawn from this source as well as from Epicurus, suggests to us that with the purging of belief we have, on the one hand, the purging of the bases of aggressiveness, intolerance, cruelty, and greed. But the Skeptic who cultivates his garden does not, like Candide, do so alongside beloved friends and family; he does not, like Epicurus, live with friends to whose good he is committed; he does not, like Lucretius' imagined pupil, love a spouse and children; he stands alone. Perhaps it is not in the case of the person or the city that one loves that one should make a demonstration of one's indifference.

[56] The word he uses, *gunaion*, can be a term of endearment (as in "the little woman'), and can also connote weakness or helplessness. The Philista story is, however, very obscure, since it is transmitted in two very different versions—see Brunschwig (1992). The Diogenes Laertius version and the longer version in Aristocles both descend from Antigonus. Aristocles' version has no negative: Pyrrho says that one *should* show indifference in such a matter, but the matter is given a rather different explanation: what Pyrrho is avoiding is getting angry at his sister for not getting everything ready for a sacrifice, so that he had to go buy the things himself. On that version, he would be showing *praotēs* to her, and saying that this is how one *should* deal with a woman.

Stoic Tonics: Philosophy and the Self-Government of the Soul

I

THERE IS, I assure you, a medical art for the soul. It is philosophy, whose aid need not be sought, as in bodily diseases, from outside ourselves. We must endeavor with all our resources and all our strength to become capable of doctoring ourselves" (Cic. *TD* 3.6). "I am writing down some healthful practical arguments, prescriptions for useful drugs; I have found them effective in healing my own ulcerous sores, which, even if not thoroughly cured, have at least ceased to spread" (Sen. *Ep.* 8.2). So first Cicero, then Seneca, display the Stoic use of the medical analogy, which is more pervasive and more highly developed in Stoic texts than it is in those of any other Hellenistic school—so pervasive, in fact, that Cicero declares he is tired of their "excessive attention" to such analogies (*TD* 4.23). The analogy can be traced back to the greatest of the Stoic philosophers, Chrysippus, who wrote, in his book on the therapeutic treatment of the passions:

> It is not true that there exists an art [*technē*] that we call medicine, concerned with the diseased body, but no corresponding art concerned with the diseased soul. Nor is it true that the latter is inferior to the former, in its theoretical grasp and therapeutic treatment of individual cases. (*PHP* 5.2.22, 298D – *SVF* 3.471)

The analogy, Chrysippus continues, has value in guiding our search for philosophical cures: "For the correlative affinity of the two will reveal to us, I think, the similarity of therapeutic treatments and the analogical relationship of the two modes of doctoring" (*PHP* 5.2.24). In this way, a study of the medical analogy will help Stoic philosophy to reach its practical goal.[1]

---

[1] The entire passage, as quoted in Galen, shows both Chrysippus' detailed interest in the analogy and his concern to show its roots in ordinary usage (*PHP* 5.2.22–28, 298–300D). Galen, following Posidonius, accepts the heuristic and justificatory value of the analogy, but claims that it actually justifies the Platonic understanding of health as a balance among separate parts. Musonius Rufus also makes a striking use of the medical analogy in "That Women Too Should Do Philosophy?"—see subsequent discussion.

The medical analogy is as important for the Stoics as for the Epicureans and Skeptics—both illustrative of philosophy's proper function and valuable in discovering and justifying a concrete account of its content, methods, and procedures. And it is clear that the Stoics, like our other two schools, wish to claim that a philosophical art of soul-healing, correctly developed and duly applied, is both necessary and sufficient for attaining the highest ends of human life. "Be convinced at least of this," Cicero's interlocutor declares, "that unless the soul [*animus*][2] is cured, which cannot be done without philosophy, there will be no end to our afflictions. Therefore, since we have now begun, let us turn ourselves over to philosophy for treatment; we shall be cured, if we want to be" (*TD* 3.13). What are these philosophical treatments? What arguments and techniques do they use? And what forms of human sickness do they claim to heal?

The Stoics share with the Epicureans and Skeptics a deep interest in human self-sufficiency and tranquillity, and in using philosophy to bring about this happy condition. But I believe that they have more adequate answers than do the other schools to some criticisms that chapters 4 and 8 have brought against that project. First, as our opening citation from Cicero already indicates, the Stoics have a high respect for each person's active practical reasoning. They give this activity great value—indeed, intrinsic as well as instrumental value. And they construct an account of philosophical therapy that does justice to this idea.

According to this account, philosophy is still a compassionate doctor, ministering to urgent human needs. "There is no time for playing around," says Seneca, attacking philosophers who devote their careers to logical puzzles. ". . . You have promised to bring help to the shipwrecked, the imprisoned, the sick, the needy, to those whose heads are under the poised axe. Where are you deflecting your attention? What are you doing?" (*Ep.* 48.8). And yet, this compassion is combined with a fundamental respect for the integrity of the reasoning powers of each person. The patient must not simply remain a patient, dependent and receptive; she must become her own doctor. Philosophy's medical function is understood as, above all, that of *toning up* the soul—developing its muscles, assisting it to use its own

---

[2] In the chapters dealing with Stoic thought, I shall translate *animus* as "soul" rather than (as in the Epicurean chapters) "mind." I do this because *animus* is unambiguously the Latin rendering of Greek *psuchē*, including whatever Greek *psuchē* is taken to include, whereas Lucretius' distinction between *animus* and *anima* breaks *psuchē* up into two pieces. Lucretius' *animus* is used interchangeably with *mens*, while emotional states are typically referred to the *pectus* or described using the emotion-terms themselves. For the Stoics, all emotions and appetites belong to *animus*.

317

capabilities more effectively (Sen. *Ep*. 15).[3] In this way, the Stoics do justice to some powerful beliefs about reason that were preserved in Aristotle's theory, but displaced (to a greater or lesser extent) in Epicureanism and Skepticism. And yet, unlike Aristotle, the Stoics combine this respect for reason with a commitment to the radical criticism of conventional belief, and to the inclusion within philosophy of all of rational humanity, wherever (in whatever class, station, gender, part of the world) it is found. We shall see how these ingredients give rise to a distinctive philosophical curriculum, one based on the ideas of rational self-government and universal citizenship.

Second, Stoicism's work on the nature and structure of the emotions goes well beyond Skepticism, and in certain ways also beyond Epicurus, both in its systematic comprehensiveness and in the precision of its concrete investigations. As a result, the Stoic account of emotion is a powerful one. We can accept it even if we object to the Stoics' conclusion that the passions should be eliminated from human life. But the Stoic analysis also yields deep and non–question-begging arguments against those who value the emotions and the attachments of external things that underwrite them. Although many elements in the Stoic condemnation of passion do, like other Hellenistic arguments we have studied, presuppose the self-sufficiency of true good and the worthlessness of externals, we shall also find in Stoic moral psychology arguments that should give serious difficulty even to someone who is initially convinced of the true worth of external-related goods like personal love and political activity. Chrysippus is explicit that this is his design. He says that Stoicism has arguments related to any major conception of the good that a pupil is likely to hold, so that, even if the pupil is not ready to accept the Stoic conception, he or she can be convinced in terms of his own conception that he has reasons to get rid of the passions (*SVF* III.474 = Origen *Contra Celsum* 1.64, 7.51). And we shall see that this design is admirably fulfilled. In particular, we shall find an argument to the effect that the ordinary person's external attachments, taken seriously in the way that many ordinary ethical views (and Aristotle's with them) recommend, commit the agent to emotional conditions that by their very nature can be neither moderated nor adjusted to the requirements of reason; indeed, that cannot reliably be stopped from taking the agent straight into an excess, a cruelty, and a monstrousness that most ordinary people (and Aristotelians) themselves condemn and flee.

---

[3] This is not just metaphor but a literal physical idea. For a general discussion of Stoic physics of mind, see Long and Sedley (1987) 313–23.

Finally, the Stoics, unlike our other two schools, have a developed political theory that both supports and is supported by their general account of philosophical therapy. They do not, like the others, turn away from politics, bringing *eudaimonia* to individual pupils (or groups of friends) by moderating their individual desires, without social change. They set themselves the task of producing a just and humane society. And they argue that this task, like (and as a part of) the private task, cannot be achieved without philosophical therapy. Their diagnosis of the diseases of passion becomes the basis for a diagnosis of political disorder; and the extirpation of passion is said to promise a new basis for political virtue.

I shall investigate each of these contributions in turn. This chapter will focus on therapeutic techniques and strategies, showing how the Stoic interpretation of the medical analogy differs from that of the other schools, and imagining the effect of all this on Nikidion's education. I shall then turn to the Stoic account of the emotions or passions,[4] and to the Stoics' arguments that the passions should be completely extirpated from human life. In both of these chapters, the attempt will be to provide a coherent and synthetic account of mainstream Stoic beliefs, drawing on both Greek and Roman sources.[5] Two further chapters will then focus more closely on Seneca and Roman Stoicism. Chapter 11 will explore the political motivations for and consequences of the Stoic account of the passions by studying Seneca's *De Ira* and its account of the role of the emotions in public life.[6]

---

[4] In what follows, I shall use these two words more or less interchangeably, making no salient distinction between them. "Emotions" is the more common modern generic term, while "passions" is both etymologically closer to the most common Greek and Latin terms and more firmly entrenched in the Western philosophical tradition. In any case, what I mean to designate by these terms is a genus of which experiences such as fear, love, grief, anger, envy, jealousy, and other relatives—but not bodily appetites such as hunger and thirst—are the species. (This corresponds to the Stoic use of the Greek *pathē*, though other Greek writers sometimes use *pathē* more broadly, to apply to any affect of the creature—preserving the general connection with the verb *paschein*.) This family of experience, which we call emotions as opposed to appetites, is grouped together by many Greek thinkers, beginning at least with Plato, and his account of the soul's middle part. The Stoics and Plato recognize the same family grouping, though Plato and Chrysippus differ on the family's proper analysis and definition, and also on the question whether these experiences are properly ascribed to animals and children; Posidonius revives the Platonic analysis.

[5] For Seneca's Chrysippan orthodoxy on the analysis of the passions, see chapter 11 and Inwood (1993). Epictetus is unquestionably a Chrysippan. See Bonhöffer (1894) for a comprehensive analysis.

[6] I shall not otherwise provide an account of Stoic political thought, a task that would require another book. But since I believe that the Stoics' most important contributions to political thought are in their account of the therapy of excessive attachments to money,

Finally, in chapter 12 I shall turn to Stoic poetry: to Seneca's *Medea*, where we shall see, both elaborated and called into question, the most powerful of the Stoic arguments against the passions.

II

Nikidion, then, arrives at the Stoa. Incompletely won over by her previous experiences, her rational and critical faculties not yet lulled by Skepticism's assault, she has decided to seek a different way of reasoning. She is still confused and vulnerable. She longs for things she does not control, and is not satisfied by the things she does control. She wants to be in charge of her own life, and she also wants to be in love. And it still seems to her that death is a bad thing—and all the more when she feels otherwise happiest and most alive.

What does she want from philosophy? To understand all this, to understand herself. For it seems to her that she must find out, must determine for and within herself, which things are worth valuing and which are not, which risks are worth the attendant pain and which are not. And she feels that even the most painful and confusing aspects of life would be made more tolerable by understanding and by choice, by the sense that she herself had drawn the boundary of herself here and not here, had formed her desires and evaluations in this way and not in this. To examine, then, and to take charge of herself.

She wants, however, something further. She wants to feel herself a member of a community, and to care for the good of all human beings in the community. (She still has a very hazy idea of what the appropriate boundaries of such a community would be; and we shall see how Stoicism shapes those conceptions.) The Epicurean community's emphasis on friendship, the emphasis on the good of the city that she has found in the teaching of Aristotle and in the poem of Lucretius—these have made her feel that life is incomplete without embracing *some* wider network of cares, and, indeed, that she is herself a being fundamentally social, bound by both similarity and attachment to that wider network and not fully herself without it.

There is something else. Nikidion really wants to do philosophy. She wants, that is, to do tough, active intellectual work, to take charge of things with her mind, reasoning and making distinctions. She wants the exhilara-

---

power, and honor, and of the related therapy of anger and other socially divisive passions, I believe that the core of their contribution will in fact be discussed.

tion of disinterested thought and sustained effort. This desire, encouraged within the Aristotelian school, was gratified in Epicureanism, with its intricate structures of argument—but only in a qualified way. For that school, it seems, did not respond to her intuition that active practical reasoning is something of intrinsic worth and dignity, something essential to her humanity. Or if it did respond, it did so in an unemphatic and equivocal way. And its asymmetrical structures of authority in reasoning encouraged her, as pupil, to receive with passive trust and to retain within her the dogmatic teachings of the master, rather than to reason actively on her own. Still, there was a sense in which Epicureanism did urge her to protect herself by reason from the confusions of life and from passivity before its events. Skepticism, as we saw, moved away from even this sort of commitment to reason, urging her to divest herself of the urge to take control of life through thought.

Moving now to the Stoa, Nikidion feels that to give up the aim of taking charge of her own life, by her very own thinking, is to give up something too deep and too essential; she feels she would not survive without it. She wants to get the better of her lassitude and confusion through the toughness and energetic activity of good reasoning. She wants to become more, not less, of a distinct self, healthier and stronger, thinking only her own thoughts, and thinking them actively, rather than being a passive vessel for the dogmas of another. She wants, in short, to tone up the muscles of her mind. She gives herself Seneca's advice:

> Without philosophy the mind is sickly. The body too, even if it has great strength, is strong only in the way that a madman's or lunatic's body is strong. Concern yourself, then, above all with this sort of health. After that, take thought as well for that second sort, which will not cost you much effort, if you want good physical health. (*Ep.* 15.1–2)

Nikidion's motivation, as I have described it so far, has two aspects, which we could call the therapeutic and the philosophical. Though they are almost inseparable in her thinking, they can in principle come apart. Nikidion wants philosophy to improve her life. She is led to philosophy in part by the feeling that something is not right with her life. But she is also drawn to it for its own sake, and its procedures seem valuable to her in their own right. She wants philosophy to be a part of her health, not just an agent of cure. As she sees it, the two aspects of her interest in philosophy are complementary. For the way she hopes to improve her life is by the control provided by understanding and reasoning. The very exercise she values in philosophy also makes her healthier. On the other hand, we can also see that there might conceivably be a tension between these two interests. Her attachment to critical independence might or might not lead in the direction of a therapeutic cure, understood in a particularly Stoic fashion. In this chapter I shall focus on philosophical procedures (though I shall not deny that the procedures have, themselves, a normative content). In the next, we shall see how, using such procedures, the Stoics commend their radical therapeutic goals. As we have already suggested, they do not assume that any pupil who agrees to follow their procedures will already agree on distinctively Stoic goals, for example, on the goal of extirpating the passions. They respect the rational independence of the pupil, and are anxious to show that participation in no way entails subservience. Nikidion can argue as they recommend, while rejecting every conclusion they put forward—if she comes up with sufficiently powerful arguments of her own. The Stoics, on the other hand, must convince her that their radical critical arguments are good and compelling arguments.

One way in which the Stoics might begin to encourage her to take the results of their radical critique of ordinary belief seriously is to remind her that she is there, as a respected pupil; this could not have been the case in Aristotle's school, which up to a point resembles their school in its commitment to practical reasoning. Aristotelian dialectic is respectful of deeply rooted convention and ordinary belief. Aristotle's school, following the conventions of its time, apparently did not admit women to study philosophy. Are these two things only accidentally linked? Stoicism conducts a radical critique of convention and ordinary belief, arguing that many deeply held ordinary beliefs will not pass appropriate tests of rationality. One belief that will not pass those tests is the belief that women cannot and should not do philosophy. Nikidion is studying there (without disguise) because this critique was carried through and its results taken seriously. In what follows, I am going to imagine her as a Roman Stoic pupil, since we know so little about the structure of education under Zeno and Chrysippus, and since so much of the material we have about therapeutic argument in the Stoa comes from Roman sources, especially from Seneca and Epictetus. But I do not believe that the position on women's education that I shall describe is at all incompatible with the views of the Greek Stoics, who insisted that in an ideal city there would be equal citizenship for all virtuous human beings, and even the removal of gender distinctions as created by differences in clothing.[7]

Let us imagine, then, the first example of radical criticism that Nikidion

---

[7] See especially DL 7.32–33. The relevant texts are translated in Long and Sedley (1987) 429–37. See now Schofield (1991).

encounters, as she prepares to become a Stoic pupil. She hears objections, let us imagine, from most Roman males of her acquaintance—and especially, if she is married, from her husband. Philosophy, they say, is a pursuit for which women are not suited by nature. Furthermore, it will turn them into bad wives: garrulous, aggressive, neglectful of household duties, weak on virtue. Most Roman males probably believed these things, at some level. And at some level, Nikidion probably believes them herself. These "arguments" are answered in a fascinating short work by Musonius Rufus (the teacher of Epictetus, first century c.e.), entitled "That Women Too Should Do Philosophy?" a work that tries to show an imagined male interlocutor that his prejudices against female higher education cannot stand the reflective scrutiny of all that he himself believes and says and wishes. The argument, briefly, is as follows. First, the belief that women have different natures does not stand up to a rational scrutiny of experience. For if we examine one by one, without prejudice, the faculties that are relevant to doing philosophy, we find that women have them all: all the five senses (which he enumerates one by one), reasoning powers (as we know by conversing with them), a sensitivity to ethical distinctions, desire, and a natural orientation to one's own good (*oikeiōsis*). What is needed is further inquiry and examination. But then all human beings alike should have the opportunity for this. So the Stoic insists that no sound reason has been given for not proceeding as though the philosophical mind is genderless. The interlocutor himself is expected to have the basis for these judgments in his own experience with women, once that experience is examined closely, without prejudice.

Next we turn to the virtues. The interlocutor objects that perhaps it is only men who need them. Musonius defends with some eloquence the idea that the same list of virtues is—and, moreover, is by the interlocutor at some level deeper than prejudice, admitted to be—the norm for both males and females, and that philosophy will promote these virtues in women as in men. Women too need practical wisdom, in order to manage prudently the affairs of the household. The control of appetite by the virtue of moderation is surely as important for women as for men; this goes by rapidly, since husbands are assumed to be concerned with this already. And justice, too, is a virtue essential to proper management of a household, and to good dealings with children, husband, friends, and family. Finally, women too face risk and danger, even if the sphere of life in which they do so is different from the male military sphere. Doesn't this man want a wife who will face childbirth, nursing, and so forth, with proper courage? Who will know not to be servile to tyrants, selling her family out in fear for her life? Well, how are these virtues best acquired? They are best acquired by the philosophical development of active practical reasoning, which will make a woman self-critical and critical of her intuitions.

Then, to the interlocutor's final protest, Musonius responds with a striking use of the medical anology:

> But by Zeus, say some people, women who have gone to study with the philosophers will be uncommonly stubborn and bold. They will let their housework go and come into the middle of the company of men and get involved in arguments and make sophistical distinctions and take apart syllogisms, while all the time they should be at home spinning the wool. But I say that it is not only philosophizing women but also philosophizing *men* who should not let go of their appropriate tasks and deal only in arguments. Whatever arguments they undertake, I say that these should be undertaken for the sake of deeds. Just as a medical argument is no use unless it brings human bodies to health, so too, if someone grasps or teaches an argument as a philosopher, that argument is no use, unless it conduces to the excellence of the human soul. (12.5–19 Hense)

In short: if you scrutinize the matter reasonably, prejudice aside, recognizing the relevant similarities and differences, you will come out with a radical conclusion about female faculties, female education, and the problems of leisure. There is no criticism of women's intellectual overindulgence that you should not apply in similar circumstances to yourself.

This remarkable work shows us something of what Nikidion could expect, as she begins her new education. We shall return to its arguments in what follows, analyzing them as examples of Stoic therapy. For now, however, we should insist on one striking feature of the text: its respect for the active reasoning and the participation of the interlocutor. Musonius argues for a radical conclusion, and argues vigorously. But he does not simply assert the conclusion, or ask the interlocutor simply to acquiesce. The structure of the argument is made unusually plain, and the interlocutor is invited to become an active participant. The emphasis is not on the view's Stoic orthodoxy (indeed, Stoicism is not mentioned), but on the fact that the radical conclusion is the only reasonable and consistent one to be found by an interlocutor who sincerely seeks to make a coherent ordering of all of his beliefs.

III

The central and guiding attitude of Stoic therapy is its respect for the dignity of reason in all human beings. Stoicism makes a very sharp distinction between humans and animals.[8] (Indeed, one might see the Stoics' somewhat disdainful attitude to animals, and their lack of concern about signs of rationality in other species, as the negative side of their deep respect for human rationality.) Reason, it is claimed, marks humans out as incomparably higher, and worthy of a boundless respect and self-respect. "From what are we separated by the reasoning element?" asks Epictetus, and answers, "From the wild beasts. And from what else? From sheep and similar creatures. Take care, then, that we do not ever act like a wild beast" (*Disc.* 2.9.2–3). The presence of reason in any creature entitles it to respect from others, and also from itself. The first and most basic injunction addressed to Nikidion will be to respect and cultivate that all-important element in herself, the foundation of her humanity. Whenever she recognizes this capacity, she should honor it; and nothing else about a person is worthy of much honor. In a moving letter, Seneca writes Lucilius about the foolishness of attending to irrelevant external characteristics, such as wealth and status, in forming our views of people:

> What is more foolish than to praise in a person that which is not really him? What is more insane than someone who wonders at items that can the next minute be transferred to someone else? . . . No person should take pride in anything that is not his own. . . . Suppose he has an attractive group of slaves and a beautiful home, a large farm and a large income. None of these things is in him, but, rather, around him. Praise that in him which cannot be given or taken away, which belongs to the man himself. Do you ask what that is? The soul, and reason fulfilled in the soul. For the human being is a reasoning animal. (*Ep.* 41.6–8)[9]

Nikidion will be taught that she owes it to her humanity that this faculty should be developed and well used—just as it is right to keep one's body healthy (cf. *Ep.* 15). And anyone who has reason is equally worthy of her respect, whether male or female, slave or free—as she endeavors to become one "who rates a human being by that part alone by which he is human" (45.9).

Reason is not just the most important thing about humans: it is also something that is fully their own, in their power to cultivate and control. So

---

[8] For a good critical discussion, see Sorabji (1993). For a general critical history of the use of "reason" to justify a sharp division between humans and animals, with related ethical consequences, see Rachels (1990).

[9] Stoic reasoning is above all, here, practical reasoning, reasoning about life and choice. And notice that for the Stoic reasoning does not *in principle* exclude emotion: emotions are housed in the soul's rational part, and are criticized not for being non-cognitive, but for being false (see chapter 10).

another basic element in Nikidion's education will be the rejection of conventional prayer and conventional religious attitudes to the things that are of importance.[10] What is truly important is already within us; since it is in our power, we do not need to pray. As Seneca writes at the opening of the same letter:

> You do something excellent, something healthful for you if, as you write, you are persisting in your progress toward a good understanding. It is stupid to pray for this, since you can obtain it from yourself. It is not necessary to raise hands to the heavens or to beg a temple doorkeeper to let us approach the ear of a statue, as if that way we could be better heard. The god is near you, with you, inside you. This is what I'm saying to you. Lucilius: a holy spirit is seated within us, a watcher and guardian of our good and bad actions. As this spirit is treated by us, so it treats us. (41.1–2)

Reasoning, on the Stoic view, is not just divine internally: it is our piece of the divinity that inhabits the whole framework of the universe.[11] This is, therefore, not in the least an atheist view. But it is a rationalist view, a view that repudiates the subservience to external anthropomorphic and capricious divinities that is a central feature of conventional Roman religion.[12]

The use of the power of reason has many aspects, some of which I shall examine later in this chapter. But Nikidion will be taught that reason is fundamentally connected with practical choice and avoidance, and the making of distinctions between good and bad in the sphere of action. The divine faculty of reason is also frequently called the faculty of *choice*, and Epictetus imagines god saying, "We have given you a certain portion of ourself, this power of pursuit and avoidance, of desire and aversion, and, to put it simply, the power to use appearances (*phantasiai*)" (1.1.12). And in a later discourse, he addresses the pupil as follows: "Consider who you are. First of all, you are a human being, that is, one who has nothing more ruling than choice, and all else subordinate to that, but that itself without slavery or subjection" (2.10.1–2). We may imagine Nikidion being daily so addressed. Her education, as she sees it, is up to her, the expression of her moral freedom.

---

[10] On the relationship between Stoic philosophy and Hellenistic culture generally, see Sedley (1980).

[11] Here we may see Platonic influence in Seneca, and in Stoicism generally.

[12] There is a serious misunderstanding on this point in Pangle (1990), who seems to think that all ancient religious views rely heavily on *fear* of the gods, an irrational motivation that keeps people in line, and keeps them from thinking for themselves. See my comments on his article in the same issue.

With Epictetus' mention of appearances, we arrive at the most general strategy of Stoic therapy: that the pupil must be watchful and critical of the way in which she sees the world. In her control is "the most powerful and dominating thing of all, the correct use of appearances" (Epict. 1.1.7). The world impresses itself upon us in many ways, through our habits of perception and belief. Nikidion's view of the way things are around her, as she goes through life, is a complex amalgam of acculturation (conventions, reports, stories) with her own personal experience. Nor are these two items really distinct: personal experience is to a large extent shaped by antecedent acculturation. These ways of seeing—usually value-laden—are so habitual with her, so deeply a part of her whole way of being and acting, that the moment an appearance presents itself to her, she can hardly help assenting to it as the truth, as the way things are. In the Stoic view, *phantasiai*—usually with a propositional content[13]—are a necessary, but not a sufficient, condition for assent and ensuing action. But for someone who is used to them, and who has no other picture to go by, they are hard to resist. How can one do otherwise, when that is the only way things look, and one has to act on the basis of some commitment to the way things are? "When, therefore, someone assents to something false," Epictetus writes, "know that he did not want to assent to something false. For every soul is deprived of truth against its will. . . . But it seemed to him that what is in fact false was true" (1.27.4–5).

This can happen in the sphere of simple sense-perception. It also happens in the sphere of action-guiding values. And it can explain, Epictetus insists, the most terrible cases of moral error. Medea is wrong to go in for revenge against Jason, wrong to kill her children. And yet, it is difficult to blame her, since she was given no opportunity to see things in any other way. She was just following, he says, the guidance of the only ways of seeing her culture had given her:

"Yes, but she was wrong." Show her vividly that she is wrong and she will not do it. Until you show her, what else does she have to follow but the appearance? Nothing. Why then are you angry with her, because the poor

[13] See Striker (1980). This fact is often obscured in translations, which tend to use words such as "mental image" for *phantasia*. I have criticized this way of translating Aristotle in Nussbaum (1978) essay 5; but I now believe that the Hellenistic material, which is unambiguous on this point, gives further support to my attack on the "mental image" reading, providing evidence that the whole word-group remained close to the root sense of "appearing." Aristotle's *phantasiai* are not exactly like those of the Stoics, since they need not be propositional, and animals and children can have them: on this, see Sorabji (1993), and further in chapter 10.

woman has gone astray concerning the most important things and has turned from a human being into a poisonous snake? Why do you not, if anything, rather feel sorry for her, the way we feel sorry for the blind and the lame? Why don't we feel the same compassion for those who are blinded and lamed in the most crucial respects? (1.28.8–9)

Philosophy's job is to prompt a searching self-examination of culture and belief that will enable Nikidion—and would have enabled Medea—to take charge of her own thinking, considering duly the available alternatives and selecting, from among them, the one that is best. We cannot expect Nikidion not to act badly if the picture of the world suffused with the cultural values that lead to revenge is the only picture she knows. She must be shown other ways, and she must be led to assess all of them critically by reason. But this she will never do if she assents immediately and habitually to the conventional view. Therefore, the first task of the philosophical teacher will be to create a space for argument—by asking Nikidion to suspend her habitual responses, and to turn her gaze upon herself, becoming watchful and critical of each impression that she is inclined to accept:

> Right from the start, get into the habit of saying to every harsh appearance, "You are an appearance, and not the only way of seeing the thing that appears." Then examine it and test it by the yardsticks you have. (Epict. *Ench.* 1.5)

So Nikidion will be asked to examine and scrutinize herself, to be on guard against her own first impulses. The job of living actively in accordance with one's own reason, rather than passively, in the grip of habits and conventions, requires vigilance and probing. The teacher's job is to awaken and assist this complex activity.

The job of philosophical teaching, so conceived, is manifold, complex, and personal. The teacher's job requires subtle psychological interaction at a deep level, which grapples with whatever memories, wishes, fears, and habits influence the pupil, constructing the ways she sees the world. If the teacher is to show her new ways of seeing, new aspects of the seen, he or she must penetrate with her into every corner of her daily life and every angle of her vision, considering nothing too secret to be viewed by the eye of reason. The teacher is a doctor—but a doctor who leads the patient in an exacting exploration of her own insides. In an odd and powerful description of this medical intimacy, Chrysippus writes:

> Just as it is appropriate for the [physician] of the body to be "inside," as they say, the affections [*pathōn*] that befall the body and the therapeutic treatment that is proper to each, so it is the task of the physician of the soul

to be "inside" both of these, in the best possible way. (*PHP* 5.2.23–24, 298D = *SVF* III.471)

In the course of this internal examination, the soul is not inert, object rather than subject. By examining itself along with the doctor, it also "shapes and constructs" itself (Sen. *Ep.* 16.3).

IV

We can now examine the characteristics of this intimate medical education, in connection with our list of medical characteristics. This examination will yield interesting results. For while the Stoics wholeheartedly endorse the medical model up to the point at which Aristotle also endorses it—and with an even stronger insistence on the personal and context-relative nature of good teaching—they reject, as Aristotle did, certain other features of the analogy, focusing on communal well-being rather than the health of isolated individuals, and constructing a symmetrical anti-authoritarian account of the teacher-pupil relationship. (In keeping with their desire to commend philosophy as the true medical "art of life," they do not drop the medical analogy, but revise it, making it fit this new sort of doctoring.) These differences from Epicurean teaching have interesting implications for the role of books and philosophical traditions in the Stoic curriculum.

1. *Practical goal.* It is clear enough from passages we have already discussed that for Stoics ethical argument is taken to have practical value in the pupil's life, and that arguments are appropriately assessed as arguments in connection with their causal power. This is true from the beginning of Greek Stoicism; but it becomes especially prominent at Rome. The point of philosophical study, for Seneca, is "that you should make yourself better every day" (5.1); and he holds, as we have seen, that philosophy is called to alleviate human misery (*Ep.* 48; cf. earlier discussion). Even to begin such a course of study already makes human life tolerable; and indeed, one cannot have a tolerable life without it (*Ep.* 16.1). Philosophy "shapes and constructs the soul, orders life, guides conduct, shows what is to be done and what omitted, sits at the helm and guides our course as we waver amid uncertainties" (16.3). Epictetus presents the same picture. The starting point of philosophy is "our awareness of weakness and incapacity in respect of the most important things" (2.1.1). The "function of one who philosophizes" is a practical function, defined in terms of the development of powers of choice. It is unnecessary to multiply examples on this point,

since nothing is as forcefully and as repeatedly stressed in the writings of all major Stoic thinkers.

This means, for the Stoics, that the rhetorical and literary dimensions of an argument are not mere incidental frills: they are part and parcel of what the business of arguing is all about. Thus the criticism that Cicero brings against the excessive compression and dryness of some of the Stoic paradoxes—if correct—is a criticism that should trouble them. On their own terms, they have failed if their arguments really do not succeed in moving and changing the soul.[14] (Most outstanding Greek prose style is, however, compressed by comparison to Cicero's Latin, so his criticism may be partisan.) Seneca is always at pains to stress that his arguments take cognizance of their practical therapeutic context and are written in a style appropriate for that context (esp. *Ep.* 40). And Arrian, setting out the words of Epictetus, even feels that he needs to apologize for the fact that he is able to give only the bare words, without the presence and voice of the man himself, which added so much to their practical power:

> When he uttered his discourses, he was clearly aiming at nothing else but to move the minds of the hearers on toward what is best. If, now, the words set down here should achieve that, they would have, I think, the property that the words of philosophers ought to have. If not, then let those who encounter them be sure that, when he used to speak them, it was necessary for the listeners to experience whatever he wanted them to experience. But if the words by themselves do not accomplish this, I may be to blame, or perhaps it is necessary for things to be this way. (Pref. 5–8)

The words themselves are valuable only insofar as they move the listener to perform valuable mental and psychological activities. But this means that any dimension of the words that has causal importance is important for their success *as philosophy*. The message Stoicism constantly brings home to the philosopher is that it is bad philosophy to slip into a self-satisfied professional jargon, neglecting the world of human beings for whom philosophy exists, and to whom, as a philosopher, one is committed. Philosophical language should be selected with care, specificity, and psychological insight. Philosophers, we might say, should "shape and construct" their

---

[14] We know very little indeed about early Greek Stoic writing styles. Chrysippus is often criticized in ancient sources for dryness of style—but he is also portrayed as a vividly dramatic philosopher, and one with a keen interest in ordinary language. The point about style remains unclear, but the interest in ordinary language, and in literature, is plain. For the evidence, see references in chapters 10 and 12, and Nussbaum (1992). On Stoic arguments in favor of poetry, see chapter 12 and Seneca Letter 108, and Nussbaum (1993a).

own souls, cultivating compassion, perception, literary skill, and responsiveness to the individual pupil.

It is important to recognize the magnitude of this task. For the guiding principle of Stoicism is respect for humanity wherever it is found. And from the recognition of humanity follows the obligation to extend to all the benefits of a philosophical education. "No one can live happily, or even tolerably, without the study of wisdom" (Sen. *Ep.* 16.1). But then, if a being is capable of the study of philosophy, it is of the utmost urgency and importance for that being to be given the opportunity to do philosophy. And this is so whether or not the being is from a privileged stratum of society, whether this being is male or female, slave or free. Musonius does not hesitate to conclude that anyone who possesses the five senses, plus reasoning power and moral responsiveness, should study philosophy. And clearly he thinks that even his traditional male interlocutor will have difficulty avoiding that conclusion—since he himself implicitly recognizes reason, and therefore humanity, in his wife by putting her in charge of his household and the raising of his children, and by communicating with her as with an intelligent and responsive being. Epictetus, himself a former slave, is equally committed to an inclusive method of teaching. Seneca insists that the philosopher has made a tacit promise to the sick, the needy, in short to all humanity. But this means that the philosopher's task is a vast one, and highly complex. If the audience for philosophy is the entire human race, not just a narrow elite, philosophical teaching and writing will have to develop many different shapes and forms, in order to reach everyone it ought to reach. Oral as well as written forms of expression will be required, and different levels and styles of writing. Epictetus' discourses are vigorous, brief, colloquial, direct—suited to a general audience from many different backgrounds, and requiring little literary or philosophical preparation—although some, as well, are concerned with the needs of pupils who have already done advanced philosophical reading.[15] Seneca's more elaborate works can be read on a number of different levels; their choice of Latin in principle opens them to a relatively broad audience, although his style is more literary and elaborate than the popular styles of Musonius and Epictetus. The fullest possible understanding of his arguments requires considerable historical and literary sophistication (though much of this

---

[15] Epictetus and Musonius both use Greek, the language of educated cosmopolitan discourse, whereas Seneca, like Cicero and Lucretius before him, undertakes the difficult task of recasting Greek philosophical ideas in Latin terms. On the other hand, Epictetus and Musonius are more popular in style than Seneca is; so it is hard to assess the social implications of language choice.

would have been the effortless possession of his contemporaries). But even without this, their effect can still be felt, as one can see by teaching them to modern undergraduates.

2. *Value-relativity.* I shall say much more about the value-relativity of Stoic arguments in the next chapter, when I examine the ways in which Stoics try to convince non-Stoics that the passions should be completely extirpated from human life. We shall see that they argue for this conclusion on the basis of intuitions about the integrity of the person and the dignity of reason that are taken to be common ground between Stoics and non-Stoics, beliefs that they think unlikely to be rejected by any reflective interlocutor. The arguments attempt to show interlocutors that if they reflect thoroughly enough they will find an inconsistency in their position, and that more superficial beliefs about the objects of the passions are in conflict with deeper and more essential beliefs about reason.

In general, from Chrysippus on, Stoicism is committed to arguing from the "common conceptions," and to using these as its touchstones and basic criteria. This is so, however, not because beliefs derived from society have any value as such, but because human beings are believed to come into the world with an innate orientation toward what is really good and reasonable—so that their deepest moral intuitions can for this reason be good guides to what is really good in the universe. As Epictetus writes:

> We come into the world without any innate conception of a right triangle or a half-tone interval, but from some sort of specialized instruction we learn each of these things. . . . But as for good and bad and fine and shameful and fitting and unfitting, and the flourishing life [*eudaimonia*] and what is proper and incumbent on us and what one must do and what not—who was not born with an innate conception of these things? (2.11.2–4)

The job, he continues, is to develop and refine what we have by nature, and to adapt it to the circumstances in which we find ourselves; in all this, there is much room for error. But nature provides a sound basis from which to start.

This is a complex topic. I shall return to the origins of error in chapters 10 and 11; and I shall not attempt to investigate the many texts relevant to the important Stoic idea of innate orientation to the good (*oikeiōsis*), the human being's complex adjustment to the design of the universe.[16] Epic-

---

[16] On *oikeiōsis*, see Long and Sedley (1987), Striker (1983), White (1979), Lesses (1989). White's paper has a good analysis of the central passage from Cicero's *De Finibus*.

tetus' account of matters here is actually rather crude. For the orthodox Stoic view (insofar as we may reconstruct it, for example, from the accounts in Cicero's *De Finibus* 3 and Seneca's Letter 121) is that the sense of what is appropriate to one's nature as a rational being evolves gradually, beginning from the child's orientation to self-preservation, and culminating in the mature adult's grasp of moral order. The awareness of one's own constitution and what it requires matures as the constitution itself matures, and "Each period of life has its own constitution, one for the baby, and another for the boy, and another for the old man. They are all related appropriately to that constitution in which they exist" (Sen. *Ep.* 121.15). Since Nikidion is an adult, the teacher can rely on her moral intuitions in a very basic way, although much work will have to be done to separate these from socially taught opinions about the application of morality to life.

Stoic value-relativity is in some important ways different from Aristotelian value-relativity. On the one hand, it is still the case here that the doctor's duty is to the actual constitution of the patient, and that good treatment is good because of its relation to the patient's constitution. In ethical terms, the teacher's goal is to get rid of false beliefs that obscure the pupil's relation to the good to which her own constitution and orientation most deeply respond. So far, this is not unlike Aristotle. And the Stoics, like Aristotle, strongly deny that there is in human beings any innate or original evil: when they go wrong, it is on account of false belief, and this is why correct teaching can play such a valuable ethical role.[17] But Aristotle insists that social and ethical excellence is a purely human matter, internal to the human form of life, a product of the combination of need and resource that characterizes that form of life. Neither beasts nor gods have the ethical virtues. For the Stoics, things are otherwise. For the universe is ruled by a *virtuous* god, whose self-sufficiency the truly virtuous life attempts to emulate. Ethics is in the heavens as well as on earth. Our orientation to virtue is not a purely human response to our needy circumstances but, rather, a piece of divine perfection lodged within us by god's providential design. Our connection to truth and virtue is not contingent, as in the Platonic position I described in chapter 1: for it is the essence of humanness to have this relation to virtue; and it is the nature of universal providence to have given it to us. In this sense it is true, in a way it could not be for Plato, that investigating the depths of human nature is a sufficient way of reaching

---

[17] On Aristotle, see *EN* VI. 13, 1144b3 ff. Aristotle does, however, acknowledge that the bodily appetites are difficult to manage and may impede the development of virtue. Another important antecedent is, plainly, the Socratic *elenchos*—whose close resemblance to the account of self-scrutiny here is especially well brought out in Vlastos (1991).

for the truly good. But this ethical good is not, as in Aristotle, defined in purely human terms; and the doctor's task is one of discovering a truth that is situated not only within us, but in the nature of things as a whole.

Given this starting point in the pupil's nature, what Stoic argument needs to do is to reach for the deepest and most indispensable moral intuitions, and to separate these from any false beliefs with which they may be inconsistent. Frequently they find such depth in beliefs about the dignity of reason and the integrity of the person as a reasoning being. But they have many other ways of searching out inconsistency and steering the pupil toward a more coherent vision. The pupil's attachment to reason is taken to include an attachment to logical consistency; it is also taken to entail a commitment to treating similar cases similarly, unless it can be shown that there is a morally relevant distinction between them. Appearances often present cases to the pupil as widely different, when on reflection the differences will not stand up as morally salient. The Stoics frequently use this idea to criticize the differential treatment of human beings based on superficial distinctions of status, class, origin, gender, wealth. They argue as Musonius does, What is the basis of our judgment that a being is a human being? What sets such a being off from the beasts? Reason. Does this creature before us possess reason? Yes. (For the interlocutor acknowledges this by speaking and interacting with him or her, and cannot consistently deny it.) Well then, what reason is there not to accord this person the respect due to all humans, "rat(ing) a human being by that part alone by which he is human" (*Ep.* 45.9)? None. If the interlocutor should persist, pointing to differences in possessions or status or appearance, the philosopher will persist too, pointing out that these are external to the person and are not really the person. (In Zeno's ideal city, recall, men and women wear similar clothing, in order to prevent some of these problems from arising.)[18] The interlocutor will eventually be forced to acknowledge this, by being shown (for example) that he would make a similar judgment in his own case: he would consider himself to be still the same human being and of the same human worth, even if he should lose his fortune. This sometimes takes a long time: in one Senecan letter the interlocutor makes the very same reply, "But they are slaves," six times, and a good number of other truculent replies as well (*Ep.* 47). But the philosopher persists, and, sooner or later, reason makes its mark.

In this way, the Stoics aim to get truth out of a combination of good initial impulses and rigorous rational examination. They know, of course,

[18] See DL 7.32–33. cited in Long and Sedley (1987). See Schofield (1991).

that a one-shot argument will not persuade Nikidion's husband or lover to give her a philosophical education, any more than it will persuade the slaveholder of Seneca's Letter 47 to perceive the natural equality between himself and his slaves. As we shall see, they evolve complex techniques of meditation and self-scrutiny to assist the work of argument, dealing with the soul's entrenched resistance. But they have enormous respect for the goodness of reason in each person. This commitment is not only part of the content of their teaching, it is also what organizes it at the deepest level. All their therapy is cognitive, and cognitive therapy is taken to be sufficient for the removal of human diseases. They really believe that prejudice, error, and bad conduct result from incorrect reasoning, not from original evil, or even original aggressiveness or lust or unruliness. And so they believe that philosophy, if it develops the right ways of approaching stubborn and prejudiced people, really can change the look of the world, the appearances these people see, removing the salience of morally irrelevant features and emphasizing those that good and consistent reasoning would endorse. The thing of cardinal importance is for reason to trust itself, to take charge of itself, to scrutinize the sloppy or inconsistent appearances through which a lax and corrupt society influences it. Daily life is not so much evil as flaccid and lazy. We get truth by toning up the muscles of the mind.

3. *Responsiveness to the particular case.* Therapeutic argument may take many forms. It may give general theoretical accounts or more concrete precepts. It may discuss the emotions one by one, or as a group. And, since the beliefs to be scrutinized form a complex system—a tangled skein, we might say—philosophical examination can begin almost anywhere, with beliefs on any topic, general or concrete. Here the Stoics are in profound agreement with the other schools in recommending that the choice of starting point and direction be made in accordance with the teacher's awareness of the pupil's concrete situation. The doctor, said Chrysippus, must be "inside" the pupil's passions and beliefs "in the best possible way." This evidently entails being keenly aware of the pupil's particular history, experiences, and immediate situation. For there are different therapies for different constitutions, Seneca observes (*Ir.* 1.6.2); and "one person is moved in one way, another in another" (Cic. *TD* 3.76). A good doctor will not send a prescription through the mail, Seneca insists, without personally examining the patient: he must feel the pulse (*Ep.* 22.1). Cicero (like our Epicurean texts) mentions the notion of *kairos*, the critical moment. Just as in diseases of body a doctor must choose the appropriate time for the administration of treatment in the particular case, so too with diseases of the soul. And "it makes a difference how the remedy is applied" (*TD*

3.79): we must think what words, what examples, will be best suited to the interlocutor with whom we are dealing. For not every sort of error and distress is treated by a single method (*TD* 4.59). We have to think whether this is the sort of person who will do best with a general or a concrete argument, and where the person's area of particular distress may be, what sort of speech will engage not only the surface, but the whole of his or her life and thought. "All speech that is employed to cure the mind has to sink down into us. Remedies are no use, unless they stay in the system" (Sen. *Ep.* 40.4).

A doctor is part of a medical tradition; as such he or she had better know well what that tradition offers. And the Stoics insist that profound knowledge of the philosophical tradition (not only the Stoic tradition, as we shall see) is essential for the good philosopher. A great part of Seneca's time, he insists, is spent in reading his predecessors. This is a delight, an enrichment, and an encouragement for him (cf. points 5 and 8). It is also a great help in his work as a teacher. "I profoundly respect the discoveries of wisdom and their discoverers; it is a delight to approach, as it were, the legacy of many predecessors" (64.7). But this material is insufficient for good doctoring, for two reasons. First, because (in Seneca's view, at any rate) the truth is, so far, incompletely discovered: more always remains to be done (7–8). But, second, because even if it *were* all discovered, the wisdom of predecessors cannot tell us how to apply it to the particular patient:

> Imagine that prescriptions have been handed down to us for the cure of eye disease: I have no need to search for others. Nonetheless, these need to be suited to the particular disease and moment. This one relieves irritation of the eyes, this one reduces swelling of the lids, this prevents sudden pain and watering, this one sharpens vision. You then have to pulverize them, choose the time, and apply the proper treatment to each case. The medicines for the soul were discovered by the ancients—but it is our job to find out how to apply them and when. Our predecessors accomplished a lot, but not everything. (64.8–9)

In this elaborate use of the medical analogy we see Seneca going beyond Epicurus, who insisted on the exceptionless truth of general dogmas, and simply pointed out that they must be applied in the right way. Seneca, in addition to claiming that philosophy's general wisdom is incomplete and still progressing (7–8), insists that in the application itself is a large part of medical expertise and medical discovery. The dignity of the doctor's work comes from the fact that, however much has been done before him, what really makes the difference between cure and disease is in his flexible hands.

What does this imply for philosophical teaching? It implies that therapeutic argument can never be fully or completely given in a treatise intended for public consumption. The paradigm of philosophical interaction is the quiet conversation of friends who have an intimate knowledge of one another's character and situation. Conversation, writes Seneca, is "more useful" than writing, even intimate letter writing, "because it creeps bit by bit into the soul" (38.1). Compared with personal conversation, "lectures prepared in advance and poured out to a listening crowd have more volume but less intimacy. Philosophy is good practical advice; nobody gives advice in a loud voice" (38.1).

This means that, for the Stoics as for the Socrates of Plato's *Phaedrus*, written texts will always be inferior to personal communication. Epictetus clearly philosophized in oral form, now addressing a group, now more concretely an individual. Much the same seems to have been true of Musonius. And Arrian is right to worry that in setting down Epictetus' discourses and publishing them, he will be losing something that played an important role in their causal efficacy. On the other hand, there are good reasons for a Stoic thinker to write. No teacher can approach very many pupils one by one. (This is even more obviously true for those Hellenistic thinkers who believed that the philosopher should also be actively involved in public life,[19] and who acted on this belief.) It is important to try to reach a broader audience, even if imperfectly, and to leave something behind as a contribution to the education of future philosophers.

A written work can give a general account of what Stoic therapy is like; it can show its reader the general ethical theory that is put to work in therapy. But how can it show the searchingly personal "inside" nature of Stoic therapy itself? Seneca finds a profound and ingenious solution to this problem. For in the greatest body of surviving Stoic therapeutic writing, his *Epistulae Morales*, he creates, within the written text, an intimate personal dialogue between teacher and pupil. Situating both his own fictionalized persona and that of the interlocutor Lucilius very concretely, in relation to their ages, to the seasons of the year, to events of many kinds, showing the teacher's intimate responsiveness to the pupil's thought and feeling, Seneca shows the reader what it is like for philosophy to be an "inside" business.[20] Both men feel that conversation would be even better than letter writing;

[19] On the participation of philosophers in politics, see M. Griffin (1989). The early Stoics did not follow their own prescriptions about political participation; the Roman Stoics are more consistent.

[20] On the historical inconsistencies of the portrait of Lucilius, and the importance of regarding him as essentially a fictional persona, see M. Griffin (1976).

but by writing frequently and candidly, they achieve the intimacy required for real therapy: "In the only way you can, you show yourself to me. I never received a letter from you, without being together with you directly" (40.1). And by making Lucilius in certain ways representative of the reader's own likely doubts and fears, Seneca can begin to conduct, as well, a therapy of the reader, as Lucilius asks advice on many topics, from the fear of death to literary style, from the liar paradox to the vicissitudes of a political career. Seneca's responses are fully personal and non-authoritarian, full of loving concern for Lucilius' whole life (see point 7). He depicts himself as himself a struggling incomplete being, not a perfected authority. This extended example of philosophical compassion shows us a great deal about what Nikidion could expect from real life Stoic teaching. It also offers teaching, in its own way, to those not fortunate enough to have such a teacher and friend.

Although Stoic teaching is in this way highly individualized, certain procedural guidelines are recommended for use by teachers in all but the most unusual cases. They are, in effect, procedures that are likely to help a teacher get at the pupil's concrete situation, whatever it may be. Two of these are of particular interest: the focus on the concrete and the use of examples. The task of teaching, we have said, is to provoke rational assessment of the ways of seeing that actually guide the pupil's actions. The most powerful among these are usually highly specific *phantasiai*; their acceptance presupposes background beliefs of a more general kind, whose removal would affect their status. But as a general rule, Stoic therapy holds that you cannot get a pupil to be critical of a more abstract or general belief, except through the medium of the concrete. Suppose, Cicero says, you have a person who is upset about being poor. Now to be sure, it would be most economical to convince this person right away that there are never any good reasons for being upset about anything, that nothing beyond our control matters, that nothing is bad except vice (*TD* 4.59, 3.77). But this person, upset as he is, will probably not be able to focus on this abstract general argument (3.77). It is more effective to focus on the specific, saying something that is appropriate to the person's preoccupation here and now, even if this means (as it clearly does with Lucilius) that teaching will have to go on for an indefinitely long time, covering the indefinitely many areas in which a human being all too concerned with externals may act and choose. (For, as Cicero says, "How far-reaching the roots of distress, how many, how bitter" [*TD* 3.83].) Seneca's practice (as we shall see in section VII) is to move from concrete context to general reflection, and back again, allowing them to illuminate one another. As the general propositions become better and better embedded, they suggest a way of seeing a new concrete case; and the new concrete case, appropriately seen, gives force and vivacity to the general proposition.[21]

These views about teaching have a further consequence: this is, that in Stoic teaching narratives and examples will play a central role. There is no moral philosophy in the Western tradition in which this is more evident; it is a constant practice, and it is also a part of the official theory (see *TD* 3.79). Since the goal is to get Nikidion to see an incident or person in a more adequate way, a crucial technique will be to tell a vivid story about a similar case, pointing out aspects that have not entered her imagination. If she is struck by the story in the *exemplum*, if she is engaged by its vividness of language, her own imagination will be helped to have a corresponding *phantasia* in her own case. And frequently the *exemplum* will be more available to her than a correct perception of her own case, since she has no bias with regard to it, no confusing surges of feeling. It is better than an abstract principle, since it is concrete enough to show her how to imagine. It is also in a way better than her life, since she is in a better position to perceive it truly. Literature provides a source of such *exempla*, as we shall see; but it must be carefully watched.

The importance of *exempla* and narrative in Stoic teaching is, then, closely connected to the importance Stoics attach to concreteness. And this itself seems to have more than one source. One, as we have seen, is motivational: we cannot really change a particular soul without engaging it in a highly personal, vivid, and concrete way. But there is, it seems, something deeper going on. For Stoicism, getting it right is not simply a matter of getting the general content of an act right. Right content by itself makes only a *kathēkon*, or acceptable act. To become a *katorthōma*, or fully virtuous act, an action must be done *as* the wise person would do it, with the thoughts and feelings appropriate to virtue.[22] And this, the Stoics hold, is a highly contextual and particular matter. General content-rules cannot guarantee a correct result, since, as Seneca says, they contain "what a person ought to do," but not "how" (*quemadmodum, Ep.* 95.4). What is needed, ultimately, is a *ratio*, a strategy of rational assessment that will in a concrete case show Nikidion "when one ought to act and how far and with whom and how and why" (*Ep.* 95.5), a procedure "whereby, whatever the particular situation, he or she can fulfill the whole gamut of appropriate acts" (95.12). *Exempla* do not by themselves contain this procedure; they

---

[21] Cf. Epict. *Disc.* 2.16.3, Sen. *Ep.* 95.12.

[22] For this distinction, see Long and Sedley (1987), Mitsis (1993), Kidd (1971a).

need to be supplemented by philosophical explication. But they show Nikidion as nothing else could what it *is* to act wisely, to get the entire rightness of motive, tone, response that go beyond, and are the source for the rightness of, the general rule.

Accordingly, Stoic *exempla* are frequent and vivid. They are embedded, for the most part, in a philosophical argument that aims at describing procedures by which any case at all might be assessed. In Seneca, however, the role of *exempla* undergoes a subtle shift. For, in the letters to Lucilius, the search for general procedures and the process of philosophical commentary on *exempla* all take place within the *exemplum*. What we are given in the *Letters* is in fact, for us, one long rich *exemplum*, an openended and highly complex story of two concrete lives. Philosophy is at the heart of those lives; so whatever they see and experience and communicate is subjected to philosophical commentary; but that is still part of the life, therefore part of the *exemplum*. The letters show us, I think, more vividly than any single story of virtue could, how the rightness of any act, any life, is in large part a function of the devotion to reason that inspires and infuses it—that we do not have two separate activities, virtuous action and philosophical reason; that much of what makes good action virtuous is the dedication to reason out of which it grows. In this sense, it should be impossible to give a really correct *exemplum* without showing, inside it, the work of philosophical argument.

And finally, the "inside" nature of philosophical teaching reaches deeper still. For, like Epicureanism, Stoicism views the soul as a spacious and deep place, a place with many lofty aspirations but also many secrets, a place of both effort and evasion. Much that goes on in it escapes the notice not only of the world at large, not only, even, of the teacher, but also of the person himself or herself. Part of the sluggishness and carelessness of everyday life as it is normally lived is its failure completely to grasp its own experiences and deeds, its failure to recognize and take stock of itself. The Stoic idea of learning is an idea of increasing vigilance and wakefulness, as the mind, increasingly rapid and alive, learns to repossess its own experiences from the fog of habit, convention, and forgetfulness. In his letter on reason as internal divinity, Seneca implicitly compares the spaciousness of the soul to a dark secluded grove, formed by overarching branches; to a cave made by fallen rocks that holds a mountain on its back; to pools that seem sacred because of their darkness or their immeasurable depth (41.3–4). The soul's challenge is to investigate these depths and to gain mastery over them. This, ultimately, it must do by itself, through its own daily practices of self-scrutiny. I shall examine these in chapter 11.

Such practices seem rather unremarkable to us today, since we are the heirs of centuries of practices of self-confrontation and self-scrutiny, from the confessional to modern psychoanalysis. In the context of the ancient world, however, they are remarkable. Aristotelian dialectic imagined the self as available to itself at all times, a flat surface, so to speak, or a clear and rather shallow pool from which one could always pick out the relevant intuitions. Stoicism, like Epicureanism, thinks differently. The self must acknowledge itself; only this brings peace and freedom. But this requires assiduous, daily litigation, in a darkened room, as the soul, in the absence of external light, turns its vision on itself (Sen. *Ir.* 3.36.1–3, discussed in chapter 11).

In short, we see in Stoicism, as in Epicureanism, a vivid sense of the personal depth of good philosophical teaching. And we see, as well, something different, something that should strike us as very unlike Epicurean practice. For Seneca does speak of doctoring and teaching. He is himself a teacher. But in the most intimate activity of self-recognition, he encounters no teacher but himself. The result of philosophical instruction is that the mind itself can bring itself before its own bar (*Ir.* 3.36.1–3), autonomous, secret, and free.

V

I turn now to our second group of medical (or anti-medical) characteristics, the ones that separated Aristotle, on the whole, from both Epicureanism and Skepticism. We find, with respect to these, a complex situation. On the one hand, the Stoics appear in many ways to side with Aristotle against the others, in their emphasis on the social nature of the human being, in their defense of the intrinsic worth of practical reason, and in their construction of a teacher-pupil relationship that is more symmetrical than authoritarian. On the other hand, in some crucial ways the Stoic *interpretations* of these features differ from Aristotle's, in such a way that they are able to make far more searching and radical criticism of existing social institutions.

4. Stoic arguments seek the health of the individual human being, to be sure. But as they do so, they never let the pupil forget that pursuing this end is inseparable from seeking the good of other human beings. For philosophy's mission, as we have seen, is not to one person or two, not to the rich or the well-educated or the prominent, but to the human race as such. And all human beings, following philosophy, should understand themselves to

be linked to all other human beings, in such a way that the ends of individuals are intertwined, and one cannot pursue one's own fullest good without at the same time caring for and fostering the good of others. Seneca writes to Lucilius:

> I am not your friend, unless whatever is at issue concerning you is my concern also. Friendship makes a partnership of all things between us. Nothing is advantageous or disadvantageous for the individual: we live in common. And nobody can live happily who considers only himself and turns everything into a question of his own utility. You must live for another, if you wish to live for yourself. This fellowship, scrupulously and reverently preserved, which makes us mingle as a human being with human beings and which judges that there is a common law of right for the human race, also makes a big contribution to fostering that more intimate fellowship of friendship of which I was speaking. For he that has much in common with his fellow human being has everything in common with his friend. (48.2–3)

In short, a life based on narrow self-interest cannot be successful, even on its own terms. Since the self is a member of the human community, promoting its fullest success includes promoting the ends of others.

The complex placement of human beings within relationships of varying degrees of intimacy, which make different contributions to their ends, was given vivid representation in a famous passage preserved from Hierocles, a Stoic of the first and second centuries C.E.[23] Each of us, he writes, is as if surrounded by a series of concentric circles. The first one is drawn around one's own self;[24] the next takes in the immediate family; then follow more remote family; then, in turn, neighbors, fellow city-dwellers, fellow countrymen—and, finally, the human race as a whole. The job of a reasonable person is to "draw the circles somehow toward the center," moving members of outer circles to the inner ones. "The right point will be reached if, through our own initiative, we reduce the distance of the relationship with each person." (Hierocles suggests some procedures for fostering this—such as calling cousins brothers, and uncles and aunts fathers and mothers.)[25]

It is especially important to consider Hierocles' outermost circle: for

[23] See the discussion of this in Long and Sedley (1987) 349.

[24] It is worth noting that for Hierocles the most central circle includes not only the soul but the entirety of the body, and "anything taken for the sake of the body."

[25] Compare the development of a similar idea in Plato's *Republic*, clearly very influential in the development of Stoic political thought.

here we reach the deepest point of difference between the Stoics and Aristotle. Aristotle thought of the basic unit as the *polis*. He did believe that one account of the good human life was valid for all human beings; but this account included no obligations to promote the good of the entire human species as such. He envisages the good person as achieving self-sufficiency "along with parents, children, wife, and in general friends and fellow citizens" (*EN* 1097b9–11). And he argues that the *polis* is the unit within which human self-sufficiency and the good life are achieved. The books on friendship do speak in passing of a broader sense of recognition and affiliation that links every human being to every other—connecting this with the experience of travel to foreign lands (*oikeion kai philon*, *EN* 1155a21–22). But this recognition seems to generate no moral obligation of any importance, certainly no sense that one's ends include the good of all humanity.

It is otherwise with the Stoics. In keeping with their strong distinction between the human and the animal, and their strong insistence on the dignity of reason in each human being, they hold, as well, that our reverence for reason is and should be a reverence for the entire species, for humanity wherever it occurs. In this sense, we are to view ourselves as citizens of a worldwide community of rational beings, "members of a community because of their participation in reason" (Ar. Did. *SVF* II.528 = Euseb. *Prep. Ev.* 15.15.3–5). And we are to regard the political community in which we are placed as a secondary and somewhat artificial matter, our first loyalty and attachment being to the whole. Seneca writes:

> Let us take hold of the fact that there are two communities—the one, which is truly great and truly common, embracing gods and men, in which we look neither to this corner nor to that, but measure the boundaries of our state by the sun; the other, the one to which we have been assigned by our birth. (*De Otio* 4.1)[26]

Sometimes this Stoic idea of the human being as a "citizen of the world" (*politēs tou kosmou*, Epict. 2.10.3 and passim) is taken to be a call for the abolition of nations and the establishment of a world state. Plutarch's account of Zeno's ideal city suggests that he may have read it this way:

> The much admired *Republic* of Zeno is aimed at this one main point, that we should not organize our daily lives around the city or the deme, divided from one another by local schemes of justice, but we should regard all human beings as our fellow demesmen and fellow citizens, and there

---

[26] See Long and Sedley (1987) 431. I use their translation.

should be one way of life and one order, just as a herd that feeds together shares a common nurturance and a common law. Zeno wrote this as a dream or image of a well-ordered and philosophical community.[27]

But it is unclear whether Zeno really wished to establish a single state; more important by far is the insistence that human beings should view themselves as linked to the human race as a whole, and take thought for the good of the whole species.[28] This idea itself has obvious political implications; but it can be compatible with the maintenance of local and national forms of political rule, and most Stoic political thought recognizes this.

Nikidion, then, will be taught that what she is *as an individual* is a member of a whole, and that this whole reaches out to include the entirety of humanity. She is to respect humanity wherever and however she encounters it; and she is to take thought, in her personal deliberations, for its overall good. This means, in educational terms, that she will do and read whatever is required in order to recognize the humanity of people distant in terms of geography or social class, learning to have empathy with their concerns and to view them, increasingly, as her brothers and sisters. Musonius, in his writing on women, takes this to require the vivid imagination of the different way of life, so that one can see how reason is realized in it. Both literary and historical texts would assist this task. Throughout, the medical concern she, and the teacher, feel for her personal health is at the same time a concern for the world of rational beings, of which she is a "principal part" (Epict. 2.10.3).[29]

I turn now to the role of practical reason in Stoic education: for here we arrive at the most distinctive part of the Stoics' conception, and the one that most profoundly shapes their idea of the philosophical curriculum. I shall treat features 5 and 7 together, and then turn to features 6 and 8.

5 and 7. Because *practical reason has intrinsic value*, Stoicism constructs a model of the teacher-pupil relationship that is strongly *symmetrical and anti-authoritarian*. I have said that the central commitment of Stoicism is to the dignity of reason in each human being. (And we shall see in the next chapter that the Stoics even define *eudaimonia* as identical with the right activity of reason.) This commitment shapes and is expressed in their idea of teaching, as one might expect. Following the Socratic idea that the unexamined life is not worth living, the Stoics view the business of teaching

[27] See Long and Sedley (1987) 431 f.

[28] The "common law" is an authoritative moral law that is normative for particular political communities.

[29] The contrast here is with animals.

as one of waking up the soul and causing it to take charge of its own activity. The passivity of the Skeptical pupil (cf. chapter 8) would, to the Stoics, be an abnegation of the essence of human identity. (We notice that the Skeptics granted the depth of those intuitions, in their metaphors of castration and divestment.) Even the subservience of the Epicurean pupil, fortified by a memorized doctrine and by the authority of a godlike supreme teacher, would not embody sufficient respect for the pupil. Stoics know that pupils are fond of authority: it is always easier to follow than to stand on one's own. Thus a central part of their effort, while offering guidance, is to repudiate subservience, to make the pupil teach himself or herself. "Become, yourself, both your own pupil and your own teacher," Epictetus insists. And he mocks the passivity of the needy pupil in rude and jarring language:

> "Yes, but my nose is running." "What have you hands for, then, slave? Isn't it so that you can wipe your own nose?" (1.6.30)

Seneca, more gently but with similar intent, discourages Lucilius from leaning on him—both by portraying himself as incomplete and struggling, and by encouraging Lucilius toward an ever greater independence of thought. In one important letter, he explicitly contrasts his Stoic attitude to teaching with the attitude of the Epicureans:

> We are not under a king: each one claims his own freedom. With them, whatever Hermarchus said, whatever Metrodorus said, is ascribed to a single source. In that band, anything that anyone says is spoken under the leadership and command of one alone. (33.4)

Although this is somewhat exaggerated as criticism of Epicurus and especially Lucretius (see chapters 5, 7, and 13), it shows us very clearly the values implicit in Stoic procedures.

And this has important implications for the role of the "great books" of the past in a philosophical curriculum. The example of Socrates, which is always of such deep importance to the Stoics, already gives guidance here: for in the *Phaedrus* (Plato's) Socrates argues that books are at best *reminders* of live philosophical teaching. They do not themselves *do* philosophy, and can never substitute for the living critical activity in the pupil's soul that *is* philosophy. At worst, they may actually impede that activity. For in one who reveres them, they may induce passivity and the "false conceit of wisdom."

Stoic teaching follows and develops these arguments. Since Stoicism is a school in which "great books" play a major role, and there is over a period of centuries a deep concern with the thought of the three great founding teachers of the school, Zeno, Cleanthes, and Chrysippus, it was particularly important for writers like Seneca and Epictetus to define carefully the use the pupil should and should not make of these and other sources of philosophical authority. This they do, repeatedly. Epictetus tells the story of a young man who comes to him saying he has made progress because he has internalized the contents of Chrysippus' treatise on choice. Epictetus tells him that he is like an athlete who boasts that he is making progress because he has a new set of training weights. He will not be congratulated. Instead, he will be told, "Show what you can *do* with your weights" (1.4.13–17). So too with books: don't just say that you have read them; show that through them you have learned to think better, to be a more discriminating and reflective person. Books are like training weights for the mind. They are very helpful, but it would be a bad mistake to suppose that one has made progress simply by having internalized their contents.

Seneca develops this idea further in two remarkable letters. In Letter 33, to which I have already referred, he warns the pupil against the danger of passivity and reverence that comes from digesting the thoughts of great men and relying on the bits of it that one recalls, as on an authority.

> "This is what Zeno said." But what do you say? "This is Cleanthes' view." What is yours? How long will you march under another person's orders? Take command, and say something memorable of your own. Bring out something from your own stock. . . . It is one thing to remember, another to know. To remember is to safeguard something entrusted to the memory. But to know is to make each thing one's own, not to depend on the text and always to look back to the teacher. "Zeno said this, Cleanthes said this." Let there be a space between you and the book. How long will you be a pupil? From now on, be a teacher also. (33.7–9)

This passage, close to the *Phaedrus*, does not repudiate the written text. In fact, it suggests a positive use for it (as we shall shortly see). But it insists that the written text contains a danger, the danger of deference to authority. This danger is clearly at its greatest when certain books have already been invested with a special importance, as was the case with the founding texts of Stoicism. Here, while Seneca clearly reveres the texts, he is particularly emphatic about the need for distance and critical autonomy.

The fullest expression of Seneca's complex position on books and reverence is in Letter 88, the famous letter on liberal education. Here he attacks traditional Roman methods of education for young gentlemen, which focused on the close and reverential study of certain canonical texts.[30] Seneca expresses grave doubts about the traditional notion of *studia liberalia*, if interpreted in its conventional meaning of "studies suited to a freeborn gentleman" (88.1–2). If such studies serve only to augment one's income, he says, they are no good at all. And even where they do have some use, they are useful only as a basis, not as the noble activity of the mind itself. The only study truly worthy of the name *liberalis* is philosophy: for that *liberates* the mind. It is good to *have had* the basic education embodied in conventional liberal studies, but philosophy is the only study whose activity is itself an exercise of human freedom.

Seneca makes a more complex set of contrasts here than he did in Letter 33. The contrast between reception and one's own activity is still important to him; and in that spirit he contrasts food that helps the body with what is really a part of the body itself and its own functioning (25). But he is also interested in a different contrast: between arts whose activity is merely preparatory and instrumental, and philosophy, the art concerned with virtue and choice, whose activity is therefore intrinsically noble. To linger too long and too obsessively in merely preparatory and ancillary studies— studies, for example, of great literary works, studies, too, of mathematics and engineering—may delude one into thinking them intrinsically important; and this mistake makes people "boring, wordy, insensitive, and self-satisfied" (37).[31] Life is too short to devote too much of it to activities that are not at the heart of what it is to be human. And, Seneca comments, this includes, as well, a great part of what is called philosophy; for metaphysical and linguistic analysis, insofar as it has no bearing on the central ethical and social questions of human life, is itself merely preparatory, and not intrinsically worthwhile (43–45).

In short, taking charge of one's own education means not only doing whatever one does in a vigilant and critical way, it means never losing sight of the most important things, the ones by which human life is really guided.

How should a pupil begin this task of self-teaching? The *rudimenta* of a traditional liberal education are very useful, Seneca concedes, as food for the developing soul. Next after this, he and Epictetus consistently ascribe great positive value to the study of the most important works of the major traditions of moral philosophy. Training weights are not exercise, but there are muscles that it is hard to exercise without them. And Seneca insists (in a

---

[30] For ancient conceptions and practices of education, see Marrou (1965).

[31] The reason, presumably, is that these studies may inspire the "false conceit of wisdom" that the *Phaedrus* already identified as a danger (275AB). The same could be said of some contemporary proposals defending a return to the "Great Books" as the core of a university curriculum.

passage I examined under point 3) that the books of the ancients are like medical texts: a young practitioner would be foolish not to study them. Even though their "prescriptions" are incomplete, and do not dictate their own application, they are worthy of enormous respect and close study (64.8–9). They should, however, be studied as wholes, and in depth:

> Get rid of the idea that by means of epitomes you can summarily taste the minds of great men: you have to look into their thought as a whole, and go over it as a whole. . . . I don't object to your examining separate limbs, so long as you examine them as parts of the whole body. (33.5)

In keeping with what we have already said, this positive use of books should always be viewed as training for one's own independent thought; and it is well for Nikidion to have a teacher and friend such as Seneca assisting the process, reminding her of the proper goal, and of the great book's incompleteness. She should not be discouraged from alluding to the book—so long as she does so by and from her very own understanding, approving of no more than what she can defend with her own reasons. Quoting to Lucilius a saying of Epicurus, which he approves but wishes to modify slightly, Seneca comments:

> There is no reason why you should judge that these works belong to Epicurus alone; they are public property. I think we should do in philosophy as they do in the senate; when someone proposes a motion that pleases me in part, I ask him to divide his motion in two, and I vote for the part that I approve. (21.9–10, cf. 8.8)

But Nikidion, we must remember, will not spend all her time in reading, writing, and conversation. Part of her every day must be spent by herself, in the reflective meditation about human life in general and the critical scrutiny of her own life that are such a deep part of the Stoic prescription for human health. For the body, moderate and simple exercise, taking up a small part of the day, is sufficient for health. But "exercise the soul both day and night—for it is nourished by moderate labor. This exercise will not be impeded by cold, or heat, or even old age" (15.5). Nikidion, in taking charge of herself, takes on a total way of life, affecting the conduct of her days, the temper of her friendships, even the content of her dreams.

6. *Value of logic.* Here we arrive at an area of considerable complexity in Stoic educational thinking. On the one hand, the Stoics' deep respect for the worth of practical reasoning leads to an associated respect for some of its excellences. Thought that is excellent is consistent, clear, precise; and a big part of taking charge of one's own thought is to strive for these excel-

lences, rooting out confusion, murkiness, inconsistency. And the Stoics believe that, given the way human thought is basically oriented, the sincere search for consistency will lead the pupil to truth. So logical virtues are a very important part of the intrinsic worth of reason.

They also have instrumental use. Getting a reasonably sophisticated training in logic, including the mastery of logical puzzles, the dissection of various forms of equivocation and sophistry—all this, Epictetus argues, is important in order that a good person, entering a complex argument, "should not conduct himself in a random or muddled fashion" (*sunkechumenōs*, cf. chapter 2), but should be able to test the argument and not be misled (1.7). But for this, he holds, formal logical training is required, a kind of disciplined mental gymnastics that the trained philosopher is the person best equipped to impart (1.8). "You see," he concludes, "that you have to become a pupil of the schools, that animal at whom everyone laughs, if in fact you want to make a critical examination of your own beliefs. And you know as well as I do that this is not the work of a single hour or day" (1.11.39–40).

This logical education will include the study of the meanings of terms (1.17.12, 2.14); it includes the study of syllogisms, which permits secure and confident arguing (2.13.21). It includes puzzles and paradoxes (2.17.27). And all of this should precede, according to Epictetus, substantive instruction in moral philosophy (1.17.4–12). An interlocutor objects that "the cure" is a more pressing business (1.17.4): but Epictetus replies that one cannot *use* the standard that measures reasoning to examine everything else, unless we have first examined the measuring standard itself, to see that it is in good order. Logic is that measuring standard (1.17.4–12). Seneca is far more guarded: but, given the prominence of logic in the Greek Stoa,[32] it would be hard for any orthodox Stoic thinker not to endorse this limited positive conclusion.

On the other hand, both Seneca and Epictetus are well aware that an interest in logic can carry the pupil away from real philosophizing, producing some of the same difficulties that were caused by misplaced deference to books: lack of sincere ethical reflection, false arrogance about one's knowledge and skill. Therefore, despite the Stoic tradition's insistence on logical training, both Epictetus and Seneca also spend time showing the pupil the futility of a pursuit of logical sophistication simply for its own sake and

---

[32] The excellence of Stoic logic has been underrated over time because of the fragmentary nature of our evidence; but Chrysippus clearly was one of the greatest logicians in the history of the subject, fully the equal of Aristotle. For some rudiments, see Long and Sedley (1987) 183–236; for a fuller account, Frede (1974); and see Brunschwig (1980).

without reference to the ethical content that gives logical training its point. Epictetus imagines a pupil who comes to him saying that his main purpose in studying philosophy is to understand the liar paradox. "If that is your plan, go hang," is his reply (2.17.34). Logic should always point beyond itself to a valuable ethical end (in which it may be a constituent part, since the end is a kind of thinking).

Seneca spends much more time on this problem, and correspondingly less on the positive value of logical training. This difference of emphasis may be explained in part by differences in the potential vices of their pupils: Lucilius is not likely to slack off intellectually. In part it may be temperamental. And in part it may be a feature of the dramatized situation of Lucilius' life, in which old age and shortness of time are central concerns. For Seneca's attacks on logical game-playing often allude to shortness of time (117.30; 111.5; 48.12; 45.5). There may also be genuine differences: for Seneca seems to see no worth at all in logical tricks such as the famous paradoxes (45.8–10, etc.); and his attitude to dissection of the meaning of terms seems far more negative than Epictetus'. Since Seneca returns to the limits of logic so frequently and at such length, I shall not be able to give a complete account of his statements here. Letters 45, 48, 111, and 117, among others, explore his positions in detail; from these one may draw representative passages together to produce a compressed summary of his views.

Many of the logical and linguistic inquiries in which philosophers pass their time, Seneca holds, have no practical benefit. Disputes about the meanings of words, verbal paradoxes—these are amusing games, but they do not always accomplish anything for life, or improve the person's command over his or her own choices (111.1; 48.1; 45.5). Often these philosophical puzzles do not correspond to any real-life problem or puzzle (48.8). They are like juggler's tricks—of no interest, once you have the trick (45). The philosopher should therefore attend to them only insofar as they serve "to lighten our ills" (48.8–9).

Why does this follow? Why should the philosopher not attend to them for their own sake, in addition to worrying about the large ethical questions? To this, Seneca has four answers. First, our life is just too short. We haven't solved the really important ethical questions, and we have so very little time as it is. "Do this," he says, "when you want to do nothing" (111.5)—but there are few times like that for a good person who wants personal mastery of the important questions. "Do we really have so much leisure? Do we already know how to live, how to die?" (45.5; cf. 48.12, etc.). Second, human beings *need* something from philosophy: philosophy has made a promise to come to the aid of the human race (48.7; cf. earlier discussion); and this it does not do by "playing around." Third, these studies are seductive: get deeply enmeshed in them, and one will have trouble getting back or getting on to other things (111.5; 45.4–5). Finally, they actually weigh the mind down, making it less able to pursue its most important concerns (48.9–10; 117.19–20); because they make the mind believe that the important questions of life are merely technical questions (48.10), they actually weaken it in its approach to these questions.

In short, logic is to be studied and used as an element in reason's self-government, with respect for one's own practical choices and those of others. The professional's love of cleverness for its own sake is to be strongly resisted—and resisted not because professional philosophy doesn't matter, but because it matters so much.

8. Nikidion will find that part of her self-government, as a Stoic pupil, will be the critical evaluation of philosophical writings from a variety of different traditions. The Stoics do not appear to go as far as Aristotle does in the direction of the idea that the truth emerges from the critical adjustment of the views of the "many and the wise." In my discussion of value-relativity I offered some reasons for this difference. But they do, like Aristotle, insist on the importance of reading with respect the works of previous (and not only Stoic) philosophers (cf. earlier discussion). And they make a point, in connection with their account of the pupil's independent self-governing character, of insisting that the pupil *should* read non-Stoic works, with the same watchful and critical eye with which she reads any work at all: "I have not sold myself as a slave to anybody; I bear no master's name. I have much confidence in the judgment of great men, but I claim something for my own judgment also" (45.4). Seneca's use of Epicurus is an extended *exemplum* of this point: for his reverent and close attention dispels the pupil's prejudice against learning from an alien source. And at the same time, his measured and critical attitude shows the caution with which any text, however excellent, should be approached. Always, the emphasis is on the view that good ideas are public property, but should be asserted only out of one's very own reflection and judgment. "Truth lies open to all; it has not yet been appropriated" (33.11).

The Stoics make a striking application of these ideas to the role of poetry in the curriculum. For unlike Epicureans and Skeptics, unlike Plato as well, they have a high regard for poetry, holding that it can play a valuable role in promoting self-recognition, and especially in confronting the spectator with the vicissitudes and uncertainties of life. But poetry frequently approaches these vicissitudes in a spirit alien to that of Stoicism. The pupil is not therefore forbidden to confront the work: but vigilance must be re-doubled. In a work that seems to be primarily Stoic in origin,[33] Plutarch expresses succinctly the nature of the Stoics' problem here, and its proposed solution:

> Shall we then, stopping the ears of the young as those of the Ithacans were stopped, with a hard and unyielding wax, force them to put to sea in the Epicurean boat, and to avoid poetry and steer their course clear of it? Or, shall we instead stand them up against some upright standard of reason and there bind them fast, straightening and watching over their judgment, in order that it should not be borne off course by delight toward what will harm them? (*How the Young Person Should Listen to Poetry*, 15D)

Critical spectatorship is encouraged by both Epictetus and Seneca, in their remarks on the drama (cf. chapter 12). It permits the pupil to derive from the poetry whatever is of real worth, and to avoid becoming passive tools of the poet's own purposes. The standard of the pupil's own trained reason prevents passivity and seduction.

9 and 10. The arguments of Stoicism are cautiously optimistic about their own power. They do not promise to bring the pupil all the way to wisdom, but they do promise progress, if the pupil works at them hard enough. "It is a large and difficult task, who doubts it? But what distinguished achievement is not difficult? Nonetheless, philosophy promises to achieve it, if only we receive her care" (Cic. *TD* 3.84, the topic being therapy of passion—see chapter 10). Even the beginnings of philosophy, as we saw, make life better; and the more one works, the better one will live. We must bear in mind here that Stoicism insists on linking this goal with the good of others: the good achievement of this hard work is not limited to oneself and one's own happiness. Seneca says he stays up nights working on philosophy, "so as to help as many as possible" (8.8). He has found his advice useful for himself, and is now writing it up for the good of others.

This optimism in Stoicism is connected, we should remind ourselves, with the fact that they refuse to trace human misery to any natural or inherent evil; instead, it is produced by ignorance, confusion, and weakness of thought. "Every soul is deprived of truth against its will." Reason, taking charge of itself, and working very hard, should be able to extricate the soul from whatever confusion society has produced. The roots of false belief go deep in the soul; so this cannot be an *easy* optimism. But optimism

---

[33] See Nussbaum (1993a).

it is, based on the deep belief that human beings are essentially reasonable, and that reason is basically just and good.

The arguments Nikidion receives increase her desire to pursue them further, and her ability also. The first steps in philosophy are "strenuous, since it is characteristic of a weak and sickly soul to fear the unfamiliar" (50.9). But once one has begun, "then the drugs are not bitter: for as soon as they are curing us they begin to be delightful. In the case of other cures, pleasure comes only after the return of health; but philosophy is at the same time health-giving and delightful" (50.9).

VI

In short, Nikidion's training, here as in the other Hellenistic schools, will be not simply academic instruction, but a way of life ordered by reasoning. In contrast to the life offered by popular religion, this will be a life committed to argument, whose god is the god within. In contrast to the life of skepticism, this life will be active, vigilant, critical, committed to truth. In contrast to the life of Epicureanism, this life is suspicious of any external authority, reverential only to reasoning itself; it is egalitarian and universalist about reason, and it commits itself to the fostering of rationality in the self, and in the world as a whole.

Stoicism is indeed, as Michel Foucault and other affiliated writers have recently insisted,[34] a set of techniques for the formation and shaping of the self. But what their emphasis on habits and *techniques du soi* too often obscures is the dignity of reason. Many forms of life in the ancient world purveyed *techniques du soi*. What sets philosophy apart from popular religion, dream-interpretation, and astrology is its commitment to rational argument. What sets Stoicism apart from other forms of philosophical therapy is its very particular commitment to the pupil's own active exercise of argument. For all these habits and routines are useless if not rational. And the basic motivation behind the whole business is to show respect for what is most worthy in oneself, for what is most truly oneself. One does not do this by anything but good argument. At the end, we have not the images of habituation and constraint so prominent in Foucault's writings, but an image of incredible freedom and lightness, the freedom that comes of

[34] Foucault (1984), vol. III; see also the different account in Hadot (1981, 1990), and the approving introduction by editor Arnold Davidson, Davidson (1990).

understanding that one's own capabilities, and not social status, or fortune, or rumor, or accident, are in charge of what is most important. The procedures of Stoic argument model a kingdom of free beings—the ancestor (in terms of both content and causal influence) of Kant's kingdom of ends, a kingdom of beings who are bound to one another not by external links of hierarchy and convention, but by the most profound respect and self-respect, and by their sense of the fundamental commonness in their ends. It is doubtful whether the view of the world contained in Foucault's work as a whole could admit the possibility of such a kingdom, or its freedom. For Foucault, reason is itself just one among the many masks assumed by political power. For the Stoic, reason stands apart, resisting all domination, the authentic and free core of one's life as an individual and as a social being. Argument shapes—and, eventually, *is*—a self, and is the self's way of fulfilling its role as citizen of the universe.

VII

Examining one case of Senecan therapy in detail will help us to see parts of this picture more clearly. I have chosen a case that does not anticipate the particular elements in Stoic normative theory (and philosophical procedure) that will be the focus of the next three chapters. Letter 44 is a rather ordinary letter, one of many that Seneca addresses to Lucilius on the subject of status and related external goods. And it is important to an understanding of the letter that its arguments are, and must be, repeated. Lucilius' education requires a formation of the soul that takes time; and in the absence of a conversation that "creeps step by step into the soul" (38.1), frequency of correspondence is essential—not just to cover all the points, but to cover any one of them well, with appropriate self-revelation (40.1) and effective exchange. Letter 44 is, then, part of an extended course of therapy for Lucilius' Roman beliefs about family and social rank.

At this point in the correspondence, Lucilius is imperial procurator in Sicily. He writes Seneca frequently (38.1; 40.1), and occasionally hears other philosophical lectures (40.2). He is making good progress (34.1–2, 37.1), but still needs urging to pursue his studies with diligence (35.1). Since there are not many books in his part of the world (45.1), he asks Seneca to send him books and other notes (39.1). But recently he has become, in his exalted position, the object of gossip and envy (43.1–3). Despite his new-found fame, or perhaps because of it, Lucilius is anxious, and has little self-esteem (*contemnas ipse te*, 43.3).

Letter 44 begins, as most do, with the fabric of Lucilius' daily life, and with his situation. In particular, Seneca starts with Lucilius' thoughts about himself, as expressed (we are to imagine) in his own previous letter: he feels himself low and insignificant, and blames both nature (birth) and fortune for preventing him from separating himself from the crowd and rising "to the greatest human happiness" (an achievement that is actually in his power, says Seneca, if only he realized it). It is a repeated complaint: "Once again you . . . call yourself an insignificant nobody," the letter opens. Lucilius, a Roman knight, conceives of human happiness in terms of political and social status; and he blames both birth and wealth for barring his access to this end. This is of course not a problem peculiar to Lucilius: most educated and relatively prosperous Romans would have similar feelings; in addressing himself to the therapy of these feelings, Seneca can expect to be treating most of his readers as well.

Seneca begins his argument by introducing philosophy, a persona whose behavior to Lucilius contrasts strikingly with his own to himself: "If there is any good in philosophy, it is this: that it does not look into genealogies." All humans, "if traced back to their first origin, come from the gods" (2). In this way, Seneca reminds Lucilius of the relative superficiality of the origins to which people attach importance, of the similarity of our ultimate origins, and also of his belief (the subject of Letter 41) that there is a kinship between human beings and the divine, forged by reason. Lucilius is reminded, then, of his view that, with respect to the divinity in themselves, human beings are all equal.

Seneca now refers in detail to some features of the status-consciousness of Roman society: the order of knights (to which Lucilius' hard work has brought him) is very exclusive; so is the Senate; so too the army. He now contrasts this entire social world with the society created by reason: "A good mind [bona mens] is open to all; in respect of this, we are all nobles. Philosophy neither rejects nor selects anyone: its light shines for all" (2–3). We have, then, a countersociety set over against Roman society. Lucilius is reminded of his belief in the existence of this other society, his allegiance to it, and the advantages that it offers its members—equality, openness, full human dignity.

Examples are now produced to illustrate philosophy's indifference to social class: Socrates was no patrician, Cleanthes was a hired gardener and water-carrier, "Plato was not received by philosophy *as* a noble, but made noble by it" (3). The first two examples are straightforward, the third complex. Since it must have been known to Seneca that Plato was in fact of noble Athenian family, he is playing in a complicated way on the word "noble." Plato really *was not* noble, not in the truest sense, even though called so by society—until philosophy conferred on him her true nobility. The world of philosophy and its rankings are now not just contrasted with, but substituted for, the rankings of Athens and Rome. This world now provides Lucilius with a genealogy: these great philosophers can be his *maiores*, he can be a part of *that* (true) nobility—if only he acts in a way worthy of them. And he will so act, if only he convinces himself at the outset that he is as intrinsically noble as any other human, in respect of real nobility (3–4). In other words, giving up Roman values and Roman class- and status-consciousness is a necessary prerequisite for achieving the worth that is most important. Lucilius has now been shown a deep conflict between his attachment to Roman social mores and his deep attachment to the worth of reason. He is asked to see that a very general aim he has for himself—to attain the summit of human life—can be fulfilled only if he gives up the former and clings to the latter.

The ensuing section deepens these reflections, by referring to the min-gling of origins in the long history of humanity: everyone ultimately goes back to a time before which there was nothing, and the whole history of the world shows a long sequence of alternations of splendor and ignominy (4–5). Again, Seneca returns to the theme of *true* nobility: what went before us is not *us* (5). "The soul confers nobility, and it is permitted to rise superior to fortune out of any situation whatever" (5).

This idea is now confirmed by a thought experiment. Imagine, Seneca says, that you are not a Roman knight, but a freedman (6). Still, you can be the only truly free person in a group of gentlemen. Lucilius is now imagined as protesting: "How?" The answer is, by independence of convention's tyranny—"if you distinguish bad and good not relying on the authority of popular opinion" (6).

Seneca now presents Lucilius with a distinction that is not only basic to good self-government but at the root of Lucilius' own confusion: the dis-tinction between things that are good in themselves and things that are merely instruments of the happy life. This general and basic philosophical distinction enters the argument as motivated by the concrete context, and returns to illuminate the context. All human beings, Seneca continues, seek the happy life, but many confuse the *instrumenta*—for example, wealth and status—with that life itself. This focus on the instrumental goods makes people get further from the happy life, rather than closer to it, since possessions and wealth cause constant unease and are thus like a sort of baggage that the person has to drag through life (7).

This argument once again asks Lucilius to see a conflict between two sets of beliefs within himself, one of which is alleged by the argument to be deeper and more fundamental than the other. On the one hand, he is expected to agree that the really worthwhile things are the activities (of virtue, etc.) that *make up* the happy life, and not the external instruments that produce it. On the other hand he has himself been very deeply attached to status. Seneca wants him to see that attachment not only as inconsistent with his allegedly deeper beliefs, but as a dead weight, an impediment. Indeed, he now goes further: the more a person pursues those things, the further he will get from what he really wants. Seneca ends his letter with an image that illustrates that more extreme judgment: "when people hurry through a maze, their very haste gets them more and more entangled" (44.7). This image clearly stands, too, for the whole of a life—for the difficulty of choosing well, for the complexity of the choices before us. How *does* one in fact find one's way through a maze? By going slowly and deliberately—the pace of good philosophy, as Seneca has written in Letter 40. ("Philosophy should carefully place her words, not fling them out, and proceed step by step" [40.7].) By following, too, a guiding thread, which is what reason offers us, as we go through life.

Thus the letter ends by indicating to Lucilius that it is only by following reason, and attending to its guidance with patient care, that he can have any hope of finding his way through the tangled maze of a human life. It has presented a forceful argument against attending to class and status, and in favor of enrolling oneself in reason's kingdom. And it has done something more: by its patient personal attention to Lucilius, by its careful choice of language and imagery, it has participated, *with him*, in the shaping of his soul.

VIII

By focusing on procedure rather than on all of the content of Stoic philosophy, I have, obviously, introduced one large and central part of that content, the emphasis on the dignity of reason. But one could, it seems, approve of what has been said here about the importance of freedom and self-formation, about the equal dignity of all human beings, about books and self-reliance, about the moral irrelevance of gender, class, and status, without being a Stoic. For the Stoics, as we shall see in the following chapter, hold that ties to items outside oneself are without intrinsic value; and it does not seem to be incumbent on the believer in rational self-determination to believe this. The Stoics, moreover, hold that all the passions should be completely extirpated from human life. And, once again, it does not seem to be necessary for the Nikidion I have described in this chapter to believe this. Indeed, one could imagine a further unpacking of the notion of practical rationality itself that would allow emotions such as love, sympathy, and grief to play a guiding role.

To some extent, these commitments really are independent of one another: one may continue to pursue many of the Stoic goals investigated in this chapter (under some description, at least) without accepting the anti-passion side of Stoicism that I shall describe in the following chapter. Indeed, certain Stoic arguments rely on this, beginning from the pupil's antecedent commitment to reason's integrity and trying to argue from that to the advisability to extirpating passion. But there is need for caution: for the Stoic argument will charge that the life of the person in question is actually inconsistent. Many people, they charge, claim that they are committed to their own integrity and practical reason, while living lives of subservience to passion that conflict with and undercut that commitment. In other words, they claim (whether successfully or not) that the commitment to rational self-determination, properly understood, actually entails the extirpation of the passions. And in the account of self-reliance that I have just given, one can already see some strong suggestions of the anti-emotion view.

Nikidion is to trust nothing and nobody but herself. But how deeply, then, can she trust and care for others? She is to be ceaselessly watchful over herself, her appearances and her impulses. But isn't this likely to put an end to the surprise and spontaneity that are so important to the passionate life? She is to value her own reason as *the* source of her humanity and her integrity, the one thing of real intrinsic worth in her life. So long as that is with her, she can go through life fulfilled. So long as that is free, she has her dignity, whatever the world may do to her. But what, then, can she consistently think of her deepest ties to other people? Of the prospect of losing them or being betrayed by them? In this way, reason's zealous hegemony, plausible and attractive though it is, points beyond itself to some of the more disturbing and controversial elements in Stoicism. Can one live in reason's kingdom, understood in the way the Stoics understand it, and still be a creature of wonder, grief, and love?

The Stoics on the Extirpation
of the Passions

I

IN ORDER to get a deeper understanding of the Stoic conception of therapy we must now turn to their account of the emotions or passions[1] and its
consequences for their picture of the "cured" person's life. I begin by
setting down, somewhat dogmatically and without detailed textual argument, certain features of the Stoic conception of the human end or good
that will play a role in the Stoics' diagnosis and treatment.[2] (This will not
prevent us from asking, later on, how the diagnosis and this conception of
health are interrelated.) According to Stoicism, then, only virtue is worth
choosing for its own sake; and virtue all by itself suffices for a completely
good human life, that is, for *eudaimonia*. Virtue is something unaffected by
external contingency—both (apparently) as to its acquisition and as to its
maintenance once acquired.[3] Items that are not fully under the control of

---

[1] On these terms and their interchangeability, see chapter 9 n. 4.

[2] Many of the pertinent ancient texts are to be found in *SVF*, especially vol. III. See, above
all, DL 7, Cic. *Fin.* 3–4, for general accounts of Stoic moral theory. On the *pathē*, *SVF*
III.377–490, DL 7.110–18, Cic. *TD* 3–4, Galen *PHP* 4–5. There is much pertinent material
in Seneca's *Moral Epistles* and *Moral Essays* (on the *pathē*, above all the *On Anger*, or *De
Ira*). On Seneca's relationship to early Stoicism, see chapter 11 and Inwood (1993). Good
general accounts of Stoic ethics that can be consulted to supplement this summary include
Rist (1969), Long (1974), Inwood (1985); for the connection of Stoic ethics with physics and
logic, see also Christensen (1962). Useful collections of articles dealing with related issues are
Long (1971), Rist (1978), Schofield and Striker (1986), Brunschwig and Nussbaum (1993).

[3] There are actually difficulties surrounding both of these claims. For since the Stoics,
beginning at least with Chrysippus, did not claim to be wise men, and clearly thought the
appearance of a wise man a rare and remarkable event, for which decent effort alone is not
sufficient, they might appear to be placing this most important matter in the control of forces
beyond the agent. They would certainly resist this inference; but it is not entirely clear what
account they give in reply. As for the losing of virtue, numerous texts insist that the Stoic
position (in contrast to that of the Peripatetics) is that virtue once acquired cannot be lost: cf.
SVF III.238 = Simplic. *In Aristot. Categ.* f. 102A, 102B; III.240 = Clem. *Strom.* 4.22; III.241
(Theognetus comicus), 242 = Alex. Aphr. *De Fato* 199.27. But DL 7.127 (*SVF* III.237)

the agent—such as health, wealth, freedom from pain, the good functioning of the bodily faculties—have no intrinsic worth, nor is their causal relationship to *eudaimonia* even that of an instrumental necessary condition. In short, if we take all these things away, if we imagine a wise person living in the worst possible natural circumstances, so long as she[4] is good—and once good she cannot be corrupted—her *eudaimonia* will still be complete.[5] She will be living as valuable and choiceworthy and enviable a life as a human being possibly could.

At this point we enter an area of considerable controversy and obscurity. For the Stoics (in order, apparently, to explain why and how the wise person will actually act in any way at all out there in the world)[6] also insist that these external goods are appropriately preferred, in many circumstances, to their opposites. The wise person will in many cases, and rightly (for the wise person never errs)[7] pursue health and not sickness, freedom from pain rather than pain, and so forth.[8] Some texts seem to suggest that these items may therefore be correctly said to have some worth, even if only a derivative or second-grade worth.[9] It is extremely difficult to tell exactly what worth (*axia*) is, and how it is related to goodness (*to agathon*), which is consistently denied to all indifferents. I do not intend to get enmeshed in

reports a difference of opinion between Cleanthes and Chrysippus, Cleanthes holding that virtue can never be lost, Chrysippus that it is lost in times of drunkenness and mental illness—times, in other words, when the entire functioning of the cognitive system is knocked out of commission. This distinction, though interesting in its own right, does not affect our argument here. For Chrysippus clearly denies that virtue can degenerate in the sense of turning into vice.

[4] The Stoics are convinced that both males and females have the potential for virtue—that, in effect, the moral and rational soul is genderless; see chapter 9. They typically use the unmarked masculine gender to refer to the wise person, but since I am following Nikidion's education and since their theory plainly admits the possibility of female virtue, I shall use the feminine throughout, marking it with brackets in citations.

[5] On the sufficiency of virtue for *eudaimonia*, see, e.g., DL 7.127.

[6] Contrast the heterodox position of Aristo of Chios who, holding that everything other than virtue is a matter of perfect indifference, left the wise man no reasons of his own for action. If he moves and acts at all, it is only in the way a stage actor does (DL 7.160–64, *SVF* I.333–403 and, for good discussion of all the evidence, Ioppolo [1980]).

[7] Cf. DL 7.121–22 = *SVF* III.549, 556; Stob. *Ecl.* 2.111,18 = *SVF* III.554, 548. The wise man does all things well—cf. *SVF* III.557–66, especially 561 = DL 7.125.

[8] For the list of "indifferents" and the claim that they are not goods (*agatha*), see DL 7.102 = *SVF* III.117, Stob. *Ecl.* 2.79, 1W = *SVF* III.118, and also *SVF* III.118–123.

[9] On the notion of worth (*axia*) and the connection of worth with the preferred indifferents, dis-worth (*apaxia*) with the dispreferred, see especially DL 7.105–6 = *SVF* III.126–27; Stob. *Ecl.* 2.83.10, 2.84.4, 2.84.18 = *SVF* III.124, 125, 128; Cic. *Fin.* 3.50–53; and in general, *SVF* III.124–39.

this difficult problem of interpretation here.[10] I shall simply record certain facts that seem to me uncontroversial, sketch several available routes out of the interpretative dilemma, and then show the significance of these observations for the issues that will concern us most.

It is quite clear, then, that for the Stoics virtue admits of no trade-offs in terms of any other good; indeed, it is not even commensurable with any other good. This ultimate good, Cicero insists, has a unique quality that is not reducible to degrees or quantities of anything else (*Fin.* 3.33–34). For this reason we cannot speak of adding other goods to virtue to get a larger total: "It is not the case that wisdom plus health is worth more than wisdom by itself separately" (*Fin.* 3.44).[11] But given that the other goods and virtue are not commensurable with one another, and given that virtue alone has the highest worth, we then cannot speak of exchanging a piece or part of virtue, however "small," for even the largest possible amount of any other good or goods. No such trade-off would ever be justified. Furthermore, it is equally clear that for the Stoics external goods are neither parts of *eudaimonia* nor necessary for *eudaimonia*. They are "things that have no power for living happily or wretchedly" (*Fin.* 3.50). Virtue by itself is self-sufficient, sufficient for *eudaimonia*.[12] But the Stoics, like Aristotle, also hold that *eudaimonia* is, by definition, inclusive of everything that has intrinsic value, everything that is choiceworthy for its own sake. Putting these claims together, we are forced to conclude, what a large number of texts in fact assert, that external goods, all goods other than virtue, have no intrinsic value at all.

At this point we might try various interpretative strategies. We might say that the preferred indifferents have a kind of second-class worth and are ordered below virtue in the sort of hierarchy that is known in contemporary philosophy as a "lexical ordering": we satisfy all the claims of virtue first, but at any time when we have satisfied them we may go on to consider the claims of the indifferents. Or we might claim that the worth of the indifferents to derive from the productive relation in which they stand to virtue in the career of the child, whose natural orientation to these exter-

---

[10] For a variety of recent treatments, see Irwin (1986), Kidd (1971a), Rist (1969), Long and Sedley (1987), Inwood (1985), C.C.W. Taylor (1987), Lesses (1989).

[11] See also *Fin.* 4.29, 5.7; Sen. *Ep.* 92.17; *SVF* III.29 = Plut. *St. Repugn.* 1039C; *SVF* III.30 = DL 7. 101. Other passages are collected and well discussed by Irwin (1986).

[12] See, e.g., DL 7.127–28 = *SVF* III.49; also *SVF* III.50–67. Diogenes reports that Zeno and Chrysippus both defended that view; he adds that the later Stoics Panaetius and Posidonius denied it, claiming that health, strength, and some means of livelihood are necessary conditions of *eudaimonia*.

nals plays a crucial positive role in the process of development. When the child's reason matures and he or she develops virtue, she does not cease to be a natural being, and she still appropriately follows the animal aspects of her natural constitution, when and as virtue permits. Various other similar solutions have been suggested.[13] But I think it is clear that what we must absolutely avoid doing, if we are faithful to the spirit of the Stoic conception, is to attach to the indifferents, to external goods, the sort of value that most ordinary people are seen to attach to them and that Aristotle explicitly accords them. That is, we must neither ascribe to them any intrinsic worth as constituent parts of the agent's *eudaimonia* nor view them as absolutely indispensable necessary conditions for the *eudaimōn* life. But most ordinary people, and Aristotle with them, do ascribe intrinsic worth to love and friendship, which are in their nature relations with unstable and uncontrolled external items. Most people, again, see themselves as social beings, for whom the loss of a country or of political privileges is the loss of an intrinsic value. Most people believe that the good human life cannot be pursued and realized without a certain amount of food, shelter, and bodily health—making these items necessary for *eudaimonia*, though not constituents of it. The Stoic is committed to denying all of this.

It is particularly important to understand that when the Stoics deny all value to items other than virtue they are including here all the items to whose presence or absence the contingencies of the external world can make a difference. This means that they are committed to denying the intrinsic worth of external worldly action and even, as they explicitly assert, the intrinsic worth of life itself (DL 7.102).[14] Not only traditional "external goods" like wealth and honor, not only "relational goods" like having children, having friends, having political rights and privileges, but also individual forms of virtuous activity, such as acting courageously, justly, and moderately, are held to be, strictly speaking, worthless, on the grounds that they can, as Aristotle has argued and as anyone knows, be cut off or impeded by accidents beyond our control. But the wise man must be self-sufficient; his life is always *eudaimōn*, no matter what happens (*TD*

[13] The first alternative is suggested by several texts; the second is argued by Lesses (1989) on the basis especially of Cic. *Fin.* 3.19ff. Kidd (1971a) and Irwin (1986) suggest still other solutions.

[14] It is, of course, odd to deny that life is necessary for virtue—especially in the absence of a belief in an afterlife in which virtuous activity is possible. The Stoics hold that the souls of the dead survive until the next conflagration, and presumably retain their virtue, but without opportunities for its exercise. One clear point is that Stoics, like Epicureans, hold that the prolongation of life is not important for virtue: more life is not always better, and can sometimes be worse (see chapter 11).

5.83).[15] The virtues are held to be states of soul (*diatheseis*—cf. DL 7.89, 98).[16] Cicero's interlocutor tells us that it is as if we said that in spear-throwing the ultimate end was to "do all one could to aim straight"—and the actual hitting of the target, even, presumably, the actual throwing action, will be no part of what is esteemed.[17] Virtue, then, is not an inert inner condition: it is imagined as a striving or straining: indeed, as Diogenes Laertius tells us, "the good person is always using his soul, which is perfect" (7.128). But, these inner activities are explicitly said to be unaffected by worldly contingency (DL 7.128); and they are held to be complete in themselves, quite apart from their emergence into the world, complete from the very moment they begin. The worldly performance is for this reason called a mere "afterbirth" (*epigennēmatikon*, Cic. *Fin.* 3.32).[18] The wise person does not need to stride out into the world at all, to open up her soul to the world, to press the exigencies of her soul upon the world. She can, as Seneca so frequently says, simply stay at home; for at home, inside herself, she has whatever she needs. In this way the Stoics not only repudiate the value of the usual list of "external goods," to which (with the exception of *philia*) even Aristotle does not ascribe intrinsic worth. They go further and break with one of the claims about human good to which, as Aristotle tells us, ordinary people will most readily give their agreement: namely, that the good life consists in activity and that this activity goes on out in the world.

We are beginning to get a picture of the radical detachment of the Stoic sage, the detachment that greets slavery and even torture with equanimity, the detachment that receives the news of a child's death with the remarkable words, "I was already aware that I had begotten a mortal" (Cic. *TD* 3.30).[19] Of this detachment and the view of the self it implies, I shall speak

---

[15] Cf. also *Fin.* 3.26, 42; Stob. *Ecl.* 2.98.17 = *SVF* III.54.

[16] Cf. also *TD* 4.34 = *SVF* III.198 (*adfectio animi*) and also the definitions of the particular virtues given by Andronicus (*SVF* III.266ff.), which characteristically use the words *hexis* and *epistēmē*, although DL 7.98 makes a clear distinction between *diatheseis* and *hexeis*, giving virtue as an example of the former. See also Plut. *Virt. Mor.* 441C, where both *diathesis* and *dunamis* are used.

[17] On this image, see Striker (1986), Irwin (1986), Inwood (1985), C.C.W. Taylor (1987).

[18] The word seems to mean that which is produced after something, as its causal product: it is not limited to contexts of birth. See, e.g., Plut. *Mor.* 637E, where the egg is the *epigennēma* of the creature's nourishment and digestion.

[19] The story is told about Anaxagoras (cf. Diels-Kranz, Anaxagoras, A33): he is being used as an example of the right Stoic response. The story occurs also in DL 2.13, and, cited by Posidonius, in Galen *PHP* 4.7.9–10, 282D. Posidonius uses this story as an example of the moral value of "prefiguring" (*praemeditatio*).

more in what follows. But this detachment has a corollary, which I must now introduce. If declaring worldly activity external and unnecessary eases the agent's ethical burden in one way, making her less dependent upon ungovernable conditions, in another way it increases it, by focusing all ethical attention on the internal doings of the heart.

Aristotelian ethics had already argued that we are morally assessable not only for our overt acts, but also for the quality of feeling and imagination that accompanies them. A person who does the correct thing from the wrong motives, or with rebellious and conflicting reactive feelings, does not perform a virtuous action. To be virtuous, an act must be done as the person of practical wisdom would do it. And yet the overt action, while not the only important thing, is still very important. Self-control, or *enkrateia*, correct action accompanied by rebellious yet temporarily frustrated feelings, is morally far better than *akrasia*, doing the incorrect thing in spite of good principles and some good feelings. (It is, of course, vastly better than doing the bad thing with harmoniously bad feelings.) The difference between *enkrateia* and *akrasia* is a large moral difference; but we can imagine that frequently the inner difference will be very small, a tiny tilting of the balance of thought and feeling. And in some cases this difference may be made not so much by some extra degree of moral strength at all, but by some feature of the circumstances over which the agent does not have full control: the absence of a supremely tempting object, the presence of some unusual pressure or temptation. Aristotle does urge us, in assessing such cases, to consider how the agent's disposition stands to the usual case. If she yields to a pressure that most good people would withstand, we judge her harshly. If she yields to extreme circumstantial pressures, we are asked for forgiveness and some indulgence of judgment (*EN* III.1). But Aristotle does not ask us simply to forget what the person has in fact done. The action is there, and it makes things morally different. Many of us will do something shameful if pressed hard enough; and yet the few who have the bad luck to be so pressed will be judged for their acts, while the rest of us will not. On the other hand, a person who forms bad thoughts and wishes, but never carries them into action for want of an occasion, will be judged harshly, to be sure, but not nearly as harshly as the person who actually does these acts.

We can see already that the Stoics would not be happy with this emphasis on the external. First, they are committed to denying the moral relevance of luck and external circumstance; so they will be committed to judging people for what their intentions and motives and thoughts are, quite apart from what happens out there, quite apart from all worldly conditions over which agents do not have full control. This means that there is no moral difference at all between the criminal who never gets a chance to commit his crime and the one who does; no moral difference between ordinary people who do vile things under circumstances of extreme pressure and you and me, who never happened to be so tempted but are right now such that we would not resist any and every temptation.[20] The only virtue we can safely applaud is a pure error-proof virtue, virtue without any counter-balancing inner forces. (We begin to see why the Stoics want to say that the only wise person is one who never errs at all, and that all others are fools.) Similarly, the only difference between self-control and *akrasia* the Stoic can recognize is the one that is actually there in the heart: that is, frequently, a very small delicate difference in the inner psychological condition, in its balance of feelings and thoughts.[21] We assess the agent for her thoughts and passions, without permitting ourselves the moral comfort of insisting that all was well in the end. It becomes difficult to distinguish the person who has but masters murderous wishes from a conflicted and reluctant murderer. The boundary between agent and world, the decisive wall that for us now separates the two, is taken away: it is permitted to have no moral relevance at all.

We can go further. On the Stoic picture, what happens internally just is an action, and is assessable as such. And a virtuous or vicious act is, we recall, complete at any moment, complete at its inception in the heart. So what for Aristotle would be described as a correct action achieved with difficulty against the pressure of angry murderous desires will in Stoic terms be described as a good inner action, accompanied by an extremely vicious inner action. Cicero makes this explicit:

> For just as it is a moral offense [*peccatum*] to betray one's country, to use violence against one's parents, to rob a temple, which are evils in result [*in effectu*], so too to fear, to grieve, to have erotic desires are each of them a moral offense, even without any result [*sine effectu*]. Truly these are of-

---

[20] There will, however, be a moral difference between the person whose bad motives are checked by good motives and the person who lacks such inhibiting motives—see chapter 12.

[21] A question that naturally comes up at this point is: what about the difference made by circumstances to one's desires and thoughts? Not only the expression of desire in action but also the formation of desires and intentions themselves seem to some extent to be affected by factors we do not control. Are people who never desired to harm others, but were not so error-proof that they could not have been led to form those desires under certain circumstances, any better morally than people of similar strength who actually did form such desires? This thought suggests one more reason why the Stoics wanted to insist that all who were not absolutely error-proof were fools.

fenses not in their subsequent consequences, but straight from the start. So too, the things that proceed from virtue are to be judged morally right on the basis of their first inception, not their completion. (*Fin.* 3.32)

And since virtue is not a matter of degree, but an absolute, we will find it hard to distinguish the bad inner act of the self-controlled murderer from the bad act that actually gets by into the world. A single failure in thought and passion can have, directly, the direst possible consequences for the agent's whole moral condition. If philosophy must make itself a therapy of passion, we begin to see why this should be so: the cost of failure in passion is higher here than in any other school.

One further observation, before we examine the Stoic passions. The Stoic virtues are all forms of knowledge; the inner activity of these dispositions is some form of practical reasoning or wise thinking. This being the case, it follows that the art that pursues wisdom has the structure of an art whose activities are (once we reach a sufficiently high level) ends in themselves. Cicero reminds us that some arts, like navigation and doctoring, aim at ends that are separate from the activities of the artist and can be fully characterized without reference to his activity. In others, like dancing and acting, the art activities are themselves ends (*Fin.* III.24). Wisdom is of the latter sort. And yet, Cicero immediately reminds us, it is quite unlike all the other arts in this: that its performance is entirely unified and self-contained: each exercise of wisdom is an exercise of all virtue. Thus philosophy is not only a road to *eudaimonia*: practiced at its highest, it is our human end, and the whole of it, not simply a part. *Phronēsis*, wise and virtuous thinking, just is *eudaimonia*.[22]

II

Among the most notorious and paradoxical theses in the history of philosophy is Chrysippus' thesis that the passions are forms of false judgment or false belief.[23] On its face this claim seems bizarre indeed. For emotions

---

[22] Plutarch, *St. Rep.* 26, 1046D = *SVF* III.54: Chrysippus held that "*Phronēsis* is nothing other than *eudaimonia* in anu of itself, but just is *eudaimonia.*"

[23] Chrysippus seems to have used both the word *doxa*, usually translated "belief" or "opinion," and the word *krisis*, usually translated "judgment": the latter more often in general assertions (the *pathē* are *kriseis*), the former more often in concrete definitions ("grief is a fresh *doxa* that something bad is present"). *Hupolēpsis*, "supposition," is sometimes used as well. (See, e.g., DL 7.111, where in reporting Chrysippus' view Diogenes shifts from *krisis* in the statement of the general view to *hupolēpsis* in particular examples.) Most of the

such as fear, grief, anger, pity, and erotic love seem to us (and seem to the Stoics too, when they write about them concretely) to be (as their name implies) violent motions or upheavals in the soul, quite unlike the calm graspings and placings of reason. To equate passion with belief or judgment seems, furthermore, to ignore the element of passivity that installed the term "passion" as another generic name. For judgments seem to be things that we actively make or do, not things that we suffer. In short: to feel love or fear or grief or anger is to be in a condition of tumult, violent movement, and vulnerability. Nikidion will ask: how can this condition possibly be equivalent to judging that such and such is the case?

We can readily see why the Stoics might have wished to defend this strange claim. For it helps them in no small measure to establish the necessity and efficacy of philosophy as the art of life. If passions are not subrational stirrings coming from our animal nature, but modifications of the rational faculty, then, to be moderated and eventually cured they must be approached by a therapeutic technique that uses the arts of reason. And if judgments are all that the passions are, if there is no part of them that lies outside the rational faculty, then a rational art that sufficiently modifies judgments, seeking out the correct ones and installing them in place of the false, will actually be sufficient for curing Nikidion of the ills that are caused by the passions.[24] False beliefs can be altogether removed, leaving no troublesome trace behind them. If, in addition, the curing of the passions (which, as we shall see, means their total extirpation) is the central task for which Nikidion requires an art of life, then philosophy, in showing that it can cure them, will establish its own practical sovereignty. So the analysis of the passions and the description of a philosophical therapy go hand in hand. Chrysippus wrote, we are told, four books on the passions. In the first three he argued for his analysis of passion and gave his accounts and definitions of the particular passions. The fourth book turned from this theoretical basis to the practice of curing. It was called the *thera-*

---

canonical definitions use *doxa*. The Latin sources show the same pluralism of use: *iudicium* occurs alongside both *opinio* and *opinatio*. (Cic. *TD* 3.61 uses *opinio et iudicium* in defining grief.) Since the Stoics are unusually careful to say exactly what sort of cognitive activity they have in mind, this does not cause a problem for their argument.

[24] Later Stoics who reject Chrysippus' view and posit a natural irrational part of the soul are led to the view that philosophy must be supplemented by music (understood in a rather non-cognitive way) which alone can tame this animal part. See especially the fragments of Diogenes of Babylon *On Music* in *SVF* III, pp. 221–35. Early Stoics value poetry, but on cognitive grounds. Seneca follows the approach of Chrysippan Stoicism: see chapter 12. On all of this see Nussbaum (1993a).

peutikon, the therapeutic book, and also the *ēthikon*, the one concerned with ethical practice. Clearly this book required and rested on the analysis for which the first three books had argued.[25]

But it is one thing to see why a certain thesis is important to a philosopher, quite another to assess its truth. A closer analysis shows, however, that the apparently strange thesis is not merely a handy theoretical tool imposed by force upon the experience of life. It is one of the most powerful candidates for truth in this area; and it is also far less counterintuitive than we might at first think.

These two issues—intuitive acceptability and truth—are closely linked in most contemporary ethical thought. They were also closely linked in the thought of Chrysippus. It would be surprising indeed if he had completely missed the mark where ordinary belief and experience are concerned. For more than any other ancient philosopher, with the possible exception of Aristotle, he is constantly, deeply, and almost obsessively concerned with the close investigation of ordinary thought and language. It is clear that his book on the emotions is no exception to this general policy. Aristotle characteristically begins an inquiry with a brief dialectical summary of ordinary beliefs and sayings on a topic. Chrysippus goes further,[26] filling

---

[25] On the four-book structure of Chrysippus' *Peri Pathōn*, see *PHP* 5.6.45–46, 336D = *SVF* III.458, and 5.7.52, 348D = *SVF* III.460. In citing from the fourth book, Galen sometimes calls it the *therapeutikon*, sometimes the *ēthikon* (once *therapeutikon kai ēthikon*, 5.7.52). Here Galen says that the fourth book was written "apart" from the other three, "added on" (*epigraphomenon*) "on its own" (*idia*). But he consistently speaks of the work as a single four-book whole, or *pragmateia* (e.g., 272D); and his citations from the therapeutic book make clear its closeness to the others in argument and purpose. Indeed, from the surviving fragments it is difficult to see any clear difference—though presumably the final book would have included detailed material on the treatment of the passions that does not survive because Galen is not interested in it. Galen describes the purpose of the fourth book as "to know all the causes" of irrational action (272D); later he says that the fourth book sets out to describe the proportion or harmony according to which the soul is said to be healthy or diseased (304D). One further remark of Galen's is probably misleading. In a different work (*De Loc. Affect*. 3.1 = *SVF* III.457) he uses Chrysippus' books to illustrate his own distinction between the *logikōtera*, i.e., "those that going beyond use examine the nature of things as they are in their own being," and writings intended for use. But a Chrysippan Stoic would be unlikely to make this distinction in this sphere (cf. chapter 9.) In any case, the surviving quotations show us that the fourth book contains a lot of theory, and that the earlier books discuss the emotions in a way that is highly relevant to practice. Judging from Galen's remarks about the relative length of Chrysippus' books and his own, the *On Passions* must have been fairly long: about 250 printed pages in a standard typeface.

[26] Chrysippus and Aristotle seem to be close here. But I think that their reasons for interest in ordinary use are subtly different. For Chrysippus, language reveals a rational structure that exists in the universe; it is important as a sign of that independently existing reality. For

much of his four-book work with scores of observations on ordinary usage, on common expressions, on literary passages used as evidence for ordinary belief, and even on our gestures as evidence of our common conceptions. He clearly thinks that our language and our daily practices reveal truth, and that philosophical theory ignores these data at its peril. Some of the examples recorded by Galen seem tendentious or naive; many more seem, to me at least, to reveal a subtle and careful attention to the nuance of what we say and the conceptual structure revealed in what we say. And it is very clear indeed that Chrysippus thought that his theory of the passions was the one to which everyday intuitions gave strongest support. Galen sometimes objects to his arguments on the grounds that experience refutes them. But more often, and revealingly, he mocks Chrysippus for spending too much time on what non-experts and poets say, too little on the theories of the philosophical experts.[27] This all indicates that we cannot claim to have understood Chrysippus' theory unless we have seen not only how it coheres with his other theories, but also how it might be defended, and commended to a non-Stoic Nikidion, on intuitive and experiential grounds.

As we have seen, there is in Greek thought about the emotions, from Plato and Aristotle straight on through Epicurus, an agreement that the emotions are not simply blind surges of affect, stirrings or sensations that are identified, and distinguished from one another, by their felt quality alone. Unlike appetites such as thirst and hunger, they have an important cognitive element: they embody ways of interpreting the world. The feelings that go with the experience of emotion are hooked up with and rest upon beliefs or judgments that are their basis or ground, in such a way that the emotion as a whole can appropriately be evaluated as true and false, and also as rational or irrational, according to our evaluation of the grounding belief. Since the belief is the ground of the feeling, the feeling, and therefore the emotion as a whole, can be modified as a modification of

---

Aristotle, use is itself more intimately connected with truth, since (or so I think) the reality use reveals does not exist as a set of distinct items in nature, independently of the demarcating activities of mind. However, when we remember that the Stoic universe is itself a rational animal, and that the structure revealed by *logos* is itself, in this way, a homoiomorphic conceptual structure or *logos* (and not only similar in structure, but the larger whole of which this *logos* is a part), the difference becomes far subtler. Neither thinker believes that the universe has a structure apart from *logos* and reason's conceptualizing activity; and this is one reason why, for both, the study of the conceptual structures of discourse is of the highest importance.

[27] See, e.g., *PHP* 3.5.23, 204D: Galen has so far criticized only "all the arguments that have some plausibility and do not invoke the testimony of women, non-experts, etymologies, motions of the hands, upward or downward movements of the head, or poets."

belief. We have seen how these ideas provided Aristotle with accounts of emotions like anger and pity; we have seen how they were put to work in Epicurean therapy.

Two further elements of continuity in the tradition prepare the way for Chrysippus' move. First, the beliefs on which emotions are based prominently include our evaluative beliefs, our beliefs about what is good and bad, worthwhile and worthless, helpful and noxious. To cherish something, to ascribe to it a high value, is to give oneself a basis for the response of profound joy when it is present; of fear when it is threatened; of grief when it is lost; of anger when someone else damages it; of envy when someone else has it and you don't; of pity when someone else loses such a thing through no fault of his or her own. Second, as chapter 3 argued, the evaluative beliefs on which the major emotions rest all have something in common. They all involve the ascription of a high value to vulnerable "external goods"—to items that are to some extent not in the full control of the agent, items that can be affected by happenings in the world. They presuppose, then, the non–self-sufficiency of the most valuable things (or some of them). They embody a conception of the agent's good according to which the good is not simply "at home" inside of him, but consists, instead, in a complex web of connections between the agent and unstable worldly items such as loved friends, city, possessions, the conditions of action. They presuppose that we have hostages to fortune. In this sense, we notice that there is a remarkable unity among the emotions. They share a common basis, and appear to be distinguished from one another more by circumstantial and perspectival considerations than by their grounding beliefs. What we fear for ourselves we pity when it happens to another; what we love and rejoice in today engenders fear lest fortune should remove it tomorrow; we grieve when what we fear has come to pass. When others promote the vulnerable elements of our good, we feel gratitude; the same relation to an external good gives rise to anger, should the action of others prove maleficent.

In all these cases the emotion will not, Aristotle stresses, get off the ground unless an evaluative belief ascribes not only worth, but also serious or high worth, to the uncontrolled external item. Fear requires the thought that important damages can happen to us through no fault of our own; anger, again, requires the thought that the item slighted by another is of serious value. I do not go around fearing that my coffee cup will break; I am not angry if someone takes a paper clip. I do not pity someone who has lost a toothbrush. My breakfast cereal does not fill me with joy and delight; even my morning coffee is not an object of love.

These examples suggest a further thought, one that will be exploited by Stoic therapy. The damages of fortune, when they are seen as trivial or light, and thus prove insufficient to ground an emotion, are frequently seen this way because the object damaged or promoted is itself seen, with respect to its value, as replaceable. Coffee cups and paper clips are rarely reasons for grief, because we don't care which one we use. There is a readily renewable supply, and all alike serve the function for which we value the item. If we try to imagine a case where the loss of a coffee cup would be an occasion for grief, we find ourselves imagining a case in which the particular item is endowed by the owner with a historical or sentimental value that makes it a unique particular. This suggests that the removal of the sense of particularity and specialness, in big things as well as small, might contribute to the eradication of fear, anger, and even love, should we wish to effect their eradication.[28]

This tradition of Greek thought about the emotions seems, so far, to be not bizarre, but intuitively quite plausible. If Chrysippus does indeed end up in a counterintuitive position, he starts from a basis that seems to articulate our intuitions about the emotions as well as any philosophical reflection on this topic ever has. Chrysippus places himself within this tradition; but he also makes a radical departure from it. To see what he has done, we need to distinguish four theses that are defended within this tradition about the relationship between belief or judgment and passion.

1. *Necessity.* The relevant belief[29] is necessary for the passion.
2. *Constituent Element.* The belief is a (necessary) constituent element in the passion.
3. *Sufficiency.* The belief is sufficient for the passion.
4. *Identity.* The belief is identical to the passion.

To be precise enough, this classification would need several refinements. First, we would need to distinguish occurrent passions from entrenched dispositional states. Stoic theory does this well, as we shall later see. Second, we would need to get clear in each case about exactly what level of belief we are working with, and about how the different levels interact. Generic beliefs that at least some external uncontrolled items have high value; more concrete beliefs that there are serious damages that I may suffer by another's agency, through no fault of my own; the very concrete belief

---

[28] For a typical example of a Stoic therapeutic exercise focusing on this idea, see Epict. *Ench.* 3. And see also Sen. *Ep.* 63.11, cited later. There may be antecedents of this therapy in Plato's *Symposium*: see Nussbaum (1986a) chapter 6.

[29] Of course it may also be a complex family of beliefs.

that X has wronged me in such and such a way just now—all of these are at work in the passion of anger; they need to be distinguished and their role in the passion assessed. Again, the Stoics thought carefully about this. For now, however, I shall be thinking of a specific occurrent evaluative belief (for example, "X has seriously damaged an important element of my good life just now") that is the basis for a concrete episode of passion; this specific belief of course presupposes the more general ones, and would be removed with their removal.

To put things roughly and somewhat crudely: Plato and Epicurus hold (1) and possibly none of the other theses—though their position on (2) is unclear, and Epicurus might be prepared to grant (3).[30] Aristotle, I have argued, holds (1) and (2). His position on (3) is unclear, but his rhetorical strategies rely on the *usual* sufficiency of belief for passion. Zeno, Chrysippus' predecessor, seems to have held (1), in a causal form that is incompatible with (2), and also (3). He says that the belief reliably causes a fluttering feeling, and that this feeling, not the belief, is what the passion itself is. He appears to deny (2); and yet there is need for caution here. For it appears that he individuates and defines passions at least partially via their causes, the beliefs; and it seems to be his view that the very same feeling not only could not be caused in another manner, but would not, if it were otherwise caused, count as that pathos.[31] All of these people, then, defend a close and intimate connection between passion and belief; but this connection stops short of identity.

[30] See also Galen *PHP*, 240D, who identifies Epicurus' position as (3) and links it with Zeno's.

[31] For Zeno's position, see *SVF* I.205–15; the relevant passages of Galen are I.209, 210. See also Galen *PHP* 4.3.1–2, 246D; 5.1.4, 292D; 4.2.6–7, 240D. Galen consistently insists on the difference between Zeno and Chrysippus. There is some evidence, on the other hand, that Zeno on occasion did identify passion and judgment—see, e.g., Cic. *TD* 3.74–75 = *SVF* I.212, where Zeno is said to have added "fresh" (cf. subsequent discussion) to the definition of distress as *opinio praesentis mali*. The general classification of the *pathē*, along, perhaps, with the canonical definitions, is ascribed to Zeno (and Hecato) by DL 7.110–11. Just after this, Diogenes Laertius writes, "They believe that the *pathē* are judgments as Chrysippus says in his *Peri Pathōn*." "They" presumably means "Stoics": but it is significant that Diogenes Laertius saw no significant shift of ground here. At any rate, it is clear that both Zeno and Chrysippus had "one-part" views of passion; neither recognized an independent emotional part of the soul. I do not agree with Inwood (1985) that the difference makes no difference, for there are important intuitive differences, as we shall see; and we should emphasize that to preserve intuitions was one of Chrysippus' goals and achievements.

The substantial literature on the possible differences between Zeno and Chrysippus is summarized in Inwood (1985). Some major contributions are Pohlenz (1938, 1970), Voelke (1965), Glibert-Thirry (1977), Rist (1969), Lloyd (1978).

III

Now we want to know: what leads Chrysippus to take the final step?[32] We might have thought that the Zenonian and/or the Aristotelian position would have been sufficient to defend whatever picture of philosophical therapy the Stoics wish to defend. Now clearly Chrysippus does not ignore or deny the affective and kinetic aspects of passion—for he says that the judgment that is identical with the passion is itself a *pleonazousa hormē*, an excessive inclination.[33] But he wants to say that the sort of tumultuous movement it is, is a judgment; and that its seat is the rational soul. Why does he want to say this?

Here we frequently get a superficial answer. The Stoics, we are reminded, recognize only a single part to the soul, namely the rational part. They reject Plato's division of the soul into three distinct elements. Hence they have to make all psychological conditions conditions of this one element, no matter how odd or implausible this might seem.[34] This seems to me quite inadequate as an answer. It was not an item of unargued dogma for the Stoics that the soul has just one part; it was a conclusion, and a conclusion of arguments in moral psychology, prominently including arguments about the passions. Galen tells us that Chrysippus argued first for the existence of some *alogos dunamis*, some irrational capability, in the soul, and then went on to consider the relative merits of a view that separates passion from judgment and the view he finally adopted, arguing against a pluralist psychology and in favor of his own one-part account of passion, as the view that best explained human irrationality.[35] Posidonius,

[32] Major discussions of Chrysippus' theory include Frede (1986), Lloyd (1978), Inwood (1985); see also Pigeaud (1981), and the works cited in the previous note. On Posidonius' criticisms of Chrysippus, see Kidd (1971b).

[33] Cf. Plut. *Virt. Mor.* 449C = *SVF* III.384, and especially Galen *PHP* 4.8.2–18, 240–42D = *SVF* III.462. Chrysippus writes as if he is explicating the traditional Zenonian definition.

[34] This answer is first given by Galen (drawing perhaps on Posidonius), who thinks that all intuitive evidence about the *pathē* points in the direction of the tripartite view. It recurs in many accounts. Lloyd (1978) concludes that Chrysippus could not have really had the view that emotions are simply judgments: he must have meant "judgments that lead to irrational feelings." But this seems to go against the evidence of Galen, which says that Chrysippus argued against the view that passions are things supervening on judgments and in favor of the view that they are the judgments.

[35] Galen, *PHP* 4.1.14ff., 4.3.1ff. Galen reproves Chrysippus for not considering Plato's view, but arguing instead only against the view that passions are irrational items that supervene on or follow on judgment. But it is not clear that we should believe this. Chrysippus may not have spent time quoting Plato; but he clearly produced, by Galen's own account, a great

a perfectly good Stoic, takes the opposite course, restoring the three parts of the soul and placing emotion in an irrational part, because he felt that this gave Stoicism its best account of human irrationality.[36] So what needs explaining is precisely the fact that is being invoked as an explanation—namely, why Chrysippus decides to make all passional states the conditions of a single part or faculty, and the same faculty that does our practical reasoning. Why does he think this the best and most plausible account?

We must begin by noting that a judgment, for the Stoics, is defined as an assent to an appearance.[37] In other words, it is a process that has two stages. First, it occurs to Nikidion, or strikes her, that such and such is the case. (Stoic appearances are usually propositional.) It looks to her that way, she sees things that way—but so far she hasn't really accepted it. She can now go on to accept or embrace the appearance, commit herself to it; in that case, it has become her judgment. She can also deny or repudiate it: in that case, she is judging the contradictory. Or, like the Skeptic she was in chapter 8, she can live with it without committing herself one way or the other. Recall Aristotle's similar analysis. The sun strikes Nikidion as being about a foot across.[38] (That's the way it looks to her, that's what she sees it as.) But if she has acquired a belief, to which she is committed, that the sun is larger than the inhabited world, she will reject the appearance. She distances herself from it, she does not accept or embrace it—though of course it may go on looking that way to her. She says to herself, "That's the way it looks to me, but of course that's not the way things really are." In this simple perceptual case there seems to be nothing odd about saying both that the appearance presents itself to her cognitive faculties and that its acceptance or rejection is the work of those very faculties. Embracing or acknowledging an appearance, committing oneself to it as true, seems to be a task that requires the discriminating power of cognition. And unless we have an anachronistic Humean picture of cognition, according to which it is motionless, performing calculations without commitment, it seems in no way strange to say that it is reason itself that reaches out and takes that

---

deal of intuitive and literary evidence in favor of his view and against the view that the passions inhabit a separate irrational part. For a fine discussion of Chrysippus' use of literary examples, see Gill (1983).

[36] See Kidd (1971b), who, however, insists that Galen is not to be altogether trusted in his assimilation of Posidonius to Plato, and who shows that Posidonius retains many essential points of Chrysippus' view.

[37] See also Frede (1986).

[38] *Insomn.* 460b19. On *phantasia* and belief, and Aristotle on the emotions of animals, see chapters 3 and 8, and also Sorabji (1993).

appearance to itself, saying, so to speak, "Yes, that's the one I'll have. That's the way things are." The classic way of distinguishing humans from other animals, from Aristotle on, is, in fact, to point to the fact that animals just move in the way appearances cause them, without making judgments.[39] They move the way things strike them, without commitment. The extra element of selection, recognition, and commitment that sets us apart from the beasts is taken to be the contribution of reason. In fact, we might say that this is paradigmatically what reason is: that faculty in virtue of which we commit ourselves to a view of the way things are.

Let us now examine a different case.[40] A person Nikidion loves very much has died. It strikes her, it appears to her, that something of enormous and irreplaceable value that was there a short time ago is there in her life no longer. If we want to display the appearance pictorially—a conception of appearing that some Stoic texts occasionally suggest—we might think of a stretch of daily life with a big empty space in it, the space that the loved person used to fill by his presence. In fact, the representation of this evaluative proposition, properly done, might require a whole series of picturings, as she would notice the person's absence in every corner of her existence,[41] notice the breaking of a thousand delicate and barely perceptible threads. Another sort of picturing would also be possible: she could see that wonderful beloved face, and see it both as enormously beloved and as irretrievably cut off from her. What we must insist on, however, is that the appearance is propositional: its content is that such and such is the case; and it is evaluative. Whether pictorially displayed or not, it represents the dead person as of enormous importance, as unlike anything or anyone else in the world.[42]

So far, we are still at the stage of appearing. Now several things might happen. She might reject or repudiate the appearance, push it away from

---

[39] Cf. Aristotle, *EN* 1147b3–5, *Metaph.* 980b25–28. On this view of reason and belief, see also Burnyeat (1980a).

[40] Grief and mourning were central examples for Chrysippus—cf. *PHP* 4.7.

[41] I have depicted the grief as self-referential: strictly speaking, there seem to be two aspects here. I mourn the dead person both as a part of my existence and experience, and also for his own sake, mourning the loss of life and activity to him. It is not clear that the Stoics make this distinction.

[42] Strictly speaking, the recognition of qualitative uniqueness does not seem to be necessary—for I might believe that each and every human life is of enormous importance and value, no matter how like or unlike humans are to one another in both intrinsic and historical/relational characteristics. But the ascription of an extremely high value to a particular object is frequently connected with, and also nourished by, the thought that the object is irreplaceable.

her—if, for example, she decides that it is a nightmare or a morbid imagining. She might, if she is still a Skeptic, get herself into an attitude of complete neutrality about it, so that she neither commits herself to it nor rejects it. But suppose that she embraces it, really accepts or assents to it, commits herself to it as the way things are. Is a full assent to the idea that someone tremendously beloved is forever lost to her compatible with emotional equanimity? Chrysippus' claim is that it is not. She cannot really perform that act of recognition without profound upheaval. Not if what she is recognizing is that proposition with all its evaluative elements. Suppose she says, quite calmly, "Yes, I know that the person I love most is dead and I'll never see him again. But I feel nothing; it does not disturb me at all." (Remember Cicero's story about the father who says, on learning of his son's death, "I was already aware that I had begotten a mortal.") Chrysippus will say, This person is in a state of denial. She is not really assenting to that proposition. She may be saying the words, but there is something in her that is resisting it.[43] Or if she is assenting to something, it is not to that same proposition. She may be assenting to the proposition that a mortal human being has died: even (just possibly) to the proposition that X (the man she loves) has died; what she has not assented to is the proposition, that the person whom she loves and values above all others,[44] has died. For to recognize this is to be violently disturbed.

Notice the crucial importance of getting clear about which proposition we have in mind here. Some of the literature about Chrysippus' view makes the salient proposition one without any evaluative element, say, "Socrates is dead." We have already seen that the beliefs or judgments that are hooked up with emotion in the pre-Stoic tradition are judgments about value: cherishings and disvaluings of external uncontrolled items. We should now insist that the appearances that the Stoic agent either acknowledges or does not are, similarly, appearances with a marked evaluative element. To be more precise, in order to be equivalent to a passion they must have three features. First, they must make a claim about what, from the point of view of that agent, is valuable and fine, or the contrary. The

---

[43] Cf. Aristotle on the akratic: he mouths the words of the correct proposition, but doesn't really activate it in his life. He is like an actor, or like a drunk reciting the words of Empedocles. Aristotle adds that it is like this with a pupil who recites a lesson, but can't be really said to have, as yet, the relevant knowledge: it must "grow to be a part of him, and this requires time" (*EN* 1147a10–24).

[44] I do not intend to suggest that loving implies high *moral* evaluation; I mean only to say that it implies thinking of the object as of tremendous importance, however that importance is to be understood.

texts speak always of the "opinion of good and bad," the "supposition of good and bad"—both in giving the general theory and in defining particular passions (e.g., *SVF* III.385, 386, 387, 391, 393, 394).[45] And we should insist here that the propositions express not simply the agent's desires and preferences, but his or her values: the scheme of ends believed choiceworthy, by which she chooses to live. Thus several texts insist that the agent not only believes that something bad is at hand, but believes that it is the sort of bad thing about which it would be right to be upset.[46] This added element of affirmation shows us that we are not talking about mere desiderative whim and caprice.

Second, the propositions ascribe to the item in question not only some value, but a serious or very high value (or disvalue).[47] Chrysippus tells us explicitly that the mistake, and the passion, come not in thinking the things in question to be good, but in thinking them to be much better than they are—in fact, to be the most important things (cf. *PHP* 5.5.20–22, 262D = *SVF* III.480; compare Galen's paraphrase, which adds the word *megista*, "greatest"—264D). Similarly, accounts of the dispositional conditions that underlie particular episodes of passion make them equivalent to a belief that something is very worth pursuing (*valde expetenda*, Cic. *TD* 4.26 = *SVF* III.427, Sen. *Ep.* 75.11 = *SVF* III.428; the Greek has *sphodra*, cf. *SVF* III.421), although that thing is in fact either only slightly choiceworthy or not choiceworthy at all. Again, a passage of Posidonius, reporting Chrysippus, speaks of a conviction that a thing contains a "great

---

[45] There are several roughly equivalent ways in which we could express the proposition, and its evaluative element. The definition of *lupē* (grief or distress) is "a fresh belief that a bad thing is present." This suggests that in my example the proposition about the lover's death should be, "A very horrible event is here at hand." The evaluative element would be the strong disvalue of that event. I have instead placed the evaluative element on the other side, so to speak, by attributing high positive value to the lover who is said in the proposition to be irretrievably lost. The texts insist (cf. section IV) that it should not matter which conception we adopt. For if something has a very high positive value for us we view its destruction or loss as a correspondingly bad thing. One might dispute the connection in a number of ways. For example, Epicurus would say that to value highly the life of a friend will not, in rational people, lead to the judgment that the friend's death is bad—not for him at any rate, and possibly not for you. But the Stoic equivalence view does seem to capture well the structure of most people's desires.

[46] Cf. *SVF* III.391.

[47] Frede (1986) seems to take this element of seriousness or intensity to be not a part of the content of the proposition itself, but rather to be a way this proposition has of appearing to a certain agent. Although it is true that *phantasiai* contain more than their strictly propositional contents, the textual evidence strongly and without any exception I know of supports the view that the intensity of concern with the object is part of the propositional content.

benefit" (fr. 164 E-K). The belief that money is a good thing is said to turn into a chronic infirmity only "when one holds that money is the greatest good and even supposes that life is not worth living for the man who has lost it" (*PHP* 4.5.25, 264D).[48]

Finally, the belief must have a certain content: it must be concerned with vulnerable external things, things that can fail to be present, that can arrive by surprise, that are not fully under our control. This is common ground between Chrysippus and the pre-Stoic tradition. The Stoics do not explicitly include this in their definitions, though they repeatedly underline the connection between passion and a concern with external goods, and emphasize that a person who ceases to be concerned with externals will be free of passion. For this failure to be explicit they are reproached by Posidonius, who points out that the wise man ascribes the highest possible value to his wisdom, and yet does not feel fear for its loss, longing for its presence, and so forth (fr. 164 E-K, 266D).[49] Again, sometimes the texts speak as if the relevant group of judgments was identified by its falsity, relative to Stoic moral theory. This seems to be a strategic error too, since the Stoics claim to be able to persuade pupils like Nikidion, who start out with another conception of good. The passion-beliefs all share, as the more concrete definitions make clear, a subject matter; and they can and should be identified and defined with reference to that subject matter. This would answer Posidonius' worry and make more perspicuous the motivations behind the theory and the call for extirpation.

So far we have gotten only to thesis 3 on our list. We have argued that a judgment is an embracing of an appearing proposition; and that the real embracing of or assent to a certain sort of evaluative proposition is sufficient for being moved emotionally. It entails the emotion; if emotion is not there then we are entitled to say that real acknowledgment of the proposition is not (or not yet) there. But all of this—though it goes against Aristotle's claim that the belief-component of the emotion is independent of the feeling—could, apparently, be satisfied by a causal picture like Zeno's, in which the belief of necessity produces the passion, which is still seen as a distinct item. We still need to know, then, what leads Chrysippus to make

[48] This is actually Galen, imagining how Chrysippus would develop his view further in reply to objections. He is staying close to Posidonius' account of the orthodox Stoic view.

[49] Posidonius also considers the attitude of the person who is making progress toward wisdom. Here it is less obvious that the attitude in question could not be a *pathos*—given the elusive character of wisdom and the absence of sufficient conditions for its acquisition. But it is clear that the Stoics are committed to saying that it is not.

the emotion itself a function of reason, and to make it identical with the assent that is the judgment.

First, then, why should the upheaval be seen as a state of reason? Well, what is it that gets the terrible shock of grief? Nikidion thinks of the person she loves—she embraces in her mind the fact that that extraordinary person will never be with her again—and she is shaken. Where, she asks herself? Is the grief a fluttering off in her ear, or a trembling in her stomach? Is it a movement in some animal appetitive nature that she shares with rabbits and birds?[50] No, these answers seem wrong. It seems clear that we don't want to relegate the grief itself to such trivial and undignified seats as these. We want to give it a seat that is specifically human, and discerning enough, complex enough, to house such a complex and evaluatively discriminating response. What part of me, she asks, is worthy of grieving for the person I love? Perhaps we could invent a special emotional part of the soul to house it. But in order to be capable of housing it, this part would have to be capable of conceiving of the beloved person in all his beauty and specialness; of comprehending and responding to the evaluative proposition on which the grief is based, even of accepting it. It would have to be able to know and properly estimate the richness of their love for each other; to insist on the tremendous importance of that love, even in the face of Stoic arguments belittling it; and so forth.[51] But then it will need to be very much like reason: capable of the same acts of selection, evaluation, and vision that are usually taken to be the works of reason. It then begins to seem peculiar to redouble faculties. If we have a faculty on hand that can perform this job, we surely would do best to make the grief a state of that same faculty. The point is, once we make the emotions as cognitive and selective as Chrysippus, building on his tradition, argued that they must be, Reason looks like just the place to house them.

But, one might object, this is not yet clear. For if it is true that emotion's

[50] Galen and Posidonius treat it as obvious that animals and young children have the same *pathē* that we do, and they use this as a point against Chrysippus. I believe that they are correct only insofar as it would also be correct to ascribe to children and to certain animals complex cognitive attitudes. Seneca and other Chrysippans regard it as obvious that animals do not have full-fledged passions: see, e.g., *Ir.* 1.3.6–8.

[51] Chrysippus stressed this element of deliberate evaluation and even deliberate rejection of contrary arguments, in distinguishing between *pathē* and other errors of reason. Passionate people have cognitive commitments; when they knowingly go against the correct Stoic course, it is not because some force just blows them away. They are led by a contrary view of things, they (often consciously) disobey reason—something that the tripartite people often say, but which their view cannot explain, since it makes the "disobeying" part too brutish even to understand the opposing argument. Cf. *PHP* 4.2 and 4.6, passim.

seat must be capable of many cognitive operations, there also seems to be an affective side to emotion that we have difficulty housing in the soul's rational part. We have already begun to respond to this point by stressing the fact that Stoic reason is dynamic, not static. It moves, embraces, refuses. It can move rapidly or slowly; it can move directly or with hesitation. We have imagined it entertaining the appearance of the loved person's death and then, so to speak, rushing toward it, opening itself to take it in. So why would a faculty this dynamic, this versatile, be unable to house, as well, the disorderly motions of the ensuing grief? Sophocles' Creon, confronted by the death of his only son, says, "I accept this knowledge and am shaken in my reason" (*Antigone* 1095). What Chrysippus wants us to see is that this can happen; reason is capable of that. But if this is so, why push off the affect into some corner of the soul more brutish, less discriminating, less closely connected with the cognitive and receptive processes that we have seen to be involved in grieving? "I recognize this and (incidentally) I am shaken in my gut." Here we lose the close connection between the recognition and the being shaken that Chrysippus' analysis, and Creon's speech, give us. No, we want to say, the recognizing and the upheaval belong to one and the same part of her, the part with which she makes sense of the world.

I have spoken of the recognition and the "ensuing" upheaval. The final stage in Chrysippus' argument is to tell us that this distinction is wrong and misleading. When Nikidion grieves, she does not first of all coolly embrace the proposition, "My wonderful lover is dead," and then set about grieving. No, the real, full recognition of that dreadful event is the upheaval. It is like putting your hand straight down on the sharp point of a nail. The baneful appearance sits there, asking her what she is going to do about it. If she goes up to embrace it, if she takes it into herself, opens herself to receive it, she is at that very moment putting the world's knife into her own insides.[52] That's not preparation for upheaval, that's upheaval itself. That very act of assent is itself a wrenching, tearing violation of her self-sufficiency and her undisturbed condition. The passion is a "very violent motion" that carries us along, "pushing us violently" toward action (*SVF* III.390). But this does not imply that it is not a form of recognition. For, as Chysippus insists, "It is belief itself that contains the disorderly kinetic element" (*SVF* III.394). Knowing can itself be violent.

Seneca adds a useful distinction. Sometimes, he says, the presence of an appearance might evoke a reaction even when the appearance itself is not accepted or taken in, but, so to speak, just strikes against your surface.

---

[52] For related imagery in Seneca, see chapter 12.

Sudden pallor, a leap of the heart, sexual excitation—all of these bodily movements may be caused by the appearance alone, without assent or judgment.[53] But these are not passions: these are mere bodily movements.[54] It is only when the appearance has been allowed in, that we get—in the very act of recognition—the tumult of the mind that is the passion (*Ir.* 2.3).

In short: we have here a dynamic conception of practical knowing or judging, in which a judgment is not a cool inert act of intellect set over against a proposition, but an acknowledgment, with the core of my being, that such and such is the case. To acknowledge a proposition is to realize in one's being its full significance, to take it in and be changed by it. On this conception—which seems to me to be a powerful one—there is every reason to insist that passion and judgment do not come apart: rather, the passion is itself a certain sort of assent or acknowledgment: an acknowledgment of the tremendously high importance of something beyond my control, an acknowledgment appropriately called "excessive" because it transgresses the limits prescribed by right reason for our relation to things external.[55]

Chrysippus adds one further significant element to his account. The judgment, to be equivalent to a passion,[56] must be *prosphaton*: not yet spoiled or digested, "fresh." This word, used frequently of food, and also of corpses newly dead,[57] implies that no decomposition has yet set in—the item in question still has its pristine character. The point of this seems to be to allow for certain sorts of affective distancing, especially over time, compatibly with the retention of the same belief or judgment. When the person Nikidion is mourning has been dead for a long time, she will no longer have the violent recognition of his death that is identical with grief. Without the supplement, Chrysippus would then have been required to say that she no longer judges or believes that he is dead; or, equally implausible, that this

[53] See chapter 3 on Aristotle's *MA* chapter 11.

[54] For a convincing defense of the view that Seneca is an orthodox Chrysippan on this point, see Inwood (1993).

[55] For this interpretation of "excessive" as "transgressing the limits set by right reason," see also Inwood (1985), with a convincing discussion of Chrysippus' use of the phrase *logou summetria*, the balance or commensurateness of reason.

[56] Strictly speaking, "freshness" is involved in the definitions only of passions relating to the present, not the future: *SVF* III.391.

[57] Representative examples: of corpses, Hom. *Il.* 24.757, Hdt. 2.89, 2.121–24; of food and drink, Ar. *HA* 520b31, *PA* 675b32; Ps.-Ar. *Probl.* 924b28; of actions and events, Aes. *Cho.* 804, Soph. fr. 130, Ar. *HA* 509b31, *GA* 764a6, *Rhet.* 1375b27, 1376a7, Ps.-Ar. *Probl.* 907b25; of emotions and thoughts, Lys. 18.19, Ar. *EE* 1237a24, *MM* 1203b4; and see LSJ s.v.

cool and distant recognition is itself identical with grief. He does not wish to say either of these things. For there are many ways to acknowledge an irreplaceable loss, and over time those ways naturally transform themselves. When, like food, the loss has been assimilated or digested, she will still have the same judgment and the same recognition, but it seems wrong to say that she still has the passion. Loss of "freshness" is usually portrayed in the texts as a temporal matter; though we might be able to imagine other factors that might distance her from passion without entailing a refusal to recognize or admit the proposition.

It may seem that here Chrysippus gives the game away. For isn't he admitting after all that there is something more to grieving than believing that . . . ? And isn't this something, this "freshness," an irrational element that has nothing to do itself with grieving? Yes, and no. Yes, having a certain belief is not, we now see, sufficient for grieving (though we should remember that Chrysippus advances this point with uncharacteristic tentativeness, saying that the phenomenon is "hard to understand" [*asullogiston*]). No, because the difference is itself a cognitive difference—a difference in the way that proposition is active in, received by, the self; above all, a difference in its relation to other propositions. The "fresh" acceptance is something tearing and wrenching. Since it concerns her deepest values and projects, it upsets everything in me, all the cognitive structures of hope, cherishing, and expectation that she has built up around those values.[58] But when the proposition has been there for a long time, when the element of surprise and tearing is gone, it has lost its extreme sharpness, its intrusive cutting edge, since she has by that time adjusted her life and the rest of her beliefs to fit with it. It does not assault the other beliefs, it sits alongside of them. For example, she doesn't any longer look forward to happy times that she will share with her lover. She doesn't have the belief that he will be with her tonight, or expect to see his face when she opens the door. These, however, are cognitive changes. It was the discrepancy of the death-proposition with so many others that gave grief its bite, and time removes this discrepancy—not because the grief-proposition changes, but because other related propositions change. As Chrysippus says in this very passage, "Things don't present the same appearances."[59]

---

[58] This shows us a further reason why a Stoic will not grieve: through the practice of *praemeditatio* she will have accepted bad things before they happen and will adjust her hopes and expectations to the knowledge of life's tremendous uncertainty. For just a few of the hundreds of references to this technique in Stoic texts, see Cic. *TD* 3.29–34, 4.57; Epict. *Disc.* 1.4.20; *Ench.* 21; Sen. *Ep.* 4.6; 14.3; etc.

[59] *SVF* III.466 = Galen *PHP* 4.7.12ff. Chrysippus says that the opinion that remains is that

Chrysippus' picture has interesting implications for the analysis of ethical conflict. On the parts-of-the-soul view, conflict is viewed as a struggle between two forces, different in character and simultaneously active within the soul. Reason leads this way, desire pushes that way. The outcome may or may not be a matter of sheer strength; what is crucial is that both forces are active together, until one wins. Suppose that Nikidion is mourning for the person she loves; suppose she is also, at the same time, striving to be a good Stoic, distancing herself from grief with the thought that virtue is sufficient for happiness. The parts view will say that her irrational element is doing the grieving, while the rational part is thinking philosophical thoughts and endeavoring to restrain her from grief. Chrysippus would urge us, instead, to regard the conflict as an oscillation of the whole soul between recognition and denial. He speaks of the soul "turning and shifting as a whole," "not the conflict and civil war of two parts, but the turning of a single reason in two different directions, which escapes our notice on

---

"a bad thing is present"—i.e., I still judge the death to be a bad thing, not just to have been at one time a bad thing. (See also Cicero's explanation of *recens* at *TD* 3.74ff.) Freshness figures only in the definitions of the present passions. Inwood connects loss of freshness with ceasing to accept the proposition that it is appropriate to be upset. There seems to be no evidence for this; and we have seen that that opinion is really a part of the evaluative content of the main proposition.

Two further suggestions have now been made in Duncan (1991), a very subtle treatment of this entire topic. First, he notes that when a bad event such as a death is recent, many cues in my environment will call the relevant impression to mind; as time goes on, I have fewer occasions for thinking about it. This seems true, but not likely to be an explanation of Stoic "freshness," which has to concern some change in the way the proposition itself strikes me, not just the number of times it strikes me. Duncan's second suggestion is, however, a valuable alternative to my interpretation. He points out that over time, as memory fades, the particular value my lover (for example) had for me becomes vague, and the corresponding propositional appearances likewise. "Particular experiences, we claimed, gave rise to particular types of value. Without a continual supply of such experiences to nourish it, the true character of valuations perhaps fades for want of sustenance." He adds that, when memory brings back that full particularity, we are often thrown back into "the pronounced disorder of our initial grief."

Finally, in my 1993 Gifford Lectures (Nussbaum, forthcoming a), developing a quasi-Stoic theory in my own way, I argue that over time the proposition alters with respect to its eudaimonistic content, as I reshape my life and goals. It was once true that "a person who is absolutely central to my life has died." Over time, the centrality shifts into the past tense, as I find myself able to go on living without that person, and adopt other attachments. Studies of disordered mourning—e.g., in Bowlby (1980)—show that the failure of grief to fade over time is usually connected to a failure to reformulate a conception of what is most important in one's life: the person remains fixed on the lost object as still of central, even paramount, importance for her entire life.

account of the sharpness and swiftness of the change" (*SVF* III.459 = Plut. *Virt. Mor.* 441C, 441F).[60] At one moment, she assents (her whole being assents) to the idea that an irreplaceable wonderful person has departed from her life. At another moment, she distances herself from that knowledge, saying, "No, you will find someone else." Or, "that is just one person like many others." Or, in the words of Seneca: "You have buried the one you love; go look for someone to love. It is better to replace your love than to weep for him" (*Ep.* 63.11). Then the thought of her lover, with his particular eyes, his ways of moving and talking, overwhelms her, and she assents, once again, to the thought that something has gone from her life that she can never replace. Chrysippus claims that this story of oscillation and shifting perspective is a more accurate account of the inner life of mourning than the story of battle and struggle. The oscillation may of course be extremely rapid; his point is that in this rhythm of embracing and denial, this uneven intermittance of vision, we have a more accurate analysis of the struggle of mourning than the parts model can provide. When she denies the evaluative proposition about her lover's specialness, at that moment she really is not grieving. When she is fully acknowledging that irreplaceability, she is not at the same time committing herself to a Stoic view of the good. We cannot fully comprehend the complex agony of these conflicts if we downplay their cognitive content, thinking in terms of contending forces. They must be seen as urgent struggles of reason with itself concerning what is valuable and fine in the universe, concerning nothing less than how to imagine the world. To struggle against grief is to strive toward a different view of the universe, in which that face does not appear, luminous and wonderful, on every path; in which places, no longer seen as habitations for that particular form, flatten out and lose their agonizing sharpness.

The picture of oscillation can explain one further feature of the experience of mourning that the parts model fails to notice. In my example, the thought of the Stoic attitude toward loss and the relapse into grief were not accidentally connected; one can be seen to have been, in a strange way, the cause of the other. It was the fact that Nikidion noticed herself looking for someone else to love—she caught herself saying Seneca's cold words about replacing—that threw her back, so to speak, into the arms of her grief. It was the cognitive content of one picture that reminded her violently of the

---

[60] For an excellent treatment of this part of Chrysippus' view, with reference to his interpretation of Euripides' *Medea*, see Gill (1983); see also Campbell (1985). For this interpretation of Euripides' *Medea*'s conflict, see also Epict. *Disc.* 1.28.7.

opposing picture: the very suggestion of other replacements that prompted the return of that one face—as the ebbing tide is followed inexorably by the flood. The parts model cannot explain this rhythm, except to say that sometimes one force, sometimes the other, wins the upper hand. Chrysippus' view strikingly anticipates the account of mourning in Proust, when it suggests that the explanatory connections are tighter, and work through the very cognitive content of the opposing pictures. Just as it is the thought of making love with other women that awakens Marcel's grief and love for Albertine, until that love, like a raging lion, takes over the heart with its own violent view of the world, so here it is the vision of undifferentiated flatness that summons the vision of the single point, which returns with triumphant force as, in pain, she embraces it.

Notice that we have here, subtly delineated, two conceptions of mourning: the mourning of time, which is compatible with the retention of recognition and acknowledgment, and the mourning of denial, which cuts short the natural process of grief's digestion by veering over to a different view of the world. If Nikidion mourns in the first way, the way most people mourn, she will find her grief diminishing gradually, as her judgment loses its "freshness." She will eventually stop grieving altogether, but she will continue to retain the very same judgment.[61] She never tells herself that the person who died was not uniquely beloved. She never alters her fundamental commitment to that love. She may in time find another love; but she will not for that reason give up her thought that the first person was unique and irreplaceable; she will not go over to Seneca's flattened view, and she will probably continue to find it a shocking view. This means that she will be likely to see her new love, too, as a unique and irreplaceable individual, qualitatively distinct from the other, and indeed from all other people in the universe. So she will still be loving in a way that leaves her vulnerable to loss in the future. Because she has not altered her judgments, she remains the sort of person for whom grief is possible and natural. If she mourns in the second way, the way described in my example, the extinction of grief is the result of a more fundamental restructuring of her cognitive commitments. The grief is extinguished by the refusal of the evaluative proposition and the acceptance of a contradictory proposition. By the time that grief is gone, she will have denied the value of something she once valued supremely; and her attitude to a new love can hardly fail to be different in

---

[61] If we accept Duncan's proposal, however (see n. 59), the judgment will remain the same only in its general outlines, and will shift in its degree of concreteness. If we accept my Gifford Lecture proposal, the tenses in a part of the judgment will shift.

consequence. (Proust, mourning in the second way, comes to understand that each beloved woman is simply an instantiation of the "general form" of his needs and desires, and that love has, really, nothing to do with the individuating qualities of the loved one.) She will be removed in a global way, from the possibility of future grief. As Chrysippus would say (recommending the second way),[62] she will be that much closer to being really cured. We shall shortly see how he argues for the second way.

IV

As we by now expect, the Stoic passions will be very close to one another, resting, as they all do, on some kind of high evaluation of externals. And they are classified accordingly in the formal definitional accounts that become canonical in the school, with reference to two distinctions: the distinction between good and bad, and the distinction between present and future, as these opposites figure in the propositions to whose content passion is a response.[63] Thus, there are four basic emotions: (1) judgment that what is presently at hand is good: called delight (*hēdonē*); (2) judgment that something still in the future is good or valuable: called longing or appetition (*epithumia*); (3) judgment that what is presently at hand is bad: called distress (*lupē*); and (4) judgment that what is still in the future is bad: called fear (*phobos*).[64] (Note that to recognize that a possible or future

---

[62] Chrysippus suggests, however, that the two sorts of mourning can be connected: for when grief has lost freshness one may also hope that "reason will make its way in and take up its place, so to speak, and expose the irrationality of the affection" *PHP* 4.7.26–28, 286D = *SVF* III.467.

[63] There is some evidence that the Stoics (or some of them) regarded the two future emotions as prior in some way: they "lead off" (*prohēgeisthai*); the present species are the "subsequent" responses to the results of our longings and fears, "pleasure occurring when we get what we desire or escape what we try to avoid and pain when we miss what we desire or run into what we fear" (see Arius Didymus in Stob. *Ecl.* 2.88–89, translated and discussed in Inwood [1985] 146). Epictetus makes a similar remark about the relationship among the four, though without any claim of priority. The claim seems to be (*pace* Inwood) no more than a straightforward remark about temporal sequence: for any imagined good or bad event (relative to my scheme of values) it will be in the future for me, and so an object of fear or longing, before it is (if it ever is) in the present for me.

[64] I have used "delight" and "distress" to translate *hēdonē* and *lupē*, rather than the more obvious "pleasure" and "pain." I have done so because these are genera that have as their species only specifically human emotions, and not the bodily feelings and reactions that we share with animals. I believe that the Stoics were not giving a surprising analysis of bodily feeling, or denying that animals feel simple bodily pleasures and pains, such as thirst and

item is good or valuable is ipso facto to reach out for it; that's what it is really to have that recognition.) There are in each case numerous sub-species, depending upon the specific subject matter of the content of the proposition. Pity is distress at the undeserved sufferings of another; envy is distress at the good fortunes of another, viewed as a bad thing for me; mourning is defined as distress at the untimely death of a beloved person; and so forth.[65]

In some cases as well, we find the definition mentioning the specific kinetic character of the recognition or judgment: depression (*achthos*) is a distress "that weighs us down"; exasperation (*enochlēsis*) is "a distress that coops us up and makes us feel that we haven't got enough room"; confusion (*sunchusis*) is "an irrational distraction that scrapes away at us and prevents us from seeing what is at hand" (DL 7.112 = *SVF* III.412; cf. Andron. in *SVF* III.414). These wonderful phenomenological descriptions show us that the Stoics are not neglecting the way passions feel. What they insist is that, in each case, the thing that feels like this is an act of assent or acknowledgment. Some recognitions feel like embracing a nail; others like rubbing yourself across a rough, grating surface; other propositions "cut" differently, so other acceptances have a different phenomenological content.

These emotions, we have said, are concrete episodes of passion, to be identified with highly specific evaluative beliefs about one's situation. But we have also said that the Stoics recognize the importance of more general beliefs in generating the passions: the entrenched beliefs about the value of certain sorts of externals that, internalized in a person's ongoing concep-

---

hunger. They were using these words in a rather special sense, for want of any better generic words. Cicero remarks on this double use at *Fin*. 3.35: "what, giving a single name to both a bodily and a psychological phenomenon, they call *hēdonē*." Cicero himself removes the ambiguity where *lupē* is concerned, using *aegritudo* rather than *dolor* for the emotion genus. In the case of *hēdonē*, he is again at pains to indicate that it is not the ordinary sense of *voluptas* that is meant here: he speaks of *voluptas gestiens, id es praeter modum elata laetitia* (*TD* 3.24). At other times he simply uses *laetitia* (4.14). On the double sense of *voluptas*, see also Sen. *Ep.* 59.1.

[65] For the canonical definitions, see DL 7.110–14; Cic. *TD* 4.14–22; Andronicus *Peri Pathōn* 2–5 = *SVF* III.397, 401, 409, 414. The reader of these lists will be struck by the prevalence of terms designating angry and hostile feelings. Under *lupē* we find jealousy, envy, spite, annoyance; under longing, we find hatred, love of quarreling, anger (*orgē*), wrath (*mēnis*), resentment—and only two other species. Even under delight we find hostility: one of the four species mentioned is malevolent joy at another's sufferings, *epichairekakia*. If one were to inquire into the motivations behind the Stoic condemnation of the passions on the basis of these lists alone, one would have to conclude that worries about malice and anger are central. The rest of the evidence confirms this.

tion of value, are the stable basis for concrete outbursts of passion. This level of belief figures, as well, in their formal theory, which here relies explicitly on the medical analogy. The soul of an ordinary person says Chrysippus, is like a body that is prone to various diseases, some large, some small, which may arise from chance causes (*PHP* 5.23, 294D). These diseases are diseased conditions of belief. A *nosēma* or chronic illness of the soul is a stable condition of the personality that consists in accepting a value-judgment that leaves its holder susceptible to passions. It is defined as "a belief in the desirability of something that gets strengthened into a disposition [*hexis*] and hardens, according to which they take things that are not choiceworthy to be strongly choiceworthy" (Stob. *Ecl.* 2.93.1 = *SVF* III.421; cf. DL 7.122). The belief that money is extremely important, the belief that passionate love is extremely important, these would be *nosēmata*.[66] So too, presumably, would be the more concrete belief that X is extremely important—an entrenched belief that could become the basis for a concrete episode of love, fear, or grief. Chrysippus added that when such an illness is deeply enough entrenched and generates psychological weakness, we should call the condition of *nosēma* plus weakness an *arrhostēma*, or infirmity.[67]

What this schema implies, among other things, is that (if we confine ourselves to the big generic categories and some especially prominent subspecies) Nikidion cannot have one emotion without letting herself in for many others: perhaps even, given the fullness of time, for all the others. Once she has hostages to fortune, the very course of life will bring her now to grief, now into fear, now into intense joy. "Those same things in whose presence we experience distress are objects of fear when they are impending and approaching" (Cic. *TD* 3.14; cf. 4.8). "If the wise man should be open to distress, he would also be open to anger . . . and also to pity and envy" (3.19–20). "Where you take greatest joy you will also have the greatest fear." Just as there is a unity among the virtues, all being forms of correct

---

[66] Examples in Diogenes Laertius are love of fame and love of pleasure. Stobaeus adds love of women, love of wine, love of money—and also the hatreds corresponding to each of these.

[67] One further category is *euemptōsia*, or susceptibility to a particular passion. Examples given include irascibility, enviousness, fearfulness. It is not entirely clear how these tendencies are supposed to be related to the beliefs that are the *nosēmata*. I shall not discuss here the problems raised by Cicero's confused and careless account of these categories at *TD* 4.23ff. He expresses irritation with Chrysippus' extended probing of the medical analogy (*nimium operae consumitur*, 4.23), and concludes that we may neglect the fine points of the medical analogy and occupy ourselves with the main outlines of the argument. This leads him into confusion.

apprehension of the self-sufficient good, just so there is a unity to the passions—and also to their underlying dispositional states. But this means, too, that there is a unity to the cure of the passions. "You will cease to fear, if you cease to hope. . . . Both belong to a soul that is hanging in suspense, to a soul that is made anxious by concern with the future" (Sen. *Ep.* 5.7–8). The world's vulnerable gifts, cherished, give rise to the passionate life; despised, to a life of calm. "What fortune does not give, she does not take away" (Sen. *Ep.* 59.18).

V

The Stoics teach Nikidion that the passions should be not moderated but extirpated. Indeed, they view this as one of the greatest differences between their therapeutic teaching and that of their Aristotelian/Peripatetic rivals. "It is often asked," writes Seneca, "whether it is better to have moderate passions or none. Our people drive out the passions altogether [*expellunt*]; the Peripatetics moderate them" (*Ep.* 116.1 = *SVF* III.443). They must be pulled out root and branch (Lactantius, *SVF* III.444, 447). We must, that is, not only cut out the external manifestation but also tear out the roots of the passion that go deep into the soul (Cic. *TD* 3.13ff.; cf. 61–63). Since they are beliefs, and not organic parts of our innate constitution, they can be so extirpated (3.31, etc.). Indeed, nature herself demands their removal, saying, "What is all this? I brought you into the world without longing, without fear, without religious anxiety, without treachery and these other plagues; leave the way you came in" (Sen. *Ep.* 22.15).[68]

[68] The passions are present in almost all human beings. The Stoics must have a good explanation for this, since they deny their natural origin and their presence in animals and children. Chrysippus apparently offered two explanations for the prevalence of error (DL 7.89 = *SVF* III.228; *PHP* 5.5.12–20, 320D = *SVF* III.229a). He seems to have granted that even if children were raised by a philosopher and never saw or heard any examples of vice, nonetheless they would not necessarily turn out philosophers in the end. One reason for this is "the conversation of most men" (*PHP*; cf. DL, "the conversation of those around them"). Here presumably Chrysippus is envisaging a situation in which the child, while without examples of vice, still mingles with the surrounding culture enough to encounter the value system that grounds the passions. A child whose only conversation was with a philosopher and who was without paradigms of such viciousness as exclusive love and concern (these two requirements would be hard to combine) might escape. (For this explanation, see also Sen. *Ep.* 115.11–12 = *SVF* III.231; Sen. *Ep.* 94.53 = *SVF* III.232; and *SVF* III.233–35.) The second explanation, as stated in the sources, is obscure. Diogenes Laertius says "through the persuasiveness of external things"; Galen, "through the persuasiveness of appearances," and

So the Stoic does not hesitate to describe the wise person as totally free from passion (*apathēs*; cf. DL 7.117). Free, that is, from fear, distress, pity, hope, anger, jealousy, passionate love, intense joy, and all of the many relatives and subspecies of these.[69] Free, as Seneca etymologizes, from all vulnerability and passivity toward the world (*Ep.* 9.2–4). The wise person is totally self-sufficient. "Distress never befalls [her]: [her] soul is serene, and nothing can happen that would cloud it" (*Clem.* 2.5.4; cf. DL 7.118, Cic. *TD* 4.10ff.). External happenings merely graze the surface of her mind (Sen. *Ep.* 72). Indeed, her spirit is "like the country on the other side of the moon: it is always calm there" (*Ep.* 59.16). Our task must now be to understand the reasons for this extreme view of the goal of therapy. What, then, could possibly persuade Nikidion to take up this militant and obsessive opposition to the passions? Let us pursue this question by imagining her an Aristotelian; for it is the Aristotelian view that is the Stoics' primary target here, and it is that view which serves as their surrogate for the ordinary beliefs to which it is closely related.

The first thing that we must tell Nikidion is that, in Stoic terms, the judgments with which the passions are identical are *false*. Externals do not have such great value; indeed, they have no intrinsic ethical value at all. If one had only true evaluative judgments, both general and particular, one would never have any of them. This is evident from the account we have given of the Stoic theory of value. But this, in a sense, does not take us very far. For the very judgments that are false according to the Stoic theory of value are true inside the Aristotelian theory, which appears to be closer to our intuitions. So far, then, we have no reason why someone not independently convinced of the truth of Stoic theory should wish to extirpate the

---

elaborates, "pleasure throws forward the persuasive appearance that it is good and pain that it is bad." We must not interpret this in any way that makes use of a notion of innate or natural attraction or aversion. How, then, to grasp the cause of the appearance? (Posidonius apparently found Chrysippus unclear here.) A long passage in Chalcidius' commentary on the *Timaeus* offers an interesting and possibly correct explanation (*SVF* III.229). The idea seems to be that a new baby finds the experience of birth a painful one, on account of the sudden transition from a warm moist environment to a cold dry one. But as soon as it cries the doctor hurries to assuage it, washing it in warm water and simulating the pleasant environment of the womb. This gives the child already the idea that in this world pain is something to be avoided and pleasure pursued. This idea is acquired so early (long before the child grasps propositional judgments) that it seems natural: things just look that way. But nonetheless, this appearance is learned, and once learned it shapes the propositions the child will form. On this topic, see also Kerferd (1978). For a different and more plausible account in Seneca, see chapter 11.

[69] On love and marital affection, see further in chapter 12.

passions. And it is also clear that, although the Stoics certainly do defend their account of value with arguments (including a complete view of the universe) that are in many ways independent of their analysis of passion, they view the account of passion as offering serious support to the theory of good. One of the major reasons repeatedly adduced in favor of going over from the Aristotelian to the Stoic theory is that it will free us from the domination of our passions.[70] We recall that Chrysippus went to some pains to insist that his arguments could treat people who continued to cling to a false conception of good; Cicero's statements about therapy tell the same story. Indeed, Epictetus goes so far as to say that if he discovered that the belief that the external is nothing to us was false, and the arguments that support it deceptions, he would still cling to that deception, since from it he is likely to live in a smooth and undisturbed way (*Disc.* 1.4.27). We need to find out, therefore, whether the Stoics really have what they claim they have: independent arguments for extirpation, arguments that would be powerful even to an Aristotelian Nikidion.[71]

A second Stoic claim takes us a little further. This is that the passions are not as important as the Aristotelian thinks in motivating virtuous action. Insofar as anger is defended on the grounds that without it patriotic or other-defending action would be either non-existent or weak, the Stoics are able to answer that a healthy mind can be motivated to correct action by the thought of virtue and duty alone—indeed, that these are far more secure and reliable than the motivations that come from passion. Aristotle describes the man without anger as a man who will allow himself to be trampled down in a slavish manner, who will not fight to defend his country or those he loves. Seneca's *On Anger (De Ira)* vividly rebuts this contention:

> "What then?" he says. "The good man will not be angry, if he sees his father slaughtered, his mother raped?" No, he will not be angry; but he will avenge them, he will protect them. Why, moreover, are you afraid that *pietas* is too slight a motivation without anger? . . . The good man will fulfill his duties undisturbed and unafraid; and he will do what is worthy of a good man in such a way so to do nothing that is unworthy of a man.

---

[70] Cic. *TD* 3 is an especially clear example of this line of argument. It is pervasive in Seneca's *Epistulae Morales* as well.

[71] I choose the Aristotelian position in what follows because, compared with its major philosophical rivals, it is the most committed to the positive value of items over which we do not have full control; and it is also the one that seems closest to ordinary intuitions about these values, both ancient and modern.

... My father is being slaughtered: I shall defend him. He is slaughtered: I shall pursue the murderer—because it is appropriate, not because I am in pain. (*Ir.* 1.12.1–2)

The good man's actions, he later says, are like the operations of the law: secure, constant, reliable, passionless—and reliable because passionless, and therefore maximally capable of rational self-determination (1.16.6).

This argument has something to say to Nikidion insofar as, in following Aristotle, she has built her case for the passions on their importance as forces motivating to correct action. But an Aristotelian is bound to feel at this point that the main point has been missed.[72] Nikidion will, first of all, dispute the Stoic claim that emotional motives are unstable and unreliable, and she will be right to ask for more and better argument here. But, more important, she will insist that the moral value of an action depends in part upon its motives and upon the other reactive feelings accompanying it; and that motives of passion are in many cases more morally valuable than motives of duty, as revealing cares and commitments that are themselves ethically valuable. As showing a recognition of the proper and high importance of certain externals. She will insist that an action, in order to be really virtuous, must not only have the same content as the virtuous man's action; it must be done in the way that the person of practical wisdom would do it, with those very motives, those very reactive feelings. The person whom Seneca describes is not only less praiseworthy than one who is moved to anger by the rape of a mother and the murder of a father; he is actually failing to perform a virtuous action. Anger is the right motive here; grief and pity will be the right accompanying reactions. Right, because these passions are acknowledgments of the importance of family love in a correct view of the good human life. So it appears that this Stoic argument, like the first, rests, after all, on the prior acceptance of a Stoic view of value, and can do little work independently of it. I shall discuss this argument further in chapter 11.

A third argument is only partially circular. It concerns the intensely painful feeling of the experience of the passions. In making the case for seeing the passions as sick conditions of the personality, their underlying dispositional bases as forms of chronic illness, the Stoics like to point out that, after all, passions are felt, more often than not, as violent pains and upheavals of the organism; moreover, the person subject to them feels herself to be in a chronic condition of weakness and lassitude. Stoic writ-

[72] For related argument against Kantian positions that resemble Stoicism on this point, see Blum (1980).

ings continually put before us the discomforts of anxiety, the raging disorder of anger, the agony of fear, the torments of love. Treatises on particular passions characteristically begin with a description of the painful phenomenology of the passion in question, destined to convince even those who might think the passion an appropriate response that its cost in pain and upheaval is too great to bear. Consider, for example, this description of an angry person from the opening section of Seneca's *On Anger*:

> His eyes blaze and sparkle; his face is red all over as the blood surges up from the lowest depths of the heart; his lips tremble, his teeth are clenched, his hair bristles and stands on end, his forced breath makes a creaking sound, his joints make a cracking sound from twisting; he moans and bellows, his speech bursts out in hardly comprehensible words; he keeps striking his hands together and pounds the ground with his feet; his whole body is aroused, "and performs the great threats of anger." It is a disgusting and horrifying sight of swelling and distortion—I don't know whether this vice is more detestable or more hideous. (1.1.3–5)

Even the allegedly positive emotions, these writings stress, have a phenomenology of upheaval and disruption. Joy of the intense sort is experienced as a giddy inflation, a dangerous uplift that is never without the vertiginous sense that at any moment we may be dashed to the ground. It feels thin, ungrounded, terribly exposed and fragile. Love of the intensely passionate sort (as opposed to the calm affection that is aimed at friendship, which Stoics approve and foster—cf. chapter 12) feels uncertain, scary, unpredictable. And Chrysippus perceptively insists that lovers demand this element of surprise and unpredictability, rejecting a more solid relation (*SVF* III.475 = *PHP* 4.6.29, 276D). But spontaneity brings with it the possibility of upset, and therefore a continued enervating anxiety. In general, the dispositional state of a person who is prone to strong passions is a state that feels infirm, debilitated, lacking in solidity. It is the psychological analogue to the physical state of a person who is lacking in muscular tone, effete, neurasthenic. (And of course, given Stoic psychological theory, it is just such a physical state.) Epictetus tells us that this feeling of psychological weakness is felt as disease even by those who have not yet learned from philosophy that their beliefs about externals are false. They are led to seek out philosophy in the first place by "an awareness of weakness and incapacity" concerning the things that they consider most important (*Disc.* 2.1.1).

Here, I think, the Stoics begin to have a case against Nikidion's Aristotle. To some extent, it is the sort of circular argumentation already familiar to us from the Skeptics of chapter 8. For unless Nikidion is already convinced of the ethical value of freedom from disturbance and anxiety, she will be less than overwhelmed by the obvious fact that passions are disturbing. However, the Stoics' detailed and careful work on the phenomenology of particular strong passions does forcefully remind Aristotelians of the magnitude and the terror of these disturbances of the personality. It asks them whether having these forces around, with their ability to shatter reflection, to invade and shake up other areas of life, is not too great a price to pay for the ethical satisfactions they afford. The claim that uncontrolled externals have serious ethical value was defended by the Aristotelian not with any knockdown or even by any very detailed or systematic argument, but only by pointing directly to intuitions about value that most ordinary people seem to share. Those intuitions may begin to weaken if we confront Nikidion vividly enough with the agony of passion and the disruption it leaves behind it. Especially in the case of anger—and especially when Stoic writers depict its baneful influence in the public sphere—the case for extirpation made through this line of argument begins to look pretty strong. Does Nikidion want Nero to feel "appropriate" Aristotelian anger when she sees truly how ghastly a disturbance of personality anger is? Does she want leaders and wise men whose souls are always being cut through by knives, even if she does have a view of the good that endorses this agony as a correct response?

The Stoics add to this argument two others that are even more impressive. The first, an argument from integrity, contains an element of circularity, but is still powerful internally against the Aristotelian position. The second, the argument from excess, seems free of even this limited circularity. Since the deeper exploration of these arguments will be the business of chapters 11 and 12, I shall here describe them only briefly.

The argument from integrity reminds Nikidion that as an Aristotelian she herself is committed to a good life that is, for each agent, "one's own and hard to take away" (*EN* 1095b25–26). She defines her selfhood, her identity, in terms of the planning and ordering of such a life. Identified with several intrinsically good ways of acting and living, and with the practical reason that arranges for the orderly enactment of these,[73] she views an impediment to these actions or to this reasoning as a diminution and even an invasion of her sphere of selfhood, of her person. She has, then, a deep abhorrence for the condition of slavery, a condition in which her own actions and relations are not under his own control, but are dictated by

---

[73] For the identity of person and practical reason, see *EN* I.7 and IX.4, 1166a16–17.

externals over which he has no control. It was on grounds such as these that Aristotle himself argued against ascribing supreme value to external items such as wealth or fame and in favor of ascribing such value to virtuous action. He too, then, wants to be "at his own disposal, not someone else's" (Epict., passim, e.g. *Disc.* 4.7.9). But then doesn't Nikidion have to grant that by opening herself up to external goods such as love and the other grounds of the passions, by valuing in such a way as to be living a passionate life, she opens his personality, the core of her self, to the possibility of invasion and control by the world—therefore to a possible loss of personal dignity and integrity? Distress, *lupē*, Chrysippus etymologizes, gets its name from the verb *luō*, "dissolve": it is a dissolution of the entire person (Cic. *TD* 3.61; cf. Plato *Crat.* 419C). The self of the Aristotelian agent is extended out over parts of the world of change. Happenings in that world can then lacerate it, even rip it limb from limb. It can be enslaved, raped, even devoured by another. To cultivate such attachments, and the conception of the self that goes with them, is to go about inviting rape and enslavement, violations that abase and humiliate because they damage what is most intimately one's own. This spectacle of violation is just as repellant to the Aristotelian as it is to the Stoic; but she does not move to close off that possibility. The Stoic self, by contrast, feels external happenings as things that merely graze the surface of his skin (Sen. *Ep.* 72). They can never penetrate to the core. He and his good are safely at home together. "He retreats into himself and lives with himself" (Sen. *Ep.* 9.17). As Seneca puts it, his highest good "seeks no equipment from outside. It is cultivated at home, and is entirely developed from within him. He begins to be the subject of fortune, the minute he looks for some part of himself outdoors" (*Ep.* 9.15); again, "all his good begins and ends inside him— and he can say, 'All my goods are with me'" (9.18). Philosophy builds an impregnable wall around the self, fortifying it against all possible assaults of fortune (*Ep.* 82.5).

To some extent, once more, this argument is circular. That is, unless Nikidion accords the enormous value the Stoics do to self-sufficiency and rational control, it will not seem to be a fatal objection to the passionate life that it opens her to violation by fortune. Again, unless she believes that virtue is the supreme good, she will not be disposed to grant that the Stoic does have all good things at home with her. But the argument has force against the Aristotelian nonetheless. For even if she does not ascribe supreme value to self-sufficiency and freedom from external control, Nikidion does ascribe considerable value to it—far more, it appears, than is compatible with her endorsement of the passionate life. She is charged with not having considered seriously enough the cost of her scheme of value in terms of her own conception of integrity. The suggestion is that once she considers this she will realize that the values she most seriously prizes can only be found within a Stoic life.

Finally, the Stoics charge the Aristotelian with naive optimism about the extent to which passion can be moderated and controlled. Nikidion seems to believe that a good upbringing and good habits can make love and anger into moderate, discerning, self-governing elements of good character, choosing just the occasion and degree of expression that reason also approves. The Stoics reply that if we really enter into the inner life of passion, we will understand that this is not the case. Passions have in their very nature a propensity to ungovernable excess. In a long passage of *On Passions* quoted by Galen, Chrysippus invents a vivid metaphor. When a person is walking, the impulse of the limbs can be checked and changed as he wishes. But if he is running, it is no longer this way. The movement carries itself further, by its own impetus—so that even if she should wish to stop or change course, she will be unable to. The impulse of her motion will take her on ahead of the point at which she wished to stop. That is the way passion is. The true judgments of Stoic reason, like walking, are governable by our will; anger, fear, and love, even when they can be stopped, cannot be reliably stopped at the place where virtue would want. They carry us further than our wish (*SVF* III.462 = *PHP* 4.2.13–19, 240–42D).[74]

There are actually two subtly different points made by this set of arguments. One concerns the internal structure of each passion taken singly. Love leads on to excessive love, anger to excessive anger. Nikidion cannot say, "I shall have anger in my life, but I shall educate myself so that anger will always manifest itself in the right way at the right time toward the right people in the right degree." No, say the Stoics, that is not possible; for the passion is tumultuous and gets ahead of your plan. As Seneca vividly expresses this point:

> There are certain things whose beginnings are in our power, but which later carry us away by their force and leave us no way of turning back. As when people's bodies are dropped headlong from a height they have no control over themselves and, once thrown down, are unable to hold back or delay, but the irrevocable speed of the fall cuts away all reflection and all second thoughts, and they are not permitted to avoid arriving at a place

---

[74] Chrysippus seems to have been fond of the runner metaphor: see also *SVF* III.476 = *PHP* 4.4.24–26, 256D, and *SVF* III.478 = *PHP* 4.6.35–36, 276–78D, both direct quotations from Chrysippus.

toward which they would once have been permitted not to go, so the soul—if it hurls itself into anger, love, and the other passions—is not allowed to check its impetus: the very weight and the downward nature of the vices must carry it away and take it to the very bottom. (*Ir.* 1.7.4)

And Chrysippus has insisted that it is in the very nature of passion that those who are in it disdain planning and control. Absence of control is, indeed, a part of what people value in the experience of passion. Nikidion doesn't want lovers who obey a rational principle at all times. She likes them to fling caution to the winds, to ignore sound advice, to follow their love in an "uncalculated" spontaneous way. In short: to be carried away by love (*SVF* III.475 = *PHP* 4.6.29, 276D). Such lovers, Chrysippus says, should have as their motto the lines from Menander: "I took my good sense and stuffed it into a jar." For that is what it means to have those values and those beliefs about the good.

This rejection of limit and measure is most unfortunate in the case of anger: for the excesses of that passion are not just silly and wasteful, they are harmful, both to self and to others. In anger, Chrysippus observes:

> We stand so far from ourselves and get so far outside ourselves and are so completely blind in our difficulties that sometimes if we have a sponge or some wool in our hands we raise it up and throw it, as if by doing this we could accomplish some end. If we had happened to have a knife or something else of the sort, we would have used it in the same way. (*PHP* 4.6.44–45 = *SVF* III.478)[75]

Seneca, too, insists that anger cannot reliably be stopped short of cruelty and murderousness (*Ir.* 2.5.3). The politics of his time lend support to these contentions. Nero's career is not a reassuring spectacle for even the most determined Aristotelian.

This argument is complicated and strengthened by the view we have already mentioned, concerning the close interrelationships among the passions. Suppose Nikidion tries to reply by conceding a part of the Stoic argument. All right, she says, I shall extirpate anger, and jealousy, and any

---

[75] The extracts that Galen quotes immediately after this one are also of interest: "Often under the influence of this kind of blindness we bite our keys and thump against the door when it is not opened right away. And if we stub our toe on some stones we take our revenge on them, breaking them up and hurling them who knows where. And each time we use the most inappropriate language" (*PHP* 4.6.45, 280D). And, following this, "From such examples one can discern the unreasonableness of people gripped by passion, and how blinded we are in such moments, as if we had become different people from the ones who were previously exchanging reasoned arguments" (*PHP* 4.6.46, 280D).

other passions whose excessive form is likely to be especially brutal and dangerous. But surely I need not extinguish love, or pity—or perhaps even fear. For the first two may have no harmful excess; and the excess of the third is surely harmful to me alone. The Stoic now points out that this is neither plausible nor even consistent with Nikidion's own position. The very same evaluations that ground one group of passions ground—given a change of circumstances or a different temporal perspective—the others as well. She cannot love without being liable to hate and anger; unless she is extraordinarily lucky she cannot love without actual hate and anger. For her love may have an obstacle; another person may take from her the one she cherishes; and then the love itself provides anger with most exquisite fuel. Nor can she be the sort of person who feels intense joy without being frequently immobilized and tormented by fear; without sometimes suffering all the agonies of grief. Seneca writes to Nero reproving the emotion of pity (*Clem.* 2.4.4, 2.5.4, 2.6.4; cf. DL 7.123). If the Aristotelian thinks this a moral and political error, she had better reflect further on the connections between that emotion and murderous rage. She will find them if she looks.

These seem to me to be the most powerful of the Stoic arguments against Aristotelians. For they tell them that they cannot have forms of evaluation and action that they cherish, without committing themselves to what they themselves abhor. If there is any argument that would persuade those among us who cherish our passions to rethink those commitments—to persuade Nikidion if she considers turning from Aristotle to the Stoic way—it would, I believe, be the argument that it is only in the Stoic life of self-containment that we can have stable gentleness and beneficence, the avoidance of terrible acts. ("Wise men are harmless: for they do no harm, either to others or to themselves" [DL 7.123].) I shall therefore devote chapters 11 and 12 to the further exploration of these claims.

VI

What is Nikidion left with, if she completes the Stoic therapy? As far as the passions themselves go, she has, as Zeno put it, the scars of her former condition, though the wound itself is closed (*Ir.* 1.16.7). Seneca interprets this to mean that she will "feel certain suggestions and shadows of the passions, but from the passions themselves [s]he will be entirely free" (*Ir.* 1.16.7).[76] She will, on the other hand, be permitted to keep three so-called

---

[76] These scars and shadows will include, presumably, the natural animal responses that are

affective responses (cf. DL 7.115 = *SVF* III.431; Cic. *TD* 4.12–14 = *SVF* III.438). These items, called *eupatheiai*, are not passions and are not identified with any high evaluation of externals. But they are motivations that will help Nikidion steer her way among things indifferent. There is no good affective form corresponding to distress: in other words, no good way to register negatively the presence of a bad state of affairs. A response of prudent caution (*eulabeia*) is, however, approved toward future negative possibilities. In other words, without ascribing to externals any intrinsic value at all, while keeping one's responses exactly in accordance with reason's judgment about their value,[77] one can still appropriately be motivated to avoid death and other dispreferred indifferents. If they come, one will not mind; but one can sensibly avoid them. Toward their future opposites one can move under the guidance of rational wish (*boulēsis*).[78] And finally, if the good externals should arrive as one wishes, Nikidion is permitted to have a certain sort of joy (*chara*), namely the sort that is defined as "rational uplift" (*eulogos eparsis*).

So it is a further point in the Stoic battle against Aristotelianism to insist that they have not done away with the thing that people value most in the emotional life. There is joy here; joy without enervating uncertainty, joy without fear and grief, a joy that really does move and lift up the heart. "Do you think that I am now taking many pleasures from you," Seneca asks Lucilius,

> when I remove things that come by chance, when I insist that hopes, those extremely sweet delights, must be avoided? No, on the contrary: I do not want you ever to lack gladness [*laetitiam*]. I want it to be born in your home; and it is born, if only it is inside of you. Other cheerful things [*hilaritates*] do not fill the breast, they simply relax the brow; they are

---

sometimes erroneously taken to be the passions themselves—such as the tendency to start when alarmed, to be sexually aroused by appropriate stimuli, etc.

[77] Cf. *SVF* III.480 = *PHP* 4.5.21–22, 262–64D, Galen quoting Chrysippus' therapeutic book: "For these infirmities, we say, do not lie in the judgment that each of these things is good, but in inclining to them in excess of what is in accordance with nature." Chrysippus, Galen reports, defined *orexis* as "a rational impulse for something pleasant to the extent that it should be found pleasant" (*SVF* III.463 = *PHP* 4.2.4, 238D). *Orexis* is first named in the classification of the *eupatheiai* reported in Andronicus—but *boulēsis* is defined as *eulogos orexis*; and Galen may be mistakenly reporting as a definition of *orexis* what is actually a definition of *boulēsis* or of one of its species. Epictetus contrasts passion with a *summetros orexis* for the choiceworthy things (*Disc.* 4.1.84).

[78] Inwood (1985) argues persuasively that a central idea here is that of "reservation": I want X, but with the proviso that it is in accordance with Zeus' will. See for example Epict. *Ench.* 2.2; *Disc.* 4.7.12; Sen. *Tranq.* 13.3, *Ben.* 4.34.4, 4.39.4.

superficial [*leves*]—unless perhaps you believe that a person who laughs has joy [*gaudere*]. The soul must be brisk and confident, raised up above everything. (*Ep.* 23.3)

Interpreters sometimes point to passages such as this in order to argue that Stoic extirpation is not the radical move against our emotional life that we might initially think. For though the tumult is undone, much happy affect still remains.

But I believe that we should not be lulled by this sort of Stoic rhetoric into thinking that extirpation will leave much of Nikidion's happiness where she is accustomed to find it, while merely getting rid of many difficulties and tensions. The state that Seneca describes is indeed called joy. But consider how he describes it. It is like a child that is born inside of one and never leaves the womb to go out into the world. It has no commerce with laughter and elation. For wise people, we know, are harshly astringent, *austēroi*,[79] intolerant of idle pleasure in themselves and in others (DL 7.117); and it is difficult to laugh if one is never caught off guard.[80] Indeed, the letter goes on,

> Believe me, true joy [*gaudium*] is a stern matter [*res severa*]. Or do you think that one can with a carefree expression, or one that . . . is full of humor, despise death, open one's home to poverty, hold pleasures in check, contemplate the endurance of pain? The person who reflects on these things in himself is in a condition of great joy [*gaudio*]—but not a sweetly agreeable joy. It is this joy that I want you to possess; it will never fail you, if once you have discovered where to seek it. . . . The joy of which I speak, to which I am trying to lead you, is something solid. . . . Therefore, I beg you, my dearest Lucilius, do the one thing that can make you really happy [*felicem*]: cast away and trample underfoot everything that shines on the outside, everything that is offered you by another or from another. Look to the true good and take joy only in that which comes from what is your own. What do I mean by "from what is your own"? I mean you yourself and your own best part. (23.4–6)

In the following chapters we shall examine further the motivations that we all may have for going over to this joy. But we can see already that the

---

[79] On the notion of austerity, see *SVF* III.637–39. Chrysippus mentions that he has elsewhere discussed the causes of laughter—apparently in close connection with the *pathē* (*SVF* III.466 = *PHP* 4.7.17, 284D). His rejection of surprise may well have played a role in the analysis.

[80] Compare Epictetus' advice: each person making progress away from diseases of passion "keeps guard over himself, as if he were an enemy lying in wait" (*Ench.* 48.3).

change to Stoic joy from Nikidion's own is vast. It is the change from suspense and elation to solid self-absorption; from surprise and spontaneity to measured watchfulness; from wonder at the separate and external to security in that which is oneself and one's own. To follow Seneca's sexual metaphors, it is the change from passionate intercourse, giving birth, and child-rearing to parthenogenetic conception, followed by the retention of the conceived child forever inside the womb. It is a change that leaves no part of life untouched. She is promised great good; and for this good she is asked to give up what are now to her the most precious things, the very bases of her daily life. Epictetus imagines speaking to Medea, the unhappy heroine of chapter 12. He gives her one simple formula for happiness. "Stop wanting your husband, and there is not one of the things you want that will fail to happen" (*Disc.* 2.17.22). Nikidion sees that this is not casual modification. Indeed, it is not modification at all. It is what the Stoics said it was. It is extirpation.

Seneca on Anger in Public Life

In THE SPRING of 1991 I visited the U.S. Military Academy at West Point, lecturing to the required cadet ethics course on the topic of moral dilemmas. After my lecture I ate with the officers in their club overlooking the Hudson River, where leaves were unfolding on the banks and a stiff breeze sent ripples glinting across the water. The clean beauty of the April day made blood, sand, and brutality in the Gulf seem like distant dreams. And I thought about the young cadets, now calmly doing moral philosophy on the banks of the Hudson, but someday in some place, perhaps, to order untold deaths, rage and hatred and fear filling the place in their hearts now occupied by the arguments of Kant and Aristotle. As we ate, the officers and I, we began, therefore, to talk about rage, about the debate between Stoics and Aristotelians concerning the role of anger in public life. As we talked we told each other stories of public, and especially military, anger, arguing from *exempla* much as Seneca does in the *De Ira*, returning obsessively, as he does, to images of public anger both (apparently) justified and hideous—and sometimes both together. I want to begin my approach to this difficult text with three of these stories, similar to Seneca's examples in the range of concerns they explore, but taken from our own time. For in a Senecan dialogue, the reader is also the interlocutor; and, as Seneca says, preparing to launch into recent Roman history, "Would that this rage had been confined to foreign examples" (3.18). (As we shall see, that wish itself is an accomplice of anger; and admitting that anger is not so confined is a crucial step in anger's therapy.)

1. An American platoon enters a Vietnamese village, looking for hidden Viet Cong soldiers, helpers, supplies. When the inhabitants of the village refuse to cooperate, the commanding officer, enraged at the 'gooks' who are, to him, all enemies and not fully human, orders his men to open fire. Coming after months of frustration and suffering in the jungle, the invitation to revenge is delightful. Anger floods over them, sweet as a reward. They shoot children and old men. Women they rape and mutilate first. Finally they set the huts on fire, leaving nothing behind them. (This story is told with reluctance by officers who know it as a communal nightmare that philosophy, at West Point, has not managed to exorcise.)

2. As the fighting in the Gulf nears its conclusion, which is presented to the American people as an occasion of immense pride and satisfaction, General Norman Schwarzkopf appears on the news to discuss new evidence regarding the torture of civilians in Kuwait. (I tell this story, remembering how I heard him on the radio in my car, somewhere between Providence and Attleboro.) He speaks with contagious anger in his voice. He says that he does not know how to speak about the people who did these horrible acts. He can only say that, whatever they are, they do not seem to be of the human species that we know and recognize.

3. The colonel who heads the West Point philosophy department now tells a story that was told to them by Elie Wiesel on a visit to the academy a few weeks before. Wiesel was a child in one of the Nazi death camps. On the day the Allied forces arrived, the first member of the liberating army he saw was a very large black officer. Walking into the camp and seeing what was there to be seen, this man began to curse, shouting at the top of his voice. As the child Wiesel watched, he went on shouting and cursing for a very long time. And the child Wiesel thought, watching him, now humanity has come back. Now, with that anger, humanity has come back.

These stories, taken together, bring forward what I believe to be the central problem with which Seneca grapples in the *De Ira*—with which we, in turn, grapple as his readers and interlocutors. On the one hand, anger is closely connected to brutality and a delight in vengeance for its own sake. Seeing others as anger sees them—as people who ought to suffer—is a way of distancing oneself from their humanity; it can make it possible to do terrible things to them. And this ferocity is, in turn, a diminution of one's own humanity. Much of Seneca's argument, as we shall see, focuses on these points, and on examples that support them.

On the other hand, *not* to get angry when horrible things take place seems itself to be a diminution of one's humanity. In circumstances where evil prevails, anger is an assertion of concern for human well-being and human dignity; and the failure to become angry seems at best "slavish" (as Aristotle put it), at worst a collaboration with evil. Wiesel's soldier was no Stoic. But it was just on account of the extremity of his justified rage that the child Wiesel saw him as a messenger of humanity. Seneca's treatise urges the extirpation of anger. It ends with the famous injunction, "Let us cultivate humanity," *Colamus humanitatem*. Can the Aristotelian have rage without losing humanity? Can the Stoic have humanity while losing rage?

Our second example compounds the problem. For if the Aristotelian tries to say that we can have appropriate and justified anger while removing that which is excessive and unjustified, the Schwarzkopf example should

403

trouble him. For it shows how very easy it is to slip from the one to the other. General Schwarzkopf begins, in effect, like Wiesel's soldier, with (apparently) justified rage at horrible acts of brutality. But he ends up, and rather quickly, not too far from Lieutenant Calley. For the force of his statement as a whole seems to be to say, "Look, these Iraqis are no better than animals. They are not up to our standards of civilization, they don't really belong to the same species. So it was good that we killed as many of them as we did, wasn't it? And it will be fine at any time to kill a lot more." This anger asserts the importance of human moral concerns; but at the same time it debases its object and summons against the object energies that can all too easily be used for Calley-style brutality.

This doubleness in anger is an old story, old even for Seneca and his interlocutor. For Achilles' wrath,[1] sweeter than honey, brought thousandfold pains upon the Achaians; and it led him to treat the corpse of his enemy in a base and dehumanizing manner.[2] It is only when, with Priam, he puts aside his anger that he is able to recognize the equal humanity of his foe.[3] And yet the same reader who fears Achilles' wrath cheers the anger of Odysseus that sets to right the damage to his house, cheers as the evil and not fully humanized suitors and their allies are shot, strung up, humiliated, hacked to bits. For this is made to seem to the reader like Wiesel's story, in which rage restores a sense of moral order and humane concern. But how

---

[1] It is clear that the Stoics are concerned with this example: for *mēnis*, hardly a common word in the Hellenistic world, is prominent in the definitions of passions. (It is defined as "anger that stores itself up for a long time"—see *SVF* III.396–97.) Stoic references to Homer are very numerous; see Fillion-Lahille (1984) 1ff., 69–70, and Nussbaum (1993a). It is worth noticing how many different species of anger are recognized in these definitions, far more than for any other major emotion besides distress (*lupē*). Under the genus *orgē* are ranged *thumos* ("incipient anger"), *cholos* ("swollen anger"), *pikria* ("anger that breaks out suddenly"), *mēnis*, *kotos* ("anger that awaits the right time for vengeance"); close relatives are *misos* ("longing for things to go badly for someone, with eager intensity"), *dusnoia* ("longing for things to go badly for someone for his own sake"), and *dusmeneia* ("*dusnoia* that bides its time and does bad things"). The Latin lists contain far fewer words here: *ira* (*orgē*), *excandescentia* (*thumos*), *odium* (defined as *mēnis* is defined, though it would appear to be a verbal translation of *misos*), *inimicitia* (defined as *kotos* is defined, though perhaps a translation of *dusmeneia*), and *discordia* ("anger of a rather bitter sort that is conceived deep in the soul and heart")—see Cic. *TD* 4.21. It is worth bearing in mind the close association between anger and hatred: the main difference seems to be that the definition of hatred does not mention a prior offense as the occasion.

[2] Today in Boston, the *Iliad* is used in a therapeutic program for disturbed Vietnam veterans suffering from postcombat stress syndrome—I am grateful to Jonathan Shay for discussion on this point.

[3] On *Iliad* 24, see J. Griffin (1980), MacLeod (1982), Nussbaum (1992).

far apart, really, are the two stories? And can't the pleasure of anger itself lead us straight from one into the other? Can we, then, cultivate humanity in public life either with anger or without it?

II

Seneca's *De Ira* is a therapeutic argument. Its addressee is the philosopher's brother, a non-philosophical public man who is depicted as having characteristic Roman concerns about military strength and success, about the safety and dignity of one's family and home, about strength and dignity and manliness and greatness of soul generally.[4] Novatus (and the speaker inside the text who, intervening simply with *inquit*, may or may not be identical with Novatus) is characterized in such a way that he stands in for many readers and voices anxieties that would be likely to vex any good Roman beginning to take an interest in Stoic positions on anger. At the same time, with its composition at the start of a new regime,[5] with its references to Claudius' own semi-philosophical writing on anger and its frequent allusions to the angers and crimes of Caligula, the treatise reaches beyond the interlocutor to address the new emperor as well, and general Roman concern for the future of public life.[6] Its therapy is thus both individual and broadly social. We shall see that the two aims are profoundly linked—that Seneca's prescription for public life depends on getting each individual to recognize the deficiencies of his or her own soul.[7] Since its therapeutic structure is so personal, I shall permit Novatus to replace Nikidion in this chapter, although we should not ignore the fact that his preoccupations are likely, in some form, to be hers as well.[8]

The structure of the *De Ira* has frequently been criticized as haphazard,

---

[4] On Novatus, and Seneca's family generally, see M. Griffin (1976).

[5] The date is probably 41 C.E., the first year of Claudius' reign.

[6] See Fillion-Lahille (1984). Explicit references to Caligula are at 1.20, 2.33, 3.18–19, 3.21. A general reflection on recent Roman crimes is at 2.8–9, on which see further discussion. On Claudius' edict distinguishing between *ira* and *iracundia*, see Fillion-Lahille (1984) 273ff. On Roman Stoicism generally, see Boyancé (1963).

[7] On Roman concerns about anger, see Fillion-Lahille (1984) 1ff.; on Virgil, see M. Putnam (1985) and, on the relationship between Seneca and the *Aeneid*, M. Putnam (forthcoming).

[8] For the concern of Roman wives of the same social class with honor and courage, see Musonius Rufus, "Should Women Too Do Philosophy?" Roman historians offer many examples of women's concern with the "manly" military virtues: one might consider, for example, Tacitus' portrait of Agrippina, wife of Germanicus.

405

lacking in rational sequence.[9] Rabbow calls it a veritable "durcheinander," a topsy-turvy mélange of heterogeneous material.[10] Bourgery goes still further, speaking of "désordre extraordinaire, excedant vraiment toute licence"; and concludes, "Que l'on s'y prenne comme on voudra, on n'arrivera pas à mettre dans cette oeuvre de l'ordre et de la clarté."[11] To Cupaiuolo, Seneca's argument "obeys only a single necessity, that of filling the blank page, without considering whether a question should be treated in a different place or whether it has already been introduced."[12] Janine Fillion-Lahille responds to these attacks,[13] finding in the treatise a good deal of order—but only by imposing on it an excessively simple chronological schema. In her view, Book 1 responds to Aristotelian criticisms of the Stoic position on anger; Book 2 turns to Epicurean positions, attacking Philodemus' idea of a "natural anger" in the wise man; and Book 3, turning to more practical and Roman concerns, addresses itself to and builds upon the work of Seneca's near contemporaries, Sextius above all. Although Fillion-Lahille's historical claims have some interest, the sort of order they give the work is odd indeed, based on arbitrary chronological considerations that have no interesting connection to the therapy of the interlocutor, or to the development of a compelling philosophical position.

I cannot attempt here a comprehensive structural analysis of the three books of *De Ira*. My aim is to grapple with one central piece of the philosophical therapy it offers; and the task of showing how each and every piece of the work contributes to its therapeutic purpose must wait for another occasion. But I suggest that we begin to have a far more just appreciation of Seneca's enterprise if we keep in mind throughout that his argument is, in fact, a therapeutic argument addressed to a decidedly non-Stoic interlocutor. On the one hand, this interlocutor comes to the text ready to hear what Seneca will have to say. For he has, it seems, demanded of Seneca, with some urgency (*exegisti a me*, 1.1) a written account of how anger may be modified (*quemadmodum posset ira leniri*); and Seneca claims to know that he has an intense fear of this passion (*pertimuisse*, 1.1). Later on, the attempt to "cut anger out of our minds or certainly to rein it in and curb its impetus" is characterized as "what you have longed for above all, Novatus" (*quod maxime desiderasti*, 3.1).

[9] For a comprehensive survey of opinions, see Fillion-Lahille (1984) 29ff., 222ff., 283ff.

[10] Rabbow (1914) 141.

[11] Bourgery (1922) 39–40, 100.

[12] Cupaiuolo (1975) 68, cited in Fillion-Lahille (1984) 283, my translation of Fillion-Lahille's French.

[13] Fillion-Lahille (1984).

On the other hand, however, the interlocutor, being an ambitious and self-respecting Roman public man, is convinced that anger is an important part of a self-respecting public response to evils, and of a strong manly military life. Such considerations cannot, in real life, be easily dispelled by logical argument; they are seated deep in the soul, and obdurately voice their resistance. It is this resistance, I suggest, that, above all else, dictates the structure of Seneca's argument. Again and again, the anonymous third-person voice speaks forth—from, it seems, deep in Novatus' soul itself. Again and again it brings up the connection of anger with dignified punishment of wrongdoing, with military honor, with greatness of soul. Again and again it protests that anger may in fact be moderate and self-contained. "What are you saying? Isn't punishment sometimes necessary?" (1.6) "Anger lifts up hearts and inspires them, and nothing grand can be done in war by courage, unless this flame is kindled under it" (1.7). "But some people control themselves in anger" (1.8). "But angry people are self-consistent and self-controlled" (1.8). "But anger is necessary against the enemy" (1.11). "What are you saying? Will a good man not be angry, if he sees his father slaughtered and his mother raped?" (1.12) "Anger is useful, because it makes better fighters" (1.13).

The resistance of the interlocutor drives the argument. But such resistance is not likely to emerge in perfect philosophical order, with a neat systematic agenda. As the examples I have given show, it emerges— sometimes spontaneously and sometimes in response to what Seneca says—in a tumultuous and multiform way, pouring out its repeated and heterogeneous objections. Seneca's task is first to draw out and then to grapple with this resistance—which can be expected to be in the reader as well, in much the same way. An elegant neatly ordered logical argument would not accomplish this task. Argument must follow the heterogeneous promptings of the interlocutor's heart, and must repeat itself as obsessively as the resistance itself does, bringing forward example after example even long after the first argument on a given point has been successfully stated, answering each anxious question with psychological aptness and, in this way, forcing the Stoic lesson down into the depths of the interlocutor's soul. The real structure of *De Ira* is, I suggest, the drama of this therapy—no neater than any real-life struggle with complex psychological obstacles.

Such an approach to the *De Ira* can also explain another feature of the text that has puzzled critics: the fact that Stoic positions emerge gradually and unsystematically, in a way that we would not expect of a treatise that set out to clarify and to argue for the Stoic account of anger. One can read very far into the work without agreeing to anything distinctively Stoic; and one can read almost to the end without being confronted with what is perhaps the most controversial element in Stoic morality for this interlocutor, namely the worthlessness of externals. The Stoic material is introduced gently, gradually, and also minimally, in a way that maximizes the terrain of agreement between Seneca and his interlocutor, and draws the interlocutor into the process of therapy without asking him first to give up any cherished goal. All this is odd if what we expect from *De Ira* is systematic Stoic moral philosophy. But the Stoics claimed to have arguments that could convince those not antecedently Stoic to embark on a Stoic program of passion-extirpation; and it is not at all odd that a therapeutic treatise directed to a non-Stoic interlocutor should focus on such arguments, making, at first, only exiguous and minimal use of anything like Stoic premises.

Finally, approaching the text as a therapeutic argument enables us to make sense of the historical facts noted by Fillion-Lahille, but in a more organic and less arbitrary way. It is no surprise that the philosophers most prominent in Book 1 should be Aristotle and Theophrastus; for, as we shall see, their views lie very close to the interlocutor's own intuitions. By the time we get to Book 2, the interlocutor is ready for some more detailed semi-technical discussion of Stoic passion theory, and thus Seneca can introduce the claims of rival Stoic views. (Unlike Fillion-Lahille, I see no reason to suppose that Epicurean views are in evidence here.) Finally, in the third book, when an already convinced interlocutor is ready to put the view of anger into practice in his own life, it is no surprise that we should find a much greater concentration of *exempla*, and a focus on Roman material.[14]

The course of Novatus' therapy, briefly described, is as follows. At the opening of the work, he confesses to a fear of anger and asks Seneca to tell him how it might be *moderated* (not extirpated). At this point, his views seem to lie close to the views of Aristotle and Theophrastus that are brought forward: he thinks it is possible to moderate anger without removing it completely; he thinks anger useful and even necessary as a motivating force; he believes that it is right for a good man to get angry at damages done to himself and his own; he believes that one ought to get angry at people who do bad things. (Indeed, when Theophrastus becomes an inter-

---

[14] Thus Fillion-Lahille ([1984] 250ff.) is perfectly right to stress the importance of Sextius and other Roman figures for Book 3, and for Seneca's philosophical education generally (on which see also M. Griffin [1976]). But the idea of bringing the argument closer to home has a philosophical and therapeutic motivation. On structure generally in Senecan dialogues, see also Abel (1967).

locutor in 1.12 and 1.13, what he "says" is simply a paraphrase of what the interlocutor has said or will say.) In this part of the work, the interlocutor speaks very frequently, voicing many objections to Seneca's claims. And Seneca, in replying, leads him into therapy gently, relying on very few Stoic premises that an Aristotelian would not also accept. He stresses the closeness of his definition of anger to Aristotle's (1.3.3); he relies heavily on views about the natural tendency to goodness in human beings that an Aristotelian would also share (1.5);[15] and he addresses his arguments to Aristotelian claims about motivation that can to some extent be separated from the overall Aristotelian position.

By the opening of Book 2, the interlocutor has begun to take a more serious interest in the Stoic position; for he has been at least temporarily convinced that it accommodates many of his intuitions about duty and military rectitude better than he thought. He is now ready to engage in a more detailed and serious study of the Stoic view of the passions; Seneca therefore presents him with some arguments against taking passions to be lodged in a separate irrational part of the soul, and with a distinction between irrational reflex movements and passions that is essential to upholding that claim.[16] The interlocutor now participates more fully in the philosophical search for understanding. ("*Inquis*" now begins to replace "*Inquit*," showing perhaps a more direct personal engagement in the process of therapy: instead of emerging as anonymous voices from within, the objections are now stated by Novatus himself in his own persona.) His interest in philosophy now begins to become apparent: when he asks, "What is the relevance of this inquiry?" he gets back the answer, "That we should know what anger is" (2.2); and this answer does not at all deter him. The voices of resistance are now heard less frequently—though they do burst out still from time to time, saying "An angry orator is sometimes better," (2.17) and "A soul that lacks anger is languid" (2.17).

Seneca now feels able to broach the topic of remedies for anger (2.18); the rest of the book is occupied with questions of education. The last outbreak of resistance is recorded near the end of the book, when the interlocutor reveals a deep personal interest in punishing to which he had not confessed before: "But anger has some pleasure, and it is sweet to return pain for pain" (2.32). He also speaks, again for the first time, of his own deeply personal sense of honor and self-esteem: "We shall be less despised, if we avenge a wrong" (2.33). We seem at this point to have

[15] See *EN* VI.13.

[16] For a compelling analysis of this part of the treatise, see Inwood (1993).

reached all the way down into Novatus' soul, to have elicited the deepest sources of his resistance to the eradication of anger. And with Seneca's repeated and emphatic responses to these concerns, we arrive at the end (for the time being at any rate) of the interlocutor's objections.

Book 3 begins with an interlocutor who now longs (if with some slight qualification) to have anger totally removed from his soul (3.1). His interventions are now on Seneca's side: "There is no doubt that it is a great and pernicious force: therefore show how it is to be cured" (3.3). Aristotle now appears as the opponent of both Seneca and Novatus, and Novatus can see how far his current perceptions are from the Peripatetic intuitions with which he began. The focus is now on examples that show both the badness of anger when uncontrolled and the possibilities for its removal. In this book for the first time, we see introduced, apparently with the interlocutor's approval, some central elements of Stoic doctrine about the instability of fortune, the worthlessness of externals, the need to live so as not to be damaged by Fortune (3.5, 6, 11, 25, 30, 34). The interlocutor is convinced that the cultivation of *humanitas* in himself and in others requires the removal of anger. To this conclusion, and its bearing on our original question, we shall shortly return.

III

Seneca's central line of argument to Novatus has three parts: an account of anger that shows it to be non-natural and non-necessary, an artifact of judgment; an argument that anger is not necessary or even useful as a motivation for correct conduct; an argument from excess, showing Novatus that the angry person is prone to violence and cruelty. In other words, Seneca does not rely on showing that the beliefs of the angry person about the importance of injury are false; and, as we shall see, the desire not to confront the interlocutor openly on this point is a source of considerable complexity in the argument.

The account of anger lies, as Seneca remarks, very close to the Aristotelian account ("desire to return pain for pain," 1.3.3). His own definition, which can be reconstructed from Lactantius' report of this lost section of the work, seems to have been "desire to avenge a wrong" (*cupiditas ulciscendae iniuriae*); he also approves the Posidonian definition, "desire to punish one by whom you believe yourself to have been wronged" (1.2.3b). Thus he conforms to the Greek Stoic account, as reported with slight

410

variations in Andronicus, Stobaeus, and Diogenes Laertius.[17] Seneca makes it very clear that he approves the original Greek Stoic view, according to which this *cupiditas* (*epithumia*) is itself a judgment (2.1ff.).[18] But even before he asks the interlocutor to accept this, he is anxious above all to get him to accept the view (which might be held independently of a Chrysippan analysis)[19] that anger does not stem from a natural aggressive

[17] Andronicus: *epithumia timōrias tou ēdikēkenai dokountos*; Diogenes Laertius: *epithumia timōrias tou dokountos ēdikēkenai ou prosēkontōs;* Stobaeus: *epithumia [tou] timōrēsasthai ton dokounta ēdikēkenai para to prosēkon* (*SVF* III.395–97). Strictly speaking, the additions in Diogenes Laertius and Stobaeus may seem redundant—for the idea of "being wronged" seems, by itself, to include the notion that what has occurred is "inappropriate"— even if we translate *ēdikēkenai* as "to have wronged" or "injured," rather than more strongly as "to have committed injustice." The purpose of the additions may be to take account of cases, such as that of merited punishment, where the person doesn't get angry because he knows he deserved it. But it is unlikely that such a punishment would be called an *adikēma*, even in the widest sense.

[18] 2.1 asks whether anger begins *iudicio an impetu*, by judgment or by impulse, and then asks, more precisely, whether, on the appearance (*species* = *phantasia*) of a wrong, one is moved to anger with or without the assent of reason. He asserts that anger requires *assent* (2.1, 2.3), though he agrees that the mere *species* may provoke certain bodily responses, such as trembling, pallor, tears, genital excitation, sighing, etc. (2.3). These, however, are not passions, and they do not have the connection to action that passions do. Here he agrees not only with Greek Stoic traditions, but also with Aristotle—see *DA* III.9, *MA* 11 (on which see Nussbaum [1978] commentary ad loc.).

In 2.4, Seneca divides anger into three stages: a non-voluntary movement (the bodily reflexes he has already discussed, which follow directly on the *species* and precede assent); a movement that is voluntary but not "stubborn," which consists in the judgment (assent to the *species*) "that it is right for me to take revenge since I have been wronged," or "it is right for this person to be punished, since he has done a wrong." Third is "an already controlling motion, which does not want to take revenge if it is right, but in any way at all, and conquers reason." The course of Seneca's argument here shows clearly that the *second stage* is already anger, and it is what the wise man *must not have*. So it is no solution to the problem I shall raise to say that the wise person should stop at stage 2. Indeed, it is at the stage that we arrive at the very *definiens* of anger, as Book I has already established it. The second stage, Seneca believes, will lead automatically to the third, unless some countervailing reasoning enters in to stop it. The point of distinguishing the two stages is to show that the judgments in which anger consists *can* be modified by judgment (*qui iudicio nascitur, iudicio tollitur*)—but not once things have gone too far.

[19] It *is* so held by both Aristotle and Epicurus—see chapters 3, 7. And indeed, the idea of innate aggressiveness is very rare in ancient texts. It *may* be implicit in Posidonius' division of the soul, and Posidonius may believe it implicit in Plato—but Plato's *thumoeides*, though present in children, is an "ally of belief," and is connected to ideas of honor that would have to be taught. On the other hand, quite a few ancient thinkers believe that the general course of life almost inevitably gives rise to this passion and its problems through rivalry for scarce

instinct in human nature, that the human being is by nature inclined to sociability and mutual aid, and not to hostility. In a very effective rhetorical passage, he personifies anger as an alien being, no part of what it is to be human:

> Whether or not it is according to nature will be evident, if we examine the human being. What is gentler than the human being, when he is in a right state of mind? But what is more cruel than anger? What is more loving to others than the human being? What more hostile than anger? The human being is born for mutual aid, anger for destruction; the one wants to join together, the other to rend asunder, the one to help, the other to harm, the one to come to the aid even of strangers, the other to attack even those nearest and dearest; the one is ready to spend himself for the well-being of others, the other to plunge into danger, so long as it can drag others along. (1.5.2)

Seneca is not altogether explicit at this point concerning the judgments that are at the root of this non-natural passion; and we shall soon see how difficult it is for him to be so. But, given that even the Aristotelian position makes judgments of a certain sort necessary conditions for anger, he is, with this interlocutor, on safe ground: anger is in some way or another a social artifact, a product of what we are taught to believe and judge, for which any non-cognitive bodily predisposition (cf. 2.17ff.) will prove insufficient.

This being established, the argument focuses on what I have called the motivational argument and the argument from excess. To the interlocutor's repeatedly voiced concerns that anger is useful and perhaps necessary as a motivation for behaving well in war, and even in the defense of one's own in private life, Seneca replies (as we have already seen in chapter 10) that the motivations supplied by anger are not necessary: for one can be moved to action by the thought of virtue and duty alone. *Ratio* is by itself sufficient, in war, in defending one's own, even in punishing offenders (1.8.5, 1.9.1, 1.10.1, 1.11.2, etc.). Furthermore, the motives supplied by anger are not dependable: to rest the safety of others on the vicissitudes of one's own pain seems to be a foolish and irresponsible thing to do (1.10.1, 1.11.1, 1.12.1ff., 1.13.3, etc.).

This argument is strengthened by our familiar argument from excess.

---

goods and beliefs about their importance—see chapter 7. Anger would in that sense be "natural," as being a more or less universal outgrowth of the human condition. We shall see that it is this position that Seneca, too, will defend.

One way in which anger is a bad motivational force to rely on is that it is prone to exceed the boundaries set by reason. Thus in turning ourselves over to anger we become out of our own control, unable to stop where we wish. Anger is like a body hurled headlong from a height (1.7.4; cf. chapter 10): its impetus will carry it straight to the bottom, and nothing can be done to call it back. The impulses of anger are "violent and lacking in foresight" (1.10.1). Contrary to what Aristotle says, anger is not like a useful weapon: for a good weapon, like virtue or reason, is "firm constant obedient," not, like anger, "double-edged and capable of being turned against its master" (1.17.2).

These claims about anger are bolstered throughout the work by a sequence of examples, illustrating the military and political effectiveness of the non-angry—the ruses of Fabius *cunctator*, dear to every Roman's memory, the prudent delays of Scipio, the patience of the other Scipio in front of Numantia (1.11), the clemency of Julius Caesar (1.23), the gentle moderate behavior of Augustus (3.23, 40)—and also the horrendous excesses of public anger, including the impiety and cruelty of Caligula (1.20; 2.33; 3.18–19, 21), the crimes of Sulla (1.34, 3.18), the mass killings of Volesus (2.5), the murderous anger of Alexander (3.17),[20] and many others, with a crescendo of ugliness and horror that culminates, in Book 3, in ghastly tales of mutilation and torture (3.17–18).

The confrontation between anger and prudent non-anger reaches its climax in 3.40, where Vedius Pollio, angry because a slave has broken a single crystal goblet, is about to have him killed by throwing him to the eels. The slave throws himself at the feet of Augustus Caesar, who happens to be a guest, asking only to be given a less awful form of death. Augustus, "shocked by such an innovation in cruelty," commands that the slave be let off, that all the crystal goblets should be broken before his eyes, and that the fish-pond should be filled in. The emperor now delivers a singularly Stoic speech:

> Do you order men to be snatched away from a banquet and tortured with new forms of punishment? If your goblet is broken, will the bowels of a human being be torn apart? Are you so arrogant that you will order a man to be led to death in the presence of Caesar? (3.40.4)

Seneca concludes that the "ferocious inhuman bloodthirsty" power of anger can only be assailed by the power of reason, the only power (like the emperor) strong enough to make it tremble.

---

[20] Alexander is seen in a better light in 2.23, where he fails to believe a letter warning him against his doctor.

IV

These are the central arguments. How effective are they? There are some evident problems. First, Seneca's motivational arguments rely heavily on the claim that the non-angry person will be able to have the same reasons for action as the angry person. He will respond to injury by inflicting merited punishments, including punishments that cause the death of the offender (1.15). He will pursue the enemy with vigor and dedication in war. He will avenge the murder of his father, the rape of his mother; he will defend himself and his own (1.12). In such passages Seneca might be read as saying that the difference between the angry person and the non-angry person is a non-cognitive difference: they both have the same reasons and judgments, but one has a kind of furious passionate motivation that the other does not. This, however, cannot be a correct interpretation, if Seneca is consistent. For it is, of course, his view that anger is a certain kind of judgment, that its furious impetus is the impetus of a type of reasoning about externals.[21] So the difference between the two people must, after all, be a difference in judgments; and if this is so, we must ask what this difference actually is, and whether the person's reasons for acting, given the difference, will really remain the same. Let us consider the following, representative, passage:

> "What then?" he says. "The good man will not be angry, if he sees his father slaughtered, his mother raped?" No, he will not be angry; but he will avenge them, he will protect them. Why, moreover, are you afraid that *pietas* is too slight a motivation without anger? . . . The good man will fulfill his duties undisturbed and unafraid; and he will do what is worthy of a good man in such a way as to do nothing that is unworthy of a man. My father is being slaughtered: I shall defend him. He is slaughtered: I shall pursue the murderer—because it is appropriate, not because I am in pain. (1.12.1–2)

What are the judgments of the good person in this example? It would appear that they include the following: a deliberate and culpable wrong

[21] Remember that the judgment that so-and-so should be punished because he wronged me is already anger, even before it gets out of hand. The non-angry person may still judge that a person ought to be punished—viewing the punishment in a deterrent or reformatory light. What he cannot do is to hold that the wrong done to him ought to be avenged by the punishment. And that is what Seneca's allegedly non-angry person does think, in the example to follow.

has been done to someone who is important to me, someone whom I am obliged to protect. This person ought to be punished, ought to suffer for what he has done. But what, then, are the judgments of the angry person? Again, they seem to include the belief that a deliberate wrong has been committed, that the wrong is in some way important, and that it will be good for vengeance to come to the wrongdoer. These judgments, it appears from both Seneca's account and other Stoic accounts, are sufficient for anger; indeed, on the Chrysippan view, which Seneca accepts, they are what anger *is*. But then, if the good person really has these judgments, he is angry, whether he foams at the mouth and rolls his eyes or not. The measured and diligent pursuit of revenge described here looks precisely like a type of anger—a type, moreover, that may jeopardize Seneca's attempt to link anger to excess and lack of control. If, on the other hand, the good person does not really have the judgments characteristic of the angry person, then it seems to be still an open question whether and to what degree he will pursue the offender and take risks to protect his own.

The Stoic, in short, has to come clean about the extent to which his good man will be detached from ordinary judgments about wrongdoing and its importance. On the one hand he can try, as here, to make the good man as close as possible to the good Roman of the interlocutor's imagination: but then, in giving him good Roman judgments, he seems to have no evident way of stopping him short of anger (albeit anger of a measured and non-furious kind). On the other hand he can make the good man a more evidently Stoic figure, a figure who believes in his heart that family ties are without true worth and that the only thing of real importance is virtue, a figure who goes through the motions of the conventionally appropriate action like a play-actor, without really deep commitment to the issues at stake, simply carrying out his role in the overall scheme of things. Such a person will really be different in judgments from the ordinary Roman. He will, it seems, really be able to take revenge without anger. But is this a person whom Novatus could respect, a person whose conduct in private and public life satisfies a Roman's deep demand for commitment, constancy, and risk-taking loyalty? A person who will always do what the person of Roman virtue would do, even when great obstacles are in the way?[22]

Let us consider Wiesel's American soldier. This soldier judged that a hideous wrong had been done, and that the people who had done it should

---

[22] For related concerns, see Murphy (1990) and Murphy's chapters in Murphy and Hampton (1988).

be punished. His anger was an acknowledgment of the importance of the wrong, and therefore of the human values against which it had offended. By his anger the soldier aligned himself with Wiesel and his fragile humanity. He also, we can add, aligned himself with a kind of optimism for humanity more generally: for his outrage expressed the judgment that things need not be this way, that one must expect better of human beings. What, by contrast, would be the judgments and actions of a Stoic soldier? According to Seneca, he would be moved to pursue the offender. But what, in his heart, would he think? If a true Stoic, he will think that none of this matters very much anyhow, that such evils are bound to come about in human life, that it's all what one should expect. This being the case, it's not worth his while to get very upset about it and cry out. If he pursues the Nazis, on the battlefield or in the lawcourts, it will be not because he attaches any intrinsic value to the righting of these wrongs, but because he has come to believe that this is what the universe requires of him right now. But why, one might inquire, does the universe require it, if it is of no true importance? And might the person who believes it has no true importance not be likely to waver concerning what the universe actually requires, especially if the vindication of the wronged requires prolonged labor and risk? Seneca's deeply ambiguous and incomplete portrayal of the good man avoids the issue, making him seem like any other Roman, without coming clean as to whether he has judgments about the worth of externals that would seem to Novatus indispensable, but must seem to any Stoic false.

Nor, if Seneca had produced the orthodox Stoic reply, would it have solved his problem. The Stoic, he could say, allows that all these items have (in a certain sense) worth (*axia*) and are appropriately *preferred* on account of their relation to one's natural constitution (see chapter 10). But the *kind* of worth they have must, as we recall, be carefully circumscribed. They do not have a worth that is either necessary for or a part of one's own *eudaimonia*; without them, one's life is still complete. One will therefore have no reason for grief at damage to them, or for fear at a threat. Nor is the worth in any sense comparable to or commensurable with the worth of one's virtue: never will one even consider putting any amount of them, however great, ahead of one's own virtuous thinking, or even beside it. There is just no competition at all. Nor is it the case that they, in turn, have a *sui generis* worth that is, symmetrically, non-comparable with that of virtue: the situation is completely and radically asymmetrical. It is difficult to believe that this account of devotion to friend, family, and country would satisfy Novatus, or justify (without elaborate circumnavigation *via* Stoic

416

teleology) the sort of risk-taking action in defense of others that he needs to endorse.[23]

Seneca has an answer at this point; and it is an answer to which he returns with increasing frequency as his argument develops, and as his interlocutor becomes more and more prepared for Stoic interpretations of the world. The answer makes use of the medical analogy. The good man is concerned about his fellow citizens in the manner of a doctor. When he administers a punishment for wrongdoing, he does so not because he himself takes any personal interest in the infliction of pain, but in order to improve the offender. "On all these things he looks as benignly as a doctor on his patients" (2.10), believing that "it is better by far to cure a wrong than to avenge it." In public life this means that he will use all the conventional forms of punishment—but without the inner pain of being personally wronged, and without any eager desire for the suffering of the wrongdoer. "For he does not harm, but he administers medical treatment in the guise of harming" (1.6). Just as some bodily afflictions respond to a gentle alteration in daily regimen, so too the character of some offenders can be treated by "rather gentle words" (1.6.3). If this does not work, he will employ harsher speech, "which warns and reproves." Finally he moves to punishments—first "light and reversible," then, for the most recalcitrant and deepest wrongs, the penalty of death (1.6.4).

This is a good response for the Stoic to make to our problem. For it shows a way in which the non-angry person can still care intensely about humanity, and be motivated on its behalf, while failing to share the judgments of the angry person. But at the same time it reveals how far the Stoic actually is from the good Roman avenger of father and mother, and also from the soldier who restored humanity to Wiesel's death camp. The Stoic views the punishment as justified, not on account of the importance of the wrong done, not on account of the pain and injustice suffered by the victim, and certainly not because *he* cares about what has happened in any personal way, but solely on account of the well-being of the offender. (And Seneca takes this to a very extreme point, defending even capital punishment on the grounds that death is in some cases a good for the person who dies [1.6, 1.14–15].) Are these, however, the motives we, with Novatus, would wish in a person whose father has been murdered, whose mother has been raped? Don't we want a response that acknowledges the impor-

---

[23] This does show, however, that the Stoic account does not involve the total detachment from commitment produced in Skepticism. One may still concern oneself with others because of certain beliefs about the universe and one's position in it.

tance of their death and suffering, that wants the punishment of the offender just because it has caused that pain and suffering? Don't we want, in Wiesel's case, the response the American soldier actually had, when he burst out against the horrors he saw, without for a moment thinking of how or whether Hitler's life might be improved, without allowing any thought for the reform of Germans to deflect him from the suffering of their victims?[24] Don't we want a response that acknowledges one's own fellow feeling with the sufferer, one's own deep implication in the lives and vulnerabilities of others, rather than the somewhat detached and superior response of the Stoic doctor?

And as we reflect in this way, we even begin to lose hold of the conception of merited punishment itself. For if the sufferings of the victim are of no real importance in the overall scheme of things, then the act that caused them seems to lose its serious badness. The good person thinks of the events of fortune as things that merely graze the surface of his skin; but how bad can it be to graze the surface of someone else's skin? And if the offender's act is not serious, for what disease, then, is the medicine of punishment being meted out? Seneca to some extent conceals these problems, particularly in the first book, by not spelling out in very great detail the beliefs of the good person concerning what has importance and what does not. But they are always there beneath the surface of his argument: and if he cannot resolve them he cannot, in the end, convince an interlocutor who has Roman and Aristotelian intuitions.

A second and closely related problem arises, if we consider the argument from excess. One of Seneca's key claims in his debate with the Aristotelian is that anger cannot reliably stop short of excess and cruelty. In establishing this claim he does indeed present many examples of the excesses of anger, examples in which a pleasure in returning pain for pain oversteps all bounds of humanity. But need this always be so? When we considered the person avenging his father and mother, we found that it was very difficult to distinguish the angry person from the non-angry person that Seneca depicts, by referring simply to Seneca's official account of anger in terms of judgment: for it seemed perfectly possible to have all the requisite judgments and still pursue one's duties in a measured way. Seneca, however, repeatedly denies this possibility, and more or less defines anger in terms of its excessive propensities: "If it listens to reason and follows where reason leads, then it is no longer anger, whose peculiar property [*proprium*] is

---

[24] See Murphy (1990).

obstinate rebellion" (1.9.2; cf. 2.5.3, 3.12, etc.).[25] Similarly, in personifying anger, he invariably chooses images that portray it as in its very nature excessive and uncontrolled: it is "inflamed, raging with lust" (1.1); it is a soldier who will not listen to the signal for retreat (1.9), an infernal monster with serpents and flame (2.35), the very image of Bellona and Discordia (2.35).

By what right, however, does Seneca declare that a *proprium* of anger is resistance to reason, given that he has defined it in terms of belief alone? By what right does he describe it using images that connote excess and cruelty, when all his argument has yet established is that it is a certain sort of judgment? It is, of course, possible for there to be a species of judgment that is by its very nature especially deep-seated and resistant to modification by other judgments; but if Seneca wants to claim this he will have to present an argument and tell us the nature of the barrier to reasoning. This, I think, he will find it difficult to do without mentioning the deep commitments to the well-being of oneself and one's own around which anger weaves its fabric: for it is, it seems, the depth of these commitments that makes an angry person plunge into extremes of reactive fury, resisting dissuasive arguments. It is because offenses are felt at the core of one's being that revenge seems so urgent and so necessary, its pleasure so seductive. But, once again: can Seneca tell Novatus they really are not important, without removing from him something essential not only to his Romanness, but also to his humanity?

There is, however, more to be said than this on Seneca's behalf: for an argument that we have not yet considered will shed considerable light on these two objections and their force, showing the relative detachment of the Stoic in a more attractive light.

V

We can begin to approach this crucial argument by noticing a tension in Seneca's account of the human being and human nature. On the one hand,

---

[25] This may seem to contradict 2.4, where Seneca gave the person an anger that was not yet *contumax*, at stage 2 (see n. 18). But I think that the two passages can be rendered consistent by a consideration of 2.5.3, which says that anger *becomes* ungovernable and cruel "by frequent exercise." Seneca wishes to stress both that anger can be removed by reasoning and that it is terribly difficult to do this, once it takes root in the soul. Certainly by then its impetus can't be checked by a single opposing judgment, but only by the *adsidua meditatio* he recommends and constructs (2.12).

as we have seen, Seneca repeatedly denies that there is in human nature an innate and irremediable aggressive instinct. He presents this thesis early in the treatise (1.5, cited previously), and returns to it frequently in the three books. Anger is not "according to human nature" (1.6); it lifts the angry person "beyond all human forms of thinking" (1.20), casting out "all human compacts" (2.5). It is a "foul and execrable force of harming, most alien to the human being, by whose influence even wild animals are tamed" (2.31), and it can be removed "by continual reflective practice" (2.12). Immediately after narrating the most shocking of his *exempla*, the mutilation and torture of Telesphorus by Lysimachus (3.17), he observes that, although the mutilations made their victim look unlike a human being, "far more unlike a human being was the one who inflicted the torture" (3.17). The final injunction to "cultivate humanity" is closely linked to the advice to extirpate anger and aggression.

On the other hand, throughout the text Seneca also dwells on the pervasiveness of vice, especially of aggression and the desire to inflict harm on others. The person who pardons a wrong is "giving indulgence to the human species" (2.10); every part of life is filled with crime and vice (2.9). In fact, our life is very much like a gladiatorial contest, or, worse still, a "gathering of wild beasts"—except that wild beasts do not devour their own kind (2.8). Anger and aggression "omit no time of life, exempt no race of human beings" (3.22); they occur among the best brought-up, the most balanced (3.4); nobody should judge himself safe from them (3.5). "We are all bad," *omnes mali sumus* (3.26).

What is going on here? It seems unlikely that Seneca is simply being inattentive and sloppy, since the denial of the naturalness of anger and related vices is such a central part of his argument, of Stoic arguments generally. And the claims for an aggression-free human nature are mixed in among the reminders of the pervasiveness of vice as though Seneca feels no problem for his argument arising from the combination. I believe that this is right: that the best explanation of his remarks concerning human badness do render them consistent with the remarks about human nature. The key, I think, lies in 2.9–10, where Seneca tells us some crucial facts about vice and its origins. The wise person, he says, is not surprised at the omnipresence of aggression and injustice, "since he has examined thoroughly the circumstances of human life" (*condicio humanae vitae*, 2.10). Circumstances, then, and not innate propensities, are at the origins of vice. And when the wise person looks at these circumstances, he understands that "among the other difficult circumstances of human life is this one: confused and blurred thinking, and not so much the necessity of erring as the love of erring" (2.9). Human life is like a ship leaking at the seams: and is it surprising that such a ship should take on water (2.10)? These remarks, together with the rest of Seneca's argument, suggest the following picture. Human beings do not come into the world with evil or aggressive instincts. On the contrary, their initial impulses are those of love and concord. But the world into which they come is a rough place, that confronts them with threats to their safety on every side. If they remain attached to their safety and to the external goods that protect it, that very attachment to the world—universal and in a certain sense according to their first nature— will almost certainly, in time, lead to aggressions that will rupture the "compact of humanity." For when goods are in short supply and people are attached to them, they fight one another for them. Thus aggression grows not inside our nature, but out of an interaction between nature and conditions that is likely to be universal, unless and until philosophical education removes the darkness from human thought. This, I believe, is the strongest and most consistent interpretation, not only of the argument here,[26] but of many other passages that trace the origin of vice to a desire for that which we do not have (e.g. *Ep.* 90, *Clem.* 2.1).[27] It brings his argument very close to the arguments of Lucretius that I discussed in chapter 7.

What this means, in effect, is that life, if we attach ourselves to it, alienates us from our own humanity. A baby is not born hard, aggressive, vicious. It opens its arms gladly to the beneficence of its parent. Its nature is indeed "mild," "loving of others," "born to mutual aid" (1.5). But the softness and mildness of this baby almost invariably turn to a hardness, as

---

[26] In 2.10 there are some images that may suggest natural aggression: why should one be surprised that brambles do not grow fruit (2.10.6), nobody gets angry when "nature protects the vice" (2.10.6). But these are reminders of the universality of the *condition* that prompts vice; and the claim *vitiam natura defendit* should, I think, be read very precisely, as the claim that nature (i.e., the *condicio* the world puts us in) *supports* the growth of vices of aggression and competitiveness.

[27] *Clem.* 2.1 traces the origin of "all evil of the soul" to the *cupido alieni.* Epistle 90, similarly, refers to greed and lust for the belongings of others as the forces that disrupted a previously harmonious era (90.3, 16, 36—they are described as arriving on the scene in a somewhat mysterious manner—*inrupit*, etc.). The letter is difficult, since these forces are said to have disrupted a previously "golden age"—without its being made terribly clear whether a change in material conditions prompts the shift. But Seneca's golden age is not the material golden age of tradition in which external goods are readily available (see chapter 12), it is a *moral* golden age (90.44—*egregia, carens fraude*; cf. chapter 12), a time when people were not culpably attached to (scarce) externals. It would not be surprising if such a condition— purely hypothetical in a world of scarcity and said by Seneca to result from the innocence of ignorance (90.45)—should be disrupted by desire once people were aware of scarcity and of possibilities of helping themselves to others' belongings in order to protect themselves.

life itself, and the care for that which supports one's life, turns the child, in time, against itself and the roots of its bonds to others. We become, with time, less human; and we encounter one another from day to day under a form of life that shows us to one another as combatants in gladiatorial shows, as vicious monsters rather than gentle humans.

Seneca now uses this view as the basis for his strongest argument against anger. Given the omnipresence of aggression and injustice, if we look around us every day with the attitudes typical of the angry person— determined, that is, to consider injustice and aggression important bad things, worth getting upset about, then we will never cease to be angry, for everything we see will upset us:

> The wise person will never cease to be angry, if he once begins: for everything is full of crime and vice. Much more is done than can be cured by restraint. People compete in a huge contest of wickedness. Every day there is more lust for crime, and less shame. Casting aside all thought for what is better and more just, their lust now hurls itself wherever it wants. Nor are crimes even hidden any longer: they are before our very eyes, and wickedness has such public status and such strength in the hearts of all that innocence is not so much rare as non-existent. (2.9)

Seneca now lists recent Roman offenses, especially those connected with the recent times of civil strife: betrayals, killings of one's own family members, poisonings, burnings of cities, tyrannies, secret plots, subversion of the state, sexual offenses,[28] plunder, false oaths of nations, broken treaties, theft and fraud of all sorts. He concludes: "If you want the wise man to be as angry as the baseness of the crimes demands, he must not only be angry, he must go mad" (2.9).

Here, we notice, Seneca grants the importance of these offenses, and in a sense grants that anger might well be an appropriate response to them. Notice that they are not simply offenses against one's own security and reputation,[29] but in most cases injustices, most of them public, at which it seems reasonable to be angry. What he suggests, however, is that this course is not without its consequences for the human spirit. For a person who notes and reacts to every injustice must, in reacting to them all with anger, become, in the end, similar to the raging and furious people against whom he reacts. Anger hardens the spirit and turns it against the humanity it sees.

---

[28] Here Seneca mentions rape and promiscuity.

[29] Some of the therapeutic material in Book 3 is of this sort, but this is because the focus is now Seneca's own, and the pupil's own, mundane daily life.

And in turning against humanity, in evincing the rage and disgust of the angry, one then becomes perilously close to the cruel and aggressive types who arouse the disgust. Thus, in Seneca's *exempla*, we find acts of horrifying vindictiveness and cruelty committed by those whose anger is in the first place justified, according to an ordinary Roman sense of justice. Sulla's crimes were initially directed against legitimate enemies: but they led him to murder innocent children (2.34). Caligula was in a certain sense right to be angry over the imprisonment of his mother: and yet he turned to cruelty, destroying a villa and much else besides (3.21). Cambyses had cause of battle against the Ethiopians: but in his rage for restitution he led his men on a fatal campaign that ended in cannibalism (3.20). How much wiser Plato, who, when he had cause of complaint against a slave, turned the actual punishment over to Speusippus, saying, "I am angry: I shall do more than is appropriate, I shall do it with pleasure. Let this slave not be in the power of someone who is not in his own" (3.12). Anger, however justified, turns us against the face of our humanity. If we see before us only a disgusting beast, then we have no way of guaranteeing that we shall behave toward it as to a human being.

Consider again our Norman Schwarzkopf example. It seems to be just what Seneca has in mind. In one sense, it is right for Schwarzkopf, looking at scenes of brutal torture, to get angry and to try to make his audience angry. On the other hand, anger hardens the angry against the wrongdoer. It says what Schwarzkopf in fact said: these people are not really human, we do not have to feel gentle and protective toward them, we can treat them as we like. And this hardening against a group is a first step toward brutality, a breaking, itself, of the "human compact."

Seen in this light, the Stoic injunction to withhold ourselves from anger seems not so much a way of detaching us from human needs and the importance of human safety, as a strategy to solidify our underlying bonds with our fellow human beings, to preserve something of the child's natural open and loving demeanor toward others, something of the nature to which human beings are born before they see the world. And in this way, we can see various pieces of Stoic advice—the advice to meditate on future evils, the advice not to consider injuries as terribly important, the advice to take up a medical attitude to the wrongdoer—not as strategies of insulation and detachment from others, but as necessary tools toward a truly humane and gentle public life. Thus, I think, Seneca's ambivalent attitude to externals in this treatise: he does not directly deny their importance; he never assails head-on the popular beliefs according to which family and city have enormous importance. He shows, on the other hand, that a policy of medical detachment from that importance is a wise policy, more profoundly consistent than strong attachment is with other goals to which Novatus, being a lover of humanity, is deeply attached.

A central element in anger is a severing of the angry person from the object of anger. In getting angry I set myself over against the one who wronged me, preparing to take pleasure in his hurt. In so doing, I usually think, "This person is beneath me," "This person has done what I would consider unworthy of myself," and even, with Schwarzkopf, "This person (unlike me) is not really human." Anger contains, in this way, as Seneca says, an excessive love and exaltation of oneself (2.31). In our examples, a crucial part of the anger of both Calley and Schwarzkopf is clearly a segmentation of the world into good and bad, a segmentation that falsely exalts American virtue and debases the foreign offender. Accordingly, a central element in Seneca's prescription for Novatus is that he should remind himself at every turn that he himself is capable of the failings he reproves in others. "If we want to be fair judges of all things, let us persuade ourselves of this first: that none of us is without fault. For it is from this point above all that anger arises: 'I did nothing wrong,' and 'I did nothing.' No, rather, you don't admit to anything" (2.28).

The fair judge examines the wrongdoings of others along with a searching critical scrutiny of himself, searching out the roots of wrongdoing in both self and others, seeing them as both pervasive and not deriving from an evil nature (2.28, 30; 3.12). Seeing vice as something with a causal history, and something whose causal chain runs also in oneself, saying at each point, "This you yourself did also," (2.28; cf. 3.26), the judge becomes no more alienated against another's wrong than he is against himself and his own. And it is, indeed, another benefit of the non-angry attitude that one can remain gentle toward oneself, rather than raging against one's own aggression, violent toward one's own desires.

Here we arrive at the deepest reason why Seneca's treatise moves the interlocutor gradually from more remote and foreign examples to recent and Roman examples—why, in Book 3, so much time is spent establishing that anger dwells among us and our own. This argument reaches its climax in 3.36, when Seneca uses himself as *exemplum*, showing Novatus a new way of life, based on searching self-inspection and medical gentleness to both self and others:

All your senses must be effectively led to a condition of firm endurance; by their nature they are enduring, if they are no longer corrupted by the mind—which must be called to account every day. That is what Sextius used to do: at the close of the day, when he retired to his nightly rest, he used to pose questions to his mind: "What fault of yours have you cured today? What defect have you resisted? In what way are you better?" A person will cease from anger and be more moderate if he knows that every day he has to come before himself as judge. What therefore is more wonderful than this habit of unfolding the entire day? How fine is the sleep that follows this acknowledgment of oneself, how serene, how deep and free, when the mind has been either praised or admonished, and as its own hidden investigator and assessor has gained knowledge of its own character? I avail myself of this power, and plead my cause daily before myself. When the light has been removed from sight, and my wife, long since aware of this habit of mine, has fallen silent, I examine my entire day and measure my deeds and words. I hide nothing from myself, I pass over nothing. For why should I fear anything from my own errors, when I can say, "See that you don't do that again, this time I pardon you." (3.36)

There follows an extended example of such minute self-confrontation, in which Seneca shows both the patience and the particularity with which the doctor of the mind or soul approaches his task.[30]

In this remarkable passage we see a new attitude to the self being forged. No longer is Novatus to consider himself as simply an agent in the outer world of the contest for honor and achievement. He is to think of himself as a person with rich inner depths, a person who is to some extent hidden from himself until he turns on his doings and thoughts the patient light of medical reason.[31] Seeing the complexity and fallibility of his own acts, seeing those acts as the product of a complex web of highly particular connections among the goodness of nature, the circumstances of life, and the complicated psychological reactions life elicits from the mind, he will learn to view others, too, in this light, as people whose every act and thought is worthy of keen attention, as people whose errors emerge from a highly complex narrative history rather than from a simply evil nature (cf. also 3.24); he will moderate his rage toward their injustices and intensify his commitment to human solidarity and mutual aid.[32] Where groups and nations are concerned, he will see them as composed of many selves, selves

[30] Given the Pythagorean connections of Seneca's teacher Sextius, the practice described may not be altogether Stoic (or Senecan) in origin.

[31] Compare the reading of Epistle 40, in chapter 9.

[32] On the relationship between taking up the narrative attitude and getting rid of anger, see also Nussbaum (1993c) and also "Perception and Revolution," in Nussbaum (1990a).

each with a complex history, selves each of whom, so far as basic nature goes, he himself might have been. Thus this most private part of the *De Ira* is also extremely public, central to its prescription for public action. In a world in which emperors mutilate their enemies for fun, looking into oneself is an act of public courage, and of humanity.

VI

The soul of the Greek Stoic wise man is a hard soul that protects itself from all impulses that would sway it from the strict path of virtue and duty. "All wise men are severe" (*austēroi*, DL 7.117 = *SVF* III.637). They "never permit their soul to give way or to be caught by any pleasure or pain" (Clem. *Strom.* 7.7 = *SVF* III.639). And this hardness cordons them off from any yielding response to the defects of another: the wise man does not forgive those who err, and he never waives the punishment required in the law (Stob. 2.7 = *SVF* III.640, cf. DL 7.123 = *SVF* III.641). An unyielding judge, he does exactly what strict legal justice requires, and rejects the idea of *epieikeia*: the idea, that is, that one might waive strict punishment as a result of a concrete understanding of the particular case (*SVF* III.640).

And here we encounter, I think, a deep tension in the Greek Stoic position. On the one hand, the Stoics are deeply committed to the analogy between wise philosophical treatment and medical therapy; and they accept, as well, the Aristotelian claim that good medical treatment in ethics is searchingly particular, devoted to a deep understanding of each concrete case. On the other hand, the Aristotelian tradition links this medical model with a strong commitment to *epieikeia* in public life. Indeed, *epieikeia* means for Aristotle both the searching particularity of good judgment, which goes beyond the generality of law, and also a tendency to mitigation of strict legal punishment in the light of a causal understanding of the particular case. It is, says Aristotle, "equitable [*epieikes*] to forgive human things" (*Rhet.* 1374b10).[33] The connection between the two meanings of the *epieikes* seems, in fact, to be forged by the medical analogy: for if one approaches a case with the doctor's sympathetic interest in its particularities, one will be more likely to take an interest in the prospects of the offender as a human being, to notice any mitigating factors, and, in general,

---

[33] For earlier chapters in the history of this connection, see Nussbaum (1993b).

not to use the hardness of the law as a way of dividing oneself off from the offender.[34]

Seneca, more consistent here, I think, than the Greek Stoics, allows his adherence to the medical way of looking at human defects to carry him away from the harsh rigor of the Stoic wise man and toward the Aristotelian tradition of *epieikeia*. A commitment to mildness and to the waiving of strict judgment is held, here, to be the only way to avoid constant insane rage against oneself and all human beings; and the particularism inherent in the medical attitude is made a central structural feature of the Stoic's attitude to both self and others, as a searching examination of circumstances, coupled with an acknowledgment of the magnitude of the obstacles to virtue, leads to a forgiving and non-angry attitude to deficiencies. Anger, as we have seen, has a we-them mentality, raging at a defect and holding oneself, at the same time, aloof from it; rarely does anger acknowledge that the same fault is in oneself. The harsh rigor of the Greek Stoic looks, from this point of view, strangely like a kind of anger: an aggression against the defects and passions of human beings, born of the exalted hope of perfect blameless virtue. Senecan *clementia* does not fail to judge vice: this is constantly stressed in the *De Clementia*, as here. Mercy is not acquittal. But, looking at oneself and at the circumstances of humanity, one comes to understand how such things have happened. And this medical understanding leads to mercy.[35]

Mercy, *clementia*, is even defined in a manner that makes its difference from Greek Stoic harshness evident: for it is an "inclination of the soul to mildness in exacting penalties," and also "that which turns its course away this side of that which could be justly determined" (*Clem.* 2.3). The Greek Stoic soul, by contrast, never bends aside, never inclines away from hardness. And, given that the opposite of mercy is cruelty (2.4), and that cruelty is a reflex of anger, we can also say that mercy is opposed at one and the same time both to strictness in exacting penalties and also to anger, as if that strictness does, indeed, lie very close to anger in the heart. As Seneca says, "It is a fault to punish a fault in full," *culpa est totam persequi culpam* (*Clem.* 2.7, fr.).

The politics of the *De Ira* is a politics of mercy and of gradualism. By the

---

[34] On the two dimensions of the concept of equity, see Lawless (1991), Nussbaum (1993b). For a comprehensive history of the concept and its role in the law, see D'Agostino (1973).

[35] For a related argument that extends the position to moral responsibility itself, arguing that one is not responsible for bad actions if one's upbringing has prevented one from becoming able to respond to ethical reasoning, see Wolf (1990).

standards of Aristotelianism, Seneca's proposals, like many Stoic proposals, are radical: for they ask Novatus to give up a rather central part of
traditional morality, of which Aristotle offers only moderate criticism. On
the other hand, the proposals do not neglect the difficulty of making any
radical change in human life. For Seneca reminds Novatus that excessively
high expectations and utopian ambitions are all too often a recipe for rage
(3.30, his diagnosis of the murder of Julius Caesar by his associates). The
hope of a complete change in the human being and in human social life may
have been the force behind the famous radical utopian works of Greek
Stoic political theory, the *Politeiai* of Zeno and Chrysippus. For these
works did indeed imagine a city all of whose citizens are virtuous: and it
imagined the removal of many of the constraints that the absence of virtue
now makes necessary in human life.[36] Seneca's more cautious and humane
approach insists that we cannot and should not expect the leaky vessel of
human life to be made anew. Instead we patch it and keep it going as best
we can, working patiently each day for each day's small improvement,[37]
neither disgusted nor discouraged if the task proves as difficult as human
life is. "Evils that are continuous and prolific require slow patient
resistance—not in order that they should cease, but in order that they
should fail to conquer" (*Ir.* 2.10.8). As doctors of ourselves, doctors of
human life, we try, quite simply, to fill the short space of our years with as
much goodness as possible and as little rage—including, and especially,
rage against rage itself.[38]

---

[36] See Schofield (1991).

[37] Seneca's work always stresses the need for continued improvement, denying that any
living person is wise and stressing the moral worth and dignity of striving itself—see, e.g.,
Epistles 88, 90. Epistle 90 even argues that there could be no genuine virtue in the golden age
that preceded vice: the art of philosophy is necessary for genuine virtue, and this is a creation
of human need. *Non enim dat natura virtutem: ars est bonum fieri*, and this art would not
have existed had vice not existed, and the conditions that prompt it (90.45).

[38] On mercy, see Murphy and Hampton (1988), who argue for a rather narrow understanding of the concept, restricting it to juridical and institutional contexts and contrasting it
with forgiveness, the broader moral notion. Seneca understands mercy as a broad notion,
applicable in both private and public dealings—although he is concerned with the assignment of punishments rather than with the determination of guilt. Although mercy does have
special prominence in the legal realm, it requires only the possibility of punishing. Mercy does
not entail *ignoscere*, forgiving or pardoning, since, as Seneca stresses, one may be severe
about the crime and still mitigate the punishment (*Clem.* 2.7). See Nussbaum (1993b) for
further discussion of these points.

Especially important is the distinction between mercy and pity or compassion, *misericordia* (Gk. *eleos*). The latter involves acknowledgment of one's own weakness and vulnerability, and as such is forbidden the Stoic—cf. *Clem.* 2.5. Seneca argues that *misericordia*

Seneca concludes his argument for mercy by reminding Novatus that there is simply too little time in human life to waste it on anger:

> Soon we shall breathe our last. Meanwhile, while we endure, while we are among human beings, let us cultivate humanity. Let us be a cause of fear, of danger, to no one. Let us despise harms, injustices, abuses, and taunts and bear with a large soul our brief inconveniences. While we look back, as they say, and turn around, death is upon us. (*Ir.* 3.43)

Here the injunction not to care for external happenings enters the argument not as a way of detaching Novatus from the world and from ties to others, but as a strategy for *humanitas*, removing barriers that stand between oneself and one's fellow citizens. Detachment from one's own wrongs is necessary for mercy; and mercy is, as Nietzsche once said in a Senecan mood, the "self-overcoming of justice."[39]

Is mercy merely a strategy to keep the self pure from rage? Or is it also supposed to be the correct attitude to the offender? Seneca's argument begins by insisting on the former goal; but by the end of the *De Ira*, and in the entirety of the *De Clementia*, he seems to endorse the latter view as well. It is appropriate to judge, to blame, to convict in law; but then, in the assignment of penalties, it is appropriate to think of the whole course of a human life, and of the fact that even the most heinous wrongs are the products not of an initially evil will, but of a network of circumstances, psychological, social, and natural. When one sees all this, mercy is not just prudent, it is just. *Epieikeia* as correct situational perception leads to *epieikeia* as merciful mitigation.[40]

VII

Seneca's argument is powerful; and yet it leaves us with some disturbing questions. First, any modern reader of the *De Ira* and the *De Clementia* is likely to be startled by the rather large amount of violent punishment that is allowed and fostered in the name of mercy. The medical defense of capital punishment as a good for the person who dies raises large Epicurean

---

is a condition of weakness, a form of depression, a yielding to fortune. Here the Stoics seem to differ from Epicureans, who endorse compassion—and here I find a major weakness in Stoic political theory.

[39] Nietzsche, *Genealogy of Morals* 2.10; on the connection of Nietzsche's critique of pity to Stoic arguments, see Nussbaum (1993c).

[40] For further discussion of this connection, see Nussbaum (1993b).

questions: and its strained character reveals just how committed Seneca is to the preservation of the death penalty, even when the logic of his argument does not seem to support it. Beyond this, we discover, nestling at the heart of *exempla* of mildness, actions that strike us as horrible in their cruelty. Plato, for example, is praised because he did not beat his slave in anger. But what *did* he do? He simply turned the job of slave-beating over to the non-angry Speusippus (3.12). It never occurred to him to ask whether slaves ought to be beaten. So much, one might feel, for mercy. The reader here will simply have to put a great deal down to cultural differences, reminding herself that the text also contains many examples of mercy that would in their time have seemed radical enough: Augustus' intervention that freed the slave from punishment, his genial behavior to a person who had insulted him (3.23, 40). Once again, however, these seem extraordinary only because public morality is so bad, because Seneca's reader is so accustomed to slaves being tortured and killed, to emperors beheading those who criticized them. All this might make us think that Senecan gradualism sets its sights rather low, and puts up with, even makes a virtue of, much that should not have been accepted. Its general pessimism about the behavior of human beings and its strategic advice to prepare oneself for the worst in order to avoid the surprise of anger when the worst happens— aren't these in a certain sense hostile to the cultivation of humanity, since they are preparations for tolerating what is worst in the human being?

Seneca's answer would be, I think, that the objector has to some extent misunderstood the purpose of his argument. His strategies of preparation for the worst and of focusing on the universal badness of human life are aimed not at making us callous toward evil but at being patient in the fight against evil. Setting one's expectations too high, whether in politics or in love, is a recipe for anger and cynicism when things go wrong. Armed with a Stoic view of the obstacles to goodness, one will continue patiently to aid human beings, seeing them not as bestial and ugly but as weak, struggling against almost insuperable odds. And this means that one will not grow angry with them or dismiss them, but will continue in the slow path of mercy:

> For, tell me, do you think one should be angry with those who walk with stumbling footsteps in the darkness? At people who do not follow orders because they are deaf? At children, if, neglecting concern for their duties they turn to the games and foolish play of their companions? Would you be angry at those who are ill, aged, weary? (2.10)

The claim is that seeing human beings in this medical way is the best, perhaps the only, alternative to a rage that forfeits all humane concern.

But this leads us to what is perhaps the deepest question raised by Seneca's argument. How far, indeed, is the evil done by human beings to one another a thing worth caring about? And doesn't the Stoic, after all, step back too far, in the very act of trying not to step back? Seneca claims that his strategy cultivates humanity, allowing us to remain deeply involved with one another's good and ill, without reactions that would break the bonds of that concern. And throughout his argument—in a manner that may or may not be fully consistent with orthodox Stoicism—he allows the events of the world to have real weight and importance. He grants that the murder of a father, the rape of a mother, are things of real significance, worthy of a response. And he clearly wishes the interlocutor to feel horror at the incidents of cruelty he narrates, thinking of them as significant damages. Here the advice not to get angry comes in, as I have suggested, more as a strategy of mildness than as a dismissal of the real horror of the crimes.

And yet, at the same time, the Stoic is not to behave like Wiesel's soldier, acknowledging the importance of damages in a way that shows his own deep personal involvement in human affairs. Instead, the Stoic, in order to avoid anger for the reasons Seneca has given, must cultivate what some-times does seem to be an alarming degree of detachment, hardly compati-ble, it would seem, with the full acknowledgment of the sufferings of vic-tims, the crimes of the cruel. "Step back quite far and laugh," Seneca tells us (3.36).[41] But what would we think of Wiesel's soldier, what would the child Wiesel have thought, had the soldier entered the death camp and laughed? Surely this is a person who is, in his careful and deliberate *hu-manitas*, not quite fully inside the human race, not a part of its sufferings

---

[41] This is in a context where Seneca urges detachment from slights to one's own reputation—but similar advice is given in 2.10, in connection with the serious public crimes and injustices that Seneca there enumerates. He describes the contrasting behavior of Her-aclitus and Democritus, one of whom wept at human failings, the other of whom always laughed, since "none of the things that were done seriously seemed serious to him." The main purpose of this story is to present both Heraclitus and Democritus as superior to the person who gets angry: "Where is there room here for anger? Everything must either be laughed at or wept at." Nonetheless, it would appear that Seneca's argument makes Democritus' response preferable to Heraclitus': for a wise person should have neither grief nor compassion, and it seems difficult to weep without these. Cf. also 3.11: "Quite a few things can be turned into occasions for jest and amusement," and the accompanying story of Socrates' joke when struck on the head.

and joys. Again, Seneca tells us that the anti-anger strategy requires a deliberate avoidance of knowledge: "It is not expedient to see everything, to hear everything. For many wrongs [*iniuriae*] pass us by, and the person who does not recognize them is not touched by many of them. You don't want to be prone to anger? Don't be curious" (3.11).[42] While we are on the subject of the death camps, this advice reminds us chillingly of the actual behavior of all too many people in that time—who avoided anger, no doubt, but whose failure to be curious cost them their humanity. Seneca's goal, the preservation of sympathy for all human beings, may be worthy enough. And he may well be right that the curious risk forfeiting humanity in another way. But can the solution really be to fail to intervene on behalf of others, because one has avoided knowledge of their plight? If Seneca were willing simply to say that none of these things matters anyhow, his position would be, if objectionable, at least consistent.[43] But he is not willing to say this: he wants to defend public courage and sacrifice and *pietas*. Doesn't he then undercut his own concerns, by advocating the refusal of public knowledge?

This tension about detachment emerges throughout this text in various ways—but nowhere, I think, more clearly than in the passages of Book 3 where Seneca discusses the appropriate response to a tyrant's crimes against one's family. Book 1, we recall, had given these cases special prominence, as instances where it will be particularly important for a good person to get involved, pursue the offender, do justice to family love. We wondered whether this could in fact be done without the beliefs charac-

---

[42] Again, the immediate examples have to do with the avoidance of knowledge of insults to oneself—but this is part of a perfectly general program for the elimination of the tendency to anger, and the advice is expressed in unambiguously general language. In the following section we find the story of Plato, Speusippus, and the slave. Here the slave's offense must be serious, since Seneca judges a beating the appropriate punishment. Immediately after this are the stories of Praexaspes and Harpagus, which show what it is to look the other way under tyranny; thus the advice is connected with Seneca's most complex and serious reflections on political life. In addition, 2.9–10, focusing on serious public crimes, gives similar advice; and quite a few of the *exempla* dealing with serious public matters have a similar moral: e.g., 2.23, where Alexander is praised for overlooking a threat to his life. One might try to deal with the problems presented by this advice by saying that Seneca offers it only ad hominem, to an interlocutor prone to err in the other direction. But I think that this would not be sufficient: there is no sign that Novatus is any more prone to excessive curiosity than anyone else, and Seneca makes it clear that the avoidance of rage really does require a refusal to become cognizant of evils that are all around one.

[43] He comes close, however, in 3.34: "None of the things that we do with such sadness [*tam tristes*] is serious, none of great importance. This is the source of your anger and madness, that you think tiny things worth a lot."

teristic of anger; and now, in Book 3, we will see Seneca granting that the avoidance of anger, in such cases, does in fact require a kind of detachment from the event that seems objectionable even to Seneca himself. It is one thing for Cato to hold his ground when a mocker spits in his face (3.38). It is quite another, we feel, for Pastor to attend a banquet "with a joyful expression," as ordered by Caligula, on the very day when Caligula had murdered his son. Seneca quickly explains and justifies this instance of non-anger in a way that satisfies us: "Do you ask why? He had another son" (2.33). Suppression of an otherwise appropriate response is necessary in order to prevent a further atrocity, a further loss. Not so easy, however, either for us or for Seneca himself, is the story of Praexaspes and Cambyses, introduced in Book 3 ostensibly in order to show that it is possible to refrain from anger in even the most extreme circumstances.

Cambyses the king was too fond of wine; so Praexaspes, one of his closest friends, advised him to drink more sparingly, saying that drunkenness was shameful in a king, who was the object of the eyes and ears of all. To this Cambyses said: "Just so that you will know that I never lose control of myself, I will prove to you that my eyes and my hands, after drinking, can still do their duty." He then drank even more extravagantly than ever, taking larger cups. And when he was already heavy and drunken he ordered the son of his critic to walk to the other side of the threshold and stand there with his left hand held above his head. Then he took aim with his bow and shot the young man straight through the heart—for it was at this that he said he aimed. And cutting open his breast he showed the father the arrow sticking straight into the heart, and asked him whether he had a sufficiently steady hand. But he replied that Apollo himself could not have shot more unerringly. May the gods curse such a man [di illum male perdant], a slave in soul even more than in circumstances. He praised something that it was too much even to witness. The breast of his son torn into two parts, the heart still beating in the wound—this he thought an occasion for flattery. He ought to have contested the boast with him, and called for another shot, so that the king might have shown in the person of the father himself an even more unerring hand. O bloody king! O one worthy of being the object of the arrows of all of his followers! Though we may abominate [execrati] him for finishing a banquet with punishment and death, nonetheless it was more criminal to praise that shot than to make it. We shall shortly see how a father ought to behave, standing over the body of a son of whose death he was both the witness and the cause. But the point under discussion is clear: that it is possible to suppress anger. He did not curse the king, he let slip no word of anguish, although he saw his own heart pierced together with his son's. (3.14)

And lest we think that the peculiarities of this passage are isolated and atypical in Seneca's text, he follows this story up with a very similar one, with similar complexities:

> I don't doubt that Harpagus gave some such advice to his king, the king of the Persians—taking offense at which the king gave him his own children to eat at a banquet and kept asking whether he liked the recipe. Then, once he saw that he was sufficiently filled with his own ills, he ordered the heads of the children to be brought in and inquired what Harpagus thought of his entertainment. The poor man did not lack words, his mouth was not sealed. "At the home of the king," he said, "any dinner is delightful." What did he accomplish by this flattery? He escaped being invited to eat what was left. I do not say that a father must not condemn an act of his king, I do not say that he should not seek to give such an atrocious monster [*tam truci portento*] an appropriate punishment—but for the moment I draw this conclusion, that it is possible to conceal the anger arising from a great evil and to compel oneself to words that give the opposite impression. (3.15)

In these two stories we find Seneca wrestling with the tensions in his own position. Ostensibly these stories are put in to show that one can conceal anger. And it is the official advice of this part of the text that one should in fact do so, even in great evils where one cannot possibly avoid feeling some anger. (Notice that Seneca never seriously doubts that a parent will *feel* anger inside himself at these incidents, nor does he even try to suggest that it would be a good thing if he didn't.) Throughout Book 3 there are quite a few examples of people not getting into political trouble because they refrained from displaying anger; and this is officially supposed to be a good thing. But Seneca cannot fully accept his own advice. He can't really say that these parents were right to detach themselves that much, to give way to the demand for flattery as if it didn't really matter. He himself shows how much he thinks the incidents matter, in the dramatic character of his language, in the vehemence of his condemnations of Cambyses and the Persian king, which uses very angry words (*di illum male perdant, execrati, truci portento*, etc.). And, very significantly, he judges that Praexaspes, in his deferential avoidance of anger, is even worse than Cambyses, even more to be cursed by the gods. No longer a mild doctor, Seneca wishes ill to the wrongdoer: *di male perdant* is far from a medical response. Like Wiesel's soldier, Seneca here is forced to curse at what he sees, asking the gods to damn the man's slavishness, his indifference to his son's still beating heart.

What then should a father do in such circumstances? Seneca has promised us an answer to that question. If a life of detachment is in certain circumstances too vile, if a life of anger, on the other hand, is pernicious to one's *humanitas*—what remedy does this text then offer for those who live in times when not to see monstrosity is slavish? The answer is given, shortly after the Harpagus story.

> We shall not give consolation to such a sad chain gang of slaves, we shall not urge them to do the bidding of those butchers. We shall show them that in every servitude a road lies open to liberty. Such a person is sick in soul and wretched by his own fault, since it is possible for him to end his troubles and himself at the same time. To the man whose fortune it is to have a king who aims his arrows at the breasts of friends, and to the man whose ruler stuffs fathers with the guts of their children, I shall say: "Why are you moaning, madman? Why do you wait for some enemy to avenge you by the destruction of your nation, or a powerful king to fly to your rescue from a distance? Wherever you look, there is an end to your troubles. Do you see that precipice? That way you can descend to liberty. Do you see that sea, that river, that well? Liberty sits there in the depths. Do you see that tree, stunted, blighted, barren? Liberty hangs from its branches. Do you see your throat, your gullet, your heart? They are escape routes from slavery. Are the exits I show you too difficult, requiring too much courage and strength? Do you ask what is the straight road to liberty? Any vein in your body." (3.15)

Seneca here adheres to a Stoic tradition regarding suicide.[44] It is not my intention here to discuss the entirety of that tradition, or whether the beliefs that underlie the decision to end one's life in that tradition are or are not fully consistent with other Stoic doctrines concerning the worthlessness of externals. I believe that there are in fact deep problems for any Stoic here. But my concern is with Seneca, and with the way in which the advice to commit suicide emerges from a specific tension in his argument. On the one hand, he does not wish the person living under butchery and tyranny

---

[44] On Stoic suicide, see, among others, Rist (1969), Long and Sedley (1987), the excellent and comprehensive discussion in M. Griffin (1986), Bonhöffer (1894). On Seneca in particular, see Tadic-Gilloteaux (1963) and the excellent account in Englert (1990). Griffin stresses Seneca's Stoic orthodoxy; Englert finds Seneca orthodox about the conditions under which suicide may be chosen but, in my view correctly, finds something new in Seneca's rich account of connections between suicide and freedom.

to live a life of anger. On the other hand, he is forced to acknowledge that a detached and mild response is in some extreme circumstances disgustingly slavish. His first instinct, advising the bereaved father, was to incite him to something that looks very much like angry resistance: for he told him to reply by courting a second shot from the tyrant's bow. But now, in keeping with his insistence that anger is never necessary, he gives him a different alternative—and insists that without this extreme response his life will be a life on the sad chain gang of slaves. The two routes to death are not different in their result; the crucial difference seems to be that suicide preserves *humanitas* free from corruption in a way that angry resistance does not.

We wonder, however, whether Seneca does not attach too much importance to an ideal of purity and integrity that is, if one considers it, more than a little egocentric. For the person who reacts to tyranny by leaping into a well does not do anything for others; and he protects his gentle involvement with humanity at the price of a selfish sort of non-involvement. Wiesel's soldier, the whole allied liberation army, might have gone straight out and jumped into the North Sea: but what, then, would have become of the child Wiesel and his kindred victims? Even when one's own death is likely to follow an act of resistance, that one act may accomplish something for humanity. And even if it does not, its very existence makes a statement on behalf of social justice that suicide, even Stoic suicide, does not seem to me to make.

What we see, furthermore, is that this strategy of purity is, even on its own Stoic terms, unsuccessful. For suicide does not show, cannot possibly show, that the world and what happens in it do not matter. In the very act of deciding for suicide, the Stoic has become as deeply implicated in the world and its evils as the angry person. For he judges that the *condicio humanae vitae* (note the repetition of this term in the Praexaspes story) really does, in this case, matter too much, that some things cannot be lived with, cut too deeply to permit continued life. In so judging he has granted that, in order not to be a slave, he has to live in the world as a human being, and be *of* that world, deeply caring about murders to children and shameful commands of tyrants, his heart pierced with the arrow that took his son's life. And really, notice, the beliefs characteristic of this suicide are in effect a kind of anger: for they include the judgment that a grave injustice has been done, and also the judgment that it ought to be punished. The only difference is that the suicide refuses, whether through impotence or through exaggerated purity, to get personally involved in the punishing: but he too knows that life with this tyrant is a disgusting base life, and he cares so much about those externals that he punishes the tyrant in the most effective way he believes he can, cheating the tyrant of the pleasure of his own murder.

Throughout most of this work Seneca has tried to depict a life of gentle patient involvement with humanity, in which a certain detachment protects the agent from hardness and cruelty. Now, in confronting the extreme events of his own time, he allows his own ambivalence about the right response to injustice to become palpable. The official conclusion is that it is always possible to avoid anger, whether by mild detachment or by suicide. But the twistings and turnings of the text contain a far more complex message. For "step back and laugh," "don't see too much," is hardly the advice Seneca gives, when the chips are down in an extreme case of family love and honor. These things matter, and it is slavish not to let them matter. Whether in angry resistance or in the quasi-anger proper to suicide, he confronts them, curses ready to hand, more Wiesel's soldier than his own incurious hero.

The importance of this passage for Seneca's thought is reinforced by our knowledge that he took his own advice. Years later, when things under Nero got too bad and his advice was useless, he did not excuse himself, Praexaspes-like, before the angry emperor. First, in fact, he did attempt political resistance: for he was implicated in the conspiracy of Piso. When the conspiracy failed and the emperor accused him, he did not seek to evade the charge by obsequiousness. Instead he wrote a letter that, while moderate, resisted by refusing to flatter: "For," comments the historian Tacitus, "his mind was not facile in flattery. And nobody knew this better than Nero, who had had more experience of Seneca's liberty than of his servitude" (*Annales* 15.61). And by the courage and dignity of his own death he punished the emperor, cheating him of the pleasure of watching his own suffering and humiliation.[45] Whether we call this anger or not, it was some condition of deep involvement with human affairs. He opened his veins; but since he was an old man the blood did not flow quickly. He therefore got on with his work. "Even in his last moments his eloquence did not fail him. He called scribes in and dictated a good deal, which, since it is published in his collected works, I shall not bother to adapt" (15.63).[46]

In this way, perhaps, Seneca managed to make a coherent whole of all the complex tensions of his philosophical position: reacting against tyranny

---

[45] Seneca had no choice about whether to die: had he not committed suicide he would have been executed. On the other hand, he showed great courage in his political life before that, and the manner of his death showed deliberateness and courage.

[46] On Seneca's suicide, see M. Griffin (1976, 1986), who stresses its enactment of Stoic norms, and especially its links with the image of Socrates in the *Phaedo*.

with courage and quasi-anger, and yet cultivating *humanitas* by producing, to the end, writings expressing medical compassion. Even as he looked around, death was, in fact, upon him.

I have spoken of anger and non-anger in the public context. But Nikidion might accept the complex Stoic argument about the importance of avoiding anger in this sphere, while still believing that we ought to keep our private loves and permit ourselves, in these cases, a deeper implication with the world. (It is no accident that the cases that show the limits of Senecan detachment are deaths of children.) She might remember that the Stoic wise person is permitted (after a fashion) to fall in love (*SVF* III.650–53; see chapter 12 n.3). And she might well wonder what this love is, and whether the Stoics could permit the deep passions of unregenerate *erōs*, with the conflicts and pains those may entail. To this question, as well, and to its deepest psychological complexities, Seneca is no stranger.

✳ CHAPTER 12 ✳

Serpents in the Soul: A Reading
of Seneca's *Medea*

O bed of women, full of turmoil, how many bad things you have
already done to mortals.

> Euripides, *Medea* 1290–92

Stop wanting your husband, and there is not one of the things you
want that will fail to happen.

> Epictetus [addressing Medea], *Disc.* 2.17.22

The wise man ought to love his wife deliberately, not passionately. He
controls the impulse to pleasure and is not led headlong to intercourse.

> Seneca, *On Marriage* [fragment]

Madness will come to you too.

> Cassandra, in Seneca, *Agamemnon* 1012

I

IMAGINE, first, the ending, staging it in your mind as the audience for
Seneca's recitation-dramas would have staged it:

She appears on the steep slope of the palace roof. The man she loves
stares up at her. He sees her looming over him (995), radiant and boiling,
wrapped in the red light of her grandfather Sun.[1] (She wrapped his helpless
bride in a cloak that ate her flesh with snaking flames [818–19].) She will
not die of this light. Fire is her patrimony, as snakes are her familiars. She
calls down to him to lift his swollen eyes her way (1020)—knowing, perhaps, that never has her beauty appeared to greater advantage. He is witnessing a triumph. It is the triumph of love. And now bleeding innocent
limbs of children come hurtling through the air, the last "votive offering"
(1020) of passion.

It is his passion too. For although the Chorus prefers to acquit him,

---

[1] Medea's relation to the Sun is given much emphasis in the play: cf. 28–36, 207–10, 510–
12, 570ff. For a good discussion of this, see Fyfe (1983) 82.

describing him as "accustomed in fear, and with a reluctant right hand, to caress the breasts of an unbridled partner" (103–4), Jason knows, or should know, otherwise. Only a moment before, in a desperate attempt to save the last child, he appealed to her in the name of the desire that bound and binds them. "By our flight together," he calls. (For love they robbed her father, killed her brother.) "By our bed—to which I have not been unfaithful" (1002–3)—insisting that his erotic life has been with her alone, and not with the virtuous person who died. Her reply acknowledges that they have indeed been intimate very recently—even while he was contracting marriage with a decorous virgin (whose body her arts alone managed to violate); even, in fact, while she was deploying the "whole tribe of snakes" (705) to get rid of this person. For Medea thinks it possible that she may even now be pregnant by him. She proposes a simple gynecological experiment to ascertain the facts, and to correct them:

If even now in my uterus [*matre*][2] there lies concealed some safety deposit [*pignus*] from you, I shall examine the inside of my abdomen with a sword and draw it out on the iron. (1012–13)

She is not suggesting that she might make a cut across her abdomen; she is too victorious, too defensive, for self-harm. No, enraged by the knowledge that he has been in her, that he might even now be in her, maddened by the thought of a piece of him (of their love) lodged in her own body, feeding on it, she retaliates with the wish for a murderous vaginal penetration, one that will pierce where he pierced, cancel his penetration with one controlled and managed by her alone; one that, ridding her body of love's tumorlike growth, will restore her to the health of self-sufficiency. "My kingdom has come back," she exults. "My stolen virginity has come back. . . . Oh festal day, oh wedding day" (984–86). Married to her own aggression, safely sealed against external harm. Both of them have extended themselves out into the uncertain world. Both have valued undependable things. Now she stabs him in the body of his living child (cf. 550); he stabs her by placing in her a possible new child, a pledge of *erōs*—a pledge that can be redeemed only by violence. Neither preserves integrity; neither is free of pain; neither is free of evil.

And then, flying through the bright air, a chariot appears for her, drawn by two scaly snakes equipped with wings (1023–24). "This is the way I

---

[2] For the figure, see also Costa (1973), F. J. Miller (1917), Ahl (1986). The word picks up the literal use of *mater* at 1007: "Seek the beds of virgins, abandon mothers."

make my escape," she calls, taking the reins (1022). "A road in the heavens is open for me." Charioteer and serpents, they ascend. Eyes streaming, swollen, he looks after her, weeping for his wife, for his children, for all that he has loved and she has killed. Weeping, too, if he is that honest, for the murders they have done together, for the passion he felt and feels. "Go aloft through the deep spaces of heaven," he calls to her, for the last time. "And bear witness that where you travel there are no gods" (1026–27).

What does this awful nightmare have to do with us? Seneca's claim is that this story of murder and violation is our story—the story of every person who loves. Or rather, that no person who loves can safely guarantee that she, or he, will stop short of this story. The Aristotelian holds that we can have passionate love in our lives and still be people of virtue and appropriate action: that the virtuous person can be relied upon to love the right sort of person in the right way at the right time, in the right relation to other acts and obligations.[3] Medea's problem is not a problem of love per se, it is a problem of inappropriate, immoderate love. The virtuous person can avoid this problem. The women of the Chorus in Euripides' *Medea*, who persistently treat their heroine as an abnormal being, doomed to live out the fate

---

[3] For Seneca's relation to Aristotelianism, see chapters 10 and 11, where I argue that Aristotle provides him not only with an opposing philosophical position, but also with a view close to many of the intuitions of his interlocutor concerning the role of emotions in the good life. Here I mean to describe a general Aristotelian position on love, analogous to Aristotle's explicit position on anger (see chapter 3). That it is close to Aristotle's position concerning *philia* that has an erotic component has been successfully shown by Price (1989). The Stoics clearly credited the Peripatetics with a general across-the-board position that emotions should be moderated, not extirpated (see especially Sen. *De Ira* 1, Cic. *TD* 4). The closeness of the "Aristotelian" position to that of Euripides' chorus confirms its popular credentials.

For Greek Stoic views of *erōs*, see *SVF* III.397–99 and 650–53. The definitions reject the form of *erōs* that is a mere longing for intercourse without friendship, but permit the wise man a form of physical erotic love that is combined with the hope of friendship. Cicero mocks and denounces this inconsistency in the assault on passion (*TD* 4.70–76). Seneca's *On Marriage* (fragments in Haase [1897–89]) condemns all erotic passion toward one's spouse (see epigraph and n. 48). Married people should have intercourse for reproduction only. Musonius Rufus joins in the attack on passion, holding that pleasure should never be the goal of marital intercourse. But he paints a more favorable picture of marriage as a "partnership" (*koinōnia*) and "living-together" (*sumbiōsis*) in which man and woman "strive together and breathe together." He urges marriage on the philosopher. (See "On the Goal of Marriage," and "Is Marriage an Impediment to Philosophy?" in Hense [1905].)

belonging to an overly intense nature, subscribe to this comforting thought:

> Excessive passions, when they come, bring neither good fame nor virtue to men. But if Aphrodite comes in the right way at the right time, there is no other god who is so delightful. (627–31)[4]

Seneca sternly tells us here that this distinction is empty. There is no erotic passion that reliably stops short of its own excess. That very way of caring about an external uncontrolled object yields uncontrol in the soul: in Medea's soul, strong and heroic; in Jason's, split (as most souls are) between love of passion and fear of morality.

Again, the Aristotelian tells us that we can have love in our lives and still get rid of cruelty and murderous rage. Euripides' Chorus prays to Aphrodite not to stir up hostility and aggression, but to "honor beds without strife" (639–40). The Aristotelian virtuous person is mild, not prone to vindictiveness (*EN* IV.5, especially 1126a 1–3). Seneca's argument will tell us that this, too, is a hollow prayer. Given the nature of the beliefs that ground the passions, and given the contingencies of life, one can never safely guarantee that love will not give birth to murder. For the love may come to have an impediment; someone may assail or oppose or damage it. And then love itself—its own evaluative exaltation of its object—provides rage with its most exquisite fuel. *Veniet et vobis furor.*

Finally, the Aristotelian claims that you can have an acceptable amount of personal integrity inside a life of love. You can form passionate attachments and still regard yourself as your own to govern, your selfhood as inviolate. Seneca will argue that this, too, is evasion. Love itself is a dangerous hole in the self, through which it is almost impossible that the world will not strike a painful and debilitating blow. The passionate life is a life of continued gaping openness to violation, a life in which pieces of the self are groping out into the world and pieces of the world are dangerously making their way into the insides of the self; a way of life appropriately described in the imagery of bodily violation, implosion, explosion; of sexual penetration and unwanted pregnancy.

This play explores these arguments and the connections among them. In so doing it shows us the shape of the life of passion and its characteristic

---

[4] For a similar wish, see Pindar *Nem.* 8: "Divine youthful bloom, herald of the ambrosial love pleasures of Aphrodite, you who sit on the eyelids of young girls and of boys, one person you lift up with the gentle hands of necessity, others with other hands. It is welcome if, not wandering from the appropriate occasion for each thing, one is able to get hold of the better sort of erotic love."

conception of the self; and, over against these, the structure of Stoic self-sufficiency, seen as the cure for such a life. It claims to be our story; this claim must be assessed in connection with the Stoic claim that the basic assessable action is not a movement in the outer world, but a movement in the world of the heart, a movement of thought, of wish, of desire. The play claims, then, that none of us, if we love, can stop ourselves from the wish to kill; and that a wish to kill is itself a murder. The erotic soul of Plato's *Phaedrus*, inspired by desire for its beloved, ascends toward truth and knowledge, a winged chariot driven by a charioteer and drawn by two powerful horses. Passionate love creates a beautiful harmonious movement, as the noble character of the horse representing the soul's emotions forms a partnership with reason and gives reason new motivational and cognitive power.[5] Seneca's winged chariot (absent from Euripides, but prominently stressed in this play) reveals to us, he claims, the true nature of the erotic: the human agent is drawn along toward heat and fire by two scaly serpents, whose sinuous and ignoble movements mimic the movements of the two lovers' bodies in the grip of passion, whose silent murderous ferocity is emblematic of the murderous wish of passion itself.

Such arguments against Aristotelianism can be found in Stoic prose works as well; but they are worked out with particular power and vividness in the plot and the language of this tragedy. And the Stoics, unlike the other Hellenistic schools, have a high regard for tragedy, giving it cognitive

---

[5] Plato's *Phaedrus* is a work well known and much valued by Roman Stoics. Cicero, for example, shows a detailed knowledge of one of its arguments at *TD* 1.53. Seneca paraphrases it (naming Plato), at *Tranq.* 17.10 (referring to 245A), and possibly also at *Ben.* 4.33.1 (the phrase introduced by *ut ait Plato* may paraphrase 246A). He also makes detailed reference to *Theaetetus, Phaedo, Republic, Timaeus,* and *Laws* (see the passages collected in Motto [1970]). At *Ep.* 24.6, Seneca points out that Cato, his paradigmatic Stoic hero, read Plato's *Phaedo* just before his death; and M. Griffin (1976) chapter 11 shows that Seneca, too, modeled his own death on the death of Socrates. This shows us that Seneca's relation to Plato was so deep and internal that the text became a way of expressing the most profound commitments of his life. For other Stoic or Stoic-related uses of the Platonic chariot and horses, see Plut. *Virt. Mor.* 446E: Ar. Did. *Ecl.* 2.89.4–90.6; Posidonius frr. 31, 166; Philo *Leg. Alleg.* 2.94, 3.118; Galen *PHP* 4.2, 244D, 4.5.18, and cf. 3.3.15, 3.3.5–6. (See the discussion of these passages in Inwood [1985] 462.) For an account of the motivational and cognitive role of emotion in the *Phaedrus*, see Nussbaum (1986a) chapter 7 and Price (1989). On Posidonius' use of the *Phaedrus* to defend his tripartite conception of the soul, see Nussbaum (1993a). Although Plato does distinguish between the appetitive and the emotional horse, he stresses that even the former is kept in line by reason, and the whole moves as a *sumphuton dunamis*, a "grown-together capability." Posidonius seems to think that the appetitive part, too, can be reformed and educated.

importance,[6] arguing that it can frequently display the human significance of a philosophical argument more clearly than prose writing. Cleanthes defends the philosophical value of poetry using a striking image: "Just as our breath produces a sharper and more focused sound when it passes through the long, narrow passage of the trumpet and pours out by a hole that opens at the end, so the narrow constraint of poetic form makes our meanings sharper and more focused" (Seneca, *Ep.* 108.10). Being sharper and more focused, poetry can graphically depict to the wavering soul the risks and crimes of love, probing its latent sympathies and tacit ambivalences, confronting it with a story of guilt that it cannot help acknowledging as its own. Epictetus argues that among the literary forms tragedy is the one best suited to arguing against the passions. "For what else are tragedies but the sufferings of human beings who have been wonderstruck by external things, set down and displayed in the customary meter?" (*Disc.* 1.4.26) And again, "Look how tragedy comes about: when chance events befall fools" (2.26.31). Such poems can toughen our souls by showing in an unavoidable way the consequences of the life of external wonder.

In the spirit of Stoic therapy, then, I turn to Seneca's *Medea*, looking there for a clear expression of the strongest and least circular of the Stoic arguments against passion; looking for an argument capable of engaging the heart in an unsettling scrutiny of its own commitments. After introducing the play's plot and central issues, I shall spend some time examining the depiction of passion in the play, arguing that it does indeed both conform to and develop Chrysippus' account. I shall then examine the way in which Seneca's treatment of Medea's story works out the argument from integrity and the two arguments from excess. I shall examine the play's depiction of the audacious self of passion and the closed self of Stoic self-sufficiency. Finally, I shall ask whom these arguments could convince, and how someone who is attached to love might answer them—how Seneca's own ambivalence begins to answer them. And I shall be led to some concluding

---

[6] This is true of Chrysippan Stoicism and its later continuers, especially Seneca (see chapters 10, 11 with references) and Epictetus. Posidonius, because of his belief that the soul has a separate irrational part, seems to have adopted a non-cognitive view of the moral importance of poetry and music. See also the fragments of Diogenes of Babylon's *On Music* preserved in Philodemus' polemic (*SVF* III, pp. 221–35). The evidence on Stoic views of poetry is assembled usefully in De Lacy (1948); but he does not make the very important distinction between a cognitive and a non-cognitive attitude to poetic education. I discuss this question thoroughly in Nussbaum (1993a). Seneca points out that much actual poetry is harmful, in that it contains, and reinforces, the false value structure of daily life (*Ep.* 115.12). This point, which had been made at least since Plato's *Republic*, appears to require not so much the rejection of poetry as its radical reform.

reflections about the limits of the Aristotelian position; about the ways in which love does indeed require the lover to go beyond the gods of morality.

The self-examination demanded by this play is a wrenching business. We are asked to confront our deepest feelings and to see that they contain the perpetual risk of chaos and of evil. Seneca chooses a way of approaching us with this knowledge that is violent, confrontational.[7] He thrusts ugliness before us and says: all this is you and yours. It seems to me that we do not take up the therapeutic challenge of this play unless we take up, as well, the challenge of its style. This means, I think, that the interpreter should seek, toward herself and toward her interlocutors, the same immediacy, the same bluntness, the same willingness to confront the horrible and to cause it to be confronted, that Seneca's play requires and exemplifies. This immediacy is not self-explanatory: it stands in need of philosophical commentary. But it must be there, or we will have cut ourselves off from some of the possibilities of understanding that this play makes available.

II

She is justified: yet she does monstrous things. From the play's opening lines, this doubleness is stressed. Medea calls, first, on the gods of lawful marriage; on Juno Lucina, guardian of the marriage bed, protector of childbirth (1–2); and upon all the gods by whom Jason swore binding oaths to her. Then, "with ill-omened voice," (12) her anger invokes a darker group of deities: "chaos of endless night, kingdom of the world below, unsanctified spirits of the dead" (9–10). Last of all, with a cry in which the demand for justice is inseparable from the lust for revenge, she calls the Furies:

> Now, now be near, goddesses who avenge crime, your hair foul with writhing serpents, grasping the black torch in your bloody hands—be near—as once, dread spirits, you stood about my marriage bed. Bring death to this new wife, death to her father, to all the royal line. (13–18)

We cannot avoid feeling the justice of her anger. She calls the Furies because she has a right to call them. She has loved Jason long and loyally. She has risked for him; she has sacrificed home and family; she has even committed crimes. They have lived together for years; she has borne him legitimate

---

[7] Seneca stresses the value of theater for recognition of self and "confession of truth" (*confessionem veritatis*) in *Ep.* 108.8–12.

children. And now he betrays his oaths, his lawful marriage, his wife, for the bed of a rich and well-connected younger woman. Well might the Furies bear a black and bloody torch to that marriage feast. It is, as she says, *fas*[8]—lawful and right—that she should call awful penalties down upon their union.

And yet we cannot help feeling, too, the foulness of this revenge, the awfulness, especially, of calling out powers of hell against Jason's new bride, whose only crime was to agree to receive Jason's disloyal affections. The Furies, by themselves, evoke this double response. For as described they are legitimate avengers of a real guilt; yet they are also foul and hideous. They bring their blackness, their serpents, to the soul of the one who, with whatever justice, invokes them.[9] Later, as she invokes the whole tribe of serpents to give her poison to use against Creousa, Medea herself becomes similar to these Furies—as, hair loosed, neck arched, and head darting, she calls once again upon Hecate (800–801).

This mingling of justification and horror is essential to Seneca's plot—indeed, to several of his plots. His heroines are not criminals to begin with; they are made criminals by love. His tragedies parade before us a series of loyal loving wives who are abandoned in middle age by opportunistic husbands—usually for a younger woman, sometimes for money, always with callous disregard for the wife's long years of service. The wife's intense, unabated love then produces an upheaval that leads to tragedy—usually through evil action by the wife against rival, or husband, or both. Deaneira, Phaedra, Clytemnestra, Medea—by leading us again and again through variants on this same plot, obsessively reworked, Seneca forces us to see that it is the one who loves properly, loyally, the one who really understands what it is to value a commitment to an external object, who will be most derailed by a loss. That it is precisely because these women genuinely care about that external item, stake their whole being on it, that they are driven mad by grief and anger. He shows us that a betrayal that comes from outside, though through no fault of the woman's own, can still produce evil in the woman's soul. And by dwelling on the plight of the aging wife, the collapse of a marriage of long standing, he reminds us that, the structure of erotic passion being as it is, such betrayals and such losses will frequently occur to people who have passion in their lives.

Medea lives out this general story of betrayal and derangement. But she differs from other Senecan heroines in her strength and greatness of spirit. We know that the Stoics were unusually interested in her story. Chrysippus is said to have copied out almost the whole of Euripides' play in one of his

---

[8] For excellent treatment of the ambiguities of this speech, see Fyfe (1983).

[9] On the connection between furies and moral darkness in Virgil, see M. Putnam (1990).

works.[10] Although his critics charged him with doing it to pad out the list of his writings, we can assume some stronger motivation. Epictetus, who reveres Chrysippus above all other Stoic writers and thoroughly knows his work, gives us an account of his own interest in Medea that may well derive from Chrysippus himself. Medea, he tells us (2.27.19) is an example of a "great-natured" person who has had the misfortune to become attached to external things. Here is a soul of great power and force; the magnitude of her revenge shows us, he says, that she has "the proper impression of what it means for someone not to get what he or she wants" (2.27.20). In other words, she lives out the Aristotelian life as well as it can be lived, with a soul of great strength and a proper understanding of the worth of her commitments. She is a good case of Aristotelian virtue. Indeed, she is by the same token excellent raw material for the Stoa.[11] She displays the elements of virtue that are common ground between the two schools: strength of purpose, greatness of soul,[12] intelligence, spirit, a proper sense of the worth of valuable things. The trouble is that she has the wrong values. If we see the way in which she is led into monstrousness in spite of her worth, by a single simple mistake about the value of a single man, and see how easily she might instead have been an outstanding Stoic figure, we will have understood far more clearly the differences between the two conceptions of virtue. And we can then understand that the crimes people commit from love need not result from some deficiency in love or Aristotelian virtue; they are possibilities for the best—and perhaps for the best more than the

[10] DL 7.180. The criticism of Chrysippus for including too many quotations was widespread; Galen goes on about this at length, and Diogenes reports that Apollodorus of Athens, an Epicurean, attacked Chrysippus' dependence on the poets, saying, "If one were to strip Chrysippus' books of all extraneous quotations, his pages would be left empty." For Chrysippus' interest in the poets and in everyday use, see chapter 10; for his attitude to literature in general and Medea in particular, see Gill (1983) and Nussbaum (1993a). On Chrysippus' own use of a dramatic and rhetorical style, cf. Fronto *Ant.* 2, p. 68 = *SVF* 2.27, which records that, not content with exposition, he "gives description, makes divisions, introduces characters, and puts what he has to say in other people's mouths." For Seneca's relation to this aspect of Chrysippus, see Wright (1974).

[11] The Stoics will not be upset, as Euripides' characters are and as many Greek thinkers would be, by the fact that a woman is here displaying masculine virtues, such as courage and greatness of soul. On the equal capability of women for the virtues, see chapter 9, and especially Musonius Rufus, "That Women Too Should Do Philosophy?" and "Should Sons and Daughters have the Same Education?" (in Hense 1905), cited there. To stress further the side of moral justification, Seneca even permits Medea to use official religious language as she takes her revenge—see 562, and Costa (1973) ad loc., Henry and Henry (1985) 159.

[12] Rosenmeyer (1989) also argues that she has many properties of the Stoic hero (48), though I think he is wrong to suggest that for the Stoic hero "life has meaning only as a performance, as an aesthetic experience."

worst—in that universe of precious undependable things. "Poor woman," says Epictetus, "because she made a mistake about the most important things, she has been transformed from a human being into a poisonous snake" (*Disc.* 1.28.8–9).

Seneca's treatment of Medea, I believe, is like this. For he displays her as shrewd, strong, regal, honest. He links her in the choral lyrics with great explorers and heroes of the past—with Orpheus, Hercules, Meleager, and others. He gives her speeches expressing an accurate sense of the wrong done to her and a determination that her proud spirit will respond to calamity in an appropriate way. "Fortune can take my wealth, but not my soul" (176)—a statement that conjures up a whole tradition of Stoic heroism. She sees her murderous acts as Epictetus sees them, as appropriate, in some sense correct, responses to her loss: "Do it now, my soul—you must not lose your virtuous act in secrecy" (976–77, just before killing the children). And above all, he depicts her as one who understands how deeply her own virtue, her selfhood, is identified with externals—in such a way that, injured and invaded by fortune, she is not herself any longer. She can be made Medea again only by a revenge that removes the obstacle. "Medea," the Nurse calls to her as she suffers. "I shall become Medea," she answers (171). And when, rejecting all her previous crimes as petty, she conceives of a great deed to bear the power of her grief, she then can say, "Now I am Medea: my wits have grown through suffering" (910). In suffering she has understood what it means to lose what she wants, and therefore has understood what she herself is and stands for. At the end, throwing the murdered children down, she calls out to him, "Do you recognize (or acknowledge) your wife [*coniugem agnoscis tuam*]?" (1021) Several passages link her name alliteratively with other words; the list reveals a nature poised between greatness and monstrosity. We have *monstrum, maius, mare, malum, magnum, immane.* The greatness and the evil seem more than incidentally linked. The Stoic values Medea for her greatness: he would like to teach her to have that greatness without the evil. Epictetus thinks that this is possible; Seneca, as we shall see, has a more complicated view.

III

If we are going to read this play as a relative of Stoic ethical arguments,[13] we need to begin by establishing that its representation of the passions

---

[13] There have been many attempts to trace these connections. See, e.g., Marti (1945, 1947), Pratt (1948, 1983), Egermann (1940), Dingel (1974), Rosenmeyer (1989). Marti's approach (claiming that the plays are an ordered pedagogical sequence) is too rigid, and not supported

is indeed Stoic. And in fact, if Nikidion were to use this play as a casebook of examples illustrating Chrysippan theory, she would be richly supplied.

As we have already seen, Medea's emotions—love, grief, anger—fundamentally involve the assignment of high value to external objects and situations. Her love for Jason, for her children, for her power and position, all these are the mainsprings of her action. The point is made just as clearly in the characterization of Jason, who considers his children to be his very "reason for living, the comfort of my heart, exhausted by care. Sooner could I part with breath, with limbs, with the light" (547–49). This judgment is, of course, the basis for his ensuing grief. As Medea says when she hears it, "He is trapped: there is a space wide open for a wound" (550).

But this much is common to all ancient thinkers on passion; we need to do more to show the play's Chrysippan credentials. And we can do more. The identity of emotion with belief or judgment is in fact prominently stressed. Medea's passions are not shown as coming from some part of her character to which the rational judging part is opposed. They are inclinations of her thought or judgment itself—of her whole personality, conceived of as housed in the rational part.[14] When the Nurse urges her to keep her ill wishes hidden, she replies: "Light is the grief that can deliberate prudently and conceal itself: great sufferings do not hide" (155–56). Grief is depicted as an entity capable of deliberation, of choice whether to hide or not; it is not something that stands in a certain relation to thought, it is a

---

by historical evidence; Pratt starts off from the weakly argued theory that Seneca is rejecting Chrysippus and following Posidonius; thus he cannot do justice to the dramas' cognitive content. More promising is Dingel, who has interesting things to say about Senecan tragedy's ambivalent relationship to some items of Stoic doctrine. The best accounts of the thought of Seneca's plays are the accounts that respond precisely and sympathetically to the plays' internal structures and are willing to be moved by them—above all Regenbogen (1930) and Henry and Henry (1985). Briefer pieces that capture the spirit of Senecan writing well are Herington (1966) and Segal (1983a and b). Segal's book (1986a) is less helpful, I think, on account of its rather rigid use of the terminology of Lacanian psychoanalytic theory. Seneca was a greater psychologist that Lacan, and everything that needs to be said about his play can be said by talking about the play. See also Hadot (1969), on Seneca's relation to traditions of psychotherapy. For a balanced introduction to other problems connected with the understanding of Senecan tragedy, see Fantham (1982). Rosenmeyer's (1989) project of linking the tragedies with Stoic physics is a fruitful extension of Regenbogen's work, though I do not think it removes the need for an ethical and psychological understanding. Especially valuable are Rosenmeyer's discussions linking these two levels. See also M. Putnam (forthcoming).

[14] See Gill (1983) and Knox (1977) on Euripides' play, and chapter 10, section III. Chrysippus apparently found Stoic psychology in Euripides; Seneca's drama presents the Chrysippan view in a far more explicit way.

form of thought. Later she speaks of her "angry soul" as "decreeing" or "judging" something "within her" (917–18).

Conflict, too, is shown in the Chrysippan way—not as the struggle of contending forces, but as an oscillation or fluctuation of the whole personality. The most remarkable example of this approach is in Medea's long speech of deliberation at 893ff. First she goads her soul to anger, reminding herself of Jason's wrongs (893–909). When she has fully embraced the judgment that she has been wronged, she declares herself identical with her anger: *Medea nunc sum* (910). Anger now shows her the way: the final stroke of vengeance must be the killing of the children. But the thought of the children now causes her heart to change its course. "Horror strikes my heart, my limbs are numb with cold, my breast trembles. Anger has left its place; the angry wife is driven out, and the mother has entirely come back [*materque tota coniuge expulsa redit*]" (928). She pours out her horror at child-murder. Then the thought that they are Jason's children returns. Now the oscillations become extremely rapid:

> Let them die, they are not mine, let them perish.—They are my own,[15] they are free of crime and fault, they are innocent—I acknowledge it— and so was my brother. Why, soul, do you totter back and forth [*titubas*]? Why is my face wet with tears, and why do anger and love draw now here now there [*nunc huc nunc illuc*] my oscillating self [*variam*]? A double tide tosses me; I am uncertain of my course—as when rushing winds wage savage war, and from both sides conflicting currents lash the sea, and the fluctuating waters boil, even so is my heart tossed on the waves [*fluctuatur*]. Anger puts love to flight, mother-love anger. Grief, yield to mother-love.

The oscillation continues. She embraces her beloved children. Then the tide of anger returns with the thought of Jason's wrong. "Again grief grows and hate boils, and the Fury of old takes my hand. Anger, where you lead I follow" (951–53).

This is not only a marvelous account of a deep torment; it is also a

---

[15] I have punctuated this utterance slightly differently from the way chosen by Zwierlein (1986a and b), Costa (1973), and F. S. Miller (1917), who all write: "occidant, non sunt mei; / pereant, mei sunt, crimine et culpa carent, . . . etc." Ahl (1986) translates that punctuation. On that reading, the shift takes place later, after *sunt*, and the thought is, "Let them die because they now belong to Creousa, and let them perish just because they are mine [and therefore also Jason's]." I find this less plausible, because throughout Medea has linked anger and the desire for revenge with the thought that the children are Creousa's, love and shrinking from vengeance with the thought that they are hers (cf. 920–25, 929–30).

compelling argument for the intuitive rightness of the Chrysippan view. The depth of Medea's conflict is shown in the fact that it is, precisely, an oscillation between two positions of the mind and heart, each of which represents a way in which Medea sees the world, and her children in it. One minute they appear to her as inexpressibly dear and wonderful; as innocent, as special, as hers. The next minute they strike her as pieces of their father and tools to wound him with. Her entire soul is tossed back and forth; it rocks, it verges now this way, now that. In two other scenes of deliberation, the Chorus' *nunc huc nunc illuc* is literally acted out, as Medea's physical pacing back and forth mimes the turnings of her soul. She "runs now here now here (*huc et huc*)" with a frenzied motion (385); she "turns her step now this way now that, like a tigress robbed of her young" (862–63). We become convinced that Medea's conflict is grave precisely because her whole soul is carried on the flood; what is going on here is a struggle of reason concerning what to view as most important. The account is intuitively compelling; it is also too emphatic in its emphasis on Chrysippus' view to be accidental.

But more strange and striking yet, and our most conclusive proof of this play's Chrysippan origins, is its depiction of relationships among the passions. To someone who reads this play straight through for the first time, nothing is more shocking and surprising than the way in which the names of different passions replace each other—unpredictably, indiscriminately, almost as if they are synonyms—or as if the characters themselves did not quite know what emotion they were feeling or seeing. Jason describes Medea this way: "And see, at the sight of me she starts up, she bursts into rage, she displays her hate before her—the whole of her grief is in her face" (445–46). Later, in the passage we have just discussed, Medea says of her own feelings: "Anger puts mother-love to flight, mother-love anger; grief, yield to mother-love" (943–44). In both of these passages the word "grief" appears where we should expect "anger"—or, rather, the anger and the grief are so close, so commingled, that what first manifests itself as one shows itself a second later as the other.[16] The Loeb translator F. J. Miller,

---

[16] This closeness of the passions, evident in other Latin poetic texts as well (in Virgil above all) has even affected the sense of the word *dolor*, so that in quite a few passages it appears to mean "being wounded" in the sense of "feeling resentment," and thus lies very close to anger. See, e.g., *Aen.* 1.25, 5.608, 7.291, 2.594, 9.66, 8.220, 8.501. This complicates my point, but does not remove it. We would expect the Stoic thesis to link what ordinary non-technical discourse keeps separate only if it were a theory very much at odds with ordinary beliefs and life. I have argued that it is not. The fact that non-technical discourse has the same tendency for *dolor* to hook up, on occasion, with *ira* should, I think, be taken as evidence of the

perplexed, translates *dolor* in the second passage by "wrath." But such passages (and they are by no means unusual in Seneca's plays)[17] should not be normalized. For it is not surprising that love, anger, and grief are this close, if the Stoics are right about what these passions are. Medea's passionate love, her anger, and her grief, are all identical with judgments that ascribe high and non-replaceable value to Jason. They differ only in the precise content of the proposition. Grief focuses on the fact that this beloved man is lost to her; anger, on the fact that he is gone because he has betrayed his oaths and deserted her; love, simply on how valuable he is. It is not surprising, in Medea's situation, that these judgments should lie close to one another in the heart.

What we see as we watch her is that one basic condition—the condition of ascribing so much importance to this unstable external being—naturally takes on a kaleidoscopic multiplicity, as she goes through the various judgments that are part of this condition. The Nurse describes it well:

> Her cheeks flaming, she draws deep sighs, she shouts aloud, she weeps floods of tears, she shines with joy; she shows the form of every passion. She stops: threatens seethes complains groans. Where will she incline the weight of her soul? Where will she place her threats? Where will this wave break? Madness swells beyond all bounds. (387–92)

The soul in love has gone outside of its own bounds into the world. It is swollen up like a wave that can break now on the side of joy, now on that of murderous rage or of grief. (And her joy here may be joy at the thought of murder.) Once she cares about this man that much, there is no passion into which she will not go. The change from grief to love, from anger to joy—this is hardly in her power, but lies with him, with the power she has given him over her life and thought. (Indeed, the only way she can get from grief to joy without his help is to do several murders.) And the play's claim is that the same is true of the relation between love and anger. If he and Creousa

---

intuitive strength of the view. I am grateful to Michael Putnam for discussion on this point; and I have been helped by the subtle account of *dolor, amor,* and *ira* in M. Putnam (1985). See also M. Putnam (1987, 1990).

[17] For just a few pertinent examples, see *Phdr.* 360ff., 1156; *Ag.* 131ff., *HO* 249ff. (on which see Regenbogen [1930]), 295ff. I would say, both in these cases and in the cases brought forward by Putnam (n. 16) that it is usually right to translate *dolor* as "grief" or "pain"—but to recognize how quickly pain leads to retaliation. At *HO* 249ff., the "forms" of *dolor* are complaints, implorings, and groans (*queritur implorat gemit*); but it is also clear that they are closely associated with threats (249); and 295 insists that *dolor* demands revenge.

act so as to threaten what she values most in the world, then the very commitment of soul that is her love will turn into rage and hate directly.

I have said that these points are evidence of Stoic doctrine. I have also said that I find them compelling and psychologically true. There is too much highly specific use of Stoic ideas to be mere coincidence, especially since our author is a Stoic philosopher. But the play is not a mere tract or handbook, nor is Seneca just paying lip-service to an idea. The conviction and power of this dramaturgy is the work of someone who has found in the Stoic doctrine a true way of seeing human life.

IV

So much for the depiction of passion. Now we must see how Seneca uses this psychology to construct a case against love—a case that might even convince the Aristotelian, antecedently convinced of its high value. I have argued in chapter 10 that one could accept the Stoic analysis and depiction of passion without accepting their case for extirpation—though clearly the analysis helps them both to show that extirpation is possible and to convince us that it is necessary. Seneca has accepted the analysis; he also presses in a powerful way the case for extirpation, developing the strongest of the Stoic anti-Aristotelian arguments.

No confirmed Aristotelian who reads this play will be convinced that Medea's love is simply an error of judgment, an acceptance of beliefs about Jason that are false. Seneca has not rested his case upon falsity—and chapter 10 has shown us that this is wise. Indeed, in order to persuade the reader that the argument is evenhanded, he has, if anything, shown Jason to be a more appealing figure than he was in Euripides. By stressing that his motive was sincere love for his children and fear for their safety, not greed or callousness, Seneca gives him a new humanity and dignity. Both here and in the continual reminders of his past heroism and strength, we see a figure who is believably worthy of Medea and her judgments, worthy of her loving wish for his life: "May he live on—if possible, my Jason, as he was— if not, still may he live remembering me, and keep safely the life I gave him" (140–41). Indeed, as we have already suggested, Jason is a figure who in many ways invites our identification. Like most members of the audience, he is a split being with a double allegiance. On the one hand, he shows a sensitivity to morality and a fearfulness before moral laws that Medea increasingly loses. His first and final speeches are about the gods of morality (431ff., 1026–27). He speaks of moral shame (504), of loyalty (*fides*,

1003), of a desire for reasonable discourse and an end to anger (537, 558–59). It is as a moral being that he shrinks (or so the Chorus sees it) before Medea's ferocious passion (102–4). On the other hand, he is a hero, and as such is persistently linked with *erōs* and *audacia*, with bold exploits that have Medea as their fitting prize (364), since they break through the laws of nature. In both aspects, Jason wins the reader's sympathy; we are convinced both by his erotic nature and by his moral concern; and we sense the same double allegiance in ourselves.[18]

Seneca grants, then, that this is a good case of love, no obvious delusion or distortion. But here his argument has only begun. For all three of the non-circular arguments against Aristotle are here worked out with subtlety. If we study them in the order in which chapter 10 introduced them, we should remember that much of the drama's force derives from the way they are interwoven.

First we have, throughout, ample evidence of the painful and debilitating feeling of passion. Love, anger, and grief are repeatedly described as very violent movements, stronger than "any force of fire or of swelling gale" (579ff.). This violence of movement results in a weakened and unstable condition of the soul. This weakness is most evident in the case of Jason, who, from his first entrance, has clearly lost the vigor and intensity of his heroic days. He is a man exhausted, drained, burned out: "I yield," he says, "worn out by troubles" (518). And the same is true of his wife. Medea, from the time when she first appears, is enervated, longing for "the ancient vigor" of her spirit (41–42).[19] She feels that she is being drawn here and there in a way she does not comprehend: "unstable, distracted as I am, I am carried in every direction" (123–24). She is riding a wave; nobody knows where it will break (392). Above all, she feels an agonizing passivity; she is "snatched away headlong by mad passion" (850–51), she does not know "what my fierce soul has decreed within me" (917–18); "I follow," she says to her anger, "where you lead" (953). Passages like these show the experience of emotion to be a disturbing and awful one for the person who, in Aristotelian fashion, is attached to practical reason, planning, and control. How can a figure this commanding, this capable of heroic virtue, endure to be at the mercy of forces like these, her soul blown before the wind?

The repeated suggestion that the passions may operate beneath the level

---

[18] On Jason's character, see Maurach (1966), Pratt (1983) 25, Herington (1966).

[19] For these symptoms of passion, cf. *Phdr.* 360ff., especially 374–78: "She goes with an unsteady step, wasted now in strength. Her energy is not the same, and the ruddy glow of health does not shine on her bright face."

of consciousness deepens Seneca's argument against Aristotle; for can the experience of a life in which the most important things are decided at a level to which the agent has incomplete access be anything but excruciating to one who is trying to live a life "in accordance with practical reason"? Aristotle has let the emotions into the good life without understanding how they operate, without understanding how little they are transparent—how much passivity, therefore, they bring to the life that lets them in. The Stoic, on the other hand, watches over himself "like an enemy lying in wait" (Epict. *Ench.* 48.3)—for his zeal for his moral perfection, taken together with his belief in the moral relevance of thought and desire, means that he cannot afford to let down the guard of moral scrutiny for even a moment.[20]

This leads us directly to the argument from integrity. Medea, like a good Stoic hero, values control; she defines her selfhood in terms of certain aims and activities that are very important to her, and she views it as a diminution of her selfhood if these things should be invaded or controlled by another. But she loves. And any person who loves is opening in the walls of self a hole through which the world may penetrate. Seneca's tragedies are full of images of the loss of bodily integrity—images in which, through an agent's loves and needs, pieces of the external world get taken into the self, there to exert an uncontrolled disturbing power.[21] Thyestes, victim of Atreus' revenge, eats his children and discovers inside his own entrails a horrible substance that both is and is not his own and himself:

> What is the uproar that stirs up my entrails [*viscera*]? What just trembled inside? I feel a burden I cannot carry, and my breast groans with a groaning that is not my own [*meumque gemitu non meo pectus gemit*]. (999–1001)

His boundaries have been invaded by the consequences of *erōs* and anger. Seneca's interlocking word order (*meum . . . non meo*) shows us the horrible confusion of self and not-self that these attachments bring about. Oedipus, who could have had a tranquil life had he not killed in anger, had he not felt erotic passion, discovers his crime and feels that he must dig into himself to root out the eyes in which these passions have lived: he digs out (*scrutatur*) his eyes with "hooked fingers" (965), snatching them from "their furthest roots deep within" (968). In language unmistakably laden

---

[20] Cf. Rabbow (1954), who perceptively speaks of the Stoics' "Wille zur ethischen Totalität."

[21] In what follows I am much indebted to Segal (1983a) whose translations I follow for *Thy.*, *Oed.*, and *Phoen.*; see also Henry and Henry (1985).

with the imagery of his sexual penetration of the woman from whose womb he came, he tears "the hollows and empty recesses," his "hand fixed deep inside." In the *Phoenissae* he goes still further: he wishes to reach beyond the eye into the brain itself: "Now dip your hand into brain; complete your death in that part where I began to die" (180–81). Desire is so deep in his insides that only a fatal assault on his own brain can restore his self-sufficiency. The invasions and corruptions of self that come with passion can be corrected only by further violations. Desire is the beginning of the death of the self.

In the Medea we see these remarkable visceral images worked out with consistency and power. Seneca's language, far more graphically physical than the language of Greek tragedy, reminds us that a life given over to love cannot avoid having holes in it. And once there is a hole, there is, as Medea says, "a space wide open for a wound" (550). Later on, her sword does in fact enter the body of the still-living child; it enters Jason at the same time. "Here, where you forbid me, where you suffer pain [*qua doles*], I shall plunge my sword" (1006). On her side, as we have seen, the sexual love she still feels for Jason is felt as an unwanted pregnancy; her desire is to root it out, to destroy the piece of him that grows in her. Her image of success is the fantasy of restored virginity.

Seneca's violence forces us to confront the issue of integrity in a way that no calm didacticism could. For it reminds us of the physical feeling of passion and of pain—of the way we do feel struck by the external world in a very physical way, as a piercing of our private bodily space. Struck, therefore, when things go wrong, with a pain that is from the world but yet indwelling—that has enormous power, therefore, of dislocation, mutilation. Can the Aristotelian—can any of us—bear this? And Seneca does something more. By showing us these characters' violent response to the violation of bodily integrity, he makes a connection between this argument and the argument from excess that is not, to my knowledge, made in Stoic prose works at all.

The argument goes something like this. The person who leads an Aristotelian life values the passions and their objects; she also values her own personal integrity, her freedom from invasion or violation. Because she values integrity, she will respond to a violation with anger—appropriately, given her value conception—and with some attempt to remove the invading external stimulus, to set the world to rights. Love almost inevitably leads to wounds; so love will lead to anger and to a reactive attempt to root out the source of the disorder, restoring the boundaries of the self. But these attempts are almost always violent. They involve digging out what is other in oneself, assailing the source of pain. And, furthermore, they may also be self-defeating. For love, reacting as anger, moves to seal off the wounds or holes that make love possible. So in the end, what we get is the sealed self that the Stoic has had all along; only the road to this self must be through violence. Virginity once lost can be restored only by the sword. If you see with the open eyes of love, you must blind yourself to remove the evil that has entered. Once the soul's universe is violated, it can be set to rights only by a reactive campaign that disturbs the entire universe. "I shall assault the gods and shake up everything" (424–45), she says.

The Aristotelian likes to imagine herself as stably balanced by good character, taking steady aim at the target of virtuous action. Seneca argues that if the passions and the commitments that ground them remain inside this life, it cannot have this constancy. Instead, it must be in a dangerous oscillation between gaping passivity and a violent rejection of intrusive externals; between raw bleeding skin and tough scar tissue, between rape and violent abortion, being mutilated and mutilating.

And lest we think that reactive passion, once aroused, can be made moderate or gentle, Seneca saturates this drama with evidence of passion's excesses. Only a light grief, Medea has told us, can be ruled by reason (155); since she has loved intensely, she will know no moderation, no mean (*modum*) in hate (397–98). "How difficult it is to turn the soul from its anger when once it is aroused," she says in language that recalls Chrysippus (203–4). The Nurse, observing, describes her: "It is monstrous how her grief grows and feeds its own fire" (671–72).

Two images that recur throughout the play make the Chrysippan idea clear: the image of the bridle, and the image of the wave. Medea's sexuality, said the Chorus, is "unbridled."[22] Later on, they realize that this implies an equal excess in reactive anger: "Medea does not know how to bridle her anger or her love" (866–67). And in the great ode in which the Chorus compares the anger of disappointed love to all the most violent of natural forces, they conclude, "Blind is the fire of love when fanned by anger; it does not want to be ruled, it does not tolerate the bridle" (591–92). If the image of the bridle emphasizes the ardent speed and force of the passions, the wave image emphasizes the inexorability of their violence, once begun. Her wave will surely break (392), her mad passion "overflows" (*exundat*, 392). The Chorus adds to the imagery of water images of fire, wind, and flood-bringing rain (579ff.).

---

[22] On connections between being a proper bride and bearing a bridle, see Aelianus, *De Natura Animalium* 12.33, and other references gathered in Bonnefoy (1991), 97. Aristotle *HA* 578a8 makes the mare model of a greedy female, eager for lovemaking.

We have seen how the play draws the different passions together; we have seen how Seneca's version of the argument from integrity draws them even closer. We have seen Medea's excesses. Seneca completes his argument by showing that—as we by now expect—the excesses of passion are mixed excesses. What we have here is a love that has itself, while still being love, turned murderous. "Where is this blood-stained maenad carried headlong by ferocious love [*praeceps amore saevo*]?" the Chorus asks (849–50). Medea herself makes an even more paradoxical claim. Speaking of the past, of her murder of her brother, she says, "And no crime did I do out of anger [*irata feci*]; it was unhappy love that raged [*saevit infelix amor*]" (135–36). The text has frequently been emended by critics who are troubled by the conjunction of love and ferocity.[23] It is deliberate.

Later the Chorus generalizes the point, in a passage to which we have referred:

> No violence of fire or swelling gale, no fearful force of hurtling spear, is as great as when a wife, bereft of her marriage, burns hot with love and hate [*ardet et odit*]. . . . Blind is the flame of love when fanned by anger. It cannot be ruled, it does not endure the bridle. (579ff.)

In such passages we are confronted with a love itself turned violent. Anger is only a stimulus. The primary strength of frenzy comes from love itself, unhappily blocked. Love is not a gentle, lovely passion (or not only that—for we should not forget Medea's wish for Jason's good); it is the strongest form of violence in nature, a fire that burns now for our wonder, now for terror. The difference is made by fortune; we are passive to it. Nor can we, if we once give ourselves to that flame, in any way prevent it from consuming innocent others. Now we know the deepest reason why the Aristotelian cannot say, "I shall have love in my life, but I shall get rid of murderous rage." It is because it is love itself that rages and does murder.

V

We can now confront the play's central image—the image of the snake. Snakes are, from the beginning of the play, the emblems of Medea, of her love, of the crimes of her love. We see them first writhing in the hair of the

---

[23] See Zwierlein (1986a, 1986b); he keeps *saevit*, defending it against various proposed emendations (such as *suasit, movit,* and *fecit*), with references. Especially pertinent is Virg., *Aen.* 4.531–32: "Ingeminant curas rursusque resurgens / saevit amor magnoque irarum fluctuat aestu."

Furies who, having avenged against Medea the earlier crimes of her love, are now prepared to help her bring destruction to Creousa her rival (13ff.). Her imagination depicts a vengeance that is itself snakelike: "wounds and slaughter and death creeping along the limbs." And (as often in Latin poetry) the thought of the snake is linked with the thought of flame—alike in its lethal suddenness, in its fluid supple shape. The destruction of Corinth is to come by flame; and its witness will be Medea's grandfather the Sun (28ff.). Later in the play, as we have seen, Medea herself becomes a maenad with snakelike neck and loosened hair (752ff., 800–81). The play's central episode is the long scene of incantation, in which Medea calls forth all the snakes on earth and in the heavens. Fierce, powerful, forked tongues darting, winding their coils, they leave their hidden places at the sound of her songs and gather to do the will of her ferocious love. Out of their bodies she extracts poisons that contain "hidden seeds of fire" (832). These devour Creousa's vital organs, as "the snaking flame burns her inmost marrow" (818–19). At the play's end, after being hounded by the angry Furies of her brother, bearing whips made of snakes (958–61), she escapes through the aid of other snakes. The snake-drawn chariot that carries her toward the sun is, as we have seen, Seneca's ironic replacement for the *Phaedrus*' stirring and beautiful image.

But what are snakes here? We have said that they represent her love; her anger; the anger of her love: its cycle of passion, crime, and retribution; its final triumph. But how do they represent it? What does the image of the snake—or the dual image of snake and flame—tell us about Seneca's view of this love? Snakes are a pervasive source of imagery in Latin poetry, as Bernard Knox showed in his classic article "The Serpent and the Flame."[24] And Seneca explores many of the traditional associations: the ferocity of snakes, their silent deadly power, the concealed nature of the threat they pose to innocent life.[25] (The Chorus tells us that not even Idmon, who knew fate well, could guard against a serpent's sudden bite on the Libyan sands [653].) Snakes are sinuous and indirect in motion; they come out from hiding and touch their victim all at once, intrusively, tongue hungrily

[24] Knox (1958), who collects many examples of snake imagery and of the linking of images of snake and flame. He refers also to the "serpent catalogue" in Virg. *Georg.* 3.414–39, and to the elaborate description of a serpent in *Culex* 163–97.

[25] For other references to snakes in Seneca, see Motto (1970). The passages in the prose works stress the poisonous character of snakes, their ferocity, their unpredictability (e.g., *Ir.* 1.1.5–6, 1.16.5, 1.17.6; *Clem.* 1.25.4; *NQ* 2.31.2). But *Clem.* 1.17.1 says of a different sort of animal, "No animal is more recalcitrant of temper, no other needs such skill in handling." That animal is the human being.

darting. They are a most appropriate symbol of erotic passion as this play depicts it. Three centuries later, Augustine tells us why the devil, bringing sin into the Garden of Eden, chose the serpent as his bodily form: "because, being slippery, and moving in tortuous windings, it was suitable for his purpose" (*Civ. Dei* 14.11)—his purpose, of course, being the awakening of sexual desire in the Garden's previously virtuous and will-governed inhabitants. The snake is the suitable form for the threat posed by erotic desire to the will and to morality.[26] It is appropriate that Lucan's poem depicts the snake as the deadliest foe of the Stoic hero Cato, as in the remarkable "catalogue of snakes" he records the dangers faced by Cato in the desert.

In our play, Seneca, far more explicitly than Virgil or Lucan, plays upon the snake's sexual associations, both female and male. Transforming Medea into a snake, he links the serpent with woman's hair, and with her writhing movement. And in the great catalogue of snakes in the incantation scene, he reminds us that the snake is also an emblem of the sexual power of the male. Making her serpentine offering to Hecate, Medea includes "the members that rebellious Typhoeus bore when he attacked the power of Jove" (773–74). F. J. Miller translates *membra* with "these serpent limbs." And in fact if we look to the mythographer Apollodorus (a likely source for Seneca in this and other passages), we find these limbs described as follows. "And growing from his thighs he had extremely large snakes, whose coils, stretching out and up toward his head, sent forth a great deal of hissing" (1.6.3ff.). So, at the moment when she prepares the murder of her rival, she is haunted, as if in a dream or hallucination, by the image of Jason's erotic power—which she depicts as something wondrous and at the same time dangerous, linked with mythic strength and with guilt, something that rebels violently against the gods of morality. To Hecate she offers these members.

Up to a certain point, then, Seneca is true to Stoic tradition in his depiction of the snake (and, through it, of love) as undependable, violent, lethal, the deadliest enemy of virtue and order. Most of the snakes in the catalogues are dangerous foes of the gods and heroes. The Hydra was Heracles' most difficult labor; Python dared to attack Apollo and Diana when they were still innocent babies in the womb (a prefiguring of Medea's fantasized abortion); Typhoeus assailed Zeus himself. And yet, when we read this catalogue we feel that the serpents of this play are not the same as that hideous tribe who threatened Lucan's Cato in the desert. There the vile

---

[26] See also Freud (1900–1901) VI E, which argues for a universal significance for snake imagery. The multiple meanings of the Roman snake imagery are paralleled in the remarkable catalogue of snakes in the *Mahabharata*. For one excellent account of snake imagery in Indian erotic traditions, see Doniger (1973, 1986).

properties of each variety of serpent are given a detached naturalistic description, and we see them come to life vividly as actual base animals, with no higher power or function. Here, by contrast, snakes take on a mythic and quasi-divine power; and they have a beauty that we cannot in any simple way despise. Medea's magic, working through and with snakes, has been able to change the laws of nature, to alter the seasons, to reorder the heavens. It has created not chaos, but a counterorder. And the snakes that answer to her songs are no mean or vulgar beasts: "Now now," she cries, "it is time to set in motion something higher than common crime" (692–93).

In the lines that follow, she calls down the snakes of heaven and of age-old myth: the constellation Draco, coiling its way between the two bears; the immense power of Ophiouchos; the daring of Python; the snake-heads of Hydra, cut off by Hercules "which renew themselves with their own slaughter" (*succisa serpens caede se reparans sua*, 702); and finally, the serpent who guarded the Golden Fleece. The presence of these snakes of legend suggests to us that the power of *erōs* is no petty evil, but an age-old cosmic power, a divine force connected with regeneration and birth, as well as death and slaughter. (Knox finds this same doubleness in Virgil's imagery.)[27] It is, we might say, a force that comes from a countercosmos set outside of, but just as powerful as, the cosmos of the gods, a cosmos that claims our reverence as well as our fear. It is the image of *erōs* that we find, in fact, in Euripides' *Medea*; and memorably in Sophocles' *Antigone*, where *erōs*, though capable of inspiring injustice, is "seated from the beginning of things beside the great laws of right" (797–800).

We might think at this point that Seneca is simply recalling to us the age and the power of irrationality and its attendant evils, telling us that such ugliness creates ongoing and powerful obstacles to virtue in any human life. But I think that matters are not so simple. For these snakes, unlike Lucan's, are not—or not all—hideous. The winged chariot at the play's end soars into the bright air with grace and power. We are, I think, to imagine it as brilliantly colored, gleaming in the sun.[28] The first snake who answers Medea's incantations has properties both hideous and wonderful:

[27] Knox (1958) 380: "Besides suggesting the forces of destruction, it may also stand for rebirth, the renewal which the Latin poetic tradition associated with the casting-off of the serpent's old skin in the spring." He refers to Ovid *Met.* 9.266, *AA* 3.77, Lucr. III.614, Tibullus 1.4.35, and others: and this is a crucial feature in his own interpretation of *Aeneid* 2, where Troy's death and its (more glorious) rebirth are seen to be inseparable. On the connection between creativity and destruction in the *Medea*, see also Fyfe (1983) 83.

[28] The emphasis of her speeches in this final scene is all on light and openness. Just as in the opening she invokes the Sun as her forefather, "sower of our family," and speaks of the Sun's chariot (with its flaming horses) as "racing through the accustomed spaces of pure heaven"

Here a fierce snake [*saeva serpens*] draws his huge body along; he darts out his forked tongue and seeks those to whom he can come bringing death; hearing her song he stops in awe, wraps his swollen body into writhing knots and compels them to coil in circles [*cogitque in orbes*]. (686–90)

This snake is lethal and erotic; he also has an affinity for poetry or song. (Seneca's alliterative poetry has, too, an affinity for him.) And, as he silently winds himself into *orbes*—Seneca's frequent word for cosmic order [29]—compelling fluid matter to take on form, we feel we are present at the creation of a world. The world it creates, Medea's countercosmos, is, furthermore, fertile and benign. When she describes how she has altered nature there are no images of blight. Instead there is harvest in winter, flowers in summer, light in the forest, sun and moon blazing together. Here, clearly, the snake has stood for birth and flourishing. [30]

Finally, consider the snake Draco, lying "like a vast rushing river" (694) in the starry heavens. What we are to imagine as Medea says of him "let that serpent descend" (695), what we would have to see before us if ever this scene were to be visually represented, is the sudden descent into Medea's earthly room of a snake whose tremendous body is made out of the stars of heaven. We would see its winding splendor shooting down toward us. And then the entire room, our entire world, would explode

---

(30), so now (her "kingdom" restored from the darkness of the middle of the play and its nocturnal ponderings) she speaks of being "borne through the open air"; a "way to the heavens lies open" (1022, 25). Jason sees her as flaming (996–97), and as soaring "aloft" (*sublime*) into the "open spaces of the ether." When we add to this the fact that she speaks of this as a wedding day, a day of recovery of royal power and of her paternal power (982–84), we can see that there is reason to associate the serpent chariot with the sense of brightness and openness that dominates the whole scene, and with the fiery brightness of the paternal chariot of the opening. A good stage director (or rather lighting designer) would develop these hints; the reader's or listener's imagination does also.

[29] The word, according to Busa and Zampolli (1975), occurs in Seneca's works 165 times, of which 45 occurrences are in the *Naturales Quaestiones*. The singular most often occurs in the phrase *orbis terrarum*, meaning "universe"—and a universe as ordered, not in the process of breaking up into chaos. The plural usually refers to some heavenly body's "circuits," again with the emphasis upon order and design. In the *Medea* the word occurs in four other passages. At 5 it is the natural world order as recipient of the sun's light. At 98, it designates the circle made by the horns of the moon as they enclose a full circle of light; at 372 it is used of the entire world of nature, now traversable by human daring; at 378, of the new "worlds" that will be discovered by that daring.

[30] This aspect of Seneca's portrait of the erotic life is neglected by the otherwise impressive analyses of Regenbogen (1930) and Henry and Henry (1985), who lay all stress on disorder and chaos.

around her, around us, in a blaze of flickering light. It is an unmistakable and extraordinary image of sexual pleasure. It captures the beauty and value, as well as the intensity, of erotic experience. And by putting the snake of heaven before the spectator or listener, in her room (so to speak) as well as Medea's, it makes the experience hers, it recalls to her that it is hers. There is nothing like this in Lucan, where disgust remains supreme and Cato's straightness distances itself ever more from the snake's subversive power. Seneca has invited the power of the snake into the heart of his play. It has arrived, illuminating the world with irresistible splendor, creating (subversively) a counterworld to the world of Stoic virtue. He lets us know that these beauties are inseparable from the snake's death-dealing properties; but he shows as well that a virtue that leaves this out leaves out something for which one would, perhaps, commit a murder. In short: he allows the spectator to see, and be gripped by, the value of *erōs*. She is suddenly bitten; the "snaking flame" penetrates to her inmost marrow.

This reading is confirmed by the play's final lines. Medea triumphs: this is itself a subversive thought. For in a universe ruled, as the Stoic universe is ruled, by right reason, such audacity should not go off scot-free. (Seneca is very fond of, and elsewhere obsessively retells, the stories of Icarus and of Phaethon, whose unhappy endings give a properly moral warning against such ambitiousness.)[31] But the ending is given by the traditional plot; so perhaps we should discount it. What we cannot discount are Jason's final lines, lines that have been found anomalous and shocking even vis-à-vis the Greek and Roman mythic tradition; and which surely are far more so placed at the end of a Stoic drama. "Go aloft through the deep spaces of heaven," he calls, "and bear witness that where you travel there are no gods" (1026–27). Here Jason expresses, of course, his sense of injustice: her triumph seems incompatible with the gods' judgment on her acts. Since he is only partially encased within the narrow world of Stoic moral judgment—since, indeed, he mirrors the likely position of the spectator, caught between that moralism and an intuitive human sense of the worth of externals—he cannot help seeing her escape as a triumph and cannot help feeling that this matters. But the way Senaca chooses to have him express this thought is very strange. Costa remarks, "*Nullos esse deos* is not a characteristic complaint in Greek tragedy, even in Euripides: rather the

---

[31] For Icarus, *Ag.* 506, *Oed.* 892ff., *HO* 686; for Phaethon, *Phdr.* 1090, *HO* 677, 854, and the Chorus at *Medea* 599. At 826, Medea tells us that she got her fire from Phaethon: so she is his survivor, so to speak. On Virgil's use of the Icarus story in *Aeneid* 6, with some very pertinent reflections on *dolor* and pity, see M. Putnam (1987).

sufferer asks, 'How can the gods allow these things to happen?' "[32] T. S.
Eliot writes, "The final cry of Jason to Medea departing in her car is
unique; I can think of no other play which reserves such a shock for the last
word."[33] The shock is, of course, deepest within a Stoic view of the world.
For in that view, god is everywhere. There is no space in the universe that is
not inhabited by divine reason. No matter where Medea goes, her rage and
her love will be judged bad by reference to the will of god, which is to say,
with reference to perfect moral virtue. The universe is thoroughly moralized, and everything must be either good or evil; if not good, therefore
evil. And Seneca explicitly told us that the region beyond the moon is as
serene—and as good—as a wise man's heart (*Ep.* 59.16). Jason's line, by
contrast, tells us that the moral universe has a space in it. Not every place is
full of gods. For the serpent chariot takes the loving soul to a realm in
which god and god's judgment on passion do not exist. A place, then,
beyond virtue and vice, health and disease—a place, as Nietzsche would
say, beyond good and evil.

VI

Seneca's play now begins to have the suddenness, as well as the passion, of
the snake; it takes us by surprise, weaving its path between the moral world
and the world of love. Like the poetic snake who loved Medea's song, it
arranges its coils into a cosmos, it creates a world—and, like that snake, it
has a forked tongue, and asks to whom it should come bringing death. We
do not know whether its intended victim is passion, or Stoic morality itself.
To conclude our depiction of the play's serpentine doubleness, and make
the case for finding these ambiguities in it stronger still, we turn to the
Chorus and its remarkable ode on the golden age and humanity's fall from
purity. Unlike the Euripidean Chorus, Seneca's is not sympathetic to
Medea. Throughout it is the sober voice of Stoic morality, counseling the

[32] Costa (1973) 159–60. Rosenmeyer (1989) oddly translates as "the gods are dead"; but
his remarks about the relationship between her passion and an upheaval in the world order
(200–201) are suggestive and apposite.

[33] Eliot (1951) 73. Cf. Pratt (1983) 89, who remarks, perceptively, that Medea has become
"anti-god." This is much better, I think than Lawall's (1979) association of Medea with chaos
and unshaped wild nature. Dingel (1974) 108ff. argues that since the gods support Medea
they cannot be real gods. Fyfe (1983) argues that we are meant to see Jason as deluded: Medea
is an instrument of the natural order's vengeance. I find this the least successful part of her
otherwise valuable paper.

extirpation of passion, the containment of daring, a life that stays at home with its own virtue, never overstepping the limits of nature. Yet I believe that we will find that the very language Seneca gives it for its central sermon contains a critical judgment upon that morality; and in this judgment is contained a profound criticism of traditional portraits of the Stoic hero. Like the ode on the human being in the *Antigone*, though apparently without that ode's admiring side, this chorus begins with a story of humanity's invention of the art of sailing.

> Too daring [*audax nimium*], the one who first in a fragile bark broke through the treacherous seas and, seeing his lands disappear behind him, entrusted his life to the light winds: who, cutting the waters in a doubtful path, could trust to a slender plank, drawing too slight a line between the circumstances of life and death. (301–8)

Soon this account of human daring is contrasted with a purer and more moral world:

> Pure [*candida*] were the ages our fathers saw, crime being far removed. Each person inactive [*piger*], keeping to his own shore, grew old in his ancestral fields, rich with only a little, knowing no wealth except that which his fatherland bore. (329–34)

Both before and after this portrait of a "golden age," the Chorus goes on to indict the daring (*ausus*) of early explorers who broke through limits previously set up in the laws of Nature (*foedera mundi*, 335), wrote new laws for the winds, and afflicted the sea (depicted, in Stoic fashion, as a living, morally demanding presence) with blows (337); the chronicle of excessive exploration culminates in its observation that the prize for the Argo's voyage was Medea, a danger worse than the sea (*maiusque mari Medea malum*, 363). The ode concludes with a bitter reflection that appears to move from the mythical times of the play straight into Roman contemporary life:

> Now, in our time, the sea has ceased resistance and suffers any law we give it. . . . Any little bark now wanders anywhere on the deep. Every boundary has been removed [*terminus omnis motus*]; cities have set their walls in new lands, and the world, now open to travel throughout [*pervius orbis*], has left nothing in its earlier seat. . . . There will come a time in the distant future when Ocean will loose the bonds of things, when the huge earth will be revealed, when Tethys will uncover new worlds [*novas orbes*], and Thule will not be the limit of the lands. (365–79)

This ode[34] presents us with a contrast between two conceptions of the good life and two associated conceptions of the self, one of which it apparently blames and one of which it apparently praises. On the one side we have the audacious life of the human being who values external goods and who expends effort and ingenuity to get to the objects of his or her desires. Since this life is clearly linked with Medea and her scheme of value, and with the erotic Jason of the old days, we might call it the erotic life. This life values unstable things like possessions, love, worldly achievement, renown. It is imagined in terms of outward movement, of adventuring. The *audax* self is dynamic, extending itself beyond itself, spreading exuberantly out over pieces of the world. Its relation to nature and natural law is frequently adversarial—it bursts through boundaries, it joins lands that are supposed to be separate, it lets no limit stand.[35]

On the other side is a purer self: this self stays at home content with few externals because it does not value these things. It is morally unsullied, pure white (*candida*); crime is far off.[36] It is the Stoic self, which has all its goods at home, because all good is placed in virtue. It respects, because it doesn't want not to, the limits in nature.

Most commentators have seen this passage as a depiction of an ideal "golden age." Costa, for example, says that it "clearly belongs in the category of the many accounts of that ideal early existence which we find in Greek and Latin literature." He mentions Hesiod, Virgil, Ovid.[37] But we can see, if we examine these sources (and others) that Seneca is criticizing these traditional stories in a predictably Stoic fashion. The typical stress of golden age stories is on the ready availability, without risk or labor, of valued external goods. The earth itself bears fruit; it is spring all year long;

[34] On this choral ode, see especially Henry and Henry (1985) 51–52, Segal (1983b), Lawall (1979). Lawall's reading of the Chorus' tone as one of "happy optimism" about human progress, and its dream here as one of "unlimited progress and harmony between man and nature" seems peculiar. To be sure, he does see something that is really beneath the ode's surface, a certain attachment to *audacia* and the erotic life; but at the price of missing the surface argument, which is surely far more pessimistic. His view that the vision of progress is opposed to Medea's daring (he links her with raw nature as opposed to art) is equally odd.

[35] Again, however, we see no sign that this self is committed to chaos. Instead, it pursues orderly projects, discovers new spheres for human practical reason.

[36] Cf. *innocuae vitae*, *HFu* 125ff., on which see further discussion, and *vitio carens* of Hippolytus' praise of the woodland life free from greed (*Phdr.* 482ff.).

[37] See Virg. *Georg.* 1.125 (notice that this golden age contains no poisonous snakes); Hes. *Op.* 109ff., Aratus *Phaen.* 110–11, Catullus 64.6ff., 38ff.; Ovid, *Met.* 1.94ff., Tibullus 1.3.37ff. See Costa (1973) ad loc; Lovejoy and Boas (1935), especially 263ff.; Konstan (1977); Blundell (1986).

abundance requires no toil; there are no diseases, no old age, no pain. The age is golden because people have all good things at home with them—but the good things are the usual externals, and the myth therefore requires an alteration in the behavior of nature. There is no seafaring here not because, as in Seneca, there is no desire for the goods that are achieved by seafaring, but because nature herself gives these very same goods in abundance right where we are. Of course to a Stoic this emphasis upon the value of externals is deeply misguided. The thing that is wrong with human life, the thing that prevents people from having all good things with them as they are, is vice; so the only way to imagine a golden age correctly is to imagine an age without vice, without passion, without the false belief in the value of externals. This is what we have here.[38] These people stay at home inactive because they do not misguidedly long for the things that are far away.

What we must, however, notice as we read the ode again is the ambivalence with which this ideal existence is depicted. The word *piger* is not a term of praise in Roman literature. It is consistently pejorative, and opposed to *labor* and to *virtus*. Seneca uses the word (with its relatives, *pigritia* and *pigrescere*) fifty-six times in his writings.[39] It is neutral only in a few cases, where it has a complement introduced by *ad* and means "slow to do X," "sluggish at X-ing"—where X is not always something good. But without *ad*, *piger* is pejorative. When it designates sluggish movement in non-human nature, or in the physical life of human beings, there is almost always, even here, something ominous going on. A sluggish river has water that damages the fertility of crops (*Phdr.* 15); sluggishness of limbs is a sign of plague (*Oed.* 182); fresh air prevents a stagnant sluggish atmosphere from forming (*NQ* 5.18.1); the air beneath the earth is sluggish and foul, so that, released by earthquakes, it causes plague (*NQ* 6.27.2); an oozing swamp surrounds a sluggish or stagnant pool (*Oed.* 547). And so forth: "stagnant" is frequently the best translation. In the moral world, things are clearer still, as Seneca consistently reproves stagnation of soul. "I will give no pardon to the sluggish [*pigris*], to the careless, to the babblers," he proclaims [*Ir.* 3.24.2]. "Morally vicious [*inhonesta*] is all timidity and worry, is sluggishness [*pigritia*] in any action" (*Ep.* 74.30). Mix *pigritia* in with a virtuous act and it loses its virtuous character (*Ep.* 66.16). The job of a philosophical teacher is to draw forth mental powers that were previously hidden and sluggish (*Ben.* 6.16.7). So *piger* in Seneca, as in other Roman

---

[38] And cf. also Horace *Carm.* 1.3, much closer to this passage than other golden age descriptions are; and *Ep.* 16 should be compared as well.

[39] Cf. Busa and Zampolli (1975) s.v.

writers, Stoic and non-Stoic, is a word unambiguously opposed to major virtues, especially those connected with work and striving. It is a word that the Stoic, in order to have a convincing conception of virtue (especially at Rome) needs to be able to set over against his own idea.

But can he consistently do so? Our passage suggests deep doubt. The presence of *piger* on the side of Stoic virtue suggests to us that the Stoic ideal, while pure and blameless, is strangely lacking in effort, daring, and activity—qualities deeply valued by the entire Roman tradition of virtue. The life of a Stoic paradise is indeed a sluggish or lazy life—as it must, perhaps, be, if it cares deeply for nothing outside itself.

The one other apparently positive use of *piger* in Seneca confirms this story. The Chorus in the *Hercules Furens* has praised the simple life of the country, where needs are few and people "have the undisturbed quiet [*tranquilla quies*] of a life free from harming [*innocuae vitae*]" (159–60). They have contrasted this life with the "immense hopes and trembling fears" (162–63) of the city, where people live for unreliable external goods. They have, once again, praised *secura quies* (175) and reproved the "too brave heart" of Hercules [*nimium . . . pectore forti*, 186]. They now give a summary of their moral advice:

> Let glory speak of someone else to many lands. Let babbling report praise him through every city, and lift him up, an equal to the stars of heaven. Let someone else go lofty [*sublimis*] in a chariot. As for me, let my land protect me beside an unknown hearth. The inactive [*pigros*] live on to old age; and the mean lot of a small house rests in a lowly but secure place. But high-spirited virtue falls from a lofty height [*alte virtus animosa cadit*]. (192–201)

Again, being *piger* is linked with Stoic goals of security and quiet, and with a lack of blameworthy concern with externals. Again, it is connected with moral blamelessness, again opposed to heroic daring.[40] But here, even more clearly than in the *Medea*, we discover what the ideal of moral purity rejects: the courage of Hercules, the glory of great deeds out in the world, and high-spirited virtue itself.

Seneca, in these plays, sees more deeply than most Stoic writers when he comprehends that you cannot have traditional Roman heroism and have Stoic virtue too. Stoic writers would like to think that you can, and they

---

[40] The odd reference to riding lofty (or aloft) in a chariot (*alius curru sublimis eat*) might make us think of Medea's exit per *alta . . . spatia sublime aetheris*; though the reference is more likely to be a general one, invoking the thought of living rulers and leaders—among whom, perhaps, we might discover Seneca himself.

write as if these elements can be combined. Lucan's Cato, ever watchful, effortful, *audax*, exemplifies, along with his Stoicism, some elements of Roman virtue to which any reader of the poem will be deeply attached. "The virtue of Cato, unwilling to stand still, dares [*audet*] to entrust his men to unknown lands" (9.371–72). His *audax virtus* (302) does not know how to keep inactive (294–95). In crossing the Libyan desert he hopes to get the better of Nature (302). "I seek as my comrades," he says, "those who are attracted by danger itself." Without these qualities Cato could hardly be a Roman hero. Seneca's point here (directed, presumably, not only at others but at some of his own views) is that this sort of heroism is not available to the good Stoic, even though they like to think that it is. The good Stoic may not be altogether inactive; but because he lacks the passionate love of externals he will not undertake bold projects out in the world, or endure labor and risk for their sake. Instead of the grand old words *audax* and *labor*, we must now honor the words *candidus* and *piger*—the latter now assuming a new positive meaning. This is a profound change in the ideal of the hero. A later ode denounces for excessive daring and boundary violations a whole list of heroes usually thought great—the Argonauts first, then Hercules, Meleager, several Homeric heroes. The good Stoic wants none of this life.

But when the spectator sees how limp and unheroic this newly bounded life is, contrasted with her intuitive images of greatness, she is likely to be ambivalent toward it, and erotically drawn to Medea's greatness of soul. (Jason the erotic voyaging Argonaut, is a far more sympathetic figure than the tame and moralizing Jason we see in most of this play; indeed, it is clearly Seneca's intent to juxtapose these two Jasons, not always to the advantage of the latter. We might add that the only time when the stage figure of Jason inspires love is when he declares his love of his sons, his grief on their account, his fear on their behalf. These are not Stoic sentiments.) Nor can we, further, escape the fact that this very ode—unlike, for example, Horace's condemnation of progress in *Odes* 1.339—depicts the *audacia* it condemns with unmistakable élan. The lines about future exploration allegedly depict a nadir to which our audacity will eventually lead us. But they have an exuberant tone that sits ill with Stoicism. In the margin of his copy of the play, Ferdinand Columbus wrote, "This prophecy was fulfilled by my father Christopher Columbus in the year 1492."[41] He feels in the lines not moral condemnation, but a prophecy of high achievement. I think he saw something that is really there.

[41] See Costa (1973) ad loc.

We can venture even further, following the argument of chapter 11. In this Stoic golden age, characterized by moral blamelessness, we do not even get a very rich conception of moral virtue. *Candida saecula* have no dark blot; but it is not clear what else they do have. The image makes us think of a blank space. *Procul fraude remota*, too, is negative and weak. (Compare *vitio carens*, *Phdr.* 483; *innocuae vitae*, *HFu* 159. The wise man is free from wrongdoing, *ablabēs*—DL 7.123.) We see here no positive concern for social justice, no generosity to one's fellow human beings, no courage for friends or country. For—as Aristotle keenly saw when he told us that the gods lack moral virtue—the great moral virtues all require some high evaluation of uncontrolled external things. What courage can there be, if poverty, slavery, loss of loved ones, and even death are not to be counted evils and there is no fear to manage? What commitment to justice can there be, if the goods distributed within society have no real human worth? Again, what generosity? The only virtue that can exist here fully is, perhaps, *sōphrosunē*—construed as knowing and keeping one's proper place in the scheme of things. The traditional anthropomorphic gods cannot have the virtues because they control all good things; like the men of the traditional golden age, they want these goods, but they command them fully. The Stoic, this play suggests, has a similar problem with the virtues, because what he doesn't control he defines as non-good and learns not to want. The result is the same; the Stoic is indeed godlike. This life, then, begins to look strangely *piger* not only in terms of traditional standards of heroism, but also with regard to its own ostensible scheme of valued ends. Virtue, it seems, may itself be erotic.

What we have discovered, then, is that there are two selves, two pictures of selfhood in the world; two pictures, even, of morality; and that we must choose between them. This choice is not simple, but tragic. If we go for *erōs* and *audacia*, we get crime and murderous anger; if we go for purity, we get flatness and the death of heroic virtue. We get the death of tragedy too, since what tragedy is, we recall, is "the sufferings of human beings who have been wonderstruck by external things." This play can be a tragedy only by having characters who are not Stoics;[42] and I think we can say that even then it succeeds in being tragic only because it shares to some extent their loves and their wonder—only because it depicts the choice to follow Stoicism as itself a certain sort of tragedy inside of us, brought about by the

---

[42] In a fragment of the *On Marriage*, Seneca writes, "Everything that fills up tragedies, everything that overturns cities and kingdoms, is the struggle of wives and mistresses" (Haase [1897–98]).

demand of our moral being for unsullied purity and lives free from harming.

Who, then, is Seneca, we feel like asking. And what is Senecan tragedy? Seneca is, as would be no surprise to anyone who has worked on him, an elusive, complex, and contradictory figure, a figure deeply committed both to Stoicism and to the world, both to purity and to the erotic. A figure who sits at home and who is carried lofty in his chariot. The tensions between his career and his thought are many and famous. They have been set forth with convincing precision of argument by Miriam Griffin in her fascinating study.[43] What is less frequently discussed is the fact that these tensions surrounding the value of worldly striving work themselves into the writing as well. Griffin perceives the writing's paradoxical character: "If one were asked to characterize as briefly as possible the distinctive Senecan outlook, one would probably point to his morbid asceticism and his realistic humanity.[44] We have seen already in chapter 11 how Seneca's intense interest in progress and striving made him attach to the work and effort of philosophy a value that is hard to reconcile with Stoicism. What we are saying now is that this interest in daring, courage, and striving—which itself has deep roots in (especially Roman) Stoicism—actually turns out, and is here seen by Seneca to be, in a deep and tragic tension with some fundamental principles of Stoic morality. This tragedy discovers and explores this tension, taking Seneca further in his criticism of Stoic purity than he is willing to go in any prose work.[45]

It is, perhaps, no accident that it is in poetry that this ambivalence should have come out most powerfully; no accident that it was in tragedy that this critique should have been made. For tragedy is, as Plato, banning it, already saw, profoundly committed to the values that Plato and Stoicism wish to reject. It is a dangerous form for the Stoic to attempt. Like Medea's serpent, it has a way of sneaking up on Stoic morality with its own sense of drama, its own ways of appealing to the imagination and memory of its audience, its own scheme of values. The real danger posed by literature to philosophy is nowhere more evident than here, inside this play: for in the very act of turning tragedy into a Stoic argument, Stoicism has bitten itself.

[43] M. Griffin (1976).

[44] M. Griffin (1976) 177.

[45] This might be a chronological point, but it certainly does not need to be, especially in light of the fact that philosophical writing and action-guiding belief are in continuing tension, it seems, throughout Seneca's life (see M. Griffin [1976]). The dating of the tragedies is highly uncertain in any case. And changes of feeling and thought about important matters are not always unilinear; we recall Seneca's account of the heart's oscillations.

471

VII

The Aristotelian[46] wants to reply. For Seneca has placed before us a tragic dilemma: give up a great value, or run the constant risk of harming. But any tragic dilemma is only as convincing as are the force and inevitability of its two sides. The Aristotelian acknowledges the value of love. She needs still to be convinced about the risk of murder. Moved and horrified by this tragedy, she may still be unwilling to accept it as a story that pertains to her—or, just as important, to good characters educated in the Aristotelian way. We need to listen to her objections.

Surely, she begins, Seneca is not accurate when he claims, if he does, that this story is the story of every person who loves. This is a very extreme story. Very few lovers become murderers; fewer still kill their own children. This story seems, in fact, so strange in its excesses that it is an open question whether we ought to care about it at all.

To this the Stoic has, I think, several interesting answers. His first move will be to point out that the Aristotelian is either naive or willfully blind if she does not see how much actual harm is done to people every day in the name of passionate love. The number of killings may be relatively small. But consider the whole terrain of marriage, and especially of divorce, and you will not easily avoid the conclusion that passion and cruelty frequently go hand in hand. Consider the many acts of physical abuse, especially of women and children; consider the acts of betrayal; consider the ingenious vindictive reprisals of the betrayed toward former lover and toward rival, the manipulation of children's lives and emotions, the financial warfare, the excessive litigation—consider these things and you will discover that the risks and uncertainties associated with erotic passion do indeed produce a great deal of bad and destructive action.[47] But if the people whom one daily sees abusing one another and their innocent children—and these are not just distant newspaper reports, they are frequently our friends and ourselves—if these people had gone into marriage in the Stoic way, extir-

---

[46] Once again, I refer here to a hypothetical position, with deep roots in popular intuitions, not to Aristotle's explicit arguments.

[47] This argument is close to an argument in the fragments of Seneca's *On Marriage.* Criticizing modern Roman marriages, he praises the orator Varius Geminus for coining the saying, *Qui non litigat, caelebs est* (If you're not involved in litigation, you're single). Musonius remarks that a failed marriage is far worse than "desolate solitude" (*erēmia*) ("The Goal of Marriage").

pating passion,[48] how much less cruelty there would be all round, how much securer, especially, the lives of young children would be.

Such harms are not universal in erotic love. Possibly they are not universal even in broken erotic love. (Though it is difficult to find a divorce that does not contain an element of cruelty; and the protestation that this is the sort of thing that happens only to others is likely to sound, in time, like the protest of Euripides' Agamemnon, who confronts Hecuba's actions with the observation that only foreigners kill out of revenge.)[49] But it would still be excessively sanguine to think that a person could take up an erotic life with a secure expectation that such things would not take place. You cannot promise yourself, "I will have love in my life, but I will never hurt my children." For whether or not *erōs* in fact leads you into a dilemma in which the further pursuit of love entails child-harming or some other sort of harming—this is very much a matter of chance. The Euripidean Chorus seems to have gotten it right when, hearing the sounds of child-murder within, they call out, "Do you hear, do you hear the cry of the children? O poor woman, o unlucky woman." The English translation by Rex Warner says here, "O you hard heart, o woman fated for evil." But it seems important that the Greek mentions neither fate nor evil. The cruelty she does is seen as her bad luck. And so, in the Aristotelian world of that play, it must be. Some lovers avoid it and some don't; you yourself can only hope. But is that a satisfactory way to live and to raise children?[50]

The Aristotelian must acknowledge these facts. Yet she will try to insist at this point that a person of good character, committed to generosity,

[48] From Seneca's *On Marriage*, a story of a man who loved his wife passionately: "The source of that love was decent enough, but its size was ugly and monstrous. It doesn't matter from what decent cause one goes mad. That's why Sextius used to say, 'That man is an adulterer who loves his wife too passionately.' Indeed, any love of someone else's wife is disgraceful, but so is excessive love of one's own. The wise man ought to love his wife deliberately [*iudicio*], not passionately [*adfectu*]. He controls the impulse to pleasure and is not led headlong to intercourse. Nothing is more disgusting than to treat one's wife like an adulterer. Let those who say that they make love with their wives and have children for the sake of the Republic and the human race at least imitate cattle—and, after the wife's belly is swollen, let them not damage their sons. Let them show themselves not the lovers of their wives, but the husbands."

[49] Euripides' *Hecuba*; see Nussbaum (1986a) chapter 13.

[50] The emphasis on not just begetting but also raising children as a primary end of marriage for both spouses is, it seems, new in this period—see Musonius, "The Goal of Marriage," "Is Marriage an Impediment to Philosophy?" and also the anti-infanticide work, "Should One Raise All the Children That Are Born?" (Hense [1905]).

473

justice, and family love, will usually be able to stop short of the really bad forms of cruelty. She will insist on driving a wedge between grief and anger here: a life with passionate love in it cannot count on avoiding grief, but it can safely avoid anger. When two important values, such as passion and the love of children, collide by chance in a life dedicated to both, there may be no avoiding some harm to someone, if it is a harm to be left alone or to be separated from those one loves. But a good person will do the harm with reluctance, without anger, as an unfortunate necessity. He will do everything possible to promote the neglected good later on, to make reparations. (In contemporary terms, to pay alimony generously, to see and help one's children.) The person who receives the harm, the betrayed person, is in an even safer position. For she need face no conflict at all between passion and duty; she can accept the loss of passion with grief, and avoid the revenge that turns grief into harm. Neither one of them, furthermore, will ever do the really terrible things that Medea does; neither, surely, will ever maim and kill.

The idea that there is a morally appropriate way of leaving one's family and children strikes the Stoic as quite self-serving. These things are bad.[51] And the conflict of values that gives rise to the bad actions involved in divorce would not have arisen at all had the person not valued *erōs*. So all this talk of unavoidable necessity (so frequently heard at these times) is so much self-serving cant. There are well-known and efficacious ways of changing one's disposition toward *erōs*, of forming a truly rational marriage. If a person doesn't take them up, he is surely responsible for whatever wrongs ensue. As Phaedra says in Seneca's version of her story, "It is mind, not chance, that produces infidelity" (*Mens impudicam facere, non casus, solet*). And as for the poor wronged person, two things can be said. First, that the habits of mind that ground the great grief of lost love are the same ones that ground betrayal and make marriages unstable. The innocent one cannot take pride in her innocence, for she might equally well have been the guilty one. (Medea kills her brother for Jason's sake before she herself is wronged.) Furthermore, it seems quite implausible to say that a person who has staked her entire life on *erōs* will feel only grief. Grief itself is bad enough—an invasion of one's personal space, a tearing of one's integrity. But grief and anger lie close in the heart. And if you lose the one you love not through death but through betrayal, it will be not only likely, it

---

[51] The Roman Stoics are strong opponents of adultery for both men and women: for a vehement assault on the prevalent sexual double standard, see Musonius, "On Intercourse." On this and related issues, see Foucault (1984).

will, given the Aristotelian picture, be right, that you will feel anger at that betrayal and wish to undertake some harmful action against its cause.

This leads the Stoic to make one more very important observation. The Stoic has argued that the core of assessable action is what takes place in the privacy of the heart. The external act is but an "afterbirth" of the real act, which is a movement of thought, of desire, of will (cf. chapter 10). Suppose, then, we were to view the murderous acts of this play not as acts done out in the world, but as murders of wish, of fantasy. We are encouraged to take up this viewpoint by a number of strange features of the tragedy—quite apart from our knowledge of this Stoic doctrine. The blame of Medea is almost always focused upon her psychological states—her audacious temper, her mad furor, the unstable vicissitudes of her passion. The physical murder of the children is characterized as a "votive offering" to her *dolor*—as if the *dolor* itself was the really important and ruling thing, the thing toward which our attention should really be directed. The murder of Creousa suggests this interiority even more strongly. For how is Creousa murdered? Not by straightforward worldly action on Medea's part, but by magical incantation. We do not see Medea walk up to her rival and assault her. Instead, we see her standing in a room alone, praying and saying her charms, calling forth the snakes who by this time in the play have already become identified with her own erotic wishes and desires. What better dramatic representation could there be of the way in which love silently, obsessively broods over the death of its obstacle, menacing it with all the power of its thought? Creousa dies of venom: but Medea appears, in this very scene, as a murderous snake, whose poisons are the thoughts and feelings of love. This scene of murderous thought and desire occupies fully one-fifth of the play, if we include the Nurse's report and the Chorus' commentary.[52] Indeed, this is the biggest difference between this play and Euripides': that so much of the external action is replaced by internal action. This scene is only part of the story; elsewhere too, much of the play is occupied by inner doings of Medea's heart, so much so that the commentator Costa writes, at line 893, "Once more she is in the dark tortured world of her own mind."[53]

Add to all this, finally, the fact that these serpents and monsters—even if the plays were to be staged—would not appear flat-footedly before the audience like so much clumsy baroque stage machinery. They would ap-

---

[52] Zwierlein (1966) advances this as one argument against believing that the plays were staged. See also the comments of Henry and Henry (1985).

[53] Costa (1973) ad loc.

pear to her imagination and to the spectator's, in a way that suggests that they are creatures of the mind's eye, extensions of passionate thought. And if, as is more likely, these plays were not meant for staging,[54] the internality grows still more pronounced. For now, in addition to the fact that the murders are represented in the text as crimes of thought and wish, we have the fact that the whole of the representation is itself being staged within each solitary listener's or reader's mind. And each person who hears Medea say, "This is what my mind ponders within," would become aware that the whole nightmare of Medea's inner world is, even now, the pondering of hers.

So we now can read the claims of the play against the Aristotelian in a stronger light. Seneca is saying: even if you should stop short of evil external action in unhappy love, you will never be safe from thinking violent and angry thoughts, forming fantasies of murder and evil, against your former lover and/or your rival. You will still, almost in spite of yourself, be likely to find yourself weaving murderous spells, wishing for horrors. These thoughts are not under the control of right reason and good character. They have a life of their own, like flames, like snakes. Born out of the heat of love itself, they go their own way in the soul, so silent that they surprise even the most watchful, even the one who takes most pride in knowledge of the heart. (Even Idmon, who knew fate well, was bitten on the Libyan sands.) You may suppose yourself pure, capable of loving "without strife." And then some day, some night in a dream, some morning when you are going about your life, you will feel in your heart the bite of an evil wish. Or, in the image of Typhoeus' membra, the wish for another's harm may enter you in the sexual act itself; so that to permit that penetration of yourself (and remember that this sexual act, too, could be an act in thought, so far as the play's moral argument is concerned), to permit this is to let in a swollen snake that may by its very internal presence defile you. There is no reliable goodness of heart, there is no safe purity of intention, if once you open your mind to desire. *Veniet et vobis furor*: Cassandra's prophecy, always true, always disregarded.

Here the Aristotelian will interrupt, insisting that we must maintain the moral importance of the distinction between inner wish and outer act. The Stoic directs all assessment toward the inner world; a murderous wish seems to become as bad as murder. But surely we do not think this. Wishes and intentions are relevant to the assessment of a crime; but if there is no external act, there is no crime. Our laws, and even our moral judgments,

---

[54] For helpful discussions of this difficult issue, see Zwierlein (1966) and Fantham (1982).

permit people to have murderous thoughts. So long as they control themselves out in the world, they may say whatever incantations they like.

This is surely, however, an insufficient answer. First of all, it is inaccurate about the Stoic position. The Stoic will still in fact be able to make a distinction between external and internal, though in a different and, he would argue, more morally relevant way. The intention is indeed all; we do not think that a would-be murderer who is prevented from crime by external constraints alone is less morally awful than the one who succeeds. More often, however, the inhibition is produced by opposing desires and wishes, by an oscillation of the heart that does not permit the evil thought to hold the mastery long enough to generate action. But this is something that the Stoic can and does take into account. He can say that an oscillating heart is in a certain way less evil than one wholly given over to rage.[55] What he still insists, however, is that such a heart is not virtuous, is not pure—is, in fact, quite bad. And here the Aristotelian must agree. For she too takes the presence of appropriate motives and reactive feelings to be essential to virtue and virtuous action. She too thinks of desires as assessable elements of the soul. She too refuses to say that an act is virtuous if it is not done from thoroughly, harmoniously virtuous desire. So she must, it seems, concede that the person who loves cannot guarantee the purity of his virtue against wishes that would defile it. And for the Aristotelian, who wishes virtue to be entirely stable and reliable, wishes the person of practical wisdom to be someone who can be counted upon to act at the right time in the right way, this is bad enough. It means that either the person of practical wisdom must give up the erotic life, or else that such a person, reliably virtuous in thought and response as Aristotle describes him, cannot really exist.

This accords, I think, with our moral intuitions. For however much we distinguish between the inner wish and the outer act, we do not approve of those who wish for the death of innocents, and we do not approve of violent wishes in ourselves. Let us think of Medea, for the moment, as a woman who simply wishes for Creousa's death; who fantasizes about it, who dreams of it, who exults in her heart when (let us say) it does in fact take place, though through some other means. And let us suppose her a person of good character, in whom the murderous wishes have arisen not because of a habit of malice but only out of the desperate intensity of her desire for the man whom Creousa now possesses—in whom, therefore, the bad wishes and the exulting coexist with a good deal of appropriate good

---

[55] But the Stoics are reluctant to recognize that evil has degrees, given their insistence that the line between the wise man and the fool is absolute.

wishing and, should harm befall Creousa, with appropriate grieving. We might even suppose the murderous thoughts to be, or most of them, unconscious, since her character will not tolerate them, pushes them down. This woman will not be tried for murder; she will even get a lot of sympathy. But we will judge her still; and, more important, if she is the person we have described, she will judge herself. On awakening to the presence of evil inside of her, she will indeed believe herself invaded by a snake; and she will have a hard time not connecting the presence of this snake with the presence of love itself. Horror at her own aggression may well lead her to wish for Medea's ending: a return to virginity, a sealing of all holes.

But so far we have not given the Aristotelian the strongest possible case. For we have so far omitted from our account a feature that is central and, in Aristotle's view, necessary if any relation is to deserve the name of love.[56] This is a concern for the beloved person for that person's own sake—a concern free of selfish possessiveness. If Medea really loves Jason deeply, in the best and most genuine way, says the Aristotelian, she will love him for himself, for his good and his happiness, even at some cost to her own. This sort of devotion is evident in her earlier sacrifices, and even after the desertion, in her wish for his good (140–42). If she consistently kept up and carried through that attitude, then, even when Jason left her, her justified anger and resentment should have been eclipsed by that real love for him, and this love should have restrained her from attempting, and even from wishing, acts of aggression against him. The fact that this does not happen here shows us that we do not have here a good case of genuine love—but only some more mixed and self-serving passion. We can, then, imagine a love that is more personal, more erotically intense than Stoic marriage, but which is still free of Medea's angry jealousies.

I think that this view would be difficult to sustain against the evidence of life. It has some truth in it: for there are some kinds of love, for example the love of parent for child, that have built into their very structure a willingness to let the other party go off and live a separate life. When a child leaves the home there is grief, but not, unless things go badly wrong, anger and resentment, even in wish and fantasy. But erotic love—as this play depicts it and as most of us now live it—involves other pledges, other hopes. Even when it is not pathologically possessive and jealous, it involves the hope of sharing a life—or a long part of a life.[57] And when this does not happen, it

---

[56] For Aristotle on love (and the relationship between love and friendship in Aristotelian *philia*), see Nussbaum (1986a) chapter 12, Price (1989).

[57] This is also a Roman norm—see Musonius, "On the Goal of Marriage," on which see n. 3.

is the one who loves deeply and appropriately, as we have said, who is going to find that loss wrenching and disabling. And if the disabling event was inflicted upon her by the other's wrongdoing, then anger will be both a natural and appropriate response. This wrongdoing, discovered, may actually cause love to cease—for this sort of love must be based in some sort of evaluation of the object, and the discovery that the other person is not what we took him to be may derail it. But even when this does not take place, even when the love of the person and the wish for his good persists, this love will naturally and appropriately be tainted by anger. To insist upon a soft and gentle response to such a wrong would be, I think both unrealistic and wrong; it would impose upon the Aristotelian conception a Christian idea of turning the other cheek that probably is deeply incompatible with the whole Aristotelian world outlook, with its entire stance toward the value of external worldly goods. The Christian conception will not satisfy the person who deeply values erotic love: indeed, the Christian's determination to avoid retributive anger helps to explain Christianity's suspiciousness and hostility toward a passion that seems to lie so close to the roots of anger. But this conception, which cuts back both *erōs* and anger together, is at least consistent. What is not consistent is to value love in what I have called the Aristotelian way and then to turn around and insist upon Christian detachment at its end. That is, I think Aristotle is right to say, too "slavish" a response. There is another part of the Christian picture that is far more promising, one that the Christians discovered in Seneca; I shall return to it shortly.

We could at this point go somewhat beyond the Aristotelian account and insist upon the importance, in the best kind of personal love, of a tenderness and gentleness that are only rarely to be seen in Medea's fierce passion—a spirit that would help as much as any passionate dedication to the loved one's good to keep the loved one safe from harm. Medea, the argument goes, is all along the sort of person who might do murder, because all along she is tigerish and without gentleness. If we imagine another type of literary lover—say, Dante's Francesca with her defense of the sort of erotic flame that is "quickly kindled in the gentle heart"—we have a much more difficult time thinking of love as generating murder, even in wish. Dante depicts his lovers, in fact, as doves: animals who are apparently incapable of cruelty, though they are capable of suffering and a sense of loss.

This reply contains a partial truth, and I shall return to it. But it does not seem to be enough to solve altogether the problem of wounded or broken love. Doves may be doves to one another in good circumstances, and then become serpents when abandoned, while still remaining, so to speak, the same people. (Paolo and Francesca, though in hell, had the good fortune to die together, united.) Or rather, normal and good people who believe themselves to be doves through and through may discover themselves to be inhabited by hidden serpents. And it is in the very nature of good and tender love, of the intensely erotic sort, that this should be so. By so much as she was tender and loving toward Jason, by so much Medea will and should feel resentment at his desertion. Tenderness toward him while he celebrates his new marriage would seem, and be, a pathological response. And if this is so in the case of the man she loved, it is much more so in the case of the blameworthy rival—a figure toward whom even dovelike Francesca has the bitterest of evil wishes. ("Caina waits for the one who took our lives"—not just a statement of fact.) And we feel, if we sympathize with her love, that she is right to have that anger, to wish him frozen, unabsolved, in the lowest depths.

VIII

The message to the Aristotelian is, then, that there is no safe way of combining deep personal love (especially, but probably not only, erotic love) with spotless moral purity. If you are determined to be a person who cherishes all the virtues, whose every act is done justly and appropriately, toward the right person in the right way at the right time, you had better omit erotic love, as the Roman Stoics do. And you had better omit, too, any form of love in which you and your good are deeply vulnerable, any love on which you have staked your *eudaimonia*. If you admit such love, you will almost surely be led outside the boundaries of the virtues; for this one constituent part likes to threaten and question all the others. And then the very perfectionism of the Aristotelian, who so wants all of life to fit harmoniously together, will be likely to produce rage upon rage—angry violence toward one's own violence, a sword aimed at one's own aggression.

On the other hand, if we leave love out, as the play also teaches us, we leave out a force of unsurpassed wonder and power, whose beauty is incommensurable with and no less than that of morality. It can never reside harmoniously inside morality, as one component inside a harmonious life-plan; but leave it out and you will have a life that is not complete, therefore not *eudaimōn*. So, either way we live, we will be, it seems, imperfect.

The Aristotelian and the Stoic are both forced to see, then, that not all beauty and wonder can be dragooned into an orderly arrangement for the perfect, the healthy life. The Aristotelian's emphasis on balance and health, on getting clear about the pattern of one's target and then reliably hitting it, ignores the fact that some great goods are in their nature not susceptible of such domestication, some great values require us not to care for health above every other thing. These goods may not be forms of disease, as the Stoic has said; but they require us, if we admit them, to take our stand outside of the opposition between disease and health—at least in the sense that one does not obsessively punish oneself for every divergence from virtue. I shall have love so long as it is a part of health, so long as it comes at the right time in the right relation to my target: this wish is not only unlikely to be realized, it is a wish not to have love itself in one's life. For love, the play suggests, cannot be thoroughly moralized; nor can it coexist with militant punitive moral scrutiny.

What this play suggests, in the end, is a conception of the ethical stance that turns its back—at least some rare times and in some ways—on one aspect of the medical analogy, its tireless insistence on perfect health; a conception in which a full human life is conceived not as Aristotle's target, but as Medea's snake, who sometimes settles his coils into orderly rings, and sometimes glides off in search of someone to murder. Murderous impulses may continue to be judged wrong—but if they become the focus of obsessive guilty scrutiny and self-punishment, as the medical analogy sometimes seems to recommend, the capacity to love may itself be destroyed.

This brings us back to the argument from integrity. For on this issue, too, a related criticism of Aristotelianism seems to be required. Aristotle cares too much about self-sufficiency and rational control to admit love in all of its terribleness. He permits many risks, but he despises slavery too much to admit to intrinsic value a kind of relation in which we are so completely within the power of another, inhabited, intertwined, with no hard core to our natures. The Stoic remedy is a contraction of boundaries. But if we refuse this remedy, we must, it seems, learn to imagine ourselves with new images: not as safe house-dwellers in the solid edifice of our own virtue, but as beings soft and sinuous, weaving in and out of the world, in and out of one another.

As we develop this ethical conception and these images, we are in fact very much assisted by another aspect of the medical analogy: its particularism, its empathetic concern for the causal history of each case. This narrative attitude supplied Seneca with his (partial) remedy for rage at human imperfection. In mercy, the soul turns itself away from the strict punishment of each defect, even where a fault is present, understanding the difficulties the person faced in his or her efforts to live well. Here we have sympathetic understanding without detachment; here we have a source of gentleness to both self and other that can modify one's passions even where there is wrongdoing and even where there is both anger and ill-wishing. Nikidion our pupil will be urged to assume this merciful attitude toward the lover who has wronged her—imagining patiently and vividly (in the manner of one watching a play) the difficulties and obstacles, both social and psychological, that contributed to his wrongdoing, until rage gives way to narrative understanding. She will also, and just as urgently, be urged to take up this attitude toward herself, understanding the reasons for her resentments and her evil impulses, and relaxing the harsh punishments she is inclined to mete out to her own soul, seeing in the nature of human life itself grounds for mitigation.

The attitude that engenders mercy is, I argued, an empathetic narrative attitude. If Nikidion were to become a pupil of an ethical view committed to the worth of both love and mercy, she would spend much of her time as both Aristotle and the Stoics recommend, thinking philosophically, getting clear about her values. But her teacher would also create, in this dialectical life, certain spaces in which stories would be told and heard—to let them be there in their mystery, in their character that is neither that of sickness nor that of health. This play might well be one of these stories. We would want, too, to have happier love stories—in which a great passion flourished, for once, without evil; or at least in which the mutual love of the lovers was itself not tarnished by events. And we would want comedies as well as tragedies: for in comedy, too, we find an acceptance of a mixed human life. But we would insist on confronting Nikidion with this particular story; for in a story like this certain limits of Aristotelian and Stoic morality can be especially well seen.

Listening to these stories, being moved by them, Nikidion would see the limits of the human aspiration to perfect virtue, and learn—if it is possible to teach such things to a person so eager for the perfection of her own practical reason—to moderate her demand for her own moral safety, to wait with a certain humility before unpredictable things. I shall therefore end this chapter by telling Nikidion a story. It will be the story of the end of Seneca's play, the story with which we began—but retold so as to bring out the transmoral ambiguities that we have discovered in the meantime beneath its moralizing surface. I tell it, in parting, to this Nikidion who has all through this book desired so anxiously to learn how to live well; who wants so very much to be always in the right; who wants, as her name implies, a little bit of victory over disorder and evil, just so much as is compatible with a perfect balanced attachment to everything that has true value. To Nikidion, then I retell the end of Medea's story.

She appears on the steep slope of the palace roof. The man she loves stares up at her. He sees her looming over him, radiant and boiling, wrapped in the red light of her grandfather Sun. That light both threatens and transfigures. The straight order of the daily world, imperiled, shines with amazing beauty. In terror, in passionate desire, he lifts his swollen eyes to the snakelike flames; for never has her beauty appeared more wonderful. And now, flying through the bright air, a chariot approaches, drawn by two scaly snakes equipped with wings. He sees their sinuous and sudden movements, their noiseless coils glistening. As she takes the reins, their twisting motion becomes one with her hair and with the movement of her body. Jason sees them as the doubles of her body and of his own, wrapped around one another in passion. Excessive winged fluid lethal, symbols at once of death and potency, of murder and of birth.

Charioteer and serpents, anti-Platonic symbols, they ascend. Medea, fully identified with her passion, goes off from our world into the sun, from the place of moral judgment to the place where there are no gods. Jason, pulled equally by morality and by love, by identification and by judgment, by the compunctions of piety and the splendor of the serpent, is as if split into two, as the mind of the spectator is also split in two. The moral Jason weeps, condemns, repudiates. He distances himself from Medea's flight, saying, "Where you travel, there are no gods." But now we recall, we see in our mind, that there are two serpents in the sky. The serpent Jason, twining in ecstasy around his partner, moves himself, winged, reborn, beyond the gods, beyond the Stoic universe in which gods dwell everywhere. Deep in the cosmos, in that once silent country beyond the chaste Stoic moon (while children die on the earth), there now appears a flickering hot light, an irregular, snaking motion. We are witnessing a triumph. It is the triumph of love.

✳ CHAPTER 13 ✳

The Therapy of Desire

> To say more than human things with human voice,
> That cannot be; to say human things with more
> Than human voice, that, also, cannot be;
> To speak humanly from the height or from the depth
> Of human things, that is acutest speech.
>
> Wallace Stevens, "Chocorua to Its Neighbor"

So philosophy, in these schools, makes itself the doctor of human lives. What should we make of their achievements? A comprehensive philosophical appraisal would require nothing less than answering the fundamental questions of human life. We would need to get clear about what the death of a human being is, and whether it is ever right to fear it; about what forms of attachment to undependable external things a human life needs in order to be complete, and whether one can have these without debilitating uncertainty; about how much uncertainty and need a person can endure, while retaining integrity and practical reason; about whether it is good to love at all, given the pain that love can inflict; about whether virtue itself needs love, and whether, if it does not, it is still sufficient for a complete life; about whether society should be based on love, need, and compassion, or on respect for the dignity of reason; about whether, in order to avoid slavishness, we must allow ourselves angers that can corrode the heart, alienating us from our enemy's humanity and our own. Much of the distinction of Hellenistic ethics lies in the complexity of its description of these problems, and in the fertility of the questions it thus continues to provoke.

It is likely that there will remain deep division—among human beings and, perhaps, within each human being—over these questions. For vulnerability is indeed painful, and the life of passionate attachment to externals a perilous and, at times, a harmful, unjust life. On the other hand, it is difficult to dismiss the thought that these attachments contribute something without which life—and perhaps even virtue itself—is not complete. I am not sure that it is philosophically good to believe that one has an exhaustive once-and-for-all solution to these problems. If one can lucidly describe their difficulty and one's own perplexity before them, criticizing inadequate accounts and making a little progress beyond what was said in the more adequate, this may stand, perhaps, as a Socratic substitute for arrogant certainty. And that sort of philosophical work should be a good preparation for the complex particular confrontations of life—not in the spirit of skeptical equipoise and indifference, but in that of the Socratic search for truth and excellence—which retains awareness too, however, of the limitations of human wisdom concerning matters so mysterious and many-sided.[1] (Here I side methodologically neither with the Skeptics nor with the more confidently dogmatic of the Epicureans and Stoics, but with the open-endedness of the Socratic *elenchos* and of Aristotelian dialectic; but this approach is paralleled, I think, in the most complex and Socratically humble of Stoic ethical writings, and in the more dialectical portions of Lucretius.) This Socratic inquiry has been carried on throughout the book, and it would be false to my purpose (as well as beyond my abilities) to offer, here, a sudden answer to all difficulties. Instead, I want to conclude with some unsystematic reflections about several themes that link the book's various chapters and sections.

I. Methodological Achievement of Therapeutic Arguments

I have argued that a conception of philosophy's task as medical, dedicated to the relief of human suffering, leads to a new conception of philosophical method and procedure; that choices of method and procedure are not, as some might suppose, content-neutral, but closely bound up with a diagnosis of human difficulties and an intuitive conception of human flourishing. I have tried to show that in each case the procedures embody complex conceptions of disease and health—and, as well, of friendship and the structure of community. On the other hand, I have tried to show that this fact does not make the entire enterprise question-begging: for the different elements in the conception support and reinforce one another, in such a way that justification, while holistic, is not therefore just a joke. But what, more specifically, do I take the methodological achievements of the schools to have been, both to their own historical context and to our own concerns about how moral philosophy should work?

1. First and centrally, one must, I think, point to the *new attention to questions of need and motivation* that we see in the schools' attempts to grapple medically with concrete human lives. Ancient Greek and Roman

---

[1] See Vlastos (1985, 1991).

philosophy tends to be more sensitive to these questions than contemporary moral philosophy in any case; for asking how to live is never, in the Greek traditions, a merely academic exercise, nor philosophy a merely academic subject. It is prompted by real human perplexities, and it must address these in the end. But the Hellenistic schools move well beyond Aristotle, and even beyond Socrates and Plato, in their fine-tuned attention to the interlocutor's concrete needs and motives for philosophizing. They design their procedures so as to engage those deepest motivations and speak to those needs. The different schools do this in different ways, with rather different conceptions of the diseases that lead the pupil to seek the philosophical doctor. Yet from all of these attempts contemporary moral philosophy has much to learn, if it wishes to move beyond the academy to take its place in the daily lives of human beings.

2. Closely connected with this, and a major source of the excellence of these philosophical works, is their *careful attention to the techniques of philosophical speech and writing*.[2] Rigor and precision, they feel, are, while necessary, not sufficient, if philosophy is to communicate to more than a narrow elite. For rigor and precision couched in dry or fussy or jargon-laden academic language will not engage the pupil in the search for truth, will not penetrate deeply enough into her thought about what matters in life to draw from her an acknowledgment of what she really thinks and what is troubling her. Literary and rhetorical strategies enter into the methods at a very deep level, not just decorating the arguments, but shaping the whole sense of what a therapeutic argument is, and expressing, in their stylistic concreteness, respect for the pupil's need. In the course of writing this book I have become more and more concerned with this aspect of Hellenistic procedure; and this has, of necessity, led me more and more to Rome rather than to Greece, since there are whole literary works to be examined. In chapters 5 through 7, 11, and 12, especially, I have found in Lucretius and in Seneca remarkable models of philosophical-literary investigation, in which literary language and complex dialogical structures engage the interlocutor's (and the reader's) entire soul in a way that an abstract and impersonal prose treatise probably could not.

In attending closely to the pupil's needs, these writers are the heirs of Socrates' oral practice.[3] And in chapter 4 I brought forward evidence that the oral practice of argument in the Epicurean tradition, at least, had

---

[2] The Skeptics seem to be exceptions here, although they do carefully consider how to engage the particular pupil.

[3] On Hellenistic attitudes to Socrates, see Long (1988).

enormous rhetorical complexity and particularity. But, unlike Socrates and like Plato, Lucretius and Seneca have to grapple with the fact that their audience is diverse and at a distance. This they do by the creation of an internal surrogate for the reader, and by the use of language well designed to engage the imagination of the sort of reader they address. Form and content are not just incidentally linked, as they are so frequently in philosophical writing today. Form is a crucial element in the work's philosophical content. Sometimes, indeed (as with the *Medea*), the content of the form proves so powerful that it calls into question the allegedly simpler teaching contained within it. More frequently, the relationship is simpler and more harmonious.

Historians of philosophy, who have usually turned to Lucretius and Seneca as the source for arguments that they can use to reconstruct the Greek Epicurean and Stoic positions, should recognize that they cannot without violence to the overall philosophical enterprise—indeed, without missing some of what is actually being argued—remove the "arguments" from the entire context of their expression. Classical literary scholars, who frequently attend to the literary form of these works without bothering much with the philosophical arguments, should recognize that the form is not separable from the philosophy and can be fully understood only as philosophical expression. There is a lot more work to be done along these lines, on writers as diverse as Lucretius and Cicero, Seneca and Plutarch.[4] And from all of this, contemporary moral philosophy, whose formal choices are now frequently dictated by academic convention—by the policies of established journals, for example) rather than by human need, has a great deal to learn.

3. In all of their procedures, the Hellenistic moral philosophers develop further Aristotle's interest in *particular perception as an ingredient in good choice.* The way in which they do this diverges to some extent from Aristotle, as chapter 4 argued: for on the whole particularity takes center stage when the doctor is seeking to treat a patient's disease, not when she is articulating the norm of health itself. On the other hand, it is *in* the particular that the norm must, if at all, be realized; and all the schools recognize this. For the Stoics, furthermore, it is the particular circumstances in which an action is chosen that give it its moral status. And the medical therapeutic attention of the teacher/doctor is to be applied by each person to herself in the struggle to examine one's motives and to live well each day. Thus for the Stoics as for Aristotle, particular perception is an essential moral ability,

---

[4] For examples of new contemporary work along these lines, see Nussbaum (1990d).

crucial in any reasonable enactment of a general conception, and of moral worth in its own right.[5] Here is one more way in which the conception of moral inquiry as therapeutic leads the Hellenistic schools to a rich exploration of an element in ethics that contemporary moral theory has less often made central.

Further work on Stoic ethics would also offer valuable guidance concerning the relationship between particularism and relativism, showing clearly that an ethics that values the keen perception of particular contexts and holds this to be criterial of good choice need not in any sense be relativistic—any more than good doctoring need have a situation-relative idea of health. As I argued in chapter 1 and subsequent chapters, the norm of health itself must respond to something in real human beings, and in particular to some of their deepest needs and desires, or it will not be a norm of *health*. But this in no way entails subjectivism or even relativism— for all these schools argue powerfully that human beings at some level have similar deep needs and similar underlying goals of flourishing. Those goals must be realized in a way that suits each context and each history, each particular set of impediments to flourishing. But they are still, in their most general form, universal human goals.

4. Central among the methodological achievements of Stoicism and Epicureanism is their *recognition that existing desires, intuitions, and preferences are socially formed and far from totally reliable.* This is connected, of course, with one of their greatest substantive achievements, their powerful analyses of desire and emotion. And it is one example of the manner in which content and procedure are fruitfully and not question-beggingly related. Modern moral philosophy, on the whole, has tended to treat existing preferences and intuitions as a reliable basis for argument. This is true explicitly and methodologically of the simpler (especially the economic) forms of Utilitarianism; more complex philosophical Utilitarians, who insist on some correction of preferences at the heart of their theory, do not always worry about this in their practice of arguing with their readers.[6] It is true as well, in both theory and practice, of some contemporary moral philosophers who think of themselves as heirs of the ancient Greek virtue-centered traditions.[7] For they believe that the advice of these traditions is to

[5] The Stoics, however, intellectualize this ability far more than Aristotle does.

[6] Exceptions to this, with profound methodological considerations, are Hare (1981) and Parfit (1984); see also Brandt (1979). For a valuable recent critique of the reliance on uncorrected preferences, see Sunstein (1991).

[7] See, for example, Williams (1985); for a comparable procedure without reference to Greek traditions, see Nagel (1979). The position or positions of MacIntyre (1981, 1988) on

trust to the intuitions and emotions; and in a sense they are (so far as Aristotle is concerned) correct. But they, to some extent, neglect the subtle insights of Aristotle himself concerning the deformation of preferences and desires in existing societies; and they certainly neglect the radical challenge of the Hellenistic schools.

Nothing is trickier than to balance the recognition that preferences are unreliable against the wish for the interlocutor to be an active self-governing participant in the process of argument. It is easy enough to bypass the pupil's preferences if one simply discards the whole idea of arguing and brainwashes the pupil instead, or induces, through non-argumentative means, some sort of "conversion" experience. Such procedures have more in common with religious and political manipulation than they do with philosophy; to the extent that the Hellenistic schools turn to them, they risk ceasing to be philosophical. I shall say more about this shortly. On the other hand, the best of the arguments I have considered here do show a recognition that the work of criticism must be undertaken from within the pupils own beliefs and desires, and by a process of rational critical argument. If techniques of a more manipulative sort are used, their results can generally be validated by appeal to cogent arguments, impressive for the way in which they bring the allegedly unreliable preferences of the pupil into conflict with other things she believes and wants, clarifying for her the nature of her alternatives. Lucretius on anger and love and fear, Seneca on love and anger—these are arguments that radically challenge what most people will say if asked to state their current intuitions. Yet their conclusions are reached by argument, and by argument that slices deeply into the pupil, drawing up hidden and deeper beliefs.

This issue has complicated my own task in writing the arguments of this book. And I have more than once been aware that my conclusions, especially where critical of Hellenistic therapies, might be accused of being biased by my own culturally formed (or deformed) preferences, preferences that I expect many of my readers to share, but which are not validated simply by their ubiquity. It is difficult to be confident that one has probed deeply enough into oneself, or looked critically enough at one's society, to satisfy the demands of Hellenistic therapy. Where I have been able to discover a tension or inconsistency in the Hellenistic view itself—as with

---

ordinary belief and intuition are complex. On the one hand, MacIntyre does urge a return to a society such as he believes Greece to have been, in which ordinary intuitions about what to do were reliable and harmonious; on the other hand, he believes that this return is impossible without first principles that are secured by religious or quasi-religious authority, which informs preferences by a thoroughgoing ordering of life and practice.

Lucretius on fear and Seneca on anger—this gives me some confidence that the intuitions I bring forward in criticism are deep and worthy of respect. The only way to proceed here, I think, is to put oneself on the line with as much sincerity and accuracy as possible, showing what one takes to be truly deep and pertinent; and I shall be content if the reader judges (there and elsewhere) that I have done this.

5. Finally, the Hellenistic schools are the first in philosophy's history in the West to *recognize the existence of unconscious motivations and beliefs.* This innovation—again both substantive and methodological—leads, as I have argued, to a radical change in the methods of Aristotelian dialectic. Methods must now be designed to draw these unconscious views to the surface for inspection and, as well, to ensure that the true beliefs get lodged at a deep enough level that they can, in Epicurus' words, "become capable" in the soul. This means that philosophy cannot be conducted simply in an academic fashion, occupying only a small part of one's life. It requires long and patient effort, a careful attention to each day and each part of each day, and, too, the support of philosophical community and philosophical friendship.

Epicureans place the emphasis, here, on the role of the wise teacher, who demands the pupil's trust and "confession," and sometimes uses techniques (such as memorization and repetition) that do not require the pupil's own critical activity. Skeptics go much further, engineering the methods of philosophy to cut away the pupil's active cognitive contribution, leaving her more and more in the grip of motivating forces that do not involve belief.[8] Of all the schools it is the Stoics, I think, who most effectively combine recognition of depth in the soul with respect for the pupil's active practical reasoning, producing a picture of philosophical friendship that combines intimacy with symmetry and reciprocity, a picture of self-scrutiny that supplements, and does not displace, dialectical philosophical procedures. (Lucretius seems to capture this combination in many of his arguments, both forming that sort of friendship with the reader and making friendship an end in itself; he may to this extent diverge from the authoritarianism of what seems to have been the common Epicurean procedure.)

As for the arguments in favor of recognizing the unconscious, these are not above criticism—no such argument could be—but in the case of Lucretius on fear they are extremely impressive. The central problem here is

---

[8] The Skeptics do not explicitly recognize the unconscious—and of course to have any theory of the structure of the mind is contrary to their procedure.

490

that the arguments are relatively local and unsystematic, not linked to any clear developmental theory of infancy. The Hellenistic thinkers are in some ways the parents of modern psychoanalysis, but they have not done the empirical work with actual children that would make such a practice well grounded in a developmental way.[9] There is rich material in Lucretius, I think, for a theory of infant emotional development and the ensuing repression of anxiety. Such an account, if fully developed would stand comparison with the best of psychoanalytical theories. In some respects it would be on stronger ground than mainstream Freudian theory, since it would start from the very general and certainly (in some form) universal experience of need and the lack of self-sufficiency, rather than from the problematic and rather narrow notion of infantile sexuality. The work of Melanie Klein and the object relations school develops some of these insights.[10]

6. We now must confront some of the potentially more problematic methodological consequences of using therapy as a norm. First of all, I have been troubled throughout by the possibility that the schools, in their passion for health, might *subordinate truth and good reasoning to therapeutic efficacy.* I argued that it was not unreasonable to define ethical truth (to some extent at least) in terms of the deepest needs and desires of human beings. All ethical theories make the connection between truth and desire somehow. In the case of an extreme form of Platonism, the link is contingent, through recollection. But in the case of Aristotle's theory, an ethical proposal will be rejected as false if it is too far out of line with the deepest wishes and desires of the participants in the inquiry. I argued that it is still appropriate to speak of truth here—in part because of the insistence of such a theory on broad consistency and fit, in part because the demand for consistency will also constrain the ethical theory from without, as it fits itself to results in psychology and physics. The Stoic theory clearly meets these constraints, and it seems perfectly appropriate for it to claim truth. In fact, as I argued in chapters 9 and 10, the Stoic theory is in a sense less anthropocentric and more externally realist than the Aristotelian theory, since human desires are good guides just in case they are the ones that harmonize with the rational order of the universe. (However, for those who cannot accept Stoic teleology, the Stoics, I argued, also offer independent arguments for the extirpation of passion that are good dialectical arguments in the Aristotelian sense—see point 7 in this section.) We may add that the Stoics, unlike the other schools, make practical reasoning a

---

[9] See Brunschwig (1986).
[10] See, e.g., Klein (1984, 1985), Fairbairn (1952), Bollas (1987).

major intrinsic value; in no way do they subordinate it to the good of *apatheia*.

At the other end of the spectrum, the Skeptics clearly do jettison truth, and even good reasoning, on the way to *ataraxia*. They cheerfully admit, even insist, that they do this; so to point this out is not a knockdown criticism of their practice. The criticism in chapter 8 came from a comprehensive look at what a life without truth and norms of good reasoning is really like. I argued that it is an impoverished life.

The case of the Epicureans is, on this point, the subtlest, the most difficult to describe correctly. For on the one hand the Epicureans do offer powerful and compelling arguments in favor of their positions. The quality of the arguments is important to them, and the arguments do construct a comprehensive view of the universe, or at least of all those aspects of it that bear on any question pertaining to our *ataraxia*. On the other hand, it appears that this reasoning is given a purely instrumental value, albeit a very high instrumental value. And scientific inquiry here, by contrast to Aristotle's school, is pursued only for the sake of an ethical end. It is not altogether clear, then, that physics can offer ethics the independent support that seems important if we are to think of ethical truth as a (partly) desire-independent notion. The broad coherence and fit of Epicurean ethics and physics may themselves suffice to give the view a claim to truth, especially when we add to this the (alleged) correspondence of the view to the deepest of human needs and desires. But the instrumentality of reason remains a troubling element in the Epicurean procedure, compounded by the procedure's failure to consider the opinions of the "many and the wise" in Aristotelian dialectical fashion. *Ataraxia* is somewhat dogmatically put forward as an end; and this end is then used to shape other arguments, and even to determine which judgments and arguments will be considered. (Some of Lucretius' arguments fared better in this regard.)

7. This leads directly to my second area of concern: the *tension between critical autonomy and causal manipulation in the treatment of the pupil.* The schools want the pupil to achieve *eudaimonia*, and all of them (even the Skeptics, or so I argue) operate with some definite conception of what this end is. They all, as well, view existing society as diseased in its beliefs and preferences, and the pupil as infected with those diseases. This naturally leads to a desire to *intervene* in the pupil's rational thought processes, to cut beneath what society has imparted in order to get at the sounder judgments that are, they hold, buried beneath this material in the soul. (Or, in the case of the Skeptics, to knock out *all* the belief-material, leaving nothing in its place.) Aristotle solves the problem of the pupil's autonomy

by beginning with pupils who have already had a good moral education (which relies on habituation and other forms of non-philosophical, though certainly not non-intellectual, teaching). With such a pupil he can safely use open-ended dialectical strategies, since he can rely on their producing—in interaction with those relatively healthy preferences—an ethically reliable result. The Hellenistic schools cannot do this: and all, to a greater or lesser extent, restrict the pupil's free consideration of alternatives, manipulating the outcome.

Here, once again, the Skeptics produce by far the most disturbing result, since they quite frankly apply their arguments to the pupil as behavior-manipulating devices, not as arguments to be critically assessed. The strength of the argument, indeed, is calibrated precisely to meet the strength of the pupil's disease. The pupil is discouraged from playing any active or critical role, and becomes, increasingly, a passive recipient of forces. The teacher is like this too, so authoritarianism is not the problem. The problem is, in effect, the complete disappearance of subjecthood and agency. This may bring nothing but joy to the Skeptic; I have argued that it it is, however, a bad result for social and personal life.

The Epicurean community has, as well, some disturbing aspects. The pupil is encouraged to mistrust herself and to rely on the wisdom of the teacher, the saving power of the Epicurean doctrine. Separated from the city and its cognitive influence, subjected to a daily regimen of memorization, repetition, and confession, denied the evenhanded consideration of alternative views, the pupil does not have very much autonomy. Nor is autonomy recognized as a valued end by the Epicurean doctrine. It is striking that in Roman Epicureanism things seem to be subtly different. Arguing with Romans who are deeply attached to their own integrity, who live, moreover, at Rome with other Romans, Lucretius moves his interlocutor gradually to a position of greater autonomy and maturity. His attitude to opposing views is still contemptuous and shrill, far from dialectical. But he asks the pupil to take on himself the job of arguing and assessing. For this pupil will not live in a tranquil Epicurean community, celebrating the hero-feast of Epicurus and relying on the support of Epicurean friendship. He must go home to his family and friends, and play his role as a political and military man in a world in which most people he meets will be non-Epicureans. Lucretius does not leave him unprepared.

The Stoics, I think, solve these problems in the most attractive way. For, first of all, they recognize that they will not always be dealing with pliant Stoic or pre-Stoic pupils. Thus, though they are happy to expound their system and to show how it coheres as a whole, they are also eager to offer arguments to interlocutors who are not Stoics—as Seneca, for example, so frequently does. This entails arguing seriously and dialectically against Peripatetic and Epicurean positions. Moreover, since they hold that active practical reasoning is intrinsically valuable, they encourage the pupil not to defer to anyone's authority (neither teacher nor book), but to take charge of her own life. And this means, in effect, doing away with the asymmetry between teacher and pupil that is suggested by the medical model, as the teacher goads and assists, but leaves the conclusions to emerge from the pupil's own thought. Entrenched social beliefs still need to be subverted: and the teacher is ready to offer the pupil some very powerful arguments and some vivid rhetoric to that end. But he is not an authority: the reason of the pupil is the only true authority. This means that *self*-criticism and *self*-recognition take the place of Epicurean "confession" as the central critical and diagnostic activity. Here the Stoics follow very effectively the example of Socrates, who with his ironic distance from the pupil and his stinging challenge to unexamined belief places the pupil's autonomy ahead of her comfort, and even her adherence to the correct view.[11]

I suggested in discussing Epicurus that the open-endedness of Aristotelian dialectic stood in contrast to the dogmatism of Hellenistic "medical" thought, and that no thoroughly medical conception could have Aristotle's flexible capacity for self-scrutiny and self-revision. The Stoics call this into question. For while their method is, to be sure, not officially dialectical and in fact quite dogmatic, they are so deeply committed to the integrity of practical reason that they deny the pupil the shelter that dogmatic authority would afford. Nothing is reliable, except (insofar as one is rational) oneself. Thus it is not surprising that out of that procedural commitment we get the examples of self-questioning and apparent revision of Stoicism that we have found in chapters 11 and 12; no surprise that in Seneca we find not the inflexible announcement of a creed, but a resourceful and deeply personal grappling with ongoing problems.

II. TENSIONS IN THE MEDICAL MODEL

The medical model yields a rich portrait of the philosopher—sympathetically concerned and yet free from disturbing gusts of emotion, expert in skill and yet close to each suffering patient. In this portrait there arise two tensions that we must now confront. First is the apparent tension between

---

[11] See Vlastos (1991) chapter 1 for a related discussion of Socrates.

compassion and freedom from disturbance. The medical philosopher is apparently led to philosophy by the urgency of human need, and is depicted as moved by some sort of compassionate response to that need. And yet for none of the schools is compassion (pity)[12] an appropriate motivation; for all insist that the wise person is free from all (or, in the Epicurean case, most) emotions. How, then, can they explain the doctor's choice to be a soul-doctor—presumably not the easiest and least upsetting course a person could follow?

The Skeptics here are, if implausible, still consistent—for they insist that the teacher has no emotional motivation, only the habit of following a trade and whatever perceptions and feelings are left when all belief is removed. This does not yield a very rich account of the alleged *philanthrōpia* of the teacher, nor explain very well why someone would go in for teaching *others* in the first place, rather than just using his trade to cure himself. But perhaps the Skeptic became a teacher before being a full-fledged Skeptic—and kept at it even when belief dropped away. Or maybe he makes his living that way. Here as elsewhere, these are hardly motives to rely on, in constructing a society. But the Skeptic is not in the business of being reliable.

The Epicureans face a very complex tension, which is a version, really, of the tension in their whole position on questions of friendship and love. Unlike the other schools, they do not repudiate *all* emotion, so they can and do permit some compassion (cf. chapter 7); and their view of the human goal, which allows them to believe that in general pain and disturbance are bad, gives a basis for compassion, when another's pain is encountered. On the other hand, the end for each person is supposed to be his or her own *ataraxia* and *aponia*, and, as we saw, the good of others comes into it above all instrumentally, though possibly also via the intrinsic worth of certain sorts of interaction with friends (cf. chapter 7). This does not seem sufficient to explain why Epicurus runs his school, and leaves a will providing for its future; why Diogenes of Oenoanda erects an elaborate inscription aimed at strangers and people of the future; why Lucretius wishes to leave behind for others a work on which he has expended much labor. Even if all altruism to the living could be explained as based upon the (largely, but not entirely) instrumental principles of Epicurean friendship, that will not explain any sort of concern for strangers and people of the future. And yet

---

[12] The Greek and Latin words—*eleos* and *misericordia*—do not have the associations with condescension that the English word "pity" sometimes does, though "pity" is the most common translation for the words in the modern version. The French philosophical use of *pitie* (as, e.g., in Rousseau) follows the Greek and Roman usage closely.

Epicureans clearly have this concern, and rely on it for the genesis of their work.

The Stoics have, here, the problem they have with all altruism: they have to explain why the good of others matters to someone who has eliminated all the attachments on which the emotions are based. And they have a further problem as well: they must explain why, if virtue is self-sufficient, needing nothing from without in order to realize and maintain itself, virtuous people will judge that other people need their help. These problems they handle by their complex account of the preferred indifferents (see chapter 10), which may or may not be sufficient to explain the actions in question. (Certainly it denies the philosopher all motives based on pity or compassion; I think this is a considerable loss here, as also in the case of material goods and their distribution.) In addition, they hold that philosophical activity is of intrinsic worth—so the person who philosophizes hardly *needs* a justification for doing so (though that by itself does not explain why it is done to and for others). Above all, however, they rely, here, on the self-activating work of each pupil, thinking of doctoring as, above all, *self*-doctoring, of argument as scrutiny of oneself. The question is whether all these answers, put together, are really sufficient to explain the sort of altruism to which the interlocutors of Stoic arguments (especially at Rome) are profoundly attached. And it is not surprising that here, as in Epicureanism, we should find cases of philosophical involvement with the world that go beyond what the official position allows—as when Seneca curses the slavish parent, as in the passionate attachment with his pupil's good that Seneca more than once seems to reveal, as in the ambiguities within the *Medea*'s portrait of *erōs*.

A second tension in the medical analogy is harder to describe; it played a major role in chapter 11. On the one hand, the conception of the philosopher as doctor creates a strong asymmetry of expertise and places the pupil far from the teacher. This leads, in the case of some of the Greek Stoics and Epicureans, to a rather severe posture, in which the doctor watches and judges the pupil with keen perception, but without fellow feeling. On the other hand, the particularism inherent in the medical model leads, on its side, to an interest in understanding the patient's whole history. And this narrative emphasis leads, in Seneca, to a turning away from harshness, to empathetic fellow feeling, and to mercy. The two approaches are in principle consistent, since expert perception can be particularistic; but in practice they lead to different attitudes and to different philosophical techniques. The emphasis on expertise leads to hard dogmatism; the emphasis on narrative leads to flexible judgment that diverges from fixed rules, or at least turns aside from the punishments they recommend. Much hinges here on the attitude the doctor takes up to him or herself: for the distant and judgmental stance is likely to be associated with the idea that one is far wiser than the pupil, the merciful stance, as Seneca makes explicit, with the recognition that one is oneself imperfect in ways similar to the offender.

The Skeptics do not concern themselves with the distinction between moral judgment and mercy, preferring the limitless flexibility of the teacher who suspends all judgment. In Epicureanism things are more complex: to some extent the distant asymmetrical relation of moral judgment prevails (though with greater mutuality in Lucretius); at the same time, however, compassion for human weakness is an approved sentiment, and one that guides the teacher's practice. The Greek Stoics appear to have opted for distance and austerity of judgment. But it remained for Seneca—drawing, probably, on both Aristotelian and Roman traditions—to develop the idea of mercy, connecting it with a perception of one's own imperfection and the intractability of the "circumstances of life." I think that this is an advance of major proportions for moral philosophy, both substantively and (as the end of chapter 12 argued) methodologically.

III. Nature and Finitude

Each of the schools claims to give the pupil a life according to nature. All make claims about nature, deriving them from some sort of scrutiny of the human being, its needs and capabilities. In all, the notion of nature is normative rather than simply descriptive, a notion of unimpeded flourishing connected with the removal of certain obstacles imposed by (usually social) diseases. And in all cases the claim to give us a life according to nature is connected with an idea of recognizing our finitude as mortal beings, giving up socially induced longings that take us beyond those limits. On the other hand, in all three schools as well there is a claim to give us a *godlike* life—usually in connection with the claim to remove disturbances that most vex a mortal life. Here we see, in each case, a tension or series of tensions between the repudiation of transcendence and the attempt to achieve another sort of transcendence. How does each of the schools deal with this issue?

The Skeptics have, among the three, the most reductive idea of nature— one that really does confine the "naturally" human to the level of animal impulse plus habit, as the pupil is urged "to divest" herself utterly "of the human being." And it is this very life that they also defend, somewhat rhetorically, as blessed and godlike—for it is that life, they argue, that exemplifies the blessed end of *ataraxia*. In the Greek tradition, the beast and the god lie close to one another in certain ways (cf. chapter 7): for neither has ethical and other-related concerns, neither has the virtues. The Skeptic's divinity is of this negative and quasi-bestial sort, the freedom from disturbance that comes from having no cares and no commitments. Their "nature" is still a normative idea of freedom from impediment; the impediments are, as in the other schools, traced to that which society and teaching impose. But in their zeal to remove these impediments, and through their relentless assault on normative commitment itself, they take away what has seemed to all other Greek philosophers—and to most ordinary people—to be, in normative terms, an essential part of our human flourishing.

In Epicureanism the tension between "nature" and divinity is far more complex. For the gods are exemplars of invulnerability and self-sufficiency, and they serve explicitly as norms for the pupil. On the other hand, as we have seen, much of the detailed and excellent philosophical work of the arguments consists in leading the pupil to understand herself, in a way free from conventional religious longing, as a finite mortal being. The rich normative conception of nature includes an idea of accepting one's membership in a world of finite living things. And it also appears to include friendship as an item of intrinsic value—at least in Lucretius and possibly in Epicurus as well, making the flourishing person ungodlike in her need for others. In Lucretius' treatment of anger, community and friendship, and in much of his account of love, that finitist idea predominated, as Lucretius offered the pupil a human way of inhabiting both love and risk, "yielding to human life," forgoing the longing for divine life, for perfect safety. These results may not be fully consistent with the official Epicurean demand for *ataraxia* as goal; and yet Lucretius does not in these cases pursue that goal at the expense of the mortal goods his argument has identified. (He does not, for example, like Epicurus, counsel the philosopher against marriage and children, nor does he urge the avoidance of political life, with its possibilities for anger.) In the arguments against death, however, and in the love arguments' refusal of any erotic connection that is more passionate than a sexualized friendship, we see the tension between mortal and divine, safe and vulnerable, arise within Lucretius' position itself. I have on the whole preferred the finitist strain in his argument, and I think the Epicurean can have a consistent anti-transcendence position by focusing on this strand—but only by weakening, as Lucretius appears to, the commitment to perfect *ataraxia*.

The Stoics have, among the three, the richest normative conception of nature, one that permits the life according to nature to include practical reasoning as an intrinsic good, and even reasoning about the rational order of the universe. Thus there seems to be no tension in their position between the aspiration to live in accordance with nature and the aspiration to live in a godlike manner. Our nature *is* a godlike nature: for what is most godlike is to seek comprehensive understanding. Thus through reason we both fulfill ourselves and join Zeus.

On the other hand, this rather one-sided picture of nature, with its obsessive focus on the intellectual, does raise some serious questions about the rest of what Aristotle (again, speaking normatively of that which is most important in human life) would have called our nature, all the part that reflects our finitude. Our mortality, our needs for one another as lovers, friends, spouses, fellow citizens, our needs for food and drink and support for our health—is our life to be "in accordance with" all this, as well as with our intellect? The Stoics give, as we have seen, a complicated answer. For they do acknowledge that such things are in most cases rightly preferred, and preferred, it would seem, on account of their role in our first "nature." On the other hand, our commitment to them is not to be so deep as to compromise *apatheia*, freedom from passion—and this shallowness of commitment Aristotle would think *unnatural* for a being who is affectionate, finite, and "disposed to live with others." They are not differing about matters of empirical, value-neutral fact, since for both of them the notion of nature is a normative notion. But they are differing in a fundamental way about what a human life needs in order to be complete. As in the case of Epicurus, I have preferred those Stoic works that acknowledge the pressure of the Aristotelian position, recognizing, especially, the depth of ties to others in a truly reasonable and complete life. It seems to me a major contribution of Hellenistic ethics to have urged us to think humanly, like the finite beings we are. I believe that this insight should have moved the argument, in some cases, away from *apatheia* and toward both *erōs* and compassion.

IV. COMMITMENT AND ATARAXIA

We must now confront directly the central problem with which many of these chapters have grappled: how far does the attachment of these schools to various versions of freedom from pain and disturbance allow their pupils to form commitments to *anything* outside their own virtue? And how complete is the life that results?

The Skeptics divest their pupil of *all* commitments, including cognitive commitments, on the grounds that *any* commitment to the world, even a commitment to the fact that it *is* this way or that, puts the pupil at risk. (Thus they see a remarkable fact: that the philosophical pursuit of truth, praised by the Platonist tradition as the most stable and risk-free life of all, is actually not so free from danger—for it makes our good depend on the way a reality is outside ourselves, and on the ability of a finite mind to grasp that reality.) Far less does the pupil have any commitment to loved ones or country or even to her own past, her character, her tastes. These things are *there*, and they exert their causal force—but if they happen not to, the pupil does not go after them. This gives her a life of remarkable safety; but it impoverishes the self and makes the self untrustworthy for others.

The Epicurean seems to understand *ataraxia* itself in a more active way than the Skeptic—not just as the absence of disturbance, but, in positive terms, as the healthy and unimpeded functioning of all our faculties, including, probably, some uses of our cognitive faculties,[13] and possibly including the interactive mutuality of friendship. This means that even the end may include certain sorts of commitment to others; but the instrumental requirements of the end import far more commitments. First there are the cognitive commitments of Epicurean philosophy, through which the pupil has a stake in the world's being a definite way, a way that might be falsified by experience. That imports an element of risk—though not great risk, the teacher will insist, since the Epicurean position is elaborated in such a way as to have a persuasive answer for every question and challenge. Second are the requirements of virtue and virtuous action—which are chosen only as means to *ataraxia*, but which are, apparently, binding as rules on the pupil, even when, in a particular case, virtuous action is not advantageous.[14] Here again, the pupil incurs some risk because of a commitment. And the risk may be considerable. Finally there are the commitments of friendship—instrumental above all in Epicurus, and excluding marriage, sexual love, children, and the political community. Commitments extend more broadly and deeply in Lucretius to embrace these excluded spheres, endowing them, it would seem, with more than instrumental value. In this way risk and sacrifice become likely parts of the good person's life.

The Stoics' dilemma on this point I have discussed at length—as *apatheia* and its cognitive basis would seem to be at odds with the sort of risk-taking loyalty and courage a Stoic hero is said to possess. Stoic friends and

---

[13] Though not their *philosophical* use—see chapter 4.

[14] See Mitsis (1988a), Goldschmidt (1977).

spouses must live in such a way that the death or departure of the other will not cause grief. Though *pietas* and reverence for duty may produce much loyal and quasi-committed action, the Stoic goes through the motions like one playing a role. He entrusts no part of his good to any other. This lack of deep love and openness may seem, to us as to Seneca's *Medea*, to render that life impoverished and incomplete.

So far I have focused above all on commitments to friends, loved ones, and fellow citizens, where the Hellenistic positions are deeply controversial. But in another area these schools make a major contribution. The societies they encountered are dominated by the competition for wealth, power, and luxuries. People feel committed to the pursuit of these goods, as if they had some sort of intrinsic value. And this leads, as all three schools document in their own way, to antagonisms and frenetic striving, to acts of cruelty, to the rupturing of ties that bind families, cities, the community of human beings. The injunction to live in accordance with nature is, in large part, the injunction to drop the frenzied pursuit of these pseudo-goals, and to reform one's desires and preferences in the light of the recognition that they are at best highly limited tools of human functioning. With probing arguments Epicureans and Stoics both show that the pupil's deepest and most consistent conception of human flourishing makes these items mere instruments, without intrinsic value. And by their analysis of connections between these false ends and socially divisive desires, they provide a further consequentialist argument in favor of their reform of preferences.

These are arguments that contemporary social life and, above all, contemporary economic thinking, need to take to heart. For if the Hellenistic thinkers are correct, the behavior of individuals who seek to maximize wealth and other satisfactions—far from being either natural or rational—is the product of a diseased form of social teaching. (For Lucretius it is still worse—the consequence of a false and self-deceptive belief that one can defeat one's own death by accumulation.) Such behavior will not be chosen by fully informed human beings, when they have duly scrutinized the alternatives through a process of critical argument.

Nothing seems more urgent in contemporary society than the reasoned critique of limitless wealth-maximizing and power-seeking. And yet these goals are rarely approached head on by moral philosophers, especially those in capitalist countries. Economic Utilitarians officially endorse wealth-maximizing as a rational end. Other Utilitarians modify the picture in various ways, but rarely as much as the Hellenistic argument requires. Even the contemporary Kantian theory of John Rawls includes wealth and income as among the "primary goods" of which more is always better.[15] Only theories with a clear affiliation to the ancient Greek world—such as the neo-Aristotelian theory of Amartya Sen[16]—clearly state that these financial goods are only means to human functioning. The vigorous and detailed critique of the Stoics and Epicureans still needs to be heard.[17]

V. Politics

Hellenistic approaches to the therapy of human life focus on self-sufficiency. And where the pupil's needs make her dependent on a world that does not always meet those needs, they alter needs to meet the world, rather than altering the world to meet human needs. Sometimes one suspects that the account of what has intrinsic worth in human life is tailored to meet the philosopher's knowledge of what can be readily and reliably secured, so that the claim of the uncertain goods that politics distributes is not fairly acknowledged. Do these philosophers want so much to establish philosophy as *the* art of life, providing everything needed for *eudaimonia*, that they underrate the worth of political distribution? And doesn't this mean that, in their focus on the souls of individuals, they lose sight of another task that philosophy had previously performed, that of the education of legislators for just and humane public service?

This worry has been with us from the beginning; and it is indeed possible to make a stark contrast between Aristotelian and Hellenistic thought along these lines. Aristotle, who insists that certain "external goods" are necessary for *eudaimonia*, turns to political planning to bring the world to people; the Hellenistic thinkers, instead, make people adjust their aims to fit the uncertainties and injustices of the world. Such a contrast would, however, be far too simple. This book has not attempted a comprehensive account of Hellenistic social and political thought;[18] and yet we have seen enough of the schools' views about community and self-sufficiency to begin to bring the true complexities of the picture to light.

[15] See Rawls (1971).

[16] See Sen (1982, 1985), and Crocker (1992).

[17] In pursuing this critique we would want, at least for purposes of inquiry, to distinguish the psychology of moneymaking from that of power-seeking: for both Adam Smith and Samuel Johnson have argued, in different ways, that the person who is occupied in making money is a relatively innocuous character whose virtues will include frugality and self-discipline, and who will not be likely to be given to acts of fanatical hatred or brutality. Such a character may also do good for society as a whole. These arguments need to be carefully considered.

[18] See now Schofield (1991) for one part of that project.

The simple picture fits the Skeptics well: for they have no interest at all in modifying the world, and focus entirely on the project of getting the pupil to be less pained by the way things go in it. Even bodily pain they do not expect entirely to remove; so they will not consider an insufficiency of material goods incompatible with *eudaimonia*, so long as the pain caused by the absence of these goods is moderate. Beyond that (in a situation, say, of famine) they make no recommendation, political or philosophical, and leave it to the natural responses of the organism to cope as best it can. It is likely to cope selfishly. As for psychological pains caused by social evils such as slavery, injustice, loss of friends, their remedy is to remove the belief that these things are bad. Their pupil will thus (to use their own image) be a eunuch with respect to political change, having no desire, not even one that has to be resisted, to seek social remedies for injustice.

With the Epicureans, things are already more complicated. Epicurus himself strongly discourages active involvement in the political community, and treats justice as merely instrumental to one's own freedom from disturbance. But he is at the same time very much concerned with the body and its needs, defining all pain as bad and *eudaimonia* as requiring its absence. And he is also very concerned with structures of community, and the ways in which these can help human beings meet their needs. Some of these ways involve simply being distracted from the pain that is occurring; but we have reason to suppose that the Epicurean community *was* concerned with the bodily well-being of its members, as well as their spiritual freedom from care. The very fact that Epicurus insists on the physical nature of all reality, including the reality of the human soul, is salient: for no longer (as in Platonism) can bodily ills be dismissed as harmless because they do not affect the "real me." The limits of his approach are, however, plain: not only in the instrumental conception of justice—well enough, perhaps, in a community of friends but less than adequate for a wider world—but also in the narrow boundaries of the world itself, its absence of concern for all but a few nearby people. The whole world cannot organize into little Epicurean communities; such communities are always parasitic upon the economic and political life of the larger world. How, then, is that world to live? Epicurus does not say.

Lucretius takes on this task, however, in his Roman context. We do not find a developed account of political distribution, or of the best political order. But we do find Epicurean arguments about our limited need for material goods, and attacks on unlimited material accumulation, explicitly used in a political context. And we find reflections about the social compact and about compassion that are of real political significance. Lucretius, furthermore, does much to show how the major ills of political life in his day have, in fact, psychological roots, in the anxiety and greed that make people seek to amass more and more property, in fierce competition with their neighbors.

Here, I think, Epicureanism, especially as developed in Lucretius, shows clearly how much a distinctively Hellenistic approach via the psychology of the individual has to offer to politics. For Lucretius sees something that has only recently been rediscovered in Western political thought: that the personal—the life of the emotions and one's own intimate associations, including erotic associations—is political, formed by society and having its fruits in society in turn. Politics is not simply, then, a matter of distributing the usual goods and offices. It involves the whole soul, its loves and fears and angers, its gender relations, its sexual desire, its attitudes to possessions, to children, to family. Epicureans see to what extent these allegedly "private" aspects of life have been warped by the traditions of an unjust and accumulative society; and they commend their personal therapy to us by asserting that individuals so warped can become good social agents in no other way.

The Stoics have, far more than the other schools, a developed political theory—or theories, since accounts of the best community vary between Greece and Rome and within Roman Stoicism itself. I have not studied those accounts here. They make it plain that the Stoics are deeply interested in the circumstances in which virtue is nurtured in the world—since virtue, if self-sufficient when once attained, still needs to be educated (even if external goods are not supposed to be strictly *necessary* for its formation). Furthermore, and, I think, more important, the Stoics have, like Lucretius, an elaborate account of the social/political nature of that which appears to be personal and innate—anger, the fear of death, passionate love, one's attitudes to food and money and sex. The personal self-inspection of each Stoic agent is also a profoundly political act, as chapter 11 has argued, a rooting out of socially formed preferences that deform interpersonal life at all levels, and a cultivation of *humanitas* that bears fruit (in Seneca at any rate) in a politics of gradualism and mercy.

Stoic politics is built, to a great extent, on ideas not of human incompleteness but of human dignity and self-government. This emphasis, especially when combined with Stoic universalism about the potential for virtue, puts the Stoics in a position to make a strong contribution to accounts of human rights and human freedom.[19] Their insistence on the equal

---

[19] See Burnyeat (forthcoming a).

humanity of slaves and women is especially striking—even if not combined with any very robust interest in altering the political realities of slaves' and women's lives. On the other hand, their firm repudiation of pity or compassion as a political motive undoes a tradition that played in the Greek world, and can still play in ours, a major role in appeals for beneficence and for the recognition of human fellowship and equality. To respect a slave as a human being is, as Stoic texts make clear, perfectly compatible with perpetuating and endorsing the political institution of slavery. By contrast, compassion, which makes the slave's pain real for oneself and acknowledges its significance, would naturally lead in the direction of material and institutional change. But the Stoics deny themselves compassion precisely because it ascribes significance to such external circumstances, as if human dignity were not self-sufficient. Both slaves and masters ought, instead, to see that slavery is no big deal, given our inalienable dignity and freedom. Wisdom by itself, and wisdom alone, makes one truly free.

Stoic political thought seems to me, for these reasons, to be a very mixed achievement: profound and perceptive in its analysis of the politics of the passions and the limits of materialism, profound again in recognizing the dignity of humanity across differences of social class, ethnic membership, and even gender, harsh and dogmatic when it comes to the bearing of material circumstances on *eudaimonia*. It is one thing to recognize that even in conditions of slavery human beings retain an inalienable worth on account of which enslaving them is unjust and morally repugnant. It is quite another to claim that this dignity is the only thing of true importance to human flourishing, and that it is so rock hard that slavery doesn't touch it—so that it really doesn't matter to *eudaimonia* whether one is a slave or not. Here it is Aristotle and not the Stoics who seems to set political thought in the right direction: since functioning matters, and since functioning has material and institutional necessary conditions, material and institutional conditions matter, and matter enormously.

The Hellenistic thinkers all recognize that people are shaped by the institutional and material conditions in which they live. In fact, it is the deforming effect of institutions upon desire and functioning that is their starting point. And yet—this is the central difficulty—they seem to take as their task the production of perfect people, one by one, as if perfect people could in fact be produced without profound changes in material and institutional conditions. To some extent the philosophical communities themselves create conditions different from those of the surrounding society. But that does not go very far, as they themselves recognize. And yet at the same time they do not want to acknowledge to what extent the full success of their enterprise, where people are concerned, awaits and requires political and social alterations. For this would make human beings dependent on circumstances for flourishing, and most emphatically dependent on something other than philosophy. This the schools, with their teaching of self-sufficiency and their grand claims to be *the* art of life, would rather not acknowledge. The fact is that their own thought about the deformation of desires and preferences naturally leads in the direction of a call for partnership between philosophy and politics: for it is only in conjunction with efforts out in the world that the life of thought and desire can really change in any meaningful way. Imagine, for example, what would have happened had the U.S. civil rights movement insisted on ridding people of racist desires and thoughts before moving on to laws and institutions; what would happen if women, rather than demanding equality from laws and institutions, had insisted, first, on perfecting the consciousness and the desires of men. We can conjecture that desire and thought themselves would have made less progress under such a program than in the present state of things, where, frequently, laws and institutions lead the way and thought and desire reluctantly knuckle under—perhaps to be truly changed in future generations. We can forgive many of these thinkers for not achieving much in and through politics: for the times in which they lived were difficult times, and it is never easy for philosophers to know how to do any good in politics. What we cannot and should not forgive them for is that they did not more often *call* for such changes, that they implied, indeed, that we could produce the kingdom of reason on earth simply by perfecting individuals one by one, and then permitting these perfected people to create the world.[20]

One further element in Stoic thought makes a major political contribution to the contemporary world; it will enable me to end this section on a positive note. This is the idea that each of us is a citizen of the entire universe, a *kosmou politēs*. From its Greek beginnings, Stoic thought is anti-sectarian and anti-nationalist, turned firmly against the narrow loyalties that make politics focus on competition between groups rather than on rational deliberation about the good of the whole. In chapter 9 we have seen how each Stoic pupil is to view her good as interconnected in complex ways with that of others, taking the interlocking order of the entire world as the basic subject of deliberation. This does not mean endorsing a world state; it does mean thinking of one's fundamental membership as not a

---

[20] I owe some of the formulations in this paragraph to conversations with John Roemer.

local or sectarian one, but a truly global one, and of one's fundamental family as that of all human beings. This attitude to politics is still too rare in the modern world. Even our major theories of justice—for example, that of John Rawls[21]—take the nation as their basic unit, and say little about international justice or international concern.[22] For the more relativistic among such theories there may be nothing to say, in that all norms of justice derive from traditions internal to a particular community,[23] Stoicism offers a non-relative concern for human flourishing, together with a keen awareness of the interlocking interdependence of the world order. It thus offers a promising basis for deliberation about some of the urgent problems of the contemporary world—such as hunger, ecology, population, the status of women—issues that will not be well handled unless they are approached with an eye to the good of all human beings, and, indeed, of the entire world.

VI. THE PASSIONS

The central topic of this book has been the passions. And it is now finally time to assess what we have found. One thing, I think, is indisputable: that the analyses of emotions offered by Stoic and Epicurean texts have a subtlety and cogency unsurpassed by anything on the topic in the history of Western philosophy. Aristotle's accounts were valuable predecessors, clearly. But the Hellenistic thinkers go beyond Aristotle, I believe, in the detail and power of their analyses of the relationship between emotion and belief, in their accounts of the evaluative element in emotion, in their suggestions concerning the interrelationships among the emotions, and, finally, in their connection of the emotional life with a very general view of the world, one in which we have hostages to fortune. Whatever one thinks of their arguments against the passions, and whatever one finally decides about the Stoic identification of passion with belief or judgment, these accounts are indispensable starting points for any future work. Philoso-

[21] Rawls (1971).

[22] But see the very interesting application of Rawlsian principles to international justice in Pogge (1989).

[23] This emerges clearly, for example, in some of the work of Michael Walzer (1983) and of Richard Rorty (1982). But international morality and justice are also little discussed in the work of some non-relativist thinkers who derive moral and political norms from historical traditions—e.g., Charles Taylor (1989). (Taylor's current work addresses this gap.) For related arguments, see Nussbaum (1990b and forthcoming b).

phers once knew this, and the best work on emotion in the seventeenth and eighteenth centuries—that of Descartes, Spinoza, and Adam Smith—owed them a huge debt, and perhaps in certain ways fell short of them. Today, however, the accounts are almost always ignored in philosophical writing on emotion,[24] which, therefore, has to reinvent laboriously (and usually falls well short of) what was clear there. The detailed analyses of particular emotions, moreover, are just as impressive as the general theory. Again, contemporary analyses of love, anger, and fear neglect them to their cost.

Epicurean emotion theory is in certain ways less elaborate (so far as we know) than Stoic theory: it does not make fully clear the relationship between belief and passion, discriminating between necessity and sufficiency and between both of these and identity. On the other hand, Lucretius adds something of great value: the idea of a connection between emotion and *narrative*.[25] The cognitive content of an emotion such as love does only not arrive via a grasp of abstract propositions—or, even, only through highly concrete propositions about one's own life. Instead, we internalize culturally narrated scenarios that give us the dimensions, pace, and structure of the emotion. And these scenarios are then enacted in our own lives, as we cast ourselves and others in the roles created by them. This account leads to a new appreciation of the role that literary narrative might play in moral philosophy, as indispensable to a full understanding of one of its most central elements—but also to an understanding of some ways in which the power of conventional narrative might deform human relationships.

What of the arguments for extirpation of passion? Here I shall not say any more about the fear of death, since I have given my own view on this in chapter 6, and further comparative discussion seems unnecessary. Where pity or compassion is concerned, it should also be clear by now that I approve of the Lucretian tendency to leave it in human life as a basic source of communal affiliation, rather than to banish it in the name of self-sufficiency, as the Stoics do. So I want in this final section to focus on the two passions that have, for my argument, been the most fundamental and the most problematic: anger and love.

Anger is, in a sense, the central topic of this book and its raison d'être. For I was drawn to the Hellenistic philosophers not only by the power of their analyses of passions, but also by sympathy with their arguments for

---

[24] For just one especially striking example, see Murphy and Hampton (1988), a (fine) book on anger, forgiveness, and mercy that contains no reference either to Seneca or to Stoicism. The one area in which there has not been such neglect is the fear of death, where the Epicurean arguments have been recognized as philosophically central—see chapter 6.

[25] A closely related proposal is made in De Sousa (1987).

extirpation, where this one passion is concerned. In *The Fragility of Goodness* I had portrayed the best human life as one that takes on the risk of loss and grief. I had not accepted or even (except in a chapter on Euripides' *Hecuba*) much considered the idea that the best life runs the risk of corrosive anger. The Hellenistic thinkers did confront this question—in a way that led them to reject *all* the passions. A motivation for me in writing about them was to discover whether it was possible to accept their arguments about the elimination of anger, while still rejecting their more general attack on passions such as love, fear, and grief.

To a great extent, this attempt failed. Some Hellenistic ways of removing anger—such as decreasing the attachment to money and possessions— were perfectly compatible with keeping some love in one's life, but not love of those things, and only insofar as the potential for anger itself remained as well, wherever love remained. The connection they allege between love and the possibility of anger is powerfully demonstrated, in a way that both vindicates Aristotle's claims about the connections between deep attachment and anger and calls into question, for that reason, his claim that the life of a virtuous person will contain no wrongdoing, and nothing to regret. This means that one must make a choice: either give up both love and anger, as the orthodox Stoics do, or run the risk of harming.

Here both Seneca and Lucretius have complex and ambivalent positions, in both the public and the private sphere. Lucretius' attempt to describe the bases of community shows, at the same time, and retains, the basis for anger on behalf of oneself and one's own. This legitimate anger is not free of potentially disturbing consequences, and chapter 7 saw Lucretius attempting a difficult balancing act, as he tried to create a community in which individuals both protect themselves and cherish their friends. Seneca, too, has great difficulty describing a community that is both self-respecting and free from anger. His analysis makes a powerful case against anger and in favor of a medical attitude toward injury and wrongdoing. But in cases where a tyrant damages someone whom one loves, detachment gives way to cursing.

Where the attachments of erotic love are concerned, things become even more complex. Lucretius imagines a stable marriage free from the risk of anger and jealousy: but only by in effect removing *erōs*, and imagining the relationship as a friendship with sexual pleasure added in. His recommendation is similar to the Stoic ideal of marriage described in Musonius Rufus (chapter 12)—though the Stoics attach less importance than Lucretius does to sexual pleasure. I have argued that these balanced and sanitized relationships leave something out: while claiming to yield to human life,

Lucretius does not follow that advice far enough. The omitted dimension is stirringly and horrifyingly depicted in Seneca's *Medea*, which shows the value of *erōs* as well as its dangers. To some extent, we can combine the Hellenistic norm with Seneca, insisting that erotic love is most valuable when it does occur between people who respect one another's characters as friends do and who share commitments and a way of life together. And perhaps in this sort of love there would be somewhat less risk than elsewhere of the most destructive sort of resentment and rage, since mutual respect counts for something, even in agony.

But this doesn't really remove anger from the erotic life, it only circumscribes it a little. Certainly it does not go far enough to satisfy the Stoics—for good character, as chapter 12 argued, may inhibit harmful action without removing harmful wishing. Here, I think, we must turn, with Seneca, to mercy and to narrative—trying to respond to what has taken place without strict punishment, asking the watchful eyes of wisdom to look with narrative understanding into the complexities of another's motivation and one's own. The bold Stoic attempt to purify social life of all its ills, rigorously carried through, ends by removing, as well, its finite humanity, its risk-taking loyalty, its passionate love. Abandoning the zeal for absolute perfection as inappropriate to the life of a finite being, abandoning the thirst for punishment and self-punishment that so frequently accompanies that zeal, the education I recommend looks with mercy at the ambivalent excellence and passion of a human life.

* Philosophers and Schools *

(For further historical information about figures discussed in this book, the reader may consult Long and Sedley [1987] vol. I, Long [1974], Sedley [1980].)

Academy. — School of philosophy at Athens founded by Plato, dominated by Skepticism in the Hellenistic period (then called the New Academy).

Aenesidemus. — Formerly a member of the New Academy, then, after a break with the Academy, founder of the neo-Pyrrhonist movement in the first century B.C.E.

Arcesilaus. — Skeptical philosopher, head of the New Academy from c. 273 to 242 B.C.E.

Aristotle. — 384–322 B.C.E. Major Greek philosopher, founder of the Peripatetic school at Athens.

Aurelius, Marcus. — Roman emperor 161–80 C.E. and Stoic philosopher, author of *Meditations* (in the Greek language).

Carneades. — Fourth head of New Academy, mid-second century B.C.E.; retired 137, died 129.

Chrysippus. — c. 280–206 B.C.E. Leading Stoic philosopher, third head of the school, beginning 232. Author of a large number of works in logic, metaphysics, philosophy of language, philosophy of mind, moral and political philosophy. He was probably the most philosophically able of the early Stoics, and certainly the most prolific. His influence in the Hellenistic and Roman worlds equaled that of Plato and surpassed that of Aristotle. Along with Zeno, he is the inventor of propositional logic and, to all intents and purposes, of the philosophy of language in the Western tradition, as well as one of its most profound writers about the nature of emotion and desire, and of moral judgment. No complete work of his survives, but we have copious summaries in Cicero, Diogenes Laertius, Plutarch, and other writers, the evidence of his Roman followers Epictetus and Seneca, and many citations. His theory of the passions is attested in especially ample citations and summaries in Galen.

Cicero, Marcus Tullius. — 106–43 B.C.E. Leading Roman orator, statesman, and philosopher. Toward the end of his life he wrote a large number of works, most of them dialogues, and most of them surviving, in which he explained the views of the major Hellenistic schools and subjected them to critical scrutiny. He is a major source for reports and citations of the views of leading philosophers, as well as a thinker in his own right. He also made a concerted effort to render Greek philosophical terminology into Latin, and is the primary source for the subsequent Latin philosophical vocabulary. His importance in the education of both philosophers and generally cultivated people from the Renaissance until this century can hardly be overestimated. Along with Plutarch, Epictetus, Seneca, and Marcus Aurelius, he is among the major sources for later centuries' knowledge of Hellenistic thought; and he is one of the ancient writers most read by the American Founders.

Cleanthes. — 331–232 B.C.E. Stoic philosopher and poet, second head of the school at Athens, from 262. Of the three major early heads of the school, he seems to have been the least analytically inclined, and to have had the least influence on the development of the school's philosophical views.

Colotes. — Epicurean philosopher, active between c. 310 and 260 B.C.E. His reverence to Epicurus is well documented (see chapter 4). He was attacked by Plutarch in the anti-Epicurean work *Against Colotes.*

Cynic School. — School of philosophers founded by Diogenes of Sinope in the mid-fourth century B.C.E. Claiming to follow Socrates, they led unconventional and deliberately shocking lives, insisting on their indifference to wealth, comfort, and convention.

Cyrenaic School. — School of philosophers founded by Aristippus of Cyrene, active in the fourth and early third centuries B.C.E. They professed hedonism, but differed from Epicurus in their focus on immediate bodily sensations.

Democritus. — Mid to late fifth century B.C.E. Atomist philosopher, associated with Leucippus. Epicurus began as a follower of his philosophical views, which stressed the importance of a calm state of well-being.

Diogenes of Babylon. — Head of Stoic school in early to mid second century B.C.E. He wrote on many familiar Stoic topics, including rhetoric and poetics.

Diogenes Laertius. — Early third century C.E. Writer about the lives and doctrines of Greek philosophers, a major source for our knowledge of the Hellenistic schools. The earliest published work of Nietzsche was a rigorous historical examination of the sources for his work.

Diogenes of Oenoanda. — Wealthy Epicurean philosopher of the second century C.E. who had an account of Epicurus' philosophy inscribed on a stone in a public colonnade in what is now central Turkey.

Epictetus. — c. 55–c. 135 C.E. Major Stoic philosopher at Rome, a former slave. His lectures (in Greek) were transcribed by his pupil Arrian, and are among our major sources for Roman Stoic philosophy.

Epicurean School. — School of philosophers founded by Epicurus, influential in both Greece and Rome. Its major philosophers include Epicurus, Metrodorus, the Romans Lucretius and Philodemus, and Diogenes of Oenoanda.

Epicurus. — 341–271 B.C.E. Leading Greek philosopher and founder of the Epicurean school. Author of a very large number of books. Three lengthy letters and a collection of maxims, cited in Diogenes Laertius, preserve his own account of his central doctrines. Copious citations and summaries in ancient sources and a large number of papyrus fragments of his major works contribute to our evidence, as does the poem of his follower Lucretius.

Galen. — Greek doctor, medical writer, and philosopher, late second century C.E. He is a central source for Chrysippus' theory of the passions, of which he is a very hostile critic.

Hierocles. — Stoic philosopher, active around 100 C.E.

Lucretius. — Early to mid first century B.C.E. Roman poet and philosopher, follower of Epicureanism, author of the six-book didactic poem *De Rerum Natura* (*On the Way Things Are*), an account of Epicurean views on the universe, mind, death, sexuality, and political community.

Metrodorus of Lampsacus. — c. 331–278 B.C.E. Epicurean philosopher and close associate of Epicurus. Epicurus' will makes provision for the support of his children.

Musonius Rufus, Gaius. — Roman Stoic philosopher, active in the first century C.E., teacher of Epictetus. His surviving works (in Greek) include arguments in favor of equal education for women, arguments against the sexual double standard in marriage, arguments against infanticide, arguments that the philosopher ought to marry and to take part in the life of the community.

Nausiphanes. — Democritean philosopher, teacher of Epicurus.

Panaetius. — c. 185–110 B.C.E. Stoic philosopher from Rhodes, head of the school from around 129. His views, which in some respects appear to have modified the original Greek Stoic doctrines, were very influential at Rome.

Peripatetic School. — School of philosophers founded by Aristotle, later headed by Theophrastus and Strato. Less influential in the Hellenistic period than Epicureanism, Skepticism, and Stoicism.

Philodemus. — Epicurean philosopher of the first century B.C.E., whose works were influential in Roman intellectual circles. Extensive papyrus fragments of his writings have been found at Herculaneum.

Plato. — c. 429–347 B.C.E. Major Greek philosopher, founder of the Academy.

Plutarch. — Late first to early second centuries C.E. Leading Greek writer and thinker. His lives of Greek and Roman figures are animated by a moral purpose, and his extensive writings on philosophical matters, grouped together as the *Moralia*, are among our major sources of information about Hellenistic thought. A Platonist, he writes extensive critical accounts of both Epicureanism and Stoicism, and his criticisms are frequently philosophically acute. He remained a very widely read figure throughout much of the history of modern Western culture; for example, he was one of the central classical influences on the American Founders, and one of their central sources for Hellenistic thought.

Posidonius. — c. 135–c. 50 B.C.E. Stoic philosopher, based in Rhodes, a pupil of Panaetius. Heavily influenced by Plato as well as by Stoicism, he differed from Chrysippus about the structure of the soul, the nature of the emotions, and the proper use of music and literature in education. His views on these matters survive primarily through reports and citations in Galen, who prefers them to the views of Chrysippus.

Pyrrho. — c. 365–270 B.C.E. Founder of the Skeptical movement in philosophy, and legendary sage-figure for later Skeptical philosophers. Diogenes Laertius' account of his life is among our major sources for the views of the Skeptics. The report that he visited India with Alexander the Great has at least some plausibility, given the close relationship between some Skeptical patterns of argument and contemporary arguments in Indian philosophy. (See Flintoff [1980].)

Pyrrhonist School. — School founded by Aenesidemus, active from the first century B.C.E. until at least 200 C.E. Sextus Empiricus belonged to this school.

Seneca, Lucius Annaeus. — c. 1–65 C.E. Major Roman Stoic philosopher and poet, writing in the Latin language. He was also active in politics, serving as tutor and advisor to the young emperor Nero. On his life see M. Griffin (1976). Seneca's drama had a major influence on the development of Elizabethan tragedy. His philosophical works were extremely widely read from the Renaissance to the present century, and had a major influence on thinkers such as Descartes, Spinoza, the American Founders, Kant, and Nietzsche.

514

Sextus Empiricus. — Pyrrhonist Skeptical philosopher, active in the second century C.E. He was apparently a doctor of either the Empiricist or the Methodist school. His writings are our central source for Pyrrhonist and other Skeptical doctrines, as well as for the views of the schools whom he attacks.

Socrates. — 469–399 B.C.E. Athenian philosopher who wrote nothing; his views are portrayed in works of Plato and Xenophon, and described by Aristotle. His life and activity have a major influence not only on Platonists, but also on Cynics, Stoics, and Skeptics, all of whom appeal to him in some manner as a model and source.

Stoic School. — The most influential philosophical school of the Hellenistic period. Founded by Zeno of Citium, and later headed by Cleanthes and then Chrysippus, its early phase lasted from 300 to 130 B.C.E. Panaetius and Posidonius introduced some modifications, and their period is sometimes called "Middle Stoicism." At Rome, Stoicism is represented by Musonius Rufus, Seneca, Epictetus, Marcus Aurelius, and Hierocles.

Timon of Phlius. — c. 325–c. 235 B.C.E. Skeptical philosopher and poet, follower of Pyrrho.

Zeno of Citium. — 334–262 B.C.E. Stoic philosopher, founded of the Stoic school. Along with Chrysippus, the originator of the school's most important philosophical views and arguments. It is very difficult to tell to what extent, if any, Zeno and Chrysippus differed philosophically, but Zeno appears to have had an independent theory of the passions.

* *Bibliography* *

Abel, K. (1967). *Bauformen in Senecas Dialogen.* Heidelberg.

Ackrill, J. (1980). "Aristotle on *Eudaimonia.*" In A. Rorty (1980) 15–33.

Ahl, F., trans. (1986). *Seneca: Medea.* Ithaca.

Annas, J. (1980). "Truth and Knowledge." In Schofield, Burnyeat, and Barnes (1980) 84–104.

Annas, J. (1986). "Doing without Objective Values: Ancient and Modern Strategies." In Schofield and Striker (1986) 1–30.

Annas, J. (1992). *Hellenistic Philosophy of Mind.* Berkeley.

Annas, J. and Barnes, J. (1985). *The Modes of Scepticism: Ancient Texts and Modern Interpretations.* Cambridge.

Arnim, H. von. (1903–5). *Stoicorum Veterum Fragmenta.* 3 vols. Leipzig.

Arrighetti, G. ed. and trans. (1960) *Epicuro Opere.* Turin.

Aubenque, P. (1957). "La définition aristotélicienne de la colère." *Revue philosophique de France et de l'étranger*: 300–317.

Austin, J. L. (1961). "*Agathon* and *eudaimonia* in the Ethics of Aristotle." In *Philosophical Papers*, by J. L. Austin, 1–31. Oxford.

Bailey, C., ed. (1900). *Lucreti De Rerum Natura.* Oxford Classical Text. Oxford.

Bailey, C., ed. and trans. (1926). *Epicurus: The Extant Remains.* Oxford.

Bailey, C. (1938). "The Mind of Lucretius." *American Journal of Philology* 61: 278–91, and in Classen (1986): 3–16.

Bailey, C., ed. (1947). *Titi Lucreti Cari De Rerum Natura*, with Prolegomena, Critical Apparatus, Translation, and Commentary. 3 vols. Oxford.

Barnes, J. (1982a). "Medicine, Experience and Logic." In *Science and Speculation*, ed. J. Barnes, J. Brunschwig, M. Burnyeat, M. Schofield, 24–68. Cambridge and Paris.

Barnes, J. (1982b). "The Beliefs of a Pyrrhonist." *Proceedings of the Cambridge Philological Society* 29: 1–29.

Betensky, A. (1980). "Lucretius and Love." *Classical World* 73: 291–99.

Blum, L. (1980). *Friendship, Altruism, and Morality.* London.

Blundell, S. (1986). *The Origins of Civilization in Greek and Roman Thought.* London.

Bollack, J. (1975). *La pensée du plaisir.* Paris.

Bollack, M. (1978). *La raison du Lucrèce.* Paris.

Bollas, C. (1987). *The Shadow of the Object: Psychoanalysis of the Unthought Known.* London.

Bonhöffer, A. (1894). *Die Ethik des Stoikers Epictet.* Stuttgart.

Bonnefoy, Y. (1991). *Greek and English Mythologies.* Trans. under direction of W. Doniger. Chicago.

Bourgery, A., ed. (1922). *Seneca. De Ira.* Paris.

Bowlby, J. (1980). *Loss: Sadness and Depression*. New York.

Boyancé, P. (1963). "Le stoicisme à Rome." In *Actes du VIIIᵐᵉ Congrès de l'Association G. Budé*, 218–55. Paris.

Boyle, A. J., ed. (1983). *Seneca Tragicus*. Victoria, Australia.

Brandt, R. B. (1979). *A Theory of the Good and the Right*. Oxford.

Brieger, A. (1908). Review of W. A. Merrill's edition of Lucretius. *Berliner Philologische Wochenschrift*: 1621–25.

Brock, D. (1986). "Justice and the Severly Demented Elderly." *Journal of Medicine and Philosophy* 13: 73–99.

Brock, D. (1993). "Quality of Life Judgments in Health Care and Medical Ethics." In Nussbaum and Sen. (1993) 95–132.

Brown, R. D. (1987). *Lucretius on Love and Sex*. Leiden.

Brueckner, A., and Fischer, J. M. (1986). "Why Is Death Bad?" *Philosophical Studies* 50: 213–21.

Brunschwig, J. (1980). "Proof Defined." In Schofield, Burnyeat, and Barnes (1980) 125–60.

Brunschwig, J. (1986). "The Cradle Argument in Epicureanism and Stoicism." In Schofield and Striker (1986) 113–44.

Brunschwig, J. (1992). "Pyrrhon et Philista." In *"Chercheurs de sagesse": Hommage à Jean Pépin*, Paris. 133–46.

Brunschwig, J., and Nussbaum, M., eds. (1993). *Passions & Perceptions: Proceedings of the 5ᵗʰ Symposium Hellenisticum*. Cambridge.

Burnyeat, M. F. (1980a). "Can the Sceptic Live His Scepticism?" In Schofield, Burnyeat, and Barnes (1980) 20–53, and in Burnyeat (1983) 117–48.

Burnyeat, M. F. (1980b). "Aristotle on Learning to Be Good." In Rorty (1980) 69–92.

Burnyeat, M. F. (1982). "The Origins of Non-deductive Inference." In *Science and Speculation*, ed. J. Barnes, J. Brunschwig, M. Burnyeat, M. Schofield, 193–238. Cambridge.

Burnyeat, M. F., ed. (1983). *The Skeptical Tradition*. Berkeley.

Burnyeat, M. F. (1984). "The Sceptic in His Place and Time." In *Philosophy in History*, ed. R. Rorty, J. B. Schneewind, and Q. Skinner, 225–254. Cambridge.

Burnyeat, M. F. (forthcoming a). "Greek Freedom."

Burnyeat, M. F. (forthcoming b). "Carneades."

Busa, R., and Zampolli, A. (1975). *Concordantiae Senecanae*. 2 vols. Hildesheim.

Buxton, R. G. A. (1982). *Persuasion in Greek Tragedy: A Study of Peitho*. Cambridge.

Campbell, K. (1985). "Self-mastery and Stoic Ethics." *Philosophy* 60: 327–40.

Caston, V. (1992). "Aristotle on Intentionality." Ph.D. diss., University of Texas at Austin.

Caston, V. (forthcoming). *The Problem of Intentionality in Ancient Greek Philosophy*. Cambridge.

Cavell, S. (1969). "Knowing and Acknowledging." In *Must We Mean What We Say?* by S. Cavell, 238–66. New York.

Cavell, S. (1979). *The Claim of Reason*. Oxford.

Charles, D. (1984). *Aristotle's Philosophy of Action*. London.

Chen, M. (1983). *A Quiet Revolution: Women in Transition in Rural Bangladesh*. Cambridge, Mass.

Chilton, C. W. (1960). "Did Epicurus Approve of Marriage?" *Phronesis* 5: 71–74.

Chilton, C. W. (1967). *Diogenes Oenoandensis*. Leipzig.

Chilton, C. W. (1971). *Diogenes of Oenoanda: The Fragments*. London and New York.

Chilton, C. W., ed. (1976). *Epicurus' Letter to Mother*.

Christensen, J. (1962). *An Essay on the Unity of Stoic Philosophy*. Copenhagen.

Classen, C. J. (1968). "Poetry and Rhetoric in Lucretius." *Transactions of the American Philological Association* 99: 77–118, and in Classen (1986) 331–74.

Classen, C. J., ed. (1986). *Probleme der Lukrezforschung*. Hildesheim.

Clay, D. (1976). "The Sources of Lucretius' Inspiration." In *Études sur l'epicurisme antique*, ed. J. Bollack and A. Laks, 203–27. Lille.

Clay, D. (1983a). *Lucretius and Epicurus*. Ithaca.

Clay, D. (1983b). "Individual and Community in the First Generation of the Epicurean School." In *ΣΥΖΗΤΗΣΙΣ: Studi sull' epicureismo greco e romano offerti a Marcello Gigante*, ed. G. Macchiarolli, 255–79. Naples.

Clay, D. (1984a). "The Cult of Epicurus: An Interpretation of Philodemus *On Epicurus* (P Here 1232) and Other Texts. In *"Atti del XVII Congresso Internazionale di Papirologia*, Naples. 677–79.

Clay, D. (1984b). Review of Frischer. (1982). *American Journal of Philology* 105: 484–89.

Clay, D. (1986). "The Cults of Epicurus." *Cronache Ercolanesi* 16: 11–28.

Collins, S. (1982). *Selfless Persons: Imagery and Thought in Theravada Buddhism*. Cambridge.

Commager, H. S., Jr. (1957). "Lucretius' Interpretation of the Plague." *Harvard Studies in Classical Philology* 62: 105–18.

Copley, F. O. (1956). *Exclusus Amator: A Study in Latin Love Poetry*. Monographs of the American Philosophical Association, 17. Baltimore.

Costa, C. D. N., ed. (1973). *Seneca. Medea*. Oxford.

Costa, C. D. N., ed. (1984). *Lucretius De Rerum Natura V*. Oxford.

Crocker, D. (1992). "Functioning and Capability: The Foundations of Nussbaum's and Sen's Development Ethic." *Political Theory*, 20: 584–612.

Cupaiuolo, G. (1975). *Introduzione al "De ira" di Seneca*. Naples.

Davidson, A. (1990). "Spiritual Exercises and Ancient Philosophy: An Introduction to Pierre Hadot." *Critical Inquiry* 16:475–82.

D'Agostino, F. (1973). *Epieikeia: Il tema dell'equità nell'antichita Greca*. Milan.

De Lacy, P. (1948). "Stoic Views of Poetry." *American Journal of Philology* 69: 241–71.

De Lacy, P. (1958). "*Ou mallon* and the Antecedents of Ancient Scepticism." *Phronesis* 3: 59–71.

De Lacy, P., ed. (1978–80). *Galen, De Placitis Hippocratis et Platonis.* Corpus Medicorum Graecorum. Berlin.

De Sousa, R. (1987). *The Rationality of Emotion.* Cambridge, Mass.

De Witt, N. W. (1954). *Epicurus and His Philosophy.* Minneapolis.

Diano, C. (1974). *Epicuri Ethica et Epistulae.* Florence.

Diels, H., and Kranz, W., eds. (1968). *Fragmente der Vorsokratiker.* 3 vols. Dublin and Zürich.

Dingel, J. (1974). *Seneca und die Dichtung.* Heidelberg.

Doniger, Wendy. (1973). *Siva: The Erotic Ascetic.* Chicago.

Doniger, Wendy. (1986). "Horses and Snakes in the Adi Parvan of the *Mahabharata.*" *Aspects of India-Essays in Honor of Edward Cameron Dimock*, ed. Margaret Case and N. Gerald Barrier. New Delhi.

Dover, K. J. (1974). *Greek Popular Morality in the Time of Plato and Aristotle.* Oxford.

Dover, K. J. (2nd ed. 1989). *Greek Homosexuality.* Cambridge, Mass.

Drèze, J., and Sen, A., eds. (1989). *Hunger and Public Action.* Oxford.

Duncan, C. M. (1991). "Diseases of Judgment: The Emotions in Stoic Psychology and Ethics." Undergraduate honors thesis, Department of Philosophy, Brown University, April.

Düring, I. (1966). *Aristoteles.* Heidelberg.

Edelstein, L. (1967). "Empiricism and Scepticism in the Teaching of the Greek Empiricist School." In *Ancient Medicine*, ed. L. Edelstein. Baltimore.

Edelstein, L., and Kidd, I. G., eds. (1972). *Posidonius.* Vol. 1, *The fragments.* Cambridge.

Egermann, F. (1940). "Seneca als Dichterphilosoph." *Neue Jahrbücher für Antike und deutsche Bildung* 3: 18–36.

Eliot, T. S. (1951). "Seneca in Elizabethan Translation" and "Shakespeare and the Stoicism of Seneca." In *Selected Essays.* London.

Englert, W. (1988). *Epicurus on the Swerve and Free Action.* American Classical Studies, 16. Atlanta.

Englert, W. (1990). "Seneca and the Stoic View of Suicide." Paper read to the meeting of the Society for Ancient Greek Philosophy, December.

Fairbairn, W.R.D. (1952). *Psychoanalytic Studies of the Personality.* London.

Fantham, E. (1982). *Seneca's Troades: A Literary Introduction with Text, Translation and Commentary.* Princeton.

Fauth, (1973). "Divus Epicurus: Zur Problemgeschichte philosophischer Religiosität bei Lucrez." In *Aufstieg und Niedergang der römischen Wettt*, ed. H. Temporini and W. Haase, I. 4: 205–25. Berlin.

Feinberg, J. (1977). "Harm and Self-Interest." In *Law, Morality, and Society: Essays in Honour of H.L.A. Hart*, ed. P.M.S. Hacker and J. Raz, 284–308. Oxford.

Fillion-Lahille, J. (1970). "La colère chez Aristote." *Revue des etudes antiques* 72: 46–79.

Fillion-Lahille, J. (1984). *Le De Ira de Sénèque et la philosophie stoicienne des passions*. Paris.

Fish, S. (1989). *Doing What Comes Naturally: Change, Rhetoric, and the Practice of Theory in Literary and Legal Studies*. Durham.

Fitzgerald, W. (1984). "Lucretius' Cure for Love in the *De Rerum Natura*." *Classical World* 78: 73–86.

Flintoff, E. (1980). "Pyrrho and India." *Phronesis* 25: 88–108.

Fortenbaugh, W. (1975). *Aristotle on Emotion*. London.

Foucault, M. (1984). *Histoire de la sexualité*. Vol. 3, *Le souci de soi*. Paris.

Fowler, D. P. (1989). "Lucretius and Politics." In M. Griffin and Barnes, (1989) 120–50.

Frede, M. (1974). *Die Stoische Logik*. Göttingen.

Frede, M. (1979). "Des Skeptikers Meinungen." *Neue Hefte für Philosophie* 15–16: 102–29. Translated as "The Skeptic's Beliefs." In *Essays in Ancient Philosophy*, by M. Frede, 179–200. Minneapolis, 1987.

Frede, M. (1982). "The Method of the So-Called Methodical School of Medicine." In *Science and Speculation*, ed. J. Barnes, J. Brunschwig, M. Burnyeat, and M. Schofield, 1–23. Cambridge and Paris.

Frede, M. (1983). "Stoics and Sceptics on Clear and Distinct Ideas." In Burnyeat (1983) 65–94.

Frede, M. (1984). "The Sceptics' Two Kinds of Assent and the Question of the Possibility of Knowledge." In *Philosophy in History*, ed. R. Rorty, J. Schneewind, and Q. Skinner, 255–78. Cambridge.

Frede, M. (1986). "The Stoic Doctrine of the Affections of the Soul." In Schofield and Striker (1986) 93–110.

Freud, S. (1900–1901). *The Interpretation of Dreams*. London.

Frischer, B. (1982). *The Sculpted Word*. Berkeley.

Furley, D. J. (1967). *Two Studies in the Greek Atomists*. Princeton.

Furley, D. J. (1978). "Lucretius the Epicurean on the History of Man." In *Lucrèce. Entretiens sur L'Antiquité Classique* 24: 1–37. Geneva. Reprinted in Furley, *Cosmic Problems*. (1989). Cambridge.

Furley, D. J. (1986). "Nothing to Us?" In Schofield and Striker (1986) 75–91.

Fyfe, H. (1983). "An Analysis of Seneca's *Medea*." In Boyle (1983) 77–93.

Gigante, M. (1975). "*Philosophia Medicans* in Filodemo." *Cronache Ercolanesi* 5: 53–61.

Gill, C. (1983). "Did Chrysippus Understand Medea?" *Phronesis* 28: 136–49.

Glibert-Thirry, A. (1977). "La théorie stoicienne de la passion chez Chrysippe et son évolution chez Posidonius." *Revue philosophique de Louvain* 75: 393–435.

Glidden, D. (1983). "Skeptic Semiotics." *Phronesis* 28: 213–55.

Godwin, J., ed. (1986). *Lucretius: De Rerum Natura IV*. Warminster.

Goldschmidt, V. (1977). *La doctrine d'Epicure et le droit*. Paris.

Graver, M. (1990). "The Eye of the Beholder: Lucretius on Perceptual Relativity." In Nussbaum (1990d) 91–116.

Green, O. H. (1982). "Fear of Death." *Philosophy and Phenomenological Research* 43: 99–105.

Griffin, J. (1980). *Homer on Life and Death.* Oxford.

Griffin, M. (1976). *Seneca: A Philosopher in Politics.* Oxford.

Griffin, M. (1986). "Philosophy, Cato and Roman Suicide: I and II." *Greece and Rome* 33: 64–77, 192–202.

Griffin, M. (1989). "Philosophy, Politics and Politicians at Rome." In M. Griffin and Barnes (1989) 1–37.

Griffin, M., and Barnes, J., eds. (1989) *Philosophia Togata.* Oxford.

Grimal, P. (1963). "Lucrèce et son public." *Revue des études latines* 41: 91–100.

Guthrie, W.K.C. (1975). *Plato: The Man and His Dialogues, Earlier Period. A History of Greek Philosophy.* Vol. 4. Cambridge.

Haase, F., ed. (1897–98). *L. Annaei Senecae Opera Quae Supersunt.* 3 Vols. Leipzig.

Hadot, I. (1969). *Seneca und die griechische-römische Tradition der Seelenleitung.* Berlin.

Hadot, P. (1981). *Exercises spirituels et philosophie antique.* Paris.

Hadot, P. (1990). "Forms of Life and Forms of Discourse in Ancient Philosophy." *Critical Inquiry.* 16: 483–505.

Halliwell, S. (1986). *Aristotle's Poetics.* Chapel Hill.

Halperin, D. (1986). "Plato and Erotic Reciprocity." *Classical Antiquity* 5: 60–80.

Halperin, D. (1989). "Plato and the Metaphysics of Desire." *Proceedings of the Boston Area Colloquium for Ancient Philosophy* 5: 27–52.

Halperin, D. (1990). *One Hundred Years of Homosexuality and Other Essays on Greek Love.* New York.

Hardie, P. (1986). *Cosmos and Imperium.* Oxford.

Hare, R. M. (1981). *Moral Thinking: Its Levels, Method, and Point.* Oxford.

Harris, W. (1990). *Ancient Literacy.* Cambridge, Mass.

Henry, D., and Henry, E. (1985). *The Mask of Power: Seneca's Tragedies and Imperial Rome.* Warminster.

Hense, O., ed. (1905). *C. Musonii Rufi Reliquiae.* Leipzig.

Herington, C. J. (1966). "Senecan Tragedy." *Arion* 5: 422–71.

Hershbell, J. P., ed. (1981). *Pseudo-Plato, Axiochus.* Chicago.

Hossenfelder, M., intro. and trans. (1968). *Sextus Empiricus. Grundriss der Pyrrhonischen Skepsis.* Frankfurt.

House, D. K. (1980). "The Life of Sextus Empiricus." *Classical Quarterly* 30: 227–38.

Housman, A. E. (1972). "Lucretiana." In *The Classical Papers of A. E. Housman,* ed. J. Diggle and F.R.D. Goodyear, 2:432–35. Cambridge.

Hume, D. (1739–40). *A Treatise of Human Nature.* Oxford.

Hutchinson, D. (1988). "Doctrines of the Mean and the Debate Concerning Skills in Fourth-Century Medicine, Rhetoric, and Ethics." *Apeiron* 21:17–52.

Humphries, R., trans. (1968). *Lucretius: The Way Things Are.* Bloomington.

Inwood, B. (1985). *Ethics and Human Action in Early Stoicism.* Oxford.

Inwood, B. (1987). "Goal and Target in Stoicism." *Journal of Philosophy* 83: 547–56.

Inwood, B. (1993). "Seneca on Emotion and Action." In Brunschwig and Nussbaum (1993) 150–83.

Ioppolo, A. M. (1980). *Aristone di Chio e lo Stoicismo antico*. Naples.

Irwin, T. H. (1986). "Stoic and Aristotelian Conceptions of Happiness." In Schofield and Striker (1986): 205–44.

Jackson, H. (1920). "Arisotle's Lecture Room and Lectures." *Journal of Philology* 35: 191–200.

Jaeger, W. (1934). *Aristotle: Fundamentals of the History of His Development*, trans. R. Robinson. Oxford.

Jaeger, W. (1957). "Aristotle's Use of Medicine as Model of Method in His Ethics." *Journal of Hellenic Studies* 77: 54–61.

Kenny, A. (1963). *Action, Emotion, and Will*. London.

Kenny, A. (1973). "Mental Health in Plato's *Republic*." In *The Anatomy of the Soul*, by A. Kenny, 1–27. Oxford.

Kenney, E. J. (1970). "Doctus Lucretius." *Mnemosyne*, ser. 4, 23: 366–92, and in Classen (1986) 237–65.

Kenney, E. J., ed. (1971). *Lucretius, De Rerum Natura, Book III*. Cambridge.

Kenney, E. J. (1977). *Lucretius. Greece and Rome* New Surveys in the Classics, 11. Oxford.

Kerferd, G. B. (1978). "The Origin of Evil in Stoic Thought." *Bulletin of the John Rylands Library of Manchester* 60: 482–94.

Kidd, I. G. (1971a). "The Stoic Intermediates and the End for Man." In Long (1971) 150–72.

Kidd, I. G. (1971b). "Posidonius on Emotions." In Long (1971) 200–215.

Klein, M. (1984). *Envy, Gratitude, and Other Works, 1946–1963*. London.

Klein, M. (1985). *Love, Guilt, and Reparation and Other Works, 1921–45*. London.

Knox, B.M.W. (1958). "The Serpent and the Flame.," *American Journal of Philology* 38: 379–400.

Knox, B.M.W. (1977). "The *Medea* of Euripides." *Yale Classical Studies* 25: 77–93.

Konstan, D. (1973). *Some Aspects of Epicurean Psychology*. Leiden.

Konstan, D. (1977). *Catullus' Indictment of Rome*. Amsterdam.

Kosman, L. A. (1976). "Platonic Love." In *Facets of Plato's Philosophy*, 53–69. *Phronesis* Supplement Vol. II. Assen.

Laursen, J. C. (1992). *The Politics of Skepticism*. Leiden.

Lawall, G. (1979). "Seneca's *Medea*, The Elusive Triumph of Civilization." In *Arktouros: Hellenic Studies Presented to B.M.W. Knox*, ed. G. Bowersock et al., 419–26. Berlin and New York.

Lawless, J. (1991). "Equity Argumentation in Isaeus." Ph.D. diss., Brown University.

Lazarus, R. (1991). *Emotion and Adaptation*. New York.

Lefkowitz, M. (1986). *Women in Greek Myth*. Baltimore.

Leighton, S. R. (1982). "Aristotle and the Emotions." *Phronesis* 27: 144–74.

Lesses, G. (1989). "Virtue and the Goods of Fortune in Stoic Moral Theory." *Oxford Studies in Ancient Philosophy* 7: 95–128.

Lieberg, G. (1962). *Puella Divina. Die Gestalt des göttlichen Geliebten bei Catull im Zusammenhang der antiken Dichtung.* Amsterdam.

Lloyd, A. C. (1978). "Emotion and Decision in Stoic Psychology." In Rist (1978) 233–46.

Lloyd, G.E.R. (1981). *Magic, Reason, and Experience.* Cambridge.

Lloyd, G.E.R. (1983). *Science, Folklore, and Ideology: Studies in the Life Sciences in Ancient Greece.* Cambridge.

Lloyd, G.E.R. (1989). *The Revolutions of Wisdom.* Berkeley.

Locke, J. (1690). *An Essay Concerning Human Understanding.* Ed. P. H. Nidditch. Oxford, 1975.

Logre, J. B. (1946). *L'anxiété de Lucrèce.* Paris.

Long, A. A., ed. (1971). *Problems in Stoicism.* London.

Long, A. A. (1974). *Hellenistic Philosophy.* London.

Long, A. A. (1981). "Aristotle and the History of Greek Scepticism." In *Studies in Aristotle,* ed. D. J. O'Meara, 76–106. Washington, D.C.

Long, A. A. (1988). "Socrates in Hellenistic Philosophy." *Classical Quarterly* 38: 150–71.

Long, A. A., and Sedley, D. (1987). *The Hellenistic Philosophers.* 2 vols. Cambridge.

Longo Auricchio, F. (1978). "La scuola di Epicuro." *Cronache Ercolanesi* 8: 21–37.

Lovejoy, A., and Boas, G. (1935). *Primitivism and Related Ideas in Antiquity.* Baltimore.

Luper-Foy, S. (1987). "Annihilation." *Philosophical Quarterly* 37: 233–52.

Luria, S. (1970). *Demokrit.* Leningrad.

Lutz, C. (1988). *Unnatural Emotions.* Chicago.

MacLeod, C. W., ed. and comm. (1982). *Homer: Iliad 24.* Cambridge.

MacIntyre, A. (1981). *After Virtue.* Notre Dame.

MacIntyre, A. (1988). *Whose Justice? Which Rationality?* Notre Dame.

McPherran, M. (1987). "Skeptical Homeopathy and Self-Refutation." *Phronesis* 32: 290–328.

Mahabharata. (1973). *Vol. 1, Of the Beginning.* Trans. J. van Buitenen. Chicago.

Marrou, H.-I. (1956). *A History of Education in Antiquity.* Trans. G. Lamb. London.

Marti, B. (1945). "Seneca's Tragedies: A New Interpretation." *Transactions of the American Philological Association* 76: 216–45.

Marti, B. (1947). "The Prototypes of Seneca's Tragedies." *Classical Philology* 42: 1–16.

Marx, K. (1841). *Difference between the Democritean and Epicurean Philosophy of Nature.* In *Collected Works,* Vol. 1, by Karl Marx and Fr. Engels, 25–74. London and Moscow, 1975.

Maurach, G. (1966). "Jason und Medea bei Seneca." *Antike und Abendland* 12: 125–46.

Mill, John Stuart (1961). "Nature." In *Three Essays on Religion*, in *The Philosophy of John Stuart Mill*, ed. M. Cohen. New York.

Miller, F. (1976). "Epicurus on the Art of Dying." *Southern Journal of Philosophy* 14: 169–77.

Miller, F. J., ed. and trans. (1917). *Seneca's Tragedies*. 2 vols. Loeb Classical Library. London and Cambridge, Mass.

Mitsis, P. (1988a). *Epicurus' Ethical Theory: The Pleasures of Invulnerability*. Ithaca.

Mitsis, P. (1988b). "Epicurus on Death and Duration." *Proceedings of the Boston Area Colloquium for Ancient Philosophy* 4: 303–22.

Mitsis, P. (1993). "Seneca on Rules and Precepts." In Brunschwig and Nussbaum (1993) 285–312.

Morrison, D. (1990). "The Ancient Sceptic's Way of Life." *Metaphilosophy* 21: 204–22.

Motto, A. L. (1970). *Seneca: A Sourcebook*. Amsterdam.

Murphy, J. G. (1976). "Rationality and the Fear of Death." *Monist* 59: 187ff.

Murphy, J. G. (1990). "Getting Even: The Role of the Victim." *Social Philosophy and Public Policy* 7: 209–25.

Murphy, J. G., and Hampton, J. (1988). *Forgiveness and Mercy*. Cambridge.

Nagel, T. (1979). "Death." In *Mortal Questions*, by T. Nagel, 1–10. Cambridge. Originally published in *Nous* 4 (1970): 73–80.

Newman, W. D. (1887–1902). *Aristotle: Politics*. 4 vols. Oxford.

Nietzsche, Fr. (1887). *On the Genealogy of Morals*. Trans. W. Kaufmann. In *The Basic Writings of Nietzsche*, ed. W. Kaufmann, 439–579. New York, 1966.

Nietzsche, Fr. (1888). *Twilight of the Idols*. Trans. W. Kaufmann. In *The Viking Portable Nietzsche*, 463–563. New York, 1968.

Nussbaum, M. (1972). "*Psuchē* in Heraclitus, II." *Phronesis* 17: 153–70.

Nussbaum, M. (1978). *Aristotle's De Motu Animalium*. Princeton.

Nussbaum, M. (1986a). *The Fragility of Goodness: Luck and Ethics in Greek Tragedy and Philosophy*. Cambridge.

Nussbaum, M. (1986b). "Therapeutic Arguments: Epicurus and Aristotle." In Schofield and Striker (1986) 31–74.

Nussbaum, M. (1990a). *Love's Knowledge: Essays on Philosophy and Literature*. Oxford.

Nussbaum, M. (1990b). "Aristotelian Social Democracy." In *Liberalism and the Good*, ed. R. B. Douglass, G. Mara, and H. Richardson, 203–52. New York.

Nussbaum, M. (1990c). "Therapeutic Arguments and Structures of Desire." In *Differences* 2: 46–66. *Society and Sexuality in Ancient Greece and Rome*, ed. D. Konstan and M. Nussbaum.

Nussbaum, M., ed. (1990d). *The Poetics of Therapy: Hellenistic Ethics in Its Rhetorical and Literary Context. Apeiron* 23, no. 4.

Nussbaum, M. (1991a). Review of Mitsis (1988a). *Philosophy and Phenomenological Research* 51: 677–87.

Nussbaum, M. (1991b). Review of Vlastos (1991). *New Republic*, September: 34–40.

Nussbaum, M. (1992). "Tragedy and Self-Sufficiency: Plato and Aristotle on Fear and Pity." *Oxford Studies in Ancient Philosophy* 10: 107–59. A shorter version in *Essays on Aristotle's Poetics*, ed. A. Rorty, 261–90. Princeton.

Nussbaum, M. (1993a). "Poetry and the Passions: Two Stoic Views." In Brunschwig and Nussbaum (1993) 97–149.

Nussbaum, M. (1993b). "Equity and Mercy." *Philosophy and Public Affairs*.

Nussbaum, M. (1993c). "The *Oedipus Rex* and the Ancient Unconscious." In *Freud and Forbidden Knowledge*, ed. P. Rudnytsky and E. H. Spitz. New York.

Nussbaum, M. (forthcoming a). *Upheavals of Thought: A Theory of the Emotions.* Gifford Lectures 1993. Cambridge and New York, 1996.

Nussbaum, M. (forthcoming b). "Aristotle on Human Nature and the Foundations of Ethics." In *World, Mind, and Ethics: Essays on the Philosophy of Bernard Williams*, ed. J.E.G. Altham and R. Harrison. Cambridge.

Nussbaum, M., and Rorty, A., eds. (1992). *Essays on Aristotle's De Anima*. Oxford.

Nussbaum, M., and Sen, A., eds. (1993). *The Quality of Life*. Oxford.

Oatley, K. (1992). *Best Laid Schemes*. Cambridge.

Olivieri, A., ed. (1914). *Philodemus: Peri Parrhēsias*. Leipzig.

Owen, G.E.L. (1986). *Logic, Science, and Dialectic: Collected Papers in Greek Philosophy*. Ed. M. Nussbaum. London and Ithaca.

Pangle, T. (1990). "The Classical Challenge to the American Constitution." *Chicago-Kent Law Review* 66: 145–76.

Parfit, D. (1984). *Reasons and Persons*. Oxford.

Partridge, E. (1981). "Posthumous Interests and Posthumous Respect." *Ethics* 91: 243–64.

Patin, M. (1883). *Études sur la poésie latine*. Paris.

Pease, A. S., ed. and comm. (1955). *M. Tulli Ciceronis de Natura Deorum liber primus*. Cambridge, Mass.

Perelli, L. (1969). *Lucrezio Poetà dell' Angoscia*. Florence.

Pigeaud, J. (1981). *La maladie de l'âme: Étude sur la relation de l'ame et du corps dans la tradition medico-philosophique antique*. Paris.

Pitcher, G. (1984). "The Misfortunes of the Dead." *American Philosophical Quarterly* 21: 183–88.

Pogge, T. (1989). *Realizing Rawls*. Ithaca.

Pohlenz, M. (1938). "Zenon und Chrysipp." *Nachrichten der Gesellschaft der Wissenschaften zu Göttingen*, phil.-hist. Kl. Fach. 1, no. 2: 173–210.

Pohlenz, M. (1970). *Die Stoa: Geschichte einer geistigen Bewegung*. 2 vols. 4th ed. Göttingen.

Pomeroy, S. B. (1975). *Goddesses, Whores, Wives, and Slaves: Women in Classical Antiquity*. New York.

Pratt, N. T. (1948). "The Stoic Base of Senecan Drama." *Transactions of the American Philological Association* 79: 1–11.

Pratt, N. T. (1983). *Seneca's Drama*. Chapel Hill.

Price, A. W. (1989). *Love and Friendship in Plato and Aristotle*. Oxford.

Price, A. W. (1990). "Plato and Freud." In *The Person and the Human Mind*, ed. C. Gill, 247–70. Oxford.

Putnam, H. (1981). *Reason, Truth, and History*. Cambridge, Mass.

Putnam, H. (1993). "Objectivity and the Science-Ethics Distinction." In Nussbaum and Sen (1993) 143–57.

Putnam, H. (forthcoming). "Pragmatism and Moral Objectivity." In *Human Capabilities: Women, Men and Equality*, ed. M. Nussbaum and J. Glover. Oxford.

Putnam, M.C.J. (1985). "Possessiveness, Sexuality, and Heroism in the *Aeneid*." *Vergilius* 31: 1–21.

Putnam, M.C.J. (1987). "Daedalus, Virgil and the End of Art." *American Journal of Philology* 108: 173–98.

Putnam, M.C.J. (1990). "Anger and Blindness in Virgil's *Aeneid*." In Nussbaum (1990d) 1–40.

Putnam, M.C.J. (forthcoming). "Senecan Tragedy and Virgil's *Aeneid*."

Rabbow, P. (1914). *Antike Schriften über Seelenheilung und Seelenleitung auf ihre Quellen untersucht*. Vol. 1, *Die Therapie des Zorns*. Leipzig.

Rabbow, P. (1954). *Seelenführung*. Munich.

Rachels, J. (1990). *Created from Animals*. New York and Oxford.

Rawls, J. (1971). *A Theory of Justice*. Cambridge, Mass.

Rawls, J. (1980). *Kantian Constructivism in Moral Theory: The Dewey Lectures*. *Journal of Philosophy* 77.

Regenbogen, O. (1930). "Schmerz und Tod in den Tragödien Senecas." *Vorträge der Bibliothek Warburg, Vorträge 1927–1928*, ed. F. Saxi, 167–218. Leipzig and Berlin. Reprinted in *Kleine Schriften*, 411–64. Munich, 1961.

Reynolds, L. D., ed. (1977). *Seneca: Dialogi*. Oxford Classical Text. Oxford.

Reynolds, L. D., ed. (1965). *Seneca: Ad Lucilium Epistulae Morales*. Oxford Classical Text. Oxford.

Richardson, H. (1992). "Desire and the Good in *De Anima*." In Nussbaum and Rorty (1992) 382–99.

Rist, J. M. (1969). *Stoic Philosophy*. Cambridge.

Rist, J. M. (1972). *Epicurus: An Introduction*. Cambridge.

Rist, J. M., ed. (1978). *The Stoics*. Berkeley.

Rodis-Lewis, G. (1975). *Epicure et son école*. Paris.

Rorty, A., ed. (1980). *Essays on Aristotle's Ethics*. Berkeley.

Rorty, A. (1983). "Fearing Death." *Philosophy* 58: 175–88.

Rorty, R. (1982). *Consequences of Pragmatism*. Minneapolis.

Rosenbaum, S. (1986). "How to Be Dead and Not Care: A Defense of Epicurus." *American Philosophical Quarterly* 21: 217–25.

Rosenbaum, S. (1987). "The Harm of Killing: An Epicurean Perspective." In *Con-*

temporary Essays on Greek Ideas: The Kilgore Festschrift, ed. Baird et al., 207–26. Waco.

Rosenmeyer, T. G. (1989). *Senecan Drama and Stoic Cosmology*. Berkeley.

Russell, B. (1953). *The Conquest of Happiness*. New York.

Sainte Croix, G.E.M. de. (1981). *The Class Struggle in the Ancient Greek World*. London.

Salkever, S. (1989). *Finding the Mean*. Princeton.

Sandbach, F. H. (1975). *The Stoics*. London.

Santayana, G. (1910). *Three Philosophical Poets*. Cambridge.

Schofield, M. (1991). *The Stoic Idea of the City*. Cambridge

Schofield, M., and Striker, G. eds. (1986). *The Norms of Nature*. Cambridge.

Schofield, M., Burnyeat, M. F., and Barnes, J., eds. (1980). *Doubt and Dogmatism: Studies in Hellenistic Epistemology*. Oxford.

Schrijvers, P. H. (1969). "Eléments psychagogiques dans l'oeuvre de Lucrèce." *Actes du VIIᵉ Congrès de l'Association G. Budé*, 370–76. Paris.

Schrijvers, P. H. (1970). *Horror ac Divina Voluptas: Etudes sur la poétique et la poésie de Lucrèce*. Amsterdam.

Scruton, R. (1986). *Sexual Desire*. New York.

Sedley, D. (1980). "The Protagonists." In Schofield, Burnyeat, and Barnes (1980) 1–19.

Sedley, D. (1983a). "The Motivation of Greek Skepticism." In Burnyeat (1983) 9–30.

Sedley, D. (1983b). "Epicurus' Refutation of Determinism." In *ΣΥΖΗΤΗΣΙΣ: Studi sull' epicureismo greco e romano offerti a Marcello Gigante*, ed. G. Macchiarolli, 11–51. Naples.

Segal, C. P. (1983a). "Boundary Violation and the Landscape of the Self in Senecan Tragedy." *Antike und Abendland* 29: 172–87.

Segal, C. P. (1983b). "Dissonant Sympathy: Song, Orpheus, and the Golden Age in Seneca's Tragedies." In Boyle (1983) 229–51.

Segal, C. P. (1986a). *Language and Desire in Seneca's Phaedra*. Princeton.

Segal, C. P. (1986b). "War, Death and Savagery in Lucretius: The Beasts of Battle in 5.1308–49." *Ramus* 15: 1–34.

Segal, C. P. (1988). "Poetic Immortality and the Fear of Death: The Second Proem of the *De Rerum Natura*." *Harvard Studies in Classical Philology* 92: 1–19.

Segal, C. P. (1989). "Poetic Immortality and the Fear of Death: The Second Proem of the *De Rerum Natura*." *Harvard Studies in Classical Philology* 92: 193–212.

Segal, C. P. (1990). *Lucretius on Death and Anxiety*. Princeton.

Sen, A. (1982). "Equality of What?" In *Choice, Welfare, and Measurement*, by A. Sen, 353–69. Oxford.

Sen, A. (1985). *Commodities and Capabilities*. Amsterdam.

Sherman, N. (1989). *The Fabric of Character: Aristotle's Theory of Virtue*. Oxford.

Shibles, W. (1974). *Death*. Whitewater, Wis.

Sihvola, J. (1989). *Decay, Progress, the Good Life? Hesiod and Protagoras on the Development of Culture.* Societas Scientarum Fennica. Helsinki.

Silverstein, H. (1980). "The Evil of Death." *Journal of Philosophy* 77: 401–17.

Simon, B. (1978). *Mind and Madness in Ancient Greece.* Ithaca.

Sinaiko, H. (1965). *Love, Knowledge, and Discourse.* Chicago.

Sorabji, R. (1980). "Aristotle on the Role of Intellect in Virtue." In Rorty (1980) 201–20.

Sorabji, R. (1983). *Time, Creation and the Continuum.* London.

Sorabji, R. (1993). *Man and Beast.* Townsend Lectures, Cornell University, 1991. Ithaca.

Stevens, W. (1954). *The Collected Poems.* London.

Stewart, Z. (1958). "Democritus and the Cynics." *Harvard Studies in Classical Philology* 63: 179–91.

Stough, C. (1984). "Sextus Empiricus on Non-Assertion." *Phronesis* 29: 137–63.

Striker, G. (1980). "Sceptical Strategies." In Schofield, Burnyeat, and Barnes (1980) 54–83.

Striker, G. (1983). "The Role of *Oikeiosis* in Stoic Ethics." *Oxford Studies in Ancient Philosophy* 1: 145–68.

Striker, G. (1986). "Antipater, or the Art of Living." In Schofield and Striker (1986) 185–204.

Striker, G. (1988). Comments on P. Mitsis, "Epicurus on Death and Duration." *Proceedings of the Boston Area Colloquium in Ancient Philosophy* 4: 322–28.

Sudhaus, S. (1911). "Epicur als Beichtvater." *Archiv für Religionswissenschaft* 14: 647–48.

Sumner, L. S. (1976). "A Matter of Life and Death." *Nous* 10: 145–71.

Sunstein, C. (1991). "Preferences and Politics." *Philosophy and Public Affairs* 20: 3–34.

Sykes Davies, H. (1931–2). "Notes on Lucretius." *Criterion* 11: 25–42, and in Classen (1986) 273–90.

Syme, R. (1964). *Sallust.* Berkeley.

Tadic-Gilloteaux, N. (1963). "Sénèque face au suicide." *L'antiquité classique* 32: 541–51.

Taylor, Charles. (1989). *Sources of the Self: The Making of Modern Identity.* Cambridge, Mass.

Taylor, Charles. (1993). "Explanation and Practical Reason." In Nussbaum and Sen (1993) 208–31.

Taylor, C.C.W. (1980). "All Perceptions Are True." In Schofield, Burnyeat, and Barnes (1980) 105–24.

Taylor, C.C.W. (1987). Review of Schofield and Striker (1986). *Oxford Studies in Ancient Philosophy* 5: 235–45.

Usener, H. (1887). *Epicurea.* Leipzig.

Vlastos, G. (1941). "Slavery in Plato's Thought." *Philosophical Review* 50: 289–304, and in Vlastos (1973).

Vlastos, G. (1973). *Platonic Studies*. Princeton.

Vlastos, G. (1983). "The Socratic Elenchus." *Oxford Studies in Ancient Philosophy* 1: 27–58.

Vlastos, G. (1985). "Socrates' Disavowal of Knowledge." *Philosophical Quarterly* 35: 1–31.

Vlastos, G. (1991). *Socrates: Ironist and Moral Philosopher*. Cambridge.

Voelke, A. J. (1965). "L'unité de l'âme dans l'ancien stoicisme." *Studia Philosophica* 25: 154–81.

Walzer, M. (1983). *Spheres of Justice: A Defense of Pluralism and Equality*. Cambridge, Mass.

White, N. P. (1979). "The Basis of Stoic Ethics." *Harvard Studies in Classical Philology* 83: 143–78.

Whitehead, D. (1975). "Aristotle the Metic." *Proceedings of the Cambridge Philological Society* 21: 94–99.

Whitehead, D. (1977). *The Ideology of the Athenian Metic*. PCPS Supp. Vol. 4. Cambridge.

Whitman, W. (1973). *Leaves of Grass*. Norton Critical Edition. New York.

Wilke, C. (1974). ed. *Philodemi De Ira liber*. Leipzig.

Williams, B.A.O. (1962). "Aristotle on the Good: A Formal Sketch." *Philosophical Quarterly* 12: 289–96.

Williams, B.A.O. (1973). "The Makropulos Case: Reflections on the Tedium of Immortality." In *Problems of the Self*, by B.A.O. Williams, 82–100. Cambridge.

Williams, B.A.O. (1985). *Ethics and the Limits of Philosophy*. Cambridge, Mass.

Winkler, J. J. (1990). *The Constraints of Desire: The Anthropology of Sex and Gender in Ancient Greece*. New York.

Winkler, J. J. (forthcoming). Martin Classical Lectures, 1988. Princeton.

Wolf, S. (1990). *Freedom within Reason*. New York.

Wormell, D.E.W. (1960). "Lucretius: The Personality of the Poet." *Greece and Rome* 7: 54–65.

Wright, J.R.G. (1974). "Form and Content in the *Moral Essays*." In *Seneca*, ed. C.D.N. Costa. London.

Young, C. (1988). "Aristotle on Temperance." *Philosophical Review* 97: 521–42.

Yourgrau, P. (1987). "The Dead." *Journal of Philosophy* 84: 84–101.

Ziegler, Konrat (1936). "Der Tod des Lucretius." *Hermes* 71: 421–40.

Zwierlein, O. (1966). *Die Rezitations-dramen Senecas*. Meisenheim-am-Glan.

Zwierlein, O., ed. (1986a). *Seneca: Tragoediae*. Oxford.

Zwierlein, O. (1986b). *Kritischer Kommentar zu den Tragodien Senecas*. Mainz-Stuttgart.

* Index Locorum *

I would like to thank Dion Gray for her assistance in preparing the index locorum.

General Index *

This index contains subject references and references to the most substantive discussions of the secondary literature. It is not a complete catalogue of all footnote references. I am enormously grateful to Margaret Graver for her generous help in the preparation of this index.

For enquiries or renewal at
Quarles LRC
Tel: 01708 455011 – Extension 4009